ADOLESCENT BRAIN DEVELOPMENT

VULNERABILITIES AND OPPORTUNITIES

ANNALS OF THE NEW YORK ACADEMY OF SCIENCES
Volume 1021

ADOLESCENT BRAIN DEVELOPMENT

VULNERABILITIES AND OPPORTUNITIES

Edited by Ronald E. Dahl and Linda Patia Spear

The New York Academy of Sciences
New York, New York
2004

Library of Congress Cataloging-in-Publication Data

Adolescent brain development : vulnerabilities and opportunities / edited by Ronald E. Dahl and Linda Patia Spear.
    p. cm.— (Annals of the New York Academy of Sciences ; v. 1021)
  "This volume is the result of a conference entitled Adolescent Brain Development: Vulnerabilities and Opportunities, which was sponsored by the New York Academy of Sciences and held September 18–20, 2003 in New York, New York"—Contents p.
  Includes bibliographical references and index.
  ISBN 1-57331-506-0 (cloth : alk. paper) — ISBN 1-57331-507-9 (pbk. : alk. paper) 1. Developmental neurobiology—Congresses. 2. Brain—Growth—Congresses. 3. Adolescent psychology—Congresses. 4. Cognition in adolescence—Congresses. I. Dahl, Ronald E. II. Spear, Linda P. III. Series.
  Q11.N5 vol. 1021
  [QP363.5]
  500 s—dc22
  [616.89/008

                            2004012348

GYAT / PCP
Printed in the United States of America
ISBN 1-57331-506-0 (cloth)
ISBN 1-57331-507-9 (paper)
ISSN 0077-8923

ANNALS OF THE NEW YORK ACADEMY OF SCIENCES

Volume 1021
June 2004

ADOLESCENT BRAIN DEVELOPMENT

VULNERABILITIES AND OPPORTUNITIES

Editors
RONALD E. DAHL AND LINDA PATIA SPEAR

Conference Organizers
RONALD E. DAHL, LINDA PATIA SPEAR, ANN E. KELLEY,
RICHARD R. CLAYTON, AND RASHID A SHAIKH

This volume is the result of a conference entitled Adolescent Brain Development: Vulnerabilities and Opportunities, which was cosponsored by the New York Academy of Sciences and the University of Pittsburgh School of Medicine, Center for Continuing Education, and held September 18–20, 2003 in New York City .

CONTENTS

Part II. Brain Development during Puberty and Adolescence

Part III. Hormone, Behavior, and Affect Interrelationships during Adolescence

Part IV. Cognitive Development, Decision Making, and Behavioral Choices

Part IX. Short Papers

Human Studies

This conference was organized in collaboration with:

- **THE ROBERT WOOD JOHNSON FOUNDATION**
- **TOBACCO ETIOLOGY RESEARCH NETWORK (TERN)**

We gratefully acknowledge additional support from:

- **NATIONAL CANCER INSTITUTE**
- **NATIONAL INSTITUTE ON DRUG ABUSE, NIH**
- **NATIONAL INSTITUTE OF MENTAL HEALTH, NIH**
- **NATIONAL INSTITUTE OF CHILD HEALTH AND HUMAN DEVELOPMENT, NIH**
- **ADAPT RESEARCH NETWORK**

Preface

RONALD DAHL,[a] LINDA PATIA SPEAR,[b] ANN KELLEY,[c] RASHID SHAIKH,[d]
AND RICHARD CLAYTON[e]

[a]Psychiatry and Pediatrics, University of Pittsburgh Medical Center,
Pittsburgh, Pennsylvania 15213, USA

[b]Psychology Department, State University of New York at Binghamton,
Binghamton, New York 13902, USA

[c]Department of Psychiatry, University of Wisconsin-Madison Medical School,
Madison, Wisconsin 53719, USA

[d]New York Academy of Sciences, New York, New York 10021, USA

[e]Tobacco Etiology Research Network (TERN), Kentucky School of Public Health,
Lexington, Kentucky 40504, USA

This volume of the *Annals* contains the proceedings of an interdisciplinary conference entitled Adolescent Brain Development: Vulnerabilities and Opportunities, which was convened under the auspices of the New York Academy of Sciences and held at The Lighthouse Conference Center in New York, September 18–20, 2003. This conference brought together a distinguished group of scientists to address a wide range of questions about neurobehavioral, psychological, and social changes during adolescent development. The presentations and discussions addressed a compelling set of issues, with emphasis on the clinical and social policy relevance of this area of research.

The primary objective of this conference was to examine and integrate current evidence that suggests that adolescence represents a key period in the development of a wide range of behavioral and emotional health problems emerging in adolescence—particularly with respect to the onset of nicotine dependence, alcohol and other substance use, risk taking, and emotional problems including adolescent depression and suicide. A working premise was the value of bringing together preclinical, clinical, and social policy perspectives on adolescence to help promote a fruitful interdisciplinary dialogue—one with the long-term goal of informing early intervention and prevention strategies for youth.

The initial conceptualizing of this conference came out of work from a transdisciplinary research network, the Robert Wood Johnson Tobacco Etiology Research Network (TERN), which supported several phases of the early planning and development of the conference. A meeting was convened by the New York Academy of Sciences that included Dick Clayton, Ron Dahl, Rashid Shaikh and a three-member ad hoc committee, assembled by the Academy, consisting of Bruce McEwen (Rockefeller University), Michael I. Posner (then at Weill Medical College of Cornell University), and Theodore Shapiro (Weill Medical College of Cornell University), along with Israel Lederhendler (NIMH) and Craig Ferris (University of Massachusetts Medical School), who were planning a companion conference on early childhood

Ann. N.Y. Acad. Sci. 1021: xi–xii (2004). © 2004 New York Academy of Sciences.
doi: 10.1196/annals.1308.067

and mental illness. The final organizing committee for this conference consisted of Ron Dahl, Linda Spear, Ann Kelley, Rashid Shaikh, and Dick Clayton.

It is also essential to acknowledge and express sincere gratitude to several sponsors, who provided the essential financial support that turned these ideas into a reality. This included a grant from the Robert Wood Johnson Foundation, support from the National Cancer Institute, and an NIH conference grant that was jointly supported by the National Institute on Drug Abuse, the National Institute of Mental Health, and the National Institute of Child Health and Human Development. In addition, the ADAPT research network (NIMH R24 MH67346) supported travel awards for several young investigators who presented posters at the conference. The Robert Wood Johnson and the Tobacco Etiology Research Network committed additional funds for the development and maintenance of an outstanding Academy website, in the form of an eBriefing, which immediately followed the conference, but preceded this volume.

We invite you to visit this site <http://www.nyas.org/ebrief/abd>, which richly complements this volume in presenting a research agenda (including compelling reasons to enter the field), an overview of the conference, audio transcripts and slides, links to related resources and other articles written by the presenters, and a list of open questions that still need to be addressed in this new, but very important field of research.

Adolescent Brain Development: A Period of Vulnerabilities and Opportunities

Keynote Address

RONALD E. DAHL

Psychiatry and Pediatrics, University of Pittsburgh Medical Center, Pittsburgh, Pennsylavania 15213, USA

ABSTRACT: This article introduces and summarizes the goals of the symposium. It also provides an overview of a conceptual framework for understanding adolescence, which emphasizes how the very nature of this developmental transition requires an interdisciplinary approach—one that focuses on brain/behavior/social-context *interactions* during this important maturational period. More specifically it describes a set of neurobehavioral changes that appear to be linked to pubertal development, which appear to have a significant effect on motivation and emotion, and considers these puberty-specific changes in affect in relation to a much larger set of developmental changes in adolescence. This framework is used to argue for the need for a transdisciplinary dialogue that brings together work in several areas of neuroscience (including animal models) and normal development with clinical and social policy research aimed at early intervention and prevention strategies.

KEYWORDS: adolescence; puberty; neuroplasticity; high-risk behavior; interdiciplinary studies

INTRODUCTION AND GOALS

One of my first goals in this opening address is to try to convey some of the excitement that has been generated among the organizers of this conference—Linda Spear, Ann Kelley, Dick Clayton, Rashid Shaikh, and myself—in the months of planning that led up to this meeting. In part, this enthusiasm emerged directly from the prospects of hearing about and discussing the many rapid advances that will allow us to gain greater understanding of the development of the adolsecent brain. Even further, we were excited at the prospect of bringing together investigators from a wide range of backgrounds and scientific disciplines in order to *create a broader interdisciplinary dialogue.*

This, we believe, is one of the key issues for the field: stronger scientific bridges need to be built across disciplines that will allow previously separate bodies of knowledge to be linked and more effectively applied to the large-scale problems af-

Address for correspondence: Ronald E. Dahl, M.D., Staunton Professor of Psychiatry and Pediatrics, University of Pittsburgh Medical Center, 3811 O'Hara St., Rm. E-724, Pittsburgh, PA 15213. Voice: 412-246-5878; fax: 412-246-5880.

dahlre@msx.upmc.edu

Ann. N.Y. Acad. Sci. 1021: 1–22 (2004). © 2004 New York Academy of Sciences.
doi: 10.1196/annals.1308.001

fecting youth. It is essential, we believe, not only to deepen our understanding of specific neurobiological changes during adolescent development, but also to broaden our knowledge of how behavioral, familial, and social influences *interact,* in multifaceted ways, with the development of the biological systems of interest.

The stakes are high: the problems affecting adolescents in our society are both enormous and complex. On one hand, there are reasons to be optimistic about the prospects of contributions from current and future scientific advances in these areas: We are entering a period of rapid progress in research aimed at many aspects of adolescent development, including several areas of basic and clinical research. These studies are beginning to provide new insights about adolescence as a unique developmental period. These include normal developmental studies of cognitive, emotional, and social maturation in adolescence; clinical research focusing on the development of a broad range of behavioral, emotional, and substance abuse problems in adolescence; and advances in using animal models to understand both neural and behavioral aspects of development during puberty and adolescence. In addition, many conceptual and methodological advances have been made in studies of adults—including rapid progress in cognitive and affective neuroscience as well as the use of structural and functional neuroimaging tools and molecular and genetic methods—that can now be applied to questions about adolescent maturation. Several of these areas of investigation are creating invaluable contributions that have direct relevance to understanding a variety of dimensions of adolescent development. There is every reason to predict that the rapid growth in many of these fields will continue to accelerate.

On the other hand, rapid growth along several different lines of investigation introduces new challenges as well as opportunities. A key part of the difficulty in this field is the tendency toward fragmentation—insularity within disciplines working on related and somewhat overlapping areas of investigation. There is often a shortage of effective bridges between disciplines: Stronger links need to be forged between animal and human investigations of adolescence, and developmental and clinical approaches need to be better integrated, as do biological and social frameworks, for understanding adolescent development. More generally, we need to promote *trans*disciplinary dialogues as well as better conceptual integration of many of the separate lines of investigation.

This is, in many ways, the *primary goal* of this conference (and a key goal for this *Annals* volume as well as its eBriefing on the Academy's web site <http://www.nyas.org/ebriefreps/main.asp?intSectionID=189>). We seek to establish connections—scientifically, conceptually, and through personal relationships—that will help counteract the tendency towards insularity within disciplines.

This emphasis on integrating a diversity of scientific backgrounds began at the level of the organizing committee for the conference, which included individuals from basic and behavioral neuroscience, clinical research in pediatrics and child psychiatry, and the social sciences and prevention research. We have attempted to organize this symposium in ways that are consistent with this trans-disciplinary goal, as will be seen in the eight sessions reported here. The format for each section includes an introduction by the organizer who selected each presenter for that session, followed by two or three papers that juxtapose basic research with other more clinical or social approaches, followed by a discussant who provides some integration of the different papers or points to particular lines of research needed to advance future understanding.

We believe that promoting such trans-disciplinary dialogue represents a crucial step toward the long-term goal of achieving a deeper understanding of adolescence as a unique period of development. In this opening address I want to sketch a conceptual framework for adolescence that emphasizes how the very nature of this developmental transition requires an interdisciplinary approach. I wish to underscore how a set of neurobehavioral changes at puberty represents *part* of a much larger set of maturational changes in adolescence, and how these require an approach that focuses on brain/behavior/social-context *interactions* during this important maturational period.

FRAMING THE BIG QUESTIONS: THE HEALTH PARADOX OF ADOLESCENCE

Adolescence presents a striking paradox with respect to overall health statistics. This developmental period is marked by rapid increases in physical and mental capabilities. By adolescence, individuals have matured beyond the frailties of childhood, but have not yet begun any of the declines of adult aging. Compared to young children, adolescents are stronger, bigger, and faster, and are achieving maturational improvements in reaction time, reasoning abilities, immune function, and the capacity to withstand cold, heat, injury, and physical stress. In almost every measurable domain, this is *a developmental period of strength and resilience.*

Yet, despite these robust maturational improvements in several domains, overall morbidity and mortality rates *increase* 200% over the same interval of time. This doubling in rates of death and disability from the period of early school age into late adolescence and early adulthood is not the result of cancer, heart disease, or mysterious infections. Rather, the major sources of death and disability in adolescence are related to *difficulties in the control of behavior and emotion.* It is the high rates of accidents, suicide, homicide, depression, alcohol and substance abuse, violence, reckless behaviors, eating disorders, and health problems related to risky sexual behaviors that are killing many youth in our society. These problems are documented as frequently in the popular media as they are in the medical or epidemiologic literature. Adolescence is strongly associated with an increase in risk-taking, sensation-seeking, and reckless behavior—all of which which lead, far too often, to actions with dire health consequences.

These high rates of "reckless" behavior in adolescence also highlight a second level of paradox: In most measurable ways, adolescents have developed *better* reasoning capabilities and decision-making skills than children. Older teenagers can perform at (or very near to) adult levels in their abilities to understand, cognitively, the consequences of risky behavior. Adolescents are much better than children at the mental processes that underpin making logical and responsible choices. Yet, despite these cognitive improvements, adolescents appear to be more prone to erratic—and, as I will argue, *emotionally influenced*—behavior, which can lead to periodic disregard for the risks and consequences.

These striking paradoxes—high rates of morbidity and mortality despite robust physical health, and increasing rates of reckless behavior despite improved capacities for decision making—provide part of the framework regarding the importance of research into the neurobehavioral underpinnings of these developmental changes.

Compelling scientific questions lurk within these mysteries and seeming contradictions. Achieving a deeper understanding of adolescent neurobehavioral development can, in the long run, contribute to the pragmatic goals of early intervention to address these large-scale problems.

ACKNOWLEDGING THE COMPLEXITY OF THE PROBLEMS

On one hand, there are compelling reasons to believe that neuroscientific research can ultimately help to delineate underlying developmental processes in ways that can inform more effective early interventions and social policies to promote healthier adolescence. On the other hand, there are equally compelling reasons to believe that complex behavioral and social factors are so intertwined with biological development as to make simplistic or reductionist goals untenable.

Examining neurobehavioral contributions in the developmental pathways leading toward these problems does *not* equate to a reductionistic approach; the goal is not to try to reduce those complex problems to the level of brain mechanisms or biological interventions. Investigators working in basic research in these areas must collaborate closely with their colleagues in clinical and social sciences. And for their part, the clinical and social scientists must seek collaboration with basic scientists without fearing that a mechanistic understanding of some aspects of these problems implies any diminished role for the social, cultural, and familial influences on these developing biological systems. Rather, it is important to emphasize how a mechanistic understanding of biological processes can actually *enhance* the importance of behavioral or social policy interventions.

To provide a simple example of this principle of collaboration between both ends of the scientific spectrum, consider the effect of scientific progress in understanding the biologic mechanisms contributing to genetic vulnerability to skin cancer. This set of insights about biological processes has not led to "blaming" the problem on the genes *or* ignoring the role of behavior and context (i.e., the role of excessive sun exposure and sunburn leading to skin cancer). Instead, mechanistic understanding of how fair-skinned children are at high risk for ultra-violet skin damage has *promoted* adaptive behavior: parents of fair-skinned children are now more highly motivated to use sunscreen and protective clothing for these children to prevent the biological vulnerability (genetically low levels of melanin in the skin) from leading to skin cancer in adulthood.

A second example—a bit closer to our focus on brain development— is the "0 to 3" campaign that has raised awareness about the importance of brain development in the first few years of life. This emphasis on biological processes has *not* been reductionistic, and has not been viewed this way by policy makers. Evidence of brain plasticity in the early years of life has not led to the conclusion that parenting and social experience are unimportant during this maturational period, but rather to its opposite: Developmental psychologists, neuroscientists, and policy makers are more likely to emphasize the value of social policies that protect and support infants and toddlers during this important period of brain development. There are, I believe, parallel opportunities regarding interdisciplinary approaches focusing on puberty and adolescent brain development.

I believe that these are crucial issues for our field. Basic neuroscientists, developmental psychologists, clinical investigators, and social scientists must work together to understand adolescence. A conceptual framework must be constructed that emphasizes the *interactions* of brain, behavior, and social context in the developmental pathways to positive and negative outcomes in youth. We need to examine, scientifically, specific components of these processes, without forgetting the complex nature of the problems.

WHY IS ADOLESCENCE A TIME OF SO MANY COMPLEX PROBLEMS?

Part of the problem of adolescent tendencies toward irrational, emotionally influenced behavior has been recognized throughout human history. As Aristotle noted more than twenty centuries ago:

> Youth are heated by Nature as drunken men by wine.

Or, in Shakespeare's words:

> I would that there were no age between 10 and 23, for there's nothing in between but getting wenches with child, wronging the ancientry, stealing, fighting... *(The Winter's Tale,* Act III*)*

Yet, there are also important differences in how we can approach understanding adolescents' problems in contemporary times. Today we can begin to parse these complex problems into empirical questions about adolescent development. We can now move beyond age-old observations and negative characterizations of impulsive and "hot-headed" youth, and start to ask specific scientific questions: What is the empirical evidence that adolescents are "heated by Nature"? Are these changes rooted in biology? Are some of these changes simply a function of greater freedoms and social influences? Are there neurobehavioral underpinnings to some of these adolescent tendencies that are universal across cultures? Are some of these changes related directly to increases in specific hormones? Are they linked to maturational changes in specific neural systems in adolescence? Which aspects of these developmental changes and problems can be modeled in animal studies? Are there unique types of neural "plasticity" during puberty and adolescence, when a particular set of individual experiences can have longstanding effects on the trajectory of development? How do these periods of plasticity create *vulnerabilities* that in turn contribute to the high rate of serious problems and disorders emerging in adolescence? How might this same type of plasticity create unique *opportunities* to intervene in positive ways at this point of development?

An analogy can illustrate the key principle: Consider the natural developmental window for learning fluency in a second (or third) language. While, a person *can* learn a new language at any age, the process of becoming easily fluent in a new language changes significantly after puberty. For an adult to achieve an even modest level of proficiency in a new language requires a great deal of motivation, special training, drills, persistent efforts, and an enormous amount of time. It is also exceedingly difficult to speak without a strong accent for persons who have learned a language as an adult. In contrast, during childhood and early adolescence, a simple immersion in an environment with a new language can result in mastery with little or no formal teaching, and a gradual loss of an identifiable accent. (A good example of this is the contrast between Henry Kissinger, who came to the U.S. as an 15-year-old, and his brother, who was 3 years younger when the family moved to this country. His brother speaks English without a noticeable accent, while Kissinger, a brilliant man who has developed a masterful command of the English language, speaks with a heavy accent and retains a consistent set of speech patterns that identify him as someone who did not learn this language during the optimal developmental window.)

This concept of *plasticity* in underlying neural systems forms the basis of several crucial questions regarding puberty and adolescence—and in ways that are likely to have great clinical relevance. For example, is there an analogous natural window of plasticity for learning *emotional* regulation? Is there a developmental period when an individual can—with the right kinds of experience—easily achieve social and emotional fluency? And if something prevents or interferes with this emotional learning process during this natural period of development, is it fundamentally more difficult to achieve such refined or fluent control at a later point?

Human and animal studies are being conducted that are providing empirical data to address questions about the unique opportunities in this interval of development. The findings are likely to have enormous implications about clinical and social policy regarding the impact of early interventions. The pay-off for interventions that are implemented before these windows of plasticity become narrowed, or closed, may be much greater than the same interventions provided later in adulthood (when the underlying neural systems may be slower to adapt to change). We are at a very early point in the curve of scientific understanding of these complex issues, but a great deal of evidence exists that points toward unique opportunities, and vulnerabilities, that emerge in adolescence.

A PERIOD OF STORM AND STRESS?

Nearly 100 years ago, the pioneering psychologist G.S. Hall performed a body of work that began the modern study of adolescence. His work emphasized this developmental interval as a period of "heightened storm and stress," a phrase that has long been an influential metaphor for understanding adolescence. In the 1960s and '70s attempts were made to understand these problems in terms of "raging hormones." Those early investigations contributed some understanding of the role of pubertal hormones in some adolescent behavioral and emotional changes, but it also became clear that many models of these hormonal effects were overly simplistic. Pubertal hormones do not seem to *cause* behavioral problems or emotional turmoil: many of the youth with the highest levels of these hormones showed little or no problems with stress, emotions, or behavior.

J.J. Arnett[1] wrote a thoughtful review of these issues in 1999, asking what the empirical evidence is regarding stress, hormones, and puberty. His review provides a nice counterweight to many oversimplified views of these complex issues. First, many, and perhaps most, adolescents navigate this transition with minimal difficulties. Perhaps up to 80% of youth have little or no major problems during these "tumultuous" times. Arnett's paper, along with other influential papers by Steinberg *et al.* and Masten *et al.* (1999) over the past decade, reminds us to be careful not to over-generalize the (sometimes) dramatic problems in some adolescents. In fact, most adolescents get along quite well with their parents and teachers most of the time, succeed in school, have positive relationships with peers, do not become addicted to drugs or alcohol, and become productive and healthy adults. However, there is also evidence that a significant proportion of adolescents *do* experience great stress, struggle, and emotional turmoil. As stated earlier, this developmental period shows a sharp increase in morbidity and mortality related to a wide range of types of behavioral and emotional problems. In addition, it is also a time when trajectories are set (or altered) in ways that lead to difficulties in adulthood. Adolescence often contains the developmental roots of lifetime problems with nicotine dependence, alcohol and drug use, poor health habits, relationship difficulties, and failure to develop skills and knowledge leading to a productive job or career. Trajectories are set in adolescence that can have a major impact later in life, and there are reasons to believe that altering these trajectories in positive ways prior to adulthood can have a larger scale effect than the same intervention applied later in the lifespan.

A NATURAL TENDENCY TOWARD RISK TAKING, SENSATION SEEKING, AND STRONG EMOTIONS?

Part of the vulnerability (and opportunity) in this period of development may be linked to a set of biologically based changes in neural systems of emotion and motivation, which contribute to what appears to be a natural increase in tendencies toward risk taking, sensation seeking, and some emotional/motivational changes during pubertal maturation. On one hand, these appear to be normative changes that affect most adolescents to some degree; on the other hand, in some individuals and in some social contexts, these normative tendencies can lead to serious problems— as will be discussed in greater depth as this book unfolds.

It is valuable, therefore, to examine and better understand the neurobehavioral underpinnings of these normative affective changes, which may represent more than just simply adolescent brooding, moodiness, and romantic inclinations. There seems to be a natural biologic proclivity toward high-intensity feelings that emerges at puberty. Some emotional states—specific types of feelings—may be triggered more quickly and/or with greater intensity as a function of the biological changes attendent on pubertal maturation. For example, the tendency for increased parental conflict in early adolescence can be understood, at least in part, in relation to an increase in the *intensity* of emotion that is aroused during pubertal maturation.[2]

There is a second, somewhat related, set of observations about adolescent emotional development. Pubertal maturation is associated with a greater inclination to *seek* experiences that create high-intensity feelings. For example, studies of sensation seeking—a measure of how much an individual *wants* to experience risks, thrills, excitement, and intensity—reveal a similar developmental increase that is linked to puberty.[3]

Adolescents *like* intensity, excitement, and arousal. They are drawn to music videos that shock and bombard the senses. Teenagers flock to horror and slasher movies. They dominate queues waiting to ride the high-adrenaline rides at amusement parks. Adolescence is a time when sex, drugs, *very* loud music, and other high-stimulation experiences take on great appeal. It is a developmental period when an appetite for adventure, a predilection for risks, and a desire for novelty and thrills seem to reach naturally high levels.

While these patterns of emotional changes at puberty are evident to some degree in most adolescents, it is also important to acknowledge the wide range of individual differences during this period of development. For some adolescents this tendency to activate strong emotions and an affinity for excitement can be subtle and easily managed. In others, these inclinations toward high-intensity feelings can lead to emotionally charged and reckless adolescent behaviors, and at times to impulsive decisions by (seemingly) intelligent youth that are completely outrageous.

ADOLESCENT EMOTIONAL BEHAVIOR:
AN ILLUSTRATIVE ANECDOTE

A young guy scanning the crowd at a party notices a girl who he finds strikingly attractive. Immediately smitten, he approaches her and launches a shower of compliments. She tries to rebuff his flattery but finds something about the young man quite appealing. Romantic feelings kindle quickly. As he departs, with a kiss followed by a second kiss, emotions are flaring.

On the basis of one brief meeting, a conversation of less than a hundred words, and two kisses, the emotional lives of two adolescents have been turned upside-down. Each cannot stop thinking about the other. These two are obsessed with a desire to meet again. They manage a clandestine late-night rendezvous. Passionate feelings now accelerate at a feverish pitch. Their motivation to be together quickly rises above all competing priorities. They are willing to spurn friends and family, disregard dangers, ignore pain, and begin to act as if being together is more important than life itself—though they just met four days previously and barely know each other.

If evaluated by a psychiatrist who did not understand youthful passions, these two could easily be judged as meeting diagnostic criteria for serious mental disorders or cognitive impairments. Previously learned abilities to think logically and behave rationally seem to have evaporated in a matter of hours. When viewed with a sense of emotional detachment—without some feeling for the heat and power of young love—this scenario of adolescent behavior would appear simply ludicrous.

Yet the story of *Romeo and Juliet* has moved audiences to tears for centuries. The basic elements of the story date back to the Greek novelist, Xenophon. An Italian version of the story written in 1535 by Luigi da Porto placed the scene in Verona and named the feuding families Montecchi and Capellati. Then followed an English poem by Arthur Brooke in 1562 titled *The Tragical History of Romeus and Juliet.* But it was Shakespeare's adaptation in 1595 that made this tale what is probably now the most successful drama in history.

This story of two adolescents in love has evoked sympathetic responses across many translations and cultures because of a nearly universal human appreciation for the emotional intensity—and potential for tragedy—from rapidly igniting adolescent passions. It is also illuminating to reflect on Juliet's age: in the Luigi da Porto's version, Juliet (Giuletta) was 18 years old and the courtship developed over a few weeks. In contrast Shakespeare made Juliet only 13 years old and he compressed the action into four days.

One can only speculate why Shakespeare created a heroine so young in this romantic tragedy. It seems likely that for dramatic effect he intentionally juxtaposed adult-like passions with the naïveté of a very young teenager. As a shrewd observer of human nature Shakespeare recognized early adolescence as a time of life that creates a natural tinderbox for igniting passions.

So the emotional changes in adolescence have been generally recognized for many centuries. But over the past 50 years studies in developmental psychology have added considerable scientific substance to our knowledge of adolescent cognitive and emotional development. And, most recently, the tools of modern neuroscience as well as the use of animal models are empowering an even deeper understanding of this developmental period.[9] These advances are generating new insights into some of the roots of emotional, motivational, and behavioral changes that emerge at puberty. However, before turning to address some of these findings, it is first necessary to consider some broader questions about how we should best conceptualize, and *define,* adolescence.

WHAT *IS* ADOLESCENCE?

Adolescence has been defined in different ways by different groups of investigators and it is sometimes difficult to reach any convergence of opinion. This lack of clear definition becomes ever more challenging when attempting to bridge between animal and human models of puberty and adolescence. Yet, these are crucial issues for our field. In part, the difficulties reaching a clear consensus are related to ambiguities regarding how best to *conceptualize* the notion of adolescence. Other contributors to this symposium will present several perspectives on these issues.

I will begin this discussion by offering some opinions, including a definition that our research group has found useful, along with a brief introduction of a conceptual model of adolescence—one that reflects the work of our NIMH-supported interdisciplinary research network called ADAPT (Adolescent Development Affect-Regulation and the Pubertal Transition Research Network). Our research group[2] presents a more detailed account of this model and its relevance to using affective neuroscience to investigate the developmental psychopathology emerging in adolescence.

Let us then provisionally define adolescence in humans as *that awkward period between sexual maturation and the attainment of adult roles and responsibilities.* This defintion has proven useful in several ways. It captures the concept that adolescence begins with the physical/biological changes related to puberty, but it ends in the domain of social roles. It encompasses the transition from the social status of a child (who requires adult monitoring) to that of an adult (who is him- or herself responsible for behavior).

In other words, the end of adolescence and onset of adulthood cannot be understood solely on the basis of physical changes. To illustrate this point, consider the maturational classification of a girl, like Juliet, who is physically mature in every measurable way—fully grown in height, adult bone age, adult levels of hormones, sexually and reproductively mature, and highly intelligent, but who is 13 years old and in 7th grade. No one would argue that this individual should be considered an adult. Being an adult is not simply a matter of completing a certain category of physical development—it involves attaining a broader set of skills and knowledge that is part of the larger process of taking on adult roles and responsibilities.

Adolescence involves transitions in social roles (from that of a child to that of an adult) interposed with a multitude of pubertal changes in body and brain. Thus, it is optimal to have a working definition of adolescence that is consistent with a conceptualization of adolescence, which is, by its very nature, best understood at the level of *interactions* between biological, behavioral, and social domains.

Since, in this conceptualization, adolescence begins in the domain of physical changes (puberty) but ends in the domain of social context (adult roles), efforts to understand the transition period *must* entail interdisciplinary approaches. The very nature of this transition involves interactions between the biological, behavioral, and social domains. Understanding this transition will therefore require conceptual and methodological approaches that reflect the cross-disciplinary nature of the problem. While many scientific investigations will perforce focus on specific aspects or components of adolescence, it is equally important to place these elements within the framework of this larger perspective.

THE ONSET OF ADOLESCENCE: BIOLOGICAL CHANGES OF PUBERTY

One place to begin within the complex suite of maturational processes that we call adolescence is to focus on the biologic changes that occur at puberty. These are striking in several ways: First, puberty brings dramatic changes in body size and composition (including alterations in muscle and fat, as well as increased rate of growth and metabolic rate). Second, puberty leads to the physical changes of sexual maturation—breast or phallic development and the development of secondary sexual characteristics, including pubic and axillary hair, skin and odor changes, and deepening of the voice and development of facial and body hair in boys. Third, the physical changes of puberty lead directly to alterations in many aspects of social experience. The world treats an individual differently when he or she begins to look like an adult. (A fourth domain of changes—cognitive, psychological, and emotional changes linked to puberty—will be discussed later.)

Thus there are several interrelated processes that contribute to the physical, emotional, and social changes that are encompassed by physical maturation. Even within this relatively narrow focus on physical changes at puberty (within the much broader set of developmental changes that stretch across adolescence) it is clear that there are still several component processes that can be considered separately. At least three sets of pubertal changes can be linked to specific sets of hormonal changes. For example, rapid physical growth and increased height is strongly linked to changes in growth hormone (GH) and the upstream neuroendocrine changes that result in very high rates of GH secretion in mid-puberty (with some added contribution by sex hormones).

In contrast, a second neuroendocrine axis, which leads to the *gonadarche*, works through the pulsing of gonadotrophins, which ultimately causes the onset of phallic or breast development at puberty. Gonadarche begins with the pulsing of gonadotrophin-releasing hormone (GnRH) in the hypothalamus of the brain, which stimulates the pituitary to release the hormones LH and FSH into the blood, where

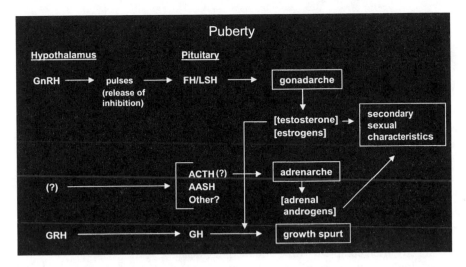

FIGURE 1. The neuroendocrine aspects of puberty include three components: gonadarche, adrenarche, and the pubertal growth spurt.

they then continue the cascade of changes by stimulating the gonads. Once the gonads are activated by LH/FSH, there is a sharp increases in estrogen in females and testosterone in males. The rising level of estrogen causes breast development in the female and the rising levels of testosterone lead to phallic growth, increased muscle mass, and voice changes in the male.

A third neuroendocrine axis, which leads to *adrenarche*, involves hormones released by the adrenal gland, including DHEA and DHEAS. These hormones often begin to rise by 6–9 years of age, but continue to increase throughout adolescence and typically peak in the early 20s. These adrenal hormones are often considered "weak" versions of sex hormones, and they bind to different receptors in the body, which contributes to adolescent changes in skin (e.g. acne) and the development of pubic and axillary hair (FIG. 1).

Clearly, puberty is *not* one process—it is a suite of changes that occur in relative synchrony. Moreover, as is apparent to those who have worked in a pediatric endocrine clinic, there is not only a wide range of variations in the precise sequence and timing of these various components, but also many types of disorders that can result in turning on a single component within this complex system. For example, some individuals can show premature adrenarche without any other sign of puberty; in other cases a girl may show premature breast development without any other sign of pubertal or adrenarchal maturation, while in some cases an individual may show an extremely early but otherwise normal spectrum of all elements of precocious puberty. Most importantly, these pubertal changes are only one set of maturational processes within the broader scope of adolescence, which includes the development of cognitive, emotional, and social skills and knowledge, as well as the maturation of judgment.

SOME ASPECTS OF ADOLESCENT DEVELOPMENT HAVE BEEN OCCURRING EARLIER

It is crucial to consider the various components of adolescence because there have been recent historical changes in the timing of (at least some aspects) of development, there now being an earlier onset of pubertal processes, particularly in females. FIGURE 2 provides data summarized by Rutter and colleagues[4] showing a great deal of historical evidence for changes in the *average* age of pubertal onset over the past century.

As shown, the age of menarche in Finland, Sweden, Norway, Italy, the UK and the United States between 1860 to 1960 has increased fairly markedly. (It is important to note here that menarche is a relatively *late* event in female puberty.) Individuals are usually at Tanner Stage 4 by the time menarche occurs, so the biological cascade has begun years earlier. Thus, when we talk about adolescence, we're not just talking about teenage years, but about this interval that often begins with a cascade of hormone changes by 9–12 years of age, with most of the physical changes of puberty often complete by the middle of the teen age years.

FIGURE 3 shows some more recent data in the U.S. on the early start of pubertal maturation. This study by Herman-Giddens and colleagues examinined a representative sample of 17,000 girls in pediatric practices. FIGURE 3 shows the number of girls at age 7 and 8 years of age that were at Tanner Stage 2 or above in breast or pubic hair development. It shows that by 7 years of age 7 % of European American, and 27% of African American, were already at Tanner 2—a stage that the level of estrogens or adrenal androgens had caused the body to develop breast tissue and/or pubic hair. By 8 years of age 47% of the African American girls were at Tanner 2! Therefore, when we talk about adolescence as an interval of development that begins with pubertal maturation, it is quite misleading to use the common convention of interchanging the word "teenager" and adolescent.

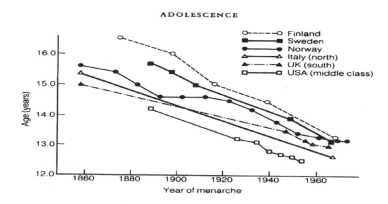

FIGURE 2. Age at menarche, 1860–1970. (Data from Tanner.[9])

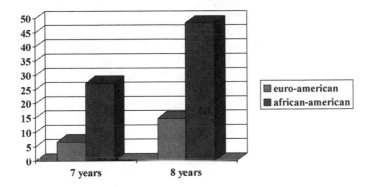

FIGURE 3. Percentage of girls who have reached at least Tanner State 2 of breast and/ or pubic hair by ages of 7 and 8.

ADOLESCENCE: AN ANTHROPOLOGICAL PERSPECTIVE

The past 150 years have witnessed a quiet revolution in human development that still sweeps across the globe today: children nearly everywhere are growing faster, reaching reproductive and physical maturity at earlier ages, and achieving larger adult sizes than perhaps ever in human history.
—CAROL M WORTHMAN, PH.D.

In our conceptualization of adolescence as the interval beginning with the physical changes of puberty and ending with the assumption of adult social roles, it becomes clear that this period of adolescent development has undergone a notionally major expansion in recent history. Adolescence is much broader and longer than the teenage years alone. It now stretches, in many cases across more than a decade, with pubertal onset often beginning by 9 to 12 years of age and adult roles delayed until the early twenties.

These changes have been well recognized and discussed by many people in the field, including Carol Worthman, an anthropologist who has studied puberty around the world. Also, Alice Schlegel and Herbert Barry[5] quantified basic aspects of puberty, adolescence, and the transition to adult roles in 187 different societies and summarized their findings in a book that is a fascinating read for anyone interested in adolescent development. Their book, in addition to being rich in anecdotes and cross-cultural observations about adolescence, also contains quantified summaries of key variables using well-defined measures. These data show that the majority of these societies have a developmental period that we could recognize as adolescence—conceptualized as a transition from the status of a child to that of an adult. Moreover, in many societies, the end of childhood was clearly demarcated by some sort of ritual. The onset of adult status in traditional societies was usually defined in terms of marriage, work roles, hunting, owning property, becoming a parent, or taking on some other specific adult role.

They found that in most traditional societies the interval between puberty and achieving adult status was relatively brief. Marriage among girls occurred within 2 years of the onset of puberty in 63% of the 186 societies studied. Among boys, where the ability to take a wife could require a specific level of achievement, such as making a first kill on a hunt, or developing a specific set of skills that increased the economic ability to provide for a family, the interval was significantly longer than for females, but still 64% of the males were married within 4 years of puberty. Thus, the adolescent interval between puberty and adult roles typically occupied a 2- to 4-year period in the majority of these societies.

Puberty versus Adult Social Roles in Contemporary Society

The situation in many contemporary societies is in sharp contrast to the data from traditional societies. While puberty is occurring earlier in many industrial societies, marriage and other adult roles are often delayed. In the U.S., the average age of menarche is now at age 12, while the average age of first marriage is 26—a 14-year transition, as opposed to the 2–4-year interval typical in females in the majority of traditional societies. This temporal elongation reflects not only the increasingly earlier development of puberty over the past 100 years, but also the increasingly longer time to marriage. In 1970 in the U.S. the timing of first marriage was age 21 for women and 23 for men; by the 2000 census, this had changed to ages 26 and 27, respectively.

A similar set of changes have occurred in other contemporary societies. In Japan, for example, the average age of menarche has decreased 4 years over the past century (from an average of 16.5 years in 1875 to an average of 12.2 years in 1975), while the average age at first marriage in Japan has increased to 26 years for women and 28.4 for men.

This is not simply a matter of changing attitudes about marriage. If one looks at other indices of adult social roles—starting careers, owning a home, choosing to become parents—it is apparent that these are also occurring more than a decade after puberty in most cases.

So, for most of human human history, adolescence has occupied a relatively brief time in individual and societal human development, lasting typically 2 to 4 years. Currently, however, it has stretched out into period that lasts 8 to 15 (or more) years in many contemporary societies.

This expansion of the period of adolescence has some advantages: Several types of opportunities are created by this prolonged interval—it permits adolescents more time to learn complex skills and to develop a variety of capabilities prior to taking on the constraints and demands of adult responsibilities. More time is available for formal education, for learning sports and arts, and for exploring a range of possible career choices; and it allows an individual more opportunities to explore different friendships, peer groups, and romantic relationships that may or may not lead to marriage. But stretching out these developmental processes does not come without costs and vulnerabilities, including the broad range of behavioral and emotional health risks that have an impact on so many youth.

HISTORICAL CHANGES IN ADOLESCENCE:
IMPLICATIONS REGARDING THE BRAIN

These historical changes and the relative temporal expansion of the period of adolescence has important implications for understanding the component processes of adolescent brain development. The earlier onset of puberty results in a relatively earlier activation of *some* neurobehavioral changes, raaising several provocative questions about the interrelationship with components of adolescent development that occur on a different time scale—particularly those aspects of adolescent brain development that continue to undergo important maturational changes long after puberty is over. In other words, it appears that the rapid prolongation of adolescence as a developmental period has also contributed to alterations in the timing and interrelationship of components of adolescent brain maturation.

The key principle here can be illustrated by a couple of clinical cases. Consider the cognitive development of an 8-year-old girl with a simple case of precocious puberty. There is no reason to expect that the early activation of reproductive maturity would create a parallel advance of cognitive development; even if physical development, sexual maturation, and bone age are consistent with those of a 14-year-old girl, she will still still have an 8-year- old's level of experience, reasoning ability, logic, and other mental capabilities. In a similar way, consider the relative cognitive development of two otherwise normal 15-year-old boys, if one has already progressed physically through puberty and looks like a mature young man, while the other is still pre-pubertal with the physical development of a young boy. Is there any basis for assuming the more physically mature 15-year-old would show any specific areas of mental ability superior to the prepubertal boy's? In fact, there is a fairly extensive clinical literature that shows that most patients who are clinically delayed in the onset of puberty—or even among those who fail to go through puberty at all because of an endocrine disorder or physical intervention, as done to the *castrati* to provide high voices for a church choir—most aspects of mental development proceed in a completely normal manner. In other words, most elements of cognitive development show a trajectory that follows age and experience rather than the timing of puberty.

This principle has direct implications regarding the recent historical changes in pubertal timing. While some neurobehavioral changes (such as drives and emotional changes at puberty) are occurring at earlier ages, many other aspects of neurocognition progress slowly, and continue to mature long after puberty is over. Thus, the recent expansion of the adolescent period has also stretched out the interval between the onset of emotional and motivational changes activated by puberty, and the completion of cognitive development—the maturation of self-regulatory capacities and skills that are continuing to develop long after puberty has occurred.

PUBERTY AND BRAIN DEVELOPMENT

Given these changes in the timing of puberty and the expansion of adolescent maturation more broadly, it is important to consider what is known about puberty and brain development. First we know that some brain changes *precede* the pubertal increases in hormones. Pubertal maturation *starts* in the brain, some neural changes leading directly to the hormonal cascade at the beginning of puberty. I will refer to these as *upstream* changes as they occur prior to pubertal changes in the body.

Second, clearly there are some brain changes that are the *consequence* of pubertal processes. Once these hormone levels increase in the body, there is some feedback to specific brain systems, what I will call *downstream* changes since they occur as a consequence of the physical development and accompanying increase in hormone levels affecting the brain. One recent area of research regarding pubertal hormone effects on the brain has focused on the discovery of a new type of estrogen receptor in several regions of the brain—the beta-estrogen receptor; this will be discussed in much greater detail by Judy Cameron in Part 3 of this book. This system appears to be the mechanism for some of the behavioral or emotional changes resulting from the increased reproductive hormones of puberty, such as changes in serotonergic regulation mediated by beta-estrogen.[6]

Third, some aspects of adolescent brain maturation and cognitive development appear to be independent of pubertal processes and continue long after puberty is over.

The existence of these three different categories of links—upstream changes, downstream changes, and puberty-independent maturational changes—makes it clear that changes in pubertal timing create the *potential for internal dys-synchrony* among the components of adolescent brain maturation.

This also highlights the importance of considering *puberty-specific changes* in neurobehavioral maturation within a broader range of developmental changes across adolescence, which has important conceptual as well as methodological implications. In most studies in adolescents, these domains become confounded in ways that do not allow investigators to disentangle these effects. Many studies do not contain any measures of puberty; and even among those that collect some data about level of reproductive maturity, these measures of pubertal development, age, and social experience can be correlated in ways that make it impossible to examine the effects of age versus [ubertal maturation. There are, however, some interesting and provocative exceptions— studies that have been designed to disentangle puberty-specific changes that point to important issues and questions. Examples of research showing puberty-specific changes in affective domains are discussed next.

PUBERTY-SPECIFIC CHANGES IN AFFECTIVE DOMAINS

A study that has found behavioral changes that are specifically linked to puberty is that of Martin and colleagues,[7] who investigated the development of smoking and other risk-taking behaviors in adolescents. They included a measure of sensation seeking as well as measures of pubertal maturation in a sample with a relatively narrow age band: most subjects were 11 to 13 years old. Interestingly, within this age range, there were no significant correlations between age and sensation seeking— the older kids were no more likely to rate themselves as higher in their desire for thrilling or exciting experiences. However, there was a *significant positive correlation between pubertal maturation and sensation seeking* in both the boys and girls, and this was associated with greater risk taking and smoking. Among individuals of similar age, those who were more advanced in puberty were more likely to seek exciting experiences and to show risk-taking behavior.

TABLE 1. Developmental   domains   having   evidence   for   puberty-specific maturational changes

- romantic motivation
- sexual interest
- emotional intensity
- changes in sleep/arousal regulation
- appetite
- risk for affective disorders in females
- increase in risk taking, novelty seeking, sensationseeking (reward-seeking)

There are several developmental domains where there is evidence for *puberty-specific* maturational changes (TABLE 1). It is important to emphasize the need for more studies that are designed to examine (and disentangle) age and pubertal effects. However, from the handful of studies that have succeeded in examining some of these issues, some themes are emerging. The existing evidence indicates that there are several domains that seem to link more strongly to puberty than age during adolescent development, and most of these are *affective* measures—related to emotion, motivation, arousal, and appetitive or drive systems. These include pubertal changes in romantic and sexual interests, mood lability, emotional intensity, reward seeking and/or sensation seeking, changes in sleep/arousal regulation, increased appetite, and risk for affective disorders among girls.

Some important caveats should be mentioned here: Remember that there is a wide range of individual differences with respect to these pubertal changes. Many adolescents show very subtle changes in the direction of sensation seeking, and these problems are easily managed without any reckless behavior or emotional problems. On the other hand, taken together, this pattern of findings suggests that the primary puberty-specific changes are related to activation of the strong drives, appetites, emotional intensity, and sensation seeking that occurs at puberty. In addition, this set of adolescent changes is occurring relatively earlier as puberty is occurring relatively earlier. In contrast, most aspects of cognitive development—including reasoning, logic, and capacities for self-regulation of emotions and drives—are still developing slowly, and continue long after puberty is over.

STARTING THE ENGINES WITH AN UNSKILLED DRIVER

This metaphor—of an early activation of strong "turbo-charged" feelings with a relatively unskilled set of "driving skills" or cognitive abilities to modulate strong emotions and motivations—has been used a great deal by our ADAPT Research Network.[8] This metaphor is one way to capture the relatively earlier timing of these "igniting passions" at puberty—passions that refer not only to romantic and sexual interests, but also to the intensification in many kinds of goal-directed behaviors that emerge in adolescence. Early adolescence is a time when many teenagers become passionate about a particular sport, hobby, music, art, or literature. It is also a time of passionate commitments to idealistic causes.

These motivational and emotional changes at puberty represent a relatively understudied aspect of adolescent development. Yet, this is an enormously important dimension of understanding the neurobehavioral underpinnings of vulnerability in adolescence. It is crucial because this early activation of intense motivations and passions, which can be channeled into a wide range of activities and types of pursuits, can be shaped by the particular experiences at this point of life. Moreover, when these passions flare up to intense levels, these young peoplet often have not yet developed the skills that can harness these strong feelings (nor have they yet achieved the neural maturation of underlying control systems).

Being a responsible adult requires developing self-control over behavior and emotions to appropriately inhibit and modify behaviors—despite strong feelings— to avoid terrible consequences. It requires that individuals be capable of initiating and carrying out a specific sequence of steps toward a long-term goal even though it may be difficult (or boring) to persist in these efforts. Adolescents need to learn to navigate complex social situations despite strong competing feelings. Skills in self-regulation of emotion and complex behavior aligned to long-term goals must be developed. These self-regulatory processes are complex and mastering behavioral skills involves neurobehavioral systems served by several parts of the brain. The ability to integrate these multiple components of behavior—cognitive *and* affective—in the service of long-term goals involves neurobehavioral systems that are among the last regions of the brain to fully mature. This point is a central focus of this symposium.

We come back to the question of what happens to cognitive development when puberty occurs earlier. A strong body of work suggests that most measures of cognitive development correlate with age and experience—not sexual maturation. Measures of planning, logic, reasoning ability, inhibitory control, problem solving, and understanding consequences are probably not puberty-linked, but depend on age and experience. And these abilities clearly continue to develop long after puberty is over as many aspects of brain development continue to occur long after puberty is over. Jay Giedd and other presenters in Part 2 describe these issues in much greater detail. Elizabeth Sowell and her colleagues at UCLA also have contributed a great deal of data (and conceptual and methodological advances) in these areas. Taken together, a large body of work has shown that structural maturational changes in the brain are continuing long after the interval of puberty is over.

So we return to the metaphor of turbo-charging the engines of a fully mature "car" beloinging to an unskilled driver, whose navigational skills are not yet fully in place. The pubescent youth has several years with a sexually mature body and brain systems that are activated for sexual and romantic interest and passions, but a relatively immature set of neurobehavioral systems for self-control and affect regulation. This "disconnect" predicts risk for a broad set of behavioral and emotional problems, and not just through recklessness, risk taking, and sensation seeking, but also in just navigating complex social situations and attempting to master strong emotions. The affective disorders of adolescence are as informed by this model as are more impulsive and externalizing disorders. Adolescence proves to be a difficult period to develop positive abilities to use strategies, make plans, set goals, learn the social rules, and navigate ambiguous situations as the cognitive and emotional systems are integrated.

THE DEVELOPMENT OF AFFECT REGULATION

I would like to mention here the links to one line of investigation—the development of affect regulation in adolescence—which has been the focus of investigation in my laboratory and of the ADAPT nterdisciplinary research network. First, it is important to delineate what is meant by the term *affect regulation.* It is not simply the process of experiencing and/or expressing emotions, but rather involves controlling one's feelings—modulating them in *adaptive* ways in order to achieve goals, to act with the norms of social rules and expectations and in ways that *support* rather than interfere with decision-making. Several investigative teams are beginning to address some of these issues of emotion and decision-making, including the role of strong emotions during adolescence. The term "hot cognition" refers to the process of thinking under conditions of high arousal and/or strong emotion, as opposed to "cool cognition," thinking under conditions of low arousal and calm emotions.

Adolescents often appear to be relatively good at making decisions under conditions of low arousal and cool emotions, this same highly intelligent youth, under intense emotional arousal, can have a much more difficult time making a responsible can experience a much more difficult time making a responsible choice. This leads, then, to another set of pragmatic questions: at what age (or based on what maturational criteria) should society *expect* individuals to make reliable independent decisions?—and be held legally responsible for these choices? As will be discussed later, Laurence Steinberg and several of his colleagues have been grappling with legal and scientific aspects to these questions. What if the average 15-year-old is capable, under "cool" conditions, of understanding the consequences of his behavior in a way that is comparable to that of adults, but is more emotionally reactive to irrational influences under conditions of "hot" cognition? How should we interpret data that show that a particular 16-year-old has adult capabilities to use logic and understand the consequences of his behavior, if we observe him, when in a group of friends, making reckless choices that the average 9-year-old would say was a pretty dumb thing to do? The point is that the age at which one has the ability to understand cognitively that a particular course of action is wrong may not be the same age as having reliable self-control over his strong emotions "hijacking" his decision-making.

There is much ambiguity and controversy in state, national, and even international policies about when society should allow individuals to make which type of decisions as adults. Why is that a young person is not able to drive a car until 16, vote until 18, drink alcohol until 21, rent a car from a commercial agency until 25, but, in some states, can stand trial for murder at age 12 or 13? At what age should youth be free to make decisions about their own health risks—such as smoking or having (or refusing) an operation, or having an abortion? At what age should he or she be able to decide to quit school, join the armed services, or get married? At what age should he or she be free to make potentially self-destructive choices such as body piercing, tattoos, acting in pornographic films, or gambling?

Leaving aside the personal and political controversies that such questions often stir up, the compelling issue for this symposium focuses on the potential for *science* to contribute to these important debates. Scientific study can shed light and offer rational approaches to these questions. If science can provide clear evidence for an immaturity of neural systems that affect decision making or abilities to regulate affect in adolescence—and if there are objective criteria for assessing the level of maturation that are not simply based on an arbitrary number of birthdays—science can be said to be making very important contributions to the legal, ethical, and moral questions about adolescent responsibility.

SOCIAL CONTEXTS AND ADULT SCAFFOLDING OF ADOLESCENT EXPERIENCE

During this period of gradual and inconsistent emergence of skills and knowledge needed to take on adult roles and decisions—and the still maturing neurobehavioral systems that undergird these skills—there is a need for a social context that can provide the appropriate amount of support to adolescents. It is crucial for adolescents have the appropriate social *scaffolding*—the right balance of monitoring and interest from parents, teachers, coaches and other responsible adults—in which to develop the skills of self-control while still being afforded sufficient support and protection. Ideally this scaffolding should, gradually fade, allowing adolescents to make increasingly independent decisions without placing them in situations that they are not yet ready to handle. Clearly, this is an ideal scenario that far too many adolescents— especially those in high-risk social contexts—never experience. Ann Masten has noted that adult monitoring is all too frequently and too prematurely withdrawn during this vulnerable period, leaving the adolescent to have to navigate situations alone or with peers at a relatively early age. This kind of mismatch between biological maturity, without equivalent cognitive-emotional maturity, in a sometimes dangerous social context and with only minimal adult supervision, plays a part in creating a great deal of vulnerability for youth in our society.

At the conference on which this book is based, we had the opportunity to view excerpts from a recent movie called "Thirteen" that illustrate these issues. This movie was co-written by a 13-year-old (who is also one of the actors in the film) along with the director. It captures, among other things, the intensity and abruptness, of making the transition from a period of playing with Barbie dolls and stuffed animals to an urban world of a teenager plunging into a confrontation with drugs, sex, and the exciting, but highly destructive allure of reckless adventure. It is a distressing clip— and a disturbing movie— which is worth seeing by anyone who wants to witness an example of the real-world difficulties facing so many early adolescents in contemporary society—a movie that raises many provocative questions about the dangers of this period of suddenly igniting passions that we have been talking about.

THE ADOLESCENT BRAIN: A NATURAL TINDERBOX

The natural adolescent inclinations toward novelty, arousal, and excitement that emerge in association with puberty create an emotional tinderbox in which passions—both negative and positive—are ignited. This creates both a great deal of vulnerability among the young as well as a great opportunity to harness these emotions in the service of positive goals. And young people are often eager to face a great deal of risk to achieve the high-intensity feelings that can be so appealing in adolescence.

Puberty itself seems to increase the appetite for a specific type of emotional experience: surges of arousal and cravings for exhilaration. This type of appetite even seems to feed on itself, as it moves behavior toward seeking yet more and more arousal and stimulation.

Fortunately, these emotional and motivational changes at puberty—these igniting passions—do not lead only to to bad outcomes: Sex, drugs, loud music, and reckless behavior are not the *only* ways to activate the kinds of high-intensity feelings that are so appealing to adolescents. The efforts necessary to achive a goal or to face a challenge can also become sources of positive, high-intensity feelings. And struggling to overcome adversity or to master a skill can also lead to inspired actions and the high-intensity feeling that can come from achieving a much-desired goal.

So these igniting passions can be aligned in *healthy* ways—in the service of higher goals. Feelings of passion are rooted in the same deep brain systems as biologic drives and the primitive elements of emotion. Yet passion intertwines with the highest levels of human endeavor: passion for ideas and ideals, passion for beauty, passion to create music or art. And the passion to succeed in a sport, business, or politics, and passion toward a person, activity, object, or pursuit can also inspire transcendent feelings.

One of the most important questions facing parents, teachers, clinicians treating adolescents, political leaders, and those of conducting science that can inform social policyis: *how* are adolescent passions being captured in modern society? How are these new intense motivational systems in the adolescent brain being shaped in ways that are healthy or unhealthy? For example, the emergence of religious zeal in adolescents can fuel positive humanistic efforts to feed the poor and care for the sick, yet, it can also lead to dogmatic attitudes, intolerance, or rash polical action. Igniting passions can lead to idealistic efforts by youth who strive to make the world a better place or these passions can be captured by a negatively charismatic figure like Adolf Hitler or Osama bin Laden, who instead inspire destructive, despairing and evil deeds.

IGNITING PASSIONS IN ADOLESCENCE: A PERIOD OF SCIENTIFIC OPPORTUNITIES

These questions about emotional and motivational changes in adolescence have profound implications for the future of youth in our society, and represent part of the reason greater scientific detail is needed to understand these maturational processes and to provide further insights regarding the types of experiences needed to shape these igniting passions in ways that serve larger humanistic goals.

This igniting of passions—this activation of overwhelming levels of emotion that can transiently block the capacity to think, reason, and proceed logically according to consequences—has an underlying neural circuitry. There are several important scientific questions about the neurobehavioral changes underpinning this temporary loss of the ability to plan and to reason. Adolescence is a developmental period when new links are established in the brain that create connections between affective and cognitive processes. For example, adolescence is a time for developing a new sense of self and identity along with the cognitive ability to imagine oneself in the future in ways that can create positive emotions (picturing oneself as highly successful) as well as linked to negative affective appraisals (imaging the consequences of failure or humiliation). This cross-temporal processing of thoughts and images can create strong feelings in adolescence that are capable of altering motivation. Most importantly, many of these more complex cognitive-emotional experiences are happening for the first time in adolescence. These new experiences are creating new patterns of neural connections. Understanding more of the details of how and when these are occurring can create opportunities for investigators to identify ways to intervene in high-risk youth at a time when some of these systems are more plastic to change. Scientific knowledge can thus be brought to bear in preventing some of the destructive negative spirals that can begin in adolescence.

Adolescence thus offers a period of scientific opportunity: it's a chance to identify key developmental processes in puberty and adolescence that are amenable to intervention. We need to learn what *kinds* of interventions will work with *which* problems and what is the best *time* to apply them. Increasingly, the advances in basic neuroscience, genetics, developmental psychology, and the use of animal models will be combined with clinical and social policy work to implement change and point to the key questions that should be priorities for the more basic investigators. My hope for this symposium is that it will spark a series of dialogues across these disciplines to integrate current knowledge, refine our conceptual models, and to focus the directions of future work that will—in the long run—have a large positive impact on the health and well being of the youth in our society.

We search, on our journeys,
for a self to be, for other selves to love,
and for work to do...
We find by losing. We hold on by letting go.
—FREDERICK BUECHNER

REFERENCES

1. ARNETT, J.J. 1999. Adolescent storm and stress, reconsidered. Am. Psychol. **54:** 317–326.
2. STEINBERG, L. *et al.* 2004. The study of developmental psychopathology in adolescence: integrating affective neuroscience with the study of context. *In* Handbook of Developmental Psychopathology. D. Cicchetti, Ed. John Wiley. New York.
3. MARTIN, C.A. *et al.* 2002. Sensation seeking, puberty, and nicotine, alcohol, and marijuana use in adolescence. J. Am. Acad. Child Adolesc. Psychiatry **41:** 1495–1502.
4. RUTTER, M. 1993. Developing Minds: Challenge and Continuity Across the Life Span. Harper Collins. New York.
5. SCHLEGEL, A. & H. BARRY. 1991. Adolescence: An Anthropological Inquiry. The Free Press. New York.
6. BETHEA, C.L. *et al.* 2002. Diverse actions of ovarian steroids in the serotonin neural system. Front. Neuroendocrinol. **23:** 41–100.
7. DAHL, R.E. *et al.* 2003. ADAPT Research Network. University of Pittsburgh: Pittsburgh. R24 MH 67346.
8. TANNER, J.M. 1989. Foetus into Man, 2nd ed. Castelmead Publications.
9. SPEAR, L.P. 2000. The adolescent brain and age-related behavioral manifestations. Neurosci. Biobehav. Rev. **24:** 417–463.
10. MASTEN, A.S., J.J. HUBBARD, S.D. GEST, *et al.* 1999. Competence in the context of adversity: pathways to resilience and maladaptation from childhood to late adolescence. Dev. Psychopathol. **11:** 143–169.

Adolescent Brain Development and Animal Models

LINDA PATIA SPEAR

Psychology Department, State University of New York at Binghamton, Binghamton, New York 13902, USA

ABSTRACT: Research examining brain development during adolescence is escalating rapidly along multiple dimensions, as illustrated by the remarkable diversity of trans-disciplinary work shown in this symposium. Ontogenetic transitions characteristics of adolescence are common among mammalian species. Although no other species demonstrates the full complexity of brain and behavioral function seen in human adolescents, adolescence appears to be a highly conserved developmental stage, its characteristics sculpted to meet common evolutionary pressures that include the avoidance of inbreeding at this time of sexual emergence. Numerous similarities are found between human adolescents and adolescents of other species in terms of developmental history and genetic constraints, as well as neurobehavioral and physiological characteristics. These similarities provide face and construct validity to support use of animal models as tools for the study of adolescence and the unique opportunities and vulnerabilities afforded by this developmental transition.

KEYWORDS: adolescent brain development; puberty

This is an exciting time for research in the area of adolescent brain development. Owing to recent achievements in technology, advances in neuroscience, and policy support, research into adolescence and the transformations occurring in the adolescent brain is escalating rapidly. The Web of Science citations on these topics over the past decade and a half (FIG. 1) show that adolescent-related publications began an upward trajectory beginning in the early 1990s that continues today. Publications focusing on the adolescent brain likewise began to increase in the early 1990s, with a second escalation beginning around 1998. It is hoped that the research presented at this symposium will serve as a catalyst for further advances in our understanding of brain development during adolescence and of the unique vulnerabilities and opportunities this important ontogenetic transition presents.

It is our hope that the reader of this book can sense the excitement that was generated at the meeting upon which this volume is based. During the course of the meeting, points of similarity emerged and synergies were created, sometimes unexpectedly, across the divergent fields of research. The papers in this volume attest to the considerable breadth of inquiry and to the exciting progress being made.

Address for correspondence: Linda Patia Spear, Ph.D., Psychology Department, Box 6000, Binghamton University, New York, NY 13902-6000. Voice: 607-777-2825; fax: 607-777-6418. lspear@binghamton.edu

Ann. N.Y. Acad. Sci. 1021: 23–26 (2004). © 2004 New York Academy of Sciences.
doi: 10.1196/annals.1308.002

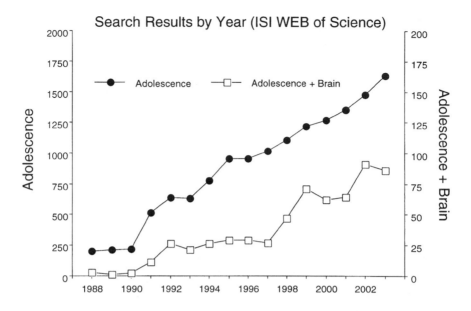

FIGURE 1. Yearly number of publications listed in the Web of Science under the key words "adolescence" (*left axis*) and "adolescent + brain" (*right axis*).

As emphasized by Ron Dahl in his keynote address,[1] an important underlying premise of this meeting is its trans-disciplinarity. Within each of the areas of focus, research was included that dealt with human adolescents as well as a variety of animal models. Implicit in this approach is the recognition that developing mammals of many species undergo a similar transition from the dependence of youth to sexual maturity and the (relative) independence of adulthood. During this transition, puberty occurs and adolescents are faced with the challenge of acquiring the necessary skills to permit survival away from parental caretakers, and of acquiring the social circumstances to permit propagation of the species. As demonstrated throughout this volume, there are sometimes surprising coherences between the fundamental neurobehavioral characteristics of human adolescents and adolescent animals of other species undergoing this developmental transition.

Although ontogenetic transitions characteristic of adolescence can be identified in non-human animals ranging from primates to rodents, no other species demonstrates anywhere near the full complexity of human brain and behavior during adolescence (or at any other time in life, for that matter). Numerous areas of adolescent functioning in humans are not amenable to study in animal models (to mention but two: the impact of advertising on body image, and cultural differences in perception of adolescence as a life stage). Hence the appropriateness of any given animal model varies considerably with the aspect of human adolescence under investigation. Studies in laboratory animals provide the opportunity for systematic experimental manipulation of environmental and genetic variables, yet the simplicity of these variables, the dependent measures of focus and their neural substrates can challenge applicability to human adolescents. Nevertheless, considerable similarities are seen between human adolescents and adolescents of other mammalian species in terms of developmental history and genetic constraints, as well as their behavioral, neural and hormonal characteristics, similarities that provide sufficiently promising evidence of face and construct validity to support the use of animal models as tools for the study of applicable aspects of this developmental transition (see Ref. 2 for review).

A number of adolescent-typical behaviors—as well as their neural modulators—are seen across adolescents of a number of species, and may represent highly conserved, developmentally expressed genetic features.[2] Among the common hallmarks of adolescence are changes in the focus of social interactions, with adolescents of a variety of species showing increased social interactions with peers, sometimes associated with increases in parental conflict.[3-5] Adolescents from a broad range of species including humans also exhibit increases in behaviors classified as risk taking or sensation seeking.[6-8] These behaviors may serve to facilitate the adolescent transition to maturity. For example, peer-directed interactions serve to develop new skills and social support,[9,10] whereas increases in risk taking have been suggested to serve a number of potentially adaptive functions, including increasing the possibility of reproductive success in males of a variety of species, including humans.[11] Risk taking and shifts toward greater peer affiliation may also serve to facilitate the emigration of sexually maturing adolescents away from adults to whom they are genetically related. Such emigration is common to adolescents of one or both sexes of most mammalian species, and may have served evolutionarily to avoid the lower viability often associated with "inbreeding depression" or the expression of recessive genes that are lethal or otherwise reduce fitness in offspring produced from genetically related individuals.[12,13] The potential evolutionary significance of these behaviors could explain why risky behaviors have been conserved during adolescence despite the high cost, with mortality rates during adolescence (primarily driven at this age by these risky behaviors) greater than at most other ages across a variety of species including humans.[14,15]

As in human adolescence, it is difficult to determine the precise boundaries of adolescence when using animal models of this developmental transition, given the absence of single precipitating and terminating events. Likewise, as in humans, the timing of adolescence in various non-human species is influenced by maturational index as well as strain of animals and growth rate.[16] Even among the articles in this volume, you will see some variation across laboratories in the age ranges targeted for assessment during adolescence in a given species. For example, whereas the age range of postnatal days (P) 28–42 is often considered prototypic adolescence in the rat,[2] researchers interested in the earliest precursors of adolescence (that emerge first in female rats) may begin procedures as early as the conventional day of weaning, P21, while other researchers may extend the adolescent range for several weeks (to P55–60) based on criteria related to the last remnants of pubertal maturation in male rats.[17] To some extent, this variation in defined age ranges of adolescence may reflect the use of conservative age ranges when researchers want to assure that assessments are being conducted during the adolescent age range, with broader age ranges used when the intent is to ensure coverage across the entire breadth of adolescence. Adolescence is a time of multiple transitions, and young adolescents may differ in important ways from older adolescents within any of a variety of species.

What is clear at this early point in the study of adolescent brain development is that the brain undergoes considerable sculpting and remodeling during adolescence. What remains a challenge is to detail the extent of this restructuring, its functional ramifications, and the opportunities and vulnerabilities provided by this unique transition for the adolescent. To meet this challenge, converging data from a variety of trans-disciplinary approaches and study populations are needed. The work summarized in this book provides a good jump-start in this direction.

REFERENCES

1. DAHL, R.E. 2004. Adolescent brain development: a period of vulnerabilities and opportunities. Ann. N.Y. Acad. Sci. 1020: 1–??.
2. SPEAR, L.P. 2000. The adolescent brain and age-related behavioral manifestations. Neurosci. Behav. Rev. 24: 417–463.
3. CSIKSZENTMIHALYI, M., R. LARSON & S. PRESCOTT. 1977. The ecology of adolescent activity and experience. J. Youth Adolesc. 6: 281–294.
4. PRIMUS, R.J. & C.K. KELLOGG. 1989. Pubertal-related changes influence the development of environment-related social interaction in the male rat. Dev. Psychobiol. 22: 633–643.
5. STEINBERG, L. 1989. Pubertal maturation and parent-adolescent distance: an evolutionary perspective. In Advances in Adolescent Behavior and Development. G. R. Adams, R. Montemayor & T.P. Gullotta, Eds.: 71–97. Sage Publications. Newbury Park, CA.
6. ADRIANI, W., F. CHIAROTTI & G. LAVIOLA. 1998. Elevated novelty seeking and peculiar d-amphetamine sensitization in periadolescent mice compared with adult mice. Behav. Neurosci. 112: 1152–1166.
7. TRIMPOP, R.M., J.H. KERR & B. KIRKCALDY. 1999. Comparing personality constructs of risk-taking behavior. Pers. Individ. Dif. 26: 237–254.
8. DOUGLAS, L.A., E.I. VARLINSKAYA & L. SPEAR. 2003. Novel object place conditioning in adolescent and adult male and female rats: effects of social isolation. Physiol. Behav. 80: 317–325.
9. GALEF, B.G., JR. 1977. Mechanisms for the social transmission of food preferences from adult to weanling rats. In Learning Mechanisms in Food Selection. L.M. Barker, M. Best & M. Domjan, Eds.: 123–148. Baylor University Press. Waco, TX.
10. HARRIS, J.R. 1995. Where is the child's environment? A group socialization theory of development. Psychol. Rev. 102: 458–489.
11. WILSON, M. & M. DALY. 1985. Competitiveness, risk taking, and violence: the young male syndrome. Ethol. Sociobiol. 6: 59–73.
12. BIXLER, R.H. 1992. Why littermates don't: the avoidance of inbreeding depression. Annu. Rev. Sex Res. 3: 291–328.
13. MOORE, J. 1992. Dispersal, nepotism, and primate social behavior. Int. J. Primatol. 13: 361–378.
14. CROCKETT, C.M. & T.R. POPE. 1993. Consequences of sex differences in dispersal for juvenile red howler monkeys. In Juvenile Primates. M.E. Pereira & L.A. Fairbanks, Eds.: 104–118, 367–415. Oxford University Press. New York.
15. IRWIN, C.E., JR. & S.G. MILLSTEIN. 1992. Correlates and predictors of risk-taking behavior during adolescence. In Self-regulatory Behavior and Risk Taking: Causes and Consequences. L.P. Lipsitt & L.L. Mitnick, Eds.: 3–21. Ablex Publishing. Norwood, NJ.
16. KENNEDY, G.C. & J. MITRA. 1963. Body weight and food intake as initiating factors for puberty in the rat. J. Physiol. 166: 408–418.
17. ODELL, W.D. 1990. Sexual maturation in the rat. In Control of the Onset of Puberty. M.M. Grumbach, P.C. Sizonenko & M.L. Aubert, Eds.: 183–210. Williams and Wilkins. Baltimore, MD.

Risk Taking and Novelty Seeking in Adolescence

Introduction to Part I

ANN E. KELLEY, TERRI SCHOCHET, AND CHARLES F. LANDRY

Department of Psychiatry, University of Wisconsin-Madison Medical School, Madison, Wisconsin 53719, USA

ABSTRACT: Risk taking and novelty seeking are hallmarks of typical adolescent behavior. Adolescents seek new experiences and higher levels of rewarding stimulation, and often engage in risky behaviors, without considering future outcomes or consequences. These behaviors can have adaptive benefits with regard to the development of independence and survival without parental protection, but also render the adolescent more vulnerable to harm. Indeed, the risk of injury or death is higher during the adolescent period than in childhood or adulthood, and the incidence of depression, anxiety, drug use and addiction, and eating disorders increases. Brain pathways that play a key role in emotional regulation and cognitive function undergo distinct maturational changes during this transition period. It is clear that adolescents think and act differently from adults, yet relatively little is known about the precise mechanisms underlying neural, behavioral, and cognitive events during this period. Increased investigation of these dynamic alterations, particularly in prefrontal and related corticolimbic circuitry, may aid this understanding. Moreover, the investigation of mammalian animal models of adolescence—such as those examining impulsivity, reward sensitivity, and decision making—may also provide new opportunities for addressing the problem of adolescent vulnerability.

KEYWORDS: adolescence; reward; prefrontal cortex; development

Adolescence is the developmental period in animals during which the body and brain emerge from an immature state to adulthood.[1,2] This phase varies in length depending on the species, spanning from days or weeks in rodents to many years in humans. Adolescence traditionally has been primarily categorized by the distinct changes in secondary sexual characteristics that accompany puberty and sexual maturation. The organizational and activational effects of hormones and neuroendocrine events on development and behavior are relatively well characterized in mammals. However, what has received less attention are the specific alterations in brain development that accompany these neuroendocrine changes. Many dynamic cellular, molecular, and

Address for correspondence: Ann E. Kelley, Department of Psychiatry, University of Wisconsin-Madison Medical School, 6001 Research Park Boulevard, Madison, WI 53719. Voice: 608-262-1123.
aekelley@wisc.edu

Ann. N.Y. Acad. Sci. 1021: 27–32 (2004). © 2004 New York Academy of Sciences.
doi: 10.1196/annals.1308.003

anatomical modifications are taking place during this stage, contributing to the formation of the adult state. Moreover, this period of transition is marked by pronounced changes in cognition, behavior, and temperament.

Perhaps the greatest behavioral change observed in adolescence is in risk taking and novelty seeking, the focus of this section. These behaviors clearly have adaptive benefits but also render the adolescent more vulnerable to harm. In most mammalian species, the adolescent period is necessary to bridge the gap between complete dependence on parental protection and independence. Young animals venture out from the nest, motivated by a strong exploratory drive, an increased need for social and environmental stimulation, and the possibility of novel resources or opportunities. Behavioral changes and particular experiences that occur during this time may serve to provide juveniles with adaptive skills necessary to survive away from the protection of parents.

However, one of the greatest paradoxes of adolescence is that despite being a time of peak health and strength, it is associated with strongly increased morbidity and mortality compared to the rest of the life span.[3] During adolescence and young adulthood there is a disproportionately high mortality rate, caused primarily by automobile accidents associated with a higher likelihood of risk taking while driving. Indeed, fully three-quarters of deaths among teens are due to preventable causes.[4] Male adolescents and young adults are particularly at risk; young males are three times as likely as young females to die of preventable causes. This is also a time when novel experiences involving drugs, alcohol, and sexual behaviors are sought, and in a substantial majority of teens, risky behavior is viewed as exciting and rewarding. However, it is also clear that during this period young people become more susceptible to depression, suicide, eating disorders, and addiction. There are many determinants of the level of risk taking, ranging from individual personality, social or peer input, and environmental stressors. Although these behaviors may put adolescents at considerable risk for emotional and behavioral disorders, it is important to note that they may not be an entirely negative aspect of adolescent behavior, as increased risk taking and an altered response to novelty can be beneficial in learning new strategies for survival independent of the parents.

The adolescent behavioral profile involving risk taking and reward- or novelty seeking suggests that during this period there are critical developmental changes in brain pathways controlling emotional expression, cognitive and attentional functions, and reward sensitivity. Such a behavioral profile would likely involve corticolimbic circuitry, including prefrontal cortex, amygdala, ventral striatum, and the dopaminergic innervation of these structures (FIG. 1). Functions of the prefrontal cortex (PFC) in particular deserve focus. This brain region plays a key role—via interactions with other structures such as amygdala, striatum, and hypothalamus—in attention, decision making, emotional regulation, behavioral inhibition, and the ability to assess future outcomes of behavior. All of these functions are critical for decisions involving risk/reward trade-offs.[5]

There is considerable evidence for continued development in these pathways during adolescence and early adulthood.[6,7] For example, active myelination is still occurring, and the prefrontal cortex is the last brain region to undergo this process. As J. Giedd shows in this volume, connectivity is still maturing during this period: in the human prefrontal cortex there is increased myelination, declining synaptic density ("pruning"), decreasing grey-matter volumes, and increased prefrontal activa-

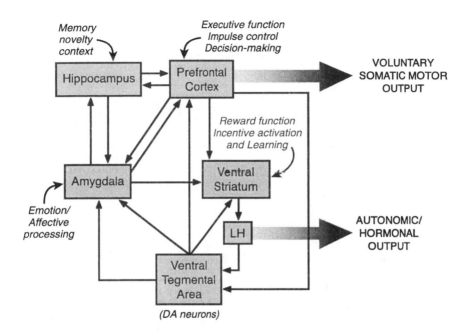

FIGURE 1. Brain pathways that play a key role in emotional regulation, cognitive function, and reward sensitivity undergo distinct maturational changes during the adolescent transition period. Altered or immature states in this neural circuitry and its inherent chemical signaling (e.g., dopamine and other monoamines, glutamate, neuropeptides, GABA) may underlie the increased risk taking and sensation seeking often associated with adolescence. Moreover, a dynamically changing substrate may be uniquely vulnerable to drugs of abuse, which can induce enduring neuroadaptive changes in these brain regions. LH, lateral hypothalamus; DA, dopamine.

tion.[8] In a monkey model, Lewis and colleagues have shown extensive synaptic pruning and distinct alterations both in the dopaminergic input and the intrinsic circuitry of the PFC.[9–11] A clear example of the dynamic anatomical alterations is further provided by the work of Cunningham and colleagues, who show that in the rat, the period corresponding to adolescence (postnatal days 25–45) is marked by a strong increase in amygdalo–prefrontal fiber innervation (FIG. 2).[12] These patterns suggest that the connectivity between a region critical for emotional learning (amygdala) and a region involved in executive decision making (PFC) is still being formed. Thus, it is clear that the teenage brain is very different from both the child and adult brain, and may display particular vulnerabilities to disruption by drugs, alcohol, and stress. Moreover, the perception and calculation of risk, with regard to risky behaviors such as drug taking, gambling, and sensation seeking likely involve a still immature substrate, particularly the PFC region and its connections. In this section, Laurence Steinberg discusses the cognitive consequences of this immature substrate, providing evidence for altered risk perception and assessment in human adolescents.[13]

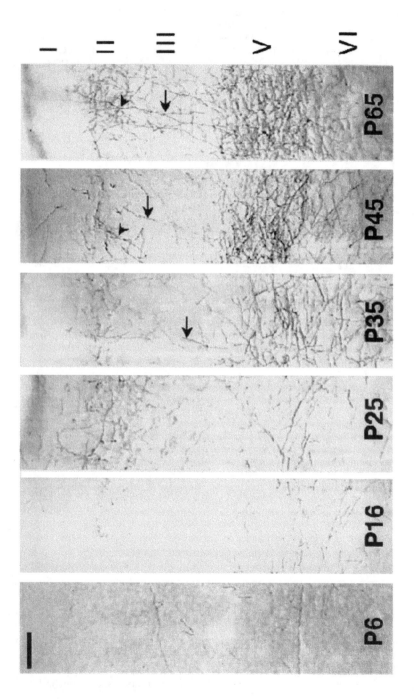

FIGURE 2. *See following page for legend.*

Animal models of adolescence can be useful in assessing behavioral and neuro-biological aspects of adolescent development. While it has yet to be extensively explored, the rat model has provided some important insights into understanding age-related behavioral and neural substrates of adolescence.[1,14] For example, like their human counterparts, adolescent rats display increased social interactions, play behavior and play fighting. They show increases in novelty seeking and hyperactivity, altered learning patterns, greater sensory sensitivity and distractibility, and altered responses and sensitivity to drugs such as nicotine and alcohol. In general, juvenile animals appear to have altered sensitivity to certain effects of amphetamine, cocaine, and nicotine.[15] For example, exposure of adolescent rodents to nicotine renders them more vulnerable to self-administering nicotine in adulthood, and such early exposure has long-lasting effects on molecular, neurophysiological, and behavioral measures.[16,17] Similar effects are found with cocaine and amphetamine.[18,19] Our own work shows that young rats are somewhat less sensitive to the long-term sensitizing and conditioning effects of nicotine compared with adults,[20] perhaps suggesting that nicotine has altered effects on neural plasticity in young rats.

An additional region of importance for neurobiological research on adolescence is the ventral striatum, also termed the nucleus accumbens. The nucleus accumbens has dense inputs from cortical regions controlling emotional and cognitive processes, such as from the amygdala and PFC, and is a major target of the mesolimbic dopaminergic system. This brain structure is critically involved in behaviors related to reward seeking, including food-, sex-, and drug-related behaviors.[21–23] A paper in this section by Rudolph Cardinal focuses on the same region in rats, suggesting that the nucleus accumbens (and presumably the circuitry in which it is embedded) plays a key role in behavioral impulsivity and "impulsive choice."[24] Rats with damage to this region tend to choose earlier, smaller rewards rather than wait for larger, delayed rewards. Further work with paradigms such as this one in adolescent animals may provide novel insights into altered reward seeking, and the development of increased self regulation over impulses. In this spirit, Michael Bardo, responding in a commentary at the end of this section, draws parallels between animal and human studies of the adolescent period, and offers questions and directions for future research on the neurobiology of this vulnerable period.[25]

REFERENCES

1. SPEAR, L.P. 2000. The adolescent brain and age-related behavioral manifestations. Neurosci. Biobehav. Rev. **24**: 417–463.

FIGURE 2. Growth of amygdalofugal fibers in the prefrontal cortex of the rat through different development stages (postnatal days 6 through 65). Image shows immunoperoxidase-labeled, biocytin-containing fibers that project from the amygdala, a brain region concerned with emotional processing and learning, to the prefrontal cortex, critical for executive control of adaptive behavior and regulation of emotions. With maturation, which occurs during the adolescent stage (in the rat approximately P35–P45), fiber ingrowth from the basolateral amygdala increases dramatically and assumes a bilaminar distribution, innervating primarily cortical layers II and V. Cortical layers are indicated by roman numerals. (From Cunningham *et al.*[9] Adapted by permission.)

2. STEINBERG, L. & A.S. MORRIS. 2001. Adolescent development. Annu. Rev. Psychol. **52:** 83–110.
3. RESNICK, M.D., P.S. BEARMAN, *et al.* 1997. Protecting adolescents from harm. Findings from the National Longitudinal Study on Adolescent Health. JAMA **278:** 823–832
4. CENTERS FOR DISEASE PREVENTION AND CONTROL. 1999. Fact sheet on adolescent injury.
5. BECHARA, A., H. DAMASIO & A.R. DAMASIO. 2000. Emotion, decision making and the orbitofrontal cortex. Cereb. Cortex **10:** 295–307.
6. GIEDD, J.N., J. BLUMENTHAL, *et al.* 1999. Brain development during childhood and adolescence: a longitudinal MRI study [letter]. Nature Neurosci. **2:** 861–863.
7. SOWELL, E.R., P.M. THOMPSON, *et al.* 1999. In vivo evidence for post-adolescent brain maturation in frontal and striatal regions. Nature Neurosci. **2:** 859-861.
8. GIEDD, J.N. 2004. Structural magnetic resonance imaging of the adolescent brain. Ann. N.Y. Acad. Sci. **1021:** 77–85.
9. CRUZ, D.A., S.M. EGGAN & D.A. LEWIS. 2003. Postnatal development of pre- and postsynaptic GABA markers at chandelier cell connections with pyramidal neurons in monkey prefrontal cortex. J. Comp. Neurol. **465:** 385–400.
10. ERICKSON, S.L. & D.A. LEWIS. 2002. Postnatal development of parvalbumin- and GABA transporter-immunoreactive axon terminals in monkey prefrontal cortex. J. Comp. Neurol. **448:** 186–202.
11. ROSENBERG, D.R. & D.A. LEWIS. 1995. Postnatal maturation of the dopaminergic innervation of monkey prefrontal and motor cortices: a tyrosine hydroxylase immunohistochemical analysis. J. Comp. Neurol. **358:** 383–400.
12. CUNNINGHAM, M., G.S. BHATTACHARYYA & F.M. BENES. 2002. Amygdalo-cortical sprouting continues into early adulthood: implications for the development of normal and abnormal function during adolescence. J. Comp. Neurol. **453:** 116–130.
13. STEINBERG, L. 2004. Risk taking in adolescence: What changes, and why? Ann. N.Y. Acad. Sci. **1021:** 51–58.
14. LAVIOLA, G., S. MACRI, *et al.* 2003. Risk-taking behavior in adolescent mice: psychobiological determinants and early epigenetic influence. Neurosci. Biobehav. Rev. **27:** 19–31.
15. ADRIANI, W., S. MACRI, *et al.* 2002. Peculiar vulnerability to nicotine oral self-administration in mice during early adolescence. Neuropsychopharmacology **27:** 212–224.
16. ADRIANI, W., S. SPIJKER, *et al.* 2003. Evidence for enhanced neurobehavioral vulnerability to nicotine during periadolescence in rats. J. Neurosci. **23:** 4712–4716.
17. SLAWECKI, C.J. & C.L. EHLERS. 2002. Lasting effects of adolescent nicotine exposure on the electroencephalogram, event related potentials, and locomotor activity in the rat. Dev. Brain Res. **138:** 15–25.
18. ANDERSEN, S.L., A. ARVANITOGIANNIS, *et al.* 2002. Altered responsiveness to cocaine in rats exposed to methylphenidate during development. Nature Neurosci. **5:** 13–14.
19. EHRLICH, M.E., J. SOMMER, E. CANAS & E.M. UNTERWALD. 2002. Periadolescent mice show enhanced DeltaFosB upregulation in response to cocaine and amphetamine. J. Neurosci. **22:** 9155–9159.
20. SCHOCHET, T., A.E. KELLEY & C. F. LANDRY. 2004. Differential behavioral effects of nicotine exposure in adolescent and adult rats. Psychopharmacology April.
21. CARDINAL, R.N., J.A. PARKINSON, J. HALL & B.J. EVERITT. 2002. Emotion and motivation: the role of the amygdala, ventral striatum, and prefrontal cortex. Neurosci. Biobehav. Rev. **26:** 321–352.
22. EVERITT, B.J., J.A. PARKINSON, *et al.* 1999. Associative processes in addiction and reward. The role of amygdala–ventral striatal subsystems. Ann. N.Y. Acad. Sci. **877:** 412–438.
23. KELLEY, A.E. 1999. Functional specificity of ventral striatal compartments in appetitive behaviors. Ann. N.Y. Acad. Sci. **877:** 71–90.
24. CARDINAL, R.N. *et al.* 2004. Limbic corticostriatal systems and delayed reinforcement. Ann. N.Y. Acad. Sci. **1021:** 33–50.
25. BARDO, M.T. 2004. High-risk behavior during adolescence: comments on Part I. Ann. N.Y. Acad. Sci. **1021:** 59–60.

Limbic Corticostriatal Systems and Delayed Reinforcement

RUDOLF N. CARDINAL, CATHARINE A. WINSTANLEY, TREVOR W. ROBBINS, AND BARRY J. EVERITT

Department of Experimental Psychology, University of Cambridge, Cambridge, United Kingdom

ABSTRACT: Impulsive choice, one aspect of impulsivity, is characterized by an abnormally high preference for small, immediate rewards over larger delayed rewards, and can be a feature of adolescence, but also attention-deficit/hyperactivity disorder (ADHD), addiction, and other neuropsychiatric disorders. Both the serotonin and dopamine neuromodulator systems are implicated in impulsivity; manipulations of these systems affect animal models of impulsive choice, though these effects may depend on the receptor subtype and whether or not the reward is signaled. These systems project to limbic cortical and striatal structures shown to be abnormal in animal models of ADHD. Damage to the nucleus accumbens core (AcbC) causes rats to exhibit impulsive choice. These rats are also hyperactive, but are unimpaired in tests of visuospatial attention; they may therefore represent an animal model of the hyperactive–impulsive subtype of ADHD. Lesions to the anterior cingulate or medial prefrontal cortex, two afferents to the AcbC, do not induce impulsive choice, but lesions of the basolateral amygdala do, while lesions to the orbitofrontal cortex have had opposite effects in different tasks measuring impulsive choice. In theory, impulsive choice may emerge as a result of abnormal processing of the magnitude of rewards, or as a result of a deficit in the effects of delayed reinforcement. Recent evidence suggests that AcbC-lesioned rats perceive reward magnitude normally, but exhibit a selective deficit in learning instrumental responses using delayed reinforcement, suggesting that the AcbC is a reinforcement learning system that mediates the effects of delayed rewards.

KEYWORDS: delayed reinforcement; impulsivity; impulsive choice; serotonin; dopamine; nucleus accumbens core; anterior cingulate cortex; medial prefrontal cortex; orbitofrontal cortex; basolateral amygdala; attention-deficit/hyperactivity disorder; drug addiction

INTRODUCTION

Adolescence is a time when people are prone to taking risks and seeking novel experiences. For the majority, this period is navigated safely and much useful experience is gained, but adolescence is a period of disproportionately high morbidity

Address for correspondence: Rudolf N. Cardinal, Department of Experimental Psychology, University of Cambridge, Downing Street, Cambridge CB2 3EB, UK. Voice: 44-1223-333587; fax: 44-1223-333554.

rudolf.cardinal@pobox.com

Ann. N.Y. Acad. Sci. 1021: 33–50 (2004). © 2004 New York Academy of Sciences.
doi: 10.1196/annals.1308.004

and mortality due to maladaptive behavior[132] (see Refs. 133 and 134). In particular, adolescents may make choices that are rewarding in the very short term, but poor in the longer term. This can be termed impulsive choice. Impulsive choice is one consequence of a failure to learn from or choose appropriately on the basis of delayed reinforcement. This chapter discusses the neurobiological systems that play a part in determining the effects of delayed reinforcement, and that may therefore contribute to impulsivity in adolescence or other pathological states in which impulsive choice features prominently.

Animals act to obtain rewards such as food, shelter, and sex. Sometimes, their actions are rewarded or reinforced immediately, but often this is not the case; to be successful, animals must learn to act on the basis of delayed reinforcement. They may also profit by choosing delayed reinforcers over immediate reinforcers, if the delayed reinforcers are sufficiently large. However, individuals differ in their ability to choose delayed rewards. Self-controlled individuals are strongly influenced by delayed reinforcement and choose large, delayed rewards in preference to small, immediate rewards; in contrast, individuals who are relatively insensitive to delayed reinforcement choose impulsively, preferring the immediate, smaller reward in this situation.[1] Impulsivity has long been recognized as a normal human characteristic[2] and in some circumstances it may be beneficial,[3] but impulsive choice contributes to deleterious states such as drug addiction[4–8] and attention-deficit/hyperactivity disorder (ADHD).[9,10]

Why are some individuals impulsive in their choices? To address these questions, the potential ways in which delayed reinforcement can affect action–outcome *learning* will be considered. Theories of instrumental *choice* involving delayed reinforcement will then be briefly considered. Interventional studies will be reviewed that examine the role of selected neurochemical systems—the serotonin and dopamine neuromodulator systems—and neuroanatomical regions—the nucleus accumbens core (AcbC), anterior cingulate cortex (ACC), medial prefrontal cortex (mPFC), orbitofrontal cortex (OFC), and basolateral amygdala (BLA)—in rats' ability to choose delayed rewards. Finally, the applications of these studies to ADHD and other disorders of impulsivity will be considered.

LEARNING TO RESPOND FOR DELAYED REINFORCEMENT

Instrumental, or operant, conditioning is a procedure in which the experimenter arranges a contingency between an animal's behavior (the operant) and a reinforcing outcome.[11] It creates multiple psychological representations, and therefore delayed reinforcement can affect learning in several ways. Early theorists considered the fundamental problem of delayed reinforcement: how a response can be strengthened by reinforcement that follows it. Hull postulated that the strength of a stimulus–response (S–R) association is inversely related to the delay between the response and the reinforcement.[12] Indeed, instrumental learning has repeatedly been shown to get worse as the response–reinforcer delay is increased.[13–15] An alternative view is that reinforcement never acts "backwards in time" to strengthen past responses; instead, reinforcement always strengthens the response that the animal is presently making. In this scenario, the effects of the delay arise because the longer the time between the response and reinforcement, the more likely it is that the animal has left the behavioral state it was in when it responded, so that some other state will be erroneously reinforced.[16–20] Moreover, since Hull's suggestion, it has been shown that when rats respond for reward, they may respond not only via a direct S–R ("habit") association—by which responses are automatically elicited by environmental stimuli as a consequence of the subject's past history of reinforcement—but also via a declarative, goal-directed system, through which the subject is aware of its goals and the actions that will lead to them.[21–24] Finally, learning can be improved if a distinctive environmental cue "bridges" the delay.[15] Such a cue, which reliably precedes delivery of the final reinforcer, can become associated with reinforcement, thereby becoming a conditioned reinforcer with the potential to affect choice on its own. Therefore, there are several systems that might be affected by delays to reinforcement. Subjects may fail to choose a worthwhile reinforcer when it is delayed because a stimulus–response, response–reinforcer, or stimulus–reinforcer association is weaker for the delayed alternative.

CHOOSING BETWEEN REINFORCERS: EFFECTS OF DELAY

Despite this potential complexity, studies of impulsive choice have produced some highly consistent results regarding the effects of delayed reinforcement in

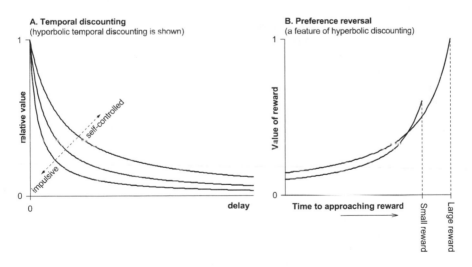

FIGURE 1. (**A**) Humans and other animals value delayed reinforcers less than immediate reinforcers; this is termed temporal discounting. The figure illustrates hyperbolic temporal discounting, governed by the equation *value = magnitude*/(1 + *K* × *delay*). Large values of *K* give the steepest curve (the most "impulsive" subjects). (**B**) Preference reversal. Given a choice between an early reward of value 0.6 and a later reward of value 1, hyperbolic discounting predicts that the larger reward will be chosen if the choice is made far in advance (toward the left of the graph). However, as time advances, there comes a time just before delivery of the small reward when preference reverses and the small reward is chosen. Figure adapted from Ainslie.[1]

well-defined choice paradigms. In a typical experimental situation, a subject chooses between an immediate, small reward or a large, delayed reward; the temporal discounting function quantifies the effect of the delay on preference. Early models of choice assumed an exponential model of temporal discounting, so that if V_0 is the value of a reinforcer delivered immediately, then the value of a reinforcer delivered after time t is $V_t = V_0 e^{-kt}$, where k quantifies an individual's tendency to "discount" the future (to value delayed rewards less). The exponential model makes intuitive sense, whether you consider the underlying process to be one in which the subject has a constant probability of "forgetting" its original response per unit time, one in which the "strength" of the response's representation decays to a certain proportion of its previous value at each time step, or one in which the subject behaves as if there is a constant probability of losing the delayed reward per unit of waiting time. Unfortunately, it is wrong; the exponential model has been emphatically rejected by experimental work with humans and other animals. Instead, temporal discounting appears to follow a *hyperbolic* or very similar discount function (FIG. 1A).[15,25–28] One interesting prediction that emerges from hyperbolic (but not exponential) models is that preference between a large and a small reward should be observed to reverse depending on the time that the choice is made (FIG. 1B), and such preference reversal is a reliable experimental finding.[29]

It is not known *why* hyperbolic discounting arises,[30] or what neuropsychological processes are responsible for it. Such discounting might, for example, result from poor knowledge of the contingencies between actions and their outcomes at long delays, or from weak S–R habits, or because subjects are perfectly aware that the delayed reward is available but assign a low value to it.[31] However, given the importance of impulsive choice in addiction[4–8] and ADHD,[9,10] a number of groups have studied the effects on impulsive choice of manipulating neurochemical and neuroanatomical systems implicated in these disorders.

NEUROCHEMICAL STUDIES OF IMPULSIVE CHOICE

Serotonin (5HT)

The suggestion that 5HT is involved in impulse control followed from the twin observations that drugs that suppress 5HT function appear to reduce behavioral inhibition, making animals more impulsive in a "motor" sense,[3,32] and that low levels of 5HT metabolites in cerebrospinal fluid are associated with impulsive aggression and violence in humans[33–36] and risk-taking behavior in monkeys.[37,38] Forebrain 5HT depletion leads to impulsive choice in a variety of paradigms[39–42] and has been suggested to steepen the temporal discounting function, such that delayed rewards lose their capacity to motivate or reinforce behavior.[39,43,44] The 5HT-depleted animal becomes hypersensitive to delays (or hyposensitive to delayed reward). As delayed rewards have unusually low value (utility), the animal consistently chooses small, immediate rewards over large, delayed rewards, a characteristic of impulsivity.[1] Conversely, increasing 5HT function with the 5HT indirect agonist fenfluramine decreases impulsive choice.[45] However, these results are not wholly clear-cut;[46,47] the effects of forebrain 5HT depletion to promote impulsive choice have sometimes been transient[41] or not observed,[48] and a nonselective 5HT antagonist has been observed to promote self-controlled choice.[49] 5HT may modulate impulsivity in different ways depending on the involvement of different receptor subtypes.[3,46] In humans, lowering 5HT levels via dietary tryptophan depletion[50–52] decreases levels of 5HT metabolites in cerebrospinal fluid,[53,54] an indirect indicator of brain 5HT levels, but although tryptophan depletion may increase "motor" impulsivity,[55] it has not been shown to increase impulsive choice in humans.[56] There are, of course, a number of substantial procedural differences between the tasks commonly used to assess impulsive choice in rats and humans (discussed below in the context of psychostimulants) and it is not presently known by what psychological mechanism 5HT depletion affects impulsive choice in rats.

Dopamine (DA)

Much of the interest in the relationship between DA and impulsivity stems from the discovery that amphetamine and similar psychostimulants are an effective therapy for ADHD.[57] Though these drugs have many actions, they are powerful releasers of DA from storage vesicles in the terminals of dopaminergic neurons, and prevent DA re-uptake from the synaptic cleft, potentiating its action.[58] Sagvolden and Sergeant have proposed that many features of ADHD, including preference for immediate reinforcement and hyperactivity on simple reinforcement schedules, are due to abnormally steep temporal discounting, and that this is due to a hypofunctional nucleus accumbens (Acb) DA system[9,10,59]—though whether ADHD is characterized by a hypodopaminergic or a hyperdopaminergic state, and how this might be "normalized" by psychostimulants, is controversial.[60–63] Many of the inferences regarding the neural abnormalities in children with ADHD have been drawn from studies of the spontaneously hypertensive rat (SHR), an inbred strain of rat that serves as an animal model of ADHD.[64–67] This rat exhibits pervasive hyperactivity and attention problems that resemble ADHD, exhibits a steeper "scallop" of responding on fixed-interval schedules of reinforcement (which can be interpreted as abnormally high sensitivity to immediate reinforcement),[65] is impulsive on measures of "execution impulsivity,"[68] and has a complex pattern of abnormalities in its DA system.[69–75]

Impulsive choice may reflect a lack of effectiveness of delayed reinforcement, and has been suggested to underlie ADHD, or at least subtypes of ADHD.[9,10,76,77] ADHD is amenable to treatment with psychomotor stimulant drugs,[57,78] suggesting that they might promote the choice of delayed rewards. In fact, the effects of acute administration of psychostimulants on laboratory models of impulsive choice have varied. Some studies have found that they promote choice of delayed reinforcers,[65,79–82] while others have found the opposite effect.[49,83,84] Indeed, the same psychostimulant can have opposite effects in different tasks designed to measure impulsivity. [82] These differences may reflect several factors. One is the presence of cues or signals present during the delay. Providing a signal during a delay to reinforcement generally increases the rate of responding during the delay in free-operant tasks,[85] and can promote choice of the delayed reinforcer.[86] One reason for this may be that the signal becomes associated with the reinforcer and acquires conditioned reinforcing properties of its own; these can affect choice.[87] We tested the effects of amphetamine on a discrete-trial task in which rats were offered the choice of a small,

immediate reinforcer or a large, delayed reinforcer (FIG. 2), and found that amphetamine promoted choice of the small, immediate reinforcer if the large, delayed reinforcer was not signaled, but promoted choice of the large, delayed reinforcer if it was
signaled.[88] This may be because amphetamine increases the effects of conditioned
reinforcers,[89–92] which in this situation would tend to promote choice of the delayed
reinforcer. This signal- or cue-dependent effect of amphetamine can explain some of
the past discrepancies in the literature.[49,79,80,82] However, conditioned reinforcement is certainly not the only procedural difference between studies that have found
differing effects of psychostimulants. Perhaps the most obvious difference between
studies of human impulsive choice and animal models is that humans can be offered
explicit choices (hypothetical or real) without prior experience of the
situation[81,93,94]—"prepackaged" action–outcome contingencies. Other animals
must learn these contingencies through experience, implying that the whole gamut
of psychological representations that contribute to their actions (including goal-
directed actions, S–R habits, and conditioned reinforcers) can influence their choices, and potentially be influenced by psychostimulants.

It should also be emphasized that few studies of the effects of psychostimulants
on impulsive choice have addressed the pharmacological basis of their effects. However, Wade et al.[80] have shown that mixed or D2-type DA receptor antagonists induce impulsive choice, while D1-type receptor antagonists do not, suggesting that
D2 DA receptors normally promote choice of delayed reinforcement, while Winstanley et al. have recently found that amphetamine appears to affect choice through
5HT as well as DA neurotransmission.[48]

NEUROANATOMICAL STUDIES OF IMPULSIVE CHOICE

In contrast to the literature on the neurochemistry of impulsivity, research into the
neuroanatomical basis of impulsive choice is a young field. We began our studies in
this area by considering the role of three candidate structures that may be involved
in regulating choice between alternative reinforcers, namely the AcbC and two of its
cortical afferents, the ACC and mPFC. These structures are firmly implicated in reinforcement processes: the Acb is a key site for the motivational impact of impend-
ing rewards[23,95–98] and many of its afferents are involved in reward-related learning,
including the ACC[99–101] and mPFC.[102–105] These regions are also important recip-
ients of dopaminergic and serotonergic afferents.[106,107] Additionally, abnormalities
of all three regions have been detected in humans with ADHD and in animal models
of ADHD. Abnormal functioning of prefrontal cortical regions, including the mPFC
and ACC, has been observed in ADHD patients.[108–110] In the SHR, differences in
DA receptor density and gene expression have been observed within the core and
shell regions of the Acb,[73–75, 111] while abnormalities of DA release have been detected in the Acb[69–71] and prefrontal cortex,[72] in addition to possible dysfunction in
the dorsal striatum and amygdala.[72,112]

Nucleus Accumbens (Acb)

We used the task described earlier (FIG. 2) to examine the effects of excitotoxic
lesions of the nucleus accumbens core (AcbC) on rats' ability to choose a delayed

reward.[113] No cues were present during the delay, to avoid any potential confounds arising from conditioned reinforcement effects, and subjects were trained preoperatively, assigned to matched groups, operated upon, and retested postoperatively, to avoid any possible effects of the lesion on learning of the task. AcbC-lesioned subjects were rendered impulsive in their choices: they exhibited a profound deficit in their ability to choose a delayed reward, and persisted in choosing impulsively even though they were made to experience the larger, delayed alternative at regular intervals. This effect was not due to an inflexible bias away from the lever producing the delayed reinforcer: AcbC-lesioned rats still chose the large reinforcer more frequent-

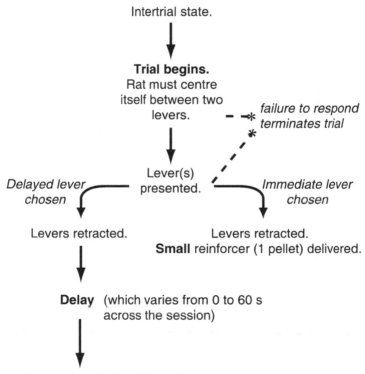

FIGURE 2. Delayed-reinforcement choice task[88,113] based on the work of Evenden and Ryan.[49] Hungry rats regularly choose between two levers. Responding on one lever leads to the immediate delivery of a small food reward (1 pellet); responding on the other leads to a much larger food reward (4 pellets), but this reward is delayed for between 0 and 60 seconds. The figure shows the format of a single trial; trials begin at regular intervals (every 100 s), so choice of the small reinforcer is always suboptimal. Sessions consist of 5 blocks. In each block, two single-lever trials are given (one trial for each lever), to ensure the animals sample the options available at that time; these are followed by ten choice trials. The delay to the large reinforcer was varied systematically across the session: delays for each block are 0, 10, 20, 40, and 60 s, respectively. In the so-called "signaled" or "cue" condition, a stimulus light is illuminated during the delay to the large reinforcer; this is absent in the "unsignaled" or "no cue" condition.

ly at zero delay than at other delays, and removal of the delays resulted in a rapid and significant increase in the rats' preference for the large reinforcer. Although a few lesioned subjects avoided the large reinforcer alternative postoperatively even when the delay was zero, this was probably due to within-session generalization from trial blocks at which delays were present (see FIG. 2). Prolonged training in the absence of delays restored a near-absolute preference for the large reinforcer in the majority of subjects—who were then much more impulsive than shams again when delays were reintroduced.[31] These results indicate that AcbC-lesioned rats are able to discriminate the two reinforcers, but prefer immediate small rewards to larger delayed rewards.

This task involves choice between reinforcers that differed in both magnitude and delay. Therefore, impulsive choice might arise as a result either of altered sensitivity to reinforcer magnitude, or delay, or both.[43] Lesioned rats might have chosen the immediate small reward because they did not perceive the large reward to be as large (relative to the small reward) as sham-operated controls did, in which case the abnormally low magnitude of the large reward would be insufficient to offset the normal effects of the delay. Alternatively, they might have perceived the reward magnitudes normally, but were hypersensitive to the delay. The latter explanation—hypersensitivity to the effects of the delay—appears more likely. AcbC-lesioned rats preferred the larger reward to the smaller,[31,113] and rats with excitotoxic lesions of the whole Acb [114, 115] or of the AcbC (Cardinal and Cheung, unpublished data) appear just as sensitive to the magnitude of reward as normal rats. Acb lesions have also produced delay-dependent impairments in a delayed-matching-to-position task.[116]

If this interpretation is correct, and AcbC lesions induce hypersensitivity to delays of reinforcement, then the effects of AcbC lesions might also extend to *learning* with delayed reinforcement, as well as choice involving delayed reinforcers. In order to learn which actions are the correct ones that eventually lead to reinforcement, some mechanism must "bridge" the delay between action and outcome. We recently examined the ability of AcbC-lesioned rats to learn a free-operant response task (FIG. 3) in which every lever press produced a food pellet, but this reinforcement was delayed by 0, 10, or 20 s in different groups. Increasing delays impaired learning in normal rats to some degree, which is a well-known finding.[13-15] Rats with AcbC lesions were unimpaired (compared to sham-operated controls) when there was no delay, but were profoundly impaired when there was a delay between action and outcome, compared to shams learning with the same delay (Cardinal and Cheung, unpublished data).

Taken together, these results suggest that the AcbC is a structure specialized for the difficult task of learning with, and choosing, delayed reinforcement. Further understanding of the mechanism by which it does so, or sometimes fails to do so, would provide insight into the pathology of a number of neuropsychiatric disorders. Given the involvement of the Acb in aversive motivation,[117,118] it will also be important to determine whether lesions of Acb induce impulsive choice in an aversive context, impairing the ability to choose a small immediate penalty in preference to a large delayed penalty.

Major glutamatergic afferents to the AcbC arrive from the ACC, mPFC, OFC, and BLA; the contribution of these structures to choice between delayed reinforcers will be considered next.

Anterior Cingulate Cortex (ACC)

Excitotoxic lesions of the ACC had no effect in this delayed-reinforcement choice task,[113] showing that the ACC is not required for rats to choose a delayed reinforcer. This finding stands in apparent contrast to previous reports of motor impulsivity or disinhibited responding in ACC-lesioned rats. For example, such rats have been found to overrespond to unrewarded stimuli,[100,101] and to respond prematurely in situations where they are required to wait.[119] However, motor ("execution") impulsivity and impulsive choice ("outcome impulsivity") are known to be dissociable.[3] Thus, these results suggest that despite findings of ACC abnormalities in disorders of impulsivity,[109,110] ACC dysfunction is not an important contributor to impulsive choice.

In the delayed-reinforcement choice task (FIG. 2),[113] subjects choose between reinforcers that differ in magnitude and delay (small immediate versus large delayed) but do not differ in probability (both are delivered with probability 1) or response effort (both require a single lever press). However, Walton *et al.*[120] found that large mPFC lesions encompassing prelimbic cortex (PrL), infralimbic cortex (IL), and ACC altered rats' preference when the two alternatives differed in magnitude, response effort, and delay (although delay was not controlled directly). Subjects were offered the choice of running down a short alley to obtain two pellets, or climbing over a 30-cm-high barrier to obtain four pellets. Large mPFC lesions substantially

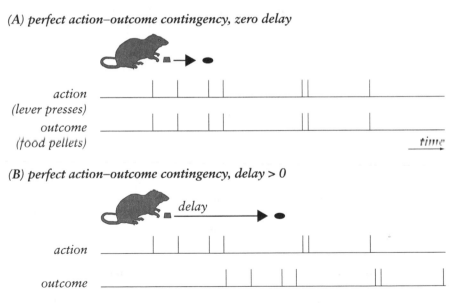

(A) perfect action–outcome contingency, zero delay

action
(lever presses)

outcome
(food pellets)

time

(B) perfect action–outcome contingency, delay > 0

delay

action

outcome

FIGURE 3. Free-operant learning with delayed reinforcement. When an animal is free to perform an action (operant) to obtain a rewarding outcome, it readily learns to do so if the action–outcome contingency (the increase in the likelihood of obtaining the outcome that is produced by performing the action) is good and if there is no delay between action and outcome (**A**). Even with a perfect action–outcome contingency, learning is impaired by imposing delays between the action and the outcome (**B**), yet animals do succeed in this task.

increased rats' preference for the small-reward, low-effort alternative. Nevertheless, lesioned subjects were capable of surmounting the obstacle if there was no low-effort alternative, and their decisions were flexible in that they responded to alterations in either the cost (effort) or the benefit of the alternatives. This effect has since been localized to the ACC: selective ACC lesions impaired performance but PrL/IL lesions had no effect on this task.[121] One interpretation of these results is that the ACC is involved in the assessment of response effort but not the delay to reinforcement.

Medial Prefrontal Cortex (mPFC)

Lesions of the mPFC (primarily PrL and IL) "flattened" the within-session shift from the large to the small reward exhibited by rats performing the delayed-reinforcement choice task shown in FIGURE 2.[113] That is, their preference for the large reward was *below* that of shams at zero delay, but *above* that of shams at the maximum delay—a regression toward indifference—although they responded appropriately when the delays were removed, preferring the larger reinforcer. There is no obvious explanation for this effect within theories of choice of delayed reinforcement, implying that the mPFC lesion resulted in some form of insensitivity to the contingencies or stimuli present in the task. One possibility is that mPFC lesions disrupted the control over behavior by the passage of time in each session. There is strong evidence that normal rats learn a session-wide temporal discrimination in this task, and that this temporal discriminative stimulus comes to control responding—in particular, the tendency to shift from the large to the small reward as the session progresses.[88] Disruption of such temporal stimulus control might be expected to produce a "flattening" of the within-session shift of the kind seen in mPFC-lesioned rats. Indeed, aspirative lesions of the mPFC have previously been shown to induce a deficit in timing ability in rats;[122] lesioned subjects showed impaired temporal discrimination in the peak procedure, an operant task that assesses the ability to time a discriminative stimulus.[123,124] Consistent with the view that mPFC lesions did not affect the basic process of choosing between reinforcers of different value in this task, combined PrL/IL lesions did not affect choice between small/low-effort and large/high-effort alternatives in the task of Walton et al.[121]

Orbitofrontal Cortex (OFC)

The OFC is a prefrontal cortical region that projects to the AcbC and is strongly implicated in the assessment of reward value. Mobini et al.[125] recently found that lesions encompassing the OFC induced impulsive choice in a task very similar to that described previously. As before, results from this task do not indicate whether the impulsive choice was as a result of altered sensitivity to reinforcer magnitude or delay. Although these lesions damaged PrL in addition to the OFC,[125] the hypothesis that OFC damage was responsible for the behavioral effect is strengthened by the finding that mPFC lesions encompassing PrL do not induce impulsive choice.[113] In contrast, Winstanley et al.[135] recently found that OFC lesions induced the opposite effect—better self-control than shams—in exactly the paradigm described previously.[113] This apparent discrepancy requires explanation. One possible reason is that subjects in the Winstanley et al. study were trained before the OFC was destroyed and retested postoperatively, while Mobini et al. trained and tested postoperatively.

Another is that Mobini *et al.* offered rats a choice between a 1-pellet immediate reinforcer and a 2-pellet delayed reinforcer, whereas Winstanley *et al.* used a 1-pellet immediate reinforcer and a 4-pellet delayed reinforcer. Differences in subjects' sensitivity to either the delay or the magnitude of reinforcement can play a role in determining preference in this task[31,43,125] and it may be that OFC lesions affect both[125]—a hypothesis for which Kheramin *et al.*[126] have found direct support. This emphasizes the necessity for quantitative analysis of delay and magnitude sensitivity[43] or the use of multiple, very different paradigms to provide independent measurements of sensitivity to delay and magnitude.[31]

Basolateral Amygdala (BLA)

Finally, Winstanley *et al.*[135] have recently found that excitotoxic lesions of the BLA promote impulsive choice in the delayed-reinforcement choice task shown in FIGURE 2. This suggests that a network including the BLA, OFC, and AcbC is involved in regulating choice between reinforcers differing in magnitude and delay; the BLA and OFC are extensively interconnected and both project to the AcbC. However, the precise manner in which the three structures interact in a choice situation is far from clear; the observations that BLA and OFC lesions can have opposite effects in exactly the same paradigm (Winstanley *et al.*[135]), and that OFC lesions can have effects on multiple aspects of reinforcer assessment,[126] suggest that any such interaction is likely to be complex.

CONCLUSIONS

The integrity of the Acb is critical for animals to tolerate delays to appetitive reinforcement.[113] This observation provides information on the neural systems through which delayed reinforcement normally affects behavior, but the observation that AcbC damage can induce impulsive choice also has implications for the understanding of ADHD and drug addiction, two clinical disorders in which impulsive choice is a factor, and potentially for impulsivity in adolescence. In addition to being impulsive, AcbC-lesioned rats are also hyperactive,[113,127] but they do not appear to be inattentive.[128,129] Destruction of the AcbC does not, therefore, mimic all the signs of ADHD, but these findings suggest that the behavior of rats with AcbC damage resembles that of humans with the hyperactive–impulsive subtype of ADHD.[130] The adolescent nucleus accumbens differs both in dopamine function and synaptic plasticity from that of the adult (see, e.g., Refs. 136–138), though whether any such differences contribute to impulsive behavior in adolescence[139] is at present unknown.

The same considerations apply to drug addiction, in which impulsive choice plays a prominent role in maintaining the selection of drugs of abuse in favor of other, longer-term rewards.[4–8] Drugs of abuse (including opiates, ethanol, and psychostimulants) can produce chronic neuroadaptations in brain regions including the Acb,[131] and chronic methamphetamine has been shown to increase impulsive choice in rats.[79] One mechanism contributing to addiction may therefore be the ability of drugs of abuse to induce damage or dysfunction in the AcbC, further promoting subsequent impulsive choice and future drug taking.

Impulsive choice may also be produced by damage to the BLA (Winstanley et al.[135]) or OFC,[125] two prominent afferents to the AcbC, though the exact contribution of these structures may be complex[126,135] and the manner in which they interact with each other and with the AcbC to determine an animal's preference among different reinforcers is not yet clear.

Interventional neuroanatomical studies of impulsive choice are clearly important for the understanding of the pathogenesis of ADHD, for they allow a causal role to be established between dysfunction of a brain region and impulsive choice. This may make it possible to distinguish the brain regions that underlie different types of impulsivity,[3] and to segregate the neural abnormalities that contribute to complex disorders such as ADHD and drug addiction and to the normal variation in impulsive behavior during adolescence. Although the ACC and mPFC have been shown to be abnormal in disorders of impulsivity,[108–110] damage to these regions does not produce impulsive choice in rats.[113] The abnormalities of structure or function observed in these regions in ADHD brains may therefore be responsible for other features of the disorder (such as inattention or motoric disinhibition),[119] or these regions may have altered as a consequence of a disease process beginning elsewhere. A clearer understanding of the neurochemical and neuroanatomical basis of disorders of impulsive choice may lead to more effective therapy.

ACKNOWLEDGMENTS

This work was supported by a Wellcome Trust Programme Grant and conducted within the UK Medical Research Council (MRC) Centre for Behavioural and Clinical Neuroscience. R.N.C. was supported by the MRC and the University of Cambridge School of Clinical Medicine. C.A.W. was supported by the MRC.

REFERENCES

1. AINSLIE, G. 1975. Specious reward: a behavioural theory of impulsiveness and impulse control. Psychol. Bull. **82:** 463–496.
2. ARISTOTLE. 1925. Nicomachean Ethics. [Originally written 350 B.C.] W.D. Ross, trans. Clarendon Press. Oxford.
3. EVENDEN, J.L. 1999. Varieties of impulsivity. Psychopharmacology **146:** 348–361.
4. POULOS, C.X., A.D. LE & J.L. PARKER. 1995. Impulsivity predicts individual susceptibility to high levels of alcohol self-administration. Behav. Pharmacol. **6:** 810–814.
5. BICKEL, W.K., A.L. ODUM & G.J. MADDEN. 1999. Impulsivity and cigarette smoking: delay discounting in current, never, and ex-smokers. Psychopharmacology **146:** 447–454.
6. EVENDEN, J.L. 1999. Impulsivity: a discussion of clinical and experimental findings. J. Psychopharmacol. **13:** 180–192.
7. HEYMAN, G.M. 1996. Resolving the contradictions of addiction. Behav. Brain Sci. **19:** 561–610.
8. MITCHELL, S.H. 1999. Measures of impulsivity in cigarette smokers and non-smokers. Psychopharmacology **146:** 455–464.
9. SAGVOLDEN, T. et al. 1998. Altered reinforcement mechanisms in attention-deficit/ hyperactivity disorder. Behav. Brain Res. **94:** 61–71.
10. SAGVOLDEN, T. & J.A. SERGEANT. 1998. Attention deficit/hyperactivity disorder—from brain dysfunctions to behaviour. Behav. Brain Res. **94:** 1–10.

11. THORNDIKE, E.L. 1911. Animal Intelligence: Experimental Studies. Macmillan. New York.
12. HULL, C.L. 1932. The goal gradient hypothesis and maze learning. Psychol. Rev. **39:** 25–43.
13. LATTAL, K.A. & S. GLEESON. 1990. Response acquisition with delayed reinforcement. J. Exp. Psychol. Anim. Behav. Processes **16:** 27–39.
14. DICKINSON, A., A. WATT & W.J.H. GRIFFITHS. 1992. Free-operant acquisition with delayed reinforcement. Q. J. Exp. Psychol. Sect. B Comp. Physiol. Psychol. **45:** 241–258.
15. GRICE, G.R. 1948. The relation of secondary reinforcement to delayed reward in visual discrimination learning. J. Exp. Psychol. **38:** 1–16.
16. KILLEEN, P.R. & J.G. FETTERMAN. 1988. A behavioral theory of timing. Psychol. Rev. **95:** 274–295.
17. SPENCE, K.W. 1956. Behavior Theory and Conditioning. Prentice-Hall. Englewood Cliffs, NJ.
18. MOWRER, O.H. 1960. Learning Theory and Behavior. Wiley. New York.
19. REVUSKY, S. & J. GARCIA. 1970. Learned associations over long delays. *In* The Psychology of Learning and Motivation, Vol. 4. G.H. Bower, Ed.: 1–84. Academic Press. New York.
20. MACKINTOSH, N.J. 1974. The Psychology of Animal Learning. Academic Press. London.
21. DICKINSON, A. 1994. Instrumental conditioning. *In* Animal Learning and Cognition. N. J. Mackintosh, Ed.: 45–79. Academic Press. San Diego.
22. DICKINSON, A. & B. BALLEINE. 1994. Motivational control of goal-directed action. Anim. Learn. Behav. **22:** 1–18.
23. CARDINAL, R. N. *et al.* 2002. Emotion and motivation: the role of the amygdala, ventral striatum, and prefrontal cortex. Neurosci. Biobehav. Rev. **26:** 321–352.
24. DICKINSON, A. 1980. Contemporary animal learning theory. Cambridge University Press. Cambridge.
25. MAZUR, J.E. 1987. An adjusting procedure for studying delayed reinforcement. *In* Quantitative Analyses of Behavior. V. The Effect of Delay and of Intervening Events on Reinforcement Value. M.L. Commons *et al.*, Eds.: 55–73. Lawrence Erlbaum. Hillsdale, NJ.
26. MAZUR, J.E., J.R. STELLAR & M. WARACZYNSKI. 1987. Self-control choice with electrical stimulation of the brain as a reinforcer. Behav. Processes **15:** 143–153.
27. RICHARDS, J.B. *et al.* 1997. Determination of discount functions in rats with an adjusting-amount procedure. J. Exp. Anal. Behav. **67:** 353–366.
28. GRACE, R.C. 1996. Choice between fixed and variable delays to reinforcement in the adjusting-delay procedure and concurrent chains. J. Exp. Psychol. Anim. Behav. Processes **22:** 362–383.
29. BRADSHAW, C.M. & E. SZABADI. 1992. Choice between delayed reinforcers in a discrete-trials schedule: the effect of deprivation level. Q. J. Exp. Psychol. B **44B:** 1–16.
30. KACELNIK, A. 1997. Normative and descriptive models of decision making: time discounting and risk sensitivity. *In* Characterizing Human Psychological Adaptations (Ciba Foundation Symposium 208): 51–70. Wiley. Chichester, UK.
31. CARDINAL, R.N., T.W. ROBBINS & B. J. EVERITT. 2003. Choosing delayed rewards: perspectives from learning theory, neurochemistry, and neuroanatomy. *In* Choice, Behavioral Economics and Addiction. N. Heather & R. Vuchinich, Eds.: 183–213, 217–218. Elsevier. Oxford.
32. SOUBRIÉ, P. 1986. Reconciling the role of central serotonin neurons in human and animal behavior. Behav. Brain Sci. **9:** 319–335.
33. ÅSBERG, M., L. TRÄSKMAN & P. THORÉN. 1976. 5-HIAA in the cerebrospinal fluid: a biochemical suicide predictor. Arch. Gen. Psych. **33:** 1193–1197.
34. LINNOILA, M. *et al.* 1983. Low cerebrospinal fluid 5-hydroxyindoleacetic acid concentration differentiates impulsive from nonimpulsive violent behavior. Life Sci. **33:** 2609–2614.
35. BROWN, G.L. & M. LINNOILA. 1990. CSF serotonin metabolite (5HIAA) studies in depression, impulsivity and violence. J. Clin. Psych. **51**(Suppl. 4): 31–41.

36. LINNOILA, M. *et al.* 1993. Impulse control disorders. International Clin. Psychopharmacol. **8**(Suppl. 1): 53–56.
37. MEHLMAN, P.T. *et al.* 1994. Low CSF 5-HIAA concentrations and severe aggression and impaired impulse control in nonhuman primates. Am. J. Psychiatry **151:** 1485–1491.
38. EVENDEN, J.L. 1998. Serotonergic and steroidal influences on impulsive behaviour in rats. Comprehensive Summaries of Uppsala Dissertations from the Faculty of Medicine. **764**.
39. WOGAR, M.A., C.M. BRADSHAW & E. SZABADI. 1993. Effect of lesions of the ascending 5-hydroxytryptaminergic pathways on choice between delayed reinforcers. Psychopharmacology **111:** 239–243.
40. RICHARDS, J.B. & L.S. SEIDEN. 1995. Serotonin depletion increases impulsive behavior in rats. Soc. Neurosci. Abstr. **21:** 1693.
41. BIZOT, J. *et al.* 1999. Serotonin and tolerance to delay of reward in rats. Psychopharmacology **146:** 400–412.
42. MOBINI, S. *et al.* 2000. Effects of central 5-hydroxytryptamine depletion on sensitivity to delayed and probabilistic reinforcement. Psychopharmacology **152:** 390–397.
43. HO, M.Y. *et al.* 1999. Theory and method in the quantitative analysis of "impulsive choice" behaviour: implications for psychopharmacology. Psychopharmacology **146:** 362–372.
44. MOBINI, S. *et al.* 2000. Effect of central 5-hydroxytryptamine depletion on inter-temporal choice: a quantitative analysis. Psychopharmacology **149:** 313–318.
45. POULOS, C.X., J.L. PARKER & A.D. LE. 1996. Dexfenfluramine and 8-OH-DPAT modulate impulsivity in a delay-of-reward paradigm: implications for a correspondence with alcohol consumption. Behav. Pharmacol. **7:** 395–399.
46. EVENDEN, J.L. & C.N. RYAN. 1999. The pharmacology of impulsive behaviour in rats VI: the effects of ethanol and selective serotonergic drugs on response choice with varying delays of reinforcement. Psychopharmacology **146:** 413–421.
47. DALLEY, J.W. *et al.* 2002. Deficits in impulse control associated with tonically-elevated serotonergic function in rat prefrontal cortex. Neuropsychopharmacology **26:** 716–728.
48. WINSTANLEY, C.A. *et al.* 2003. Global 5-HT depletion attenuates the ability of amphetamine to decrease impulsive choice on a delay-discounting task in rats. Psychopharmacology **170:** 320–321.
49. EVENDEN, J.L. & C.N. RYAN. 1996. The pharmacology of impulsive behaviour in rats: the effects of drugs on response choice with varying delays of reinforcement. Psychopharmacology **128:** 161–170.
50. BIGGIO, G. *et al.* 1974. Rapid depletion of serum tryptophan, brain tryptophan, serotonin and 5-hydroxyindoleacetic acid by a trytophan-free diet. Life Sci. **14:** 1321–1329.
51. CLEMENS, J.A., D.R. BENNETT & R.W. FULLER. 1980. The effect of a tryptophan-free diet on prolactin and corticosterone release by serotonergic stimuli. Horm. Metab. Res. **12:** 35–38.
52. DELGADO, P.L. *et al.* 1989. Neuroendocrine and behavioral effects of dietary tryptophan restriction in healthy subjects. Life Sci. **45:** 2323–2332.
53. WILLIAMS, W.A. *et al.* 1999. Effects of acute tryptophan depletion on plasma and cerebrospinal fluid tryptophan and 5-hydroxyindoleacetic acid in normal volunteers. J. Neurochem. **72:** 1641–1647.
54. CARPENTER, L.L. *et al.* 1998. Tryptophan depletion during continuous CSF sampling in healthy human subjects. Neuropsychopharmacology **19:** 26–35.
55. WALDERHAUG, E. *et al.* 2002. Lowering of serotonin by rapid tryptophan depletion increases impulsiveness in normal individuals. Psychopharmacology **164:** 385–391.
56. CREAN, J., J.B. RICHARDS & H. DE WIT. 2002. Effect of tryptophan depletion on impulsive behavior in men with or without a family history of alcoholism. Behav. Brain Res. **136:** 349–357.
57. BRADLEY, C. 1937. The behavior of children receiving Benzedrine. Am. J. Psychiatry **94:** 577–585.
58. FELDMAN, R.S., J.S. MEYER & L.F. QUENZER. 1997. Principles of neuropsychopharmacology. Sinauer. Sunderland, MA.

59. JOHANSEN, E.B. *et al.* 2002. Attention-deficit/hyperactivity disorder (ADHD) behaviour explained by dysfunctioning reinforcement and extinction processes. Behav. Brain Res. **130:** 37–45.
60. ZHUANG, X. *et al.* 2001. Hyperactivity and impaired response habituation in hyperdopaminergic mice. Proc. Natl. Acad. Sci. USA **98:** 1982–1987.
61. SWANSON, J. *et al.* 1998. Cognitive neuroscience of attention deficit hyperactivity disorder and hyperkinetic disorder. Curr. Opin. Neurobiol. **8:** 263–271.
62. SEEMAN, P. & B. MADRAS. 2002. Methylphenidate elevates resting dopamine which lowers the impulse-triggered release of dopamine: a hypothesis. Behav. Brain Res. **130:** 79–83.
63. SOLANTO, M.V. 2002. Dopamine dysfunction in AD/HD: integrating clinical and basic neuroscience research. Behav. Brain Res. **130:** 65–71.
64. WULTZ, B. *et al.* 1990. The spontaneously hypertensive rat as an animal model of attention-deficit hyperactivity disorder: effects of methylphenidate on exploratory behavior. Behav. Neural Biol. **53:** 88–102.
65. SAGVOLDEN, T. *et al.* 1992. The spontaneously hypertensive rat (SHR) as an animal model of childhood hyperactivity (ADHD): changed reactivity to reinforcers and to psychomotor stimulants. Behav. Neural Biol. **58:** 103–112.
66. SAGVOLDEN, T., M.B. PETTERSEN & M.C. LARSEN. 1993. Spontaneously hypertensive rats (SHR) as a putative animal model of childhood hyperkinesis: SHR behavior compared to four other rat strains. Physiol. Behav. **54:** 1047–1055.
67. SAGVOLDEN, T. 2000. Behavioral validation of the spontaneously hypertensive rat (SHR) as an animal model of attention-deficit/hyperactivity disorder (AD/HD). Neurosci. Biobehav. Rev. **24:** 31–39.
68. EVENDEN, J.L. & B. MEYERSON. 1999. The behavior of spontaneously hypertensive and Wistar Kyoto rats under a paced fixed consecutive number schedule of reinforcement. Pharmacol. Biochem. Behav. **63:** 71–82.
69. DE VILLIERS, A.S. *et al.* 1995. Alpha 2-adrenoceptor mediated inhibition of [3H]dopamine release from nucleus accumbens slices and monoamine levels in a rat model for attention–deficit hyperactivity disorder. Neurochem. Res. **20:** 427–433.
70. RUSSELL, V. *et al.* 1998. Differences between electrically-, ritalin- and D-amphetamine- stimulated release of [H-3]dopamine from brain slices suggest impaired vesicular storage of dopamine in an animal model of attention-deficit hyperactivity disorder. Behav. Brain Res. **94:** 163 171.
71. RUSSELL, V.A. 2000. The nucleus accumbens motor-limbic interface of the spontaneously hypertensive rat as studied in vitro by the superfusion slice technique. Neurosci. Biobehav. Rev. **24:** 133–136.
72. RUSSELL, V. *et al.* 1995. Altered dopaminergic function in the prefrontal cortex, nucleus accumbens and caudate-putamen of an animal model of attention-deficit hyperactivity disorder–the spontaneously hypertensive rat. Brain Res. **676:** 343 351.
73. PAPA, M. *et al.* 1996. Reduced CaMKII-positive neurons in the accumbens shell of an animal model of attention-deficit hyperactivity disorder. Neuroreport **7:** 3017–3020.
74. PAPA, M., J.A. SERGEANT & A.G. SADILE. 1998. Reduced transduction mechanisms in the anterior accumbal interface of an animal model of attention-deficit hyperactivity disorder. Behav. Brain Res. **94:** 187–195.
75. CAREY, M.P. *et al.* 1998. Differential distribution, affinity and plasticity of dopamine D-1 and D-2 receptors in the target sites of the mesolimbic system in an animal model of ADHD. Behav. Brain Res. **94:** 173–185.
76. KUNTSI, J., J. OOSTERLAAN & J. STEVENSON. 2001. Psychological mechanisms in hyperactivity. I. Response inhibition deficit, working memory impairment, delay aversion, or something else? J. Child Psychol. Psychiatry **42:** 199–210.
77. SONUGA-BARKE, E.J. 2002. Psychological heterogeneity in AD/HD–a dual pathway model of behaviour and cognition. Behav. Brain Res. **130:** 29–36.
78. SOLANTO, M.V. 1998. Neuropsychopharmacological mechanisms of stimulant drug action in attention-deficit hyperactivity disorder: a review and integration. Behav. Brain Res. **94:** 127–152.
79. RICHARDS, J.B., K.E. SABOL & H. DE WIT. 1999. Effects of methamphetamine on the adjusting amount procedure, a model of impulsive behavior in rats. Psychopharmacology **146:** 432–439.

80. WADE, T.R., H. DE WIT & J.B. RICHARDS. 2000. Effects of dopaminergic drugs on delayed reward as a measure of impulsive behavior in rats. Psychopharmacology 150: 90–101.
81. DE WIT, H., J.L. ENGGASSER & J.B. RICHARDS. 2002. Acute administration of d-amphetamine decreases impulsivity in healthy volunteers. Neuropsychopharmacology 27: 813–825.
82. RICHARDS, J.B. et al. 1997. Comparison of two models of impulsive behavior in rats: effects of amphetamine and haloperidol. Soc. Neurosci. Abstr. 23: 2406.
83. CHARRIER, D. & M.H. THIÉBOT. 1996. Effects of psychotropic drugs on rat responding in an operant paradigm involving choice between delayed reinforcers. Pharmacol. Biochem. Behav. 54: 149–157.
84. LOGUE, A.W. et al. 1992. Cocaine decreases self-control in rats: a preliminary report. Psychopharmacology 109: 245–247.
85. LATTAL, K.A. 1987. Considerations in the experimental analysis of reinforcement delay. In Quantitative Analyses of Behavior. V. The Effect of Delay and of Intervening Events on Reinforcement Value. M.L. Commons et al. Eds.:107–123. Lawrence Erlbaum. Hillsdale, NJ.
86. MAZUR, J.E. 1997. Choice, delay, probability, and conditioned reinforcement. Anim. Learn. Behav. 25: 131–147.
87. WILLIAMS, B.A. & R. DUNN. 1991. Preference for conditioned reinforcement. J. Exp. Anal. Behav. 55: 37–46.
88. CARDINAL, R. N., T.W. ROBBINS & B.J. EVERITT. 2000. The effects of d-amphetamine, chlordiazepoxide, alpha-flupenthixol and behavioural manipulations on choice of signalled and unsignalled delayed reinforcement in rats. Psychopharmacology 152: 362–375.
89. HILL, R.T. 1970. Facilitation of conditioned reinforcement as a mechanism of psychomotor stimulation. In International Symposium on Amphetamines and Related Compounds. E. Costa & S. Garattini, Eds.: 781–795. Raven Press. New York.
90. ROBBINS, T.W. 1976. Relationship between reward-enhancing and stereotypical effects of psychomotor stimulant drugs. Nature 264: 57–59.
91. ROBBINS, T.W. 1978. The acquisition of responding with conditioned reinforcement: effects of pipradrol, methylphenidate, d-amphetamine, and nomifensine. Psychopharmacology 58: 79–87.
92. ROBBINS, T.W. et al. 1983. Contrasting interactions of pipradrol, d-amphetamine, cocaine, cocaine analogues, apomorphine and other drugs with conditioned reinforcement. Psychopharmacology 80: 113–119.
93. RACHLIN, H., A. RAINERI & D. CROSS. 1991. Subjective probability and delay. J. Exp. Anal. Behav. 55: 233–244.
94. MYERSON, J. & L. GREEN. 1995. Discounting of delayed rewards: models of individual choice. J. Exp. Anal. Behav. 64: 263–276.
95. PARKINSON, J.A., R.N. CARDINAL & B.J. EVERITT. 2000. Limbic cortical-ventral striatal systems underlying appetitive conditioning. Prog. Brain Res. 126: 263–285.
96. ROBBINS, T.W. & B.J. EVERITT. 1996. Neurobehavioural mechanisms of reward and motivation. Curr. Opin. Neurobiol. 6: 228–236.
97. SALAMONE, J.D., M.S. COUSINS & B.J. SNYDER. 1997. Behavioral functions of nucleus accumbens dopamine: empirical and conceptual problems with the anhedonia hypothesis. Neurosci. Biobehav. Rev. 21: 341–359.
98. EVERITT, B.J. et al. 1999. Associative processes in addiction and reward: the role of amygdala-ventral striatal subsystems. Ann. N.Y. Acad. Sci. 877: 412–438.
99. BUSSEY, T.J. et al. 1997. Triple dissociation of anterior cingulate, posterior cingulate, and medial frontal cortices on visual discrimination tasks using a touchscreen testing procedure for the rat. Behav. Neurosci. 111: 920–936.
100. BUSSEY, T.J., B.J. EVERITT & T.W. ROBBINS. 1997. Dissociable effects of cingulate and medial frontal cortex lesions on stimulus-reward learning using a novel Pavlovian autoshaping procedure for the rat: implications for the neurobiology of emotion. Behav. Neurosci. 111: 908–919.

101. PARKINSON, J.A. *et al.* 2000. Disconnection of the anterior cingulate cortex and nucleus accumbens core impairs Pavlovian approach behavior: Further evidence for limbic cortical-ventral striatopallidal systems. Behav. Neurosci. **114:** 42–63.
102. BALLEINE, B.W. & A. DICKINSON. 1998. Goal-directed instrumental action: contingency and incentive learning and their cortical substrates. Neuropharmacology **37:** 407–419.
103. BECHARA, A. *et al.* 1999. Different contributions of the human amygdala and ventromedial prefrontal cortex to decision-making. J. Neurosci. **19:** 5473–5481.
104. TZSCHENTKE, T.M. 2000. The medial prefrontal cortex as a part of the brain reward system. Amino Acids **19:** 211–219.
105. RICHARDSON, N.R. & A. GRATTON. 1998. Changes in medial prefrontal cortical dopamine levels associated with response-contingent food reward: an electrochemical study in rat. J. Neurosci. **18:** 9130–9138.
106. HALLIDAY, G., A. HARDING & G. PAXINOS. 1995. Serotonin and tachykinin systems. *In* The Rat Nervous System. G. Paxinos, Ed.: 929–974. Academic Press. London.
107. FALLON, J.H. & S.E. LOUGHLIN. 1995. Substantia nigra. *In* The Rat Nervous System. G. Paxinos, Ed.: 215–237. Academic Press. London.
108. ERNST, M. *et al.* 1998. DOPA decarboxylase activity in attention deficit hyperactivity disorder adults. A [fluorine-18]fluorodopa positron emission tomographic study. J. Neurosci. **18:** 5901–5907.
109. BUSH, G. *et al.* 1999. Anterior cingulate cortex dysfunction in attention-deficit/hyperactivity disorder revealed by fMRI and the Counting Stroop. Biol. Psychiatry **45:** 1542–1552.
110. RUBIA, K. *et al.* 1999. Hypofrontality in attention deficit hyperactivity disorder during higher-order motor control: a study with functional MRI. Am. J. Psychiatry **156:** 891–896.
111. SADILE, A.G. 2000. Multiple evidence of a segmental defect in the anterior forebrain of an animal model of hyperactivity and attention deficit. Neurosci. Biobehav. Rev. **24:** 161–169.
112. PAPA, M., S. SELLITTI & A.G. SADILE. 2000. Remodeling of neural networks in the anterior forebrain of an animal model of hyperactivity and attention deficits as monitored by molecular imaging probes. Neurosci. Biobehav. Rev. **24:** 149–156.
113. CARDINAL, R.N. *et al.* 2001. Impulsive choice induced in rats by lesions of the nucleus accumbens core. Science **292:** 2499–2501.
114. BALLEINE, B. & S. KILLCROSS. 1994. Effects of ibotenic acid lesions of the nucleus accumbens on instrumental action. Behav. Brain Res. **65:** 181–93.
115. BROWN, V.J. & E.M. BOWMAN. 1995. Discriminative cues indicating reward magnitude continue to determine reaction time of rats following lesions of the nucleus accumbens. Eur. J. Neurosci. **7:** 2479–2485.
116. READING, P.J. & S.B. DUNNETT. 1991. The effects of excitotoxic lesions of the nucleus accumbens on a matching to position task. Behav. Brain Res. **46:** 17–29.
117. SALAMONE, J. D. 1994. The involvement of nucleus accumbens dopamine in appetitive and aversive motivation. Behav. Brain Res. **61:** 117–133.
118. PARKINSON, J.A., T.W. ROBBINS & B.J. EVERITT. 1999. Selective excitotoxic lesions of the nucleus accumbens core and shell differentially affect aversive Pavlovian conditioning to discrete and contextual cues. Psychobiology **27:** 256–266.
119. MUIR, J.L., B.J. EVERITT & T.W. ROBBINS. 1996. The cerebral cortex of the rat and visual attentional function: dissociable effects of mediofrontal, cingulate, anterior dorsolateral, and parietal cortex lesions on a five-choice serial reaction time task. Cereb. Cortex **6:** 470–481.
120. WALTON, M.E., D.M. BANNERMAN & M.F. RUSHWORTH. 2002. The role of rat medial frontal cortex in effort-based decision making. J. Neurosci. **22:** 10996-11003.
121. WALTON, M.E. *et al.* 2003. Functional specialization within medial frontal cortex of the anterior cingulate for evaluating effort-related decisions. J. Neurosci. **23:** 6475–6479.
122. DIETRICH, A. & J.D. ALLEN. 1998. Functional dissociation of the prefrontal cortex and the hippocampus in timing behavior. Behav. Neurosci. **112:** 1043–1047.

123. CATANIA, A.C. 1970. Reinforcement schedules and psychophysical judgment: A study of some temporal properties of behavior. *In* The Theory of Reinforcement Schedules. W.N. Schoenfeld, Ed.: 1–42. Appleton Century Crofts. New York.
124. ROBERTS, S. 1981. Isolation of an internal clock. J. Exp. Psychol. Anim. Behav. Processes 7: 242–268.
125. MOBINI, S. *et al.* 2002. Effects of lesions of the orbitofrontal cortex on sensitivity to delayed and probabilistic reinforcement. Psychopharmacology 160: 290–298.
126. KHERAMIN, S. *et al.* 2002. Effects of quinolinic acid-induced lesions of the orbital prefrontal cortex on inter-temporal choice: a quantitative analysis. Psychopharmacology 165: 9–17.
127. PARKINSON, J.A. *et al.* 1999. Dissociation in effects of lesions of the nucleus accumbens core and shell on appetitive Pavlovian approach behavior and the potentiation of conditioned reinforcement and locomotor activity by d-amphetamine. J. Neurosci. 19: 2401–2411.
128. CHRISTAKOU, A., T.W. ROBBINS &. B.J. EVERITT. 2004. Prefrontal cortico-ventral striatal interactions involved in affective modulation of attentional performance: implications for corticostriated circuit function. J. Neurosci. 24: 773–780.
129. COLE, B.J. & T.W. ROBBINS. 1989. Effects of 6-hydroxydopamine lesions of the nucleus accumbens septi on performance of a 5-choice serial reaction time task in rats: implications for theories of selective attention and arousal. Behav. Brain Res. 33: 165–179.
130. AMERICAN PSYCHIATRIC ASSOCIATION. 2000. Diagnostic and Statistical Manual of Mental Disorders, 4th ed., text revision (DSM-IV-TR). Washington, DC.
131. KOOB, G.F., P.P. SANNA & F.E. BLOOM. 1998. Neuroscience of addiction. Neuron 21: 467–476.
132. USA. 2001. Leading Causes Charts (National Center for Injury Prevention and Control, Centers for Disease Control and Prevention, <www.cdc.gov/ncipc/osp/charts.htm>).
133. KELLEY, A.E., T. SCHOCHET & C.F. LANDRY. 2004. Risk taking and novelty seeking in adolescence: Introduction to Part I. Ann. N. Y. Acad. Sci. 1021: 27–32.
134. DAHL, R.E. 2004. Adolescent brain development: a period of vulnerabilities and opportunities. Keynote address. Ann. N. Y. Acad. Sci.1021: 1–22.
135. WINSTANLEY, C.A. *et al.* 2004. Contrasting roles of basolateral amygdala and orbitofrontal cortex in impulsive choice. J. Neurosci. In press.
136. SCHRAMM, N.L.. R.E. EGLI & D.G. WINDER. 2002. LTP in the mouse nucleus accumbens is develpmentally regulated. Synapse 45: 213–219.
137. PHILPOT, R.M., S. MCQUOWN & C.L. KIRSTEIN. 2001. Stereotaxic localization of the developing nucleus accumbens septi. Brain Res. Dev. Brain Res. 130: 149–150.
138. ANDERSEN, S.L. & M.H. TEICHER. 2000. Sex differences in dopamine receptors and their relevance to ADHD. Neurosci. Behav. Rev. 24: 137–141.
139. ADRIANI, W. & G. LAVIOLA. 2003. Elevated levels of impulsivity and reduced place conditioning with d-amphetamine: two behavioral features of adolescence in mice. Behav. Neurosci. 117: 695–703.

Risk Taking in Adolescence

What Changes, and Why?

LAURENCE STEINBERG

Department of Psychology, Temple University, Philadelphia, Pennsylvania 19122, USA

ABSTRACT: Extant studies of age differences in cognitive processes relevant to risk taking and decision making, such as risk perception and risk appraisal, indicate few significant age differences in factors that might explain why adolescents engage in more risk taking than adults. The present analysis suggests that the greater propensity of adolescents to take risks is not due to age differences in risk perception or appraisal, but to age differences in psychosocial factors that influence self-regulation. It is argued that adolescence is a period of heightened vulnerability to risk taking because of a disjunction between novelty and sensation seeking (both of which increase dramatically at puberty) and the development of self-regulatory competence (which does not fully mature until early adulthood). This disjunction is biologically driven, normative, and unlikely to be remedied through educational interventions designed to change adolescents' perception, appraisal, or understanding of risk. Interventions should begin from the premise that adolescents are inherently more likely than adults to take risks, and should focus on reducing the harm associated with risk-taking behavior.

KEYWORDS: adolescence; risk taking

When my son, Benjamin, was 14, he and three of his friends decided to sneak out of the house where they were spending the night and visit one of their girlfriends at around two in the morning. When they arrived at the girl's house, they positioned themselves under her bedroom window, threw pebbles against her windowpanes, and tried to scale the side of the house. Modern technology, unfortunately, has made it harder to play Romeo these days. The boys set off the house's burglar alarm, which activated a siren and simultaneously sent a direct notification to the local police station, which dispatched a patrol car. When the siren went off, the boys ran down the street and right smack into the police car, which was heading to the girl's home. Instead of stopping and explaining their activity, Ben and his friends scattered and ran off in different directions throughout the neighborhood. One of the boys was caught by the police and taken back to his home, where his parents were awakened and the boy questioned.

Address for correspondence: Laurence Steinberg, Department of Psychology, Temple University, Philadelphia, PA 19122. Voice: 215-204-7485; fax: 215-204-1286.
 lds@temple.edu

Ann. N.Y. Acad. Sci. 1021: 51–58 (2004). © 2004 New York Academy of Sciences.
doi: 10.1196/annals.1308.005

I found out about this affair the following morning, when the girl's mother called our home to tell us what Ben had done. (Her daughter had identified the four boys.) It was especially embarrassing because the girl's mother, in addition to being a fellow parent at our children's school, happens to be my wife's gynecologist. After his near brush with the local police, Ben had returned to the house out of which he had snuck, where he slept soundly until I awakened him with an angry telephone call, telling him to gather his clothes and wait for me in front of his friend's house. On our drive home, after delivering a long lecture about what he had done and about the dangers of running from armed police in the dark when they believe they may have interrupted a burglary, I paused. "What were you thinking?" I asked. "That's the problem, Dad," Ben replied. "I wasn't."

Ben's behavior and his insightful, albeit brief, analysis illustrate why the approach that behavioral scientists have taken to the study of adolescent risk taking has yielded so little in the way of explaining the phenomenon. Cast within a primarily cognitive framework, adolescent risk taking has been approached as if it were the product of a series of reasoned decisions, involving the perception, appraisal, evaluation, and computation of the relative costs and benefits of alternative courses of action.[1] Surely we would agree that what Ben and his friends did that night falls into the category of risk taking as most of us understand the phenomenon. But there was no evidence that Ben engaged in any of the cognitive processes, at least at a conscious level, that psychologists examine when they study adolescent risk taking. Had he paused for even a moment to perceive, appraise, evaluate, or compute the costs and benefits of sneaking out, trespassing, and running from the police, he probably would not have done any of these things. The problem is not that Ben's decision making was deficient. The problem is that it was nonexistent.

Yet it is decision making that we continue to study when we attempt to explain risky behavior during adolescence. We study risk taking by giving individual adolescents questionnaires that ask them to tell us whether certain activities are risky, to estimate the probability of various events, to tell us what they would do in a hypothetical situation, and to describe how their behavior would change as a function of variations in levels of perceived risk. Under these conditions, adolescents look surprisingly similar to adults in the ways in which they process information. Indeed, a few years ago, my colleagues and I completed a study in which, as a small part of it, we asked individuals between the ages of 11 and 24 to evaluate the riskiness, dangerousness, potential harmfulness, and relative costs of each of a series of genuinely risky activities, such as riding in a car with a drunk driver, having unprotected sex, or shoplifting.[2] The 11- to 13-year-olds were more likely than any other age group to rate these activities as risky, scary, dangerous, and more harmful than beneficial. After 13, however, there were no age differences in risk perception. In other words, 14-year-olds—individuals the same age as my son when he and his friends took their risk—perceive the same amount of risk in things such as drunk driving, unprotected sex, or shoplifting as people 10 years older do. We did not include wandering around the neighborhood at two in the morning, trespassing, or running away from the police on our questionnaire, but I would bet that, had we done so, we would not have found age differences in individuals' evaluations of these activities, either. And yet, something tells me that a group of 14-year-olds is probably more likely to do what Ben and his friends did than is a group of 24-year-olds. I am not sure what questionnaires like ours are capturing—we used a widely employed measure developed by Benthin *et al.*[3]—but whatever they are measuring does not seem to capture something very important about risk taking during adolescence. Either the general proposition that adolescents are more likely than adults to take risks is wrong—in which case, the answer to the question posed by my talk, "What is it about risk taking that changes during adolescence?" is "nothing"—or there is something about the way in which we think about and study risk taking that is fundamentally flawed. As one who has been studying adolescent behavior for close to 30 years, my money is on the latter.

Our understanding of risk taking in adolescence has been hampered in several ways that I wish to draw your attention to. One important impediment is methodological. If my son's nighttime exploits were typical of the situations under which adolescents take risks, as I think they are, it is fair to say that the conditions under which psychologists study risk taking bear little resemblance to the real world in which adolescents live. First, psychologists study adolescent risk taking one adolescent at a time, yet most adolescent risk taking is a group phenomenon. Delinquency and criminal behavior, for example, are more likely to occur in groups during adolescence than they are during adulthood.[4] Drinking also is a group activity during adolescence: according to Add Health data, only 25% of adolescents who drink say they were alone the last time they used alcohol.[5] Risky driving is a group activity in adolescence, and teenagers are more likely to drive in groups than are adults.[6] And by the usual definition, sexual risk taking is an activity that involves more than one person at a time. So the first mistake we make is studying adolescent risk taking as if it were an individual phenomenon, when in reality it occurs in groups.

The second problem with the way psychologists study risk taking is that they do so mainly by asking individuals to respond to hypothetical dilemmas; but in the real world the risky, or potentially risky, situations in which adolescents find themselves are anything but hypothetical. The prospect of visiting a hypothetical girl from class cannot possibly carry the excitement about the possibility of surprising someone you have a crush on with a visit in the middle of the night. It is easier to put on a hypothetical condom during an act of hypothetical sex than it is to put on a real one when one is in the throes of passion and does not want to dampen the pleasurable feeling of sexual contact. It is easier to just say no to a hypothetical beer than it is to a cold frosty one on a summer night. Shoplifting a CD from a music store seems like a much riskier proposition when posed in the abstract than when one is staring at the actual CD whose music is blaring over the store's stereo system.

Finally, psychologists typically study risk taking under conditions designed to minimize emotional influences on decision making, yet most risk taking likely occurs under conditions of emotional arousal. Indeed, if any emotion is activated by the way we usually study risk taking, it is likely anxiety, because the procedures for studying risk taking often involve administering test-like stimuli to individuals under unfamiliar circumstances. This, I would assume, would lead to less risk taking than one would expect to see under non-anxiety-producing circumstances. Yet the emotion that serves as the backdrop for much adolescent risk taking is euphoria, either natural or drug induced. How many of our research subjects are in a state of euphoria when they complete our questionnaires about risk taking? How would their responses to these questionnaires differ if they were euphoric rather than anxious or bored when they completed them?

I noted earlier the general absence of age differences in questionnaire studies of risk perception and risk assessment, a finding that is widely reported in the literature on adolescent development. I have never been very surprised by the finding that adolescents' performance in paper-and-pencil studies of risky decision making is not that different from that of adults, especially if the adolescents are around 15 years old and if the decision making tasks are largely cognitive in nature. In a review of this literature that Beth Cauffman and I published nearly a decade ago, we concluded that the sorts of reasoning abilities activated in most decision making studies were fully developed, or nearly so, by age 16, and that the growth curve mapping these abilities reaches an asymptote at around this age.[7] By the time they have reached 15 or 16, most adolescents reason about hypothetical dilemmas as well as adults do. But 15-year-olds, on average, probably take more risks than adults do.

Assuming that adolescents do take more risks than adults and assuming that this is not due to age differences in risk perception and appraisal, what is it that changes over the course of adolescence that explains the developmental course of risk taking? My guess is that age differences in risk taking are due to two different phenomena, neither of which has anything to do with the red herrings of risk perception and appraisal. First, changes in reward sensitivity that occur at puberty lead adolescents to seek more novelty and require higher levels of stimulation to achieve the same subjective feeling of pleasure. It is as if they need to drive 70 miles per hour to achieve the same degree of excitement that driving 50 miles per hour had provided previously. Although most of the relevant brain research on this question comes from animal studies, there is some support for the notion that developments in the limbic system around puberty may account for at least part of this change in reward seeking.[8] What distinguishes adolescents from adults in this regard, then, is not the fact that adolescents are less knowledgeable about what is, and what is not, risky. What distinguishes them, I believe, is that adolescents have a higher need for the sort of stimulation that risk taking provides. This is why our attempts to educate adolescents about the risks of drugs, alcohol, tobacco, for example, have been such unmitigated failures.

The second contributor to age differences in risk taking has to do with the relatively slow development of higher-level self-regulatory capabilities. There is good reason to believe that many of the executive processes that govern such phenomena as impulse control, foresight, planning, and the like are still maturing well into middle and late adolescence, if not into young adulthood. The notion here, then, is that risk taking during adolescence is the product of an interaction between heightened stimulation seeking and an immature self-regulatory system that is not yet able to modulate reward-seeking impulses. The notion that self-regulatory competencies are slow to mature is consistent with emerging research on the development of prefrontal cortical systems.[9]

Psychologists have been loose—some might even say promiscuous—in their use of the term *self-regulation*, and this conceptual fuzziness likely has contributed to our failure to understand what it is about risk taking that changes in adolescence. Self-regulation is a multidimensional construct that my colleagues and I have been trying to unpack because, in our view, it is quite possible that different brain systems subserve different aspects of what behavioral scientists call self-regulation.

In our work, we are trying to separate three very different components of self-regulation and are in the process of developing an assessment protocol that can be used to measure them, both in the lab and, ultimately, while we are assessing patterns of brain activation. The three components of self-regulation are interrelated, but they are not all the same thing, and they involve different degrees of deliberate-versus-automatic control. The first involves interrupting a risky behavioral trajectory that is already set in motion—what we refer to as "getting off a runaway train." An example of this might be interrupting foreplay to put a condom on before having intercourse. The second involves thinking before acting. An example of failure in this aspect of self-regulation—what we call "jumping the gun"—might be diving into a lake of unknown depth. The third involves choosing between two alternative courses of action, one of which is riskier than the other. We call this "doing the right thing." An example of this might be turning down a ride from a driver who has been drinking.

We know surprisingly little about the developmental course of different aspects of self regulation and even less about their neurobiological underpinnings. One of the difficulties inherent in studying self-regulation is that it is influenced not only by cognitive factors, but by psychosocial and affective factors, including susceptibility to peer influence, future orientation, and emotional arousal. Unlike the literature on cognitive development, however, which suggests few age differences in reasoning beyond early adolescence, the literature on psychosocial development suggests that these sets of capacities continue to mature through middle adolescence, perhaps into late adolescence. One reason that adolescents take more risks than adults is that adolescents are more are susceptible to peer pressure, more oriented to the present than to the future, and less able to regulate their emotional states.[7] In our work we find that, in contrast to risk perception and appraisal, which do not appear to change during adolescence and young adulthood, resistance to peer influence and future orientation continue to increase throughout the mid- and late-adolescent years.

The difficulties adolescents have in resisting peer pressure, orienting themselves to the future consequences of their actions, and modulating their emotional states are, I believe, accentuated under conditions of high positive arousal—that is, under the conditions of euphoria that often develop when teenagers are with their friends in social situations. In other words, when adolescents are in this state, they become even more susceptible to coercion, more shortsighted, and more driven by their emotions. For reasons that I explained earlier, extant research on risk taking misses this. When we study decision making in the usual laboratory paradigms, we construct a social and emotional context that removes peers, dampens individuals' emotional arousal, and permits individuals to be more circumspect.

The logical implication of this conclusion is to try to find ways of studying adolescent risk taking under social and emotional conditions that more closely approximate the real world. This has proven enormously difficult to do. One of my current graduate students, Margo Gardner, has recently completed a study in which she attempted to do this to a small degree. She presented samples of teenagers, college students, and adults with a series of tasks designed to assess risk taking and the psychosocial components hypothesized to affect their judgment. In one of our computer-administered risk-taking tasks, subjects were given the opportunity to take chances while driving a car. The game simulates the situation in which one is approaching an intersection, sees a traffic light turn yellow, and has to decide whether to stop or proceed through the intersection. In the task, a moving car is on the screen, and a yellow traffic light appears, signaling that at some point soon a wall will appear and the car will crash. Loud music is playing in the background. As soon as the yellow light appears, participants must decide whether to keep driving or apply the brakes. Participants are told that the longer they drive, the more points they earn; but that if the car crashes into the wall, all the points that have been accumulated are lost. The amount of time that elapses between the appearance of the light and the appearance of the wall is varied across trials, so there is no way to anticipate when the car will crash. Individuals who are more inclined to take risks in this game drive the car longer than those who are more risk averse. Performance on this task was correlated with responses to the questionnaire's measure of antisocial decision making, such that individuals who took more chances in the driving game were more likely to say they would commit an antisocial act if they believed they would not be caught.

The added twist in the study was that individuals were asked to come to the lab with two of their friends and they were randomly assigned to play the computer games alone or with their friends looking over their shoulder, giving them advice on what to do. We find that there is an interesting interaction between age and peer influence, consistent with the idea that adolescents are more influenced by peers than are adults, that they take more chances in the presence of peers than when they are alone. Specifically, when individuals were alone, there were no age differences in risk taking, but when they were in groups, risk taking increased among the adolescents and college students, but not among the adults. In other words, the negative influence of friends on risk taking is still evident among individuals in their early 20s. I suspect that few college undergraduates would dispute this.

We did not find the same group effect for two other tasks employed in this study: a delayed discounting task (in which individuals are asked to choose between a larger reward given sometime in the future and a smaller reward given immediately) and a gambling task (in which individuals choose between a large reward with a low probability of attainment and a small reward with a higher probability of attainment). My suspicion is that the sort of group effect hypothesized to operate in adolescence is operative mainly in tasks in which adolescents get excited and "lost in the moment," such as our driving task. When the task starts to look too much like a decision making task (as I believe our gambling and discounting tasks did), we may miss what I believe is distinctive about adolescent risk taking—which is not, as I have suggested, best thought of as a decision-making process.

The dual contributors to adolescent risk taking—the shift in reward sensitivity that drives adolescents to seek higher levels of novelty and stimulation than they did as children, and the relatively slow maturation of the regulatory competencies that would rein in this novelty and stimulation seeking—do not operate simultaneously, and therein lies the problem. The shift in reward sensitivity occurs relatively early in adolescence, is mainly subserved by changes in the limbic system, and is probably closely tied to the neuroendocrinological changes of puberty. (This is all highly speculative.) The maturation of self-regulatory competence is ongoing even in late adolescence, is subserved primarily by changes in the prefrontal cortex, and does not seem to be closely linked to pubertal maturation; it is better predicted by chronological age and years of education. The temporal gap between these two changes creates a special window of vulnerability in adolescence—vulnerability not only to risk taking, but to other forms of psychopathology, as I have argued in a recent chapter coauthored with Ron Dahl, Dan Keating, David Kupfer, Ann Masten, and Danny Pine.[10] In theory, early-maturing adolescents—early-maturing girls in particular—should be at greatest risk, since the gap between the shift in reward sensitivity and the development of self-regulation will occur relatively later; many studies indicate that this is in fact the case.

CONCLUSIONS

I want to conclude with what I think this means for the prevention of unhealthy risk taking in adolescence. My argument is that heightened risk taking during this period is likely to be normative, biologically driven, and inevitable. There is probably very little we can do with respect to intervention that will either attenuate or delay the shift in reward sensitivity or accelerate the maturation of self-regulatory competence so that the window of vulnerability will be eliminated. But given extant research suggesting that it is not risk perception or appraisal that is the problem, it would seem to me that rather than attempting to change the way adolescents evaluate risky activities (which is, in essence, what health education programs attempt to do), a more profitable strategy might focus on limiting opportunities for immature judgment to have harmful consequences. After all, according to Add Health data, more than 90% of all American high school students have had sex, drug, and alcohol education in their schools;[5] and studies show very persuasively that educational efforts do not lead to less risk taking.[11] In contrast, one recent analysis indicates that the dramatic drop in teen smoking that occurred in the late 1990s had nothing to do with antismoking education but is attributable entirely to the increase in the price of cigarettes.[12] Thus, strategies such as raising the price of cigarettes, more vigilantly enforcing laws governing the sale of alcohol, expanding access to mental health and contraceptive services, and raising the driving age would likely be more effective in limiting adolescent smoking, substance abuse, suicide, pregnancy, and automobile fatalities than strategies aimed at making adolescents wiser, less impulsive, or less short-sighted.[13] Some things just take time to develop, and mature judgment is probably one of them.

REFERENCES

1. FURBEY, M. & R. BEYTH-MAROM. 1992. Risk-taking in adolescence: a decision-making perspective. Dev. Rev. 12: 1–44
2. CAUFFMAN, E., L. STEINBERG & J. WOOLARD. 2002. Age differences in capacities underlying competence to stand trial. Presented at the Biennial Meeting of the Society for Research on Adolescence, New Orleans, April 13.
3. BENTHIN, A., P. SLOVIC & H. SEVERSON. 1993. A psychometric study of adolescent risk perception. J. Adolesc. 16: 153–168.
4. ZIMRING, F. 1998. American Youth Violence. Oxford University Press. New York.
5. UDRY, J. 1998. The National Longitudinal Study of Adolescent Health (Add Health), Waves I & II, 1994–1996. Carolina Population Center, University of North Carolina. Chapel Hill, NC.
6. SIMPSON, H., Ed. 1996. New to the Road: Reducing the Risks for Young Motorists. Youth Enhancement Service, UCLA School of Medicine. Los Angeles.
7. STEINBERG, L. & E. CAUFFMAN. 1996. Maturity of judgment in adolescence: psychosocial factors in adolescent decision-making. Law Human Behav. 20: 249–272.
8. SPEAR, P. 2000. The adolescent brain and age-related behavioral manifestations. Neurosci. Biobehav. Rev. 24: 417–463.
9. KEATING, D. 2004. Cognitive and brain development. In Handbook of Adolescent Psychology, 2nd ed. R. Lerner & L. Steinberg, Eds.: 45–84. Wiley. New York.
10. STEINBERG, L., et al. Psychopathology in adolescence: integrating affective neuroscience with the study of context. In Developmental Psychopathology. D. Cicchetti, Ed. Wiley. New York. In press.

11. LANDRY, D., L. KAESER & C. RICHARDS. 1999. Abstinence promotion and the provision of information about contraception in public school district sexuality education policies. Fam. Plann. Perspect. **31:** 280–286.
12. CENTERS FOR DISEASE CONTROL AND PREVENTION. 2002. Trends in cigarette smoking among high school students: United States, 1991-2001. JAMA **288:** 308–309.
13. GRUBER, J., ED. 2001. Risky Behavior among Youths: An Economic Analysis. University of Chicago Press. Chicago.

High-Risk Behavior during Adolescence

Comments on Part I

MICHAEL T. BARDO

Department of Psychology and Center for Drug Abuse Research Translation (CDART), University of Kentucky, Lexington, Kentucky 40506, USA

ABSTRACT: Cardinal and Steinberg provide evidence from both laboratory animal and human studies indicating that behavior is controlled by two distinct brain systems, one activational and the other inhibitory. This conceptual framework continues to be a useful integrative framework in developmental neurobiology and psychology. Despite the conceptual framework that posits a two-system control of high-risk behavior, it is notable that the bulk of research related to this topic has focused on one system in isolation from the other. Since the activational and inhibitory systems are constructs that are amenable to investigation using both laboratory animals and human subjects, it seems that a fruitful avenue for future interdisciplinary research would be to ascertain the interactive effect of these systems across the periadolescent period.

As discussed by Cardinal[1] and Steinberg,[2] there is a confluence of evidence from both laboratory animal and human studies indicating that behavior is controlled by two distinct brain systems, one activational and the other inhibitory. Early basic research in developing rats indicated that the activational system matures first, followed by the inhibitory system.[3] The activational system was posited to involve subcortical adrenergic circuitry, whereas the inhibitory system was thought to involve cortical cholinergic circuitry. As discussed by Steinberg,[2] this conceptual framework continues to be a useful integrative framework in developmental neuro biology and psychology, even though the complex neural circuitry underlying each system cannot be explained fully by any single brain region or neurotransmitter system. As a clear case in point, contrary to the notion that inhibitory control is provided by cortical cholinergic systems, the work presented by Cardinal[1] demonstrates that dopamine-containing limbic pathways also play a crucial role.

Regardless of the exact neural mechanisms, however, Steinberg[2] makes a good case that the delayed maturation of the inhibitory behavioral system relative to the activational system leads to a period during adolescence characterized by high novelty seeking and risk taking. This can result in increased vulnerability to a number

Address for correspondence: Michael T. Bardo, Department of Psychology and Center for Drug Abuse Research Translation (CDART), University of Kentucky, Lexington, KY 40506. Voice: 859-257-6456; fax: 859-323-1979.

mbardo@uky.edu

Ann. N.Y. Acad. Sci. 1021: 59–60 (2004). © 2004 New York Academy of Sciences.
doi: 10.1196/annals.1308.006

of negative outcomes, such as drug abuse, risky sexual behavior, and physical injuries. Despite this, it is important to point out that high levels of novelty seeking during the adolescent period is not pathological, but rather adaptive because it promotes the breaking of parental bonds required for independent living. Thus, any attempt to prevent risk-related behavioral problems early in life by restricting novelty-seeking behavior is going against the tide of biology and likely to fail. A more fruitful approach would seem to involve the redirecting of novelty-seeking behavior into channels that promote healthy outcomes. In the case of drug abuse, for example, exposure to nondrug, high-sensation events may be useful.[4]

Despite the conceptual framework that posits a two-system control of high-risk behavior, it is notable that the bulk of research related to this topic has focused on one system in isolation from the other. In addition, examination of the age-related temporal maturation of the two systems in relation to risk-taking behavior has been lacking. Indeed, it is not known currently if the two systems are linked mechanistically. Rather than being independent processes, perhaps the temporal onset and strength of the activational system directly affects the maturation and strength of the inhibitory system. Further, it is not known if individual differences in the temporal pattern of development of the two systems may be related to negative outcomes related to high-risk behavior. Since the activational and inhibitory systems are constructs that are amenable to investigation using both laboratory animals and human subjects, it seems that a fruitful avenue for future interdisciplinary research would be to ascertain the interactive effect of these systems across the periadolescent period.

REFERENCES

1. CARDINAL, R.N., C.A. WINSTANLEY, T.W. ROBBINS & B.J. EVERITT. 2004. Limbic corticostriatal systems and delayed reinforcement. Ann. N.Y. Acad. Sci. **1021:** 33–50.
2. STEINBERG, L. 2004. Risk taking in adolescence: what changes and why? Ann. N.Y. Acad. Sci. **1021:** 51–58.
3. CAMPBELL, B.A., L.D. LYTLE & H.C. FIBIGER. 1969. Ontogeny of adrenergic arousal and cholinergic inhibitory mechanisms in the rat. Science **166:** 635–637.
4. BARDO, M.T., R.L. DONOHEW & N.G. HARRINGTON. 1996. Psychobiology of novelty seeking and drug seeking behavior. Behav. Brain Res. **77:** 23–24.

Integrating Research on Developmental Psychopathology and Neuroscience in the Study of Adolescence

Introduction to Part II

DANIEL S. PINE

Section on Development and Affective Neuroscience, National Institute of Mental Health Intramural Research Program, National Institutes of Health, Bethesda, Maryland 20817, USA

ABSTRACT: This chapter introduces three papers that summarize research findings in clinical and basic neuroscience. They integrate prior research on clinical aspects of developmental psychopathology, basic research on brain development in nonhuman primates, and neuroimaging research on both normal and abnormal human development. From the clinical perspective these papers call attention to the unique relationship between adolescence and psychopathology. From the basic science perspective they call attention to the sequence of events that culminates in a fully mature central nervous system.

KEYWORDS: neuroscience; psychopathology; adolescence; brain development

INTRODUCTION

This section contains three papers summarizing research findings in clinical and basic neuroscience, focusing on the manner in which research from each field might inform studies in the other. The need for such integrative research on adolescent development arises in light of three sets of findings. One set emerges from clinical research on developmental psychopathology. A second set emerges from basic science research on brain development in nonhuman primates. A final set emerges from integrative studies using techniques such as neuroimaging. Moreover, while each of the three sets of data note important avenues to pursue for future studies, a fourth important area of research is not addressed in the current section. This concerns the role of rodent experiments in attempting to extend insights from basic science to research on developmental psychopathology. Despite the absence in this volume of a paper on this topic, such studies play a unique role when one attempts to translate findings from the laboratory to the clinic. Accordingly, the current section briefly reviews the importance and unique role to be played by studies conducted in rodents.

Address for correspondence: Dr. Daniel S. Pine, M.D., NIMH-Building 15-K, Room 110, MSC-2670, Bethesda, MD 20817-2670. Voice: 301-594-1318; fax: 301-402-2010.
daniel.pine@nih.gov

Ann. N.Y. Acad. Sci. 1021: 61–63 (2004). © 2004 New York Academy of Sciences.
doi: 10.1196/annals.1308.007

From the clinical perspective, a series of findings summarized in the current volume note a unique relationship between adolescence and psychopathology. For some disorders, such as major depression or panic disorder, initial signs or key precursors for the disorder exhibit marked increases in prevalence at adolescence.[1,2] For other disorders, such as conduct disorder, adolescence marks a key transition period, where disorders can either remit or reach new levels of chronicity. Major questions arise from this set of clinical findings, each of which focuses on aspects of heterogeneity in adolescent psychopathology. For example, a high proportion of adolescent mood and anxiety disorders represent transient disturbances with relatively few long-term consequences. In other cases, adolescent mood and anxiety disorders represent the initial harbingers of serious long-term pathology.[1] Key questions arise concerning factors that distinguish among adolescents facing low or high risk for persistent disorders. Similar questions on heterogeneity arise from studies on treatment response and familial aggregation. Current measures derived from clinical sciences provide few answers to questions in this area.

From the basic science perspective, recent findings document in precise detail the sequence of events that ultimately culminates in a fully mature central nervous system. As reviewed by Lewis, studies in nonhuman primates demonstrate that this developmental process extends well into adolescence. As a result, such studies document plasticity in neural systems during the precise period when plasticity occurs in behavioral systems. Moreover, such studies in nonhuman primates demonstrate particularly marked developmental changes in adolescence within tertiary brain regions, including portions of the prefrontal cortex (PFC). The chapter by Lewis in the current volume illustrates the manner in which specific changes emerge within primate PFC regions during adolescence. These same brain regions have been implicated in the pathophysiology of psychiatric conditions that emerge or undergo marked changes in quality during adolescence.[2] The hope is that knowledge concerning aspects of adolescent brain development may ultimately be used to answer clinical questions on heterogeneity in outcome, familial transmission, or treatment.

In the third area of research, advances in genetics and brain-imaging techniques have generated considerable enthusiasm for such efforts to integrate clinical and basic findings on adolescence changes in behavior and brain function. With these methods, it is now possible to acquire data on genetic or neural factors in humans and directly relate these measures to indices of behavior. Moreover, such genetic and neuroimaging measures can be developed to index functional aspects of neural processes that have been elucidated in rodents and nonhuman primates. For the process of fear conditioning, for example, the functional role of specific brain regions, and even specific genes within these brain regions, has been precisely delineated through studies in rodents and nonhumans primates.[2,3] Parallel studies document the role of specific brain regions in human adults and adolescents, with and without psychopathology. The second and third presentations in this section review advances from the field of neuroimaging relevant to normal and abnormal development in adolescence. This includes studies of changes in brain structure as well as function.

Finally, none of the three reviews in this section considers the relevance of research with rodents for developmental psychopathology. Such research plays an invaluable role in attempting to integrate insights from basic and clinical domains. At least two major areas of inquiry appear particularly amenable to research in rodents, where studies in humans or nonhuman primates are virtually impossible to complete.

The feasibility of studying rodents derives from the long history of research in this group of animals, coupled with their relatively rapid development and ease of housing.

First, available studies in rodents provide key insights on developmental changes in the neurochemical regulation of neural circuits that exhibit robust changes during development. One of the major insights to derive from this work documents changes in the dopamine system. A compelling series of studies demonstrates a shift in the activity of the rodent dopamine system as it relates to regulation of cortically and subcortically mediated processes.[2] The overall weight of these data served as a major impetus for examining the role of dopamine in human and primate development around the period of adolescence. Moreover, such research carries potential implications for research examining the clinical effects of dopaminergic compounds, whether they are used clinically or illicitly.

Second, relative to studies in humans and nonhuman primates, studies in rodents provide a far more compelling elucidation of the role played by specific genetic and experiential factors in shaping complex behaviors, including behaviors influenced by emotion.[3] As a result, studies in rodents provide fertile ground for novel hypotheses relating genetic and environmental factors to human changes in complex behaviors. Indeed, studies in rodents demonstrate developmental changes in the influence of serotonin-related genes on anxiety-related behaviors.[4] The timing and anatomical specificity of these changes have been demonstrated far more precisely in rodents than is currently possible in nonhuman primates, let alone humans. Such data from rodents will play a vital role in efforts to use recent insights from genetic studies in humans to develop clinical advances.[5]

Cleary, studies reviewed in each of the three chapters within this section demonstrate the tremendous strides in basic, clinical, and integrative or translational research strategies, as they can be applied to research on adolescent development. Studies in rodents further reveal the breadth of these advances and their potential for revolutionizing mental health sciences. However, the progress that has been made also brings into focus another set of challenges, namely, as the complexity of research grows in each of these areas, this progress is likely to present ever increasing challenges for investigators attempting to conduct studies that truly bridge clinical and basic domains. As illustrated in the papers within this section, recent research generates considerable enthusiasm for efforts to build such bridges.

REFERENCES

1. PINE, D.S., P. COHEN, D. GURLEY, et al. 1998. The risk for early-adulthood anxiety and depressive disorders in adolescents with anxiety and depressive disorders. Arch. Gen. Psychiatry **55:** 56–64.
2. SPEAR, L.P. 2000. The adolescent brain and age related behavioral manifestations. Neurosci. Biobehav. Rev. **24:** 417–463.
3. MEANEY, M.J. 2001. Maternal care, gene expression, and the transmission of individual differences in stress reactivity across generations. Annu. Rev. Neurosci. **24:** 1161–1192.
4. GROSS, C., X. ZHUANG, K. STARK, et al. 2002. Serotonin1A receptor acts during development to establish normal anxiety-like behaviour in the adult. Nature **416:** 396–400.
5. CASPI, A., K. SUGDEN, T.E. MOFFITT, et al. 2003. Influence of life stress on depression: moderation by a polymorphism in the 5-HTT gene. Science **301:** 386–389.

Postnatal Development of Prefrontal Inhibitory Circuits and the Pathophysiology of Cognitive Dysfunction in Schizophrenia

DAVID A. LEWIS, DIANNE CRUZ, STEPHEN EGGAN, AND SUSAN ERICKSON

Departments of Psychiatry and Neuroscience, University of Pittsburgh, Pittsburgh, Pennsylvania 15213 USA

ABSTRACT: The typical appearance of the clinical features of schizophrenia during late adolescence or early adulthood suggests that adolescence-related neurodevelopmental events may contribute to the pathophysiology of this disorder. Here the role that GABA-mediated inhibition in the dorsal lateral prefrontal cortex (DLPFC) plays in regulating working memory, a core cognitive process that matures late and that is disturbed in schizophrenia, is reviewed. Recent studies are summarized that demonstrate (1) that certain pre- and postsynaptic markers of GABA neurotransmission in the monkey DLPFC exhibit striking changes during adolescence, and (2) that these same markers are markedly altered in the DLPFC of subjects with schizophrenia. The implications of these findings for treatment and prevention strategies are discussed.

KEYWORDS: schizophrenia; adolescence; GABA; dorsal lateral prefrontal cortex (DLPFC)

INTRODUCTION

Schizophrenia is one of the most severe brain disorders affecting adolescents and young adults. This disorder afflicts approximately 1% of the population throughout the world and typically produces a lifetime of disability and emotional distress for affected individuals.[1] The risk of developing schizophrenia is directly associated with the degree of genetic relatedness to an affected individual,[2] and a number of putative susceptibility genes for schizophrenia have been identified recently.[3] However, the degree of concordance for schizophrenia among individuals with the same genetic makeup (e.g., monozygotic twins) only approaches 50%,[2] indicating that genetic liability alone is not sufficient for the clinical features of the illness to appear. Thus, considerations of the etiology of schizophrenia have also included the role of environmental factors. Interestingly, many of the environmental events that have been associated with an increased risk of schizophrenia occur during the prenatal or perinatal periods of life, well before the typical appearance of the diagnostic clinical

Address for correspondence: David A. Lewis, M.D., Department of Psychiatry, University of Pittsburgh, 3811 O'Hara Street, W1651 BST, Pittsburgh, PA 15213. Voice: 412-624-3934; fax: 412-624-9910.

lewisda@upmc.edu

Ann. N.Y. Acad. Sci. 1021: 64–76 (2004). © 2004 New York Academy of Sciences.
doi: 10.1196/annals.1308.008

features of the disorder in the late teens or early twenties.[4] For example, advanced paternal age at the time of conception,[5] maternal influenza during the second trimester of pregnancy,[6] labor and delivery complications,[7] and increased population density at the place of birth and rearing[8] have all been associated with an increased risk of developing schizophrenia later in life. In addition, compared to unaffected sibling or schoolmate comparison groups, individuals who develop schizophrenia are more likely to have exhibited motor abnormalities in early childhood,[9] to have had lower IQ and academic performance in grade school[10] and to have experienced social difficulties in their early teens.[11]

Thus, the pathogenesis of schizophrenia is considered to represent the interaction of genetic susceptibility and environmental risk factors that alter the neurodevelopmental processes that precede the onset of the typical signs and symptoms of the illness.[4] Given the diverse clinical features of schizophrenia, understanding the specific roles that normal and abnormal neurodevelopmental processes play in the illness requires a focus on those aspects of schizophrenia that are central to its pathogenesis. Although psychosis is frequently the most striking clinical manifestation of schizophrenia, disturbances in certain cognitive processes are now considered to be a core feature of the illness.[12] For example, cognitive abnormalities have been observed both in the premorbid and prodromal phases of schizophrenia[13] and in the unaffected siblings of individuals with schizophrenia.[14] In addition, cognitive abnormalities represent the most disabling and persistent features of schizophrenia, and the degree of cognitive impairment may be the best predictor of long-term outcome in affected individuals.[15]

A variety of disturbances in cognition have been described in schizophrenia.[12] Many of these cognitive deficits appear to reflect alterations in executive control, the processes that facilitate complex information processing and behavior.[16] These include context representation and maintenance functions, such as working memory (the ability to keep bits of information in mind in order to guide thought processes or sequences of behavior), that are dependent on the circuitry of the dorsolateral prefrontal cortex (DLPFC).[17] Interestingly, a recent study suggested that impairments of working memory might represent a core deficit in that in individuals with schizophrenia "…the limited capacity of verbal and spatial 'on-line storage' is rate limiting in performance of other cognitive functions."[18] These impairments in working memory are associated with abnormal function of the DLPFC, as evident from the observations of decreased blood flow or glucose utilization in the DLPFC under appropriate conditions of cognitive activation.[19] The central importance of these alterations in DLPFC function to the pathogenesis of the schizophrenia syndrome is supported by the absence of such disturbances in disorders such as major depression.[20]

The potential link between these disturbances in working memory function and the pathogenesis of schizophrenia is supported by the parallels between the time course of working memory maturation and that of the appearance of the clinical features of schizophrenia. Specifically, performance on DLPFC-mediated cognitive functions appears to progressively improve through childhood and adolescence, with mature levels of performance not achieved until late adolescence or early adulthood,[21] the most common age of onset for schizophrenia. Thus, characterizing the development of the elements of DLPFC circuitry that subserve working memory may be central to understanding the pathogenesis of the schizophrenia syndrome.

The maturation of cortical excitatory neurotransmisssion is certainly important in this regard, and it has been the focus of a number of recent reviews.[22–24] However, recent *in vivo* studies in monkey DLPFC have also revealed a critical role for certain inhibitory processes during working memory. For example, GABA activity is necessary for the spatial tuning of neuronal responses in the DLPFC during working memory tasks, and GABA antagonists in the DLPFC disrupt working memory performance.[25,26] Indeed, Constantinidis and colleagues[27] have suggested two roles for inhibition in working memory tasks: (1) sharpening of stimulus selectivity through the concurrent responses of inhibitory and excitatory units, and (2) sculpting of the temporal profile of DLPFC neuron activation by inhibitory interactions between cells active at different stages of the working memory task, typically at transition points. Therefore, inhibition serves both a spatial role (which DLPFC pyramidal neurons are activated during working memory) and a temporal role (when they are active during the different phases of working memory). Thus, in this chapter we review (1) the postnatal maturation of GABA neurons and their synapses in the monkey DLPFC, and (2) the evidence that those inhibitory markers that undergo substantial changes during adolescence are preferentially affected in schizophrenia.

POSTNATAL MATURATION OF DORSAL LATERAL PREFRONTAL CORTEX GABA NEURONS AND SYNAPSES

The primate DLPFC exhibits the same general cellular and connectional organization that are found in other neocortical regions, although a number of these features show specializations that are characteristic for the region.[28] As in other cortical regions, the inhibitory GABA neurons of the DLPFC appear to form subclasses that can be distinguished on the basis of a number of molecular, electrophysiological, and anatomical properties. For example, as illustrated in FIGURE 1, the calcium-binding proteins—parvalbumin (PV), calbindin (CB), and calretinin (CR)—are, with a few exceptions, expressed in separate populations of cortical GABA neurons.[29] These subtypes tend to exhibit different membrane properties[30] and to have axons with different arborization patterns and synaptic targets.[31] For example, the PV-containing chandelier and wide arbor (basket) neurons principally target the axon initial segments and cell body/proximal dendrites, respectively, of pyramidal neurons, whereas the CR-containing double-bouquet subclass of GABA neurons tend to innervate the distal dendrites of pyramidal neurons and the dendrites of other GABA cells.[32]

At least some of these subtypes also appear to differ in their birthplace. For example, in contrast to cortical pyramidal neurons (all of which are born in the subventricular zone and migrate radially into the developing cortical plate), some cortical GABA neurons appear to arise from the ganglionic eminences and follow a tangential migration pathway to the cerebral cortex, whereas others originate in the anterior subventricular area and migrate radially.[33] These differences in developmental origin appear to be associated with at least some differences in biochemical features such that in mice and ferrets, the CR-containing class of GABA neurons originate in the subventricular zone, whereas GABA neurons that contain PV appear to be born in the ganglionic eminences.[33] Interestingly, in mice the majority of cortical GABA neurons are born in the ganglionic eminences,[34] whereas this region contributes only about a third of cortical GABA neurons in humans.[35] Together, these findings may

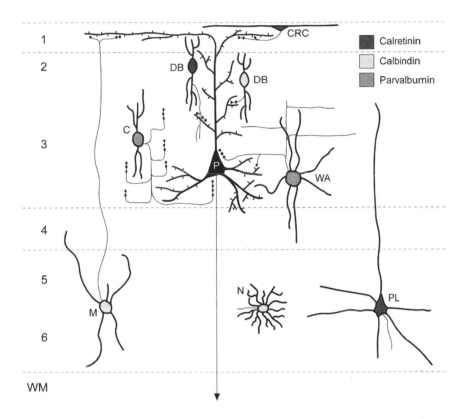

FIGURE 1. Schematic drawing of the synaptic interactions between different classes of GABA neurons and a layer 3 pyramidal neuron (P) in monkey DLPFC. C = PV-IR chandelier neuron; CRC = CR-, and/or CB-IR Cajal-Retzius neuron; DB = CR-IR (or possibly CB-IR) double-bouquet neuron; M = CB-IR Martinotti cell; N = CB-IR neurogliaform neuron; PL = CR-IR pyramidal-like neuron; WA = PV IR wide arbor ("basket") neuron (Adapted from J. Comp. Neurol. 341: 95–116, 1994.)

explain why the density of PV-positive cells clearly exceeds that of CR-positive cells in rodent cortex,[36] while in primate DLPFC CR-positive cells outnumber PV-positive cells by 2:1.[29,37] Perhaps as a consequence of these differences in developmental origin, the PV subclass of GABA neurons appears to mature much later than other subclasses. For example, in monkeys CR immunoreactivity is evident prenatally in migrating neurons in the intermediate zone, while PV immunoreactivity is not detectable until after birth.[38] Consistent with these observations, PV immunoreactivity in DLPFC wide arbor and chandelier neurons undergoes marked changes throughout postnatal development.

Wide arbor neurons (FIG. 2A), which are most common in layers 3 and 5, were named for their extensive axonal trees, which spread horizontally for up to 1 mm from the cell body.[39] These axons form terminal boutons within the local vicinity of the cell body, or within the parent cell's home column, but they appear to be special-

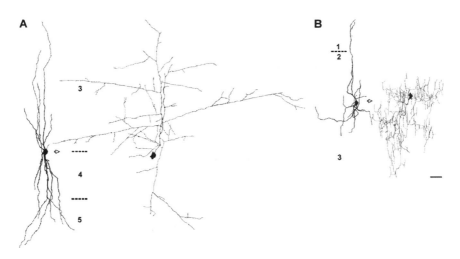

FIGURE 2. (**A**) Camera lucida drawing of a Golgi-impregnated wide arbor ("basket") neuron in layer 3 of monkey DLPFC. The dendrites (*to left*) are drawn separately from the axon (*right*). (Adapted from J. Comp. Neurol. 328: 282–312, 1993.) (**B**) Camera lucida drawing of a Golgi-impregnated chandelier neuron in layer 3 of monkey DLPFC. The dendritic field (*left*) has been drawn separately from the axon (*right*) for clarity. (Adapted from J. Comp. Neurol. 293: 599–615, 1990.) Note the much greater horizontal spread of the axonal arbor of the wide arbor neuron compared to the chandelier neuron. Laminar boundaries are indicated beside each neuron. Calibration bar equals 50 mm, and applies to both (A) and (B).

ized for providing inhibition to pyramidal cells in neighboring columns of the same cortical module.[40] The density of the PV-positive axon terminals of wide arbor neurons changes markedly during postnatal development,[41] increasing steadily in an almost linear fashion from one month of age to adulthood (FIG. 3). These developmental changes in the number of PV-positive boutons most likely reflect a shift in the detectability of wide arbor axon terminals with immunocytochemical techniques, secondary to a change in the concentration of PV protein within the terminals, since the total number of inhibitory synapses, and the axonal arbors of wide arbor cells specifically, appear to remain relatively constant over this same period of development.[39,42]

The chandelier class of PV-containing GABA neurons (FIG. 2B) also exhibits postnatal developmental changes in the expression of biochemical markers. In contrast to wide arbor neurons, the axonal arbor of chandelier neurons is restricted to a horizontal spread of approximately 250 mm, the width of a cortical column, and their axon terminals form distinctive vertical rows (termed "cartridges") that synapse along the axon initial segment of pyramidal cells.[43] These inhibitory synapses at the site of action potential generation in pyramidal neurons provide chandelier cells with a unique role in the regulation of pyramidal cell firing.[44] A typical chandelier cell may form cartridges with approximately 250 pyramidal cells,[43] and a single chandelier neuron can synchronize the firing of multiple pyramidal cells.[45] Thus, within the DLPFC, the dimensions of chandelier cell axonal arbors suggest that they serve to

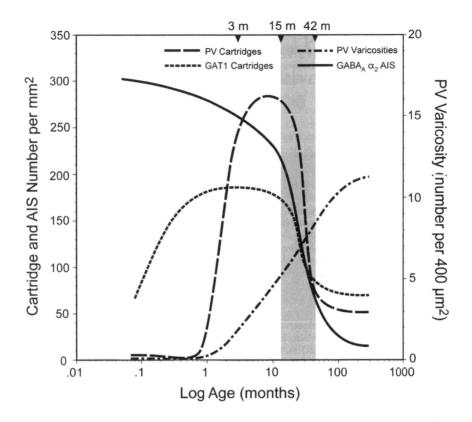

FIGURE 3. Trajectories of the densities of PV- and GAT1-labeled chandelier neuron axon cartridges and GABA$_A$α$_2$-labeled pyramidal neuron axon initial segments (AIS) across postnatal development in monkey DLPFC. Also shown are the densities of PV-positive varicosities thought to arise from axons of wide arbor neurons. *Arrowheads* demarcate the indicated ages in months, and the *shaded area* indicates the approximate age range corresponding to adolescence in this species. Note the different developmental time courses of these pre- and postsynaptic GABA markers. (Adapted from J. Comp. Neurol. 465: 385–400, 2003.)

coordinate the activity of excitatory cells within a single column, as opposed to interacting with neighboring columns, as wide arbor neurons do.

The axon cartridges of chandelier neurons can be identified with antibodies against PV or the GABA plasma membrane transporter (GAT1).[46–48] During postnatal development, the density of cartridges immunoreactive for either PV or GAT1 changes markedly in monkey DLPFC.[49] Although the precise time course differs for the two markers, the density of labeled cartridges is low in the newborn, increases to reach a peak prior to the onset of puberty, and then declines markedly to adult levels (FIG. 3). Because cartridges are readily visualized with the Golgi technique over this same time period,[39] the changes in PV- and GAT-immunoreactive cartridges likely reflect developmental shifts in the concentration of these proteins. Interestingly, the peak and subsequent decline in the density of labeled cartridges occurs prior to the age when the peak density of labeled wide arbor terminals is achieved, but appears concomitant with the pruning of intracortical excitatory connections.[50] Although the basis for this temporal coincidence remains to be investigated, it may be that the synchronous firing of a group of pyramidal cells, facilitated by inputs from chandelier neurons, is essential for promoting the maintenance of a subset of excitatory connections.

Postsynaptically, the influence of released GABA on the pyramidal cells targeted by chandelier neurons is determined by the particular type of $GABA_A$ receptor to which it binds. $GABA_A$ receptors are heteropentamers composed of two α, two β, and one γ subunit, with functional receptors containing a single type of α subunit.[51] Six different α subunits have been identified, and the distribution of these subunits shows a high degree of anatomical specialization.[52] For example, the $GABA_A$ $\alpha1$ subunit is present at approximately 85% of $GABA_A$ synapses in the adult cerebral cortex and is found at all postsynaptic domains of pyramidal cells.[53] In contrast, the $GABA_A$ $\alpha2$ subunit is localized predominantly to the axon initial segment of pyramidal neurons.[53] Furthermore, the α subunits of the $GABA_A$ receptors appear to differentially determine the effects of benzodiazepines, with the sedative effects mediated by the $\alpha1$ subtype,[54,55] and the anxiolytic effects mediated by the $\alpha2$ subtype.[56] Finally, GABA receptors including the $\alpha2$ subunit have a higher affinity for GABA, faster activation times, and slower deactivation times than receptors containing the more commonly expressed $\alpha1$ subunit.[57] Together, these features have been suggested to confer greater synaptic efficacy for GABA transmission occurring at synapses including the $\alpha2$ subunit.

Interestingly, $GABA_A$ receptors undergo changes in subunit composition during cortical development. For example, the α_2 subunit is most prevalent prenatally, and is replaced in the majority of, but not all, $GABA_A$ receptors postnatally by the α_1 subunit.[58] In the adult cortex, the majority of $GABA_A$ receptors containing the $\alpha2$ subunit are found in pyramidal cell axon initial segment.[59]

The prevalence of $GABA_A$ $\alpha2$ subunits at the axon initial segment undergoes substantial modification during postnatal development.[49] As shown in FIGURE 3, the density of pyramidal cell axon initial segments immunoreactive for the $\alpha2$ subunit is very high in the postnatal period, and then steadily declines through adolescence into adulthood. This decrease in the density of $\alpha2$-labeled axon initial segments may be interpreted as a decrease in the speed and efficacy of GABAergic transmission at the axon initial segment during postnatal maturation, rather than a reduction in the number of GABAergic synapses onto the axon initial segment, because the total number of inhibitory synapses appear to remain constant over this same time period.[42]

ALTERATIONS IN DORSAL LATERAL PREFRONTAL CORTEX GABA NEURONS AND SYNAPSES IN SCHIZOPHRENIA

The protracted postnatal maturation of these inhibitory connections in the primate DLPFC provides a series of opportunities for any disturbances, even subtle ones, to have their effects amplified as they impinge upon the trajectories of the developmental events that follow. Thus, investigations of developmentally related alterations of specific elements of DLPFC circuitry in schizophrenia, which can only be done in post-

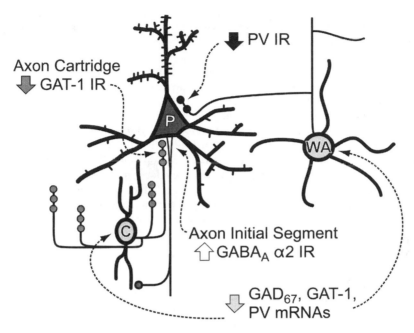

FIGURE 4. Schematic diagram summarizing the alterations in PV-containing chandelier (C) and wide arbor (WA) neuron inputs to pyramidal (P) neurons in the DLPFC of subjects with schizophrenia.

mortem human tissue, do not necessarily permit the determination of whether an observed alteration in the disease state is a primary defect, or the brain's adaptive response to some other abnormality. However, these developmental changes in the axon terminals of wide arbor and chandelier neurons, and their postsynaptic receptors, suggest that these components of DLPFC inhibitory circuitry may be particularly vulnerable in schizophrenia (see FIG. 4). Consistent with this hypothesis, the mRNAs for GAT-1 and for GAD67, a synthesizing enzyme for GABA, are not detectable in many of the GABA neurons that express PV, and the expression level of PV mRNA in these neurons is reduced below that of control subjects.[60–62] These changes are most prominent in the middle cortical layers. In addition, the density of GAT1-IR chandelier neuron axon cartridges in the middle cortical layers is reduced by 50%,[63] and the density of PV-labeled varicosities in these same layers is reduced by about 25%.[64] Together these findings converge on the idea that GABA synthesis and reuptake are reduced in the PV-containing subpopulation of GABA neurons, which include chandelier and wide arbor cells. Consistent with a reduction in synaptic GABA at pyramidal cell axon initial segments, the density of axon initial segments immunoreactive for the α2 subunit of the $GABA_A$ receptor is increased by a factor of 2 in the same subjects with schizophrenia.[65] Interestingly, the relative ratio of these markers of pre- and postsynaptic inputs to the axon initial segment of pyramidal neurons is reminiscent of that present during early postnatal development (see FIG. 3). Although it seems unlikely that the findings in schizophrenia represent an arrest of development at such an early stage, these disturbances in schizophrenia may reflect an alteration of DLPFC circuitry that makes it unable to support higher levels of working memory load, rendering the impaired performance in schizophrenia analogous to the immature levels of working memory function seen in children.[21]

The specificity of these changes for the PV-containing class of GABA neurons is supported by the observations that the overall density of GAT1-positive varicosities, a marker of all GABA terminals, including the large majority that target the dendrites of pyramidal cells, is unchanged in schizophrenia.[48] Furthermore, neither the mRNA levels nor the density of labeled varicosities for calretinin (CR), a calcium-binding protein found in about 50% of cortical GABA neurons that do not contain PV, appears to be changed in individuals with schizophrenia.[48,62] As just noted, CR expression is evident early in prenatal cortical development in primates, whereas PV expression is not detectable until the postnatal period, observations consistent with the general idea that vulnerability of neural elements in schizophrenia may be related to the timing and course of their development.

CONCLUSIONS

The acquisition of mature levels of performance for cognitive processes involving executive control, such as working memory, appears to be delayed until early adulthood in monkeys and humans. These processes depend upon the synchronized activity of neural networks in the DLPFC. *In vivo* electrophysiology studies suggest that the inhibitory regulation of pyramidal cells by fast-spiking (i.e., PV-containing) GABA neurons is essential for normal working memory function[25,26] and for the gamma-band synchronization of DLPFC neural networks[66] that appears to mediate working memory[67] and that is disturbed in schizophrenia.[68] The studies reviewed earlier indicate that two classes of PV-containing GABA neurons, chandelier and wide arbor cells, undergo refinements during a protracted period of postnatal development that parallels the time course of maturation of working memory performance in primates. In addition, PV-containing, but not other classes of DLPFC GABA neurons, are altered in schizophrenia, suggesting that the deficits in working memory in this illness may be the result of disruptions in the developmental trajectories of these neural elements. These temporal correlations may explain how a range of environmental factors (e.g., labor-delivery complications, urban place of rearing, and marijuana use during adolescence) are all associated with increased risk for the appearance of schizophrenia later in life. In addition, these findings provide a pathophysiologically based rationale for a novel and selective pharmacotherapy designed to correct the deficit in GABAergic control of pyramidal cell function.[69] Given the marked developmental changes that occur in markers of the chandelier and wide arbor cell inputs to pyramidal neurons during adolescence, this type of pharmacocological intervention may have particular value as an intervation strategy for high-risk adolescents in the prodromal phase of the illness.[70]

ACKNOWLEDGMENTS

Cited work conducted by the authors was supported by USPHS Grants MH51234, MH45156, and MH43784.

REFERENCES

1. LEWIS, D.A. & J.A. LIEBERMAN. 2000. Catching up on schizophrenia: natural history and neurobiology. Neuron **28:** 325–334.
2. GOTTESMAN, I.I. 1991. Schizophrenia Genesis: The Origins of Madness. Freeman. New York.
3. HARRISON, P.J. & M.J. OWEN. 2003. Genes for schizophrenia? Recent findings and their pathophysiological implications. Lancet **361:** 417–419.
4. LEWIS, D.A. & P. LEVITT. 2002. Schizophrenia as a disorder of neurodevelopment. Ann. Rev. Neurosci. **25:** 409–432.
5. BROWN, A.S., C.A. SCHAEFER, R.J. WYATT, *et al.* 2002. Paternal age and risk of schizophrenia in adult offspring. Am. J. Psychiatry **159:** 1528–1533.
6. MEDNICK, S.A., R.A. MACHON & M. HUTTUNEN. 1989. Disturbances of fetal neural development and adult schizophrenia. *In* Schizophrenia: Scientific Progress. S.C. Schultz & C.A. Tamminga, Eds.: 69–77. Oxford Univ. Press. New York.
7. GEDDES, J.R. & S.M. LAWRIE. 1995. Obstetric complications and schizophrenia: a meta-analysis. Brit. J. Psychiatry **167:** 786–793.
8. PEDERSEN, C.B. & P.B. MORTENSEN. 2001. Evidence of a dose-response relationship between urbanicity during upbringing and schizophrenia risk. Arch. Gen. Psychiatry **58:** 1039–1046.
9. WALKER, E. & R.J. LEWINE. 1990. Prediction of adult onset schizophrenia from childhood home movies. Am. J. Psychiatry **147:** 1052–1056.
10. OTT, S.L., S. SPINELLI, D. ROCK, *et al.* 1998. The New York high-risk project: social and general intelligence in children at risk for schizophrenia. Schizophr. Res. **31:** 1–11.
11. DAVIDSON, M., A. REICHENBERG, J. RABINOWITZ, *et al.* 1999. Behavioral and intellectual markers for schizophrenia in apparently healthy male adolescents. Am. J. Psychiatry **156:** 1328–1335.
12. ELVEVÅG, B. & T.E. GOLDBERG. 2000. Cognitive impairment in schizophrenia is the core of the disorder. Crit. Rev. Neurobiol. **14:** 1–21.
13. COSWAY, R., M. BYRNE, R. CLAFFERTY, *et al.* 2000. Neuropsychological change in young people at high risk for schizophrenia: results from the first two neuropsychological assessments of the Edinburgh High Risk Study. Psychol. Med. **30:** 1111–1121.
14. EGAN, M.F., T.E. GOLDBERG, T. GSCHEIDLE, *et al.* 2001. Relative risk for cognitive impairments in siblings of patients with schizophrenia. Biol. Psychiatry **50:** 98–107.
15. GREEN, M.F. 1996. What are the functional consequences of neurocognitive deficits in schizophrenia? Am. J. Psychiatry **153:** 321–330.
16. SHALLICE, T. 1988. From Neuropsychology to Mental Structure. Cambridge Univ. Press. Cambridge.
17. BOTVINICK, M.M., T.S. BRAVER, D.M. BARCH, *et al.* 2001. Conflict monitoring and cognitive control. Psychol. Rev. **108:** 624–652.
18. SILVER, H., P. FELDMAN, W. BILKER, *et al.* 2003. Working memory deficit as a core neuropsychological dysfunction in schizophrenia. Am. J. Psychiatry **160:** 1809–1816.
19. WEINBERGER, D.R., K.F. BERMAN & R.F. ZEC. 1986. Physiologic dysfunction of dorsolateral prefrontal cortex in schizophrenia. I. Regional cerebral blood flow evidence. Arch. Gen. Psychiatry **43:** 114–124.
20. BARCH, D.M., Y.I. SHELINE, J.G. CSERNANSKY, *et al.* 2003. Working memory and prefrontal cortex dysfunction: specificity to schizophrenia compared with major depression. Biol. Psychiatry **53:** 376–384.
21. DIAMOND, A. 2002. Normal development of prefrontal cortex from birth to young adulthood: cognitive functions, anatomy and biochemistry. *In* Principles of Frontal Lobe Function. D.T. Stuss & R.T. Knight, Eds.: 466–503. Oxford Univ. Press. London.
22. MCGLASHAN, T.H. & R.E. HOFFMAN. 2000. Schizophrenia as a disorder of developmentally reduced synaptic connectivity. Arch. Gen. Psychiatry **57:** 637–648.
23. KESHAVAN, M.S., S. ANDERSON & J.W. PETTEGREW. 1994. Is schizophrenia due to excessive synaptic pruning in the prefrontal cortex? The Feinberg hypothesis revisited. J. Psychiatry Res. **28:** 239–265.
24. LEWIS, D.A. 1997. Development of the prefrontal cortex during adolescence: insights into vulnerable neural circuits in schizophrenia. Neuropsychopharmacology **16:** 385–398.

25. RAO, S.G., G.V. WILLIAMS & P.S. GOLDMAN-RAKIC. 1999. Isodirectional tuning of adjacent interneurons and pyramidal cells during working memory: evidence for microcolumnar organization in PFC. J. Neurophysiol. **81:** 1903–1916.
26. RAO, S.G., G.V. WILLIAMS & P.S. GOLDMAN-RAKIC. 2000. Destruction and creation of spatial tuning by disinhibition: $GABA_A$ blockade of prefrontal cortical neurons engaged by working memory. J. Neurosci. **20:** 485–494.
27. CONSTANTINIDIS, C., G.V. WILLIAMS & P.S. GOLDMAN-RAKIC. 2002. A role for inhibition in shaping the temporal flow of information in prefrontal cortex. Nature Neurosci. **5:** 175–180.
28. LEWIS, D.A., D.S. MELCHITZKY & G.G. BURGOS. 2002. Specificity in the functional architecture of primate prefrontal cortex. J. Neurocytol. **31:** 265–276.
29. CONDÉ, F., J.S. LUND, D.M. JACOBOWITZ, et al. 1994. Local circuit neurons immunoreactive for calretinin, calbindin D-28k, or parvalbumin in monkey prefrontal cortex: distribution and morphology. J. Comp. Neurol. **341:** 95–116.
30. KRIMER, L.S. & P.S. GOLDMAN-RAKIC. 2001. Prefrontal microcircuits: membrane properties and excitatory input of local, medium, and wide arbor neurons. J. Neurosci. **21:** 3788–3796.
31. KAWAGUCHI, Y. & Y. KUBOTA. 1993. Correlation of physiological subgroupings of non-pyramidal cells with parvalbumin- and $calbindin_{D28k}$-immunoreactive neurons in layer V of rat frontal cortex. J. Neurophysiol. **70:** 387–396.
32. DEFELIPE, J. 1997. Types of neurons, synaptic connections and chemical characteristics of cells immunoreactive for calbindin-D28K, parvalbumin and calretinin in the neocortex. J. Chem. Neuroanat. **14:** 1–19.
33. XU, Q., E. DE LA CRUZ & S.A. ANDERSON. 2003. Cortical interneuron fate determination: diverse sources for distinct subtypes? Cereb. Cortex **13:** 670–676.
34. ANDERSON, S.A., D.D. EISENSTAT, L. SHI, et al. 1997. Interneuron migration from basal forebrain to neocortex: dependence on Dlx genes. Science **278:** 474–476.
35. LETINIC, K., R. ZONCU & P. RAKIC. 2002. Origin of GABAergic neurons in the human neocortex. Nature **417:** 645–649.
36. GABBOTT, P.L.A., B.G.M. DICKIE, R.R. VAID, et al. 1997. Local-circuit neurones in the medial prefrontal cortex (areas 25, 32 and 24b) in the rat: morphology and quantitative distribution. J. Comp. Neurol. **377:** 465–499.
37. GABBOTT, P.L.A. & S.J. BACON. 1996. Local circuit neurons in the medial prefrontal cortex (areas 24a,b,c, 25 and 32) in the monkey: II. Quantitative areal and laminar distributions. J. Comp. Neurol. **364:** 609–636.
38. CONDÉ, F., J.S. LUND & D.A. LEWIS. 1996. The hierarchical development of monkey visual cortical regions as revealed by the maturation of parvalbumin-immunoreactive neurons. Dev. Brain Res. **96:** 261–276.
39. LUND, J.S. & D.A. LEWIS. 1993. Local circuit neurons of developing and mature macaque prefrontal cortex: Golgi and immunocytochemical characteristics. J. Comp. Neurol. **328:** 282–312.
40. LEWIS, D.A. & G. GONZALEZ-BURGOS. 2000. Intrinsic excitatory connections in the prefrontal cortex and the pathophysiology of schizophrenia. Brain Res. Bull. **52:** 309–317.
41. ERICKSON, S.L. & D.A. LEWIS. 2002. Postnatal development of parvalbumin- and GABA transporter-immunoreactive axon terminals in monkey prefrontal cortex. J. Comp. Neurol. **448:** 186–202.
42. BOURGEOIS, J.-P., P.S. GOLDMAN-RAKIC & P. RAKIC. 1994. Synaptogenesis in the prefrontal cortex of rhesus monkeys. Cereb. Cortex **4:** 78–96.
43. PETERS, A. 1984. Chandelier cells. In Cerebral Cortex, Vol. 1. E.G. Jones & A. Peters, Eds.: 361–380. Plenum Press. New York.
44. KLAUSBERGER, T., P.J. MAGILL, L.F. MARTON, et al. 2003. Brain-state- and cell-type specific firing of hippocampal interneurons in vivo. Nature **421:** 844–848.
45. COBB, S.R., E.H. BUHL, K. HALASY, et al. 1995. Synchronization of neuronal activity in hippocampus by individual GABAergic interneurons. Nature **378:** 75–78.
46. LEWIS, D.A. & J.S. LUND. 1990. Heterogeneity of chandelier neurons in monkey neocortex: corticotropin-releasing factor and parvalbumin immunoreactive populations. J. Comp. Neurol. **293:** 599–615.

47. DeFelipe, J., S.H.C. Hendry & E.G. Jones. 1989. Visualization of chandelier cell axons by parvalbumin immunoreactivity in monkey cerebral cortex. Proc. Natl. Acad. Sci. USA **86:** 2093–2097.
48. Woo, T.-U., R.E. Whitehead, D.S. Melchitzky, et al. 1998. A subclass of prefrontal gamma-aminobutyric acid axon terminals are selectively altered in schizophrenia. Proc. Natl. Acad. Sci. USA **95:** 5341–5346.
49. Cruz, D.A., S.M. Eggan & D.A. Lewis. 2003. Postnatal development of pre- and post-synaptic GABA markers at chandelier cell inputs to pyramidal neurons in monkey prefrontal cortex. J. Comp. Neurol. **465:** 385–400.
50. Woo, T.-U., M.L. Pucak, C.H. Kye, et al. 1997. Peripubertal refinement of the intrinsic and associational circuitry in monkey prefrontal cortex. Neuroscience **80:** 1149–1158.
51. Barnard, E.A., P. Skolnick, R.W. Olsen, et al. 1998. International Union of Pharmacology. XV. Subtypes of gamma-aminobutyric acidA receptors: classification on the basis of subunit structure and receptor function. Pharmacol. Rev. **50:** 291–313.
52. Fritschy, J.-M. & H. Mohler. 1995. GABA$_A$-receptor heterogeneity in the adult rat brain: differential regional and cellular distribution of seven major subunits. J. Comp. Neurol. **359:** 154–194.
53. Nusser, Z., W. Sieghart, D. Benke, et al. 1996. Differential synaptic localization of two major γ-aminobutyric acid type A receptor α subunits on hippocampal pyramidal cells. Proc. Natl. Acad. Sci. USA **93:** 11939–11944.
54. McKernan, R.M., T.W. Rosahl, D.S. Reynolds, et al. 2000. Sedative but not anxiolytic properties of benzodiazepines are mediated by the GABAA receptor α1 subtype. Nature Neurosci. **3:** 587–592.
55. Rudolph, U., F. Crestani, D. Benke, et al. 1999. Benzodiazepine actions mediated by specific γ-aminobutyric acid$_A$ receptor subtypes. Nature **401:** 796–800.
56. Löw, K., F. Crestani, R. Keist, et al. 2000. Molecular and neuronal substrate for the selective attenuation of anxiety. Science **290:** 131–134.
57. Lavoie, A.M., J.J. Tingey, N.L. Harrison, et al. 1997. Activation and deactivation rates of recombinant GABA$_A$ receptor channels are dependent on α-subunit isoform. Biophys. J. **73:** 2518–2526.
58. Fritschy, J.-M., J. Paysan, A. Enna, et al. 1994. Switch in the expression of rat GABAA-receptor subtypes during postnatal development: an immunohistochemical study. J. Neurosci. **14:** 5302–5324.
59. Loup, F., O. Weinmann, Y. Yonekawa, et al. 1998. A highly sensitive immunoflourescence procedure for anlyzing the subcellular distribution of GABA$_A$ receptor subunits in the human brain. J. Histochem. Cytochem. **46:** 1129–1139.
60. Volk, D.W., M.C. Austin, J.N. Pierri, et al. 2000. Decreased GAD$_{67}$ mRNA expression in a subset of prefrontal cortical GABA neurons in subjects with schizophrenia. Arch. Gen. Psychiatry **57:** 237–245.
61. Volk, D.W., M.C. Austin, J.N. Pierri, et al. 2001. GABA transporter-1 mRNA in the prefrontal cortex in schizophrenia: decreased expression in a subset of neurons. Am. J. Psychiatry **158:** 256–265.
62. Hashimoto, T., D.W. Volk, S.M. Eggan, et al. 2003. Gene expression deficits in a subclass of GABA neurons in the prefrontal cortex of subjects with schizophrenia. J. Neurosci. **23:** 6315–6326.
63. Pierri, J.N., A.S. Chaudry, T.-U. Woo, et al. 1999. Alterations in chandelier neuron axon terminals in the prefrontal cortex of schizophrenic subjects. Am. J. Psychiatry **156:** 1709–1719.
64. Lewis, D.A., D.A. Cruz, D.S. Melchitzky, et al. 2001. Lamina-specific deficits in parvalbumin-immunoreactive varicosities in the prefrontal cortex of subjects with schizophrenia: evidence for fewer projections from the thalamus. Am. J. Psychiatry **158:** 1411–1422.
65. Volk, D.W., J.N. Pierri, J.-M. Fritschy, et al. 2002. Reciprocal alterations in pre- and postsynaptic inhibitory markers at chandelier cell inputs to pyramidal neurons in schizophrenia. Cereb. Cortex **12:** 1063–1070.
66. Blatow, M., A. Rozov, I. Katona, et al. 2003. A novel network of multipolar bursting interneurons generates theta frequency oscillations in neocortex. Neuron **38:** 805–817.

67. HOWARD, M.W., D.S. RIZZUTO, J.B. CAPLAN, *et al.* 2003. Gamma oscillations correlate with working memory load in humans. Cereb. Cortex **13:** 1369–1374.
68. SPENCER, K.M., P.G. NESTOR, D.F. SALISBURY, *et al.* 2003. Abnormal neural synchrony in schizophrenia. J. Neurosci. **23:** 7407–7411.
69. LEWIS, D.A., D.W. VOLK & T. HASHIMOTO. 2003. Selective alterations in prefrontal cortical GABA neurotransmission in schizophrenia: a novel target for the treatment of working memory dysfunction. Psychopharmacology. Published on-line Dec. 9, 2003.
70. BIRCHWOOD, M., P. MCGORRY & H. JACKSON. 1997. Early intervention in schizophrenia. Br. J. Psychiatry **170:** 2–5.

Structural Magnetic Resonance Imaging of the Adolescent Brain

JAY N. GIEDD

National Institute of Mental Health, National Institutes of Health, Department of Health and Human Services, Bethesda, Maryland 20892, USA

ABSTRACT: Magnetic resonance imaging (MRI) provides accurate anatomical brain images without the use of ionizing radiation, allowing longitudinal studies of brain morphometry during adolescent development. Results from an ongoing brain imaging project being conducted at the Child Psychiatry Branch of the National Institute of Mental Health indicate dynamic changes in brain anatomy throughout adolescence. White matter increases in a roughly linear pattern, with minor differences in slope in the four major lobes (frontal, parietal, temporal, occipital). Cortical gray matter follows an inverted U-shape developmental course with greater regional variation than white matter. For instance, frontal gray matter volume peaks at about age 11.0 years in girls and 12.1 years in boys, whereas temporal gray matter volume peaks at about age at 16.7 years in girls and 16.2 years in boys. The dorsal lateral prefrontal cortex, important for controlling impulses, is among the latest brain regions to mature without reaching adult dimensions until the early 20s. The details of the relationships between anatomical changes and behavioral changes, and the forces that influence brain development, have not been well established and remain a prominent goal of ongoing investigations.

KEYWORDS: magnetic resonance imaging (MRI); adolescence; gray matter; white matter

INTRODUCTION

It comes as no surprise to parents of teens that the brain of an 8 year old is different than the brain of a 13 year old. Yet to pin down these differences in a scientific way has been elusive. Nature has gone to great extremes to protect this most vital organ. It is wrapped in a leathery case, surrounded by a protective moat of fluid, and completely encased in bone. This has shielded the brain from falls or attacks from predators, but it has also shielded the brain from scientists. Even after the availability of X rays or CT scans, the study of the healthy teen brain remained indirect, because such techniques use ionizing radiation, which ethically precludes their use in non-ill populations.

Address for correspondence: Jay N. Giedd, M.D., National Institute of Mental Health, National Institutes of Health, Department of Health and Human Services, Room 4C110, 10 Center Dr. MSC 1367, Bethesda, MD 20892-1367. Voice: 301-435-4517; fax: 301-480-8898.
jg@nih.gov

Ann. N.Y. Acad. Sci. 1021: 77–85 (2004). © 2004 New York Academy of Sciences.
doi: 10.1196/annals.1308.009

Magnetic resonance imaging (MRI) has changed that. It provides exquisitely accurate pictures of the living, growing brain without the use of ionizing radiation and
has helped launch a new era of adolescent neuroscience. In addition to anatomical
images, MRI can also be used to assess brain function. It does so by capitalizing on
different magnetic properties of oxygenated versus nonoxygenated hemoglobin.

This chapter focuses on the first type of MRI—looking at the changing anatomy
of the brain during the teen years.

METHODS

The data for this chapter are derived from an ongoing longitudinal pediatric brain
MRI study being conducted at the Child Psychiatry Branch of the National Institute
of Mental Health. To date, the sample of healthy youths consists of 329 scans from
95 males and 66 females, with MRI scans and neuropsychological testing acquired
at approximately 2-year intervals.

Once the images are acquired, they are analyzed by a variety of automated and
manual tracing techniques through collaboration with several imaging centers
throughout the world. Further details of the testing and screening of this sample and
the methods of image analysis have been published elsewhere.[1–4]

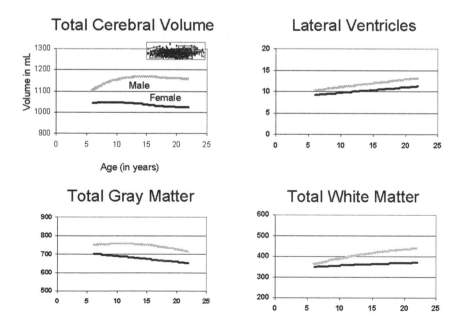

FIGURE 1. Total size of the brain.

ANATOMICAL CHANGES IN THE TEEN BRAIN

Total Brain Volume

The total size of the brain is already approximately 90% of its adult size by age six years (FIG. 1). This is counterintuitive to anyone who has seen a child trying to wear an adult's hat. The discrepancy is accounted for by the fact that head circumference does change throughout childhood (approximately, 2.0 inches in boys and 1.9 inches in girls from ages 4 to 18 years),[5] but the increase is due mostly to an increase in skull thickness not brain size.[6]

In our sample, male brains are approximately 12% larger on average than those of females. This difference remains statistically significant, even when controlling for height and weight. Of course, gross size of structures may not reflect sexually dimorphic differences in neuronal connectivity or receptor density. Given the myriad parameters influencing brain size, size alone should not be interpreted as imparting any sort of functional advantage or disadvantage.

Although the total size of the brain remains relatively stable across the ages of 6 to 20 years the various subcomponents of the brain undergo dynamic changes.

On an MRI image white matter, gray matter, and fluid have different signal strength, and these different tissue types are often used to categorize different brain structures or regions.

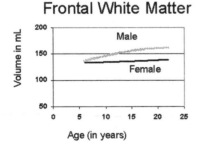

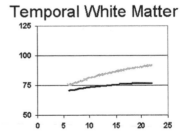

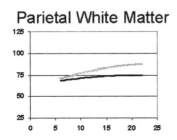

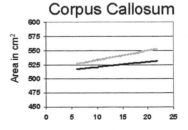

FIGURE 2. White matter in brain relative to age.

White Matter

Regional Volumes of White Matter

On MRI scans white matter indicates myelinated axons. Myelination is the result of oligodendrocytes wrapping neuronal axons in a fatty sheath that speeds up transmission between neurons—up to 100 times the speed of unmyelinated neurons. The greater speed of neuronal processing may facilitate cognitive complexity and the ability to adeptly combine information from multiple sources.

The amount of white matter in the brain generally increases throughout childhood and adolescence (see FIG. 2). The white matter increases are roughly linear, and the slope of increase is approximately the same in the four major lobes of the brain (frontal, temporal, parietal, and occipital).

Myelinated axons can be (1) *projectional,* connecting the brain to the spinal cord; (2) *associational,* connecting one type of brain part to another; or (3) *commissural,* connecting similar parts of the brain in the left and right hemispheres. A relatively new type of MRI called Diffusion Tensor Imaging (DTI) may help discern these different types of white matter connections.

The corpus callosum (CC) comprises the third type of myelinated axons, and is by far the most conspicuous white-matter component of the brain. It consists of approximately 180 million myelinated axons[7] connecting similar parts of the left and right cerebral hemispheres. The connections generally take the shortest route, so a certain topography of the brain is preserved on the CC, with anterior sections consisting of fibers connecting frontal brain areas, middle sections connecting middle cortical areas, and posterior sections connecting posterior cortical areas. There is some controversy as to just how tightly these spatial relationships of the cortex are maintained in the CC, but for some of the areas studied, such as the somatosensory regions, the spatial representation is highly preserved.[8,9]

With the notable exception of marsupials and monotrenes, most mammals from insectivores to higher primates have a CC, and it appears to have evolved in parallel with the neocortex.[10,11] The CC integrates activities of the left and right cerebral hemispheres, such as organizing bimanual motor output[12] and unifying the sensory fields,[13,14] but is also involved in memory storage and retrieval,[15] attention and arousal,[16] language and auditory functions,[17] and perhaps in the perception of consciousness.[18] Creativity and intelligence are linked to interhemispheric integration,[19] and the more complex the cognitive task, the more critical interhemispheric integration becomes.[20,21] These functions subserved by the CC continue to improve during childhood and adolescence, highlighting interest in the structural changes shown to progress during that developmental period.[22] Further developmental interest stems from CC anomalies reported for several neuropsychiatric disorders of childhood.[23–30]

In our sample the midsagittal CC size increased on average 1.3% per year. However, when individual children are followed longitudinally, the changes in specific subcomponents of the CC are shown to occur much more dramatically.[31] The CC changes occur in a front-to-back direction, with the anterior sections reaching adult sizes sooner than the posterior sections. This was somewhat surprising, because in general frontal regions of the brain are thought to mature later.

Another white-matter area that undergoes substantial changes during the teen years is the left arcuate fasiculus, which connects Wernicke's area (reception of speech) with Broca's area (production of speech).[32]

A postmortem study in 164 psychiatrically normal individuals, ages newborn to 76 years, revealed white matter providing connections between the hippocampus and the frontal cortex was particularly active during the teen years.[33] Speculatively, this may suggest an increasing ability to draw upon memories of past events when making decisions.

Gray Matter

The two major categories of gray-matter subdivision are cortical (on the outer surface of the brain) and subcortical (inside the cortex).

Subcortical Gray Matter

Basal Ganglia. The basal ganglia consist of the caudate, putamen, globus pallidus, subthalamic nucleus, and substantia nigra. The caudate nucleus is currently the only of these structures that we have been able to reliably quantify. The basal ganglia have a central role in control of movement and muscle tone, but are also involved in circuits mediating higher cognitive functions, attention, and affective states.

Caudate volumes decrease during the teen years and are relatively larger in females. This sexual dimorphism is interesting in light of smaller caudate nucleus volumes reported for male predominant disorders, such as ADHD[34–36] and Tourette's syndrome.[37–39]

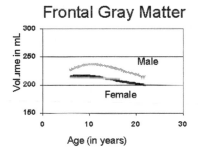

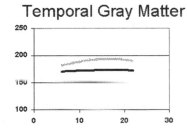

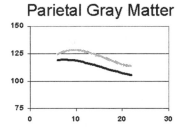

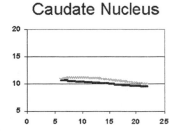

FIGURE 3. Gray matter relative to age.

Amygdala and Hippocampus. The temporal lobes, amygdala, and hippocampus are integral players in the arenas of emotion, language, and memory.[40] Human capacity for these functions changes markedly between ages 4 and 18,[41–43] although the relationship between the development of these capacities and morphological changes in the structures subserving these functions is poorly understood.

The amygdala and hippocampus have not been quantified for the longitudinal sample. In a previous report from a cross-sectional sample subset of the NIMH sample, amygdala volume increased significantly only in males, and hippocampal volume increased significantly with age only in females.[44] This pattern of gender-specific maturational volumetric changes is consistent with nonhuman primate studies indicating that the amygdala contains high numbers of androgen receptors[45] and a smaller number of estrogen receptors,[46] while the hippocampus contains higher amounts of estrogen receptors.[47]

Influence of estrogen on the hippocampus is further supported by both rodent and human studies. Gonadectomized female rats have a lower density of dendritic spines and decreased fiber outgrowth in the hippocampus, which can be alleviated with hormone replacement.[47,48] In humans, women with gonadal hypoplasia have smaller hippocampi.[49] An MRI study of 20 young adults also showed proportionately larger hippocampal volumes in females.[50]

Adolescent behavior is often attributed to "raging hormones," but it should be noted that although hormones can affect brain structure and function, particularly in the amygdala and hippocampus, they are only part of a larger realm of brain changes influencing adolescent behavior.

Cortical Gray Matter

Early cross-sectional pediatric neuroimaging studies showed a general decrease in the amount of cortical gray matter during childhood, beginning at the earliest ages of the study design, which was often around age 5 years.[51–54] So it was somewhat of a surprise when data from scans acquired longitudinally, by having people return for scans at approximately two-year intervals, indicated an "inverted U" pattern (see Fig. 3). In further contrast to the linear pattern for white-matter changes, the gray-matter developmental curves differ in the major lobes. For instance, in the frontal lobes, involved in planning, organizing, strategizing, and other "executive" functions, the cortical gray matter reaches its maximal thickness at 11.0 years in girls and 12.1 years in boys.[2] Temporal lobe cortical gray matter peaks at 16.7 years in girls and 16.2 years in boys. Parietal lobe cortical gray matter peaks at 10.2 years in girls and 11.8 years in boys.

The thickening and thinning of cortical gray matter is thought to reflect changes in the size and complexity of neurons, not a change in the actual number. The increasing size may reflect a process called arborization in which the cells grow extra branches, twigs, and roots, thereby growing "bushier" and making a greater number of connections to other cells. The decreasing amount of gray matter may reflect the process of pruning where certain connections are eliminated.

The forces guiding these processes of arborization and pruning are an area of intense investigation. Genetics, nutrition, toxins, bacteria, viruses, hormones, and many other factors have been shown to have an effect. One hypothesis for the pruning phase is the "use it or lose it" principle, in which those connections that are used will survive and flourish, whereas those connections that are not used will wither and die. If this hypothesis is correct, the activities of the teen may have a powerful influence on the ultimate physical structure of the brain.

To examine cortical gray matter development with greater regional specificity we examined the change in gray-matter density on a voxel-by-voxel basis in a group of 13 subjects who had each been scanned four times at approximately two-year intervals.[55] (An animation of these changes is available at http://www.loni.ucla.edu/~thompson/DEVEL/dynamic.html).

Cortical-gray-matter loss occurs earliest in the primary sensorimotor areas and latest in the dorsolateral prefrontal cortex (DLPFC) and superior temporal gyrus. The general pattern is for those regions subserving primary functions, such as motor and sensory systems, to mature earliest and the higher-order association areas, which integrate those primary functions, to mature later. For instance, in the temporal lobes the latest part to mature is the superior temporal gyrus/sulcas, which serves as a heteromodal association site integrating memory, audiovisual input, and object-recognition functions (along with prefrontal and inferior parietal cortices).[56-58]

DISCUSSION

The relatively late development of the DLPFC, not reaching adult levels until the 20s, is intriguing in light of the behavioral data presented elsewhere in this volume. The DLPFC is linked to the ability to inhibit impulses, weigh consequences of decisions, prioritize, and strategize. Speculatively, the DLPFC is still "under construction" for a decade after the throes of puberty and may therefore be related to some of the behavioral manifestations of the teen years. However, direct data on the relationship between the brain changes shown here and behavior changes of the type described for teens has not been established.

In fact, straightforward relationships between volumes of a particular structure and performance on a particular cognitive task are elusive. Even simple tasks eventually involve the majority of brain systems, and the diversity of afferent and efferent connections to the many distinct nuclei of most structures as well as the intricacy of their various neurochemical systems further complicate functional correlates of gross volume size.

In conclusion, brain structure goes through explosive changes during the teen years. The connection between these structural changes and behavioral changes is only beginning to be elucidated.

REFERENCES

1. GIEDD, J.N. et al. 1996. Quantitative magnetic resonance imaging of human brain development: ages 4-18. Cereb. Cortex 6: 551–560.
2. GIEDD, J.N. et al. 1999. Brain development during childhood and adolescence: a longitudinal MRI study [letter]. Nat. Neurosci. 2: 861–863.
3. ZIJDENBOS, A.P., B.M. DAWANT & R.A. MARGOLIN. 1994. Automatic detection of intracranial contours in MR images. Comput. Med. Imaging Graphics 18: 11–23.
4. CHUNG, M.K. et al. 2001. A unified statistical approach to deformation-based morphometry. Neuroimage 14: 595–606.
5. NELLHAUS, G. 1968. Head circumference: girls and boys 2-18 years. Pediatrics 41: 106.

6. SHAPIRO, R. & A.H. JANZEN. 1960. The Normal Skull. Hoeber. New York.
7. TOMASCH, J. 1954. Size, distribution and number of fibers in the human corpus callosum. Anat. Rec. 119: 119–135.
8. INNOCENTI, G.M., T. MANZONI & G. SPIDALIERI. 1974. Patterns of somesthetic messages transferred through the corpus callosum. Exp. Brain Res. 19: 447–466.
9. SPIDALIERI, G., G. FRANCHI & P. GUANDALINI. 1985. Somatic receptive-field properties of single fibers in the rostral portion of the corpus callosum in awake cats. Exp. Brain Res. 58: 75–81.
10. KAPPERS, C.U.A., G.C. HUBER & C.C. CROSBY. 1936. The Comparative Anatomy of the Nervous System of Vertebrates Including Man, Vol. 2. Macmillan. New York.
11. RAPOPORT, S.I. 1990. Integrated phylogeny of the primate brain, with special reference to humans and their diseases. Brain Res. Rev. 15: 267–294.
12. ZAIDEL, D. & R.W. SPERRY. 1977. Some long-term effects of cerebral commissurotomy in man. Neuropsychology 15: 193–204.
13. BERLUCCHI, G. 1981. Interhemispheric asymmetries in visual discrimination: a neurophysiological hypothesis. Doc. Opthalmol. Proc. Ser. 30: 87–93.
14. SHANKS, M.F., A.J. ROCKEL & T.P.S. POWEL. 1975. The commissural fiber connections of the primary somatic sensory cortex. Brain Res. 98: 166–171.
15. ZAIDEL, D. & R.W. SPERRY. 1974. Memory impairment after commissurotomy in man. Brain 97: 263–272.
16. LEVY, J. 1985. Interhemispheric collaboration: single mindedness in the asymmetric brain. In Hemisphere Function and Collaboration in the Child. C.T. Best, Ed.: 11–32. Academic Press. New York.
17. COOK, N.D. 1986. The Brain Code. Mechanisms of Information Transfer and the Role of the Corpus Callosum. Methuen. London.
18. JOSEPH, R. 1980. Awareness, the origin of thought, and the role of conscious self-deception in resistance and repression. Psychol. Rep. 46: 767–781.
19. BOGEN, J.E. & G.M. BOGEN. 1969. The other side of the brain. The corpus callosum and creativity. Bull. Los Angel. Neurol. Soc. 34: 191–220.
20. HELLIGE, J.B., J.P. COX & L. LITVAC. 1979. Information processing in the hemispheres: selective hemisphere activation and capacity limitations. J. Exp. Psychol. Gen. 108: 251–259.
21. LEVY, J. & C. TREVARTHEN. 1981. Color-matching, color naming and color memory in split brain patients. Neuropsychology 19: 523–541.
22. GIEDD, J.N. et al. 1996. A quantitative MRI study of the corpus callosum in children and adolescents. Brain Res. Dev. Brain Res. 91: 274–280.
23. BIGELOW, L.B., H.A. NASRALLAH & F.P. RAUSCHER. 1983. Corpus callosum thickness in chronic schizophrenia. Br. J. Psychiatry 142: 284–287.
24. GIEDD, J.N. et al. 1994. Quantitative morphology of the corpus callosum in attention deficit hyperactivity disorder [see Comments]. Am. J. Psychiatry 151: 665–669.
25. HYND, G.W. et al. 1990. Brain morphology in developmental dyslexia and attention deficit disorder/hyperactivity. Arch. Neurol. 47: 919–926.
26. HYND, G.W. et al. 1991. Corpus callosum morphology in attention deficit-hyperactivity disorder: morphometric analysis of MRI. J. Learn. Disabil. 24: 141–146.
27. NJIOKIKTJIEN, C. 1991. Pediatric Behavioral Neurology, Vol.3, The Child's Corpus Callosum. Suyi. Amsterdam.
28. PARASHOS, I.A., W.E. WILKINSON & C.E. COFFEY. 1995. Magnetic-resonance-imaging of the corpus-callosum—predictors of size in normal adults. J. Neuropsychiatry Clin. Neurosci. 7: 35–41.
29. PETERSON, B.S. et al. 1994. Corpus callosum morphology from magnetic resonance images in Tourette's syndrome. Psychiatry Res. Neuroimaging 55: 85–99.
30. ROSENTHAL, R. & L.B. BIGELOW. 1972. Quantitative brain measurements in chronic schizophrenia. Br. J. Psychiatry 121: 259–264.
31. THOMPSON, P.M. et al. 2000. Growth patterns in the developing brain detected by using continuum mechanical tensor maps. Nature 404: 190–193.
32. PAUS, T. et al. 1999. Structural maturation of neural pathways in children and adolescents: In vivo study. Science 283: 1908–1911.

GIEDD: ADOLESCENT BRAIN

33. BENES, F.M. *et al.* 1994. Myelination of a key relay zone in the hippocampal formation occurs in the human brain during childhood, adolescence, and adulthood. Arch. Gen. Psychiatry **51:** 477–484.
34. HYND, G.W. *et al.* 1993. Attention deficit hyperactivity disorder (ADHD) and asymmetry of the caudate nucleus. J. Child Neurol. **8:** 339–347.
35. GIEDD, J.N. *et al.* 1994. Quantitative morphology of the corpus callosum in attention deficit hyperactivity disorder. Am. J. Psychiatry **151:** 665–669.
36. CASTELLANOS, F.X. *et al.* 1996. Quantitative brain magnetic resonance imaging in attention-deficit hyperactivity disorder. Arch. Gen. Psychiatry **53:** 607–616.
37. PETERSON, B. *et al.* 1993. Reduced basal ganglia volumes in Tourette's syndrome using three-dimensional reconstruction techniques from magnetic resonance images. Neurology **43:** 941–949.
38. SINGER, H.S. *et al.* 1993. Volumetric MRI changes in basal ganglia of children with Tourette's syndrome. Neurology **43:** 950–956.
39. PETERSON, B.S. *et al.* 2000. Regional brain and ventricular volumes in tourette syndrome. Unpublished.
40. NOLTE, J. 1993. Olfactory and limbic systems. *In* The Human Brain. An Introduction to Its Functional Anatomy. R. Farrell, Ed.: 397–413. Mosby-Year Book. St. Louis, MO.
41. JERSLID, A.T. 1963. The Psychology of Adolescence. Macmillan. New York.
42. WECHSLER, D. 1974. Wechsler Intelligence Scale for Children—Revised. The Psychological Corporation. New York.
43. DIENER, E., E. SANDVIK & R.F. LARSEN. 1985. Age and sex effects for affect intensity. Dev. Psychol. **21:** 542–546.
44. GIEDD, J.N. *et al.* 1996. Quantitative MRI of the temporal lobe, amygdala, and hippocampus in normal human development: ages 4–18 years. J. Comp. Neurol. **366:** 223–230.
45. CLARK, A.S., N.J. MACLUSKY & P.S. GOLDMAN-RAKIC. 1988. Androgen binding and metabolism in the cerebral cortex of the deveoping rhesus monkey. Endocrinology **123:** 932–940.
46. SHOLL, S.A. & K.L. KIM. 1989. Estrogen receptors in the rhesus monkey brain during fetal development. Dev. Brain Res. **50:** 189–196.
47. MORSE, J.K., S.W. SCHEFF & S.T. DEKOSKY. 1986. Gonadal steroids influence axonal sprouting in the hippocampal dentate gyrus: a sexually dimorphic response. Exp. Neurol. **94:** 649–658.
48. GOULD, E. *et al.* 1990. Gonadal steroids regulate dendritic spine density in hippocampal pyramidal cells in adulthood. J. Neurosci. **10:** 1286–1291.
49. MURPHY, D.G.M. *et al.* 1993. X chromosome effects on female brain: a magnetic resonance imaging study of Turner's syndrome. Lancet **342:** 1197–1200.
50. FILIPEK, P.A. *et al.* 1994. The young adult human brain: an MRI-based morphometric analysis. Cereb. Cortex **4:** 344–360.
51. JERNIGAN, T.L. *et al.* 1991. Cerebral structure on MRI, Part I: Localization of age-related changes. Biol. Psychiatry **29:** 55–67.
52. PFEFFERBAUM, A. *et al.* 1994. A quantitative magnetic resonance imaging study of changes in brain morphology from infancy to late adulthood. Arch. Neurol. **51:** 874–887.
53. SOWELL, E.R. *et al.* 2002. Mapping sulcal pattern asymmetry and local cortical surface gray matter distribution *in vivo*: maturation in perisylvian cortices. Cereb. Cortex **12:** 17–26.
54. STEEN, R.G. *et al.* 1997. Age-related changes in the pediatric brain: quantitative MR evidence of maturational changes during adolescence. AJNR Am. J. Neuroradiol. **18:** 819–828.
55. GOGTAY, N. *et al.* 2004. Dynamic mapping of human cortical development during childhood through early adulthood. Proc. Natl. Acad. Sci. USA. In press.
56. MESULAM, M.M. 1998. From sensation to cognition. Brain **121**(Pt. 6): 1013–1052.
57. CALVERT, G.A. 2001. Crossmodal processing in the human brain: insights from functional neuroimaging studies. Cereb. Cortex **11:** 1110–1123.
58. MARTIN, A. & L.L. CHAO. 2001. Semantic memory and the brain: structure and processes. Curr. Opin. Neurobiol. **11:** 194–201.

Neuroimaging of Developmental Psychopathologies

The Importance of Self-Regulatory and Neuroplastic Processes in Adolescence

ALEXANDRA L. SPESSOT,[a] KERSTIN J. PLESSEN,[a,b] AND BRADLEY S. PETERSON[a]

[a]Columbia University College of Physicians & Surgeons and the New York State Psychiatric Institute, New York, New York 10032, USA

[b]Center for Child and Adolescent Mental Health, University of Bergen, Bergen, Norway

ABSTRACT: Normal brain maturational and developmental processes, together with plastic reorganization of the brain in response to experiential demands, contribute to the acquisition of improved capacities for self-regulation and impulse control during adolescence. The frontal lobe is a main focus for these developmental and plastic processes during the transition from adolescence into adulthood. Tourette syndrome (TS), defined as the chronic presence of motor and vocal tics, has been increasingly conceptualized as a disorder of impaired self-regulatory control. This disordered control is thought to give rise to semicompulsory urges to perform the movements that constitute simple tics, complex tics, or compulsions. Neuroimaging studies suggest that the expression of the genetic diathesis to TS is influenced by genetic and nongenetic factors affecting activity-dependent reorganization of neuroregulatory systems, thereby influencing the phenotype, illness severity, and adult outcome of tic disorders. Similar developmental processes during adolescence likely determine the phenotype and natural history of a broad range of other complex neuropsychiatric disorders of childhood onset, and they likely contribute to the acquisition of improved self-regulatory capacities that characterize normal adolescent development.

KEYWORDS: adolescence; brain; development; Tourette syndrome; neural plasticity; compensation

NEURODEVELOPMENT AND PLASTIC PROCESSES

Although adolescence is a time of immense cognitive, social, and emotional change, it actually represents the culmination of maturational and developmental processes that begin in fetal life and early childhood. During fetal development, neu-

Address for correspondence: Bradley S. Peterson, M.D., Columbia College of Physicians & Surgeons and New York State Psychiatric Institute, Unit 74, 1051 Riverside Drive, New York, NY 10032. Voice: 212-543-5330; fax: 212-543-5522.
PetersoB@childpsych.columbia.edu

Ann. N.Y. Acad. Sci. 1021: 86–104 (2004). © 2004 New York Academy of Sciences.
doi: 10.1196/annals.1308.010

rons proliferate from early precursor cells that migrate radially outward from the ventricular zone to establish the normal cellular architecture that composes the cerebral cortex. Dendrites and axons then arborize massively, forming initial intercellular communications and synapses. This vast overproduction of neurons, axons, and synapses is followed in the second half of gestation by a selective apoptosis that results in the loss of up to 50% of all cortical neurons.[1] Activity-dependent processes and afferent connectivity during this time determine whether a neuron survives this process of cellular elimination.[2]

Subsequently, during early postnatal brain development, synaptic density increases dramatically, reaching approximately 140% of adult levels at its peak.[3] Although this process of synaptogenesis is largely under genetic control, activation of these genes and the molding of synaptic connections depends on patterns of neural activity, which in turn are a product of environmental and experiential input.[4] During adolescence, more than 40% of all synapses are eliminated through this activity-dependent, massive pruning of primarily excitatory connections.[5,6] Levels of local GABAergic interneurons, in contrast, remain fairly stable from childhood into adulthood, suggesting that experience selectively remodels exuberant excitatory synapses into adultlike patterns of connectivity.[7,8] Regardless of the kind of synapse that is remodeled, life experiences of the developing child clearly exert a profound influence on brain architecture in adolescence.[9]

The frontal lobe in particular appears to be an important locus of maturational change during adolescence. One longitudinal MRI study of normal subjects aged 4 to 22, for example, demonstrated that gray matter of the frontal lobe increases during childhood and preadolescence, with a maximum volume occurring at approximately 11 to 12 years of age. Gray matter volumes in the frontal lobe then decline slowly through adolescence, producing a net decrease in frontal lobe volume from childhood to early adulthood.[10] Despite this decrease in gray matter of the frontal lobe during adolescence, myelination continues and volumes of frontal lobe white matter increase progressively during adolescence and into adulthood.[10–12] These imaging findings are consistent with the rapid improvement during adolescence of various functions subserved by the frontal lobe, such as response inhibition, emotional regulation, and capacities for organization and planning.[13]

Superimposed on these major maturational changes during childhood and adolescence, the brain continually reorganizes its neural elements in response to developmental and experiential demands,[14,15] a process termed *neural plasticity*. Although plasticity presumably is a general characteristic or capacity of all brain tissue, in humans it has been documented most convincingly *in vivo* within the motor cortices during the acquisition and practice of motor skills[16,17] and in the visual system after lesions to the occipital cortex.[18–20] Plasticity may be most robust in younger individuals,[21–23] but even the adult cortex is thought to undergo continual plastic remodeling.[24] Studies suggest that the motor cortex in adults may undergo plastic change during the acquisition of new motor skills in a matter of days[16] or even minutes.[25] Neural plasticity is also likely responsible for the spontaneous recovery of function following various types of brain injury.[26] Although its molecular basis is not entirely understood, the reorganization of neural tissue, either in terms of neurogenesis, modification of dendritic spines or dendritic arborization, or synaptic remodeling, is thought to require modification of gene expression and protein production within the cell.[27–31]

Plastic reorganization of brain structure and function, by definition, helps the organism adapt to changing experiential and contextual demands. One of the most salient demands of adolescence is the increasing requirement for behavioral control, or self-regulation, that occurs in the context of increasing urges to act on impulses and desires that meet with generally decreasing degrees of social and environmental acceptance. Improvement in self-regulatory control could be regarded, in fact, as a definition of forward progress in the ontogeny of human development, perhaps particularly so during adolescent development. The successful emergence from adolescence is marked, therefore, by a greatly increased capacity to control aggressive and sexual impulses and by improved ability to regulate an increasingly wide range of unpredictable changes in mood and affect.

We believe that failure of these self-regulatory systems to develop during adolescence can lead either to the new onset of a wide range of psychopathologies, to the exacerbation of symptoms that onset earlier in childhood, or to interference with the attenuation of symptoms during adolescence that is characteristic of many childhood-onset disorders. Failure of self-regulatory systems can therefore alter the typical natural history of an antecedent illness.

Neuroimaging studies have opened an invaluable new window onto the processes of brain organization and plasticity that help to define normal and pathological adolescent development. Because neuroimaging is a large and newly emergent field of inquiry, we will present one example of the ways in which neuroimaging methodologies have provided novel insights into the importance of organizational and plastic processes during adolescent development, and of the ways in which visualizing these processes illuminate understanding of the neural bases of long-recognized, but previously unexplained, clinical phenomena. The example will come from our studies of self-regulatory capacities in tic and obsessive-compulsive disorders.

NEURAL PLASTICITY AND TOURETTE SYNDROME

Tourette Syndrome: Overview

Tourette syndrome (TS) is defined by the presence of chronic motor and vocal tics that wax and wane in severity over time.[32] Examples of simple motor tics include eye blinking, head jerks, shoulder shrugs, and facial grimacing, while complex tics can include a wide variety of more semi-goal-directed behaviors, such as touching, tapping, rubbing, smelling, or licking. Vocal tics vary from simple throat clearing and guttural sounds to the uttering of speech fragments, which can include syllables, words, or whole phrases. Vocal tics that are more behaviorally complex can include utterances of obscenities and profanities (coprolalia) or repetition of others' speech (echolalia). A tic is preceded often by a "premonitory urge"—a sense of general discomfort or tension in the muscles involved in producing the tic, or a feeling of generalized anxiety that is relieved temporarily by the performance of the tic. Similar to normal stereotyped movements, such as blinking, tics can be suppressed voluntarily for a finite period of time, after which the urge to tic becomes irresistible. The ability to suppress tics voluntarily varies across individuals and situational contexts.

TS typically begins in early childhood with the appearance of one or several tics of minimal frequency and forcefulness that are regarded often by parents as simply

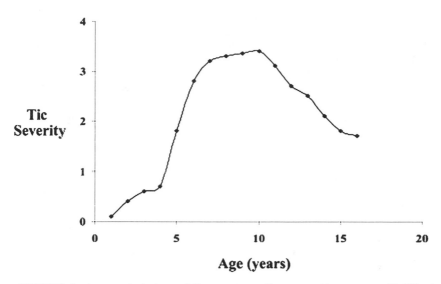

FIGURE 1. Average trajectory of tic symptoms. On average in persons with TS, tic symptoms begin in preschool or early grade school years, increase gradually during childhood, plateau as puberty begins, then decline gradually throughout adolescence before reaching stable levels by early adulthood. Tic severity on the *y* axis was measured using the Annual Rating of Relative Tic Severity (ARRTS).[35]

habits or unusual mannerisms. Tics then gradually increase in number, frequency, and forcefulness until they peak in severity at approximately 11 or 12 years of age. They then usually decline gradually in severity throughout adolescence (FIG. 1).[33] By the age of 18 years, roughly 90% of TS patients experience substantial remission of symptoms, and more than 40% will be symptom-free.[34–36] Superimposed on this gradual rise, plateau, and fall in the severity of tics across childhood and adolescence is an unpredictable fluctuation in severity over minutes, hours, days, and weeks.

Studies increasingly suggest that TS (both motor and vocal tics lasting more than one year) belongs to a spectrum of tic disorders that includes transient tics (those lasting less than one year) and chronic tic disorders (either motor or vocal tics, but not both, lasting more than one year). By definition, then, TS seems simply to be a chronic and severe form of tic disorder that includes both motor and vocal tics, rather than either motor or vocal tics appearing in isolation.[37] Indeed, transient and chronic motor tics are phenomenologically similar to, if not indistinguishable from, the tics of TS. These more benign tic disorders affect between 5 and 20% of children in the general population,[38–44] and they occur four to five times more frequently in males than in females.[45] This high prevalence of tics in the general population raises the question of whether tics may actually represent one aspect of a normal behavioral repertoire.

Tics, however, often co-occur with other behavioral and emotional problems. In clinically identified patients with TS, for example, 40–60% have comorbid obsessive-compulsive disorder (OCD), a condition that is characterized by intrusive, distressing thoughts and urges to action that are relieved, at least temporarily, by performing the action.[46] Moreover, family-genetic studies have repeatedly shown that tics and OCD occur within the same family more often than they occur in control families, even when they do not occur together in the same individual.[47–49] This co-occurrence of tics and OCD within families suggests that these two conditions are variable manifestations of the same underlying genetic vulnerability. The genetic relatedness of TS and OCD in turn suggests that although their phenotypes at least superficially seem to differ dramatically, their phenotypes might be more intimately related than their surface phenomena would otherwise suggest. The symptoms of TS and OCD, for example, might lie on a spectrum of "semicompulsory" behaviors, in which urges to execute these behaviors build until they become irresistible, at which point performing the behaviors brings relief. Symptoms with a prominent ideational component, in this scheme, may belong to OCD on the one end of the spectrum, those with little or no ideational component may belong to the simple tics of TS on the other, and complex tics might be positioned somewhere between these two extremes.

Although TS has been shown to have a strong genetic component,[50–52] penetrance of the putative vulnerability genes is only partial. Even the monozygotic (MZ) co-twins of persons with TS can be discordant either for the presence of a tic disorder or for its severity.[53] Non-genetic influences are therefore believed to be important in determining not only which genetically vulnerable individual develops TS or OCD, but also how severe the illness is if one does develop. These nongenetic influences on expression of the putative vulnerability genes for tic-related disorders are thought to include neuroregulatory and neuroendocrine factors. These factors presumably influence the expression of vulnerability genes for tics that are highly prevalent within the general population, given that tics affect as many as 20% of all boys. These regulatory and endocrine factors therefore likely determine, at least in part, who has transient tics, who has chronic tics, and who has TS or OCD. Because tics preferentially affect boys more than girls,[45] neuroendocrine factors likely either increase expression of the vulnerability genes in boys or reduce their expression in girls. This possibility is supported by reports that androgens can exacerbate tics, while androgen receptor antagonists can attenuate them.[54–56]

Neural Circuitry

Lesion and stimulation studies in animals have long suggested that disturbances in basal ganglia portions of cortico-striatal-thalamo-cortical (CSTC) circuits can cause stereotyped, ticlike behaviors.[57–62] These circuits are composed of multiple, partially overlapping, but largely "parallel" pathways that direct information from virtually all portions of the cerebral cortex to the subcortex, and then back again to specific regions of the cortex.[63] Cortical portions of CSTC circuits are thought to contribute to self-regulatory functions by modulating activity in the basal ganglia and thalamus, which in turn modulate activity in the cortex.[64–66] Each of these circuits is further subdivided into the direct and indirect pathways, both of which project from the cortex to the caudate nucleus and putamen, then to the globus pallidus, then to the thalamus, and finally back to the cortex.[67] These pathways differ, however, in their connections to differing portions of the globus pallidus and thalamus. The direct pathway projects from the caudate and putamen to the internal seg-

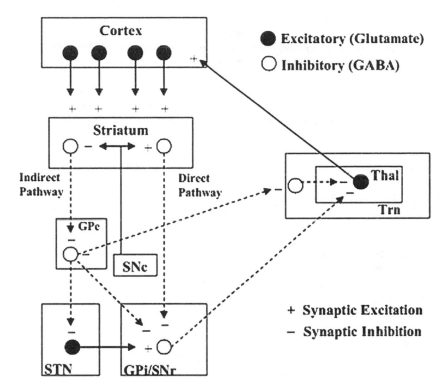

FIGURE 2. Schematic diagram of CSTC circuitry. Striatum = caudate nucleus and putamen; GPe = globus pallidus pars externa; SNc = substantia nigra pars compacta; STN = subthalamic nucleus; GPi = globus pallidus pars interna; SNr = substantia nigra pars reticulata; Thal = midline thalamic nuclei; Trn = thalamic reticular nucleus.[104]

ment of the globus pallidus (GPi) and then to the major midline thalamic nuclei. The indirect pathway, in contrast, projects from the caudate and putamen to the external segment of the globus pallidus (GPe), and then to the reticular portion of the thalamus (FIG. 2). The reticular portion of the thalamus exerts powerful inhibitory influences over the thalamic nuclei belonging to the direct pathway.[68] These inhibitory influences of the indirect pathway are thought to facilitate movement by modulating activity in the direct pathway, which itself is believed to have a primarily inhibiting influence on motor activity in the cortex. CSTC circuits thus comprise a delicately balanced system of activation and inhibition, both within each of these pathways and in the influences of each pathway on the other.

Neuroimaging Studies Suggest the Presence of Impaired Self-Regulatory Systems in Tourette Syndrome

Until the advent of neuroimaging technologies, no evidence has existed to demonstrate directly the involvement of CSTC circuits in the pathophysiology of TS. The first functional magnetic resonance imaging (fMRI) study of individuals with

TS examined the ways in which components of CSTC circuits contribute to the voluntary suppression of tic behaviors. The effects of tic suppression on activity in cortical and subcortical components of these circuits were assessed in 22 adult patients with TS.[67] Images acquired during periods of voluntary tic suppression were compared with images acquired when subjects were allowed to tic spontaneously. The magnitudes of signal change in the images were then correlated with measures of tic severity. Significant increases in signal intensity were detected in both the prefrontal area and the caudate nucleus during tic suppression, along with significant decreases in activity in the putamen, globus pallidus, and thalamus. Increased activity in the frontal cortex during tic suppression was associated with increased activity in the caudate nucleus ($r = .48$; $P = .03$), consistent with the known excitatory projections from frontal cortex to the caudate. Increased activity in the caudate nucleus was in turn associated with greater decreases in activity of the putamen ($r = .86$; $P < .001$), globus pallidus ($r = .84$; $P < .001$), and thalamus ($r = .51$; $P = .02$), consistent with the known inhibitory projections from the caudate to these other subcortical nuclei. Moreover, the magnitudes of the decreases in signal intensity in the caudate, putamen, globus pallidus, and thalamus correlated inversely with severity of tic symptoms outside of the scanner. In contrast, tic severity generally did not correlate significantly with activity in cortical regions. Given the known connections and flow of information between cortical and subcortical structures, the correlations between tic severity and activity in each of the subcortical portions of CSTC circuits were interpreted as "downstream" effects of correlations that were initially established at the point of entry into subcortical portions of the circuits, namely in the projections into or out of the caudate nucleus. The greater the dysfunction of this portion of the CSTC circuitry, the greater the escape from self-regulatory control, and the worse the individual's tic symptoms were likely to be outside of the MRI scanner.

This interpretation of the caudate nucleus as the origin of functional disturbances in CSTC circuitry and as a source of impairment in the self-regulatory control of tic behaviors is consistent with a recent anatomical MRI study of basal ganglia volumes in 154 children and adults with TS and 130 healthy control subjects.[69] Analyses indicated that volumetric abnormalities did not affect all basal ganglia structures in the TS group, but that the abnormalities were instead specific to the caudate nucleus ($P < .001$) (FIG. 3). These regionally specific effects in TS subjects moreover varied significantly with age of the subject ($P = .008$), deriving from smaller volumes of the putamen and globus pallidus volumes in adults, but not in children with TS. No significant associations were found between basal ganglia volumes and tic severity.

These anatomical findings had several important implications for our understanding of the role of the basal ganglia in the pathophysiology of TS. First, the presence of significantly smaller caudate nuclei in both children and adults suggested that hypoplasia of the caudate nucleus may represent a trait morphological abnormality in persons with TS. Second, decreased caudate nucleus volumes that persisted into adulthood implied that the caudate nucleus is not a prime target for plastic changes in response to the presence of tics, nor is it a likely candidate for the cause of the normal attenuation of tic symptoms during adolescence. Third, the decreased volumes of the putamen and globus pallidus that were detected in adults, but not in children with TS, by definition was not generalizable to the larger population of persons with TS. Thus, the findings of decreased metabolism and blood flow in the putamen and globus pallidus of TS adults[70-74] reported in positron emission tomography

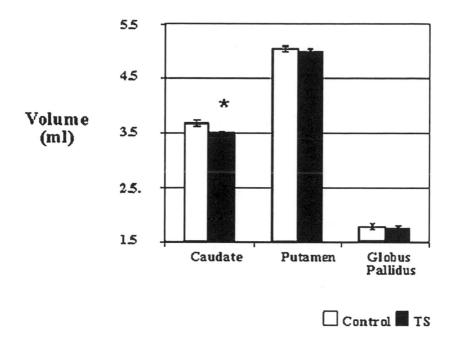

FIGURE 3. Basal ganglia volumes in TS. A significant diagnosis-by-region effect (P < .001) derived mainly from volume reductions in the caudate nuclei of TS subjects (P = .01, denoted with the asterisk).

(PET) and single-photon emission computed tomography (SPECT) studies are likely to reflect the presence of smaller volumes of these structures in adults with TS. The PET and SPECT findings thus are unlikely to be generalizable to populations of children with tics, in whom volumes of these structures are normal.

Evidence for Neural Plasticity in Tourette Syndrome

Whereas anatomical and functional studies suggest that the caudate nucleus may be the locus of trait abnormalities in children and adults with TS, these studies have also suggested that cortical portions of CSTC circuits are more important in the expression and regulation of tic symptoms in individuals who have a tic diathesis. The first study to measure the volumes of cortical regions in TS patients scanned a sample of 155 children and adults with TS and 131 normal control subjects.[75] Significant region-specific differences in cortical volumes were detected in subjects with TS compared with control subjects (P < .0001). Group differences derived primarily from larger dorsal prefrontal volumes in both TS males (P = .0004) and females (P = .01). These regional differences in the TS group varied significantly with age (P < .0001), however, in that larger dorsal prefrontal volumes were detected in children with TS, but smaller volumes were observed in adults with TS (FIG. 4). Furthermore,

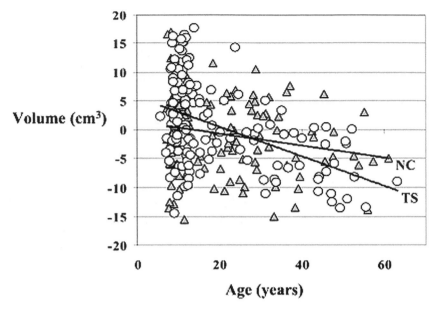

FIGURE 4. Prefrontal volumes in individuals with TS. The association of age with prefrontal volumes differed significantly by diagnosis ($P < .0001$). Volumes were larger in children with TS than in control children, but smaller in adults with TS than in adult controls.
The plotted prefrontal volumes are residuals after adjusting for the effects of whole brain
volume, sex, socioeconomic status, OCD, and ADHD. Because these are residual volumes,
they may have positive or negative values.

larger cortical volumes were significantly associated with fewer tic symptoms in
both the orbitofrontal and parieto-occipital regions (β's $< -.20$; P's $< .03$) (FIG. 5).

These inverse correlations of prefrontal volumes with tic severity suggest that the
larger volumes in children with TS could in some way be a compensatory or adaptive
process in the brains of children that helps to attenuate the severity of tics. This possibility gains further credence from the findings of the fMRI study of effortful tic
suppression, previously described, in which broad expanses of prefrontal cortices
activated robustly during the suppression of tics. The need to suppress tics at school
and in other social settings would activate these prefrontal regions repeatedly and
frequently. This repeated activation could then induce activity-dependent, plastic hypertrophy of prefrontal cortices in children and adolescents with TS. Activity-
dependent plasticity and hypertrophy within prefrontal regions would in turn help to
attenuate the severity of tic symptoms by increasing inhibitory reserve and the capacity for self-regulatory control. This interpretation of findings in prefrontal cortices from anatomical and functional MRI studies is consistent with the known role of
this region in subserving self-regulatory functions. The prefrontal region is thought
to mediate performance on tasks that require decisions of whether, when, and how
to act across a time delay, as are needed in working memory, behavioral inhibition,
and go–no-go tasks.[13] In the case of tic symptoms, prefrontal cortices inhibit across

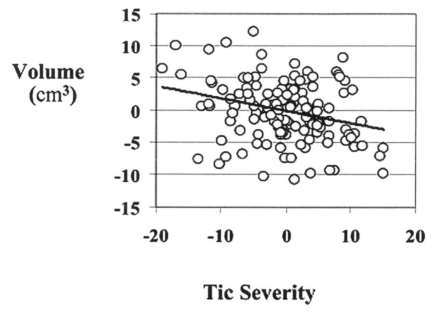

Tic Severity

FIGURE 5. Correlations of prefrontal volumes with the severity of tic symptoms. Larger prefrontal volumes tended to accompany fewer tics. Volumes and severity measures are residuals after adjusting for the effects of total brain volume and sex, and therefore may have positive or negative values.

time a behavioral response to the somatosensory urge to tic, and they likely determine when to release the tic behavior from controlled suppression. Dysfunction of prefrontal regions in TS patients is therefore likely to impair their ability to inhibit tic symptoms.

Impairment in the capacity to generate this hypothesized, activity-dependent plastic response in prefrontal regions to the continued experiential demands to control tics should in theory contribute to more severe tic symptoms. Indeed, we suspect that the failure to generate this plastic response accounts for the presence of smaller prefrontal volumes in adults with TS, a finding that is diametrically opposite the finding of larger prefrontal volumes in children with TS. Although tics usually remit or substantially improve by early adulthood, the adults who participated in these imaging studies had persistent tics that were as severe as those in the children who participated. The adults therefore represented a unique subgroup of all persons who have a lifetime history of TS, those whose symptoms fail to remit during adolescent development. We believe that the smaller prefrontal volumes in adults with TS represent a failure to induce an activity-dependent, plastic hypertrophy of prefrontal cortices in response to the presence of tics and the need to suppress them. The failure to induce this hypertrophic, compensatory response would interfere with the improvement of self-regulatory functions that the hypertrophy presumably subserves, and it would contribute to the persistence of more severe tic symptoms in adolescence and adulthood. Failure of neuroplastic responses to the presence of tics in childhood, in other words, is precisely why the tic symptoms of these adults failed to remit during adolescence.

The smaller prefrontal volumes measured in adults with TS thus likely represented an ascertainment bias in which still-symptomatic adults were recruited for the imaging study. The dramatically different findings in adults and children with TS, which are a consequence of this ascertainment bias, emphasize the caution that is needed when interpreting the findings of studies that are exclusively of adults with TS. They also emphasize the inherent difficulties and dangers in making inferences concerning the developmental trajectories and longitudinal course of an illness from cross-sectional studies alone.[76, 77] Longitudinal, prospective studies are needed to clarify the ways in which plastic responses in neuroregulatory systems affect the clinical course in individuals who have TS.

Nevertheless, when considered together, the existing MRI studies suggest that anatomical and functional disturbances in the caudate nucleus may predispose an individual to having tics, while impaired neural regulatory systems based largely within prefrontal cortices may unmask this predisposition to tic in children, adolescents, and adults who have TS. Additional preliminary, unpublished longitudinal data from our laboratory furthermore suggest that volumes of the caudate nucleus measured in childhood predict the persistence and severity of tics in late adolescence and early adulthood,[78] consistent with the hypothesized status of the caudate nucleus as a trait pathophysiological feature of TS that operates across all stages of development. Measures of prefrontal volumes and basal ganglia activity during tic suppression correlate with the severity of tics at the time of scanning, and prefrontal volumes measured in childhood seem not to predict the severity of tics later in adulthood. These latter measures therefore seem to be more important determinants of severity in the moment, in temporal proximity to the time of scan. Although prefrontal volumes do not predict the severity of tics in adulthood, those who are unable to generate a hypertrophic plastic response of prefrontal cortices seem to be unlikely to have symptoms that will remit during adolescence.

The compensatory plastic response observed in the prefrontal cortex of persons with TS may not be limited to that structure alone. The corpus callosum (CC) has been the focus of several recent imaging studies of individuals with TS, because it is believed to inhibit activity in prefrontal cortices through its major white matter pathways that connect these cortices across the cerebral midline.[79] The CC may be particularly amenable to plastic remodeling in response to experiential demands, owing to the widespread and transient overproduction of callosal projections in early childhood.[80] The involvement of callosal projections in plastic remodeling of the cortex has been demonstrated in numerous studies, including experiments of sensory deprivation in which the effects of transcallosal inhibition on behavior was shown to depend on GABAergic neurotransmission.[81]

One study examining CC size in 158 children and adults with TS and 121 control subjects[82] reported that subjects with TS had smaller overall CCs ($P < .005$). CC size correlated positively with current ($r = .247$; $P < .003$) and worst-ever tic severity ($r = .298$; $P < .0001$), indicating that the smaller CCs in the TS group accompanied fewer tic symptoms. These correlations suggested that smaller CCs, similar to the larger prefrontal cortices detected in children with TS, could be a compensatory response to the presence of tics. CC size, moreover, correlated inversely with volumes of prefrontal cortices in both the TS and control groups, suggesting that smaller CCs may normally contribute to or influence the growth of prefrontal cortices. The magnitudes of these inverse correlations, however, were significantly larger in the TS group than in controls ($P < .025$), suggesting that the normal influence of the CC on prefrontal volumes is exaggerated in persons with TS. The exaggeration of this influence in those with TS presumably serves an adaptive or compensatory purpose, given that smaller CCs and larger prefrontal cortices seem to attenuate tic severity. In other words, a normal developmental process in the CC may be co-opted for adaptive purposes in the brains of those who have TS. We speculate that the plastic processes producing a smaller CC also help to reduce inhibition of prefrontal self-regulatory control in persons with TS by reducing excitatory input from the CC to GABAergic interneurons located within prefrontal cortices.[79,83,84] Reduced inhibition of prefrontal self-regulatory functions will in turn facilitate the control of tic behaviors by the prefrontal cortices.

Neuroendocrine Factors and Brain Plasticity in Tourette Syndrome

The increased frequency of TS in boys compared with girls has prompted the search for neuroendocrine influences on the expression of the putative TS vulnerability genes. These neuroendocrine influences could confer a predisposition to developing TS in boys, or alternatively, they may afford protection from TS in most girls. Several clinical observations, in fact, have implicated the involvement of sex steroid hormones in helping to determine the expression and severity of tics.[85] First, tics typically reach a peak in severity during the prepubertal years, when gonadal androgen production increases dramatically in both males and females. Second, androgen administration in adults has been reported to exacerbate tics,[54] while androgen receptor blockade has been shown to reduce them.[55,56] Third, tic severity in some women has been associated with the estrogenic phase of the menstrual cycle.[86,87]

Finally, our recent study of sex-typed behaviors and cognitive functioning in 89 children and adults with TS and 67 control subjects found that females with TS experienced more gender dysphoria, had increased masculine play preferences, and exhibited a more "masculine" pattern of performance on spatial tasks than did female control subjects.[85] Furthermore, males with TS showed increased masculine play preferences, the strength of which was positively associated with tic severity. These findings are similar to those reported previously in children who have verifiable, pathological elevations in prenatal androgen levels. Thus, whereas manipulation of hormone levels in adults has suggested a role for postnatal sex hormone levels in the pathophysiology of tics, this latter study supports the possibility that an altered androgen-dependent sexual differentiation of the brain during fetal development may contribute to the severity of tics in later postnatal life. This hypothesized prenatal androgenization presumably establishes organizational effects in the genome and in brain architecture that are activated by either normal or elevated circulating hormone levels later in childhood and adolescence in individuals who develop tics.[56,88]

Based on these clinical findings implicating neuroendocrine influences in the pathophysiology of TS, neuroimaging studies of TS are currently underway to help define disturbances in sexual differentiation of the brain that might contribute to the expression of tic symptoms. A study of regional brain and ventricular volumes in

TS[75] has already found that normal differences between sexes in volume of the parieto-occipital cortices are reduced in individuals with TS. Whereas this region in healthy controls was larger in women than in men, its size in women with TS was similar to its size in male controls and in males with TS. Because smaller parieto-occipital volumes were associated with more severe tic symptoms in this study, a profile more like males in this region could possibly predispose TS women to having more severe tics than they would otherwise have. Recent unpublished neuroimaging data also suggest that parietal and limbic regions of females with TS are morphologically similar to those of normal males, suggesting that more "male"-typed brain structures may alter function and plasticity across adolescent brain development.[78]

CONCLUSION: MULTISTRIKE ETIOLOGIES OF ADOLESCENT PATHOPHYSIOLOGIES

Neuroimaging studies have improved dramatically our understanding of the pathophysiology of TS. Findings from these studies have replaced the simplistic one-gene, one-lesion model of pathogenesis that initially dominated this field of study[89] with a more complex, though more sophisticated, multistrike model of etiology. In this model, the development of a tic-related disorder is determined by multiple risks, none of which are necessary or sufficient for developing the illness, but which in combination determine who develops it, which of its variants are manifested, how severe it will be, and how long it will last.

Strike 1 in this model is a genetic vulnerability to developing one or more of the behaviors in the spectrum of tic disorders. This vulnerability may manifest as a trait abnormality in the morphology and functioning of the caudate nucleus that disrupts the integrated functioning of frontostriatal circuits subserving self-regulatory capacities. Disruption of self-regulatory functions in turn releases, in the form of tics and other semicompulsory behaviors, fragments of motor behaviors that probably are normally programmed within the frontostriatal circuits of all living individuals, not only in those who have tic-related symptoms.

Strike 2 is a disturbance in the structure and functioning of prefrontal cortices and other brain regions, such as the CC, that may help to support self-regulatory functions. This type of disturbance might be established by initial failures in development and organization of the prefrontal cortices in early childhood. It could also be established by failures in the plastic remodeling and functional reorganization of prefrontal cortices in later childhood or adolescence in response to an enduring need to suppress the unwanted movements in an increasingly diverse set of social circumstances. Failure to establish these compensatory responses is thought to unmask functional disturbances of the caudate nucleus, and thus the genetic vulnerability to develop tic-related disorders. Under normal circumstances, prefrontal cortices would easily compensate for these presumed subtle, trait-like tendencies toward impairments in functioning of the caudate and other basal ganglia nuclei that a great many healthy people in the general population probably share. Failure of prefrontal compensatory systems releases from inhibitory control this common predisposition to move and to perform tic-like behaviors, similar to a fast-idling car that has leaky brakes, freeing it to move first into a slow coast before it gains speed and ultimately careens out of control. Disturbances in compensatory systems thus tip a *predisposition* to tic into overt tic *behaviors*. The degree to which these compensatory systems are dysfunctional determines the severity of tic symptoms, as well as whose symptoms will remit during adolescence and early adulthood.

Strike 3 includes neuroendocrine factors that confer either additional risk for, or protection from, the development of a tic-related disorder in already genetically predisposed individuals. These factors may include elevated levels of sex steroid hormones or enhanced end-organ responsiveness to normal levels of circulating hormones or to normal fluxes in their levels. They may also include the prenatal effects of steroid hormones that can alter the organization of chromatin or neural architecture in sexually dimorphic brain regions. These organizational effects then sensitize the brain to the activational effects of steroid hormones later in life. Organizational and activational effects of sex hormones thus influence the maturational modeling and plastic remodeling of brain structure and function throughout development, presumably in regions that subserve sexual or aggressive drives and in the neural systems that help to regulate them. These neuroendocrine influences seem most to confer additional risk to genetically predisposed females by masculinizing their brain structure and function, thereby increasing their likelihood of developing a neuropsychiatric disorder that preferentially affects boys.

Additional nongenetic determinants seem to increase the risk for developing TS. These may include prior infection with Group A Beta Hemolytic Streptococcus (GABHS), the bacterium that causes strep throat. Much more rarely, GABHS can induce postinfectious, autoimmune sequelae that include rheumatic fever and Sydenham's chorea, and possibly tics, OCD-like symptoms, or hyperactivity in genetically predisposed individuals.[90–95] The presence of an exaggerated stress response is also thought to increase the risk for developing a tic-related disorder or for increasing its severity.[96–100] Stress probably worsens tics through its adverse effects on the functioning of self-regulatory systems, which would account for its status as a nonspecific risk factor for a wide range of psychopathologies.[101–103]

This model of multiple strikes conferring risk, none of which is sufficient for developing a disorder, probably is applicable generally to most, if not all, complex neuropsychiatric disorders affecting children. The processes of self-regulation and plasticity are likely to be particularly important in conferring risk or protection because they can mask or unmask diatheses for illnesses that most individuals have to some degree. The number and particular combination of risk and protective factors likely determine the phenotype, pattern of comorbidities, severity, and natural history of an illness. Self-regulatory and neuroendocrine factors seem particularly likely to determine whether an illness remits, persists, or exacerbates during adolescence. These genetic and environmental influences undoubtedly interact in complex ways at the genetic, molecular, cellular, and neural systems levels to produce a given disorder within a particular child. This interaction is further contextualized by the child's biologically and environmentally determined adaptive and self-regulatory capacities. Genetic and environmental strengths and vulnerabilities therefore help to shape brain architecture and behavior during adolescent development. These are then further shaped, conditioned, and remodeled by life experiences, thereby determining the overall burden of symptoms and adaptive competencies that the adolescent carries into adulthood.

ACKNOWLEDGMENTS

This work was supported in part by NIMH grants MH01232, MH068318, and MH59139, the Thomas D. Klingenstein & Nancy D. Perlman Family Fund, the Suzanne Crosby Murphy Endowment at Columbia University, and a grant from the Center for Child and Adolescent Mental Health, University of Bergen, Norway. We are grateful to Drs. Kenneth Hugdahl, James Leckman, and Donald Cohen for their important contributions to this program of research. Many thanks to Chaiyapoj Netsiri, Ph.D., Georgette A. Quackenbush, B.A., and Ronald C. Whiteman, B.A., for their assistance.

REFERENCES

1. GORDON, N. 1995. Apoptosis (programmed cell death) and other reasons for elimination of neurons and axons. Brain Dev. **17:** 73–77.
2. PURVES, D. & J.W. LICHTMAN. 1980. Elimination of synapses in the developing nervous system. Science **210:** 153–157.
3. ANDERSEN, S.L. 2003. Trajectories of brain development: point of vulnerability or window of opportunity? Neurosci. Biobehav. Rev. **27:** 3–18.
4. KANDEL, E.R. 2000. Brain and behavior. *In* Principles of Neural Science. E.R. Kandel, J.H. Schwartz & T.M. Jessell, Eds. Elsevier. New York.
5. RAKIC, P., J.P. BOURGEOIS & P.S. GOLDMAN-RAKIC. 1994. Synaptic development of the cerebral cortex: implications for learning, memory, and mental illness. Prog. Brain Res. **102:** 227–243.
6. HUTTENLOCHER, P.R. 1984. Synapse elimination and plasticity in developing human cerebral cortex. Am. J. Ment. Defic. **88:** 488–496.
7. CHANGEUX, J.P. & A. DANCHIN. 1976. Selective stabilisation of developing synapses as a mechanism for the specification of neuronal networks. Nature **264:** 705–712.
8. INNOCENTI, G.M. 1981. Growth and reshaping of axons in the establishment of visual callosal connections. Science **212:** 824–827.
9. HEBB, D.O. 1949. The Organization of Behavior. A Neuropsychological Theory. Wiley. New York.
10. GIEDD, J.N. *et al.* 1999. Brain development during childhood and adolescence: a longitudinal MRI study. Nat. Neurosci. **2:** 861–863.
11. SOWELL, E.R. *et al.* 2003. Mapping cortical change across the human life span. Nat. Neurosci. **6:** 309–315.
12. SOWELL, E.R. *et al.* 1999. *In vivo* evidence for post-adolescent brain maturation in frontal and striatal regions. Nat. Neurosci. **2:** 859–861.
13. FUSTER, J.M. 1989. The Prefrontal Cortex: Anatomy, Physiology, and Neuropsychology of the Frontal Lobe. Raven. New York.
14. BLACK, J.E. *et al.* 1998. Neuronal plasticity and the developing brain. *In* Handbook of Child and Adolescent Psychiatry, Vol. 6. Basic Psychiatric Science and Treatment. N.E. Alessi *et al.*, Eds.: 31–53. Wiley. New York.
15. DAWSON, G., S.B. ASHMAN & L.J. CARVER. 2000. The role of early experience in shaping behavioral and brain development and its implications for social policy. Dev. Psychopathol. **12:** 695–712.
16. PASCUAL-LEONE, A. *et al.* 1995. Modulation of muscle responses evoked by transcranial magnetic stimulation during the acquisition of new fine motor skills. J. Neurophysiol. **74:** 1037–1045.
17. UNGERLEIDER, L.G., J. DOYON & A. KARNI. 2002. Imaging brain plasticity during motor skill learning. Neurobiol. Learn. Mem. **78:** 553–564.
18. KIPER, D.C. *et al.* 2002. Vision after early-onset lesions of the occipital cortex: I. Neuropsychological and psychophysical studies [see Comment]. Neural Plastic. **9:** 1–25.
19. KNYAZEVA, M.G. *et al.* 2002. Vision after early-onset lesions of the occipital cortex: II. Physiological studies [Comment]. Neural Plastic. **9:** 27–40.

20. RAHI, J.S. *et al.* 2002. Prediction of improved vision in the amblyopic eye after visual loss in the non-amblyopic eye. Lancet **360:** 621–622.
21. CHUGANI, H.T., R.A. MULLER & D.C. CHUGANI. 1996. Functional brain reorganization in children. Brain Dev. **18:** 347–356.
22. HUBEL, D.H. & T.N. WIESEL. 1965. Binocular interaction in striate cortex of kittens reared with artificial squint. J. Neurophysiol. **28:** 1041–1059.
23. KENNARD, M.A. 1938. Reorganization of motor function in the cerebral cortex of monkeys deprived of motor and premotor areas in infancy. J. Neurophysiol. **1:** 477–496.
24. PAULSEN, O. & T.J. SEJNOWSKI. 2000. Natural patterns of activity and long-term synaptic plasticity. Curr. Opin. Neurobiol. **10:** 172–179.
25. CLASSEN, J. *et al.* 1998. Rapid plasticity of human cortical movement representation induced by practice. J. Neurophysiol. **79:** 1117–1123.
26. HALLETT, M. 2001. Plasticity of the human motor cortex and recovery from stroke. Brain Res. Brain Res. Rev. **36:** 169–174.
27. PITTENGER, C. & E.R. KANDEL. 2003. In search of general mechanisms for long-lasting plasticity: Aplysia and the hippocampus. Philos. Trans. R. Soc. Lond.—Ser. B: Biol. Sci. **358:** 757–763.
28. KANDEL, E.R. 2001. The molecular biology of memory storage: a dialogue between genes and synapses. Science **294:** 1030–1038.
29. KEMPERMANN, G. & F.H. GAGE. 2002. Genetic influence on phenotypic differentiation in adult hippocampal neurogenesis. Brain Res. Dev. Brain Res. **134:** 1–12.
30. PRICKAERTS, J. 2004. Learning and adult neurogenesis: Survival with or without proliferation? Neurobiol. Learn. Mem. **81:** 1–11.
31. LAMPRECHT, A. & J. LEDOUX. 2004. Structural plasticity and memory. Nat. Neurosci. **5:** 45–54.
32. AMERICAN PSYCHIATRIC ASSOCIATION. 1994. Diagnostic and Statistical Manual of Mental Disorders. American Psychiatric Association. Washington, DC.
33. PAPPERT, E.J. *et al.* 2003. Objective assessment of longitudinal outcome in Gilles de la Tourette's syndrome. Neurology **61:** 936–640.
34. BLOCH, M.H. *et al.* Clinical predictors of future tic and OCD severity in children with Tourette syndrome. Submitted.
35. LECKMAN, J.F. *et al.* 1998. Course of tic severity in Tourette syndrome: the first two decades. Pediatrics **102:** 14–19.
36. BURD, L. *et al.* 2001. Long-term follow-up of an epidemiologically defined cohort of patients with Tourette syndrome. J. Child Neurol. **16:** 431–437.
37. SPENCER, T. *et al.* 1995. The relationship between tic disorders and Tourette's syndrome revisited. J. Am. Acad. Child Adolesc. Psychiatry **34:** 1133–1139.
38. ACHENBACH, T.M. & C.S. EDELBROCK. 1978. The classification of child psychopathology: a review and analysis of empirical efforts. Psychol. Bull. **85:** 1275–1301.
39. KHALIFA, N. & A.L. VON KNORRING. 2003. Prevalence of tic disorders and Tourette syndrome in a Swedish school population. Dev. Med. Child Neurol. **45:** 315–319.
40. LAPOUSE, R. & M.A. MONK. 1964. Behavior deviations in a representative sample of children: variation between sex, age, race, social class, and family size. Am. J. Orthopsychiatry **34:** 436–446.
41. NOMOTO, F. & Y. MACHIYAMA. 1990. An epidemiological study of tics. Jpn. J. Psychiatry Neurol. **44:** 649-55.
42. RUTTER, M. & M. HEMMING. 1970. Individual items of deviant behavior: their prevalence and clinical significance. *In* Education, Health and Behavior. M. Rutter, J. Tizard & K. Whitmore, Eds.: 202–232. Longman. London.
43. RUTTER, M. *et al.* 1974. Children of West Indian immigrants. I. Rates of behavioural deviance and of psychiatric disorder. J. Child Psychol. Psychiatry **15:** 241–262.
44. VERHULST, F.C., G.W. AKKERHUIS & M. ALTHAUS. 1985. Mental health in Dutch children: (I). A cross-cultural comparison. Acta Psychiatr. Scand. Suppl. **323:** 1–108.
45. FREEMAN, R.D. *et al.* 2000. An international perspective on Tourette syndrome: selected findings from 3,500 individuals in 22 countries [see Comment]. Dev. Med. Child Neurol. **42:** 436–447.

46. KING, R.A. *et al.* 1999. Obsessive-compulsive disorder, anxiety, and depression. *In* Tourette's Syndrome—Tics, Obsessions, Compulsions: Developmental Psychopathology and Clinical Care. J.F. Leckman & D.J. Cohen, Eds. Wiley. New York.
47. EAPEN, V., D.L. PAULS & M.M. ROBERTSON. 1993. Evidence for autosomal dominant transmission in Tourette's syndrome. United Kingdom cohort study. Br. J. Psychiatry **62:** 593–596.
48. PAULS, D.L. *et al.* 1986. Gilles de la Tourette's syndrome and obsessive-compulsive disorder. Evidence supporting a genetic relationship. Arch. Gen. Psychiatry. **43:** 1180–1182.
49. PAULS, D.L. *et al.* 1991. A family study of Gilles de la Tourette syndrome. Am. J. Hum. Genet. **48:** 154–163.
50. WALKUP, J.T. *et al.* 1996. Family study and segregation analysis of Tourette syndrome: evidence for a mixed model of inheritance. Am. J. Hum. Genet. **59:** 684–693.
51. ANONYMOUS. 1999. A complete genome screen in sib pairs affected by Gilles de la Tourette syndrome. The Tourette Syndrome Association International Consortium for Genetics. Am. J. Hum. Genet. **65:** 1428–1436.
52. LECKMAN, J.F. *et al.* 2003. Obsessive-compulsive symptom dimensions in affected sibling pairs diagnosed with Gilles de la Tourette syndrome. Am. J. Med. Genet. **116B:** 60–68.
53. PRICE, R.A. *et al.* 1985. A twin study of Tourette syndrome. Arch. Gen. Psychiatry **42:** 815–820.
54. LECKMAN, J.F. & L. SCAHILL. 1990. Possible exacerbation of tics by androgenic steroids. N. Engl. J. Med. **322:** 1674.
55. PETERSON, B.S. *et al.* 1994. Steroid hormones and Tourette's syndrome: early experience with antiandrogen therapy. J. Clin. Psychopharmacol. **14:** 131–135.
56. PETERSON, B.S. *et al.* 1998. A double-blind, placebo-controlled, crossover trial of an antiandrogen in the treatment of Tourette's syndrome. J. Clin. Psychopharmacol. **18:** 324–331.
57. MACLEAN, P.D. & J.M.R. DELGADO. 1953. Electrical and chemical stimulation of frontotemporal portion of limbic system in the waking animal. Electroencephalogr. Clin. Neurophysiol. **5:** 91–100.
58. BALDWIN, M., L.L. FROST & C.D. WOOD. 1954. Investigation of the primate amygdala. Movements of the face and jaws. Neurology **4:** 596–598.
59. ALEXANDER, G.E. & M.R. DELONG. 1985. Microstimulation of the primate neostriatum. II. Somatotopic organization of striatal microexcitable zones and their relation to neuronal response properties. J. Neurophysiol. **53:** 1417–1430.
60. KELLEY, A.E., C.G. LANG & A.M. GAUTHIER. 1988. Induction of oral stereotypy following amphetamine microinjection into a discrete subregion of the striatum. Psychopharmacology (Berl.) **95:** 556–559.
61. MINK, J.W. 2001. Neurobiology of basal ganglia circuits in Tourette syndrome: faulty inhibition of unwanted motor patterns? Adv. Neurol. **85:** 113–122.
62. GRAYBIEL, A.M. & J.J. CANALES. 2001. The neurobiology of repetitive behaviors: clues to the neurobiology of Tourette syndrome. Adv. Neurol. **85:** 123–131.
63. ALEXANDER, G.E., M.R. DELONG & P.L. STRICK. 1986. Parallel organization of functionally segregated circuits linking basal ganglia and cortex. Annu. Rev. Neurosci. **9:** 357–381.
64. GOLDMAN-RAKIC, P. 1987. Circuitry of primate prefrontal cortex and regulation of behavior by representational memory. *In* Handbook of Physiology: The Nervous System. V. Mountcastle, F. Plum & S. Geiger, Eds.: 373–416. American Physiological Society. Bethesda, MD.
65. LEUNG, H.C. *et al.* 2000. An event-related functional MRI study of the stroop color word interference task. Cereb. Cortex **10:** 552–560.
66. PETERSON, B.S. *et al.* 2002. An event-related functional MRI study comparing interference effects in the Simon and Stroop tasks. Cognit. Brain Res. **13:** 427–440.
67. PETERSON, B.S. *et al.* 1998. A functional magnetic resonance imaging study of tic suppression in Tourette syndrome. Arch. Gen. Psychiatry **55:** 326–333.
68. PARENT, A. & L.N. HAZRATI. 1995. Functional anatomy of the basal ganglia. I. The cortico-basal ganglia-thalamo-cortical loop. Brain Res. Brain Res. Dev. **20:** 91–127.

69. PETERSON, B.S. *et al.* 2003. Basal Ganglia volumes in patients with Gilles de la Tourette syndrome. Arch. Gen. Psychiatry **60:** 415–424.
70. HALL, M. *et al.* 1990. Brain perfusion patterns with Tc-99m-HMPAO/SPECT in patients with Gilles de la Tourette syndrome. Eur. J. Nucl. Med. **16:** WP18.
71. RIDDLE, M.A. *et al.* 1992. SPECT imaging of cerebral blood flow in Tourette syndrome. Adv. Neurol. **58:** 207–211.
72. BRAUN, A.R. *et al.* 1993. The functional neuroanatomy of Tourette's syndrome: an FDG-PET study. I. Regional changes in cerebral glucose metabolism differentiating patients and controls. Neuropsychopharmacology **9:** 277–291.
73. MORIARTY, J. *et al.* 1995. Brain perfusion abnormalities in Gilles de la Tourette's syndrome. Br. J. Psychiatry **167:** 249–254.
74. KLIEGER, P.S. *et al.* 1997. Asymmetry of basal ganglia perfusion in Tourette's syndrome shown by technetium-99m-HMPAO SPECT. J. Nucl. Med. **38:** 188–191.
75. PETERSON, B.S. *et al.* 2001. Regional brain and ventricular volumes in Tourette syndrome [see Comment]. Arch. Gen. Psychiatry **58:** 427–440.
76. KRAEMER, H.C. *et al.* 2000. How can we learn about developmental processes from cross-sectional studies, or can we? Am. J. Psychiatry **157:** 163–171.
77. PETERSON, B.S. 2003. Conceptual, methodological, and statistical challenges in brain imaging studies of developmentally based psychopathologies. Dev. Psychopathol. **15:** 811–832.
78. PETERSON, B.S. 2004. Personal communication to A. Spessot, Jan. 5.
79. CARR, D.B. & S.R. SESACK. 1998. Callosal terminals in the rat prefrontal cortex: synaptic targets and association with GABA-immunoreactive structures. Synapse **29:** 193–205.
80. INNOCENTI, G.M., D. AGGOUN-ZOUAOUI & P. LEHMANN. 1995. Cellular aspects of callosal connections and their development. Neuropsychologia **33:** 961–987.
81. WERHAHN, K.J. *et al.* 2002. Cortical excitability changes induced by deafferentation of the contralateral hemisphere. Brain **125:** 1402–1413.
82. PLESSEN, K.J. *et al.* Altered interhemispheric connectivity in individuals with Tourette syndrome. Am. J. Psychiatry. In press.
83. KRNJEVIC, K., M. RANDIC & D.W. STRAUGHAN. 1966. Nature of a cortical inhibitory process. J. Physiol. (Lond.) **184:** 49–77.
84. KIMURA, F. & R.W. BAUGHMAN. 1997. GABAergic transcallosal neurons in developing rat neocortex. Eur. J. Neurosci. **9:** 1137–1143.
85. ALEXANDER, G.M. & B.S. PETERSON. 2004. Testing the prenatal hormone hypothesis of tic-related disorders: Gender identity and gender role behavior. In press.
86. KOMPOLITI, K. *et al.* 2001. Estrogen, progesterone, and tic severity in women with Gilles de la Tourette syndrome. Neurology **57:** 1519.
87. SCHWABE, M.J. & R.J. KONKOL. 1992. Menstrual cycle-related fluctuations of tics in Tourette syndrome. Pediatr. Neurol. **8:** 43–46.
88. PETERSON, B.S. *et al.* 1992. Steroid hormones and CNS sexual dimorphisms modulate symptom expression in Tourette's syndrome. Psychoneuroendocrinology **17:** 553–563.
89. PETERSON, B.S. 2001. Neuroimaging studies of Tourette syndrome: a decade of progress. Adv. Neurol. **85:** 179–196.
90. SWEDO, S.E. *et al.* 1997. Identification of children with pediatric autoimmune neuropsychiatric disorders associated with streptococcal infections by a marker associated with rheumatic fever [see Comment]. Am. J. Psychiatry **154:** 110–112.
91. SWEDO, S.E. *et al.* 1998. Pediatric autoimmune neuropsychiatric disorders associated with streptococcal infections: clinical description of the first 50 cases [see Comment][Erratum appears in Am. J. Psychiatry 1998 **155:** 578]. Am. J. Psychiatry **155:** 264–271.
92. PETERSON, B.S. *et al.* 2000. Antistreptococcal antibody titers and basal ganglia volumes in chronic tic, obsessive-compulsive, and attention deficit-hyperactivity disorders. Arch. Gen. Psychiatry **57:** 364–372.
93. LEONARD, H.L. & S.E. SWEDO. 2001. Paediatric autoimmune neuropsychiatric disorders associated with streptococcal infection (PANDAS). Int. J. Neuropsychopharmacol. **4:** 191–198.

94. SNIDER, L.A. & S.E. SWEDO. 2003. Post-streptococcal autoimmune disorders of the central nervous system. Curr. Opin. Neurol. **16:** 359–365.
95. BODNER, S.M. & B.S. PETERSON. 2003. Pediatric autoimmune neuropsychiatric disorders associated with streptococcus. Dir. Psychiatry **23:** 235–251.
96. SURWILLO, W.W., M. SHAFII & C.L. BARRETT. 1978. Gilles de la Tourette syndrome: a 20-month study of the effects of stressful life events and haloperidol on symptom frequency. J. Nerv. Ment. Dis. **166:** 812–816.
97. BORNSTEIN, R.A., M.E. STEFL & L. HAMMOND. 1990. A survey of Tourette syndrome patients and their families: the 1987 Ohio Tourette Survey. J. Neuropsychiatry Clin. Neurosci. **2:** 275–281.
98. CHAPPELL, P. *et al.* 1994. Enhanced stress responsivity of Tourette syndrome patients undergoing lumbar puncture. Biol. Psychiatry **36:** 35–43.
99. SILVA, R.R. *et al.* 1995. Environmental factors and related fluctuation of symptoms in children and adolescents with Tourette's disorder. J. Child Psychol. Psychiatry **36:** 305–312.
100. FINDLEY, D.B. *et al.* 2003. Development of the Yale Children's Global Stress Index (YCGSI) and its application in children and adolescents with Tourette's syndrome and obsessive-compulsive disorder. J. Am. Acad. Child Adolesc. Psychiatry **42:** 450–457.
101. MCEWEN, B.S. 1997. Hormones as regulators of brain development: life-long effects related to health and disease. Acta Paediatr. Suppl. **422:** 41–44.
102. MCEWEN, B.S. 2000. The neurobiology of stress: from serendipity to clinical relevance. Brain Res. **886:** 172–189.
103. MCEWEN, B.S. 2001. From molecules to mind. Stress, individual differences, and the social environment. Ann. N.Y. Acad. Sci. **935:** 42–49.
104. PETERSON, B.S. & P. THOMAS. 2000. Functional brain imaging in Tourette's syndrome: What are we really imaging? *In* Functional Neuroimaging in Child Psychiatry. M. Ernst & J. Rumsey, Eds.: 242–265. Cambridge University Press. Cambridge.

Brain Development during Puberty and Adolescence

Comments on Part II

CHARLES A. NELSON

Institute of Child Development, Department of Pediatrics and Center for Neurobehavioral Development, University of Minnesota, Minneapolis, Minnesota 55455, USA

This chapter comments on work described in this section by Lewis,[1] Giedd,[2] and Peterson.[3] All three chapters focus on the development of prefrontal cortex and have enormous implications for elucidating atypical patterns of development. David Lewis's chapter is concerned largely with the substantial and complex changes in both pre- and postsynaptic markers of GABA-mediated activity in the dorsolateral prefrontal cortex. This work has particular relevance to our understanding of schizophrenia. Giedd's and Peterson's chapters examine a different level of anatomical detail, describing the findings of MRI technology. Giedd emphasizes changes in gray and white matter across the transition to and from puberty in typically developing children and important differences in the brains of boys versus girls. Such work has implications for typical development in children, as well as for disorders such as ADD. Peterson's chapter describes changes in brain morphometry in children and adults suffering from Tourette's syndrome and includes a very insightful model of the possible etiology of this disabling disorder.

All three chapters provide extraordinary detail in their descriptions of typical and atypical changes in brain development during childhood and adolescence. Moreover, each author is very sensitive to the needs to translate basic science into clinical science. This commentary is intended to extend the work of these three outstanding investigators in ways they surely would have themselves had page limits not been imposed on them.

WHAT ARE THE ORIGINS OF ADOLESCENT BRAIN DEVELOPMENT?

A theme common to many of the chapters represented in this volume is the failure to acknowledge the role of earlier developmental stages in ushering in changes during puberty and adolescence. Adolescent brain development does not begin once the

Address for correspondence: Charles A. Nelson, Ph.D., Institute of Child Development, 51 East River Road, University of Minnesota, Minneapolis, MN 55455. Voice: 612-624-3878; fax: 612-625-1530.
canelson@umn.edu

Ann. N.Y. Acad. Sci. 1021: 105–109 (2004). © 2004 New York Academy of Sciences.
doi: 10.1196/annals.1308.011

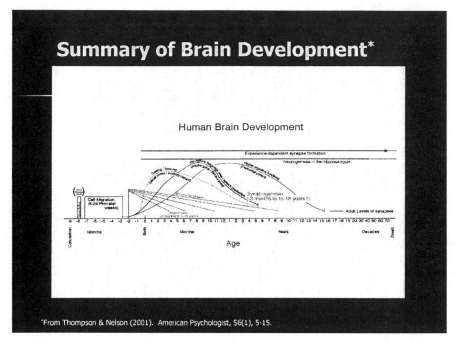

FIGURE 1. Summary of human brain development. (Reproduced by permission from Thompson and Nelson.[6])

child enters puberty; rather, there is a lengthy pre- and postnatal history that must be considered, as TABLE 1 and FIGURE 1 illustrate.

Given current models of brain development that ascribe tremendous importance to the role of experience in influencing changes in synaptic circuitry,[6–9] it is incumbent upon investigators working in this area to consider the earlier developmental stages from which the adolescent brain emerges.

HOW DOES EXPERIENCE INFLUENCE BRAIN STRUCTURE?

Numerous authors have written eloquently about the role of experience in influencing brain development during the early part of the lifespan, but what about adolescence? If we accept current thinking that synaptic pruning (which in the prefrontal cortex occurs in earnest during adolescence) is greatly influenced by experience, then can we account for nonoptimal patterns of adolescent brain development as being experience-based? If so, it is imperative that we elucidate the nature of these experiences and then posit how the structure of these experiences works its way into the structure of the brain. Doing so has enormous implications not only for understanding developmental trajectories, but for developing intervention strategies for dealing with nonoptimal patterns of development.

TABLE 1. Events in human brain development[a]

Developmental event	Timeline	Overview of developmental event
Neuralation	18–24 prenatal days	Cells differentiate into one of three layers—endoderm, mesoderm, and ectoderm—which then form the various organs in the body.
		The neural tube (from which the CNS is derived) develops from the ectoderm cells; the neural crest (from which the ANS is derived) lies between the ectodermal wall and the neural tube.
Neuronal migration	6–24 prenatal weeks	Neurons migrate at the ventricular zone along radial glial cells to the cerebral cortex.
		Neurons migrate in an inside-out manner, with later generations of cells migrating through previously developed cells.
		The cortex develops into 6 layers.
Synaptogenesis	3rd trimester–adolescence	Neurons migrate into the cortical plate and extend apical and basilar dendrites.
		Chemical signals guide the developing dendrites toward their final location, where synapses are formed with projections from subcortical structures.
		These connections are strengthened through neuronal activity, and connections with very little activity are pruned.
Postnatal neurogenesis	birth–adulthood	New cells develop in several brain regions, including: —dentate gyrus of the hippocampus —olfactory bulb —possibly cingulate gyrus; regions of parietal cortex.
Myelination	3rd trimester–middle age	Neurons are enclosed in a myelin sheath, resulting in an increased speed of action potentials.
Gyrification	3rd trimester–adulthood	The smooth tissue of the brain folds to form gyri and sulci.
Structural development of the prefrontal cortex	birth–late adulthood	The prefrontal cortex is the last structure to undergo gyrification during uterine life.
		The synaptic density reaches its peak at 12 months; however, myelination of this structure continues into adulthood.
Neurochemical development of the prefrontal cortex	uterine life–adolescence	All major neurotransmitter systems undergo initial development during uterine life and are present at birth.
		Although not well studied in humans, most neurotransmitter systems do not reach full maturity until adulthood.

[a]From White and Nelson.[5]

HOW DO WE RELATE BRAIN MORPHOLOGY TO BEHAVIOR?

The chapters by Lewis, Giedd, and Peterson describe the adolescent brain in exquisite detail. However, relatively ignored by all three authors (Peterson[3] less so than the others) is the relation between brain and behavior. For example, what are the functional correlates of changes in gray and white matter before and after puberty, and how do these morphological changes account for sex differences? Similarly, how can we relate the fine architectural detail of the dorsolateral prefrontal cortex described by Lewis to the emergence of schizophrenia?

CONCLUSIONS

The work reported by these three investigators is groundbreaking in terms of the light it sheds on adolescent brain development. The following recommendations speak to future research and are based on the strength of the research programs reported herein.

First, as our ability to peer into the adolescent brain increases (i.e., as technology improves), we should be modeling and elucidating the molecular and experiential mechanisms that drive brain development from conception onward.

Second, if we are to relate changes in brain development to changes in behavior, our knowledge of behavioral development will require the same level of detail and sophistication as our knowledge of brain development. Moreover, we need to mount a serious effort to couple brain and behavioral developmental research so that the two are better integrated.

Third, among the studies that have integrated measures of brain and behavior into the same experimental design, most are correlational—for example, they relate the volume of a particular brain structure to a particular behavior, such as the link between stress and the hippocampus. Because of the challenges in deriving cause–effect relations from correlational studies, it is incumbent upon us to change our designs so as to better explain the direction of effects—for example, do children with a genetic propensity to smaller (or in some cases, larger; see Spessot et al.[3]) prefrontal cortices lead them to develop Tourette's syndrome, or do children who develop Tourette's wind up with smaller prefrontal cortices as a result of the progression of their disease?

REFERENCES

1. LEWIS, D.A., D. CRUZ, S. EGGAN & S. ERICKSON. 2004. Postnatal development of prefrontal inhibitory circuits and the pathophysiology of cognitive dysfunction in schizophrenia. Ann. N.Y. Acad. Sci. **1021:** 64–76.
2. GIEDD, J.N. 2004. Structural magnetic resonance imaging of the adolescent brain. Ann. N.Y. Acad. Sci. **1021:** 77–85.
3. SPESSOT, A.L., K.J. PLESSEN & B.S. PETERSON. 2004. Neuroimaging of developmental psychopathologies: the importance of self-regulatory and neuroplastic processes in adolescence. Ann. N.Y. Acad. Sci. **1021:** 86–104.
4. LEVITT, P. 2003. Structural and functional maturation of the developing primate brain. J. Pediatr. **143**(4 Suppl.): S35–45.
5. WHITE, T. & C.A. NELSON. 2004. Neurobiological development during childhood and adolescence. *In* Schizophrenia in Adolescents and Children: Assessment, Neurobiol-

ogy, and Treatment. R.L. Findling & S.C. Schulz, Eds. Johns Hopkins Univ. Press. Baltimore, MD.
6. THOMPSON & NELSON. 2001. Developmental science and the media: early brain development. Am. Psychol. **56:** 5–15.
7. MONK, C.S., S.J. WEBB & C.A. NELSON. 2001. Prenatal neurobiological development: molecular mechanisms and anatomical change. Dev. Neuropsychol. **19:** 211–236.
8. NELSON, C.A. 2002. Neural development and life-long plasticity. *In* Promoting Positive Child, Adolescent, and Family Development: Handbook of Program and Policy Interventions. R.M. Lerner, F. Jacobs & D. Wetlieb, Eds.: 31–60. Sage Publications. Thousand Oaks, CA.
9. WEBB, S.J., C.S. MONK & C.A. NELSON. 2001. Mechanisms of postnatal neurobiological development in the prefrontal cortex and the hippocampal region: implications for human development. Dev. Neuropsychol. **19:** 147–171.

Interrelationships between Hormones, Behavior, and Affect during Adolescence

Understanding Hormonal, Physical, and Brain Changes Occurring in Association with Pubertal Activation of the Reproductive Axis

Introduction to Part III

JUDY L. CAMERON

Department of Psychiatry, University of Pittsburgh, Pittsburgh, Pennsylvania 15213, USA

The Oregon National Primate Research Center, Beaverton, Oregon 97006, USA

ABSTRACT: This paper summarizes the goals of this section and considers current knowledge about the association between hormonal changes that occur over pubertal development and the changes in behavior and brain function over the adolescent period. It reviews the cascade of neural and hormonal changes that occur with puberty; discusses mechanisms by which these changes can affect higher-order brain processes; reviews the current limited state of knowledge about links between puberty and changes in affect regulation in the adolescent period; identifies hurdles that have made progress in our understanding of these relationships difficult; and suggests areas for future investigation that will allow us to obtain a much more comprehensive understanding of these interrelationships. This overview of the physiological processes occurring at puberty indicates that puberty (1) encompasses changes in a number of neural systems; (2) results in altered secretion of a number of hormones; (3) involves hormones that are secreted in a pulsatile manner so that collection of a single blood sample does not clearly delineate hormone profiles; and (4) shows considerable individual variation in the rate of progression and in hormone secretion during progression. The important role that gonadal steroid hormones play throughout development and adulthood in regulating plastic changes in neuronal structure and function is noted, highlighting the need for further studies to determine the extent to which the dramatic increases in circulating steroid hormones at puberty modulate brain circuits that underlie changes in social behaviors, risk-taking behaviors, and cognitive function at adolescence.

KEYWORDS: adolescent brain development; hormones; puberty; neurotransmitters

Address for correspondence: Judy L. Cameron, Ph.D., Department of Psychiatry, University of Pittsburgh, 3811 O'Hara Street, Pittsburgh, PA 15213. Voice: 724-733-3795; fax: 724-327-1271.

cameronj@ohsu.edu

Ann. N.Y. Acad. Sci. 1021: 110–123 (2004). © 2004 New York Academy of Sciences.
doi: 10.1196/annals.1308.012

INTRODUCTION

The main goal of this section considers what we know about the association between hormonal changes that occur over pubertal development and the changes in behavior and brain function over the adolescent period. The dramatic changes that occur with the awakening of the reproductive axis at puberty, reflecting both a change in neural systems in the brain that govern reproductive function and the outpouring of gonadal hormones secondary to these changes, underlie the dramatic remodeling of the body over a relatively short period of time during adolescence, and it is compelling to consider the degree to which they also remodel the brain. Despite the great strides that have been made in the last several decades in defining the mechanisms by which the reproductive axis is activated at puberty and the general mechanisms by which reproductive hormones modulate brain systems, we still know relatively little about the extent to which these neural and hormonal changes influence the complex behavioral changes that occur in adolescence or the brain mechanisms underlying changes in social behaviors, risk-taking behaviors, and cognitive function at adolescence. This section reviews the cascade of neural and hormonal changes that occur with puberty, discusses mechanisms by which these changes can affect higher-order brain processes, reviews the current limited state of knowledge about links between puberty and changes in affect regulation in the adolescent period, identifies hurdles that have made progress in our understanding of these relationships difficult, and suggests areas for future investigation that will allow us to obtain a much more comprehensive understanding of these interrelationships.

A very difficult aspect of identifying which behavioral changes occurring over adolescence are actually linked to pubertal development is that puberty is a complex process that (1) encompasses changes in a number of neural systems; (2) results in altered secretion of a number of hormones; (3) involves hormones that are secreted in a pulsatile manner so that collection of a single blood sample does not clearly delineate hormone profiles; (4) shows considerable individual variation in the rate of progression, and hormone secretion during progression; and (5) is often tracked by monitoring physical changes that are indirect measures of the hormonal changes occurring at puberty. This section begins with an overview of the neural and hormonal changes that occur with pubertal development, and a general discussion of how these changes may influence the neural circuits that control affect regulation. Dr. Young's presentation highlights data collected in animal models and in clinical studies, providing examples of how gonadal steroid hormones influence neural circuits that underlie affect regulation. However, of note, her presentation (along with Bruce McEwen's, which, regrettably, is not included in this volume) focused on studies in adults as there is a paucity of data collected in the adolescent period examining these issues. The section concludes with a summary identifying hurdles that have impeded our progress in this area, and suggests ways for expanding our understanding of which behavioral changes in adolescence are directly linked to the physiological changes occurring at puberty.

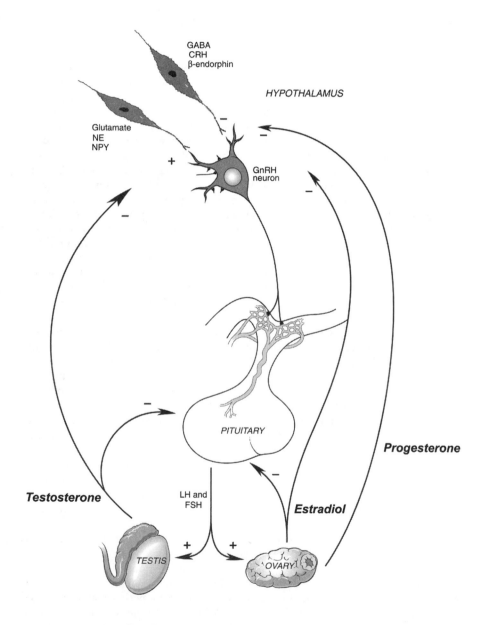

FIGURE 1. Schematic diagram of the reproductive axis, encompassing interactions between the brain, pituitary, and gonads (ovaries and testes). Interrelationships between hormones and neurotransmitters are schematically depicted as stimulatory (+) or inhibitory (−).

HORMONAL CHANGES OCCURRING WITH PUBERTAL
DEVELOPMENT ARE COMPLEX

Reproductive Function Is Governed by an Interplay between the Brain, Pituitary, and Gonads

Although reproductive function is often considered primarily a physiological function occurring at the level of the testes and ovaries, specialized neurons in the brain and hormones secreted by the "master endocrine organ," the pituitary, located just beneath the brain, play critical roles in governing reproductive function (FIG. 1).[1,2] Not only do the brain and pituitary coordinate and provide the "central drive" to the reproductive axis throughout life, but also the brain is the primary site of action for modulatory factors (such as stress, nutritional signals, and exercise) that can have a marked impact on the level of activity of the reproductive axis, and on the timing of the pubertal awakening of this axis. A population of specialized neurons in the hypothalamic region of the brain produce gonadotropin-releasing hormone (GnRH; named for its ability to release the hormones in the pituitary that provide trophic support to the ovaries and testes—the gonadotropins—luteinizing hormone [LH], and follicle-stimulating hormone [FSH]). Many neurotransmitter systems from other parts of the brain convey information to GnRH neurons.[3] These afferent systems include neurons that contain neurotransmitters that are generally stimulatory to GnRH neurons, such as norepinephrine, dopamine, serotonin, glutamate, neuropeptide Y, and galanin, as well as neurotransmitters that are generally inhibitory to GnRH neurons, such as GABA, endogenous opiate peptides, and the central hypothalamic hormone that governs the adrenal axis, corticotropin-releasing hormone (CRH). Various forms of stress can lead to a suppression of reproductive function by acting to increase inhibitory drive to GnRH neurons, often by increasing either β-endorphin or CRH input into the GnRH neuronal system.[4,5] Decreased firing of GnRH neurons leads to less GnRH stimulation of pituitary LH and FSH release, and thus less stimulation of ovarian and testicular function. Thus, with exposure to stress reproductive hormone secretion is often suppressed, and with chronic stress the reproductive axis can be completely suppressed. Changes in reproductive function also occur in psychiatric illnesses, such that changes in both reproductive function and sexual behavior are commonly reported by patients suffering from depression, anxiety disorders, and obsessive-compulsive disorders.[6,7] The drugs used to treat these disorders also have the potential of having an impact on reproductive function, because they can affect neural input into GnRH neurons, as well as treating neurotransmitter imbalances in higher cortical areas.[7,8]

GnRH stimulates both the synthesis and the release of the gonadotropins, LH and FSH, into the peripheral bloodstream. In the male, LH binds to testicular cells (Leydig cells) and stimulates the synthesis and secretion of testosterone. FSH binds to Sertoli cells in the seminiferous tubules and along with testosterone stimulates spermatogenesis. In the female, FSH acts at the beginning of each menstrual cycle on ovarian follicles to stimulate their growth and the production of estrogen. This portion of the menstrual cycle is referred to as the follicular phase and lasts about 2 weeks. In the middle of each menstrual cycle, a large surge of LH acts on the fully developed follicle to stimulate ovulation and the development of the corpus luteum (see FIGURE 2 for overview of hormonal changes during the female menstrual cycle). The corpus luteum secretes both estrogen and progesterone, which play a critical role in preparing the uterine endometrium for implantation of a developing embyro, should fertilization occur. This portion of the menstrual cycle is referred to as the luteal phase and it too lasts about 2 weeks, such that an entire menstrual cycle is about one month in length. LH and FSH are released into the bloodstream in a pulsatile manner, at rates of about one pulse every 2–3 hours in males and at rates that vary in females from one pulse every hour to one pulse every 8–12 hours at various stages of the menstrual cycle (FIG. 3).[9] The pulsatile nature of LH and FSH secretion can be a confounding factor when hormone measures are collected in clinical or epidemiological studies, in that a single blood sample may be collected when hormone levels are at the peak or nadir of a pulse. Thus, variation of LH and FSH levels within an individual can be great, making it difficult to detect group dif-

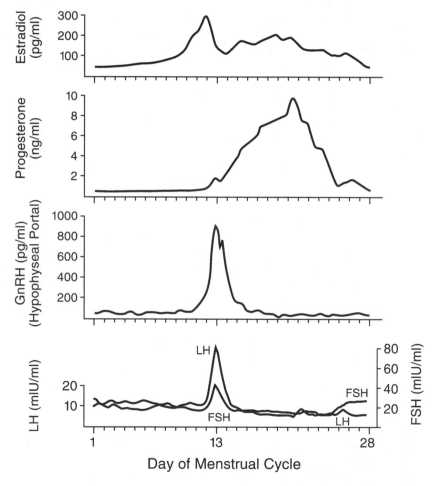

FIGURE 2. Diagramatic representation of changes in plasma levels of estradiol, progesterone, LH and FSH, and portal levels of GnRH over the human menstrual cycle.

ferences, or changes in hormone levels within an individual across time, such as during the pubertal transition.

The gonadal steroid hormones are produced in a common synthetic pathway, all derived from a common precursor, cholesterol. Although androgens are commonly thought of as "male" hormones, they are produced in both the male and female, and likewise the "female" hormone, estrogen, is present in the male as well as in the female. In males, testosterone produced by the Leydig cells of the testes can act at its target tissues by binding to testosterone receptors, or first being converted to a more potent androgen, dihydrotestosterone (DHT), by the enzyme 5α-reductase, or by being converted to estrogen by the enzyme aromatase, and acting by binding to estrogen receptors. Many of the actions of testosterone in peripheral tissues and in the brain occur secondary to conversion to either DHT or estradiol. In females, the pathway for estradiol production involves an intermediate step of androgen production, and thus the ovary is a source of low levels of androgens, principally androstenedione. The other ovarian hormone, progesterone, is produced early in the steroid hormone synthetic pathway and is a precursor for both androgens and estrogens. The gonadal hormones play very important roles at puberty in stimulating the development of secondary sexual characteristics. In the male, this includes enlargement of the penis and testis, increased muscle mass, deepening of the voice, and stimulation of adult hair growth patterns. In the female, the changes in estrogen and progesterone are responsible for the initiation of menstrual cycles, and estrogen also stimulates breast development, widening of the hips, and increased subcutaneous fat deposition. Testosterone, estrogen, and progresterone also act at the brain to play important roles in regulating the secretion of GnRH, LH and FSH by negative feedback actions at the hypothalamus and pituitary (FIG. 1). For example, the dramatic slowing of pulsatile gonadotropin release during the luteal phase of the menstrual cycle (FIG. 3) is caused by negative feedback of the high levels of progesterone secreted by the corpus luteum. Estrogen also has a positive feedback action at the hypothalamus and pi-

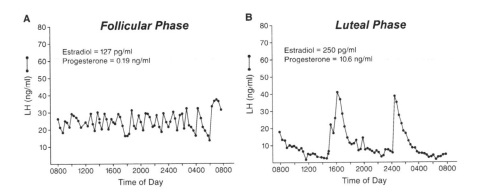

FIGURE 3. Examples of the pulsatile pattern of LH secretion in a woman during the late follicular phase (**A**) and mid-luteal phase (**B**) of the menstrual cycle. Steroid hormone levels at the two different times in the menstrual cycle are indicated on each graph. Note the dramatic slowing of pulsatile LH secretion as a result of gonadal steroid hormone negative feedback during the luteal phase. (Redrawn from Soules et al.[9]).

tuitary, and it is this positive feedback action, secondary to the rise in estradiol secreted by a rapidly developing follicle late in the follicular phase, that stimulates ovulation in the middle of each menstrual cycle.

Pubertal Activation of the Reproductive Axis Is Really a Reactivation

Early in embryonic development the components of the reproductive axis are formed and functional activity of the reproductive axis as a whole is initiated during fetal development. By midgestation circulating levels of LH and FSH reach values similar to those found in adulthood.[10,11] Later in gestational development, gonadotropin levels decline, restrained by rising levels of circulating gonadal steroids,[10,12] secreted primarily from the placenta. At birth, with a decline in steroid hormone negative feedback, there is a rise in circulating gonadotropin levels that is apparent for approximately the first year of life.[13] And then gonadotropin secretion declines between ages one and two, which appears to be due to a decrease in GnRH stimulation of the reproductive axis.[14]

Pubertal reawakening of the reproductive axis occurs in late childhood, and involves a reactivation of GnRH neurons.[14,15] One of the earliest signs of puberty is an elevation of gonadotropin and gonadal steroid hormone levels specifically at night,[16] although, since detection of this rise requires collecting blood samples at night, it is rarely examined in clinical or epidemiological studies. Changes in body habitus are the first signs of puberty that are detected by most individuals, although these emanate from increased levels of gonadal steroid hormones and are thus relatively late events in the reawakening of the reproductive axis. Likewise, in girls, menarche is a very late event, and represents the point where the adult cyclic interplay between the hypothalamic-pituitary-ovarian axis is initiated.

The trigger for renewed activation of GnRH neurons is not fully understood, but there is significant evidence that increases in stimulatory neural input into GnRH neurons and decreases in inhibitory input are both involved.[14,15,17] Low energy availability (resulting from undernutrition or very intense exercise training) can delay the onset of GnRH activity, although these signals appear to be only modulators of the pubertal process, in that puberty can only be moderately advanced by increasing energy availability.[14] Whether a genetic timing mechanism is the primary trigger for the timing of puberty, or whether other signals from the body or the brain are responsible for timing the reactivation of the reproductive axis, is unknown and awaits further research.

Most data describing the pubertal increase in reproductive hormones come from cross-sectional studies with girls and boys, and plots of the increases in reproductive hormones over time suggest that the increase in reproductive hormone secretion occurs slowly. However, this is likely an artifact of the cross-sectional design, where the probability of an individual showing increased reproductive hormone levels slowly increases, but the increase within each individual is fairly rapid. Over the past decade, detailed studies in children and monkeys (which, like girls, develop monthly menstrual cycles at puberty), collecting frequent blood samples to assess pulsatile gonadotropin secretion and using highly sensitive hormone assays, have shown that the initiation of puberty, as marked by increased gonadotropin secretion, is generally a rather rapid event occurring in the earliest stages of puberty.[18–21]

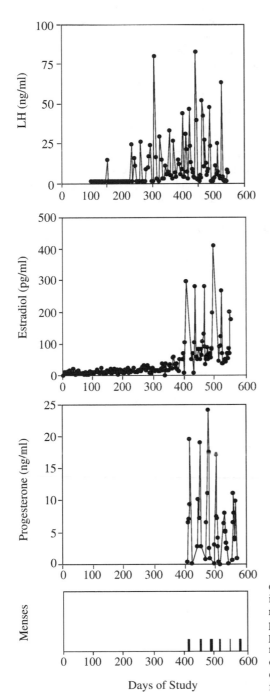

FIGURE 4. Plasma levels of LH, estradiol, and progesterone, and the incidence of menses, in one female cynomolgus monkey over an 18-month period encompassing the initiation of puberty. Blood samples for hormone measurement were collected every other day, and the monkey was checked for the presence of menstrual flow every day.

Recently, we have completed a long-term longitudinal study in 36 young female monkeys with blood samples collected every other day for 18 months to assess, in a more detailed manner than is possible in clinical studies, the relationships between changes in gonadotropin secretion, gonadal hormone secretion, and the establishment of regular, ovulatory menstrual cycles. As shown for one monkey in FIGURE 4, we have found that for most individuals the first sign of puberty is an increase in plasma LH levels, followed very shortly thereafter by a small increase in circulating estradiol levels. Within the next 4–6 months most animals show the initiation of menstrual cyclicity, with many animals immediately developing normal ovulatory menstrual cycles, while others show either irregular anovulatory cycles, irregular ovulatory cycles, or regular anovulatory cycles.

Sexual behavior is also dramatically increased at puberty. In males there is a strong correlation at this age between plasma testosterone levels and degree of sexual desire and sexual activity.[22,23] Increases in sexual desire and sexual behavior also occur in girls at puberty, but the identity of the hormones regulating this increase is controversial. Correlations have been reported between androgen levels in adolescent girls and sexual interest[24] and the initiation of coitus.[25] However, a study by Zehr et al.[26] showing that estrogen replacement alone to ovariectomized female monkeys can stimulate female sexual initiation, and earlier studies showing that in the normal menstrual cycle changes in circulating estradiol, but not androgen correlate with changes in female sexual initiation,[27] support a role for estrogen in governing female sexual behavior. In addition, there is evidence that social factors can be as important as hormonal factors in determining girls' sexual behavior.[24]

Other Hormonal Changes Associated with Puberty

A number of other hormonal changes occur in association with puberty, including an increase in androgen production by the adrenal gland (adrenarche), and changes in hormones controlling body growth.[28,29] Adrenarche is the physiological rise in the production of the weak androgen, dehydroepiandrosterone (DHEA) and its sulfated product (DHEAS). Adrenarche generally occurs several years before pubertal activation of the reproductive axis, but the developmental changes in these two endocrine systems is independent,[14] and a number of children experience increased gonadal hormone production prior to adrenarche.[30] Adrenal androgens stimulate the pubertal growth of axillary and pubic hair in both males and females. The mid-childhood growth spurt is a transient increase in the velocity of height gain, and often occurs around the same time as adrenarche, but studies have shown that these two events can be dissociated, suggesting they are not causally linked.[31] However, increased growth hormone (GH) and insulin-like growth factor-1 (IGF-1) secretion, which is under GH control, may play a role in both adrenarche and the growth spurt.[32]

MANY NEURAL CIRCUITS HAVE RECEPTORS FOR GONADAL STEROID HORMONES AND ARE RESPONSIVE TO CHANGES IN CIRCULATING LEVELS OF GONADAL STEROIDS

Gonadal steroid hormones play an important role in regulating plastic changes in neuronal structure and function throughout development and adulthood.[33–35] They influence a wide variety of neuronal processes including neurogenesis, cell migration, growth of the neuronal cell body, dendritic growth, differentiation, synapse formation, synapse elimination, neuronal atrophy, apoptosis, neuropeptide expression, the expression of neurotransmitter receptors, and neuronal excitability. Gonadal steroid hormones act early in brain development in the "organization" of neural circuits, as well as playing critical roles throughout adulthood in "activating" specific behaviors.[33–35] In many cases steroid hormones must be present both developmentally and in adulthood to elicit maximal effects on behavior. Developmental actions of steroid hormones, in particular testosterone in males, which is often converted to estrogen locally at brain cells to have its actions via estrogen receptors, causes differentiation of a number of neural circuits in the brain, resulting in sex differences in these circuits throughout life.

Steroid hormone receptors are abundant in the brain. Classical estrogen receptors (now called estrogen α-receptors) are strongly concentrated in the hypothalamus, but are also found in brain areas with strong connections to the hypothalamus.[36] In 1997, a second form of estrogen receptor (estrogen β-receptors) was identified and found to be present throughout the rostral-caudal extent of the brain, including the cerebral cortex.[37] And, in the last several years evidence has accumulated for a third form of estrogen receptor (estrogen receptor-X), as well as a number of other putative estrogen-binding proteins and variants of the identified estrogen receptors in various brain regions.[38] Specific receptors for progesterone are induced by estrogen in hypothalamic regions of the brain, and there is also some evidence for constitutive expression of progesterone receptors.[39] Androgen receptor mapping studies have shown considerable overlap in the distribution of androgen and estrogen receptors throughout the brain.[36,40]

Although early studies of the effects of gonadal steroid hormones on the brain focused on effects in hypothalamic and brainstem regions governing reproductive function and reproductive behavior, more recent studies show actions of gonadal steroid hormones throughout the brain in regions including the hippocampus, striatum, cerebellum, amygdala and cerebral cortex, and actions on many nonreproductive behaviors including spatial problem-solving ability, verbal abilities, aggression, motor activity, various aspects of learning and memory, and affect regulation.[34,35] Over the last several years, it has become clear that gonadal steroid hormones modulate activity of a number of neurotransmitter systems, including cholinergic, serotonergic, noradrenergic and dopaminergic neurons, which project throughout the brain and play central roles in regulating many higher-order brain functions, including cognitive functions and emotion regulation.[35] Although very little research has been undertaken to date examining how changes in gonadal steroid hormone levels at puberty influence activity in these circuits, there is evidence from studies in animals examining the effects of castration and hormone replacement therapy and studies in post-menopausal women with and without hormone replacement therapy, to indicate that throughout life these brain circuits remain responsive to changes in circulating levels of gonadal steroid hormones. In the basal forebrain cholinergic system, which projects to the cerebral cortex and hippocampus, the rate-limiting enzyme for acetylcholine formation, choline acetyltransferase (ChAT), is decreased after ovariectomy and increased with estrogen treatment,[41] and cyclic variations in ChAT mRNA have been reported across the estrous cycle.[42] Interestingly, treatment with tacrine, a cholinergic enhancing drug, has only been shown to be effective for women with

Alzheimer's disease if they are also on estrogen replacement therapy.[43] Serotonin neurons, which project to many regions of the brain and play an important role in many aspects of brain differentiation and development,[44] show sex differences, with females demonstrating higher serotonin levels than males.[35] In the monkey, estrogen has been shown to increase the expression of tryptophan hydroxylase (TPH), the rate-limiting enzyme for serotonin synthesis, as well as modulating expression of the serotonin transporter gene and genes for several serotonin receptors and enzymes responsible for serotonin degradation.[45] Low activity of serotonergic neurons is strongly correlated with the clinical conditions of anxiety and depression,[46,47] and estrogen has been shown to have antidepressant actions in both animal and clinical studies.[48,49] Moreover, improvement of responsiveness to the serotonergic antidepressant medication, Prozac, has been reported in women on estrogen replacement therapy.[50] Noradrenergic neurons contain estrogen receptors[51] and show changes across the estrous cycle in rats in *fos* expression.[52,53] And, dopaminergic neurons in midbrain regions are responsive to changes in circulating estrogen concentrations,[54,55] and changes in dopamine release and locomotion have also been reported across the estrous cycle in rats.[56]

STRATEGIES FOR STUDYING HOW PUBERTY CONTRIBUTES TO CHANGES IN AFFECT REGULATION DURING ADOLESCENCE

Although longitudinal studies may be considered ideal for tracking changes in complex behaviors that occur over adolescence and identifying which of these changes are specifically associated with pubertal development, such studies are rare and are not practical in many cases. They can be expensive, and retention of individuals over the prolonged period of adolescence can be difficult. Cross-sectional studies are more practical and the data reviewed above indicate several strategies that can be incorporated into cross-sectional studies that would greatly aid in answering the question of how puberty contributes to changes in various aspects of affect regulation. One strategy is at a given age to choose two groups of individuals to study: one that is clearly prepubertal and one that has progressed far enough through puberty to show changes in secondary sexual characteristics, indicating an increase in gonadal steroid hormones. Ideally, one would have the second group be as homogenous as possible (i.e., matched for a stage of pubertal development). Comparison of the outcome measures in the two groups would allow determination of the role of pubertal development in modulating the outcome under study, as the groups would be matched for age. A second strategy is to use several measures of pubertal development to more accurately characterize pubertal stage, and in particular collect accurate data on the longitudinal aspect of pubertal development for study participants, in that the effects of pubertal hormones on neural circuits may differ in adolescents who have recently experienced a rise in hormone levels compared to those who have experienced elevated hormone levels for several years. It may also be useful to use staging that monitors different aspects of pubertal development (e.g., initiation of reproductive function and adrenarche). Third, more animal studies are needed that include careful tracking of pubertal status, and in animal studies there is also the possibility of studying groups of animals before, during, and after puberty to understand the time course of changes in outcome measures as they pertain to pubertal development. Lastly, both in clinical and animal studies, a nested experimental design in which a subset of individuals are studied longitudinally, with careful assessment of pubertal measures, within a cross-sectional study, would provide a better understanding of how pubertal development contributes to changes in behavior and the neural systems that underlie behavior in the adolescent period.

ACKNOWLEDGMENTS

The work providing data presented from Dr. Cameron's laboratory was supported by a grant from the John D. and Catherine T. MacArthur Foundation Network on Health Promoting and Health Damaging Behaviors, and Grant MH50748 from the National Institutes of Health.

REFERENCES

1. STEINER, R.A. & J.L. CAMERON. 1989. Endocrine control of reproduction. *In* Textbook of Physiology. H.D. Patton *et al.*, Eds.: 1289–1342. W.B. Saunders. Philadelphia, PA.
2. GRIFFIN, J.E. & S.R. OJEDA. 2000. Textbook of Endocrine Physiology, 4th ed. Oxford University Press. London.
3. KORDON, C., S.V. DROUVA, G. MARTINEZ DE LA ESCALERA & R.I. WEINER. 1994. Role of classic and peptide neuromediators in the neuroendocrine regulation of luteinizing hormone and prolactin. *In* The Physiology of Reproduction, Vol. 1. E. Knobil & J.D. Neill, Eds.: 1621–1681. Raven Press. New York.
4. FENG, Y.J., E. SHALTS, L. XIA, *et al.* 1991. An inhibitory effect of interleukin-1 on basal gonadotropin release in the ovariectomized rhesus monkey: reversal by a corticotropin-releasing factor antagonist. Endocrinology **128**: 2077–2082.
5. NORMAN, R.L. & C.J. SMITH. 1992. Restraint inhibits luteinizing hormone and testosterone secretion in intact male rhesus macaques: effects of concurrent naloxone administration. Neuroendocrinology **55**: 405–415.
6. SHABSIGH, R., L. ZAKARIA, A.G. ANASTASIADIS & A.S. SEIDMAN 2001. Sexual dysfunction and depression: etiology, prevalence, and treatment. Curr. Urol. Rep. **2**: 463–467
7. CLAYTON, A.H. 2002. Female sexual dysfunction related to depression and antidepressant medications. Curr. Womens Health Rep. **2**: 182–187.
8. MONTGOMERY, S.A., D.S. BALDWIN & A. RILEY. 2002. Antidepressant medications: a review of the evidence for drug-induced sexual dysfunction. J. Affect. Disord. **69**: 119–140.
9. SOULES, M.R., R.A. STEINER, D.K. CLIFTON, *et al.* 1984. Progesterone modulation of pulsatile luteinizing hormone secretion in normal women. J. Clin. Endocrinol. Metab. **58**: 378–383.
10. KAPLAN, S.L., M.M. GRUMBACH & M.L. AUBERT. 1976. The ontogenesis of pituitary hormones and hypothalamic factors in the human fetus: maturation of central nervous system regulation of anterior pituitary function. Recent Prog. Horm. Res. **32**: 161–234.
11. ELLINWOOD W.E. & J.A. RESKO. 1984. Sex differences in biologically active and immunoreactive gonadotropins in the fetal circulation of rhesus monkeys. Endocrinology **107**: 902–907.
12. RESKO, J.A. & W.E. ELLINWOOD. 1985. Negative feedback regulation of gonadotropin secretion by androgens in fetal rhesus macaques. Biol. Reprod. **33**: 346–352.
13. WINTER, J.S.D., C. FAIMAN, W.C. HOBSON, *et al.* 1975. Pituitary-gonadal relations in infancy. I. Patterns of serum gonadotropin concentrations from birth to four years of age in man and chimpanzee. J. Clin. Endocrinol. Metab. **40**: 545–551.
14. PLANT, T.M. 2001. Neurobiological bases underlying the control of the onset of puberty in the rhesus monkey: a representative higher primate. Front. Neuroendocrinol. **22**: 107–139.

15. PLANT, T.M. & M.L. BARKER-GIBB. 2004. Neurobiological mechanisms of puberty in higher primates. Hum. Reprod. Update **10:** 67–77.
16. BOYAR, R.M., R.S. ROSENFELD, S. KAPEN, et al. 1974. Human puberty: simultaneous augmented secretion of luteinizing hormone and testosterone during sleep. J. Clin. Invest. **54:** 609–618.
17. OJEDA, S.R. & M. BILGER. 2000. Neuroendocrine regulation of puberty. In Neuroendocrinology in Physiology and Medicine. P.M. Conn & M.E. Freeman, Eds.: 197–224. Humana Press. Ottowa.
18. WENNINK, J.M.B., H.A. DELEMARRE-VAN DE WAAL, R. SCHOEMAKER, et al. 1989. Luteinizing hormone and follicule stimulating hormone secretion patterns in boys throughout puberty measured using highly sensitive immunoradiometric assays. Clin. Endocrinol. (Oxf.) **31:** 551–564.
19. OERTER, K.E., M.M. URIARTE, S.R. ROSE, et al. 1990. Gonadotropin secretory dynamics during puberty in normal girls and boys. J. Clin. Endocrinol. Metab. **71:** 1251–1258.
20. MANASCO, P.K., D.M. UMBACH, S.M. MULY, et al. 1995. Ontogeny of gonadotropin, testosterone and inhibin secretion in normal boys through puberty based on overnight serial sampling. J. Clin. Endocrinol. Metab. **80:** 2046–2052.
21. SUTER, K.J., C.R. POHL & T.M. PLANT. 1998. The pattern and tempo of the pubertal reaugmentation of open-loop pulsatile gonadotropin-releasing hormone release assessed indirectly in the male rhesus monkey (Macaca mulatta). Endocrinology **139:** 2274–2783.
22. UDRY, J.R., J.O. BILLY, N.M. MORRIS, et al. 1985. Serum androgenic hormones motivate sexual behavior in adolescent boys. Fertil. Steril. **43:** 90–94.
23. HALPERN, C.R., J.R. UDRY & C. SUCHINDRAN. 1998. Monthly measures of salivary testosterone predict sexual activity in adolescent males. Arch. Sex. Behav. **27:** 445–465.
24. UDRY, J.R., L.M. TALBERT & N.M. MORRIS. 1986. Biosocial foundations for adolescent female sexuality. Demography **23:** 217–230.
25. HALPERN, C.R., J.R. UDRY & C. SUCHINDRAN. 1997. Testosterone predicts initiation of coitus in adolescent females. Psychosom. Med. **59:** 161–171.
26. ZEHR, J.L., D. MAESTRIPIERI & K. WALLEN. 1998. Estradiol increases female sexual initiation independent of male responsiveness in rhesus monkeys. Horm. Behav. **33:** 95–103.
27. WALLEN, K., D.R. MANN, M. DAVIS-DASILVA, et al. 1986. Chronic gonadotropin-releasing hormone agonist treatment suppresses ovulation and sexual behavior in group-living female rhesus monkeys. Physiol. Behav. **36:** 369–375.
28. IBANEZ, L., J. DIMATINO-NARDI, N. POTAU & P. SAENGER. 2000. Premature adrenarche-normal variant or forerunner of adult disease? Endocr. Rev. **21:** 671–696.
29. TANNER, J.M. & N. CAMERON. 1980. Investigation of the mid-growth spurt in height, weight and limb circumferences in single-year velocity data from the London 1966–67 growth survey. Ann. Hum. Biol. **7:** 565–577.
30. BIRO, F.M., A.W. LUCKY, L.A. SIMBARTL, et al. 2003. Pubertal maturation in girls and the relationship to anthropometric changes: pathways through puberty. J. Pediatr. **142:** 643–646.
31. REMER, T. & F. MANZ 2001. The midgrowth spurt in healthy children is not caused by adrenarche. J. Clin. Endocrinol. Metab. **86:** 4183–4186.
32. GUERCIO, G., M.A. RIVAROLA, E. CHALER, et al. 2003. Relationship between the growth hormone/insulin-like growth factor-1 axis, insulin sensitivity, and adrenal androgens in normal prepubertal and pubertal girls. J. Clin. Endocrinol. Metab. **88:** 1389–1393.
33. COOKE , B., C.D. HEGSTROM, L.S. VILLENEUVE & S. M. BREEDLOVE. 1998. Sexual differentiation of the vertebrate brain: Principles and mechanisms. Front. Neuroendocrinol. **19:** 323–362.
34. CAMERON, J.L. 2001. Effects of sex hormones on brain development. In Developmental Cognitive Neuroscience. C.A. Nelson & M. Luciana, Eds.: 59–78. The MIT Press. Cambridge, MA.
35. MCEWEN, B.S. & S. E. ALVES. 2003. Estrogen actions in the central nervous system. Endocr. Rev. **20:** 279–307.

36. SIMERLY, R.B., C. CHANG, M. MURAMATSU & L.V. SWANSON. 1990. Distribution of androgen and estrogen receptor mRNA-containing cells in the rat brain: an in situ hybridization study. J. Comp. Neurol. **294:** 76–95.
37. SHUGHRUE, P.J., M.V. LANE & I. MERCHENTHALER. 1997. The comparative distribution of estrogen receptor-a and b mRNA in rat central nervous system. J. Comp. Neurol. **388:** 507–525.
38. TORAN-ALLERAND, C.D. 2004. Minireview: a plethora of estrogen receptors in the brain: where will it end? Endocrinology **145:** 1069–1074.
39. BETHEA, C.L., W.H. FAHRENBACH, S.A. SPRANGERS & F. FREESH. 1992. Immunocytochemical localization of progestin receptors in monkey hypothalamus: effect of estrogen and progestin. Endocrinology **130:** 895–905.
40. MICHAEL, R.P., A.N. CLANCY & D. ZUMPE. 1995. Distribution of androgen receptor-like immunoreactivity in the brains of cynomolgus monkeys. J. Neuroendocrinol. **7:** 713–719.
41. MCEWEN, B.S., V. LUINE & C. FISCHETTE. 1987. Developmental actions of hormones: from receptors to function. *In* From Message to Mind. S. Easter, K. Barald & B. Carlson, Eds.: 272–287. Sinauer Asssociates. Sutherland MA.
42. GIBBS, R.B. & P. AGGARWAL 1998. Estrogen and basal forebrain cholinergic neurons: implications for brain aging and Alzheimer's disease-related cognitive decline. Horm. Behav. **34:** 98–111.
43. SCHNEIDER, L.S., M.R. FARLOW, V.W. HENDERSON & J.M. POGODA. 1996. Effects of estrogen replacement therapy on response to tacrine in patients with Alzheimer's disease. Neurology **46:** 1580–1584.
44. WHITAKER-AZMITIA, P.M. 1991. Role of serotonin and other neurotransmitter receptors in brain development: basis for developmental pharmacology. Pharmacol. Rev. **43:** 553–561.
45. BETHEA, C.L., N.Z. LU, C. GUNDLAH & J.M. STREICHER. 2002. Diverse actions of ovarian steroids in the serotonin neural system. Front. Neuroendocrinol. **23:** 41–100.
46. RESSLER, K.J. & C.B. NEMEROFF. 2000. Role of serotonergic and noradrenergic systems in the pathophysiology of depression and anxiety disorders. Depress. Anxiety **12:** 2–19.
47. BHAGWAGAR, Z., R. WHALE & P.J. COWEN. 2002. State and trait abnormalities in serotonin function in major depression. Br. J. Psychiatry **180:** 24–28.
48. KLAIBER, E.L., D.M. BROVERMAN, W. VOGEL, *et al.* 1996. Individual differences in changes in mood and platelet monoamine oxidase (MAO) activity during hormonal replacement therapy in menopausal women. Psychoneuroendocrinology **21:** 575–592.
49. RACHMAN, I.M., J.R. UNNERSTALL, D.W. PFAFF & R.S. COHEN. 1998. Estrogen alters behavior and forebrain c-fos expression in ovariectomized rats subjected to the forced swim test. Proc. Natl. Acad. Sci. USA **95:** 13941–13946.
50. SCHNEIDER, L.S., G.W. SMALL, S.H. HAMILTON, *et al.* 1997. Estrogen replacement and the response to fluoxetine in a multicenter geriatric depression trial. Am. J. Geriatr. Psychiatry **5:** 97–106.
51. HERITAGE, A.S., W.E. STUMPF, M. SAR & L.D. GRANT. 1980. Brainstem catecholamine neurons arc target sites for sex steroid hormones. Science **207:** 1377–1380.
52. JENNES, L., M.E. JENNES, C. PURVIS & M. NEES. 1992. c-fos expression in noradrenergic A2 neurons of the rat during the estrous cycle and after steroid hormone treatments. Brain Res. **586:** 171–175
53. CONDE, G.L., R.J. BICKNELL & A.E. HERBISON. 1998. Changing patterns of Fos expression in brainstem catecholaminergic neurons during the rat oestrous cycle. Brain Res. **672:** 68–72.
54. DIPAOLO, T. 1994. Modulation of brain dopamine transmission by sex steroids. Rev. Neurosci. **5:** 27–42.
55. MCEWEN, B.S., H. CHAO & J. ANGULO. 1994. Glucocorticoid and estrogen effects on the nigrostriatal and mesolimbic dopaminergic systems. *In* Trophic Regulation of the Basal Ganglia. K. Fuxe, L. Agnati, B. Bjelke & D. Ottoson, Eds.: 67–88. Pergamon Press. London.
56. BECKER, J.B., P.J. SNYDER, M.M. MILLER, *et al.* 1987. The influence of estrous cycle and intrastriatal estradiol on sensorimotor performance in the female rat. Pharmacol. Biochem. Behav. **27:** 53–59.

Puberty, Ovarian Steroids, and Stress

ELIZABETH A. YOUNG[a] AND MARGARET ALTEMUS[b]

[a]Department of Psychiatry and Mental Health Research Institute,
University of Michigan, Ann Arbor, Michigan 48109, USA

[b]Department of Psychiatry, Weill-Cornell Medical School,
New York, New York 10021, USA

ABSTRACT: Puberty is accompanied by a number of changes, among them increased risk for development of major depression. The most common etiology of major depression is stressful life events, being present in approximately 90% of first episodes of depression. The hypothalamic-pituitary-adrenal (HPA) axis is one of the major systems involved in responses to stress, and this system is clearly influenced by ovarian hormones. Normal women demonstrate resistance to negative feedback of both cortisol in the fast-feedback paradigm and dexamethasone in the standard delayed-feedback paradigm. Depressed premenopausal women show greater increases in baseline cortisol than postmenopausal depressed women and than depressed men. Studies in rodents suggest a similar resistance to glucocorticoid feedback but suggest that estradiol can function to inhibit stress responsiveness. Studies of premenopausal depressed women demonstrate lower estradiol, which suggests that there is less inhibitory feedback of estradiol on the HPA axis, while normal progesterone continues to augment stress responses further. The onset of these reproductive hormonal changes modulating stress systems at puberty may sensitize girls to stressful life events, which become more frequent at the transition to puberty and young adulthood.

KEYWORDS: ovarian steroids; stress hormones; depression; puberty

INTRODUCTION

Numerous studies have found that stressful life events play a role in the precipitation of episoles of major depression.[1,2] Furthermore, the response to stressful life events is influenced by a number of individual characteristics known as "vulnerability."[3] Female gender is one of the clearest constituents of vulnerability. In addition to stress as a precipitant of depression, activation of the main stress hormonal system, the hypothalamic-pituitary-adrenal (HPA) axis, is seen in major depression. The HPA axis is sexually dimorphic. In this review, we will examine the influence of ovarian steroids on this axis and then speculate on how this relates to the increased role of depression at puberty.

Address for correspondence: Elizabeth A. Young, Department of Psychiatry and Mental Health Research Institute, University of Michigan, 205 Zina Pitcher Place, Ann Arbor, MI 48109. Voice: 734-936-2087; fax: 734-647-4130.
eayoung@umich.edu

Ann. N.Y. Acad. Sci. 1021: 124–133 (2004). © 2004 New York Academy of Sciences.
doi: 10.1196/annals.1308.013

"Stress" initiates a hormonal cascade by releasing corticotropin-releasing factor (CRF), which triggers the release of ACTH from the anterior pituitary corticotrope, which, in turn, triggers the release of adrenal glucocorticoids that feed back at brain and pituitary sites to turn off the stress response.[4] Studies in both rats and humans suggest that the stress response is sexually dimorphic. Studies in rats and humans suggest that gonadal steroids play an important modulatory role on HPA axis, particularly on sensitivity to glucocorticoid negative feedback. These effects may be on glucocorticoid receptors, on brain corticotropin-releasing hormone (CRH) systems, or on responsiveness to CRH.

Glucocorticoids act via multiple mechanisms at multiple sites of the HPA axis to inhibit their own release. At the pituitary, glucocorticoids have direct effects on POMC gene transcription, POMC mRNA levels, and subsequent ACTH peptide stores *in vitro* in primary pituitary cultures.[5–7] These effects involve the classic glucocorticoid receptor (GR, type II), which binds glucocorticoids, is translocated to the nucleus, and binds to sites on the DNA.[8] Studies have demonstrated that glucocorticoids interact with the CRH receptors in anterior pituitary, acutely inhibiting the binding of CRH to its receptor and chronically decreasing CRH receptor number.[9,10] Such direct effects of glucocorticoids on CRH receptors may account for some of the inhibitory action of glucocorticoids on ACTH release *in vitro*.

In addition to pituitary sites of action, glucocorticoids act at brain sites. Early work by McEwen and colleagues demonstrated a very high-affinity uptake of corticosterone, in the hippocampus of adrenalectomized rats injected *in vivo* with radio-labelled steroids.[11] These receptors were difficult to demonstrate in non-adrenalectomized rats, presumably because these sites were saturated under resting conditions.[12] These receptors were not labeled by [³H]dexamethasone, suggesting multiple types of glucocorticoid receptors.[13] The observation of receptor heterogeneity has been expanded upon by deKloet and colleagues, who have subsequently demonstrated two glucocorticoid receptor types: mineralocorticoid receptor (MR, type I), which has particularly high affinity for the glucocorticoid corticosterone; and glucocorticoid receptor (GR, type II), which preferentially binds dexamethasone.[14] The type II receptors are widely distributed throughout the brain, while the type I receptors exist predominantly in hippocampus. In addition to action at the pituitary and hypothalamus, there is strong evidence that the hippocampus is the main feedback site in the brain.

THE GLUCOCORTICOID CASCADE HYPOTHESIS

The importance of hippocampal steroid receptors in feedback regulation of stress has been demonstrated in a number of studies. Studies have demonstrated that removal of the hippocampus leads to increases in anterior pituitary secretion of β-endorphin in plasma, CRF mRNA, and a limited induction of vasopressin mRNA in parvocellular neurons.[15] Repeated stress or chronic glucocorticoid administration downregulates hippocampal steroid receptors, but not hypothalamic or pituitary receptors. Animals with downregulated hippocampal glucocorticoid receptors are slow to turn off the corticosterone response to stress, and demonstrate decreased sensitivity to glucocorticoid fast feedback.[16] This decrease in glucocorticoid receptors and insensitivity to negative feedback leads to prolonged hypercortisolism which eventually can result in atrophy in hippocampal neurons and further glucocorticoid hypersecretion.[17]

Glucocorticoid hypersecretion and hippocampal neuronal atrophy are most pronounced in aged rats, a situation analogous to the literature on human depression showing a higher incidence of HPA axis feedback abnormalities in aged individuals.[18–20] These data provide further support for the hippocampus as a site of glucocorticoid negative feedback.

BASIC STUDIES SUGGESTING SEX DIFFERENCES IN HPA AXIS REGULATION

Studies in rodents support the existence of sex differences in a number of the elements of the HPA axis. The corticosterone response to stress differs in male and female rats, with female rats demonstrating a greater overall response, faster onset of corticosterone secretion, and a faster rate of rise of corticosterone. A steeper rate of rise is necessary in female rats to elicit glucocorticoid fast feedback.[21] Corticosterone-binding globulin (CBG) is positively regulated by estrogen and thus higher in female rats; in addition, estrogen and progesterone have been demonstrated to affect the HPA axis independent of the effects of CBG. Chronic estrogen treatment enhances the corticosterone response to stress and delays the recovery from stress in estrogen-treated female rats in comparison to ovariectomized (ovx) female rats.[22] Estradiol treatment blocked downregulation of hippocampal GRs following chronic administration of RU 28362, a glucocorticoid agonist. Studies by Viau and Meaney[23] demonstrated a greater ACTH and corticosterone stress response in acute estradiol- treated rats compared with ovx female rats or estradiol plus progesterone–treated female rats after short-term (24 h) but not long-term (48 h) estradiol treatment. A partial estrogen response element is found on the CRH gene, which is able to confer estrogen enhancement of CRH expression in cell cultures,[24] providing a mechanism by which estradiol may enhance stress responsiveness in females. However, not all studies have demonstrated enhanced stress responsiveness with estradiol treatment of female animals. Studies by Young et al.[25] and Redei et al.[26] found that lower doses of estradiol, which produce estradiol concentrations in the physiological range, demonstrated an inhibitory effect of estradiol on HPA axis responsiveness. Similarly, a study by Komesaroff and colleagues[27] found similar inhibitory effects of physiological doses of estradiol. Furthermore, treatment with estradiol antagonists has been demonstrated to increase stress response.[25] Consequently, the data in experimental animals is contradictory, but recent studies using physiological doses of estradiol demonstrate inhibitory effects with treatment of several weeks.

Studies of the effect of estradiol in humans have also been contradictory. An early study by the Trier group demonstrated greater stress responsiveness in men than women and also found that treatment of normal males with estradiol led to increased stress responsiveness.[28] However, treatment of postmenopausal women with estradiol did not result in increased stress responsiveness.[29] This suggests either sexually dimorphic effects of estradiol or that estradiol treatment of men inhibited testosterone, which is also a potent inhibitory factor on HPA axis responsiveness. Further, a study by Komesaroff et al.[30] in postmenopausal women demonstrated significant inhibitory effects of 8 weeks of estradiol treatment on both HPA axis and catecholamine response to stress.

Progesterone also affects the HPA axis. In cultured rat hepatoma cells, dexamethasone and progesterone were able to bind to the same receptor, and progesterone was a clear competitive antagonist of dexamethasone binding. Progesterone had a faster binding time than cortisol for the GR, but progesterone binds at a different site on GR than the glucocorticoid binding site.[31,32] Furthermore, progesterone can increase the rate of dissociation of glucocorticoids from the GR.[31] Female rats have a greater number of GRs in the hippocampus than do male rats.[33] Progesterone modulates GR number in hippocampus.[34] *In vivo*, progesterone demonstrates antiglucocorticoid effects in intact rats.[35] While the majority of these effects are exerted at the GR, binding studies from Arriza *et al.* with expressed human MR demonstrate an affinity of progesterone for MR receptor in a range similar to that of dexamethasone.[36] Studies by Carey *et al.* found increase MR binding following progesterone treatment of female rats.[37]

Interactions between gonadal steroids and glucocorticoid feedback *in vivo* suggest that both estrogen and progesterone may play a role. Both Burgess and Handa[22] and Viau and Meaney[23] have demonstrated that estrogen treatment delays the ACTH and glucocorticoid shut-off following stress in estrogen-treated female rats in comparison to ovx female rats. Following long-term (21 days) estradiol treatment, the potent and selective glucocorticoid RU 28362 was ineffective in blocking ether-stress–induced ACTH secretion. Work by Keller-Wood *et al.* in pregnant ewes and ewes given progesterone infusions found that progesterone can diminish the effectiveness of cortisol feedback on stress responsiveness *in vivo*, complementing earlier studies demonstrating that progesterone is a GR antagonist *in vitro*.[38] Consequently, a number of mechanisms have already been described by which estradiol and progesterone may modulate HPA axis regulation.

SEX DIFFERENCES IN HPA AXIS REGULATION: HUMAN STUDIES

Given that there are a number of effects of ovarian steroids on the HPA axis, are there differences in HPA axis regulation in normal men and women and could these contribute to the excessive vulnerability to depression in women? We have observed both sex differences in response to CRH and in negative feedback in humans. The lack of a reliable robust stressor until recently has limited studies on sex differences in stress response. Studies by Kirschbaum and Hellhammer have found that oral contraceptives decrease the free cortisol response to a social stressor in women, but that treatment of normal men with estradiol for 48 h results in enhanced ACTH stress response.[28,39] A recent analysis by the Trier group of all their studies concluded that men show greater ACTH responses than do women to stress, but plasma cortisol levels are not different.[39] The saliva cortisol response is greatest in men and luteal-phase women, while follicular-phase women and women on oral contraceptives show similar responses.[39] Our studies examining sex differences in response to oCRH found a 40% greater response in women than men, again consistent with animal studies. Since oCRH is acting at the pituitary, our data support differences at the pituitary and adrenal level, as well as possibly at the level of the CRH neuron.

Infusion of cortisol "turns off" corticotroph secretion of ACTH and β-LPH/β-end within 15 min of the onset of a rise in cortisol in both premenopausal female and age-matched male control subjects. Following the termination of the infusion, men exhibited continued inhibition of corticotroph secretion for 60 min, while the women began to secrete β-LPH/β-end within this hour. This difference may be dependent upon progesterone. Women with follicular phase plasma progesterone concentrations (progesterone = 0.26 ± 0.15 ng/mL) exhibited patterns of suppression of β-LPH/β-end secretion similar to the men. However, women with progesterone concentrations typical of the luteal phase (progesterone = 6.85 ± 0.9 ng/mL), showed rebound β-LPH/β-end secretion following termination of cortisol infusion.[40] These data suggest that progesterone antagonizes the feedback effects of cortisol in humans. These conclusions agree with those of Keller-Wood et al.,[38] demonstrating a similar antagonistic effect of progesterone on the feedback effects of cortisol infusion in ewes. Combined with data demonstrating antagonistic effects of progesterone at the GR, the data suggest that progesterone is an important modulator of HPA axis function.

With respect to the influence of changes in ovarian hormones across the menstrual cycle in women, recent studies by Altemus and colleagues[41] have found increased resistance to dexamethasone suppression during the luteal phase of the menstrual cycle, as compared to the follicular phase, a change that may again be related to either increased estradiol or progesterone during the luteal phase. Furthermore, ovarian steroids influenced the expression of GR mRNA in lymphocytes, resulting in a decrease in GRs in the luteal phase compared to the follicular phase of the menstrual cycle[41] and suggesting that decreases in GRs may explain the decreased response to dexamethasone. In a design that allows investigators to distinguish the effects of progesterone from those of estrogen, Roca and coworkers[42,43] studied control women treated first with Lupron, a gonadotrophin-releasing hormone (GnRH) agonist, which causes suppression of both estrogen and progesterone secretion, and then given sequential replacement of the two hormones. They examined the response to exercise stress as well as to dexamethasone feedback and found that the exercise stress response was increased, and response to dexamethasone feedback was decreased, during the progesterone "add back" phase but not during the estrogen add-back phase. Again, these data suggest that progesterone acts as a glucocorticoid antagonist. Thus, the data from human studies suggest that ovarian steroids, and in particular progesterone, influence the HPA axis response to stress by modulating sensitivity to negative feedback. Furthermore, some data suggest that progesterone may have negative effects on mood particularly in women with premenstrual dysphoric disorder (PMDD) in which depressive symptoms occur in the luteal phase of the menstrual cycle when progesterone levels are high. Although the exact role of sex hormones in this disorder has not been established, estrogen and progesterone suppression by Lupron has been reported to produce significant symptom improvement in depression in PMDD.[43]

In humans, pregnancy is accompanied by increases in both estrogen and progesterone and thus provides another model to examine the interactions between gonadal steroids and the HPA axis. Increases in plasma CBG and cortisol during pregnancy are well known. In humans, dexamethasone challenge studies indicate resistance to glucocorticoid negative feedback during pregnancy.[44–46] The degree to which higher levels of CBG-bound cortisol contribute to the dexamethasone resistance, as manifested by higher levels of plasma cortisol following dexamethasone administration, is not completely known. Although dexamethasone itself is not bound by CBG, pregnancy could alter the metabolism of dexamethasone, resulting in less dexamethasone bioavailability. However, at least one study[46] demonstrated higher free cortisol during pregnancy, higher free-cortisol production following an ACTH infusion, decreased suppressibility of free cortisol by dexamethasone, and a normal circadian rhythm of cortisol, pointing to a change in cortisol set-point during pregnancy. These data are compatible with the data of Keller-Wood demonstrating that high circulating levels of progesterone can antagonize the effects of glucocorticoids on negative feedback.[38]

From these studies, it is clear that ovarian steroids do play a modulatory role on HPA axis regulation. However, we do not know which ovarian steroids are involved and which levels of the HPA axis are affected; the underlying mechanisms are not fully elucidated.

SEX DIFFERENCES IN HPA AXIS REGULATION IN DEPRESSION

Morning and evening cortisol hypersecretion. Our studies examining baseline cortisol secretion in the morning in 16 depressed patients and 16 age- and sex-matched control patients found increased cortisol secretion in the group as a whole, as would be expected. However, there were clear sex differences. While the male patients and their matched controls demonstrated the same plasma cortisol concentration, the female depressed patients demonstrated significantly higher mean plasma cortisol concentration (11.3 ± 0.9 µg/dL) than their matched controls (8.1 ± 0.95 µg/dL; significant by a two-tailed t-test, $P = 0.033$). Removal of glucocorticoid negative feedback by metyrapone demonstrates increased central drive in depressed patients in the evening. The response to metyrapone demonstrated sex differences; only the female depressed patients manifested rebound β-LPH/β-end secretion in comparison to their matched controls (ANOVA, $F = 8.8$, df $= 1$, $P = .01$); the males did not.

Cortisol hypersecretion and dexamethasone nonsuppression. Other studies examined whether the loss of gonadal steroids at menopause impacts HPA axis regulation in depressed women. We conducted studies using a protocol examining baseline and post-dexamethasone secretion of β-LPH/β-end and cortisol over the course of the day (8 A.M.–4 P.M.). We conducted these studies on 51 depressed women; 36 were premenopausal and 15 were postmenopausal. The premenopausal women demonstrated a significantly lower incidence of pituitary (β-LPH/β-end) nonsuppression ($n = 36$; Nonsuppressor $= 44\%$) than the postmenopausal women ($n = 15$; Nonsuppressor $= 81\%$). To determine which of a number of potential variables were associated with β-LPH/β-end nonsuppression in women, a stepwise regression analysis was done. Independent variables included: age, menopausal status, baseline β-LPH/β-end and cortisol, severity of depression as assessed by Hamilton Depression rating scores, and the number of previous episodes of depression. The dependent variable was β-LPH/β-end nonsuppression. While age had a significant effect on β-LPH/β-end nonsuppression, menopausal status was also important and, combined with cortisol, gave a correlation coefficient of 0.817. This suggests that menopausal status, in conjunction with cortisol hypersecretion, is a critical variable in the development of HPA dysregulation, as manifested by resistance to dexamethasone, and accounts for 65% of the variance. Further, the lower rate of β-LPH/β-end nonsuppression in premenopausal women suggests that gonadal steroids may modulate the HPA axis and exert some protective effect against high levels of endogenous glucocorticoids (cortisol).

The formulation of the glucocorticoid cascade hypothesis by Sapolsky suggested that stress and repeated bouts of hypercortisolemia lead to downregulation of glucocorticoid receptors, which in turn results in further glucocorticoid hypersecretion, eventually leading to loss of hippocampal neurons, that is, a "glucocorticoid feed forward cascade."[17] His studies in rats have suggested that aging is a critical variable and that aging rats demonstrate downregulation of GRs, failure to shut off stress-induced glucocorticoid secretion and hippocampal neuronal loss. Aging is also associated with HPA axis dysregulation in depression.[18–20] We were very interested whether recurrent depressive episodes with recurrent episodes of hypercortisolemia would lead to progressive HPA axis dysregulation. We divided patients into first episode vs. recurrent unipolar depression, and examined differences in rates of pituitary nonsuppression. We found no association of β-LPH/β-end nonsuppression with recurrent episodes, but within the recurrent and first-episode groups, older age was associated with a higher incidence of HPA axis dysregulation. We also used the absolute number of episodes as a continuous variable and then examined baseline hormonal measures and post-dexamethasone hormonal measures as continuous variables or nonsuppression as a categorical variable. Again, the data did not support the hypothesis that recurrent episodes of depression were associated with progressive HPA axis dysregulation, but rather that aging was the critical variable. Since 16 of the 20 subjects over 50 were women, we cannot determine whether aging is also a factor in men. However, aging is more important than absolute number of episodes in women, and, the previous analysis suggested that menopausal status was the critical variable in aging.

In summary, menopause itself is not associated with increases in plasma cortisol concentrations, but it is associated with an increase in dexamethasone resistance in depressed women. Resistance to dexamethasone suppression is strongly associated with increased baseline cortisol secretion, and thus appears to reflect the development of GR downregulation following a period of hypercortisolemia. That premenopausal women demonstrate less resistance to dexamethasone suppression suggests that they are more resistant to endogenous glucocorticoids and to GR downregulation.

SPECULATIONS ABOUT PUBERTY

The finding of an increased ACTH response to stress has very important implications for our understanding of stress and stress responsiveness in human females. It is clear that a number of diseases that have been linked to "stress" are more common in females, including depression and other anxiety disorders. Since females demonstrate resistance to negative feedback effects of glucocorticoids;[40,41,47] this suggests an exaggerated central CRH response to stress,[48] which may explain some of the susceptibilty of females to depression and other stress-related disorders. Additionally, resistance to endogenous glucocorticoids may contribute to the increased incidence of depression. If we believe Munck's hypothesis[49] that the purpose of glucocorticoids is to turn off not just the HPA axis to stress, but the entire stress response, then this resistance to glucocorticoids would further exaggerate stress responsiveness in women. Studies by Frank and colleagues clearly demonstrate that stressful life events play a role in the precipitation of depression in adolescents.[50] As girls reach puberty, these known effects of ovarian steroids on stress systems come into play. Recent studies suggest that elevated glucocorticoids can inhibit autonomic nervous system response,[51] supporting a role for glucocorticoids in terminating stress-induced activation of the autonomic stress system. This resistance to glucocorticoids may also lead to increasing levels of anxiety at puberty in girls, which may serve to "drive" the onset of depression.[52] There is evidence that the increased vulnerability to depression in women arises at puberty, when gonadal steroids would further enhance stress responsiveness. Some data suggest that following menopuase, the incidence of depression begins to decrease in women, perhaps as a consequence of increasing sensitivity to glucocorticoids. Additionally, depressed adult women demonstrate lower estradiol, which means that the inhibitory effects of estradiol on stress responsiveness are less.[53] We would expect that adolescent girls may be in a similar situation. Finally, while most effects of estradiol on serotonin systems are beneficial, decreases in 5HT 1A terminal receptors may further sensitize to depression.[54]

REFERENCES

1. BROWN, G.W. & T. HARRIS. 1978. Social Origins of Depression: A Study of Psychiatric Disorder in Women. The Free Press. New York.
2. FRANK, E., B. ANDERSON, C. REYNOLDS, et al. 1994. Life events and the research diagnostic criteria endogenous subtype: a confirmation of the distinction using the Bedford College methods. Arch. Gen. Psychiatry 51: 519–524.
3. KENDLER, K.S., R.C. KESSLER, E.E. WALTERS, et al. 1995. Stressful life events, genetic liability and onset of an episode of major depression in women. Am. J. Psychiatry 152: 833–842.
4. KELLER-WOOD, M.E. & M.F. DALLMAN. 1985. Corticosteroid inhibition of ACTH secretion. Endocrinol. Rev. 5: 1–24.
5. SCHACTER, B.S., L.K. JOHNSON, J.D. BAXTER & J.L. ROBERTS. 1982. Differential regulation by glucocorticoids of proopiomelanocortin mRNA levels in the anterior and intermediate lobes of the rat pituitary. Endocrinology 110: 1142.
6. ROBERTS, J.L., M.L. BUDARF, J.D. BAXTER & E. HERBERT. 1979. Selective reduction of proadrenocorticotropin/endorphin proteins and messenger ribonucleic acid activity in mouse pituitary tumor cells by glucocorticoids. Biochemistry 18: 4907–4915.
7. BIRNBERG, N.C., O. CIVELLI, J.C. LISSITZSKI, et al. 1982. Regulation of pro-opiomelanocortin gene expression in the pituitary and central nervous system. Endocrinology 110: 134A.
8. SAKLY, M. & B. KOCH. 1981. Ontogenesis of glucocorticoid receptors in anterior pituitary gland: transient dissociation among cytoplasmic receptor density, nuclear uptake and regulation of corticotropic activity. Endocrinology 108: 591.
9. CHILDS, G.V., J.L. MORELL, A. NIENDORF & G. AGUILERA. 1986. Cytochemical studies of corticotropin releasing factor receptors in anterior lobe corticotrophs: binding, glucocorticoid regulation and endocytosis of [biotinyl-ser1] CRF. Endocrinology 119: 2129.
10. SCHWARTZ, J., N. BILLESTRUP, M. PERRIN, et al. 1986. Identification of corticotropin releasing factor target cells and effects of dexamethasone on binding in anterior pituitary using a flourescent analog of CRF. Endocrinology 119: 2376.

11. MCEWEN, B.S., J.M. WEISS & L.S. SCHWARTZ. 1968. Selective retention of corticosterone by limbic structures in the rat brain. Nature **220:** 911.
12. MCEWEN, B.S., J.M. WEISS & L.S. SCHWARTZ. 1970. Retention of corticosterone by cell nuclei from brain regions of adrenalectomized rats. Brain Res. **17:** 471.
13. DEKLOET, R., G. WALLACH & B.S. MCEWEN. 1975. Differences in corticosterone and dexamethasone binding to rat brain and pituitary. Endocrinology **96:** 598.
14. REUL, J.M.H & E.R. DEKLOET. 1985. Two receptor systems for corticosterone in rat brain: microdistribution and differential occupation. Endocrinology **117:** 2505–2511.
15. HERMAN, J.P., M.K-H. SCHAFER, E.A. YOUNG, et al. 1989. Hippocampal regulation of the hypothalamo-pituitary-adrenocortical axis: in situ hybridization analysis of CRF and vasopressin messenger RNA expression in the hypothalamic paraventricular nucleus following hippocampectomy. J. Neurosci. **9:** 3072–3082.
16. YOUNG, E.A. & D. VAZQUEZ. 1996. Hypercortisolemia, hippocampal glucocorticoid receptors and fast feedback. Mol. Psychiatry **1:** 149–159.
17. SAPOLSKY, R.M., L.C. KREY & B.S. MCEWEN. 1986. The neuroendocrinology of stress and aging: the glucocorticoid cascade hypothesis. Endocrinol. Rev. **7:** 284–301.
18. HALBREICH, U., G.M. ASNIS, B. ZUMOFF & R.S. NATHAN. 1984. The effect of age and sex on cortisol secretion in depressives and normals. Psychiatry Res. **13:** 221–229.
19. LEWIS, D.A., B. PFOHL, J. SCHLECTE & W. CORYELL. 1984. Influence of age on the cortisol response to dexamethasone. Psychiatry Res. **13:** 213–220.
20. AKIL, H., R. HASKETT, E.A. YOUNG, et al. 1993. Multiple HPA profiles in endogenous depression: effect of age and sex on cortisol and beta-endorphin. Biol. Psychiatry **33:** 73–85.
21. JONES, M.T., F.R. BRUSH & R.L.B. NEAME. 1972. Characteristics of fast feedback control of corticotrophin release by corticosteroids. J. Endocrinol. **55:** 489.
22. BURGESS, L.H. & R.J. HANDA. 1992 . Chronic estrogen-induced alterations in adrenocorticotropin and corticosterone secretion, and glucocorticoid receptor-mediated functions in female rats. Endocrinology **131:** 1261–1269.
23. VIAU, V. & M.J. MEANEY. 1991. Variations in the hypothalamic-pituitary-adrenal response to stress during the estrous cycle in the rat. Endocrinology **129:** 2503–2511.
24. VAMVAKOPOULOS, N.C. & G.P. CHROUSOS. 1993. Evidence of direct estrogenic regulation of human corticotropin-releasing hormone gene expression. J. Clin. Invest. **92:** 1896–1902.
25. YOUNG, E.A., M. ALTEMUS, V. PARKISON & S. SHASTRY. 2001. Effects of estrogen antagonists and agonists on the ACTH response to restraint stress. Neuropsychopharmacology **25:** 881–891.
26. REDEI, E., L. LI, R.F. MCGIVERN & F. AIRD. 1994. Fast glucocorticoid feedback inhibition of ACTH secretion in the ovariectomized rat: effect of chronic estrogen and progesterone. Neuroendocrinology **60:** 113–123.
27. KOMESAROFF, P.A., M. ESLER, I.J. CLARKE, et al. 1998. Effects of estrogen and estrous cycle on glucocorticoid and catecholamine responses to stress in sheep. Am. J. Physiology **275:** E671–E678.
28. KIRSCHBAUM, C., N. SCHOMMER, I. FEDERENKO, et al. 1996. Short-term estradiol treatment enhances pituitary-adrenal axis and sympathetic responses to psychosocial stress in healthy young men. J. Clin. Endocrinol. Metab. **81:** 3639–3643.
29. KUDIELKA, B.M., A.K. SCHMIDT-REINWALD, D.H. HELLHAMMER & C. KIRSCHBAUM. 1999. Psychological and endocrine responses to psychosocial stress and dexamethasone/corticotropin-releasing hormone in healthy postmenopausal women and young controls: the impact of age and a two-week estradiol treatment. Neuroendocrinology **70:** 422–430.
30. KOMESAROFF, P.A., M.D. ESLER & K. SUDHIR. 1999. Effects of estrogen on stress responses in women. J. Clin. Endocrinol. Metab. **84:** 4292–4293.
31. ROUSSEAU, G.G., J.D. BAXTER & G.M. TOMKINS. 1972. Glucocorticoid receptors: relations between steroid binding and biological effects. Mol. Biol. **67:** 99–115.
32. SVEC, F. 1988. Differences in the interaction of RU 486 and ketoconazole with the second binding site of the glucocorticoid receptor. Endocrinology **123:** 1902–1906.
33. TURNER, B.B. & D.A. WEAVER. 1985. Sexual dimorphism of glucocorticoid binding in rat brain. Brain Res. **343:** 16–23.

34. AHIMA R.S., A.N.L. LAWSON, S.Y.S. OSEI & R.E. HARLAN. 1992. Sexual dimorphism in regulation of type II corticosteroid receptor immunoreactivity in the rat hippocampus. Endocrinology 131: 1409–1416.
35. DUNCAN, M.R. & G.R. DUNCAN. 1979. An in vivo study of the action of antiglucocorticoids on thymus weight ratio, antibody titre and the adrenal-pituitary-hypothalamus axis. J. Steroid Biochem. 10: 245–259.
36. ARRIZA, J.L., C. WEINBERGER, G. CERELLI, et al. 1987. Cloning of human mineralocorticoid receptor complementary DNA: structural and functional kinship with the glucocorticoid receptor. Science 237: 268–275.
37. CAREY, M.P., C.H. DETERD, J. DE KONING, et al. 1995. The influence of ovarian steroids on hypothalamic-pituitary-adrenal regulation in the female rat. J. Endocrinology 144: 311–321.
38. KELLER-WOOD, M., J. SILBIGER & C.E. WOOD. 1988. Progesterone attenuates the inhibition of adrenocorticotropin responses by cortisol in nonpregnant ewes. Endocrinology 123: 647–651.
39. KIRSCHBAUM, C., B.M. KUDIELKA, J. GAAB, et al. 1999. Impact of gender, menstrual cycle phase, and oral contraceptives on the activity of the hypothalamic-pituitary-adrenal axis. Psychosom. Med. 61: 154–162.
40. YOUNG, E.A. 1995. The glucocorticoid cascade hypothesis revisited: role of gonadal steroids. Depression 3: 20–27.
41. ALTEMUS, M., L. REDWINE, L. YUNG-MEI, et al. 1997. Reduced sensitivity to glucocorticoid feedback and reduced glucocorticoid receptor mRNA expression in the luteal phase of the menstrual cycle. Neurosychopharmacology 17: 100–109.
42. ROCA, C.A., P.J. SCHMIDT, M. ALTEMUS, et al. 1998. Effects of reproductive steroids on the hypothalamic-pituitary-adrenal axis response to low dose dexamethasone. Abstract at Neuroendocrine Workshop on Stress. New Orleans, LA.
43. ROCA, C.A., P.J. SCHMIDT, M. ALTEMUS, et al. 2003. Differential menstrual cycle regulation of hypothalamic-pituitary-adrenal axis in women with premenstrual syndrome and controls. J. Clin. Endocrinol. Metab. 88: 3057–3063.
44. DEMEY-PONSART, E., J.M. FOIDART, J. SULON & J.C. SODOYEZ. 1982. Serum CBG, free and total cortisol and circadian patterns of adrenal function in normal pregnancy. J. Steroid Biochem. 16: 165–169.
45. CARR, B.R., C.R. PARKER, JR., J.D. MADDEN, et al. 1981. Maternal plasma adrenocorticotropin and cortisol relationships throughout human pregnancy. Am. J. Obstet. Gynecol. 139: 416–422.
46. NOLTEN, W.E. & P.A. RUECKERT. 1981. Elevated free cortisol index in pregnancy: possible regulatory mechanisms. Am. J. Obstet. Gynecol. 139: 492–498.
47. YOUNG, E.A. 1996. Sex differences in response to exogenous corticosterone. Mol. Psychiatry 1: 313–319.
48. ALTEMUS, M., C. ROCA, E. GALLIVEN, et al. 2001. Increased vasopressin and adrenocorticotropin responses to stress in the midluteal phase of the menstrual cycle. J. Clin. Endocrinol. Metab. 86: 2525–2530.
49. MUNCK, A. & P.M. GUYRE. 1986. Glucocorticoid physiology, pharmacology and stress. Adv. Exp. Med Biol. 196: 81–96.
50. CYRANOWSKI, J.M., E. FRANK, E.A. YOUNG & M.K. SHEAR. 2000. Adolescent onset of the gender difference in lifetime rates of major depression: a theoretical model. Arch. Gen. Psychiatry 57: 21–27.
51. MCEWEN, B. 1995. Adrenal steroid actions on brain dissecting the fine line between protection and damage. In Neurobiological and Clinical Consequences of Stress: From Normal Adaptation to PTSD. M.J. Friedman, D.S. Charney & A.Y. Deutch, Eds.: 135–147. Lippincott-Raven Publishers. Philadelphia.
52. BRESLAU, N., H. CHILCOAT & L.R. SCHULTZ. 1998. Anxiety disorders and the emergence of sex differences in major depression. J. Gender Specif. Med. 1: 33–39.
53. YOUNG, E.A., A.R. MIDGLEY, N.E. CARLSON & M.B. BROWN. 2000. Alteration in the hypothalamic-pituitary-ovarian axis in depressed women. Arch. Gen. Psychiatry 57: 1157–1162.
54. LU, N.Z. & C.L. BETHEA. 2002. Ovarian steroid regulation of 5-HT1A receptor binding and G protein activation in female monkeys. Neuropsychopharmacology 27: 12–24.

Interrelationships between Hormones, Behavior, and Affect during Adolescence

Complex Relationships Exist between Reproductive Hormones, Stress-Related Hormones, and the Activity of Neural Systems That Regulate Behavioral Affect

Comments on Part III

JUDY L. CAMERON

Department of Psychiatry, University of Pittsburgh, Pittsburgh, Pennsylvania 15213, USA

The Oregon National Primate Research Center, Beaverton, Oregon 97006, USA

ABSTRACT: Adolescence is a period in life marked by change, encompassing physiological changes associated with pubertal development, changes in social status and the social stresses that an individual faces, and changes in behavioral affect regulation. The interactions between activity in the reproductive axis, the neural systems that regulate stress, hormones produced in response to stress, and neural systems governing behavioral affect regulation are complex and multifaceted. Although our understanding of these interactions remains rudimentary, we do know that stress can suppress activity of the reproductive axis, that reproductive hormones can modulate the activity of neural systems that govern the body's responses to stress, that both reproductive function and stress responsiveness can be altered in depressed individuals, and that the function of some of the key neural systems regulating behavioral affect (i.e., serotonergic, noradrenergic, dopaminergic systems) are modulated by both gonadal steroid hormones and adrenal steroid hormones. This summary reviews the central interactions discussed in this session on the interrelationships between hormones, behavior, and affect during adolescence and identifies key topics that require further investigation in order to understand the role that pubertal changes in reproductive function, interacting with increased exposure to life stresses, play in modulating behavioral affect regulation during the adolescent period.

KEYWORDS: stress; monoamines; cortisol; estrogen; psychopathology

Address for correspondence: Judy L. Cameron, Ph.D., Department of Psychiatry, University of Pittsburgh, 3811 O'Hara Street, Pittsburgh, PA 15213. Voice: 724-733-3795; fax: 724-327-1271. cameronj@ohsu.edu

Ann. N.Y. Acad. Sci. 1021: 134–142 (2004). © 2004 New York Academy of Sciences.
doi: 10.1196/annals.1308.015

INTRODUCTION

Not only is adolescence a time of remarkable change in the functioning of the reproductive axis, but also, as many of the other articles in this volume detail, adolescence is a time when persons face an increased number of challenges and life stresses. The interactions between activity in the reproductive axis, the neural systems that regulate stress, hormones produced in response to stress, and neural systems governing behavioral affect regulation are complex and multifaceted. Although our understanding of these interactions remains rudimentary at this time, we do know that stress can suppress activity of the reproductive axis, that reproductive hormones can modulate the activity of neural systems that govern the body's responses to stress, that both reproductive function and stress-responsiveness can be altered in depressed persons, and that functions of some of the key neural systems regulating behavioral affect (i.e., serotonergic, noradrenergic, dopaminergic systems) are modulated by both gonadal steroid hormones and adrenal steroid hormones. The paper by Dr. Young in this section, and that of Dr. McEwen at the conference, analyze these complex interactions in clinical studies of normal and depressed men and women and in basic animal models. This summary reviews the central interactions discussed in these presentations and identifies key topics that will require further investigation in order to understand the role that pubertal changes in reproductive function, interacting with increased exposure to life stresses, play in modulating behavioral affect regulation during the adolescent period.

MANY TYPES OF STRESS CAN MODULATE ACTIVITY OF THE REPRODUCTIVE AXIS AND THE TIMING OF PUBERTY

Many forms of stress, including psychosocial stress and a host of physical stressors (e.g., energy restriction, increased energy expenditure with exercise, temperature stress, infection, pain and injury) can lead to suppression of reproductive hormone secretion and, if sustained, to a suppression of fertility.[1-4] Stress-induced reproductive dysfunction can occur in both females and males. In adulthood, stress-induced reproductive impairment in females is characterized by a lengthening of the menstrual cycle and a suppression of ovulation, followed eventually by a loss of ovarian cyclicity and amenorrhea. In males, the reproductive impairment is characterized by a decrease in testosterone secretion and thus a decrease in spermatogenesis and hormonal support for secondary sexual characteristics, as well as a loss of libido. Chronic stress, occurring during the process of pubertal development, can impair the progression of puberty in both females and males, leading in some cases to a very marked delay in the pubertal development of reproductive capacity and the accompanying development of secondary sexual characteristics.[5] Pubertal delay resulting from undernutrition[6,7] and exercise[8,9] have been clearly documented in humans, as well as in a variety of animal species.

The primary site of disruption of the reproductive axis with all forms of stress studied in detail to date appears to be at the level of the GnRH neurons, which provide the central neural drive to the reproductive axis. Using animal models of various stresses, it has been shown for at least some stresses that GnRH secretion is impaired.[10] However, more typically, it is inferred that GnRH secretion is impaired under conditions of stress, when a suppression of pituitary gonadotropin secretion is measured. This is further supported by the finding that in all conditions of stress-induced reproductive dysfunction studied to date, administration of exogenous GnRH can stimulate the function of the reproductive axis, indicating that stress is not acting to directly suppress pituitary or gonadal activity.[11] The mechanisms by which various forms of stress impair reproductive axis activity appear to have some common elements, but there also appear to be mechanisms that are specific to each type of stress. For example, many forms of stress can activate the hypothalamic-pituitary-adrenal axis, and experimental studies have shown several mechanisms by which activation of the HPA axis can impair the central neural drive to the reproductive axis.[12,13] On the other hand, certain aspects of stress, such as decreased fuel availability, only occur with some forms of stress and are likely to impair the activity of the reproductive axis via relatively specific mechanisms.[4]

The influence of psychological and social stresses on the activity of the reproductive axis is of particular relevance to understanding the interaction between reproduction, stress, and changes in behavioral affect in adolescence. There is strong evidence, both in clinical studies and in animal models, that exposure to psychosocial stresses can impair activity of the reproductive axis. One of the best characterized forms of psychosocial stress-induced reproductive dysfunction comes from studies of women who present to infertility clinics with functional hypothalamic amenorrhea (FHA), a form of stress-induced reproductive dysfunction.[14,15] Women with FHA experience more psychological stress than other women: although they do not experience more stressful life events, they react more profoundly to the stressful events they do experience.[16] They also show increased activation of physiological systems that respond to stress, including increased HPA axis activity.[17] Treatment of these patients with cognitive behavior therapy, or with drugs that reduce the activity of some central neural systems that are activated by stress, can restore fertility, although not in all cases.[17,18] In animal studies, both acute exposure to psychosocial stresses[19–21] and exposure to chronic social stress[22] can suppress activity of the reproductive axis. However, not all persons respond to psychosocial stresses with a suppression of reproductive function, and there appear to be a number of factors underlying the individual differences in responsiveness to stress, including perception of stress, social status of the individual experiencing the stress, aggressiveness of the

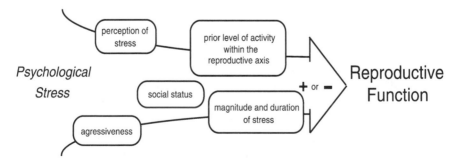

FIGURE 1. Schematic diagram of the factors that mediate the effects of psychological stress on the activity of the hypothalamic-pituitary-gonadal axis. (Redrawn from Cameron.[23])

individual experiencing the stress, the magnitude and duration of the stress, and the level of activity within the reproductive axis prior to exposure to stress (FIG. 1).[3,23]

Although the majority of studies examining the effects of psychosocial stress on reproduction have documented stress-induced suppression of reproductive function, some studies have reported that girls who have grown up under conditions of family stress (e.g., in homes in which the father is absent or there has been family conflict, or when parents have divorced) enter puberty at a significantly earlier age.[24–26] However, neural mechanisms by which such exposure to stress would advance the onset of puberty remain to be determined. It is possible that early exposure to stress does not *cause* advancement of puberty, but rather, that the likelihood of early puberty and exposure to early life family stresses may simply be correlated because they are both influenced by a common factor(s). For example, one of the factors governing the age of menarche is the age of the girl's mother at menarche.[27] Thus it is possible that mothers who experienced early menarche are more likely to have family conflict or divorce when their children are young and to have daughters who will have early menarche; but the conflict would not cause the early menarche in the daughters.

REPRODUCTIVE HORMONES INFLUENCE STRUCTURE AND FUNCTION OF STRESS-RESPONSIVE SYSTEMS IN THE BRAIN

One of the primary brain systems responding to a wide variety of stresses is the hypothalamic-pituitary-adrenal (HPA) axis, which releases the neuroendocrine neurotransmitter, corticotrophin-releasing hormone (CRH), from cells in the paraventricular nucleus of the hypothalamus to cause release of adrenocorticotropin-releasing hormone (ACTH) from the pituitary. ACTH stimulates the adrenal gland to increase synthesis and secretion of glucocorticoid hormones (cortisol in primates and corticosterone in rodents). Specific receptors for glucocorticoids are located in a number of brain regions, thus allowing glucocorticoids to have a negative feedback action to limit activation of the HPA axis as well as to influence a number of brain functions. The other brain system that is activated by exposure to stress and mediates many stress responses is the sympathetic nervous system, which involves increased release of the neurotransmitter, norepinephrine, both centrally and peripherally. Bruce McEwen has written extensively about the role of these two neural/hormonal systems in mediating allostasis (the process of adaptation to events in daily life, defined as the body processes responsible for maintaining stability, or homeostasis, through change).[28,29] These mediators of allostasis promote adaptation and play generally beneficial roles when they are released in an acute manner, but when they are released chronically, their cumulative influence leads to "wear and tear" on the body and brain that is referred to as "allostatic load."[29]

Gender differences in stress responsiveness exist. Female rats generally show higher basal levels of glucocorticoids and have greater HPA responsiveness to stress compared to males.[30] However, in human studies, males have often been shown to have greater HPA axis reactivity to stresses such as public speaking and mental arithmetic,[30] and Dorn et al.[31] reported that male adolescents have greater secretion of ACTH to an exogenous bolus of CRH. It has been proposed that at least part of this divergence between preclinical and clinical studies reflects a gender difference in humans with regard to the type of test that is perceived as stressful, and there is evidence that men show greater HPA reactivity to achievement challenges while women show greater HPA reactivity to social rejection challenges.[30] Estrogen modulation of the HPA axis reactivity to stress has been reported in both experimental animals and in humans by Dr. Young and others. In rats, short-term exposure to low doses of estrogen appears to suppress HPA axis responses to stress, while more prolonged treatment and high doses of estrogen appear to enhance HPA axis responses to stress.[32–34] In post-menopausal women estrogen has been shown to blunt HPA axis responsiveness to several forms of stress.[35,36]

High densities of glucocorticoid receptors are located in the hippocampus and the amygdala. In the hippocampus, low levels of glucocorticoids are associated with enhancement of hippocampal-mediated learning and memory tasks,[37] whereas high levels impair hippocampal functions.[38] At a structural level, stress impairs neurogenesis in the dentate gyrus of the hippocampus,[39] and reduces branching and length of several types of hippocampal neurons via glucocorticoid-mediated mechanisms.[40,41] Clinical studies by Dr. Young and others have shown that evening levels of cortisol are increased in depression,[42,43] a neuropsychiatric disease strongly linked to stress. And neuroimaging studies have found a decrease in hippocampal volume in depressed patients, related to the duration of depression.[44,45] In contrast, estrogen induces synaptogenesis on dendritic spines of hippocampal CA1 neurons.[46,47] And, whereas male monkeys and rats show CA3 neuron loss in the hippocampus upon prolonged exposure to stress, a similar loss is not found in stress-exposed females.[48,49] Female rats also do not show stress-induced atrophy of CA3 neurons,[50] and they have a larger dentate gyrus and more extensively branched CA3 neuron dendrites than male rats.[51,52] Estrogen treatment has also been shown to improve performance of ovariectomized rats in spatial memory tasks that are dependent on hippocampal function,[53] although changes in performance on spatial tasks have not been seen to vary across the ovarian cycle or in women on estrogen treatment.[54]

Taken together, there is a wealth of data to suggest that both the changes in reproductive hormones occurring with pubertal development, and increased exposure to life stresses over the adolescent period, could potentially modulate both the structure and function of neurons in the brain that make up the circuits involved in learning, memory, and detection and regulation of emotion. Since there are virtually no studies examining the effects of either gonadal or adrenal steroid hormones on these neural circuits over the adolescent period, this area is ripe for investigation.

AN INTERPLAY BETWEEN REPRODUCTIVE HORMONES, STRESS-SENSITIVE SYSTEMS, AND NEURAL SYSTEMS REGULATING BEHAVIORAL AFFECT

The interplay between reproductive hormones, neural systems regulated by stress, and the neural systems that regulate behavioral affect is multi-faceted. As discussed in the overview to this section, gonadal steroid hormones, in particular estrogen, can modulate expression of a number of genes integral to the brain monoamine systems (serotonin and norepinephrine) that play important roles in regulating behavioral affect. Moreover, there is evidence that estrogen alters responsiveness to antidepressant medications. These same systems are profoundly influenced by exposure to stress, with both systems showing activation in response to acute stress exposure,[34] but states of chronic stress exposure and a number of psychiatric diseases associated with lower activity in the serotonin system.[55,56] Glucocorticoids act on neural circuits, such as the hippocampus, in concert with norepinephrine and serotonin, and also regulate activity in these monoaminergic systems.[29] There is also evidence that activity in each of these systems may be linked to the sensitivity or resilience of an individual to stress exposure. Evidence is rapidly accumulating that indicates that an interplay between genetic factors and environmental exposure to stresses act together to influence the likelihood of an individual developing stress-related psychopathologies.[34,57] With each of these systems showing alterations in function over the period of adolescent development, and the increase in stress-associated psychopathologies such as depression showing profound gender differences in this period, much more work is needed to understand the interplay between these systems during the transition from childhood to adulthood, and the degree to which they influence changes in behavioral affect associated with adolescence.

STRATEGIES FOR FUTURE RESEARCH

As highlighted in this section, within the broader frame of understanding adolescent brain development, it is important to consider the multiple influences which pubertal maturation may have. Puberty encompasses maturational changes in at least three separate neuroendocrine axes: the reproductive axis, the adrenal axis, and the growth axis. Moreoever, each of these systems is influenced by exposure to life stresses, and many of the hormones which increase at puberty can in turn modulate the systems in the brain that respond to stress. Research to date has focused on describing the developmental processes within each of these neuroendocrine systems and understanding the mechanisms underlying maturation of each system. Other lines of research have examined the influence of hormones on the brain in adulthood, showing profound influences of these hormones on brain circuits that are integral to the processes of learning, memory, and the regulation of emotion and behavioral affect. However, there has been virtually no research examining how shifts in the function of various neuroendocrine axes at puberty modulate these brain processes over the adolescent period. A strategy for undertaking this daunting task has been proposed by Ron Dahl, a co-organizer of this meeting.[58] As discussed by Dahl, understanding how pubertal processes influence adolescent brain maturation requires consideration of the component processes of puberty including: (*a*) pubertal brain changes that *antedate* (and contribute to) the cascade of hormone changes; (*b*) pubertal brain changes that are *caused* by maturational hormonal increases; (*c*) maturational brain changes that occur relatively independent of puberty; and (*d*) maturational processes linked to puberty only in indirect ways (e.g., new experiences that occur as a result of sexual maturation). Well-controlled studies, both basic animal studies and clinical studies, are needed to directly address which aspects of adolescent development are specifically linked to which specific aspects of puberty.

ACKNOWLEDGMENTS

The work yielding data presented from Dr. Cameron's laboratory was supported by a grant from the John D. and Catherine T. MacArthur Foundation Network on "Health Promoting and Health Damaging Behaviors," as well as by NIH grants (HD26888, HD18185, HD25929, MH50748).

REFERENCES

1. LAUGHLIN, G.C.L. & S.S.C. YEN. 1978. Hypothalamic chronic anovulation. Am. J. Obstet. Gynecol. **130:** 825–831.
2. PIRKE, K.M., W. WUTTKE & U. SCHWEIGER 1989. In The Menstrual Cycle and Its Disorders. Springer-Verlag. Berlin.
3. CAMERON, J.L. 1997. Stress and behaviorally-induced reproductive dysfunction in primates. In Seminars in Reproductive Endocrinology: Brain, Behavior and Reproductive Function. S.L. Berga, Ed.: 37–45. Thieme. New York.
4. CAMERON, J.L. 1998. Fasting and reproduction in non-human primates. In Pennington Center Nutrition Series: Nutrition and Reproduction. W. Hansel, G. Bray & D.H. Ryan, Eds.: 95–109. University of Louisiana Press. Baton Rouge.
5. CARPENTER, S.E. 1994. Psychosocial menstrual disorders: stress, exercise and diet's effect on the menstrual cycle. Curr. Opin. Obstet. Gynecol. **6:** 536–539.
6. BHALLA, M. & J.R. SHRIVATAVA 1974. A prospective study of the age of menarche in Kampur girls. Ind. Pediatr. **11:** 487–493.
7. CHOWDHURY, A.K.M.A., S.L. HUFFMAN & G.T. CURLIN 1978. Malnutrition, menarche and age at marriage in Bangladesh. Soc. Biol. **24:** 316–325.
8. LOUCKS, A.B., J. VAITUKAITIS, J.L. CAMERON, et al. 1992. The reproductive system and exercise: a state-of-the-art review. Med. Sci. Sports Exercise **24:** S288–S293.
9. WARREN, M.P. & A.L. STIEHL 1999. Exercise and female adolescents: effects on the reproductive and skeletal system. J. Am. Med. Wom. Assoc. **54:** 115–120.
10. I'ANSON, H., J.M. MANNING, G.C. HERBOSA, et al. Central inhibition of gonadotropin-releasing hormone secretion in the growth-restricted hypogonadotropic female sheep. Endocrinology **141:** 520–527.
11. HOTCHKISS, J. & E. KNOBIL 1994. The menstrual cycle and its neuroendocrine control. In The Physiology of Reproduction, Vol 2. E. Knobil & J.D. Neill, Eds.: 711–749. Raven Press. New York.
12. DUBEY, A.K. & T.M PLANT. 1985. A suppression of gonadotropin secretion by cortisol in castrated male rhesus monkeys (*Macaca mulatta*) mediated by the interruption of hypothalamic gonadotropin-releasing hormone release. Biol. Reprod. **33:** 423–431.
13. RIVIER, C. & W. VALE. 1984 Influence of corticotropin-releasing factor on reproductive functions in the rat. Endocrinology **114:** 914–921.
14. REAME, N.E., S.E. SAUDER, G.D. CASE, et al. 1985. Pulsatile gonadotropin secretion in women with hypothalamic ameonorrhea: evidence that reduced frequency of gonadotropin-releasing hormone secretion is the mechanism of persistent anovulation. J. Clin. Endocrinol. Metab. **61:** 851–858.
15. BERGA, S.L., J.F. MORTOLA, L. GIRTON, et al. 1989. Neuroendocrine aberrations in women with functional hypothalamic amenorrhea. J. Clin. Endocrinol. Metab. **68:** 301–308.
16. GILES, D.E. & S.L. BERGA. 1993. Cognitive and psychiatric correlates of functional hypothalamic amenorrhea: a controlled comparison. Fertil. Steril. **60:** 486–492.
17. BERGA, S.L., T.L. DANIELS & D.E. GILES 1997. Women with functional hypothalamic amenorrhea but not other forms of anovulation display amplified cortisol concentrations. Fertil. Steril. **67:** 1024–1030.
18. BERGA, S.L., A.B. LOUCKS, W.G. ROSSMANITH, et al. 1991. Acceleration of luteinizing hormone pulse frequency in functional hypothalamic amenorrhea by dopaminergic blockade. J. Clin. Endocrinol. Metab. **72:** 151–156.

19. ROSE, R.M., T.P. GORDON, & I.S. BERNSTEIN. 1972. Plasma testosterone levels in the male rhesus: influences of sexual and social stimuli. Science **178**: 643–645.
20. COE, C.L., D. FRANKLIN, E.R. SMIT, & S. LEVINE. 1982. Hormonal responses accompanying fear and agitation in the squirrel monkey. Physiol. Behav. **29**: 1051–1057
21. NORMAN, R.L. & C.J. SMITH. 1992. Restraint inhibits luteinizing hormone and testosterone secretion in intact male rhesus macaques: effects of concurrent naloxone administration. Neuroendocrinology **55**: 405–415.
22. SAPOLSKY, R.M. 1983. Endocrine aspects of social instability in the olive baboon (*Papio anubis*). Am. J. Primatol. **5**: 365–379.
23. CAMERON, J.L. 2000. Reproductive dysfunction in primates, behaviorally induced. *In* Encyclopedia of Stress. G. Fink, Ed.: 366–372. Academic Press: New York.
24. BELSKY, J., L. STEINBERG & P. DRAPER 1991. Childhood experience, interpersonal development, and reproductive strategy: and evolutionary theory of socialization. Child Dev. **62**: 671–675.
25. MOFFITT, T.E., A. CASPI, J. BELSKY & P.A. SILVA 1993. Childhood experience and the onset of menarche: a test of a sociobiological model. Child Dev. **63**: 47–58.
26. WIERSON, M., P.J. LONG & R.L. FOREHAND 1993. Toward a new understanding of early menarche: the role of environmental stress in pubertal timing. Adolescence **28**: 913–924.
27. GRABER, J.A., J. BROOKS-GUNN & M.P. WARREN 1995. The antecedents of menarcheal age: heredity, family environment, and stressful life events. Child Dev. **66**: 346–359.
28. MCEWEN, B.S. 2003. Allostasis and allostatic load: implications for neuropsychopharmacology. Neuropsychopharmacology **22**: 108–124.
29. MCEWEN, B.S. 2003. Mood disorders and allostatic load. Biol. Psychiatry **54**: 200–207.
30. STROUD, L.R., P. SALOVEY & E.S. EPEL 2002. Sex differences in stress responses: social rejection versus achievement stress. Biol. Psychiatry **52**: 318–327.
31. DORN, L.D., E.S. BURGESS, E.J. SUSMAN, *et al.* 1996. Response to CRH in depressed and nondepressed adolescents: does gender make a difference? J. Am. Acad. Child. Adolesc. Psychiatry **35**: 764–773.
32. YOUNG, E.A., M. ALTEMUS, V. PARKISON & S. SHASTRY 2001. Effects of estrogen antagonists and agonists on the ACTH response to restraint stress in female rats. Neuropsychopharmacology **25**: 881–891.
33. CAREY, M.P., C.H. DETERD, J. DEKONING, *et al.* 1995. The influence of ovarian steroids on hypothalamic-pituitary-adrenal regulation in the female rat. J. Endocrinol. **144**: 311–321.
34. CHARNEY, D.S. 2004. Psychobiological mechanisms of resilience and vulnerability: implications for successful adaptation to extreme stress. Am. J. Psychiatry **161**: 195–216.
35. KOMESAROFF, P.A., M.D. ESLER & K. SUDHIR. 1999. Estrogen supplementation attenuates glucocorticoid and catecholamine responses to mental stress in perimenopausal women. J. Clin. Endocrinol. Metab. **84**: 606–610.
36. CUCINELLI, F., L. SORANNA, A. BARINI, *et al.* 2002. Estrogen treatment and body fat distribution are involved in corticotropin and cortisol response to corticotropin-releasing hormone in postmenopausal women. Metabolism **51**: 137–143.
37. ROOZENDAAL, B. 2000. Glucocorticoids and the regulation of memory consolidation. Psychoneuroendocrinology **25**: 213–238.
38. DIAMOND, D.M., M.C. BENNETT, M. FLESHNER & G.M. ROSE. 1992. Inverted-U relationship between the level of peripheral corticosterone and the magnitude of hippocampal primed burst potentiation. Hippocampus **2**: 421–430.
39. MCEWEN, B.S. 1999. Stress and hippocampal plasticity. Annu. Rev. Neurosci. **22**: 105–122.
40. MAGARINOS, A.M. & B.S. MCEWEN. Stress-induced atrophy of apical dendrites of hippocampal CA3 neurons: comparison of stressors. Neuroscience **69**: 83–88.
41. SOUSA, N., N.V. LUKOYANOV, M.D. MADEIRA, *et al.* 2000. Reorganization of the morphology of hippocampal neuritis and synapses after stress-induced damage correlates with behavioral improvement. Neuroscience **97**: 253–266.
42. YOUNG, E.A., R.F. HASKETT, L. GRUNHAUS, *et al.* 1994. Increased evening activation of the hypothalamic-pituitary-adrenal axis in depressed patients. Arch. Gen. Psychiatry **51**: 701–707.

43. DEUSCHLE, M., B. WEBER, M. COLLA, *et al.* 1998. Effects of major depression, aging and gender upon calculated diurnal free plasma cortisol concentrations: a reevaluation study. Stress **2:** 281–287.
44. BREMNER, J.D., M. NARAYAN, E.R. ANDERSON, *et al.* Hippocampal volume reduction in major depression. Am. J. Psychiatry **157:** 1115–117.
45. SHELINE, Y.I., M. SANGHAVI, M.A. MINTUN & M.H. GADO 1999. Depression duration but not age predicts hippocampal volume loss in medically healthy women with recurrent major depression. J. Neurosci. **19:** 5034–5043.
46. WOOLLEY, C., E. GOULD, M. FRANKFURT & B.S. MCEWEN 1990. Naturally occurring fluctuation in dendritic spine density on adult hippocampal pyramidal neurons. J. Neurosci. **10:** 4035–4039.
47. GOULD, E., C. WOOLLEY, M. FRANKFURT & B.S. MCEWEN 1990. Gonadal steroids regulate dendritic spine density in hippocampal pyramidal cells in adulthood. J. Neurosci. **10:** 1286–1291.
48. UNO, H., T. ROSS, J. ELSE, M. SULEMAN & R. SAPOLSKY 1989. Hippocampal damage associated with prolonged and fatal stress in primates. J. Neurosci. **9:** 1705–1711.
49. MIZOGUCHI, K., T. KUNISHITA, D.H. CHUI & T. TABIRA 1992. Stress induces neuronal death in the hippocampus of castrated rats. Neurosci. Lett. **138:** 157–160.
50. GALEA, L.A.M., B.S. MCEWEN, P. TANAPAT, *et al.* 1997. Sex differences in dendritic atrophy of CA3 pyramidal neurons in response to chronic restraint stress. Neuroscience **81:** 689–697.
51. ROOF, R.L. 1993. The dentate gyrus is sexually dimorphic in prepubescent rats: testosterone plays a significant role. Brain Res. **610:** 148–151.
52. GOULD, E., A. WESTLIND-DANIELSSON, M. FRANKFURT & B.S. MCEWEN 1990. Sex differences and thyroid hormone sensitivity of hippocampal pyramidal neurons. J. Neurosci. **10:** 996–1003.
53. DANIEL, J.M., A.J. FADER, A.L. SPENCER & G.P. DOHANICH. 1997. Estrogen enhances performance of female rats during acquisition of a radial arm maze. Horm. Behav. **32:** 217–225.
54. MCEWEN, B.S. & S.E. ALVES. 1999. Estrogen actions in the central nervous system. Endocrine Rev. **20:** 279–307.
55. RESSLER, K.J. & C.B. NEMEROFF. 2000. Role of serotonergic and noradrenergic systems in the pathophysiology of depression and anxiety disorders. Depression Anxiety **12:** 2–19.
56. BHAGWAGAR, Z., R. WHALE & P.J. COWEN. 2002. State and trait abnormalities in serotonin function in major depression. Br. J. Psychiatry **180:** 24–28.
57. CASPI, A., K. SUGDEN, T.E. MOFFITT, *et al.* 2003. Influence of life stress on depression: moderation by a polymorphism in the 5-HTT gene. Science **301:** 291–293.
58. DAHL, R.E. 2001. Affect regulation, brain development, and behavioral/emotional health in adolescence. CNS Spectrums **6:** 1–12.

Adolescence: Vulnerable Period for Stress-Induced Prefrontal Cortical Function?

Introduction to Part IV

AMY F. T. ARNSTEN AND REBECCA M. SHANSKY

Department of Neurobiology, Yale University School of Medicine, New Haven, Connecticut 06510, USA

ABSTRACT: Exposure to even mild uncontrollable stress impairs the cognitive functioning of the prefrontal cortex, a brain region critical for insight, judgment, and the inhibition of inappropriate behaviors. Several neurobiological factors may contribute to an exaggeration of the stress response in adolescence, for example, an increased dopaminergic projection to prefrontal cortex, and in females, increased circulating estrogen, as estrogen amplifies many aspects of the stress response and lowers the threshold for stress-induced prefrontal cortical dysfunction. These neurobiological factors may increase susceptibility to impaired judgment, drug addiction, and neuropsychiatric disorders during adolescence.

KEYWORDS: adolescence; prefrontal cortex (PFC); stress; cognitive function

INTRODUCTION

The session entitled "Cognitive Development, Decision-Making and Behavioral Choices" explored how the executive functions of the prefrontal cortex (PFC), when tested in nonemotional lab settings, develop to their full capabilities across the adolescent period in both rodents[1] and humans.[2] The PFC is critical for insight, judgment, the ability to inhibit prepotent but inappropriate responses, and the ability to plan and organize for the future.[3,4] This higher brain region, like other cortical areas, takes on its adult form during this time period, as synapses are pruned to adult levels.[5] Yet, the data also show that adolescence is a time of great vulnerability, with special sensitivity to nicotine addiction in animals and humans,[1] and eruption of stress-related neuropsychiatric disorders such as depression.[6] Thus, adolescents with well-developed decision-making abilities under nonemotional conditions may nonetheless be especially prone to impaired judgment and impulsive actions under emotionally stressful conditions. This chapter discusses some of the neurobiological factors that may contribute to heightened vulnerability to stress during the adolescent period. Finally, the relevance of these scientific findings to policies for care of

Address for correspondence: Amy F. T. Arnsten, Ph.D., Department of Neurobiology, Yale University School of Medicine, New Haven, CT 06510. Voice: 203-785-4431; fax: 203-785-5263.

amy.arnsten@yale.edu

Ann. N.Y. Acad. Sci. 1021: 143–147 (2004). © 2004 New York Academy of Sciences.
doi: 10.1196/annals.1308.017

adolescents in our society is discussed in the chapter by Cauffman.[7] There is an increasing need for policies that will protect adolescents during a biologically vulnerable time period. This is particularly important in an economy that depends on the expenditures of teenagers, and exploits their insecurities to maximize consumption. Dr. Cauffman[7] discusses the strengths and weaknesses of the scientific data, and the ethical and legal challenges in society's treatment of adolescents as adults.

STRESS IMPAIRS PREFRONTAL CORTEX COGNITIVE FUNCTION

The PFC is extraordinarily sensitive to stress. Even mild stressors can impair PFC cognitive function if the subject feels no control over the stress (a common experience for teenagers). The neurochemical bases of these impairing effects have been examined in animal studies. Research in rats and monkeys has shown that stress-induced deficits in PFC function arise from high levels of norepinephrine (NE) release engaging alpha-1-adrenoceptors, which in turn activate protein kinase C, and high levels of dopamine (DA) release engaging D1 receptors, which activate protein kinase A and CREB.[8] In contrast, stimulation of alpha-2A-adrenoceptors protects the PFC from the detrimental effects of stress, likely through inhibition of protein kinase A.[9] There are several changes that occur in the adolescent brain that may magnify these stress-induced PFC deficits.

ELEVATED DOPAMINE INNERVATION OF PREFRONTAL CORTEX IN ADOLESCENCE

Anatomical studies from the Lewis lab have examined developmental changes in the DA innervation of PFC in monkeys. These investigations have revealed higher levels of DA in the PFC of adolescent monkeys, particularly in layer III, the site of cortical–cortical interactions.[10] Given that high levels of DA released during stress impair PFC regulation of behavior and thought, these anatomical data suggest that there may be greater neurochemical potential for these impairing effects during adolescence. These data may explain why teenagers are vulnerable to loss of judgment and insight during emotional and/or stressful situations.

ESTROGEN AMPLIFIES STRESS-INDUCED PREFRONTAL CORTEX DYSFUNCTION

The rates of depression rise dramatically as girls enter adolescence,[11,12] suggesting that hormonal changes may contribute to this susceptibility. The ventromedial/orbital PFC is strongly interconnected with the amygdala and hypothalamus, and is strongly implicated in major depressive disorder.[13–15] A similar area of PFC is found in rodents, and is very sensitive to stress-induced PFC dysfunction. Our recent research in rodents shows that estrogen amplifies stress-induced PFC dysfunction in

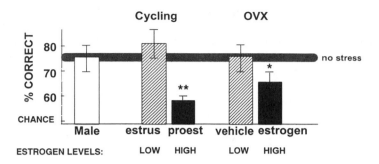

FIGURE 1. Females with high circulating estrogen are more sensitive to stress-induced PFC dysfunction. Exposure to pharmacological stress (FG7142, an anxiogenic, inverse benzodiazepine agonist) produces a dose-related impairment in delayed alternation performance, a test of spatial working memory that depends on the medial PFC in rodents. A dose of 2 mg/kg was sufficient to significantly impair delayed alternation performance in females with high circulating estrogen levels (proestrus or ovariectomy (OVX) with 10% estradiol capsule); this dose had no effect on males or females with low circulating estrogen, who required higher FG7142 doses to impair performance. Results represent mean ± S.E.M. percent correct on the delayed alternation task following 2 mg/kg FG7142; mean performance under nonstress conditions is represented by the *shaded horizontal line*. *Indicates significantly different from nonstress conditions. (Adapted from Shansky *et al.*[16] Reproduced by permision.)

females.[16] As shown in FIGURE 1, cycling females in proestrus (high estrogen) or ovariectomized females with estrogen replacement (10% estradiol capsules, blood levels similar to proestrus), are impaired by mild stressors that have no effect on females in estrus (low circulating estrogen), ovariectomized females without estrogen replacement, or males. This profile has been observed with pharmacological stress[16] and environmental stressors, including injection stress,[16] and restraint stress.[17] The marked differences in cycling animals suggest that progesterone as well as estrogen may play a role, as suggested by human studies.[18] The neurobiological basis for this enhanced sensitivity to stress is currently under investigation. Estrogen increases the expression of alpha-1 adrenoceptors[19] and decreases the expression of alpha-2A adrenoceptors,[20] and thus is in position to increase detrimental factors and decrease protective actions. Estrogen is also known to exaggerate dopaminergic transmission.[21,22] Similar effects in humans may render adolescent girls more susceptible to depression. Interestingly, recent genetic studies have linked alterations in the gene encoding for CREB1 with recurrent depression in young women, but not men.[23] These findings suggest that hormonal and genetic factors may amplify the stress response in a subset of adolescent girls, rendering them particularly vulnerable to major depressive disorder.

In summary, neurobiological factors that amplify stress-induced PFC dysfunction during adolescence may increase susceptibility to impaired judgment, drug addiction, and neuropsychiatric disorders.

ACKNOWLEDGMENTS

The research described in this paper was supported by PHS R37 AG06036 and a Ethel F. Donoghue Women's Health Investigator Program at Yale small grant to one of the authors (A.F.T.A.).

REFERENCES

1. LESLIE, F., S.E. LOUGHLIN, R. WANG, *et al.* 2004. Adolescent development of forebrain stimulant responsiveness: insights from animal studies. Ann. N.Y. Acad Sci. **1021:** 148–159.
2. YOUNG, E.A. & M. ALTEMUS. 2004. Puberty, ovarian steroids, and stress. Ann. N.Y. Acad. Sci. **1021:** 124–133.
3. STUSS, D.T., C.A. GOW & C.R. HETHERINGTON. 1992. "No longer Gage": frontal lobe dysfunction and emotional changes. J. Consult. Clin. Psychol. **60:** 349–359.
4. GOLDMAN-RAKIC, P.S. 1995. Cellular basis of working memory. Neuron **14:** 477–485.
5. BOURGEOIS, J.-P., P.S. GOLDMAN-RAKIC & P. RAKIC. 1994. Synaptogenesis in the prefrontal cortex of rhesus monkeys. Cereb. Cortex **4:** 78–96.
6. KEATING, D.P. 2003. Adolescent cognitive and brain development: the emergence of consciousness. Presented at the conference Adolescent Brain Development: Vulnerabilities and Opportunities, New York City, September 19, 3003.
7. CAUFFMAN, E. 2004. The adolescent brain: excuse versus explanation: Comments on Part IV. Ann. N.Y. Acad. Sci. **1021:** 160–161.
8. ARNSTEN, A.F.T. 2000. Stress impairs PFC function in rats and monkeys: role of dopamine D1 and norepinephrine alpha-1 receptor mechanisms. Prog. Brain Res. **126:** 183–192.
9. BIRNBAUM, S.G., D.M. PODELL & A.F.T. ARNSTEN. 2000. Noradrenergic alpha-2 receptor agonists reverse working memory deficits induced by the anxiogenic drug, FG7142, in rats. Pharmacol. Biochem. Behav. **67:** 397–403.
10. ROSENBERG, D.R. & D.A. LEWIS. 1995. Postnatal maturation of the dopaminergic innervation of monkey prefrontal cortices: a tyrosine hydroxylase immunohistochemical analysis. J. Comp. Neurol. **358:** 383–400.
11. BORN, L., A. SHEA & M. STEINER. 2002. The roots of depression in adolescent girls: Is menarche the key? Curr. Psychiatry Rep. **4:** 449–460.
12. HAYWARD, C. & K. SANBORN. 2002. Puberty and the emergence of gender differences in psychopathology. J. Adolesc. Health **30:** 49–58.
13. DREVETS, W.C., J.L. PRICE, J.R.J. SIMPSON, *et al.* 1997. Subgenual prefrontal cortex abnormalities in mood disorders. Nature **386:** 824–827.
14. MAYBERG, H.S., M. LIOTTI, S.K. BRANNAN, *et al.* 1999. Reciprocal limbic-cortical function and negative mood: converging PET findings in depression and normal sadness. Am. J. Psychiatry **156:** 675–682.
15. RAJKOWSKA, G., J.J. MIGUEL-HIDALGO, J. WEI, *et al.* 1999. Morphometric evidence for neuronal and glial prefrontal cell pathology in major depression. Biol. Psychiatry **45:** 1085–1098.
16. SHANSKY, R.M., C. GLAVIS-BLOOM, D. LERMAN, *et al.* 2003. Estrogen mediates sex differences in stress-induced prefrontal cortex dysfunction. Mol. Psychiatry. E-pub. ahead of print, Oct. 21. (Print version, May 2004.)
17. SHANSKY, R.M., K. RUBINOW & A.F.T. ARNSTEN. 2003. Sex differences in stress-induced working memory impairment. Soc. Neurosci. Abstr. 29.
18. BLOCH, M., R.C. DALY & D.R. RUBINOW. 2003. Endocrine factors in the etiology of postpartum depression. Compre. Psychiatry **44:** 234–246.
19. LEE, K., C.D. RICHARDSON, M.A. RAZIK, *et al.* 1998. Multiple potential regulatory elements in the 5′ flanking region of the human alpha 1α-adrenergic receptor. DNA Seq. **8:** 271–276.

20. KARKANIAS, G.B., C.S. LI & A.M. ETGEN. 1997. Estradiol reduction of alpha-2-adreno-ceptor binding in female rat cortex is correlated with decreases in alpha2A/D-adrenoceptor messenger RNA. Neuroscience **81:** 593–597.
21. KRITZER, M.F. & S.G. KOHAMA. 1998. Ovarian hormones influence morphology, distri-bution and density of tyrosine hydroxylase immunoreactive axons in the dorsolateral prefrontal cortex of adult rhesus monkeys. J. Comp. Neurol. **395:** 1–17.
22. BECKER, J. 2000. Oestrogen effects on dopaminergic function in striatum. Novartis Found. Symp. **230:** 134–145.
23. ZUBENKO, G.S., H.B. HUGHES 3RD, B.S. MAHER, *et al.* 2002. Genetic linkage of region containing the CREB1 gene to depressive disorders in women from families with recurrent, early-onset, major depression. Am. J. Med. Genet. **114:** 980–987.

Adolescent Development of Forebrain Stimulant Responsiveness

Insights from Animal Studies

FRANCES M. LESLIE,[a–c] SANDRA E. LOUGHLIN,[a,c] RUIHUA WANG,[a]
LILYANNA PEREZ,[b] SHAHRDAD LOTFIPOUR,[b] AND JAMES D. BELLUZZI[a,c]

[a]*Department of Pharmacology and [b]Department of Anatomy & Neurobiology,
College of Medicine, University of California, Irvine, California 92697, USA*

[c]*Transdisciplinary Tobacco Use Research Center, University of California, Irvine,
California 92697, USA*

ABSTRACT: Although initiation of drug abuse occurs primarily during adolescence, little is known about the central effects of nicotine and other abused drugs during this developmental period. Here evidence, derived from studies in rodents, is presented that suggests that tobacco use initiation during early adolescence results from a higher reward value of nicotine. The developmental profiles of the rewarding effects of other abused drugs, such as cocaine, differ from that of nicotine. Using *in situ* hybridization to quantify mRNA levels of the immediate early gene, cfos, the neuronal activating effects of nicotine in limbic and sensory cortices at different developmental stages are evaluated. Significant age changes in basal levels of cfos mRNA expression in cortical regions are observed, with a peak of responding of limbic cortices during early adolescence. A changing pattern of nicotine-induced neuronal activation is seen across the developmental spectrum, with unique differences in both limbic and sensory cortex responding during adolescence. An attentional set-shifting task was also used to evaluate whether the observed differences during adolescence reflect early functional immaturity of prefrontal cortices that regulate motivated behavior and psychostimulant responding. The finding of significantly better responding during adolescence suggests apparent functional maturity of prefrontal circuits and greater cognitive flexibility at younger ages. These findings in rodent models suggest that adolescence is a period of altered sensitivity to environmental stimuli, including abused drugs. Further efforts are required to overcome technical challenges in order to evaluate drug effects systematically in this age group.

KEYWORDS: nicotine; cocaine; limbic; sensory; cortex; cfos; attention; reward

Address for correspondence: Dr. Frances M. Leslie, Department of Pharmacology, College of Medicine, University of California, Irvine, CA 92697-4625. Voice: 949-824-6699; fax: 949-824-4855.
    fmleslie@uci.edu

Ann. N.Y. Acad. Sci. 1021: 148–159 (2004). © 2004 New York Academy of Sciences.
doi: 10.1196/annals.1308.018

INTRODUCTION

Adolescence is a critical period of vulnerability for the onset of substance abuse. Initiation of alcohol and tobacco use, in particular, does not occur beyond young adulthood, and that of other abused substances is greatly diminished.[1,2] Furthermore, those who begin drug use in early adolescence show a pattern of heavier lifetime consumption and greater difficulty quitting than those who start as older adolescents or young adults.[3–5] Epidemiological studies have characterized a progression of drug use from alcohol and tobacco to marijuana and other illicit drugs.[1] Such findings have led to the hypothesis that alcohol and tobacco may serve as "gateway" drugs,[6] although this concept has been disputed.[4]

As summarized by Spear,[7] animal studies have provided important information about adolescent brain development, particularly those detailed morphological and neurochemical aspects that cannot be studied readily in humans. Studies in both rodents and primates have shown that corticolimbic systems and their monoamine projections, which constitute the motivational circuitry implicated in drug abuse, have not fully matured by adolescence.[7–9] In particular, the structural and neurochemical maturation of prefrontal cortex is not complete.[10–13] This brain region uses representations held "on-line" to guide behavior in the absence of environmental input, and to inhibit inappropriate responses and environmental distractions.[14] Descending projections from the prefrontal cortex regulate the activity of nucleus accumbens neurons and their dopaminergic afferents,[15,16] which mediate the positive reinforcing effects of abused drugs and subsequent drug-seeking behavior.[17,18] Dysfunction of prefrontal regulatory control has been implicated in the mechanisms underlying drug abuse.[19]

Although adolescence is the principal time frame for initiation of drug use, few studies have evaluated mechanisms of drug action at this developmental timepoint. As evidence increases that critical processes in prefrontal maturation occur during adolescence, this type of analysis becomes more essential. This article summarizes ongoing animal studies of the actions of psychostimulants on forebrain motivational circuitry during adolescence, with particular emphasis on nicotine.

ARE PSYCHOSTIMULANTS MORE REWARDING IN ADOLESCENCE?

Although much work has been done to evaluate the rewarding effects of psychostimulants in adults,[20,21] only recently have studies attempted to address the issue of whether adolescence represents a period of increased sensitivity to psychostimulant reward. Such studies are technically challenging because of the short duration of adolescence in the standard rodent models. A conservative age range for the period of adolescence has been defined as the fifth and sixth postnatal weeks.[7] Thus, behavioral procedures that require long periods of training cannot be completed during rodent adolescence.

Conditioned Place Preference

Two primary approaches have been used to evaluate the rewarding effects of drugs in rodents: conditioned place preference (CPP) and self-administration. CPP does not require extensive training, and it therefore has been used to evaluate the rewarding effects of abused drugs during postnatal development.[22] In this procedure an apparatus is divided into two chambers that have unique sensory cues. During the conditioning phase, animals are given drug injections paired with one compartment and saline injections paired with the other. Animals are subsequently allowed to move freely between the two compartments in the absence of drug. Increased time spent in the drug-paired compartment is interpreted as reflecting a rewarding effect of the drug.

CPP studies have shown that the neural substrates that support drug reward are active during the neonatal period.[23] Significant CPP is generated by morphine,[24] amphetamine,[25] and cocaine[26] during the first postnatal month, although the neural mechanisms underlying the reward process may change during this period.[27] However, a loss of drug-induced CPP for both amphetamine[28] and morphine[24] has been reported to occur during mid-adolescence. All three drugs generate significant CPP in adults.[20]

In contrast to other abused drugs, nicotine does not consistently produce CPP in the adult. Preference for the nicotine-paired compartment has been shown reliably when a "biased" design is used, where the animal is given drug injections in the least preferred compartment.[29–31] Less consistent CPP has been demonstrated when an unbiased design is used, where drug injections and initial preferences are counterbalanced.[31–34] Since use of the counterbalanced methodology eliminates interpretational confounds such as anxiolytic effects,[35] the failure to demonstrate consistent nicotine preference using the unbiased test approach has led some to question the hedonic value of this drug in adults.[32,33]

Using a biased CPP design, Vastola and colleagues have shown enhanced rewarding effects of nicotine in adolescent rats as compared to adults.[36] We have recently tested rats in early adolescence (postnatal day (P) 28), mid- to late adolescence (P38), and adulthood (P90) in an unbiased, counterbalanced CPP design.[37] In older adolescents and adults, we failed to demonstrate significant nicotine-induced CPP after either one or four conditioning trials. In contrast, animals in early adolescence were uniquely sensitive to the rewarding effects of nicotine on this test, demonstrating preference for the nicotine-paired compartment after a single conditioning trial.

Self-Administration

The most commonly used methodology for an operant responding to the reinforcing effects of abused drugs is the self-administration test. The standard procedure for this test includes training to receive food reward, followed by intravenous catheterization and substitution of drug reward over a period of several weeks. Carrying out this test in adolescents presents several challenges, and has been rarely done successfully. In view of the short time frame of adolescence, the training sequence needs to be eliminated or curtailed. The small size of animals during adolescence presents unique challenges in terms of the success of intravenous catheterizations, and their rapid growth is associated with a high rate of subsequent catheter failure. Food restriction during this rapid growth phase, which is necessary for food training, may also result in growth inhibition and abnormal pubertal maturation.[38]

Despite these difficulties, studies on intravenous self-administration in adolescent rats are now being initiated. Levin and colleagues, using a less stringent definition of the duration of adolescence than that just described, have shown significantly increased rates of self-administration of nicotine in 54-day-old female rats as com-

TABLE 1. Developmental change in the self-administration of nicotine/acetaldehyde and cocaine

Treatment		Self-administering animals on Day 5		
	Age	Number	Percentage	Mean responses
Nic (30 µg) + Acet (16 µg)	P31	9/13	69.2	40.0 ± 7.0
	P41	3/6	50.0	19.0 ± 6.4
	P95	0/6	0	—
Cocaine (250–750 µg/kg/inj)	P31	0/6	0	—
	P41	2/6	33.3	50.0 ± 1.0
	P95	4/10	40.0	60.5 ± 19.6

NOTE: Data are shown for the final test day (Day 5). The criterion for responding was established as seven or more self-injections during the 3-h session.

pared to 84-day-old adults.[39] We have also undertaken studies of nicotine and cocaine self-administration during the early and late phases of adolescence in comparison to adults (TABLE 1). Using a very stringent behavioral test, in which animals were placed in operant chambers without prior training or food restriction, we have shown animals to be most sensitive to the rewarding effects of nicotine during early adolescence. In order to see this effect, however, it was necessary to combine nicotine with acetaldehyde, a constituent of burning cellulose, that is also present in substantial quantities in tobacco smoke.[40] Nicotine alone was not sufficiently rewarding to produce responses on this stringent test. In contrast to the nicotine/acetaldehyde mixture, cocaine was found to be less reinforcing in this test during early adolescence than during later adolescence and adulthood. Such findings suggest different rates of developmental maturation of the neural circuitry underlying nicotine and cocaine reward.

In mice, an oral self-administration procedure has been developed to evaluate the reinforcing efficacy of abused drugs.[41] A study of oral self-administration of nicotine in mice has produced a finding consistent with our observation in rats that early adolescence is the period of greatest reinforcing efficacy of nicotine.[72] Early adolescent animals, aged P24–35, showed a strong preference for nicotine containing water in a two-bottle task. These findings contrast with those of older adolescents, aged P37–48, who showed no preference for the nicotine bottle, and animals aged P50–61, who showed aversion. It is well established that nicotine in adults has both aversive and rewarding actions.[29,42] These self-administration data suggest that the balance between reward and aversion shifts throughout the adolescent period, with reward predominating during early adolescence but not later. A late developmental appearance of aversive effects of amphetamine also has been suggested recently.[22]

WHAT NEURAL CIRCUITRY IS ACTIVATED BY PSYCHOSTIMULANTS DURING ADOLESCENCE?

There has been substantial prior work on the influence of psychostimulants on the early phases of brain development, including the fetal and early postnatal periods.[43,44] Nicotinic receptors (nAChRs), in particular, have been shown to be transiently expressed in a number of developing brain regions and to serve unique

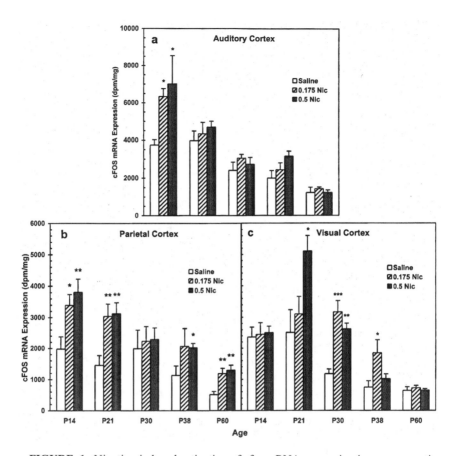

FIGURE 1. Nicotine-induced activation of cfos mRNA expression in sensory cortices at various ages from P14 to adult. Animals were injected with saline or one of two doses of nicotine 30 min prior to sacrifice. Brains were processed by *in situ* hybridization for measurement of regional levels of cfos mRNA. Data represent means ± SEM of 5–6 male rats per age group. Significantly different from saline: *, $P < .05$, **, $P < .01$; ***, $P < .001$.

developmental roles.[45–48] To date, however, very little has been done to evaluate neural mechanisms underlying psychostimulant action during adolescence.

In view of a growing body of evidence for an important functional role of nAChRs in regulating cortical development,[46,48,49] we have recently examined patterns of neural activation of developing cortex by acute administration of nicotine. The immediate early gene, cfos, was used as a marker for the functional activation of sensory and limbic cortical neurons by nicotine at different developmental timepoints ranging from P14 to adult (P60) (FIGS. 1 and 2). Although it suffers from some limitations, this approach has been used extensively to evaluate functional neuronal circuitry in adult brain.[50,51] In particular, although cfos is widely expressed in recently activated neurons, it is not a universal marker.

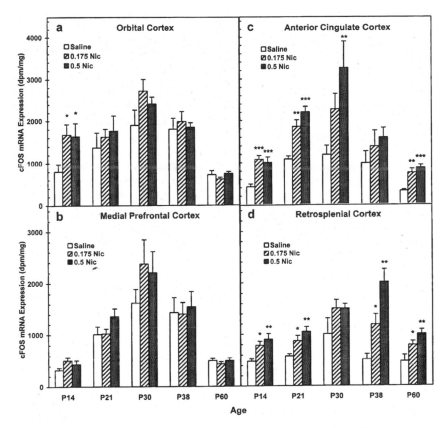

FIGURE 2. Nicotine-induced activation of cfos mRNA expression in limbic cortices at various ages from P14 to adult. Animals were injected with saline or one of two doses of nicotine 30 min prior to sacrifice. Brains were processed by *in situ* hybridization for measurement of regional levels of cfos mRNA. Data represent means ± SEM of 5–6 male rats per age group. Significantly different from saline: *, $P < .05$; **, $P < .01$; ***, $P < .001$.

Sensory Cortex

A transient expression of several nAChR subunit mRNAs has been observed during the first two weeks of sensory thalamocortical development.[45,52–54] A specific functional role to potentiate NMDA-mediated excitatory postsynaptic potentials (EPSPs) in the auditory cortex has been shown to occur during the second postnatal week, at the time of maximal nAChR expression that coincides with the peak of thalamocortical synaptogenesis and the onset of hearing.[46] Recent physiological studies have shown that, although fewer neurons in the auditory cortex are modulated by nicotine in the third postnatal week, there is a large increase in the magnitude of nicotine-enhanced EPSPs from P13 to P16.[49] Consistent with this physiological finding, nicotine-induced cfos expression in auditory cortex is evident at P14 but not at later ages (FIG. 1a).

In contrast, nicotine was found to induce cfos expression in parietal and visual cortices across a broader range of developmental timepoints (FIG. 1b and 1c). Furthermore, unique nicotine effects were observed in both regions during adolescence. Nicotine-induced neuronal activation in parietal cortex was evident at P14 and P21, and again at P38 and P60. However, there was no significant nicotine activation of this region during early adolescence (P30). The effects of nicotine on cfos expression in visual cortex emerged later than in other sensory regions, and were extremely complex. A changing dose-response relationship of nicotine effects in visual cortex was observed during the fourth through sixth postnatal weeks (P21–P38), suggestive of a change in nAChR properties. Nicotine-induced activation of cfos in visual cortex neurons was no longer evident, however, in adults. These complex changes in nicotine actions on parietal and visual cortices during adolescence may be associated with altered responsiveness to nicotine-associated sensory cues that are critical to the addiction process. Further physiological and behavioral analyses of nicotine effects on somatosensory and visual processing during adolescence would therefore seem warranted.

Limbic Cortex

Limbic cortical regions that have been implicated in drug addiction,[19] also show complex changes in cfos expression during adolescence (FIG. 2). Basal levels of cfos expression are significantly different across development, with peak levels evident at P30. This contrasts with sensory cortical regions, which showed peak basal expression levels at P14, shortly after the onset of sensory function (FIG. 1). These developmental changes in basal neuronal activity were particularly prominent in orbital and medial prefrontal cortices, and suggest that these regions may be particularly sensitive to environmental input and/or the stress of saline injection during adolescence. Although these two frontolimbic brain regions showed significant changes in baseline activity, little effect of nicotine was observed across the developmental timecourse, with the exception of activation of cfos expression in orbital cortex at P14.

The cingulate cortex plays a critical role in mood, attention, and conflict monitoring, and is activated during intoxication and craving.[55,56] It is highly interconnected with the retrosplenial cortex that is activated by emotionally relevant stimuli, and may regulate the interaction between emotion and memory.[57] Both of these limbic cortices are activated across the developmental spectrum, from P14 to P60 (FIG. 2c and 2d). However, each shows a period during adolescence in which it is unresponsive to nicotine, P30 for the retrosplenial and P38 for the cingulate cortex. Thus, these limbic cortices resemble parietal cortex in their developmental response profiles (FIG. 1b), in that they all exhibit a period of insensitivity to nicotine's effects during adolescence.

IS PREFRONTAL CORTICAL FUNCTION ALTERED DURING ADOLESCENCE?

Given evidence that the structural maturation of the prefrontal cortex is not complete by adolescence in either rodents[7–9,11] or primates,[10,12,13] it is reasonable to assume that this region is not functionally mature either. Since the prefrontal cortex has a significant role in inhibiting appetitive responding,[19] it is possible that the increased nicotine reward value during early adolescence may reflect such functional immaturity and that the later decreased drug responding occurs as a result of prefrontal executive control coming on-line. Although there is controversy as to whether there is a homologue of primate prefrontal cortex in rats,[58] recent studies have shown that animals with prefrontal hypofunction resulting from neonatal hippocampal lesions exhibit increased self-administration of cocaine.[59]

In order to test the hypothesis that prefrontal cortex is functionally immature during adolescence, we evaluated behavioral responses of rats on an attentional set-shifting task.[58,60] This test has been developed as rodent analog of the Wisconsin Card Sort Test (WCST), which is used routinely in humans as a test of prefrontal function.[61] The rodent test evaluates behavioral responding on a serial two-choice discrimination task in which the animal must choose the salient cue in pairs of stimuli across three sensory dimensions. Rats are trained to dig in bowls for food reward, and perform a series of discriminations that include reversal learning, an intradimensional shift (IDS) in which the salient stimulus (e.g., odor or digging medium) is changed within the same dimension, and an extradimensional shift (EDS) in which the formerly salient sensory dimension becomes irrelevant. Lesion studies have shown critical roles for both orbital and medial prefrontal cortices in this cognitive task.[58,60] Whereas lesions of the orbital cortex impair the ability to learn altered re-

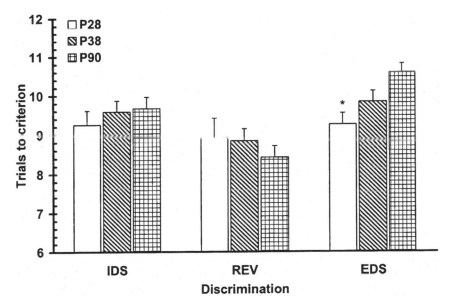

FIGURE 3. Age differences in behavioral performance on an attentional set-shifting task. Rats, aged P28, P38, or adult, were tested on a series of discriminations between relevant and irrelevant sensory stimuli until they reached the criterion of six consecutive correct responses. ABBREVIATIONS: IDS, intradimensional shift; REV, reversal; EDS, extradimensional shift. Data are means ± SEM of 12 male rats per age group. *, significantly different from P90, $P < .05$.

ward values during the reversal phase, lesions of the medial prefrontal cortex impair extradimensional set-shifting. Studies in both primates[62] and humans[63] have implicated orbital or ventral prefrontal cortex in reversal learning and dorsolateral prefrontal cortex in the EDS. Thus, although the prefrontal cortex in rodents is not organized exactly as that seen in higher species, it appears to have functional analogs.

As shown in FIGURE 3, cognitive performance on this task was enhanced in younger animals as compared to adults. Although there were no age differences in responding during the reversal or IDS trials, there was a significant enhancement of EDS in younger animals ($F_{7,33} = 3.3486$, $P < .05$). Although unexpected, this finding is similar to that of a recent study of cognitive function in humans.[64] Whereas adolescents and adults showed similar performances on a gambling task that has been associated with ventral prefrontal cortical function,[65] adolescents exhibited enhanced response on one element of the WCST.[64] Further studies will be required to evaluate the significance of these findings. Recently it has been suggested that many aspects of adolescent cognitive function may be equivalent to that of adults under "cold" laboratory situations, but may show greater deterioration under more real-life, stressful conditions.[66] This would be consistent with observed adolescent elevations in prefrontal catecholamines and their receptors,[10,67,68] which have been implicated in inhibiting the functional activity of this region during stress.[14] Alternatively, other brain regions may subserve the cognitive function of medial prefrontal cortex in adolescent rats, as has been suggested for dorsolateral prefrontal cortex in humans.[69,70]

CONCLUSIONS

There is increasing evidence that adolescence is a period of unique sensitivity of forebrain systems to environmental stimuli, including abused drugs. Given such findings, it is critical that more effort be expended in evaluating all aspects of psychostimulant action during this developmental period. Whereas this review has focused only on acute or semiacute drug effects, analysis of long-term and chronic drug effects is also warranted.[71] Further efforts will be required to overcome the technical challenges that limit systematic evaluation of drug effects in this age group. However, such efforts should be rewarded with greater insight into why adolescents initiate use of psychostimulant drugs and possible strategies for intervention.

ACKNOWLEDGMENTS

This work was supported by PHS grant DA13332.

REFERENCES

1. KANDEL, D.B. & J.A. LOGAN. 1984. Patterns of drug use from adolescence to young adulthood: I. Periods of risk for initiation, continued use, and discontinuation. Am. J. Public Health **74:** 660–666.

2. CHEN, K. & D.B. KANDEL. 1995. The natural history of drug use from adolescence to the mid-thirties in a general population sample. Am. J. Public Health **85:** 41–47.
3. BRESLAU, N. & E.L. PETERSON. 1996. Smoking cessation in young adults: age at initiation of cigarette smoking and other suspected influences. Am. J. Public Health **86:** 214–220.
4. MACKESY-AMITI, M.E., M. FENDRICH & P.J. GOLDSTEIN. 1997. Sequence of drug use among serious drug users: typical vs. atypical progression. Drug Alcohol Depend. **45:** 185–196.
5. CHEN, J. & W.J. MILLAR. 1998. Age of smoking initiation: implications for quitting. Health Rep. **9:** 39–46 (English); 39–48 (French).
6. KANDEL, D.B., K. YAMAGUCHI & K. CHEN. 1992. Stages of progression in drug involvement from adolescence to adulthood: further evidence for the gateway theory. J. Stud. Alcohol **53:** 447–457.
7. SPEAR, L.P. 2000. The adolescent brain and age-related behavioral manifestations. Neurosci. Biobehav. Rev. **24:** 417–463.
8. CUNNINGHAM, M.G., S. BHATTACHARYYA & F.M. BENES. 2002. Amygdalo-cortical sprouting continues into early adulthood: implications for the development of normal and abnormal function during adolescence. J. Comp. Neurol. **453:** 116–130.
9. CHAMBERS, R.A., J.R. TAYLOR & M.N. POTENZA. 2003. Developmental neurocircuitry of motivation in adolescence: a critical period of addiction vulnerability. Am. J. Psychiatry **160:** 1041–1052.
10. LEWIS, D.A. 1997. Development of the prefrontal cortex during adolescence: insights into vulnerable neural circuits in schizophrenia. Neuropsychopharmacology **16:** 385–398.
11. BENES, F.M., J.B. TAYLOR & M.C. CUNNINGHAM. 2000. Convergence and plasticity of monoaminergic systems in the medial prefrontal cortex during the postnatal period: implications for the development of psychopathology. Cereb. Cortex **10:** 1014–1027.
12. LAMBE, E.K., L.S. KRIMER & P.S. GOLDMAN-RAKIC. 2000. Differential postnatal development of catecholamine and serotonin inputs to identified neurons in prefrontal cortex of rhesus monkey. J. Neurosci. **20:** 8780–8787.
13. CRUZ, D.A., S.M. EGGAN & D.A. LEWIS. 2003. Postnatal development of pre- and postsynaptic GABA markers at chandelier cell connections with pyramidal neurons in monkey prefrontal cortex. J. Comp. Neurol. **465:** 385–400.
14. ARNSTEN, A.F.T. 1998. Catecholamine modulation of prefrontal cortical cognitive function. Trends Cog. Sci. **2:** 436–447.
15. CARR, D.B. *et al.* 1999. Dopamine terminals in the rat prefrontal cortex synapse on pyramidal cells that project to the nucleus accumbens. J. Neurosci. **19:** 11049–11060.
16. CARR, D.B. & S.R. SESACK. 2000. Projections from the rat prefrontal cortex to the ventral tegmental area: target specificity in the synaptic associations with mesoaccumbens and mesocortical neurons. J. Neurosci. **20:** 3864–3873.
17. DI CHIARA, G. 2002. Nucleus accumbens shell and core dopamine: differential role in behavior and addiction. Behav. Brain Res. **137:** 75–114.
18. BONCI, A. *et al.* 2003. The dopamine-containing neuron: maestro or simple musician in the orchestra of addiction? Trends Pharmacol. Sci. **24:** 172–177.
19. GOLDSTEIN, R.Z. & N.D. VOLKOW. 2002. Drug addiction and its underlying neurobiological basis: neuroimaging evidence for the involvement of the frontal cortex. Am. J. Psychiatry **159:** 1642–1652.
20. BARDO, M.T., J.K. ROWLETT & M.J. HARRIS. 1995. Conditioned place preference using opiate and stimulant drugs: a meta-analysis. Neurosci. Biobehav. Rev. **19:** 39–51.
21. KOOB, G.F. 2000. Neurobiology of addiction. Toward the development of new therapies. Ann. N.Y. Acad. Sci. **909:** 170–185.
22. TIRELLI, E., G. LAVIOLA & W. ADRIANI. 2003. Ontogenesis of behavioral sensitization and conditioned place preference induced by psychostimulants in laboratory rodents. Neurosci. Biobehav. Rev. **27:** 163–178.
23. BARR, G.A. & G. ROSSI. 1992. Conditioned place preference from ventral tegmental injection of morphine in neonatal rats. Brain Res. Dev. Brain Res. **66:** 133–136.
24. BOLANOS, C.A. *et al.* 1996. Effects of the kappa-opioid receptor agonist U-50,488 on morphine-induced place preference conditioning in the developing rat. Eur. J. Pharmacol. **317:** 1–8.

25. LAVIOLA, G. *et al.* 1994. d-Amphetamine conditioned place preference in developing mice: relations with changes in activity and stereotypies. Behav. Neurosci. **108:** 514–524.
26. LAVIOLA, G. *et al.* 1992. Ontogeny of cocaine hyperactivity and conditioned place preference in mice. Psychopharmacology (Berl.) **107:** 221–228.
27. PRUITT, D.L., C.A. BOLANOS & S.A. MCDOUGALL. 1995. Effects of dopamine D1 and D2 receptor antagonists on cocaine-induced place preference conditioning in preweanling rats. Eur. J. Pharmacol. **283:** 125–131.
28. ADRIANI, W. & G. LAVIOLA. 2003. Elevated levels of impulsivity and reduced place conditioning with d-amphetamine: two behavioral features of adolescence in mice. Behav. Neurosci. **117:** 695–703.
29. FUDALA, P.J., K.W. TEOH & E.T. IWAMOTO. 1985. Pharmacologic characterization of nicotine-induced conditioned place preference. Pharmacol. Biochem. Behav. **22:** 237–241.
30. CARBONI, E. *et al.* 1989. 5HT3 receptor antagonists block morphine- and nicotine- but not amphetamine-induced reward. Psychopharmacology (Berl.) **97:** 175–178.
31. CALCAGNETTI, D.J. & M.D. SCHECHTER. 1994. Nicotine place preference using the biased method of conditioning. Prog. Neuropsychopharmacol. Biol. Psychiatry **18:** 925–933.
32. CLARKE, P.B. & H.C. FIBIGER. 1987. Apparent absence of nicotine-induced conditioned place preference in rats. Psychopharmacology (Berl.) **92:** 84–88.
33. JORENBY, D.E. *et al.* 1990. Aversion instead of preference learning indicated by nicotine place conditioning in rats. Psychopharmacology (Berl.) **101:** 533–538.
34. SHOAIB, M., I.P. STOLERMAN & R.C. KUMAR. 1994. Nicotine-induced place preferences following prior nicotine exposure in rats. Psychopharmacology (Berl.) **113:** 445–452.
35. CARR, G.D., H.C. FIBIGER & A.C. PHILLIPS. 1989. Conditioned place preference as a measure of drug reward. *In* Neuropharmacological Basis of Reward. J.M. Liebman & S. J. Cooper, Eds.: 264–319. Oxford Univ. Press. New York.
36. VASTOLA, B.J. *et al.* 2002. Nicotine-induced conditioned place preference in adolescent and adult rats. Physiol. Behav. **77:** 107–114.
37. BELLUZZI, J.D. *et al.* 2004. Age-dependent effects of nicotine on locomotor activity and conditioned place preference in rats. Psychopharmacology (Berl.) In press.
38. DELEMARRE-VAN DE WAAL, H.A., S.C. VAN COEVERDEN & M.T. ENGELBREGT. 2002. Factors affecting onset of puberty. Horm Res. **57**(Suppl. 2): 15–18.
39. LEVIN, E.D. *et al.* 2003. Adolescent-onset nicotine self-administration modeled in female rats. Psychopharmacology (Berl.) **169:** 141–149.
40. BATES, C. *et al.* 1999. The future of tobacco product regulation and labelling in Europe: implications for the forthcoming European Union directive. Tob. Control **8:** 225–235.
41. ROBINSON, S.F., M.J. MARKS & A.C. COLLINS. 1996. Inbred mouse strains vary in oral self-selection of nicotine. Psychopharmacology (Berl.) **124:** 332–339.
42. LAVIOLETTE, S.R. & D. VAN DER KOOY. 2003. Blockade of mesolimbic dopamine transmission dramatically increases sensitivity to the rewarding effects of nicotine in the ventral tegmental area. Mol. Psychiatry **8:** 50–59.
43. LEVITT, P. 1998. Prenatal effects of drugs of abuse on brain development. Drug Alcohol Depend. **51:** 109–125.
44. SLOTKIN, T.A. 1998. Fetal nicotine or cocaine exposure: Which one is worse? J. Pharmacol. Exp. Ther. **285:** 931–945.
45. BROIDE, R.S. *et al.* 1995. Developmental expression of alpha 7 neuronal nicotinic receptor messenger RNA in rat sensory cortex and thalamus. Neuroscience **67:** 83–94.
46. ARAMAKIS, V.B. & R. METHERATE. 1998. Nicotine selectively enhances NMDA receptor-mediated synaptic transmission during postnatal development in sensory neocortex. J. Neurosci. **18:** 8485–8495.
47. ADAMS, C.E. *et al.* 2002. Development of the alpha7 nicotinic cholinergic receptor in rat hippocampal formation. Brain Res. Dev. Brain Res. **139:** 175–187.
48. MAGGI, L. *et al.* 2003. Nicotine activates immature "silent" connections in the developing hippocampus. Proc. Natl. Acad. Sci. USA **100:** 2059–2064.
49. METHERATE, R. & C. HSIEH. 2004. Synaptic mechanisms and cholinergic regulation in auditory cortex. Prog. Brain Res. **145:** 143–156.

50. KOVACS, K.J. 1998. c-Fos as a transcription factor: a stressful (re)view from a functional map. Neurochem. Int. **33:** 287–297.
51. HOFFMAN, G.E. & D. LYO. 2002. Anatomical markers of activity in neuroendocrine systems: Are we all 'fos-ed out'? J. Neuroendocrinol. **14:** 259–268.
52. FUCHS, J.L. 1989. [125I]alpha-bungarotoxin binding marks primary sensory area developing rat neocortex. Brain Res. **501:** 223–234.
53. BINA, K.G. *et al.* 1995. Localization of alpha 7 nicotinic receptor subunit mRNA and alpha-bungarotoxin binding sites in developing mouse somatosensory thalamocortical system. J. Comp. Neurol. **363:** 321–332.
54. WINZER-SERHAN, U.H. & F.M. LESLIE. 1997. Codistribution of nicotinic acetylcholine receptor subunit alpha3 and beta4 mRNAs during rat brain development. J. Comp. Neurol. **386:** 540–554.
55. CHILDRESS, A.R. *et al.* 1999. Limbic activation during cue-induced cocaine craving. Am. J. Psychiatry **156:** 11–18.
56. CARDINAL, R.N. *et al.* 2002. Emotion and motivation: the role of the amygdala, ventral striatum, and prefrontal cortex. Neurosci. Biobehav. Rev. **26:** 321–352.
57. MADDOCK, R.J. 1999. The retrosplenial cortex and emotion: new insights from functional neuroimaging of the human brain. Trends Neurosci. **22:** 310–316.
58. BROWN, V.J. & E.M. BOWMAN. 2002. Rodent models of prefrontal cortical function. Trends Neurosci. **25:** 340–343.
59. CHAMBERS, R.A. & D.W. SELF. 2002. Motivational responses to natural and drug rewards in rats with neonatal ventral hippocampal lesions: an animal model of dual diagnosis schizophrenia. Neuropsychopharmacology **27:** 889–905.
60. BIRRELL, J.M. & V.J. BROWN. 2000. Medial frontal cortex mediates perceptual attentional set shifting in the rat. J. Neurosci. **20:** 4320–4324.
61. PANTELIS, C. *et al.* 1999. Comparison of set-shifting ability in patients with chronic schizophrenia and frontal lobe damage. Schizophr. Res. **37:** 251–270.
62. DIAS, R., T.W. ROBBINS & A.C. ROBERTS. 1996. Dissociation in prefrontal cortex of affective and attentional shifts. Nature **380:** 69–72.
63. NAGAHAMA, Y. *et al.* 2001. Dissociable mechanisms of attentional control within the human prefrontal cortex. Cereb. Cortex **11:** 85–92.
64. ERNST, M. *et al.* 2003. Decision making in adolescents with behavior disorders and adults with substance abuse. Am. J. Psychiatry **160:** 33–40.
65. BECHARA, A. *et al.* 1999. Different contributions of the human amygdala and ventromedial prefrontal cortex to decision-making. J. Neurosci. **19:** 5473–5481.
66. STEINBERG, L. *et al.* 2004. The study of developmental psychopathology during adolescence. Integrating affective neuroscience with the study of context. *In* Handbook of Developmental Psychopathology. D. Cicchetti, Ed. Wiley. New York. In press,
67. ANDERSEN, S.L. *et al.* 2000. Dopamine receptor pruning in prefrontal cortex during the periadolescent period in rats. Synapse **37:** 167–169.
68. TARAZI, F.I. & R.J. BALDESSARINI. 2000. Comparative postnatal development of dopamine D(1), D(2) and D(4) receptors in rat forebrain. Int. J. Dev. Neurosci. **18:** 29–37.
69. SCHLAGGAR, B.L. *et al.* 2002. Functional neuroanatomical differences between adults and school-age children in the processing of single words. Science **296:** 1476–1479.
70. RUBIA, K. *et al.* 2000. Functional frontalisation with age: mapping neurodevelopmental trajectories with fMRI. Neurosci. Biobehav. Rev. **24:** 13–19.
71. SLOTKIN, T.A. 2002. Nicotine and the adolescent brain: insights from an animal model. Neurotoxicol. Teratol. **24:** 369–384.
72. ADRIANI, W., S. MARCI, R. PACIFICI & G. LAVIOLA. 2002. Peculiar vulnerability to nicotine oral self-administration in mice during early adolescence. Neuropsychopharmacology **27:** 212–224.

The Adolescent Brain: Excuse versus Explanation

Comments on Part IV

ELIZABETH CAUFFMAN

Western Psychiatric Institute & Clinic, University of Pittsburgh School of Medicine, Pittsburgh, Pennsylvania 15213, USA

While the papers in this volume focus on vulnerabilities and opportunities during adolescence, when viewed in historical context they also highlight vulnerabilities and opportunities of scientific research in the field.

The chapter by Leslie *et al.*[1] describes recent advances in our understanding of the behavioral and biological changes of adolescence. Leslie describes studies in which nicotine use in rats peaks during the adolescent years, and in which nicotine has a unique effect on neural system development in adolescent rats. Such findings support the view that increased sensation seeking is a normative aspect of adolescent development, and suggest that adolescence is a critical period of brain development. The research findings from Leslie *et al.* highlight the importance of understanding the brain changes during the adolescent years, as there are numerous transformations in synaptic pruning, increased function of precortical systems, and changes in gray matter.

Such work implies that adolescence is a period of developmental vulnerability, during which the brain undergoes considerable change and may be increasingly sensitive to disruption by nicotine or other psychoactive substances. Increases in sensation-seeking behavior further increase the vulnerability of adolescents (whether rodent or human) to self-destructive behavior. Yet because brain development is not yet complete in adolescence, this period may be one of opportunity, in which steps may be taken to promote positive development.

The view of adolescence as a period of significant neurological change is surprisingly new. In the 1980s, the most commonly held view was that adolescents were victims of "raging hormones" and that this was the reason for observed increases in risk taking and antisocial behavior in adolescence. In the 1990s, this popular view was supplanted (or supplemented, perhaps) by the notion that adolescent misbehavior has its roots much earlier in childhood. Brain development was believed to be completed by the age of four, and it was suggested that the promotion of positive de-

Address for correspondence: Elizabeth Cauffman, Ph.D., Western Psychiatric Institute & Clinic, University of Pittsburgh School of Medicine, Pittsburgh, PA 15213. Voice: 412-647-4713; fax: 412-647-4751.

cauffman@upmc.edu

Address after July 1, 2004: Psychology and Social Behavior Department, School of Social Ecology, 3340 Social Ecology II, University of California at Irvine, Irvine, CA 92697.

Ann. N.Y. Acad. Sci. 1021: 160–161 (2004). © 2004 New York Academy of Sciences.
doi: 10.1196/annals.1308.020

velopment during the first four years was thus of paramount importance. In the present decade, we are learning that brain development in fact continues through adolescence and possibly beyond.

Researchers, like adolescents, encounter both vulnerabilities and opportunities. The evolution of our understanding of neurological development emphasizes our vulnerability to oversimplify what is in fact an extremely complex process. The adolescent experience is influenced by the path of previous development, by hormonal changes, by continuing neurological change, and by environmental influences. Our ever-improving understanding of the relations between these factors also brings an opportunity to more effectively promote positive developmental outcomes among youth. Instead of treating the vulnerabilities of adolescence as an *excuse* for antisocial behavior, we should view our findings as providing an *explanation* that may enable more effective means of encouraging healthy development.

REFERENCES

1. LESLIE, F.M., S.E. LOUGHLIN, R. WANG, *et al.* 2004. Adolescent development of forebrain stimulant responsiveness: insights from animal studies. Ann. N.Y. Acad. Sci. **1021:** 148–159.

The Importance of Adolescence in the Development of Nicotine Dependence

Introduction to Part V

RICHARD R. CLAYTON

Tobacco Etiology Research Network (TERN) and University of Kentucky College of Public Health, Lexington, Kentucky 40504, USA

ABSTRACT: This article sets the stage for the papers in Part V by describing the research work of the Tobacco Etiology Research Network (TERN), an ititiative of the Robert Wood Johnson Foundation. Two studies coming from this matrix include one on the acquisition of tobacco use and another on the trajectories of tobacco use among college freshman.

KEYWORDS: tobacco use; tobacco dependence

As chair of the Robert Wood Johnson Foundation's (RWJF) Research Network on the Etiology of Tobacco Dependence, a transdisciplinary research "institute without walls" commonly referred to as TERN (Tobacco Etiology Research Network), I would like to begin this session with special thanks to our host and the sponsors of the Adolescent Brain Development conference. Our host, the New York Academy of Sciences, has been an outstanding partner from the initial vetting of the concept for the meeting through the myriad of strategic and logistical decisions that have resulted in this very exciting book. Although many individuals in the New York Academy of Sciences (NYAS) have participated, we all owe special thanks to Dr. Rashid Shaikh for his leadership and amazing diplomacy in getting us from there to here. We are also deeply grateful to the Robert Wood Johnson Foundation, the National Cancer Institute, the National Institute on Drug Abuse, the National Institute of Mental Health, and the National Institute of Child Health and Human Development for their generous support and encouragement.

This meeting grew out of the very creative transdisciplinary mind and thinking of Ron Dahl, who has been thinking about having such a meeting for a long time and waiting for just the right timing and venue. We all owe Ron Dahl a debt of gratitude for his persistence in developing and bringing this meeting to fruition, and for the breadth, depth, and generosity in sharing his vision with his colleagues and friends. An exegesis of the origins of this conference can be found in the interactions among Ron Dahl and his colleagues in the MacArthur Network on Psychopathology and

Address for correspondence: Richard R. Clayton, Ph.D., Chair, Tobacco Etiology Research Network (TERN), University of Kentucky College of Public Health, 2365 Harrodsburg Rd., Suite B100, Lexington, KY 40504. Voice: 859-257-5588; fax; 859-257-5592.
clayton@pop.uky.edu

Ann. N.Y. Acad. Sci. 1021: 162–166 (2004). © 2004 New York Academy of Sciences.
doi: 10.1196/annals.1308.021

Development. The proximal origins of this conference can be found in the Behavioral Aspects of Adolescent Development (BAAD) working group of TERN consisting of Ron Dahl and Robert Balster, cochairs, and the members of the group: Linda Spear, Ann Kelley, Judy Cameron, George Koob, Kathleen Merikangas, and Richard Clayton. This group explored a number of issues that led to two small grants for pilot studies by Teri Schrochet, Ann Kelley, and Charles Landry and by Cheryl Kirstein and Linda Spear. The ideas for this conference grew out of the stimulating discussions of this working group and their reports back to the TERN group.

TERN: THE TOBACCO ETIOLOGY RESEARCH NETWORK

RWJF identified the following mandates in 1996 when it established TERN: (1) identify the major gaps in the knowledge base concerning the etiology of tobacco use and dependence; (2) design and conduct innovative transdisciplinary research to fill those gaps, research that might not be funded elsewhere; (3) recruit senior and junior scientists into the field of tobacco research; and (4) develop a comprehensive transdisciplinary research agenda for the field by "thinking out of the proverbial box."

The senior members of the scientific core group were recruited over a period of about one year. The following criteria were some of those used in selecting the senior members of the TERN scientific core group. (1) We wanted at least one representative from a range of disciplines in which tobacco etiology is a relevant topic of inquiry and an overall range from cells to society. (2) We wanted individuals who are able to move comfortably away from their data and discipline and participate in discussions with a diverse set of colleagues. (3) We wanted individuals who are very curious about how other disciplines frame and study research questions. (4) We wanted a balanced mix of individuals in which about one-half had and one-half had not conducted research on nicotine/tobacco. The goal was a group in which the "interpersonal chemistry" would lead to rapport, the development of a shared conceptual framework or model, sustained collaboration across disciplines, and creative research and publications.

TERN Senior Scientists and TERN Faculty Scholars

The TERN senior scientists are: David Abrams (Brown University), Robert Balster (Virginia Commonwealth University), Linda Collins (Penn State University), Ron Dahl (University of Pittsburgh), Brian Flay (University of Illinois, Chicago), Gary Giovino (Roswell Park Cancer Center, Buffalo), Jack Henningfield (Johns Hopkins University/Pinney Associates), George Koob (Scripps Institute), Robert McMahon (University of Washington), Kathleen Merikangas (NIMH), Mark Nichter (University of Arizona), Saul Shiffman (University of Pittsburgh), Stephen Tiffany (University of Utah), and Richard Clayton, Chair (University of Kentucky).

In 2000 11 TERN faculty scholars (assistant professors when recruited) joined TERN. They include: Craig Colder (University of Buffalo), Lisa Dierker (Wesleyan University), Lorah Dorn (Cincinnati Children's Hospital), Eric Donny (Johns Hopkins University), Thomas Eissenberg (Virginia Commonwealth University), Brian Flaherty (Penn State University), Lan Liang (University of Illinois, Chicago), Mimi

Nichter (University of Arizona), Elizabeth Richardson (Brown University), William Shadel (University of Pittsburgh), and Laura Stroud (Brown University).

The senior scientists in TERN have been working together intensively for more than six years and have developed a corporate culture that has the following characteristics: (1) a high value placed on rapport, mutual respect, and affection; (2) norms that reinforce curiosity and being willing to admit not knowing; (3) a collective willingness to challenge conventional wisdom and assumptions, even those that constitute the basis for one's own research; (4) a commitment to conducting innovative research that is near the cutting edge of the scientific precipice, rather than on safer ground. In addition, TERN made a decision to publish its work in peer-reviewed journals and to facilitate the growth of young scholars by encouraging them to be the lead authors on TERN publications. This is illustrated in the two papers that emerged out of this session.

At its second meeting, in October 1997, TERN identified the following as major goals of its efforts: (1) to identify and examine the causal pathways to trajectories of tobacco use and the emergence of dependence; (2) to develop better ways to conceptualize and measure the "emergence" of dependence; (3) to measure trajectories of tobacco use and dependence in "real" time; (4) to examine the potential importance of early episodes of use in subsequent trajectories of use and dependence; (5) to explore the multilevel nature of factors (individual level and contextual level) that could explain trajectories of tobacco use and dependence; (6) to test the salience of the stress/affect pathways to tobacco use and dependence; and (7) to emphasize the importance of connecting animal to human research.

The bottom-line question addressed by TERN is: what are the pathways to individual differences in intraindividual change that may be developmentally specific and occur in nested contexts that exist at different levels?

TWO TERN STUDIES AS PREFACE TO SESSION

As a preface to the two papers in this section, one of which uses animal subjects and the other human participants, we will report briefly on two studies conducted under the auspices of TERN. Both deal with acquisition and trajectories of tobacco use.

Acquisition of Tobacco Use

A decision was made at the second TERN meeting that perhaps the best and most elegant model for measuring the behavior of human tobacco use is the animal model, in which in order to get the drug the animal pokes its nose or presses a lever. In this study, 106 male and female Sprague-Dawley rats were trained to lever press for food. They were implanted with jugular catheters and allowed to self-administer 20, 30, 60, or 90 mcg/kg of nicotine IV for 1 hour a day. Each infusion was paired with a visual stimulus. On days 1–5 the fixed ratio of reinforcement (FR) was FR1, on days 6–8 it was FR2, and on days 9–20, it was FR5. Several of these parameters were likely to minimize individual differences.

Acquisition is a learned response acquired as individuals interact with their environment. There are time- and experience-dependent changes in the frequency and intensity of behavior. While the behavior during the period of acquisition is relatively unstable, it is lawful. Most important, acquisition of drug taking behavior is a process, one that has been essentially ignored with regard to nicotine use among animals.

The findings are instructive. First, there were large individual differences in the trajectories of acquisition and use of nicotine. Some start high and trend downward, some start low and trend upward, some are largely linear, and many are curvilinear. Second, there is less variability and dispersion as the amount consumed (20, 30, 60, and 90 mck/kg) increases. Third, and perhaps most important from TERN's perspective, these data have been analyzed using latent growth modeling techniques from the social and behavioral sciences rather than ANOVA, producing a much more robust understanding of acquisition in these participants (see Donny et al.[1] and Lanza et al.[2]). From a translational perspective, these data and their analysis are important because they shed light on the process of acquisition—a process that takes place largely during adolescence in Western countries. Other papers in other sessions (see the paper by Leslie et al., this volume[3]) highlight the fact that periadolescent rats have a differential responsivity and reactivity to nicotine than do adult rats.

The Web-Based Study of Trajectories of Tobacco Use among College Freshmen

The UpTERN study was an attempt to study tobacco use trajectories in as close to "real time" as possible, the goal being a marked departure from more epidemiologically focused studies in which the behavior measured is a self-report of (1) any use in the past 30 days, (2) the number of days in the past 30 days that cigarettes were used, and (3) the number of cigarettes used per day in the past 30 days.

In this study, 4690 (80%) students in the entering freshmen class of 2002 at Purdue University completed a screening questionnaire during their summer day on campus before beginning their first year of college. This is the day for orientation and for receiving their fall-semester schedule. From these, 2001 freshmen who had some self-reported prior exposure to cigarettes, from less than a puff to more frequent use, were identified. Some 912 of these students agreed to participate in the year-long study. It involved completing a 45-minute baseline questionnaire and two longer questionnaires at the end of the first semester and at the end of the freshman year. Each week for 35 weeks, a period covering 245 days, these students were asked to complete a web-based questionnaire detailing their use of cigarettes, alcohol, and marijuana for the previous 7 days in addition to other questions (i.e., nicotine dependence measured weekly using Shiffman's NDSS [nicotine dependence symptom scale], affect, stress). On a once-a-month basis, we rotated question modules that dealt with physical activity, romantic relationships and friendships, sleep habits and body image, and stressful events.

The response rate was phenomenal: 87% of students provided weekly, and thus daily, data for the previous 7 days during the 29 weeks they were on campus; 73% provided data during the 6 weeks they were off campus—leading to a 87% response rate for all 35 weeks of the study.

It is amazing what one can find if the data are this dense. Several findings from early analyses deserve mention. First, each week there is an uptick in use that begins on Thursday, with an even larger uptick for Friday and Saturday. Tobacco use is relatively stable and lower on Sunday, Monday, Tuesday, and Wednesday. We do not yet know whether Thursday is the beginning of the weekend or just somewhat different from weekdays. Second, it is clear that smoking is proximally (and probably other ways as well) related to drinking. On the days that smoking was reported, the average proportion of cigarettes smoked while drinking was over 50% on Friday and Saturday, 46% for females and 36% for males on Thursdays, between 15% and 17% for males Sunday, Monday, Tuesday, and Wednesday, and between 16% and 22% on those days for females. Third, when we looked at each day during the first 22 weeks of the freshman year, it was possible to address the following question: what is the highest Thursday with regard to smoking. Not surprisingly, it happened to be Halloween. When we looked at the lowest smoking day during the first 22 weeks, it was Christmas Day; the highest day for smoking was 7 days later, New Year's Eve. Smoking increased during final-examination week of the first semester. Previously we had hypothesized that this reflects the desired benefits of nicotine on tracking (i.e., blocking out peripheral sights and sounds). We now believe it more likely that some students are finishing their exams early and partying a bit before they go home. This is a hypothesis that we will be testing using the daily data on trajectories of tobacco, alcohol, and marijuana use.

The above should provide you with some sense of the research work of TERN.

THE IMPORTANCE OF ADOLESCENCE IN THE DEVELOPMENT OF NICOTINE DEPENDENCE

The papers in this session were presented by two distinguished scientists and represent work funded at least partially by TERN. The first paper, Nicotine Withdrawal in Adolescent and Adult Rats, was presented by George Koob of Scripps Institute. The second paper, Individual and Contextual Influences on Adolescent Smoking, was presented by Robin Mermelstein of the University of Illinois, Chicago. In keeping with TERN's commitment to provide opportunities for younger scholars to take the lead on publications, the first author of the nicotine withdrawal paper is Laura O'Dell of Scripps; the first author of the individual and contextual influences paper is Lindsey Turner.

The respondent for this session is Kathleen Merikangas, a widely recognized genetic epidemiologist from the National Institute on Mental Health.

We in TERN are pleased to have been a sponsor of the overall conference that led to this volume and to have had the opportunity to organize this session of the NYAS conference Adolescent Brain Development.

REFERENCES

1. DONNY, E.C., S.T. LANZA, R.L. BALSTER, et al. Using growth models to relate acquisition of nicotine self-administration to break point and nicotinic receptor binding. Drug Alcohol Depend. In press.
2. LANZA, S.T., E.C. DONNY, L.M. COLLINS & R.L. BALSTER. Analyzing the acquisition of drug self-administration using growth curve models. Drug and Alcohol Depend. In press.
3. LESLIE, F.M. S.E. LOUGHLIN, R. WANG, et al. 2004. Adolescent development of forebrain stimulant responsiveness: insights from animal studies. Ann. N.Y. Acad. Sci. **1021:** 148–159.

Nicotine Withdrawal in Adolescent and Adult Rats

LAURA E. O'DELL, ADRIE W. BRUIJNZEEL, SANDY GHOZLAND,
ATHINA MARKOU, AND GEORGE F. KOOB

*Department of Neuropharmacology, The Scripps Research Institute,
La Jolla, California 92037, USA*

ABSTRACT: Previous research with animal models has demonstrated that adolescent rats display heightened sensitivity to the reinforcing and stimulant effects of nicotine relative to adult rats. Little work has focused on the response of adolescent rats to measures of nicotine withdrawal. To test the hypothesis that adolescent rats may be differentially sensitive to withdrawal relative to their adult counterparts, the present study was designed to compare precipitated withdrawal in adolescent and adult rats following chronic nicotine administration. Adult and adolescent rats were prepared with subcutaneous osmotic minipumps that delivered either saline or nicotine (9 mg/kg per day, salt; $N=12$ per group). All rats were challenged with the nicotinic receptor antagonist mecamylamine (1.5 mg/kg) on day 7 of chronic nicotine treatment. Twenty minutes after the injection, overt somatic signs of withdrawal (i.e., eye blinks, writhes, body shakes, teeth chatter, gasps, and ptosis) were recorded for 10 min. Adult rats were observed on postnatal day 73–77, and adolescent rats were tested on postnatal day 36–40. The results revealed a robust increase in mecamylamine-induced withdrawal signs in adult rats receiving chronic nicotine relative to adult rats receiving saline. In contrast, mecamylamine did not precipitate withdrawal signs in adolescent rats receiving chronic nicotine. These results indicate that there is decreased sensitivity to the somatic aspects of nicotine withdrawal in adolescent rats that may maximize the reinforcing effects of nicotine during adolescence by minimizing the aversive effects of abstinence.

KEYWORDS: adolescence; adult; rats; nicotine; withdrawal; mecamylamine

INTRODUCTION

Chronic nicotine use produces a withdrawal syndrome in humans that is of motivational significance in maintaining nicotine dependence. The syndrome is comprised of "physical" or somatic and affective components. The most common somatic symptoms include bradycardia, gastrointestinal discomfort, increased appe-

Address for correspondence: George F. Koob, Ph.D., Department of Neuropharmacology, CVN-7, The Scripps Research Institute, 10550 North Torrey Pines Rd., La Jolla, CA 92037. Voice: 858-784-7062; fax: 858-784-7405.
gkoob@scripps.edu

Ann. N.Y. Acad. Sci. 1021: 167–174 (2004). © 2004 New York Academy of Sciences.
doi: 10.1196/annals.1308.022

tite, and the affective symptoms primarily include craving, depression, irritability, anxiety, difficulty concentrating, and restlessness. It is well documented that these negative effects contribute to relapse.[1,2] A better understanding of the neurobiological mechanisms that contribute to nicotine withdrawal may lead to pharmacological treatments that alleviate withdrawal, and thus, facilitate abstinence.

Chronic nicotine administration in rats produces overt somatic symptoms of withdrawal that have been widely characterized in several laboratories.[3-6] Somatic signs of nicotine withdrawal in rats include abdominal constrictions, facial fasciculation, eye blinks, and ptosis. The emergence of the nicotine withdrawal syndrome in rats is observed after the cessation of nicotine administration (spontaneous withdrawal) or nicotinic receptor antagonist administration (precipitated withdrawal). Interestingly, the somatic signs of the nicotine withdrawal syndrome resemble those seen in opiate withdrawal, and can also be precipitated in nicotine-dependent rats using opiate antagonists as reported by Malin *et al.*[7] (however, see Watkins[8]). Support for the predictive validity of this animal model of nicotine withdrawal is provided by the finding that both the somatic and affective aspects of nicotine withdrawal are reversed by bupropion,[9] a compound that displays clinical efficacy in the treatment of nicotine dependence.[10] In addition, while the somatic signs of withdrawal are not a direct measure of changes in the brain motivational systems that drive nicotine dependence, they are sensitive to many of the same neuropharmacological agents as the affective aspects of withdrawal.[9-11] As such, somatic withdrawal syndrome provides an important index for exploring mechanisms associated with the development of dependence.

Nicotine is one of the most widely used drugs during adolescence. Although it has been argued that nicotine dependence in humans develops only after years of heavy daily smoking, recent clinical studies have observed high levels of nicotine dependence in adolescent smokers despite low cigarette exposure.[12,13] There are several factors that lead to adolescent smoking, including, but not limited to, increased risk taking, novelty seeking, and emphasis on peer interactions.[14] However, the mechanisms that lead to nicotine dependence in adolescent smokers are presently unclear.

A rat model of somatic signs of nicotine withdrawal can be used to compare physiological and behavioral differences at various stages of mammalian development. Most behavioral and physiological systems reach maximal maturation by postnatal day (PND) 60 in rats. There is general agreement that the prototypic age range for adolescence in rats conservatively ranges from PND 28–42.[14] This age range reflects a period during which age-specific behavioral discontinuities from younger and older animals are most evident.

The goal of the present study was to compare nicotine withdrawal in adult and adolescent rats. We used a model of precipitated nicotine withdrawal based on previous observations that reliable and high levels of overt somatic signs of withdrawal are observed after nicotinic receptor antagonist administration in adult rats treated chronically with nicotine. Adolescent and adult rats were challenged with the nicotinic receptor antagonist mecamylamine after 7 days of nicotine or saline administration via subcutaneous osmotic minipumps. Overt somatic signs of nicotine withdrawal were examined 20 min later during a 10-min observation period.

MATERIALS AND METHODS

Animals

Male Wistar rats (Charles River) were housed in a humidity- and temperature-controlled (22°C) vivarium on a 12-h light/dark cycle (lights off at 8 AM). This experiment was conducted in two replications with 6 animals per group for each replication (final N=12 per group). The adolescent rats arrived in the laboratory on PND 23 or 26, and the adult rats arrived on PND 60 or 64. The animals were group housed with 3–4 rats of the same developmental age group per cage. After arrival in the laboratory, the rats were handled and weighed each day during the 6-day acclimation period. Animals had *ad libitum* access to food and water throughout the course of the study except during the 10-min observation periods. All procedures were conducted in strict adherence to the *National Institutes of Health Guide for the Care and Use of Laboratory Animals*. Animal facilities and experimental protocols were in accordance with the Association for the Assessment and Accreditation of Laboratory Animal Care, and were approved by the Institute's Animal Welfare Committee.

Drugs

Nicotine tartrate and the noncompetitive nicotinic receptor antagonist mecamylamine hydrochloride were used (both purchased from Research Biochemicals International, Natick, MA). Drug doses refer to the salt form of the compound with the base in parentheses. All intraperitoneal mecamylamine injections were administered in a volume of 1 ml/kg according to body weight.

Surgical Preparation with Subcutaneous Osmotic Minipumps

Rats were anesthetized with an isoflurane/oxygen mixture (1–2% isoflurane) and prepared with Alzet osmotic minipumps (model 2ML2, 14-day; Durect Corporation, Palo Alto, CA) placed subcutaneously. The adolescent rats were surgically prepared with minipumps on PND 29 or 32, and the adults were prepared on PND 66 or 70. The minipumps were placed on the back of the animal parallel to the spine. The pumps were filled with either physiological saline or nicotine tartrate solution. The concentration of the nicotine tartrate salt solution was adjusted according to animal weight, resulting in ~9 mg/kg per day (3.16 mg/kg per day free base). There were four groups with 12 rats in each group (adolescent nicotine, adolescent saline, adult nicotine, and adult saline). The surgical wound was closed with 9-mm stainless steel wound clips (Beckton Dickson Primary Care Diagnostics, Sparks, MD) and treated with an antibiotic ointment.

Ratings of Mecamylamine-Induced Somatic Signs

The animals were tested for mecamylamine-induced precipitated withdrawal 7 days after minipump preparation. Subjects were habituated to the observation room and containers 3 times for 10 min during 3 days prior to the antagonist administration. The observation containers consisted of clear plastic cylindrical containers (30 × 29 cm) in which the animal could move freely. The adolescent rats were tested on PND 36 or 40, and the adult rats were tested on PND 73 or 77. On the test day, each

rat received an injection of mecamylamine (1.5 mg/kg, ip) and was placed in the observation container for 20 min. After 20 min elapsed, the frequency of precipitated
signs of nicotine withdrawal was recorded during the subsequent 10-min observation period. The signs recorded were eye blinks, body shakes, chews, cheek tremors,
escape attempts, foot licks, gasps, writhes, headshakes, ptosis, teeth chattering, and
yawns. These signs were derived from a standard checklist of opiate withdrawal
signs developed by Malin et al.[5] and used widely in our laboratory.[4,8] Multiple successive counts of any sign required a distinct pause between episodes. If ptosis was
present continuously, then it was only counted once per minute. The total number of
somatic signs per 10-min observation period was defined as the sum of the number
of individual occurrences of the above-mentioned withdrawal signs. One observer
was used that was unaware of whether the animal was treated with nicotine or saline,
and reliable measures were observed between the two replication studies.

Statistical Analyses

A two-way analysis of variance (ANOVA) was performed on the total number of
withdrawal signs with group (adolescent versus adult) and treatment (saline versus
nicotine) as between subjects factors. Subsequent post hoc analyses were performed
using the Fisher's PLSD Test. The total number of eye blinks was also analyzed separately to verify the pattern of results observed with the overall number of somatic
signs measures.

RESULTS

Mecamylamine administration produced a significant increase in overt somatic
signs of withdrawal in adult rats treated with nicotine relative to all other groups (see
FIG. 1). A significant age X treatment interaction effect [$F(1,44) = 11.1, P < .002$]
was observed, with adult rats receiving nicotine displaying significantly more precipitated signs relative to all other groups (Fisher's Test, $P < .001$). After mecamylamine administration, there was no difference in the signs exhibited by adolescent
rats treated chronically with nicotine or saline. A significant age X treatment interaction effect also was observed with the analyses on eye blinks [$F(1,44) = 6.1, P <
.02$], with adult rats receiving nicotine displaying significantly more eye blinks rel-
ative to all other groups (Fisher's Test, $P < .001$).

DISCUSSION

This study is consistent with previous work demonstrating that somatic signs of
nicotine withdrawal are precipitated in adult rats chronically treated with nicotine
when injected with a nicotinic receptor antagonist.[3,6,15,16] The present study extends
these previous findings by demonstrating that a nicotinic receptor antagonist does not
precipitate somatic signs of nicotine withdrawal in adolescent rats chronically treated
with nicotine using the same nicotine and antagonist doses and duration of exposure
to nicotine used in previous studies with adult rats. This conclusion is based on both
the measure of total signs of withdrawal, and on the eye blink measure.

Previous developmental studies in rats have found that adolescent rats are more sensitive to the behavioral effects of nicotine. For example, adolescent rats exhibit nearly twice as much nicotine intake in self-administration procedures relative to their adult counterparts.[17] Adolescent rats also display place preference at a low dose of nicotine that is ineffective in adult rats.[18] Enhanced sensitivity to nicotine in adolescent rats has also been observed using behavioral measures of activity.[19,20]

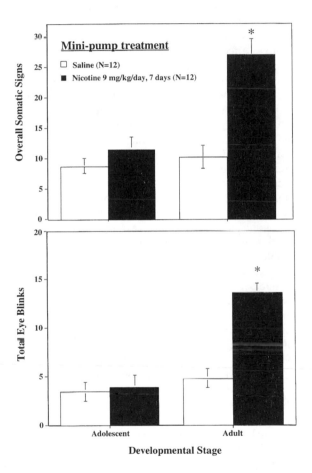

FIGURE 1. Mean total (±SEM) somatic signs of precipitated nicotine withdrawal (**top panel**) and eye blinks (**bottom panel**) in adolescent and adult rats receiving nicotine (*solid bars*) or saline (*open bars*) via subcutaneous osmotic minipumps for 7 days. All rats received mecamylamine (1.5 mg/kg, ip), and 20 min later overt somatic signs of nicotine withdrawal were recorded during a 10-min observation period. Mecamylamine precipitated robust somatic signs of nicotine withdrawal in adult rats; however, this effect was not observed in adolescent rats. The eye blinks measurement confirmed the pattern of results observed with total somatic signs of nicotine withdrawal. *Asterisks* (*) indicate a significant difference relative to all other groups (*P* < .001).

Nicotine exposure during adolescence also appears to lead to enhanced anxiolytic effects, as observed in the open field test,[21] and there is evidence that the adolescent brain is particularly sensitive to nicotine-induced alterations in cell signaling and synaptic function.[22,23] Collectively, these studies demonstrate that adolescence represents a period of enhanced sensitivity to the reinforcing and stimulant effects of nicotine.

The findings from this study demonstrate that adolescent rats do not exhibit overt somatic signs of nicotine withdrawal, at least under the conditions described. Based on the existing literature that adolescent rats appear to be more sensitive to the reinforcing and stimulant effects of nicotine and the present findings, it appears that adolescent rats are more sensitive to the positive effects of nicotine exposure and less sensitive to the negative effects of nicotine withdrawal. Support for this notion is also provided by the results from alcohol studies demonstrating that adolescent rats display place preference for doses of alcohol that are ineffective or aversive in older rats.[24] Additionally, adolescent rats display reduced sensitivity to the motor-impairing and sedative consequences of alcohol.[25] Dampened sensitivity to the negative consequences of drug use may contribute to heightened drug intake, a notion supported by the finding that alcohol-preferring rats are less sensitive to the sedative–hypnotic effects of alcohol and develop tolerance more quickly to high-dose alcohol compared to nonpreferring animals.[26]

There are well-documented changes in nicotinic receptors that are believed to contribute to precipitated withdrawal following chronic nicotine administration in adult rats (see review articles[27,28]). Developmental differences in nicotinic receptors, drug metabolism, and metabolic tolerance might contribute to the decreased nicotine withdrawal signs exhibited by adolescent rats compared to adult rats. It does not appear that a simple hypothesis of decreased nicotinic-receptor function explains our findings, because adolescent nicotine exposure elicits lasting alterations in synaptic signaling that intensify and persist during withdrawal.[22] Decreased nicotinic-receptor binding has been observed over the course of ontogeny in the rat.[29] Enhanced metabolism of nicotine may also contribute to the lack of withdrawal following chronic nicotine in adolescent rats, a notion supported by the finding that alcohol metabolism and tolerance are heightened in adolescent rats.[14] Future studies will be needed to assess whether changes in specific subtypes of nicotinic receptors and/or function contribute to the developmental effect observed in the present study.

Clinical studies have found that adolescents from age 12–18 years display a number of behaviors that may contribute to drug-seeking behavior at an early age. For example, adolescents display heightened emphasis on peer interactions, novelty seeking, and risk-taking behavior.[14] Although these behaviors can be seen as adaptive for establishing independence from the family unit, they often translate into experimentation with drugs of abuse. The present study suggests that the negative effects of withdrawal are less evident during adolescence. This finding in rats is supported widely by clinical and anecdotal evidence that negative effects of drugs of abuse, such as "hangover," are less prominent during adolescence. Taken together, the observation of enhanced sensitivity to the reinforcing effects of nicotine and resistance to the negative effects of nicotine withdrawal suggest that both of these factors contribute to the development of tobacco-smoking behavior in adolescents.

ACKNOWLEDGMENTS

This research was supported by the Robert Wood Johnson Foundation Tobacco Etiology Research Network, the Tobacco-Related Disease Research Program of the state of California (12RT-0099 to GFK, 11FT-0112 to AWB, and 12RT-0231 to AM), and the National Institute on Drug Abuse (DA11946 to AM). The authors thank Mr. Michael Arends for his excellent editorial assistance in the preparation of this manuscript. This is publication number 16341-NP from The Scripps Research Institute.

REFERENCES

1. HUGHES, J.R., S.W. GUST, *et al.* 1991. Symptoms of tobacco withdrawal. A replication and extension. Arch. Gen. Psychiatry **48**: 52–59.
2. HUGHES, J.R. 2001. Why does smoking so often produce dependence? A somewhat different view. Tob. Control **10**: 62–64.
3. HILDEBRAND, B.E., G.G. NOMIKOS, *et al.* 1997. Behavioral manifestations of the nicotine abstinence syndrome in the rat: peripheral versus central mechanisms. Psychopharmacology **129**: 348–356.
4. SKJEI, K.L. & A. MARKOU. 2003. Effects of repeated withdrawal episodes, nicotine dose, and duration of nicotine exposure on the severity and duration of nicotine withdrawal in rats. Psychopharmacology **168**: 280–292.
5. MALIN, D.H., J.R. LAKE, *et al.* 1992. Rodent model of nicotine abstinence syndrome. Pharmacol. Biochem. Behav. **43**: 779–784.
6. WATKINS, S.S., G.F. KOOB, *et al.* 2000. Neural mechanisms underlying nicotine addiction: acute positive reinforcement and withdrawal. Nicotine Tob. Res. **2**: 19–37.
7. MALIN, D.H., J.R. LAKE, *et al.* 1993. Naloxone precipitates nicotine abstinence syndrome in the rat. Psychopharmacology **112**: 339–342.
8. WATKINS, S.S., L. STINUS, *et al.* 2000. Reward and somatic changes during precipitated nicotine withdrawal in rats: centrally and peripherally mediated effects. J. Pharmacol. Exp. Ther. **292**: 1053–1064.
9. CRYAN, J.F., A.W. BRUIJNZEEL, *et al.* 2003. Bupropion enhances brain reward function and reverses the affective and somatic aspects of nicotine withdrawal in the rat. Psychopharmacology **168**: 347–358.
10. ROSE, J.E. 1996. Nicotine addiction and treatment. Annu. Rev. Med. **47**: 493–507.
11. SEMENOVA, S. & A. MARKOU. 2003. Clozapine treatment attenuated somatic and affective signs of nicotine and amphetamine withdrawal in subsets of rats exhibiting hyposensitivity to the initial effects of clozapine. Biol. Psychiatry **54**: 1249–1264.
12. HRUBA, D., L. ZACHOVALOVA, *et al.* 2003. Evaluation of the level of nicotine dependence among adolescent smokers. Cent. Eur. J. Public Health **11**: 163–168.
13. O'LOUGHLIN, J., J. DIFRANZA, *et al.* 2003. Nicotine-dependence symptoms are associated with smoking frequency in adolescents. Am. J. Prev. Med. **25**: 219–225.
14. SPEAR, L.P. 2000. The adolescent brain and age-related behavioral manifestations. Neurosci. Biobehav. Rev. **24**: 417–463.
15. MALIN, D.H., J.R. LAKE, *et al.* 1994. The nicotinic antagonist mecamylamine precipitates nicotine abstinence syndrome in the rat. Psychopharmacology **115**: 180–184.
16. MARKOU, A. & N.E. PATERSON. 2001. The nicotinic antagonist methyllycaconitine has differential effects on nicotine self-administration and nicotine withdrawal in the rat. Nicotine Tob. Res. **3**: 361–373.
17. LEVIN, E.D., A.H. REZVANI, *et al.* 2003. Adolescent-onset nicotine self-administration modeled in female rats. Psychopharmacology **169**: 141–149.
18. VASTOLA, B.J., L.A. DOUGLAS, *et al.* 2002. Nicotine-induced conditioned place preference in adolescent and adult rats. Physiol. Behav. **77**: 107–114.

19. FARADAY, M.M., B.M. ELLIOTT, et al. 2001. Adult vs. adolescent rats differ in biobehavioral responses to chronic nicotine administration. Pharmacol. Biochem. Behav. **70**: 475–489.
20. FARADAY, M.M., B.M. ELLIOTT, et al. 2003. Adolescent and adult male rats differ in sensitivity to nicotine's activity effects. Pharmacol. Biochem. Behav. **74**: 917–931.
21. SLAWECKI, C.J., A. GILDER, et al. 2003. Increased anxiety-like behavior in adult rats exposed to nicotine as adolescents. Pharmacol. Biochem. Behav. **75**: 355–361.
22. ABREU-VILLACA, Y., F.J. SEIDLER, et al. 2003. Impact of adolescent nicotine exposure on adenylyl cyclase-mediated cell signaling: enzyme induction, neurotransmitter-specific effects, regional selectivities, and the role of withdrawal. Brain Res. **988**: 164–172.
23. SLOTKIN, T.A. 2002. Nicotine and the adolescent brain: insights from an animal model. Neurotoxicol. Teratol. **24**: 369–384.
24. PHILPOT, R.M., K.A. BADANICH, et al. 2003. Place conditioning: age-related changes in the rewarding and aversive effects of alcohol. Alcohol Clin. Exp. Res. **27**: 593–599.
25. SILVERI, M.M. & L.P. SPEAR. 1998. Decreased sensitivity to the hypnotic effects of ethanol early in ontogeny. Alcohol Clin. Exp. Res. **22**: 670–676.
26. MCBRIDE, W.J. & T.K. LI. 1998. Animal models of alcoholism: neurobiology of high alcohol-drinking behavior in rodents. Crit. Rev. Neurobiol. **12**: 339–369.
27. WONNACOTT, S. 1990. The paradox of nicotinic acetylcholine receptor upregulation by nicotine. Trends Pharmacol. Sci. **11**: 216–219.
28. DANI, J.A. & S. HEINEMANN. 1996. Molecular and cellular aspects of nicotine abuse. Neuron **16**: 905–908.
29. ZHANG, X., G. WAHLSTROM, et al. 1990. Influence of development and aging on nicotinic receptor subtypes in rodent brain. Int. J. Dev. Neurosci. **8**: 715–721.

Individual and Contextual Influences on Adolescent Smoking

LINDSEY TURNER, ROBIN MERMELSTEIN, AND BRIAN FLAY

Health Research and Policy Centers, University of Illinois at Chicago, Chicago, Illinois 60608, USA

ABSTRACT: Cigarette smoking among adolescents remains one of the most important public health challenges. Despite much attention to research on the etiology of smoking, notably the examination of factors that differentiate adolescent smokers from never smokers, much less is known about factors that predict the development of dependence once an adolescent tries smoking. This paper reviews individual and contextual influences on the progression of smoking among adolescents. Highlights include a consideration of multiple levels of influence, from intra-individual factors, such as genetics, demographics, temperament and comorbidities, to social influences, such as families and peers, to the more macro, societal/cultural levels of influence, including advertising and tobacco-related policies. More recent work examining microcontextual influences through the use of Ecological Momentary Assessments is also discussed. Finally, the need to consider both developmental and transdisciplinary approaches to understanding the development of nicotine dependence in adolescents is emphasized.

KEYWORDS: adolescent; smoking; social; transdisciplinary

THE PROBLEM OF ADOLESCENT SMOKING

Cigarette smoking among adolescents remains one of the most important public health challenges. The prevalence of cigarette smoking among high school students in the U.S. increased during the 1990s, reached its peak during 1996–1997, and then began to gradually decline.[1] Despite this decline, the prevalence of adolescent smoking remains unacceptably high. The majority of youth still try smoking (57.4% by 12th grade[1]), but only a subset of those adolescents are at risk for progressing to regular daily smoking and to nicotine dependence. In 2002, 17.7% of 10th graders and 26.7% of 12th graders reported having smoked in the past month; 16.9% of 12th graders smoked daily, and alarmingly, 9.1% of 12th graders smoked at least half a pack daily,[1] a rate which suggests that nicotine dependence may already be developing in these youth. By the age of 18, almost all of those who will continue to smoke as adults have initiated smoking.[2]

Address for correspondence: Lindsey Turner, Ph.D., Health Research and Policy Centers, 1747 W. Roosevelt Road, Room 558, Chicago, IL 60608. Voice: 312-413-0479; fax: 312-996-2703.

lindseyt@uic.edu

Ann. N.Y. Acad. Sci. 1021: 175–197 (2004). © 2004 New York Academy of Sciences.
doi: 10.1196/annals.1308.023

Clearly, adolescence is the time to focus efforts on preventing and reducing smoking. As with adult smoking, adolescent smoking does not occur in a vacuum, and a variety of individual and situational factors influence adolescent behavior. While much has been learned about the various influences on adolescent smoking (e.g., Ref. 2), many fundamental questions remain unanswered, such as why some youth experiment and stop smoking, whereas others experiment and progress to dependence, or how contexts may influence these different longitudinal patterns of smoking. Our goal with this paper is to briefly highlight research in the areas of individual and contextual influences on adolescent smoking, and to suggest some promising areas of inquiry to supplement the existing knowledge base. We begin with an outline of the types of influence that will be considered, followed by a discussion of methodological issues, an overview of several known sources of influence, and suggestions for future research directions.

LEVELS OF INFLUENCE

We base our discussion of influences on the three ultimate causes of behavior proposed in the Theory of Triadic Influence (TTI),[3–5] which, as with other integrative models, emphasizes the importance of the big picture. As applied to smoking, this includes a consideration of the broad social environment in which smoking occurs, the more immediate social context surrounding smoking, the individual's characteristics or dispositions, the behavior of smoking itself, and the interaction among these forces.

For the purpose of this review, we consider three streams of influences: individual or person-level variables, immediate social or normative influences, and broader environmental and cultural influences. Genetic, biological, and fairly stable personality variables (such as temperament) fall within the individual stream of influence, as do demographic characteristics such as gender, ethnicity, and age. Influences from the TTI's social/normative stream represent the situations immediately surrounding adolescent smoking. Figuring prominently at this level are parent and peer influences, including tobacco use, attitudes, and characteristics of these important social relationships, all of which lead primarily to social normative beliefs. Finally, we consider broader environmental and cultural contextual influences, such as community characteristics, media influences, and legislative/policy issues. These lead primarily to attitudes toward smoking.

All three streams of influence start at the distal levels and contribute to specific affective/cognitive constructs at the more proximal level (self efficacy, social normative beliefs and attitudes, respectively), and each of these then contributes to determining intentions. Given the complex interaction between various levels of influence and the need to consider these reciprocal relationships, there is some overlap in discussion of these influences. For example, social context, not just the broader environmental/cultural context, shapes attitudes and expectancies. Genetic and biological forces influence the interaction between children and their parents. Even demographic variables, included in many studies, but examined in intricate detail in fewer, are highly complex and interact with context to influence behaviors such as smoking. The complexity of the etiology of adolescent smoking has been noted in many prior reviews (e.g., Ref. 4), and we again emphasize the importance of longitudinal, theoretically driven investigations that examine the complex causal links, interactions, and reciprocal relationships between various sources of influence.

METHODOLOGICAL ISSUES

Analytical Considerations

An examination of the contexts of adolescents' lives presents several analytic challenges, including the joint consideration of multiple levels of influence. As noted by Darling and Cumsille,[6] adolescents are inherently embedded within a family context, with family occurring in a diversity of forms and shapes. Families present many potential sources of influence, a number of which are interdependent. For example, there is a high degree of association between maternal smoking, paternal smoking, and sibling smoking, all of which may influence adolescent smoking independently or conjointly. The interdependence between observations gathered within families presents methodological and statistical challenges for disentangling these effects. In statistical analysis, failure to account for the clustering of observations within clusters (i.e., families, schools, communities) often violates assumptions of independence and leads to inappropriate conclusions. Techniques to adjust for clustered data have been developed under a variety of names, including hierarchical linear modeling,[7,8] multilevel models,[9] and random-effects models.[10,11] Some programs also include features allowing for structural-modeling approaches for testing latent-variable models within a mixed model framework.[12,13] Such approaches not only allow for more appropriate testing of nested data, but also for longitudinal data, where multiple observations are gathered from adolescents over a period of time. Growth-curve and mixture modeling also provide sophisticated tools for examining change over time.[14,15] The ever increasing familiarity of researchers with these approaches and the software for implementing them promises to dramatically increase the ability to model and understand the complex links between adolescent behavior and the surrounding context.

Understanding Mechanisms

A number of studies have examined differences between smokers and nonsmokers on a wide diversity of variables. Even more studies have examined possible predictors of subsequent smoking behavior. While some test complex theoretical models including specific direct and indirect paths (e.g., Ref. 16), many studies just compare the predictive utility among a group of variables. Although such direct-effects models are helpful in some regards, many conflicting results are apparent. As detailed in the following section, some studies find effects for gender, while others do not; some studies find effects for negative affect, while others do not. Differences in both study methodology and sample characteristics may well lead to disparate findings. For example, demographic variables may be moderator variables; that is, the extent of influence other variables exert on smoking outcomes are dependent on the moderator variable.[17] Furthermore, predictor relationships can be complex and include both direct effects, indirect effects, and mediated effects.[18] For our discussion, we emphasize the importance of considering such relationships, and testing models based on theoretical mechanisms of action.

Risk Models versus Trajectories and Transitions

Smoking in adolescence is a dynamic behavior; however, many studies have examined smoking behavior through cross-sectional slices. A broad literature examines the differences between youth who smoke and youth who do not smoke, and while this type of work is enormously useful in understanding descriptively how adolescent smokers differ from their non-smoking peers, these characterizations are less useful for understanding the very important question of what predicts escalation of smoking habits. Given that one goal of public health efforts is to prevent the escalation of smoking and the development of regular smoking and nicotine dependence, it is important to understand not only how adolescents who smoke differ from their never-smoking peers, but more importantly, to understand how adolescents who briefly try smoking but do not progress to regular smoking differ from those who progress to regular smoking and nicotine dependence.

PROGRESSIVE STAGES OF ADOLESCENT SMOKING

Adolescent smoking is not a"take it once and hooked for life" phenomenon. Instead, adolescent smoking is often conceptualized as progressing through a series of stages.[2,19,20] Mayhew and colleagues[20] identify six stages of adolescent smoking. The first, nonsmoking stage, is comprised of two substages, one in which the youth expresses no intention to smoke and the second, contemplation/preparation, in which the youth starts to consider smoking. Most youth go beyond the contemplation stage to trying. Subsequent stages include experimentation (smoking only occasionally, less than 100 cigarettes in lifetime); regular smoking (smoking in the past week or month and greater than 100 cigarettes in lifetime); and daily smoking and dependence.

The final stage of smoking development is nicotine dependence or addiction,[21] which occurs with the development of an internally regulated need for nicotine. Dependence is characterized by three critical factors: (a) tolerance, (b) the experience of unpleasant physiological sensations (withdrawal symptoms) upon quitting, and (c) a high probability of resuming use in the presence of challenges weeks, months, and even years after quitting. Although it has recently been suggested that among adults, tolerance is not associated with dependence, chronic tolerance appears to develop rapidly among adolescent experimenters, and dependence may soon follow.[22] Little is yet known about the developmental course of nicotine dependence in adolescence, including the patterning of symptoms or the time course from experimentation to regular use to dependence.

Researchers have only recently acknowledged that adolescents can and do become nicotine dependent;[23–25] however, the conceptualization and measurement of nicotine dependence among adolescents remain a matter of discussion. Researchers have also begun to think of nicotine dependence as a multidimensional, dynamic process (e.g., Ref. 23), and that there may be subtypes of nicotine dependence characterized by different configurations of symptoms and different trajectories of acquisition,[26] such as those who start young and rapidly accelerate or those who have a more slow and steady pace in their escalation patterns. Identifying individual and contextual differences that influence the pattern and rate of progression across stages of use and into dependence may be key to identifying youth who are at high risk for long-term smoking and negative health consequences.

TIME PROGRESSION THROUGH STAGES AND INFLUENCES ON THE COURSE OF PROGRESSION

Relatively little is also known about the time course or progression of smoking behavior after initial trials. The time interval between initial trying to regular use averages 2–3 years, with considerable variation.[27] In one prospective study, approximately half of those who experimented with smoking were smoking on a daily basis within a year.[28] Fergusson and Horwood[29] found that the rate of acceleration varied with age—rates of transition were higher in middle adolescence (e.g., 14–16 years) than in early adolescence (10–12 years). There appears to be a fair amount of both stability and forward movement among the occasional smoking group, but little de-escalation.

One of the more recent advances in understanding the progression of youth smoking has been the identification of trajectories of smoking or differential patterns of onset and escalation.[30–32] Trajectories have important implications for prevention, by potentially identifying a group of high risk youth who may be in need of specially tailored interventions, such as those who escalate early or rapidly. These youth are likely to be most at risk for developing dependence and accruing the health consequences of long-term smoking.

HIGHLIGHTS OF PRIOR RESEARCH

Thus far, researchers have learned a great deal about factors that predict the early stages of cigarette use among adolescents[2,33] but much less is known about predictors of progression from early use to nicotine dependence,[20] and even less is known about the trajectories or natural history of smoking from initiation to dependence.

Only a handful of studies have examined whether there are differential predictors of regular smoking versus initiation,[34–37] and these studies have found few differential predictors. This may suggest that the stages of transition are an artificial distinction or an artifact (see Ref. 20), and/or that the development to dependent/addicted smoking is more of a fluid continuum, as represented by trajectories rather than stages.

Given the many approaches to defining "smoking" in prior research, rather than examining the variety of predictors at each stage, we organize our review by different levels and types of influences and examine the evidence for each as an influence on different smoking stages, groupings, or trajectories.

INDIVIDUAL INFLUENCES

Demographics

Age

Social, physical and emotional development proceed at dramatically different rates for each adolescent, and a consideration of age and developmental stage is essential for understanding adolescent health behaviors such as smoking. Age is important in that adolescents who try cigarettes at younger ages are more likely to continue smoking and to be more nicotine dependent as adults.[38] However, age appears to play its most important role as a moderator of other effects—that is, altering the relative importance of various sources of influences at different ages and developmental stages, as well as different points along the smoking trajectory. In a similar vein, developmental age has been conceptualized as a type of contextual factor that influences the vector of other influences.[39] As noted throughout our review, some effects are noted among a particular age group, with different results among older or younger adolescents. For example, the effect of conduct disorder and depression differs between youths in 6th or 10th grade.[40] Furthermore, the processing of tobacco-related messages differs substantially by age.[41]

Socioeconomic Status (SES)

Although SES has been operationalized and measured in a number of ways such as parent education or household income, several reviews have noted an inverse association between SES and adolescent smoking.[33,42] On the other hand, a fair number of studies have failed to find support for this association.[43,44] Some evidence suggests that the increased rates of parental smoking among lower SES families may partially mediate the SES-adolescent smoking link.[45] It is likely that discrepant findings regarding SES depend in part on different historical contexts, conceptualizations, samples, and whether or not other variables are also considered in the statistical model.

Gender and Race/Ethnicity

Past-month smoking rates are fairly comparable for adolescent males and females;[46] however, smoking rates are higher among white adolescents than among African–American, Asian, or Hispanic adolescents.[21,46,47] A number of factors appear to be involved in these differences, many of them involving complex causal mechanisms.

Motives for smoking tend to differ by gender. Among adolescent girls, body image and eating issues are predictors of smoking initation,[48] but among boys aggression and conduct disorders appear to be fairly consistent predictors of smoking.[49]

Even more complexity arises when other causal links, such as the relationship between depression, delinquency, and smoking present differently for adolescent females than for adolescent males.[50]

Substantial racial/ethnic differences are also apparent in perceptions of smoking; although across racial/ethnic groups adolescents are similar in their reasons for smoking (e.g., image, stress management, social belonging), reasons for not smoking differ substantially.[51] Nonwhite girls, particularly African–Americans, perceive smoking to be an unladylike behavior that would cost them the respect of others, and would be incompatible with a promising future. Furthermore, ethnicity interacts with other relevant variables; for example, regardless of their parents' smoking status, nonwhite adolescents perceive smoking as disrespectful to their parents, whereas white children with parents who smoke perceive parental messages not to smoke as lacking in credibility.[51] This is consistent with other evidence suggesting that African–American parents promote stronger nonsmoking norms for their children.[47] Race functions as a moderator of other risk factors for smoking,[39,52,53] and as an indirect predictor of smoking, with effects mediated via other psychosocial processes such as family support structures[54] or acculturation.[55–57]

Physiological Differences

Genetics

Twin sudies demonstrate a substantial genetic contribution to smoking behavior[58, 59] and it has been estimated that genetic effects account for 56% of the variance in smoking initiation and 70% of the variance in nicotine dependence.[60] Animal models also provide supporting evidence for the role of genes on physiological sensitivity to nicotine,[61] as well as the development of nicotine tolerance.[62,63] Genetic influence may function through a variety of neurotransmitter pathways, including those specific to nicotine.[64] Increasingly of interest are the variety of ways in which genetic characteristics interact with environmental factors to increase the risk of initiating and continuing smoking, and this is a promising arena for additional research.[59,64]

Biology/Physiological Reactions

Adolescents' physiological responses to nicotine are a potentially important predictor of escalation.[65] Physiological differences in responses to early trials with cigarettes appear to be highly associated with the progression from initial use to regular smoking, and the sensitivity model of dependence proposes that those less sensitive to the negative effects of nicotine may have underlying physiological differences in their reactions to nicotine.[66] Among adults, regular smokers experience fewer aversive effects (e.g., dizziness, jitteriness) than do nonsmokers after smoking a cigarette,[67,68] but few, if any, controlled laboratory studies have examined the acute effects of nicotine on adolescent emotional and subjective reactions. Developing tolerance to nicotine's aversive effects may also increase the likelihood of developing nicotine dependence.[2]

Physiological reactions may also be conditioned, or moderated, by other factors such as the social setting or the individual's cognitive filters. For example, physical responses such as dizziness, which may be aversive to some, can also be labeled positively as "a buzz" or "a rush," depending on the individual's expectancies and subjective interpretation of the experience. Social settings during initial experiences may influence the progression of behavior, with evidence suggesting that adolescents who first smoke in a group are more likely to continue smoking.[69]

Smoking as a "Problem Behavior:" Association with Other Behavior Problems and Comorbidities

Adolescent drug use, including smoking, has been conceptualized as a type of unconventional, or deviant behavior,[70] and smoking initiation is related to other problem behaviors such as risk-taking, rebelliousness, and substance use.[33,71,72] Smoking is a consistent predictor of subsequent use of other substances such as alcohol and illicit drugs;[2] however, many studies have noted that substance use also predicts smoking initiation.[33] The association between deviance and smoking appears bi-directional and reciprocally reinforcing.[19] While it is quite possible that there is a causal link between smoking and other substance use, it is also entirely likely that smoking is one part of a constellation of risky behaviors,[73] or that other factors such as genetics contribute both to smoking and to other substance use.[74]

There is a well-established association between adolescent smoking and patterns of behavior characterized as psychopathology or behavior problems. Strong evidence links smoking to externalizing or disruptive disorders such as attention deficit hyperactivity disorder (ADHD), conduct disorder, and delinquency, and to internalizing disorders such as depression and anxiety.[49,75]

Attention Deficit/Hyperactivity Disorder

There is a strong link between attention decifit /hyperactivity disorder (ADHD) and cigarette smoking,[76] possibly because nicotine improves attention,[77–79] which can alleviate some of the attention and concentration difficulties of ADHD.[80] Adults with ADHD seem to use nicotine to self-medicate,[81–83] and the same also seems true among adolescents: adolescents with ADHD are more likely to smoke than are adolescents without ADHD.[84–86] In particular, adolescents with inattentiveness symptoms are more likely both to experiment with smoking and to be regular (past 30 days) smokers, even after controlling for other important correlates of adolescent smoking such as peer and family smoking.[87]

Conduct Disorder and Delinquency

Conduct disorder (CD) and delinquency are associated with smoking behavior in both cross-sectional studies,[88] and longitudinal studies predicting subsequent smoking.[49,89,90] Use of an aggressive interpersonal style to cope with conflict is also associated with smoking;[91] fortunately, intervening to reduce aggressive behavior may prevent subsequent smoking among boys.[92] The combination of both CD and ADHD poses a particular elevation of risk for substance use and dependence.[93,94]

Smoking and Depressed Mood/Negative Affect

There is growing evidence that depression and adolescent smoking are linked,[95–97] although the causal direction of this relationship is less clear.[95,98–100] Like adults, adolescent smokers commonly report that they smoke as a way to relax or manage negative moods and stress.[101,102] The stress-coping model[103] proposes that some individuals use tobacco to cope with stressful situations and as a way of self-regulating their emotions. Correlational work sugggests that high trait anxiety is associated with coping motives for smoking.[104] Indeed, a fair amount of evidence supports the association between stress or anxiety and adolescent smoking, with stress related to initiation,[105,106] increased smoking,[107–109] and decreased likelihood of quitting.[110] However, as with depression, the direction of the stress and smoking association is unclear[75,111] and conditioned by other variables. For example, evidence suggests that the negative impact of life stress on increasing adolescent substance use is buffered by characteristics such as religiosity.[112] Depression may also heighten the risk of smoking through mediational links such as increasing the susceptibility to peer influence,[113] and through an interaction between number of friends smoking and depression.[114]

Depression also maintains a complex interaction with other variables, likely in part because depression can arise from and subsequently affect the interaction between adolescents and their social environments. For instance, the combination of depression and conduct disorders has been associated with a particularly strong increase in smoking risk, although this often depends on age and gender. The combination dramatically increased the odds of smoking (43 times for girls and 12 times for boys) among 9th graders;[50] however, other work has noted a combined effect among 6th-grade boys, but an effect for conduct disorder only, regardless of depression, by 10th grade.[40] Kassel and colleagues note that the observed relationship between depression and smoking initiation may be caused by the third variable of externalizing behaviors.[75] Yet another possibility is that inadequate self-regulation and self-control underlie both internalizing and externalizing disorders and may also lead to use of nicotine and other substances.[75] Indeed, behavioral self-regulation has been associated with increased risk of smoking.[115] A key area for continued research is to understand the intersection between internalizing and externalizing disorders and the role they play at various points along the tobacco trajectory, and whether early treatment can preventing escalation of tobacco and other substance use. Further, it is important to consider tobacco use as one part of a constellation of risky behaviors and to understand how various factors combine not only to increase smoking escalation, but also to buffer risk for smoking and promote resilience (for review see Ref. 116).

Finally, with regard to individual influences, we emphasize that researchers need to better understand the acute effects of nicotine on adolescents, particularly on their emotional responses. While many adolescents perceive that smoking has a variety of positive benefits, such as helping to manage negative moods, there is surprisingly little direct evidence to date demonstrating the mood benefits of smoking among adolescents. As yet, there have been no controlled examinations of adolescents' acute response to nicotine or smoking, and such studies are necessary to understand how variation in emotional or physiological responses to nicotine are associated with subsequent progression through the stages of smoking. Beyond the lab, however, the extent to which smoking may relieve or heighten negative affect depends strongly upon the situation or context in which smoking occurs (e.g., Ref. 117). This is likely also the case with adolescents, but more work is needed in this area. Newer, sophisticated methodologies such as ecological momentary assessment[118] provide richly textured data about youth in their natural environments (e.g., Ref. 119). When used at repeated measurement points and with adolescents at varying levels of smoking vulnerability, such studies can provide valuable information about the natural progression through the stages of tobacco use. Furthermore, investigations of mood and smoking in adolescents have been almost exclusively limited to consideration of negative moods and their hypothesized amelioration due to smoking, but there has been little consideration of the positive end of the mood spectrum. There is some suggestion that positive moods may be more important to understanding youth smoking than reduction in negative moods,[120] and we suggest this as a topic for further consideration.

CONTEXTUAL FACTORS: SOCIAL RELATIONSHIPS AND ADOLESCENT SMOKING

Peer Relationships

One of the most robust findings in the literature is the link between peers and adolescent smoking.[2,33,121] Indeed, adolescent smoking is most often a social behavior. Adolescents frequently smoke in the presence of others,[69] use smoking as a way to achieve social belonging,[102,122] and are more likely to smoke if their close friends smoke.[123,124] Further, adolescents' perceptions that smoking is prevalent among their same-age peers have been linked to their own smoking behavior.[125,126] Peers can either deter or promote smoking, and their influence may be more subtle than is often assumed.[121] Adolescents rarely report direct pressure from peers to smoke, but rather, the "pressure" to smoke may be implied by being with others who are smoking and the adolescent's need to achieve a sense of acceptance or belonging.[102,122] Importantly, too, changes in peer networks may be associated with changes in smoking patterns. For example, nonsmoking adolescents who increasingly affiliate with smokers are at high risk for smoking.[127] Similarly, changes in romantic relationships may lead to changes in an adolescent's smoking patterns, depending on the partner's smoking status.[121]

Despite the plethora of research on peer influences and adolescent smoking, the mechanisms behind these influences are not well understood. It is even less clear how these influences operate "in the moment" when adolescents make decisions about smoking, or how these influences change over time through the course of adolescent development.

PARENTS, FAMILIES, AND ADOLESCENT SMOKING

An important developmental process during the adolescent years is the adolescent's growing autonomy from parents and increased orientation toward peers.[128,129] Much research has focused on the relative influence of parents and peers on adolescent smoking. Results of these studies have been mixed, with some studies finding a stronger influence for peers,[124,130,131] and others finding that parents have at least as strong an influence as peers.[132,133] Methodological differences have contributed to inconsistencies in findings.[134] For example, results differ based on whether parent smoking is classified based on current or lifetime smoking status,[135] or depending on the stage of adolescent smoking.[35,123]

Whether the relative importance of parent versus peer influence is stronger, it is clear that parents exert substantial influence on adolescent behavior through modeling with their own smoking behavior, with their messages and rules about smoking, and with their general parenting style. Parents' own smoking is one of the most widely studied influences on adolescent smoking, and much evidence supports a link between parent smoking and adolescent initiation,[33,34,136] regular smoking,[115,137,138] and the persistence of smoking into adulthood.[30,35]

Understanding mechanisms through which these effects operate is increasingly important, and many of the links between parent smoking and adolescent smoking are indirect. Parents' own smoking behavior appears to indirectly affect escalation of smoking, through increased adolescent perception of parental approval of smoking,[34] affiliation with smoking peers,[137,139] or increased availability of cigarettes, which predicts across adolescent stages of use.[138]

While parents' own smoking behavior indirectly influences children's smoking behavior, parents' overt messages and rules about smoking are also important. Household smoking bans reduce the rates of adolescent smoking.[137,140,141] Smoking-specific parenting practices, such as rules about smoking and strong anti-smoking messages are also associated with lower likelihood of adolescent smoking,[142] even if the parents themselves are smokers.[143] Smoking is less likely among adolescents who perceive that smoking would disappoint their parents or bring about punishment.[138,144] Interestingly, adolescent smoking is more associated with adolescents' perceptions of how their parents would react than parents' reports of actual reactions,[137,145] emphasizing the importance of adolescent perceptions of social control and norms. General parenting style also appears to have an influence on adolescent smoking, with an authoritative parenting style,[146] characterized by parental support and control, being associated with less likelihood of adolescent smoking.[147–150] High family autonomy and intimacy also appear protective for cigarette smoking,[151] whereas low cohesion and poor family functioning are associated with increased smoking.[43,152] Furthermore, family monitoring and support may buffer adolescents from the deleterious effects of peer smoking.[136,150,153] Parents' influence may well differ in the stages of smoking, and are a stronger predictor of regular daily smoking than smoking initiation.[154] Parent and family influences have repeatedly been found to be important for transitions to the stages beyond experimentation.[20,34,35,96,155]

In summary, a variety of parenting behaviors, including specifically parents' own smoking patterns, as well as their messages to their children, have an important role in influencing adolescent smoking behavior. However, much remains to be learned in this area. For example, it is important to understand how parents can best convey anti-smoking messages, and how the family relationship moderates which types of messages are most effective in deterring smoking. Particular types of messages may be more or less appropriate depending on the age, developmental stage, and autonomy level of the adolescent. Parent involvement and messages may function as a buffer for other risk factors for smoking initiation, such as the buffering effect of parent involvement on adolescent affiliation with problem-behaving peers.[142] Understanding more about the combined influences of family and peer factors across the stages of adolescent smoking will continue to yield valuable information for developing interventions to reduce adolescent smoking.

ENVIRONMENTAL/CULTURAL CONTEXT

Beyond individual and family level influences are the broader societal and cultural factors that also play a role in an adolescent's risk for smoking progression.

Tobacco Advertising and Media Messages

Tobacco advertising, including promotional items and paid advertising in print media, television, and movies, clearly has a substantial influence on adolescent smoking.

Adolescent smokers are most likely to smoke Marlboro, Camel or Newports, the three most heavily advertised brands;[156] they are also more likely to recall and recognize brand information than are nonsmokers.[157,158] In longitudinal studies, adolescents who own tobacco promotional items are more likely to initiate and continue smoking,[159,160] and those who approve of or are receptive to cigarette advertising are more likely to initiate smoking.[161,162] Receptivity to advertising also interacts with individual characteristics; for example, rates of smoking are highest among adolescents with high receptivity to tobacco advertising, who also have clinically significant depressive symptoms.[163] Advertising receptivity may be mediated or moderated by other variables such as novelty-seeking,[164] or parenting style.[165] Fortunately, a number of antismoking campaigns have proven effective in decreasing smoking rates (for review see Ref. 165), particularly when conducted in conjunction with school-based prevention programs.[167,168] These types of programs have also shown changes in mediator variables such as perceived smoking prevalence and knowledge of smoking's harmful effects,[169] and have noted differential success for adolescent girls and boys, or depending on the age and risk level of the target group.[166]

Taxation, Cost, and Policies

Examinations of cigarette pricing and taxation have consistently shown that higher prices discourage smoking initiation, decrease smoking rate, and encourage cessation,[170] and that adolescents are more responsive to price than are adults.[171] Compared with experimenters and lower-rate smokers, established adolescent smokers appear particularly sensitive to price.[172,173] It has been noted that price effects may occur largely through a number of contextual mechanisms,[174] such as reducing smoking rates of parents or peers,[175] and by decreasing access to cigarettes.[176] However, economic studies appear to rarely consider a combination of macro-level variables plus more proximal contextual and individual-level variables.

Laws restricting youth access to cigarettes are fairly new and compliance has been low.[177] Further, it is as yet unclear whether newer state and local laws will influence adolescent access or use of tobacco products,[178] but it seems that for such approaches to work, compliance needs to be very high.[177,179] Clean indoor air laws are relatively new and, again, their specific effect on adolescent smoking has not yet been thoroughly examined. Implementation of clean indoor air laws in California does appear to have corresponded with a dramatic increase in the number of children and adolescents living in smoke-free homes (from 38% to 82%).[180] Given that adolescents are less likely to smoke in public areas, such regulations may not affect adolescent smoking behavior directly; yet they may have an impact by changing social norms. They therefore warrant further exploration as mechanisms for decreasing adolescent smoking.

MICROLEVEL CONTEXTUAL INFLUENCES

 The research reviewed above has contributed greatly to our understanding of individual and contextual influences on adolescent smoking. However, for the most part, this prior research has relied on adolescents' self-report via retrospective and summary questionnaire methods to assess many of the key individual or contextual constructs. More recently, investigators have used Ecological Momentary Assessment (EMA)[118] methods to collect real-time data in the adolescents' every-day environments. EMA methods are ideally suited for examining the "micro-contexts" of adolescent smoking, and how the immediate context, including an adolescent's mood or subjective experience of smoking, influences future trajectories of smoking. EMA provides very rich data about both the objective (e.g., place, presence of others, in the context of other activities) and subjective (e.g., emotional and physiological responses) of smoking. Importantly, over time, EMA can answer questions about how the patterning of smoking changes and how the antecedents and emotional/subjective physiological consequences of smoking change as dependence develops. Finally, EMA allows researchers to address both between-subjects and within-subjects questions. For example, EMA data can address the question of whether adolescents who escalate in their smoking, compared to those who experiment and stop smoking, are more likely to smoke in response to negative mood states (the between-subjects question), and more uniquely, within a given adolescent, whether daily or momentary increases in negative moods prompt smoking.

Recently, Mermelstein and her colleagues[120, 181] used EMA via hand-held computers to examine whether subjective moods surrounding smoking predicted longitudinal smoking patterns among a group of adolescents ($N = 152$) early in their smoking careers (i.e., not yet regular smokers). Adolescents were randomly prompted by the hand-held computers to complete a brief interview approximately 5–7 times daily during a 7-day baseline monitoring period. In addition, adolescents "event-recorded" smoking episodes as they occurred and answered questions about mood and context both prior to and immediately after their smoking a cigarette. By examining differences in the random prompt and pre-smoke moods, Mermelstein and colleagues[120,181] addressed the question of whether adolescents smoked at times when they were less happy, more sad, or more stressed compared to random times. Adolescents who did not progress beyond a trying stage felt significantly less positive and more negative prior to smoking than at random times. However, for adolescents who eventually escalated in their smoking and moved beyond experimentation, smoking times were not necessarily preceded by mood states that were different than random times. Indeed, if anything, for these youth, smoking tended to occur at times of positive moods. Mermelstein and colleagues also examined whether adolescents' subjective mood states changed after smoking—specifically, did adolescents experience decreases in negative moods and stress, and feel better after smoking? Results indicated that adolescents who tried smoking but did not escalate failed to receive any mood benefits following smoking; however, adolescents who progressed in their smoking felt significantly more positive immediately after smoking. Taken together, these data suggest that triers (those who try but do not escalate) smoke at times of lower overall mood and fail to achieve any mood enhancements or benefits from smoking. However, adolescents who continue to smoke get substantial mood benefits from smoking. Thus, subjective mood experiences surrounding early trials of smoking may well be important in understanding the progression and development of dependence in youth.

EMA thus provides a unique opportunity to better capture the real-time contexts of youth smoking and to examine, in more detail than has been possible before, how intra-individual shifts in both objective and subjective contexts may contribute to the development of dependence. Although more stable individual differences and broad contexts clearly influence smoking trajectories, adolescents ultimately make decisions about smoking cigarettes in the presence of immediate contextual prompts and cues. EMA provides a window into understanding these micro-contexts.

SUMMARY

As previously noted, children enter adolescence with a variety of risk and protective factors, but a moderation of the impact of these factors can occur as a result of contextual variables. The critical transitions along the development of smoking trajectories are the result of a dynamic process, in which the individual's ongoing transactions with his/her environment predict individual differences in pathways of adaptation and behavior across the lifespan.[182] These intervening contexts can be the social environment, peer groups, family processes, as well as objective and subjective responses to smoking itself. Such contexts may be able to redirect a developmental trajectory set in motion. In understanding the complexities of adolescent smoking, it is clear that we need to focus both on broad, distal-level influences such as family processes, while remaining mindful of the importance of micro-level influences such as individual traits, physiological responses, and psychological characteristics.

The etiology of smoking is best conceptualized as a complex, multifactorial process, and as such, no single variable is a sufficient cause of smoking. Although certain variables examined in isolation are highly associated with smoking patterns, and single influence process models are easier to test, they are unfortunately less productive in understanding variability in individual smoking patterns. The interrelation among variables and processes is likely to be of greater importance for understanding the development of smoking trajectories than any single variable in isolation. As noted by Henningfield and Jude,[183] taking a developmental approach, and examining interactions between the psychopharmacological effects of nicotine and broad contextual issues requires "bridges across disciplines to connect what are now largely just islands of research." It is clear that we need multi-level explanatory principles to understand adolescent smoking, and collaboration across disciplines is an important step in moving this science forward.

ACKNOWLEDGMENTS

Supported by Grant #CA80266 from the National Cancer Institute and a grant from the Tobacco Etiology Research Network, funded by The Robert Wood Johnson Foundation. Additional support for the first author was provided by NIDA postdoctoral training Grant DA07293.

REFERENCES

1. JOHNSTON, L.D., P.M. O'MALLEY & J.G. BACHMAN. 2002. Monitoring the future: national results on adolescent drug use: overview of key findings, 2001. National Institute on Drug Abuse. Bethesda, MD.
2. U.S. DEPARTMENT OF HEALTH AND HUMAN SERVICES. 1994. Preventing Tobacco Use among Young People. A Report of the Surgeon General: 1-10. USDHHS. Atlanta, GA.
3. FLAY, B.R. & J. PETRAITIS. 1994. The theory of triadic influence: a new theory of health behavior with implications for preventive interventions. *In* Advances in Medical Sociology, Vol. IV: A Reconsideration of Models of Health Behavior Change. G.S. Albrecht, Ed.: 19–44. JAI Press. Greenwich, CT.
4. FLAY, B.R., J. PETRAITIS & F.B. HU. 1999. Psychosocial risk and protective factors for adolescent tobacco use. Nicotine Tob. Res. **1**(Suppl. 1): S59–S65.
5. PETRAITIS, J., B.R. FLAY & T.Q. MILLER. 1995. Reviewing theories of adolescent substance use: organizing pieces in the puzzle. Psychol. Bull. **117**(1): 67–86.
6. DARLING, N. & P. CUMSILLE. 2003. Theory, measurement, and methods in study of family influences on adolescent smoking. Addiction **98**(Suppl. 1): 21–36.
7. BRYK, A.S. & S.W. RAUDENBUSH. 1992. Hierarchical Linear Models: Applications and Data Analysis Methods. Sage Publications. Thousand Oaks, CA.
8. RAUDENBUSH, S.W. & A.S. BRYK. 2002. Hierarchical Linear Models: Applications and Data Analysis Methods, 2nd edit. Sage Publications. Thousand Oaks, CA.
9. GOLDSTEIN, H. 1995. Multilevel Statistical Models, 2nd edit. Wiley, New York.
10. HEDEKER, D., R.D. GIBBONS & B.R. FLAY. 1994. Random-effects regression models for clustered data with an example from smoking prevention research. J. Consult. Clin. Psychol. **62**(4): 757–765.
11. LAIRD, N.M. & H. WARE. 1982. Random-effects models for longitudinal data. Biometrics **38**: 963–974.
12. MUTHEN, B. 2001. Second-generation structural equation modeling with a combination of categorical and continuous latent variables: new opportunities for latent class/ latent growth modeling. *In* New Methods for the Analysis of Change. L.M. Collins & A. Sayer, Eds.: 291–322. American Psychological Association. Washington, DC.
13. MUTHEN, B. 2002. Beyond SEM: general latent variable modeling. Behaviormetrika **29**: 81–117.
14. MUTHEN, B. 2001. Latent variable mixture modeling. *In* New Developments and Techniques in Structural Equation Modeling. G.A. Marcoulides & R.E. Schumacker, Eds.: 1–33. Erlbaum. Mahwah, NJ.
15. NAGIN, D. 1999. Analyzing developmental trajectories: a semi-parametric, group-based approach. Psychol. Methods **4**: 139–157.
16. WILLS, T.A., F.X. GIBBONS, M. GERRARD, *et al.* 2003. Family communication and religiosity related to substance use and sexual behavior in early adolescence: a test for pathways through self-control and prototype perceptions. Psychol. Addict. Behav. **17**(4): 312–323.

17. BARON, R.M. & D.A. KENNY. 1986. The moderator-mediator variable distinction in social psychological research: conceptual, strategic, and statistical considerations. J. Pers. Soc. Psychol. **51**(6): 1173–1182.
18. HOLMBECK, G.N. 1997. Toward terminological, conceptual, and statistical clarity in the study of mediators and moderators: examples from the child-clinical and pediatric psychology literatures. J. Consult. Clin. Psychol. **65**: 599–610.
19. FLAY, B.R. 1993. Youth tobacco use: risks, patterns, and control. *In* Nicotine Addiction: Principles and Management. C.T. Orleans & J.D. Slade, Eds.: 365–384. Oxford University Press. New York.
20. MAYHEW, K, B.R. FLAY & J.A. MOTT. 2000. Stages in the development of adolescent smoking. Drug Alcohol Depend. **59**(Suppl. 1): S61–S81.
21. U.S. DEPARTMENT OF HEALTH AND HUMAN SERVICES. 1998. Tobacco use among high school students—United States, 1997. Morb. Mortal. Wkly. Rep. **47**: 229–233.]
22. PERKINS, K.A. 2002. Chronic tolerance to nicotine in humans and its relationship to tobacco dependence. Nicotine Tob. Res **4**: 405–422.
23. COLBY, S.M., S.T. TIFFANY, S. SHIFFMAN & R.S. NIAURA. 2000. Measuring nicotine dependence among youth: a review of available approaches and instruments. Drug Alcohol Depend. **59**(Suppl. 1): S23–S39.
24. KASSEL, J.D. 2000. Are adolescent smokers addicted to nicotine? The suitability of the nicotine dependence construct as applied to adolescents. J. Child Adolesc. Substance Abuse **9**(4): 1–36.
25. LYNCH, B.S. & R.J. BONNIE. 1994. Growing Up Tobacco Free: Preventing Nicotine Addiction in Children and Youths. National Academy Press. Washington, DC.
26. DIFRANZA, J.R., N.A. RIGOTTI, A.D. MCNEILL, J.K. OCKENE, *et al.* 2000. Initial symptoms of nicotine dependence in adolescents. Tob. Control **9**(3): 313–319.
27. LEVENTHAL, H., T. BAKER, T. BRANDON & R. FLEMING. 1989. Intervening and preventing cigarette smoking. *In* Smoking and Human Behavior. T. Ney & A. Gale, Eds.: 313–336. John Wiley & Sons. New York.
28. MCNEILL, A.D. 1991. The development of dependence on smoking in children. Br. J. Addict. **86**(5): 589–592.
29. FERGUSSON, D.M. & L.J. HORWOOD. 1995. Transitions to cigarette smoking during adolescence. Addict. Behav. **20**(5): 627–642.
30. CHASSIN, L., C.C. PRESSON, S.C. PITTS & S.J. SHERMAN. 2000. The natural history of cigarette smoking from adolescence to adulthood in a midwestern community sample: multiple trajectories and their psychosocial correlates. Health Psychol. **19**(3): 223–231.
31. COLDER, C.R., P. MEHTA & K. BALANDA, *et al.* 2001. Identifying trajectories of adolescent smoking: an application of latent growth mixture modeling. Health Psychol. **20**(2): 127–135.
32. SOLDZ, S & X. CUI. 2002. Pathways through adolescent smoking: a seven-year longitudinal grouping analysis. Health Psychol. **21**(5): 495–504.
33. CONRAD, K.M., B.R. FLAY & D. HILL. 1992. Why children start smoking cigarettes: predictors of onset. Br. J. Addict. **87**(12): 1711–1724.
34. FLAY, B.R., F.B. HU, O. SIDDIQUI, *et al.* 1994. Differential influence of parental smoking and friends' smoking on adolescent initiation and escalation of smoking. J. Health Soc. Behav. **35**(3): 248–265.
35. FLAY, B.R., F.B. HU & J. RICHARDSON. 1998. Psychosocial predictors of different stages of cigarette smoking among high school students. Prev. Med. **27**(5): A9–A18.
36. GRITZ, E.R., A.V. PROKHOROV & K.S. HUDMON, *et al.* 1998. Cigarette smoking in a multiethnic population of youth: methods and baseline findings. Prev. Med. **27**(3): 365–384.
37. ROBINSON, L.A., R.C. KLESGES, S.M. ZBIKOWSKI & R. GLASER. 1997. Predictors of risk for different stages of adolescent smoking in a biracial sample. J. Consult. Clin. Psychol. **65**(4): 653–662.
38. BRESLAU, N., N. FENN & E.L. PETERSON. 1993. Early smoking initiation and nicotine dependence in a cohort of young adults. Drug Alcohol Depend. **33**(2): 129–137.
39. JAMNER, L.D., C.K. WHALEN, S.E. LOUGHLIN, *et al.* 2003. Tobacco use across the formative years: a roadmap to developmental vulnerabilities. Nicotine Tob. Res. **5** (Suppl. 1): S71–S88.

40. MILLER-JOHNSON, S., J.E. LOCHMAN, J.D. COIE, *et al.* 1998. Comorbidity of conduct and depressive problems at sixth grade: substance use outcomes across adolescence. J. Abnorm. Child Psychol. 26(3): 221–232.
41. GRANDPRE, J., E.M. ALVARO, M. BURGOON, *et al.* 2003. Adolescent reactance and anti-smoking campaigns: a theoretical approach. Health Commun. 15(3): 349–366.
42. TYAS, S.L. & L.L. PEDERSEN. 1998. Psychosocial factors related to adolescent smoking: a critical review of the literature. Tob. Control 7: 409–420.
43. BAILEY, S.L., S.T. ENNETT & C.L. RINGWALT. 1993. Potential mediators, moderators, or independent effects in the relationship between parents' former and current cigarette use and their children's cigarette use. Addict. Behav. 18(6): 601–621.
44. FLINT, A.J., E.G. YAMADA & T.E. NOVOTNY. 1998. Black-white differences in cigarette smoking uptake: progression from adolescent experimentation to regular use. Prev. Med. 27: 358–364.
45. SOTERIADES, E.S. & J.R. DIFRANZA. 2003. Parent's socioeconomic status, adolescents' disposable income, and adolescents' smoking status in Massachusetts. Am. J. Public Health 93(7): 1155–1160.
46. GIOVINO, G.A. 1999. Epidemiology of tobacco use among U.S. adolescents. Nicotine Tob. Res. 1(Suppl. 1): S31–S40.
47. U.S. DEPARTMENT OF HEALTH AND HUMAN SERVICES. 1998. Tobacco use among U.S. racial/ethnic minority groups—African Americans, American Indians and Alaska Natives, Asian Americans and Pacific Islanders, and Hispanics: a report of the Surgeon General. USDHHS. Atlanta, GA.
48. STICE, E. & H. SHAW. 2003. Prospective relations of body image, eating, and affective disturbances to smoking onset in adolescent girls: how Virginia slims. J. Consult. Clin. Psychol. 71(1): 129–135.
49. MCMAHON, R.J. 1999. Child and adolescent psychopatholgy as risk factors for subsequent tobacco use. Nicotine Tob. Res. 1(Suppl. 2): S45–S50.
50. WHALEN, C.K., L.D. JAMNER, B. HENKER & R.J. DELFINO. 2001. Smoking and moods in adolescents with depressive and aggressive dispositions: evidence from surveys and electronic diaries. Health Psychol. 20(2): 99–111.
51. MERMELSTEIN, R. 1999. Explanations of ethnic and gender differences in youth smoking: a multi-site, qualitative investigation. The Tobacco Control Network Writing Group. Nicotine Tob. Res. 1(Suppl. 1): S91–98.
52. LANDRINE, H., J.L. RICHARDSON, E.A. KLONOFF & B.R. FLAY. 1994. Cultural diversity in the predictors of adolescent cigarette smoking: the relative influence of peers. J. Behav. Med. 17(3): 331–346.
53. SUSSMAN, S., C. DENT, B.R. FLAY, *et al.* 1987. Psychosocial predictors of cigarette smoking onset by white, black, Hispanic, and Asian adolescents in southern California. Morb. Mort. Wkly. Rep. 36(4): 11S–17S.
54. MARIN, B.V., G. MARIN, E.J. PEREZ-STABLE, *et al.* 1990. Cultural differences in attitudes toward smoking: developing messages using the Theory of Reasoned Action. J. Appl. Soc. Psychol. 20(6): 478–493.
55. KLONOFF, E.A. & H. LANDRINE. 1996. Acculturation and cigarette smoking among African-American adults. J. Behav. Med. 19(5): US, www.
56. KLONOFF, E.A. & H. LANDRINE. 1999. Acculturation and cigarette smoking among African Americans: replication and implications for prevention and cessation programs. J. Behav. Med. 22(2): US, www.
57. KAPLAN, M.S. & G. MARKS. 1990. Adverse effects of acculturation: psychological distress among Mexican-American young adults. Soc. Sci. Med. 31: 1313–1319.
58. CARMELLI, D., G.E. SWAN, D. ROBINETTE & R.R. FABSITZ. 1992. Genetic influence on smoking: a study of male twins. N. Engl. J. Med. 327: 829–833.
59. SWAN, G.E. 1999. Implications of genetic epidemiology for the prevention of tobacco use. Nicotine Tob. Res. 1(Suppl. 1): S49–S56.
60. SULLIVAN, P. & K.S. KENDLER. 1999. The genetic epidemiology of smoking. Nicotine Tob. Res. 1: 51–57.
61. MARKS, M.J., J.A. STITZEL & A.C. COLLINS. 1989. Genetic influences on nicotine responses. Pharmacol. Biochem. Behav. 33(3): 667–678.

62. COLLINS, A.C. & M.J. MARKS. 1989. Chronic nicotine exposure and brain nicotinic receptors—influence of genetic factors. Progr. Brain Res. **79:** 137–146.
63. MARKS, M.J., S.M. CAMPBELL, E. ROMM & A.C. COLLINS. 1991. Genotype influences the development of tolerance to nicotine in the mouse. J. Pharmacol. Exp. Ther. **259**(1): 392–402.
64. LERMAN, C. & W. BERRETTINI. 2003. Elucidating the role of genetic factors in smoking behavior and nicotine dependence. Am. J. Med. Genet. Part B (Neuropsychiatric Genetics) **118B:** 48–54.
65. EISSENBERG, T. & R.L. BALSTER. 2000. Initial tobacco use episodes in children and adolescents: current knowledge, future directions. Drug Alcohol Depend. **59**(Suppl. 1): S41–S60.
66. POMERLEAU, O.F., A.C. COLLINS, S. SHIFFMAN & C.S. POMERLEAU. 1993. Why some people smoke and others do not: new perspectives. J. Consult. Clin. Psychol. **61**(5): 723–731.
67. PERKINS, K.A., J.E. GROBE, C. FONTE, et al. 1994. Chronic and acute tolerance to subjective, behavioral, and cardiovascular effects of nicotine in humans. J. Pharmacol. Exp. Ther. **270:** 628–638.
68. PERKINS, K.A. 1995. Individual variability in responses to nicotine. Behav. Genet. **25**(2): 119–132.
69. FRIEDMAN, L.S., E. LICHTENSTEIN & A. BIGLAN. 1985. Smoking onset among teens: an empirical analysis of initial situations. Addict. Behav. **10**(1): 1–13.
70. JESSOR, R. & S. JESSOR. 1977. Problem Behavior and Psychosocial Development: A Longitudinal Study of Youth. Academic Press. New York.
71. COLLINS, L.M., S. SUSSMAN, J.M. RAUCH, et al. 1987. Psychosocial predictors of young adolescent cigarette smoking: a sixteen-month, three-wave longitudinal study. J. Appl. Soc. Psychol. **17**(6): 554–573.
72. LEVENTHAL, H., R. FLEMING & K. GLYNN. 1988. A cognitive-developmental approach to smoking intervention. *In* Topics in Health Psychology. S. Maes, C.D. Spielberger, P. Defares & I. Sarason, Eds.: 79–105. John Wiley & Sons. New York.
73. WAKSCHLAG, L.S., K.E. PICKETT, M.K. MIDDLECAMP, et al. 2003. Pregnant smokers who quit, pregnant smokers who don't: does history of problem behavior make a difference? Soc. Sci. Med. **56:** 2449–2460.
74. MADDEN, P.A.F. & A.C. HEATH. 2002. Shared genetic vulnerability in alcohol and cigarette use and dependence. Alcohol. Clin. Exp. Res. **26**(12): 1919–1921.
75. KASSEL, J.D., L.R. STROUD & C.A. PARONIS. 2003. Smoking, stress, and negative affect: correlation, causation, and context across stages of smoking. Psychol. Bull. **129**(2): 270–304.
76. POMERLEAU, C.S., K.K. DOWNEY, S.M. SNEDECOR, et al. 2003. Smoking patterns and abstinence effects in smokers with no ADHD, childhood ADHD, and adult ADHD symptomatology. Addict. Behav. **28**(6): 1149–1157.
77. HAHN, B. & I.P. STOLERMAN. 2002. Nicotine-induced attentional enhancement in rats: effects of chronic exposure to nicotine. Neuropsychopharmacology **27**(5): 712–722.
78. KASSEL, J.D. 1997. Smoking and attention: a review and reformulation of the stimulus-filter hypothesis. Clin. Psychol. Rev. **17**(5): 451–478.
79. STOLERMAN, I.P., N.R. MIRZA, B. HAHN & M. SHOAIB, M. 2000. Nicotine in an animal model of attention. Eur. J. Pharmacol. **393**(1–3): 147–154.
80. LEVIN, E.D., C.K. CONNERS, D. SILVA, et al. 2001. Effects of chronic nicotine and methylphenidate in adults with attention deficit/hyperactivity disorder. Exp. Clin. Psychopharmacol. **9**(1): 83–90.
81. ERNST, M., S.J. HEISHMAN, L. SPURGEON & E.D. LONDON. 2001. Smoking history and nicotine effects on cognitive performance. Neuropsychopharmacology **25:** 313–319.
82. LEVIN, E.D., C.K. CONNERS, E. SPARROW, et al. 1996. Nicotine effects on adults with attention-deficit/hyperactivity disorder. Psychopharmacology **123**(1): 55–63.
83. LERMAN, C., J. AUDRAIN, K.P. TERCYAK, et al. 2001. Attention-deficit hyperactivity disorder (ADHD) symptoms and smoking patterns among participants in a smoking-cessation program. Nicotine Tob. Res. **3**(4): 353–359.

84. BARKLEY, R.A., M. FISCHER, C.S. EDELBROCK & L. SMALLISH. 1990. The adolescent outcome of hyperactive children diagnosed by research criteria: I. An 8-year prospective follow-up study. J. Am. Acad. Child Adolesc. Psychiatry 29(4): 546–557.
85. LAMBERT, N.M. & C.S. HARTSOUGH. 1998. Prospective study of tobacco smoking and substance dependencies among samples of ADHD and non-ADHD participants. J. Learn. Disabil. 31: 533–544.
86. MILBERGER, S., J. BIEDERMAN, S.V. FARAONE, *et al.* 1997. ADHD is associated with early initiation of cigarette smoking in children and adolescents. J. Am. Acad. Child Adolesc. Psychiatry 36: 37–44.
87. TERCYAK, K.P., C. LERMAN & J. AUDRAIN. 2002. Associateion of attention-deficit/hyperactivity disorder symptoms with levels of cigarette smoking in a community sample of adolescents. J. Am. Acad. Child Adolesc. Psychiatry 41(7): 799–805.
88. BRESLAU, N. 1995. Psychiatric comorbidity of smoking and nicotine dependence. Behav. Genet. 25(2): 95–101.
89. LYNSKEY, M.T. & D.M. FERGUSSON. 1995. Childhood conduct problems, attention deficit behaviors, and adolescent alcohol, tobacco, and illicit drug use. J. Abnorm. Child Psychol. 23(3): 281–302.
90. MOLINA, B.S.G. & W.E. PELHAM, JR. 2003. Childhood predictors of adolescent substance use in a longitudinal study of children with ADHD. J. Abnorm. Psychol. 112(3): 497–507.
91. UNGER, J.B., S. SUSSMAN, C.W. DENT. 2003. Interpersonal conflict tactics and substance use among high-risk adolescents. Addict. Behav. 28(5): 979–987.
92. KELLAM, S.G. & J.C. ANTHONY. 1998. Targeting early antecedents to prevent tobacco smoking: findings from an epidemiologically based randomized field trial. Am. J. Public Health 88(10): 1490–1495.
93. FLORY, K., R. MILICH, D.R. LYNAM, *et al.* 2003. Relation between childhood disruptive behavior disorders and substance use and dependence symptoms in young adulthood: individuals with symptoms of attention-deficit/hyperactivity disorder are uniquely at risk. Psychol. Addict. Behav. 7(2): 151–158.
94. MILBERGER, S., J. BIEDERMAN, S.V. FARAONE, *et al.* 1997. Associations between ADHD and psychoactive substance use disorders: findings from a longitudinal study of high-risk siblings of ADHD children. Am. J. Addict. 6(4): 318–329.
95. BROWN, R.A., P.M. LEWINSOHN, J.R. SEELEY & E.F. WAGNER. 1996. Cigarette smoking, major depression, and other psychiatric disorders among adolescents. J. Am. Acad. Child Adolesc. Psychiatry 35(12): 1602–1610.
96. CHOI, W.S., C.A. PATTEN, J.C. GILLIN, *et al.* 1997. Cigarette smoking predicts development of depressive symptoms among U.S. adolescents. Ann. Behav. Med. 19(1): 42–50.
97. PATTON, G.C., M. HIBBERT, M.J. ROSIER, *et al.* 1996. Is smoking associated with depression and anxiety in teenagers? Am. J. Public Health 86(2): 225–230.
98. ALBERS, A.B. & L. BIENER. 2004. The role of smoking and rebelliousness in the development of depressive symptoms among a cohort of Massachusetts adolescents. Prev. Med. 34(6): 625–631.
99. DIERKER, L.C., S. AVENEVOLI, K.R. MERIKANGAS, *et al.* 2001. Association between psychiatric disorders and the progression of tobacco use behaviors. J. Am. Acad. Child Adolesc. Psychiatry 40(10): 1159–1167.
100. MARTINI, S., F.A. WAGNER & J.C. ANTHONY. 2003. The association of tobacco smoking and depression in adolescence: evidence from the United States. Subst. Use Misuse 37(14): 1853–1867.
101. DOZOIS, D.N., J.A. FARROW & A. MISER. 1995. Smoking patterns and cessation motivations during adolescence. Int. J. Addict. 30(11): 1485–.
102. MERMELSTEIN, R. 1999. Explanations of ethnic and gender differences in youth smoking: a multi-site, qualitative investigation. Nicotine Tob. Res. 1(Suppl. 1): S91–S98.
103. WILLS, T.A. & S.D. CLEARY, 1995. Stress-coping model for alcohol-tobacco interactions in adolescence. *In* Alcohol and Tobacco: From Basic Science to Clinical Practice. J.B. Fertig & J.P. Allen, Eds: 107–128. NIAAA. Bethesda, MD.

104. COMEAU. N., S.H. STEWART & P. LOBA. 2001. The relations of trait anxiety, anxiety sensitivity and sensation seeking to adolescents' motivations for alcohol, cigarette and marijuana use. Addict. Behav. **26**(6): 803–825.
105. BYRNE, D.G., A.E. BYRNE & M.I. REINHART. 1995. Personality, stress, and the decision to commence cigarette smoking in adolescence. J. Psychosom. Res. **39**(1): 53–62.
106. DUGAN, S., B. LLOYD & K. LUCAS. 1999. Stress and coping as determinants of adolescent smoking behavior. J. Appl. Soc. Psychol. **29**(4): 870–888.
107. BYRNE, D.G. & J. MAZANOV. 2001. Self-esteem, stress and cigarette smoking in adolescents. Stress Health **17**(2): 105–110.
108. KOVAL, J.J., L.L. PEDERSON, C.A. MILLS, et al. 2000. Models of the relationship of stress, depression, and other psychosocial factors to smoking behavior: a comparison of a cohort of students in grades 6 and 8. Prev. Med. **30**(6): 463–477.
109. SIQUEIRA, L., M. DIAB, C. BODIAN & L. ROLNITZKY. 2000. Adolescents becoming smokers: the roles of stress and coping methods. J. Adolesc. Health. **27**(6): 399–408.
110. SUSSMAN, S., C.W. DENT, H. SEVERSON, et al. 1998. Self-initiated quitting among adolescent smokers. Prev. Med. **27**(5): A19–A28.
111. KASSEL, J.D. 2000. Smoking and stress: correlation, causation, and context. Am. Psychol. **55**(10): 1155.
112. WILLS, T.A., A.M. YAEGER & J.M. SANDY. 2003. Buffering effect of religiosity for adolescent substance use. Psychol. Addict. Behav. **17**(1): 24–31.
113. PATTON, G.C., J.B. CARLIN, C. COFFEY, et al. 1998. Depression, anxiety, and smoking initiation: a prospective study over 3 years. Am. J. Public Health **88**(10): 1518–1522.
114. KILLEN, J.D., T.N. ROBINSON, K.F. HAYDEL, et al. 1997. Prospective study of risk factors for the initiation of cigarette smoking. J. Consult. Clin. Psychol. **65**(6): 1011–1016.
115. JACKSON, C. 1997. Initial and experimental stages of tobacco and alcohol use during late childhood: relation to peer, parent, and personal risk factors. Addict. Behav. **22**(5): 685–698.
116. BRAVERMAN, M.T. 1999. Research on resilience and its implications for tobacco prevention. Nicotine Tob. Res. **1**(Suppl. 1): S67–S72.
117. KASSEL, J.D. & M. UNROD. 2000. Smoking, anxiety, and attention: support for the role of nicotine in attentionally mediated anxiolysis. J. Abnorm. Psychol. **109**(1): 161–166.
118. STONE, A.A. & S. SHIFFMAN. 1994. Ecological momentary assessment (EMA) in behavioral medicine. Ann. Behav. Med. **16**: 199–202.
119. WHALEN, C.K., L.D. JAMNER, B. HENKER, et al. 2002. The ADHD spectrum and everyday life: experience sampling of adolescent moods, activities, smoking, and drinking. Child Dev. **73**(1): 209–227.
120. MERMELSTEIN, R., D. HEDEKER, B. FLAY & S. SHIFFMAN. 2003. Do changes in mood following smoking predict longitudinal changes in adolescent smoking patterns? Presented at the annual meeting of the Society for Research on Nicotine and Tobacco, New Orleans.
121. KOBUS, K. 2003. Peers and adolescent smoking. Addiction **98**(Suppl. 1): 37–56.
122. NICHTER, M., M. NICHTER, N. VUCKOVIC, et al. 1997. Smoking experimentation and initiation among adolescent girls: qualitative and quantitative findings. Tob. Control **6**: 285–295.
123. CHASSIN, L., C.C. PRESSON & S.J. SHERMAN. 1984. Cigarette smoking and adolescent psychosocial development. Basic Appl. Soc. Psychol. **5**(4): 295–315.
124. HU, F.B., B.R. FLAY, D. HEDEKER, et al. 1995. The influences of friends' and parental smoking on adolescent smoking behavior: the effects of time and prior smoking. J. Appl. Soc. Psychol. **25**(22): 2018–2047.
125. BOTVIN, G.J., E.M. BOTVIN, E. BAKER, et al. 1992. The false consensus effect: predicting adolescents' tobacco use from normative expectations. Psychol. Rep. **70**(1): 171–178.
126. SUSSMAN, S., T.R. SIMON, A.W. STACY, et al. 1999. The association of group self-identification and adolescent drug use in three samples varying in risk. J. Appl. Soc. Psychol. **29**(8): 1555–1581.

127. ENNETT, S. & K. BAUMAN. 1994. The contribution of influence and selection to adolescent peer group homogeneity: the case of adolescent cigarette smoking. J. Pers. Soc. Psychol. 67: 653–663.
128. ECCLES, J.S., C. MIDGLEY, A. WIGFIELD, *et al.* 1993. Development during adolescence: the impact of stage-environment fit on young adolescents' experiences in schools and in families. Am. Psychol. 48: 90–101.
129. SAVIN-WILLIAMS, R.C. & T.J. BERNDT. 1990. Friendships and peer relations. *In* At the Threshold: The Developing Adolescent. S.S. Feldman & G.R. Elliott, Eds.: 207–307. Harvard University Press. Cambridge, MA.
130. ROSE, J.S., L. CHASSIN, C.C. PRESSON & S.J. SHERMAN. 1999. Peer influences on adolescent cigarette smoking: a prospective sibling analysis. Merrill-Palmer Q. 45(1): 62–84.
131. WEBSTER, R.A., M. HUNTER & J.A. KEATS. 1994. Peer and parental influences on adolescents' substance use: a path analysis. Int. J. Addict. 29: 647–657.
132. BAUMAN, K.E., K. CARVER & K. GLEITER. 2001. Trends in parent and friend influence during adolescence. The case of adolescent cigarette smoking. Addict. Behav. 26(3): 349–361.
133. CHASSIN, L., C.C. PRESSON & S.J. SHERMAN. 1995. Social-psychological antecedents and consequences of adolescent tobacco use. *In* Adolescent Health Problems: Behavioral Perspectives. Advances in Pediatric Psychology. J.L. Wallander & L.J. Siegel, Eds.: 141–159. Guilford Press. New York.
134. AVENEVOLI, S. & K.R. MERIKANGAS. 2003. Familial influences on adolescent smoking. Addiction 98(Suppl. 1): 1–20.
135. BAUMAN, K.E., V.A. FOSHEE, M.A. LINZER & G.G. KOCH. 1990. Effect of parental smoking classification on the association between parental and adolescent smoking. Addict. Behav. 15(5): 413–422.
136. BIGLAN, A., T.E. DUNCAN, D.V. ARY & K. SMOLKOWSKI. 1995. Peer and parental influences on adolescent tobacco use. J. Behav. Med. 18(4): 315–330.
137. CHASSIN, L., C.C. PRESSON, M. TODD, *et al.* 1998. Maternal socialization of adolescent smoking: the intergenerational transmission of parenting and smoking. Dev. Psychol. 34(6): 1189.
138. JACKSON, C. & L. HENRIKSEN. 1997. Do as I say: parent smoking, antismoking socialization, and smoking onset among children. Addict. Behav. 22(1): 107–114.
139. CHASSIN, L., C.C. PRESSON, J.S. ROSE & S.J. SHERMAN. 1998. Maternal socialization of adolescent smoking: intergenerational transmission of smoking-related beliefs. Psychol. Addict. Behav. 12(3): 1189–1201.
140. GILPIN, E.A., M.M. WHITE, A.J. FARKAS & J.P. PIERCE. 1999. Home smoking restrictions: which smokers have them and how they are associated with smoking behavior. Nicotine Tob. Res. 1(2): 153–162.
141. WAKEFIELD, M.A., F.J. CHALOUPKA, N.J. KAUFMAN, *et al.* 2000. Effect of restrictions on smoking at home, at school, and in public places on teenage smoking: cross sectional study. Br. Med. J 321(7257): 333–337.
142. SIMONS-MORTON, B.G. 2002. Prospective analysis of peer and parent influences on smoking initiation among early adolescents. Prev, Sci. 3(4): 275–283.
143. SARGENT, J. & M. DALTON. 2001. Does parental disapproval of smoking prevent adolescents from becoming established smokers? Pediatrics 108: 1256–1262.
144. DISTEFAN, J.M., E.A. GILPIN, W.S. CHOI & J.P. PIERCE. 1998. Parental influences predict adolescent smoking in the United States, 1989–1993. J. Adolesc. Health 22(6): 466–474.
145. KODL, M.M. & R. MERMELSTEIN. 2004. Beyond modeling: potential psychosocial mediators of the relationship between parental smoking and adolescent smoking. Addict. Behav. 29: 17–32.
146. BAUMRIND, D. 1991. The influence of parenting style on adolescent competence and substance use. J. Early Adolesc. 11(1): 56–95.
147. ADALBJARNARDOTTIR, S. & L.G. HAFSTEINSSON. 2001. Adolescents' perceived parenting styles and their substance use: concurrent and longitudinal analyses. J. Res. Adolesc. 11(4): 401–423.

148. ADAMCZYK-ROBINETTE, S.L., A.C. FLETCHER & K. WRIGHT. 2002. Understanding the authoritative parenting-early adolescent tobacco use link: the mediating role of peer tobacco use. J. Youth Adolesc. **31**(4): 311–318.
149. JACKSON, C., D.J. BEE-GATES & L. HENRICKSEN. 2002. Authoritative parenting, child competencies, and initiation of cigarette smoking. J. Adolesc. Health **31**: 425–432.
150. SIMONS-MORTON, B., A.D. CRUMP, D.L. HAYNIE, *et al.* 1999. Psychosocial, school, and parent factors associated with recent smoking among early-adolescent boys and girls. Prev. Med. **28**(2): 138–148.
151. O'BYRNE, K.K., C.K. HADDOCK & W.S.C. POSTON. 2002. Parenting style and adolescent smoking. J. Adoles. Health **30**(6): 418–425.
152. DOHERTY, W.J. & W. ALLEN. 1994. Family functioning and parental smoking as predictors of adolescent cigarette use: a six-year prospective study. J. Fam. Psychol. **8**(3): 347–353.
153. CHASSIN, L.A., C.C. PRESSON, S.J. SHERMAN, *et al.* 1986. Changes in peer and parent influence during adolescence: longitudinal versus cross-sectional perspectives on smoking initiation. Dev. Psychol. **22**(3): 327–334.
154. MILLER, T.Q. & R.J. VOLK. 2002. Family relationships and adolescent cigarette smoking: results from a national longitudinal survey. J. Drug Issues **32**(3): 945–972.
155. PIERCE, J.P., W.S. CHOI, E.A. GILPIN, *et al.* 1996. Validation of susceptibility as a predictor of which adolescents take up smoking in the United States. Health Psychol. **15**(5): 355–361.
156. CUMMINGS, K.M., A. HYLAND, T.F. PECHACEK, *et al.* 1997. Comparison of recent trends in adolescent and adult cigarette smoking behaviour and brand preferences. Tob. Control **6**(Suppl. 2): S31–37.
157. DIFRANZA, J.R. & B.F. AISQUITH. 1995. Does the Joe Camel campaign preferentially reach 18–24 year old adults? Tob. Control **4**: 367–371.
158. GOLDSTEIN, A.O., P.M. FISCHER, J.W. RICHARDS, D. CRETEN. 1987. Relationship between high school student smoking and recognition of cigarette advertisements. J. Pediatr. **110**: 488–491.
159. BIENER, L. & M. SIEGEL. 2000. Tobacco marketing and adolescent smoking: more support or a causal inference. Am. J. Public Health **90**: 407–411.
160. PIERCE, J.P., W.S. CHOI, E.A. GILPIN, *et al.* 1998. Tobacco industry promotion of cigarettes and adolescent smoking. JAMA **279**(7): 511–515.
161. ALEXANDER, H., R. CALLCOTT, A.J. DOBSON. 1983. Cigarette smoking and drug use in school children. Int. J. Epidemiol. **12**: 59–66.
162. SARGENT, J.D., M. DALTON, M. BEACH, *et al.* 2000. Effect of cigarette promotions on smoking uptake among adolescents. Prev. Med. **30**(4): 320–327.
163. TERCYAK, K., P. GOLDMAN, A. SMITH & J. AUDRAIN. 2002. Interacting effects of depression and tobacco advertising receptivity on adolescent smoking. J. Pediatr. Psychol. **27**(2): 145–154.
164. AUDRAIN-MCGOVERN, J., K.P. TERCYAK, A.E. SHIELDS & C. LERMAN. 2003. Which adolescents are most recptive to tobacco industry marketing? Implications for counter-advertisings campaigns. Health Commun. **15**: 449–513.
165. PIERCE, J.P., J.M. DISTEFAN, C. JACKSON, *et al.* 2002. Does tobacco marketing undermine the influence of recommended parenting in discouraging adolescents from smoking? Am. J. Prev. Med. **23**(2): 73–81.
166. WAKEFIELD, M., B. FLAY, M. NICHTER & G. GIOVINO. 2003. Role of the media in influencing trajectories of youth smoking. Addiction **98**(Suppl. 1): 79–103.
167. JOHNSON, C.A., M.A. PENTZ & M.D. WEBER. 1990. Relative effectiveness of comprehensive community programming for drug abuse prevention with high-risk and low-risk adolescents. J. Consult. Clin. Psychol. **58**: 447–456.
168. TOBLER, N. & H. STRATTON. 1997. Effectiveness of school-based drug prevention programs: a meta-analysis of the research. J. Primary Prev. **18**(71–128).
169. FLAY, B.R., T.Q. MILLER, D. HEDEKER, *et al.* 1995. The television, school, and family smoking prevention and cessation project. VIII. Student outcomes and mediating variables. Prev. Med. **24**(1): 29–40.
170. LIANG, L., F. CHALOUPKA, M. NICHTER & R. CLAYTON. 2003. Prices, policies and youth smoking, May 2001. Addiction **98**(Suppl. 1): 105–122.

171. CHALOUPKA, F.J. 1999. Macro-social influences: the effects of prices and tobacco-control policies on the demand for tobacco products. Nicotine Tob. Res. **1:** S105–S109.
172. EMERY, S., M.M. WHITE & J.P. PIERCE. 2001. Does cigarette price influence adolescent experimentation? J. Health Econ. **20:** 261–270.
173. LIANG, L. & F.J. CHALOUPKA. 2002. Differential effects of cigarette price on youth smoking intensity. Nicotine Tob. Res. **4**(1): 109–114.
174. CHALOUPKA, F.J. 2003. Contextual factors and youth tobacco use: policy linkages. Addiction **98**(Suppl. 1): 147–149.
175. CHALOUPKA, F.J. & K.E. WARNER. 2000. The economics of smoking. *In* Handbook of Health Economics. A.N.J. Culyer, Ed.: 1539–1627.Elsevier Science. Amsterdam.
176. JONES, S.E., D.J. SHARP, C.G. HUSTEN & L.S. CROSSETT. 2002. Cigarette acquisition and proof of age among US high school students who smoke. Tob. Control **11:** 20–25.
177. RIGOTTI, N.A., J.R. DIFRANZA, Y. CHANG, *et al.* 1997. The effect of enforcing tobacco-sales laws on adolescents' access to tobacco and smoking behavior. N. Engl. J. Med. **337**(15): 1044–1051.
178. RIGOTTI, N.A. 1999. Youth access to tobacco. Nicotine Tob. Res. **1**(Suppl. 2): S93–S97.
179. DIFRANZA, J. 2000. Youth access: the baby and the bath water. Tob. Control **9:** 120–121.
180. GILPIN, E.A., A.J. FARKAS, S.L. EMERY, *et al.* 2002. Clean indoor air: advances in California, 1990–1999. Am. J. Public Health. **92**(5): 785–791.
181. MERMELSTEIN, R., B. FLAY, D. HEDEKER & S. SHIFFMAN. 2003. Adolescent tobacco use: trajectories and mood. Presented at the annual meeting of the Society of Behavioral Medicine, Salt Lake City, UT.
182. GRABER, J.A. & J. BROOKS-GUNN. 1999. Developmental transitions: linking human development with tobacco prevention research. Nicotine Tob. Res. **1**(Suppl.1): S73–S77.
183. HENNINGFIELD, J.E. & N.R. JUDE. 1999. Prevention of nicotine addiction: neuropsychopharmacological issues. Nicotine Tob. Res. **1**(Suppl 1): 1–15.

The Importance of Adolescence in the Development of Nicotine Dependence

Comments on Part V

KATHLEEN RIES MERIKANGAS

*National Institute of Mental Health, National Institutes of Health,
Bethesda, Maryland 20892-2670, USA*

This conference has provided a unique opportunity for scientists engaged in disparate domains of function to address this central theme (nicotine dependence) from multiple perspectives of brain function and its communication with experience. The lack of knowledge on the role of development in exposure and progression of substance use is a particularly critical gap that impedes our ability to understand, treat, and prevent substance abuse. This section on the importance of adolescence in the emergence of tobacco use and the development of nicotine dependence includes two outstanding presentations that identified common developmental differences in drug exposure from the perspectives of animal research[1] and human community-based research.[2]

EFFECTS OF NICOTINE IN ADOLESCENT VERSUS ADULT RATS

Substantial progress has been made in research on the relative effects of nicotine in periadolescent compared to adult rats. The growing knowledge of differences in brain response to experiential input as a function of development[3] has major implications for our understanding of substance use and abuse. Prior research and findings presented in other sessions of this meeting reveal that: (1) adolescent rats tend to receive greater reward from self-administered nicotine than adult rats;[4,5] and (2) alteration of *c-fos* expression in the frontal cortex of periadolescent rats by nicotine suggests that nicotine my induce deficits in executive decision making.[6] The elegant work of Koob and his colleagues taps the impact of adolescence on the development of nicotine dependence based on a withdrawal model, rather than on use as assessed by self-administration. Their article reports that periadolescent male rats seem to experience less negative effects from nicotine than adult rats. Since the attempt to reduce the negative effects of withdrawal is an important model of dependence, these findings may have major implications for our understanding of the continuation and progression beyond initial acquisition.

Address for correspondence: Kathleen Ries Merikangas, Ph.D., National Institute of Mental Health, NIH, 15K North Drive, Bethesda, MD 20892-2670. Voice: 301-496-1172; fax: 301-402-1218.

merikank@intra.nimh.nih.gov

Ann. N.Y. Acad. Sci. 1021: 198–201 (2004). © 2004 New York Academy of Sciences.
doi: 10.1196/annals.1308.024

HUMAN ADOLESCENT ACQUISITION

The study of adolescents by Mermelstein, Flay and their colleagues enhances the validity of comparisons with the elegant behavioral data collected in studies of rodents. First, the attempt to measure behavior *in vivo* through the use of personal digital assistants (PDAs), rather than through retrospective reconstruction, enhances the validity of assessment of drug use and its contextual inputs. Second, it should be noted that this approach to studying human behavioral patterns is much closer to the "gold standard" of measurement and should also be established for human behavioral researchers in order to facilitate animal-to-human collaborations. Third, classification of individuals according to smoking trajectories is far more informative than dichotomous classification of smoking behavior, its context, and consequences. Fourth, focus on the immediate proximal affective context of smoking episodes and explicit decisions not to smoke will yield information about the process of decision making in different contexts.

Similar to differences in periadolescent rats, Mermelstein and her colleagues revealed differences in adolescent exposure to nicotine, namely that positive rather than negative affective mood was associated with self-administration of nicotine. Since mood state was predictive of future trajectories of use, the lack of negative effects of nicotine may promote escalation and subsequent dependence.

COMMON THEMES FROM ANIMAL AND HUMAN RESEARCH

This work identifies several common areas of research where integration of human and animal studies may be promising. First, this research demonstrates the importance of affective states in nicotine self-administration. The primary venue for prevention in the United States is school-based, curriculum-driven, and focused on cognition rather than affect. The knowledge emerging about adolescent brain development and the differential effects of nicotine on periadolescent compared to adult brain processing may have important implications in the timing of prevention as well. Comorbidity with affective, anxiety, and substance-use disorders also require substantial transdisciplinary integration. Among both adolescents and adults there are consistent statistical relationships of depression, anxiety, and ADHD with drug use, and almost nine of ten schizophrenics are smokers. Animal studies of the core components of these states could enhance our understanding of the regulatory effects of drugs on these systems.

Second, the importance of developmental level in the experience of negative effects of nicotine should be pursued further in parallel animal and human studies. Coupled with the findings just mentioned, one of the pathways to dependence may involve experiencing more reward as adolescents from earlier episodes of nicotine self-administration, and fewer negative effects such as withdrawal. This potent combination may explain, at least in part, why a substantial proportion of adolescents who try nicotine and continue self-administration, ultimately exhibit trajectories of use that lead to chronic use and dependence. Despite this progress in discriminating neural effects of nicotine, there is still substantial research that will be required to develop adequate models of the development of human nicotine dependence.

GAPS

Despite the advances represented by this work, it is still preliminary in many respects. First, the bulk of animal research on the developmental inputs of substance use has been conducted exclusively with male animals. Since there is substantial knowledge regarding sex differences in exposure, transitions, and risk factors for drug abuse, future animal studies may provide insight on neural mechanisms underlying sex differences in the development of drug abuse.

Second, in addition to expanding our conceptualization to affective states, we also need to extend animal models of solo drug use to their human parallel of multiple substance use, both cross-sectionally and longitudinally. To date, almost all of the studies have focused on patterns of use of one drug, its correlates, and effects on the brain, body, or its social and medical consequences. While important, there is a strong need for basic science to better reflect the co-occurrence of use of various substances and the clustering of multiple problem behaviors in the same individuals, individuals who often exhibit other comorbid conditions besides drug use (see chapters in Kandel[7]). There are consistent patterns to the onset of use of tobacco, alcohol, marijuana, and other drugs, as well as consistent and moderate to stronger associations with regard to use of various drugs. There is also a strong need for transdisciplinary collaboration among social and behavioral scientists and basic scientists in designing experiments that more closely resemble how drugs are consumed in different contexts and affected by contextual as well as individual factors.

QUESTIONS FOR THE FUTURE

The two papers in this section suggest a number of important questions that could guide our future research agenda, particularly in parallel animal and human studies.

(1) What are the explanations for the differences observed in responses to nicotine among adolescents compared to adults?

(2) Are there sex differences in how individual-level and contextual-level factors influence smoking and nicotine self-administration, directly and interactively?

(3) What is the role of genetic susceptibility to initial use, early use episodes, and the trajectories of tobacco use that may or may not involve the development of dependence, and may include continued low-level use, desistence, and cessation?

(4) To what extent, and how, are patterns or trajectories of tobacco and nicotine use affected by premorbid and comorbid use of other drugs and various forms of psychopathology?

IMPLICATIONS

In terms of translation of knowledge gleaned from this initial work and future advances in our understanding of the key themes, several implications for prevention of human substance abuse have emerged. First, the exclusive basis on cognition in current programs should be shifted to include broader domains of affect and behavior. Second, the timing of onset may be critically important in prevention. Delay of onset may affect the degree to which early exposure to nicotine is rewarding. Interfering with and influencing the hiatus between adjacent-use episodes may also be important. Reducing the timing of first co-occurrence of tobacco and alcohol use and diminishing the overlapping co-occurrences may also be important.

Although there are still many questions that need to be addressed involving trajectories of nicotine use and the development of dependence, the papers in this section should be sufficient to inspire other scientists of the importance of future directions in this area. The two papers in this section provide a model for future research that adopts a transdisciplinary approach to science.

REFERENCES

1. O'DELL, L.E., A.W. BRUIJNZEEL, S. GHOZLAND, et al. 2004. Nicotine withdrawal in adolescent and adult rats. Ann. N.Y. Acad. Sci. 1021: 167–174

2. TURNER, L., R. MERMELSTEIN & B. FLAY. 2004. Individual and contextual influences on adolescent smoking. Ann. N.Y. Acad. Sci. 1021: 175–197.

3. SPEAR, L.P. 2000. The adolescent brain and age-related behavioral manifestations. Neurosci. Biobehav. Rev. 24: 417–463.

4. LESLIE, F.M., S.E. LOUGHLIN, R. WANG, et al. 2004. Adolescent development of forebrain stimulant responsiveness: insights from animal studies. Ann. N.Y. Acad. Sci. 1021: 148–159.

5. VASTOLA, B.J. & L.A. DOUGLAS. 2002. Nicotine-induced conditioned place preference in adolescent and adult rats. Physiol. Behav. 77: 107–114.

6. SCHOCHET, T.L., C.F. LANDRY & A.E. KELLEY. 2003. Differences in nicotine responsivity and prefrontal gene expression in adolescent and adult rats. Poster session presented at the New York Academy of Sciences Conf. on Adolescent Brain Development, New York.

7. KANDEL, D.B., ED. 2002. Stages and Pathways of Drug Involvement: Examining the Gateway Hypothesis. Cambridge University Press. Cambridge.

Adolescence and the Trajectory of Alcohol Use

Introduction to Part VI

LINDA PATIA SPEAR

Department of Psychology and Center for Developmental Psychobiology,
Binghamton University, Binghamton, New York 13902-6000, USA

ABSTRACT: Research in the area of adolescent alcohol use is progressing rapidly, as exemplified by the chapters in this section. Basic animal research in rodents has revealed adolescents to be more sensitive than adults to ethanol-induced disruptions in brain plasticity, although adolescents conversely are relatively insensitive to ethanol cues that serve to moderate intake. Risks for excessive alcohol consumption due to genetic background have been shown in primate research to be exacerbated by adverse early life experiences. Studies in clinical populations have revealed neurocognitive deficits evident years following adolescent alcohol abuse, along with evidence that some neural changes may predate adolescent alcohol abuse, whereas others appear to be a consequence of this abuse. Further research is needed to detail determinants and consequences of adolescent alcohol abuse and to identify potential protective factors to diminish the propensity for excessive use of alcohol during this critical developmental period.

KEYWORDS: alcohol; adolescence; brain; ethanol

Research examining alcohol use during adolescence has had a slightly longer history than some of the other topics explored in this conference on adolescent brain development. Precipitated in part by several requests for applications (RFAs) initiated by the National Institute on Alcohol Abuse and Alcoholism in the mid-1990s and exemplified by the chapters to follow, work using human adolescents as well as animal models of adolescence has progressed rapidly to examine contributors to alcohol use during adolescence, and has begun to explore consequences of that use.

Studies modeling adolescence in laboratory animals have found adolescents to be surprisingly resistant to numerous ethanol effects that may serve as cues to limit intake, including effects apparent during intoxication (e.g., ethanol-induced motor impairment,[1] sedation,[2] anxiolysis and suppression of social behavior,[3] as well as a resistance to at least some signs of "hangover."[4] Conversely, adolescents are surprisingly more sensitive than adults to certain ethanol effects that are unlikely to serve as cues to moderate intake, effects that include ethanol-induced social facilitation[3] and disruptions in hippocampal function and hippocampus-mediated behaviors (see the chapter by White and Swartzwelder[5] that follows for review). Should similar al-

Address for correspondence: Dr. Linda P. Spear, Department of Psychology, Binghamton University, Box 6000, Binghamton, NY 13902-6000. Voice: 607-777-2825; fax: 607-777-6418.
lspear@binghamton.edu

Ann. N.Y. Acad. Sci. 1021: 202–205 (2004). © 2004 New York Academy of Sciences.
doi: 10.1196/annals.1308.025

terations in ethanol sensitivity be evident among human adolescents, this combination of attenuated sensitivity to cues moderating intake, but greater sensitivity to disruptions in brain plasticity would be unfortunate, serving to increase not only the probability of "binge" drinking, but also the aversive neural consequences of that drinking.

This mosaic of ethanol sensitivities of adolescence appears related in part to differential rates of development of neural systems moderating different ethanol effects. For instance, as detailed by White and Swartzwelder in their excellent chapter in this section,[5] developmentally overexpressed NMDA receptors are unusually sensitive to ethanol inhibition early in life, contributing to the greater sensitivity of adolescent rats to ethanol-induced inhibition of long-term potentiation (LTP). In contrast, developmental immaturity in $GABA_A$ receptor systems appears to contribute to the relative resistance of young animals to the sedative effects of ethanol.[5,6]

To the extent that human adolescents are similarly resistant to effects of alcohol that normally serve to deter excessive use, it might be expected that they would exhibit relatively high levels of alcohol drinking. Indeed, human adolescents, like their counterparts in laboratory animals,[7] often consume high levels of alcohol, with over 25% of all 10th- and 12th-grade students reporting drinking of 5 or more drinks in a row during the past 2 weeks.[8] A relative insensitivity to ethanol has been shown to be a risk factor for later problematic ethanol use, as shown in studies of individuals with a family history of alcoholism.[9] A combination of genetically based and normal developmental insensitivities to ethanol cues that serve to moderate intake may be an inopportune combination for at-risk adolescents, increasing their probability of drinking excessively.

Thus, genetic background may provide one vulnerability for problematic ethanol use that may interact with a second, developmentally based vulnerability associated with ontogenetic changes in ethanol sensitivity. Prior experiences, particularly those involving stressors early in life, may provide yet another vulnerability for the development of excessive drinking. The chapter by Barr and colleagues[10] later in this section provides an outstanding example of how genetics and early life stressors may interact to increase the later risk for excessive alcohol intake in adolescent primates. In this work, male adolescent primates who exhibited increased risk taking, aggression, and excessive alcohol consumption were characterized by low brain serotonin function. In females, enhanced alcohol consumption was not only associated with genetic markers of serotonergic function, but exacerbated by poor rearing circumstances early in life.

There is emphasis throughout this volume on the substantial remodeling of the brain that occurs during adolescence; among the brain regions undergoing particularly marked alterations during adolescence are many that are alcohol sensitive (see Spear[11] for review). An important question that thus arises is whether repeated exposure to alcohol has an impact on these critical adolescent transformations of the brain. The last two chapters in this section approach this question by focusing on consequences of alcohol abuse in human adolescents. As reviewed by Brown and Talpert,[12] human adolescents with a history of heavy alcohol use exhibit poorer cognitive and brain function after weeks of abstinence, and residual deficits can be seen for years thereafter. Interestingly, some of these effects appear to be associated with withdrawal episodes during adolescence, particularly in females. To address the important issue of whether neurocognitive dysfunctions characteristic of adolescents with a history of alcohol abuse precede or are a consequence of that alcohol use, work described in the closing chapter by Hill[13] uses the strategy of imaging brains of high- and low-risk youth prior to the time of any extensive alcohol involvement. In these assessments of youth with limited prior alcohol exposure, the volume of the right amygdala was smaller in individuals with a family history of alcohol abuse relative to low-risk youth, whereas the volume of the hippocampus (previously shown to be altered following a history of adolescent alcohol abuse[12,14]) was unaffected. Thus, whereas adolescent alcohol abuse may lead to some neural alterations (such as those seen in the hippocampus), other neural characteristics of high-risk youth (i.e., amygdalar changes) may predate alcohol use and may reflect risk factors for, rather than consequences of, adolescent alcohol abuse.

Despite the rapid progress of research in the area of alcohol and adolescence, our understanding of the determinants and consequences of adolescent alcohol abuse remains rudimentary. We need to know much more about the relationship between ethanol sensitivity during adolescence and the remodeling occurring in the brain at that time, and how genetic factors and prior life experiences interact to increase the propensity for adolescent use of alcohol. Although there are intriguing hints in both basic science and clinical data that ethanol exerts sexually dimorphic effects during adolescence, potential gender-specific effects need substantial further investigation. Disconcerting evidence for neurocognitive deficits years following adolescent alcohol abuse, combined with findings suggesting that some of these neural changes may predate and others follow alcohol use, provide a strong rationale for further intensive basic research and prospective clinical studies to determine what aspects of adolescent brain development are altered by alcohol and to determine the magnitude and timing of exposure necessary to produce those effects. In addition to exploring how genetic and early adverse life experiences interact to increase risk for excessive drinking in adolescence, the opposite strategy is critical as well—that of identifying early life or contemporaneous experiences that may serve as protective factors to diminish the propensity for excessive alcohol use during adolescence and determining the substrates and mediators underlying this protection.

REFERENCES

1. WHITE, A.M., M.C. TRUESDALE & J.G. BAE, et al. 2002. Differential effects of ethanol on motor coordination in adolescent and adult rats. Pharmacol. Biochem. Behav. 73: 673–677.
2. SILVERI, M.M. & L.P. SPEAR. 1998. Decreased sensitivity to the hypnotic effects of ethanol early in ontogeny. Alcohol. Clin. Exp. Res. 22: 670–676.
3. VARLINSKAYA E.I. & L.P. SPEAR. 2002. Acute effects of ethanol on social behavior of adolescent and adult rats: role of familiarity of the test situation. Alcohol. Clin. Exp. Res. 26: 1502–1511.
4. DOREMUS, T.L., S.C. BRUNELL, E.I. VARLINSKAYA, et al. 2003. Anxiogenic effects during withdrawal from acute ethanol in adolescent and adult rats. Pharmacol. Biochem. Behav. 75: 411–418.
5. WHITE, A.M. & H.S. SWARTZWELDER. 2004. Hippocampal function during adolescence: a unique target of ethanol effects. Ann. N.Y. Acad. Sci. 1021: 206–220.
6. SILVERI, M.M. & L.P. SPEAR. 2002. The effects of NMDA and GABA_A pharmacological manipulations on ethanol sensitivity in immature and mature animals. Alcohol. Clin. Exp. Res. 26: 449–456.

7. DOREMUS, T.L., S.C. BRUNELL, R. POTTAYIL, et al. 2003. Elevated ethanol consumption in adolescent relative to adult rats. Presented at the 26th annual meeting of the Research Society on Alcoholism. Fort Lauderdale, FL, June 21–25.
8. JOHNSTON, L.D., P.M. O'MALLEY & J.G. BACHMAN. 2001. The Monitoring of the Future National Survey Results on Adolescent Drug Use: Overview of Key Findings, 2000. NIH Publ. No. 01-4923: 1–60. National Institute on Drug Abuse. Bethesda, MD.
9. SCHUCKIT, M.A. 1994. Low level of response to alcohol as a predictor of future alcoholism. Am. J. Psychiatry. **151**: 184–189.
10. BARR, C.S., M.L SCHWANDT, T.K. NEWMAN & J.D. HIGLEY. 2004. The use of adolescent nonhuman primates to model human alcohol intake: neurobiological, genetic, and psychological variables. Ann. N.Y. Acad. Sci. **1021**: 221–233.
11. SPEAR, L.P. 2000. The adolescent brain and age-related behavioral manifestations. Neurosci. Biobehav. Rev. **24**: 417–463.
12. BROWN, S.A. & S.F. TAPERT. 2004. Adolescence and the trajectory of alcohol use: basic to clinical studies. Ann. N.Y. Acad. Sci. **1021**: 234–244.
13. HILL, S.Y. 2004. Trajectories of alcohol use and electrophsiological and morphological indices of brain development: distinguishing causes from consequences. Ann. N.Y. Acad. Sci. **1021**: 245–259.
14. DEBELLIS, M.D., D.B. CLARK, S.R. BEERS, et al. 2000. Hippocampal volume in adolescent-onset alcohol use disorders. Am. J. Psychiatry **157**: 737–744.

Hippocampal Function during Adolescence

A Unique Target of Ethanol Effects

AARON M. WHITE AND H. SCOTT SWARTZWELDER

Department of Psychiatry, Duke University Medical Center, Durham, North Carolina 27710, USA and Neurobiology Research Labs, Veterans Affairs Medical Center, Durham, North Carolina, 27705, USA

ABSTRACT: Behaviors mediated by the hippocampus have long been known to be sensitive to the acute, chronic, and prenatal effects of ethanol. It has recently become clear that hippocampal function is uniquely responsive to ethanol during periadolescent development, and that alcohol affects behavior and brain function differently in adolescents and adults. We have used behavioral techniques, as well as extracellular and whole-cell electrophysiological techniques, to assess the effects of acute and chronic ethanol exposure on hippocampal function during adolescence and adulthood. Our results are consistent with the view that the hippocampus is more sensitive to the acute effects of ethanol during adolescence and may be more susceptible to the neurotoxic effects of ethanol during this developmental period. Studies of this type have yielded valuable information for prevention, education, and public policy efforts related to underage drinking.

KEYWORDS: hippocampus; adolescence; ethanol

ALCOHOL AND MEMORY

Alcohol is a potent amnestic agent. It primarily disrupts the ability to form memories that are explicit in nature, such as memories for facts (e.g., names, phone numbers) and events (e.g., what you did last night).[1] The impact of alcohol on the formation of new explicit memories is far greater than the drug's impact on the ability to recall previously established memories or to hold new information in memory for just a few seconds.

Ryback[2,3] characterized the impact of alcohol on memory formation as a dose-related continuum with minor impairments at one end and very large impairments at the other, with all impairments representing the same fundamental deficit in the ability to store new information in memory for longer than a few seconds. Consistent with this view, research indicates that the magnitude of alcohol-induced memory im-

Address for correspondence: H. Scott Swartzwelder, Ph.D., Bldg. 16, Rm. 24, VAMC, 508 Fulton St., Durham, NC 27705. Voice: 919-286-6810; fax: 919-286-4662.
hss@duke.edu

Ann. N.Y. Acad. Sci. 1021: 206–220 (2004). © 2004 New York Academy of Sciences.
doi: 10.1196/annals.1308.026

pairments increases with dose and is manifested predominantly as greater difficulty forming new memories rather than recalling existing memories. When doses of alcohol are small to moderate, such as those producing blood alcohol concentrations below 0.15%, memory impairments tend to be small to moderate, as well. At these levels, alcohol produces what Ryback[3] referred to as cocktail party memory deficits, lapses in memory that one might experience after having a few drinks at a cocktail party, often manifested as "problems remembering what the other person said or where they were in conversation." Several studies have revealed difficulty forming memories for items on word lists or learning to recognize new faces at such doses. As the doses increase, the resulting memory impairments can become much more profound, sometimes culminating in blackouts, a complete inability to remember critical elements of events, or even entire events, that transpired while intoxicated.[4]

MECHANISMS UNDERLYING ALCOHOL-INDUCED MEMORY IMPAIRMENTS: THE ROLE OF THE HIPPOCAMPUS

More than 30 years ago, both Ryback[2] and Goodwin[5] speculated that alcohol might impair memory formation by disrupting activity in the hippocampus. This speculation followed the observation that acute alcohol exposure produced a syndrome of memory impairments similar in many ways to the impairments produced by hippocampal damage. Both manipulations impaired the formation of new, long-term, explicit memories while leaving immediate recall and remote memory intact.

It is now clear that alcohol impairs memory formation, at least in part, by disrupting hippocampal function (see ref. 6 for review). Brain damage limited to neurons in a single region of the hippocampus, area CA1, markedly disrupts the ability to form new, explicit memories for facts and events.[7] In rodents, CA1 pyramidal cells often exhibit a striking behavioral correlate. Each cell tends to fire predominantly in a specific area of the environment. For this reason, these cells are often referred to as place cells, and the regions of the environment in which they fire are referred to as place fields (for review see ref. 8). Given the critical importance of these cells in the formation of memories for facts and events, and the clear behavioral correlates of their activity, they offer an ideal way to assess the impact of alcohol on hippocampal output in an intact, fully functional brain.

One recent project examined the impact of alcohol on hippocampal CA1 pyramidal cell activity in freely moving rats.[9] Alcohol decreased the output from these cells beginning at a dose of 0.5 g/kg. Doses of 1.0 and 1.5 g/kg dramatically suppressed the firing of cells in CA1, almost shutting them off entirely in some cases.

ALCOHOL SUPPRESSES HIPPOCAMPAL NMDA RECEPTOR FUNCTION AND LONG-TERM POTENTIATION

In addition to suppressing the output from pyramidal cells, alcohol has several other effects on hippocampal function. For instance, alcohol potently disrupts the establishment of long-term potentiation (LTP), an experimentally induced form of synaptic plasticity that has mechanisms in common with memory formation.[10] It is believed that an LTP-like process occurs naturally in the brain during learning (see ref. 11 for review). Because drugs that interfere with the establishment of LTP generally also cause memory impairments, many people believe that LTP serves as a good model for studying the neurobiology underlying the effects of drugs, like alcohol, on memory.

In the functioning brain, information flow, in the form of sequential activation of neurons in specific circuits, progresses in a very orderly fashion from cells in the neocortex, to cells in the dentate gyrus, to cells in CA3, to cells in CA1, and then back out to the cortex. Thus the hippocampus has reciprocal interconnections with many neocortical regions, allowing it to participate in the processing of a wide variety of sensory information. In a typical LTP experiment, two electrodes are lowered into a slice of hippocampal tissue kept alive by bathing it in oxygenated artificial cerebral spinal fluid (ACSF). The hippocampal slice, while disconnected from most neocortical inputs, preserves intact its own internal circuitry, thus allowing a precise assessment of the synaptic activity within those circuits. The first electrode is positioned near the axons coursing from CA3 to CA1. A small amount of current is passed through the first electrode, causing the neurons in this area to send synaptic signals to cells located in CA1. The second electrode, which is located in CA1, is then used to record the response of CA1 neurons to the incoming signals (see FIG.1). After a baseline response is established, a specific pattern of stimulation intended to model the pattern of activity that might occur during a learning event is delivered through the first electrode. After a delay on the order of minutes to hours, the re-

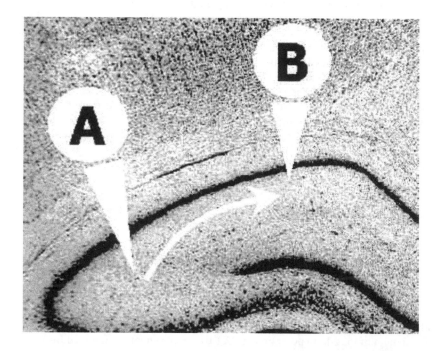

FIGURE 1. Transverse section of the hippocampal formation indicating the location of the stimulating (**A**) and recording (**B**) electrodes in area CA1 in a typical LTP experiment.

sponse of the CA1 pyramidal cells to the baseline stimulus pulse is potentiated. In other words, as a result of the patterned input, cells in CA1 are now more responsive to synaptic activation along the stimulated pathway.

Depending upon the age of the animal, and the exact nature of the preparation, alcohol interferes with the establishment of LTP beginning at concentrations equivalent to those produced by consuming just one or two drinks.[12] If sufficient alcohol is present in the ACSF bathing the slice when the patterned stimulation is given, the induction of LTP may be completely blocked.

One of the key requirements for the establishment of LTP in most hippocampal preparations is the activation of N-methyl-D-aspartate (NMDA) receptors, a glutamate receptor subtype that becomes active when neurons are strongly stimulated by excitatory inputs. Activation of the NMDA receptor allows calcium (Ca^{2+}) to enter the cell, setting off a chain of events that lead to long-lasting changes in the structure and/or function of the cell, including LTP. Alcohol interferes with the activation of the NMDA receptor, thereby preventing the influx of Ca^{2+} and the changes that follow. This is believed to be the primary mechanism underlying the effects of alcohol on the induction of LTP,[13] though other transmitter systems are probably also involved.[14]

ALCOHOL AFFECTS ADOLESCENTS AND ADULTS DIFFERENTLY

The available evidence suggests that adolescents are more vulnerable than adults to the effects of alcohol on learning and memory, though much more work needs to be done in this area. In rats, one task commonly used to assess learning and memory is called the *Morris water maze* task. This task requires rats to locate a platform submerged an inch or so beneath the surface of opaque water in a large circular tub. The ability to learn this task is very sensitive to changes in activity in the hippocampus, so it provides an easy way to assess whether drugs that disrupt hippocampal function also disrupt learning that is dependent on this structure.

A few years ago we found that adolescent rats are much more vulnerable than adults to alcohol-induced learning impairments in the water maze.[15] The rats were trained to locate the submerged platform over a period of five days and were administered either saline or 1.0 or 2.0 g/kg alcohol prior to training on each of the five test days. Adolescents exhibited learning impairments relative to saline-treated subjects at both doses. In contrast, adults were impaired only at the highest dose, indicating that lower doses of alcohol are required to disrupt hippocampus-mediated learning in adolescents compared to adults.

It is difficult to determine whether adolescent humans, like adolescent rats, are more vulnerable than adults to the effects of alcohol on learning and memory. For obvious legal and ethical reasons, this research has not been carried out in young adolescent humans. However, we were able to determine that people in their early twenties, at the trailing end of adolescence, were more vulnerable to alcohol-induced memory impairments than were those in their late twenties.[16] Subjects were tested using a variety of memory tasks, including the complex figure task. In this task, subjects are shown a line drawing and are required to reproduce the drawing immediately after it is shown to them (immediate recall) and then again 20 minutes later (delayed recall). When tested under placebo, all subjects performed similarly in both the immediate and delayed components of the task. However, when tested under alcohol (the equivalent of about 2–3 drinks), subjects in their early twenties performed worse than subjects in their late twenties on both components of the task.

POTENTIAL MECHANISMS UNDERLYING THE AGE-DEPENDENT EFFECTS OF ACUTE ALCOHOL ON MEMORY

As discussed above, the hippocampus plays a central role in learning and memory. Several studies have revealed that alcohol affects hippocampal function differently in adolescents and adults. For instance, it is quite clear that alcohol inhibits the induction of LTP[17,18] and NMDA receptor-mediated synaptic potentials[19] more potently in hippocampal slices from adolescent rats than in those from adults. These findings indicate that glutamatergic (i.e., NMDA) receptor-mediated neurotransmission in the hippocampus is inhibited more powerfully by acute alcohol during periadolescent development than during adulthood.

It also appears that the unique potency of alcohol against NMDA receptor-mediated synaptic activity is not restricted to the hippocampus. Using whole-cell recording techniques in slices of the retrosplenial cortex, we found that synaptically evoked, NMDA receptor–mediated excitatory postsynaptic currents (EPSCs) were more powerfully inhibited by alcohol in cells from juvenile rats than in those from adults.[20] Those findings illustrate three important points—developmental sensitivity of NMDA receptor–mediated currents to alcohol exists outside the hippocampus, it is observable at the level of single neurons, and it is observable at alcohol concentrations as low as 5 mM, roughly the equivalent of a single drink.

REDUCED SENSITIVITY TO ALCOHOL-INDUCED MOTOR IMPAIRMENTS AND SEDATION

In contrast to the uniquely powerful effects of alcohol against excitatory glutamatergic neurotransmission and learning in adolescence, the onset of sedation following alcohol administration is slower, and the magnitude of sedation smaller, in adolescent rats than in adult rats.[21–24] Similarly, alcohol affects motor coordination less potently in adolescents than adults.[25,26] In humans, the sedative and motor incoordinating effects of alcohol can limit the amount of alcohol an individual consumes. That is, people might find themselves incapacitated at some point during the evening and unable to continue drinking even if they desired to do so. The existing research regarding alcohol-induced sedation and motor impairments in adolescents and adults has all involved the use of rodents. If such findings extend to humans, the decreased vulnerability of adolescents to the sedative and motor-impairing effects of alcohol might allow adolescents to continue drinking for longer periods of time than adults, and perhaps achieve much higher blood alcohol concentrations, without becoming sedated. As we have seen, adolescents appear to be more vulnerable than adults to some of the cognitive impairments produced by alcohol. Thus, the reduced susceptibility to alcohol-induced sedation and motor impairments, combined with an enhanced susceptibility to alcohol-induced cognitive deficits, could potentially be a very dangerous combination of effects.

The neural mechanisms underlying the developmental differences in sensitivity to the sedative and motor-impairing effects of alcohol are unclear but are likely to involve GABA receptor–mediated inhibition. The promotion of neuronal inhibition through enhancement of $GABA_A$ receptor activation is thought to be a primary mechanism of alcohol-induced sedation[27] and has been observed in many neural circuits and regions.[28] In rats, after the polarity of $GABA_A$ receptor–mediated inhibition changes from depolarizing to hyperpolarizing by about postnatal day seven,[29,30] development of $GABA_A$ receptor-mediated neurotransmission follows a linear course. $GABA_A$ neurotransmission develops steadily, reaching adult functional levels by about postnatal day 60.[31,32] Accordingly, during the early adolescent period (postnatal days 28–36) levels of $GABA_A$ receptors increase markedly in a number of brain structures.[24] Aguayo et al.[33] have shown a developmental sensitivity of the ability of alcohol to potentiate $GABA_A$ receptor function in tissue culture. They demonstrated that $GABA_A$ receptors in 12-day cultured hippocampal cells were not potentiated by alcohol; but if left in culture for seven more days, the cells developed alcohol sensitivity. The mechanisms underlying this are not known. These findings are consistent with other studies that have demonstrated changes in the pharmacological sensitivity of $GABA_A$ receptor–mediated currents in hippocampal neurons across postnatal development.[34,35] Those studies demonstrated that $GABA_A$ receptor–mediated inhibitory postsynaptic currents (IPSCs) become progressively more sensitive to the effects of both diazepam and zolpidem across juvenile and periadolescent development, reaching adult levels of sensitivity by about postnatal day 50.

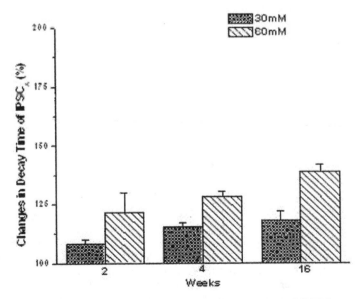

FIGURE 2. Mean (+SEM) percent change in the decay time of $GABA_A$ receptor–mediated IPSCs recorded from area CA1 of hippocampal slices from rats at 2, 4, and 16 weeks of age in the presence of 30 mM (*dense shading*) or 60 mM (*sparse shading*) alcohol.

These findings beg the question of whether the effects of alcohol on $GABA_A$ receptor function differ between adolescent and adult subjects. This has not as yet been definitively answered, but we have strong preliminary data suggesting that $GABA_A$ receptor–mediated IPSCs in hippocampal CA1 pyramidal cells become progressively more sensitive to alcohol between 2 and 16 weeks of age in the rat. FIGURE 2 shows that as rats age from 2 to 16 weeks (from the juvenile period into early adulthood) the effect of alcohol on $GABA_A$ receptor–mediated IPSCs increases steadily. This would be consistent with the behavioral findings described above indicating that juvenile and adolescent animals are markedly less sensitive to the sedating effects of acute alcohol than adults.

LONG-LASTING CONSEQUENCES OF ALCOHOL EXPOSURE IN ADOLESCENTS AND ADULTS

In addition to reacting differently to the acute, or initial, effects of alcohol, it appears that adolescents are also affected differently from adults by repeated, heavy drinking. Many adolescents engage in a pattern of chronic intermittent exposure (CIE) sometimes referred to as "binge drinking." Chronic intermittent exposure is a special case of chronic alcohol administration that involves discrete, repeated withdrawals. There is compelling evidence that it is the repeated withdrawals from alcohol that are responsible for many of the CNS effects of chronic alcohol exposure. For example, in laboratory animals, repeated withdrawals from alcohol result in a higher rate of seizures during withdrawal than are observed after continuous exposure of the same duration.[36] The association of repeated withdrawals with withdrawal seizure susceptibility is also indicated in humans. In studies of alcohol detoxification, patients with a history of previous detoxifications were more likely to exhibit seizures during withdrawal.[37] Although these data from human studies are correlational, the convergence of these findings with those from animal models strongly suggests that discrete, repeated withdrawals from alcohol exposure presents a unique risk for subsequent neurobehavioral impairments.

Our most recent behavioral studies have shown what we believe is a striking long-term effect of developmental alcohol exposure.[26] We found that CIE treatment (5.0 g/kg ip every 48 h for 20 days) during adolescence interferes with the normal increase in sensitivity to alcohol-induced motor impairments that occurs between adolescence and adulthood. As expected, under control conditions (i.e., repeated saline exposure), rats were more sensitive to the effects of alcohol on postnatal day 65 (young adulthood) than they had been on postnatal day 30 (adolescence). This is consistent with the previous reports that rats become more sensitive to the motor-impairing effects of alcohol as they progress from adolescence to adulthood.[25] However, animals that received CIE during adolescence did not show the normal pattern of increased sensitivity to alcohol as they aged into adulthood. In these subjects, the impact of acute alcohol on motor coordination remained unchanged before, two days after, and 16 days after CIE treatment. In contrast to the effects of CIE in adolescents, CIE treatment during adulthood had little impact on the subsequent effects of alcohol on motor coordination (see FIG. 3). This suggests the possibility that the chronic exposure during adolescence may have "locked in" the adolescent insensi-

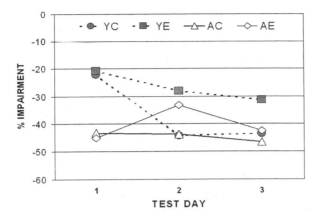

FIGURE 3. The effects of alcohol on motor coordination during three different test days (test day 1, 2, 3). The lower on the chart the data point is, the greater the impairment. Between test 1 and test 2, rats received 10 injections (one every 48 h) of either saline or alcohol. Test 3 occurred 16 days after the treatment period ended. The effects of alcohol on motor coordination in adult rats treated with saline between test 1 and test 2 (group AC) remained quite stable across the three test days. The effects of alcohol on motor coordination in adolescent rats treated with saline increased markedly between test 1 and test 2 (group YC), showing a clear increase in sensitivity to alcohol-induced motor impairments between the ages of 30 and 52 days. Note that adolescent rats treated with alcohol between test 1 and test 2 (group YE) do not show the same age-related increase in alcohol sensitivity. Note that rats in group YE continued to exhibit the same level of sensitivity shown during the first test day on test 3.

tivity to alcohol's sedative effects, or at least significantly delayed the normal progression to greater sensitivity in adulthood.

Repeated alcohol withdrawals are also associated with subsequent cognitive deficits. For example, after repeated alcohol exposures, adult rodents exhibit impaired learning in an active avoidance paradigm.[38] In addition, we have found that CIE treatment in adolescent rats results in exacerbated alcohol-induced learning deficits in adulthood.[39] In that study, adolescent and adult rats were treated with CIE (5.0 g/kg, ip every 48 h for 20 days) and then trained on a spatial memory task. All subjects acquired the task at similar rates. However, when their memory was tested under acute alcohol (1.5 g/kg), subjects treated with CIE during adolescence performed more poorly than those treated as adults. Similar results have been observed in humans. Weissenborn and Duka[40] assessed the impact of acute alcohol exposure on memory in college students. Those with a history of binge-pattern drinking performed more poorly while intoxicated than other subjects. In addition, among adult alcoholics one of the most consistent clinical neuropsychological findings is a deficit in anterograde, declarative memory, and the severity of these enduring memory deficits has been positively correlated with the number of alcohol withdrawals.[37] Finally, Brown et al.[41] observed that, among adolescents in an inpatient treatment facility, the presence of alcohol withdrawal symptoms at intake was associated with impaired cognitive functions three weeks into the program.

Cognitive impairments following repeated alcohol exposure and withdrawal may stem from neurotoxicity in the hippocampus and related structures. A study by De Bellis et al.[42] suggests that, in humans, alcohol abuse during adolescence is associated with a reduction in the volume of the hippocampus. The authors utilized magnetic resonance imagine (MRI) to assess the size of the hippocampus in subjects with adolescent-onset alcohol-use disorders and in normal control subjects. Hippocampal volumes were smaller in those who abused alcohol during adolescence, and the amount of apparent hippocampal damage increased as the number of years of alcohol abuse increased (i.e., the longer one abused alcohol, the smaller the hippocampus was). Total intracranial, cortical gray and white matter, corpus callosum, and amygdala volumes did not differ between groups. Such data suggest that the adolescent hippocampus is sensitive to the neurotoxic effects of alcohol, and that the earlier in adolescence one begins abusing alcohol, the greater the risk for producing hippocampal damage. However, whether adolescents are truly more vulnerable than adults to hippocampal damage following alcohol exposure remains to be seen.

Damage to the hippocampus following repeated alcohol exposure might stem from hyperactivity at NMDA receptors during alcohol withdrawal, which could allow intracellular Ca^{2+} levels to become neurotoxic. Repeated alcohol exposure results in an upregulation of NMDA receptors in several brain regions, including the hippocampus.[43-45] Calcium channels are also upregulated after chronic alcohol exposure.[46] Chronic exposure is also related to increased excitotoxicity of cultured neurons[47] and increased NMDA-mediated Ca^{2+} influx.[48,49] Thus, repeated alcohol exposure results in neuroadaptive changes that may increase the liability for excitotoxicity during withdrawal.

As discussed above, the available evidence suggests that adolescents might be more vulnerable than adults to brain damage and, perhaps, long-lasting cognitive deficits following alcohol exposure. Given the potential role of hippocampal neurotoxicity in these effects, it is logical to speculate that adolescents might be more vulnerable than adults to hippocampal dysfunction following repeated periods of intoxication and withdrawal. However, our most recent studies have failed to show differential neuronal death or neurophysiological indices of pathology after binge-pattern alcohol exposure in adolescent rats. For example, we have done a series of experiments in which animals were exposed to doses of 5.0 g/kg of alcohol (ip) in various patterns: once per day for six days, once per 48 hours for four days, and twice per day for five days. Some of the groups were exposed during adolescent development, and some during early adulthood. The animals were then perfused transcardially 1–3 days after the last alcohol treatment, and the brains were sectioned for subsequent staining with Flouro-Jade B (FJ-B), a marker for dying neurons. In no instance did we observe significant FJ-B staining, suggesting that at least with these relatively mild patterns of alcohol exposure there was no indication of frank neuronal death in rats of any of the ages tested. In contrast, Crews and his colleagues[50] found preferential sensitivity to brain damage among adolescent rats after a multiday, high-dose binge exposure to alcohol (four days, four doses per day, resulting in 9–10 g/kg/day of alcohol). Although they observed significant brain damage in both adult and adolescent rats after the four-day treatment period, several brain regions that had been spared in adults were damaged in the adolescents, including the frontal cortical olfactory regions and the piriform and perirhinal cortices. Sensitivity of the latter regions is particularly interesting because of their relationship to the hippocampus and other limbic structures. This study clearly indicates that younger rats are more vulnerable than adults to alcohol-induced brain damage and, coupled with our negative findings, suggests that this developmental sensitivity is not uniform, but rather depends upon the exposure paradigm, route of administration, and brain regions studied.

As detailed above, our data indicate that binge-pattern alcohol exposure (CIE) during adolescence, but not adulthood, enhances vulnerability to alcohol-induced spatial memory impairments later in life.[39] These behavioral findings suggested the possibility that the hippocampi of the animals that received CIE during adolescence may have been damaged in ways that would diminish the capacity for activity-induced synaptic plasticity and render these circuits more vulnerable to the acute effects of alcohol. Therefore, one week after the behavioral testing, we sacrificed the animals and prepared hippocampal slices to study the impact of alcohol on the induction of LTP in area CA1. We found no effect of earlier intermittent alcohol treatment on LTP induction, amplitude, or maintenance in slices from animals in either age group, with or without alcohol (20 mM) added to the ACSF (see FIGS. 4 and 5). While this does not fully address the question of long-term effects of intermittent alcohol exposure during adolescence on hippocampal function, it at least suggests that our current model of CIE produced no profound compromises of baseline LTP induction or the vulnerability of these circuits to acute alcohol exposure. Other electrophysiological indicators of hippocampal function in area CA1 were also tested, such as paired-pulse inhibition and facilitation, fiber volley amplitude, and the fiber volley/population excitatory postsynaptic potential (pEPSP) ratio. In no instance did we observe an effect of CIE during adolescence on subsequent hippocampal function in adulthood.

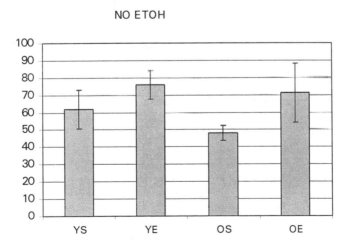

NO ETOH

FIGURE 4. Mean (±SEM) percent increase in pEPSP slope after the induction of LTP, in the absence of alcohol, in area CA1 of hippocampal slices from adult rats that had received chronic intermittent treatment with saline (YS and OS) or alcohol (YE and OE) as adolescents (YS and YE) or adults (OS and OE). There was no significant effect of either age or alcohol pretreatment on the LTP amplitude.

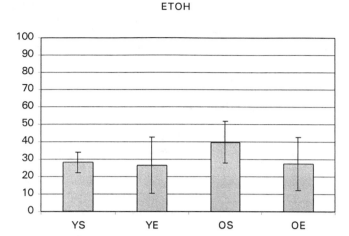

FIGURE 5. Mean (±SEM) percent increase in pEPSP slope after the induction of LTP, in the presence of 20 mM alcohol, in area CA1 of hippocampal slices from adult rats that had received chronic intermittent treatment with saline (YS and OS) or alcohol (YE and OE) as adolescents (YS and YE) or adults (OS and OE). There was no significant effect of either age or alcohol pretreatment on the LTP amplitude.

In similar studies we also found no effect of chronic intermittent alcohol exposure on epileptogenesis in hippocampal area CA3. Four treatment groups were prepared: CIE during adolescence, CIE during early adulthood, saline during adolescence, and saline during early adulthood. Beginning at either postnatal day 30 or 70, the animals got 5.0 g/kg of alcohol (or saline) ip every other day for 30 days. Twenty-four hours after the last alcohol or saline dose, the animals were sacrificed and hippocampal slices prepared. We recorded evoked extracellular responses from area CA3 in two slices from each animal. In one slice we measured pharmacologically isolated NMDA receptor–mediated pEPSPs, and in the other we recorded spontaneous epileptiform bursts generated after bath application of 7.0 mM K^+. Alcohol pretreatment did not influence the induction or amplitude of NMDA receptor–mediated pEPSPs in area CA1 in either age group, nor did it influence the time to the initial burst, the number of bursts (see FIG. 6), or the duration of individual bursts in area CA3. Thus it does not appear that intermittent alcohol exposure during adolescence or early adulthood influences hippocampal excitatory responsiveness 24 hours after the last exposure.

These "negative" findings suggest that the long-term behavioral changes observed following CIE treatment in adolescence likely involve very subtle changes in neuronal circuits that do not reveal themselves through gross measures like LTP or epileptogenesis in the hippocampus. Alternatively, the changes in brain organization and function that underlie the behavioral effects might simply take place in regions that have not yet been thoroughly examined.

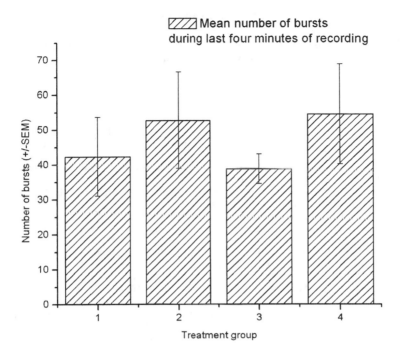

FIGURE 6. Mean (±SEM) number of epileptiform bursts recorded in hippocampal area CA3 during the final four minutes of recording in elevated K+ (7.0 mM). The *bars* represent data from animals that had received either saline (1, 3) or 5.0 g/kg alcohol (2, 4) at 48-h intervals for 30 days beginning at day 30 (3, 4) or 70 (1, 2) of age.

SUMMARY

There is mounting evidence that alcohol affects adolescents and adults differently in a variety of important ways. Adolescents appear to be more sensitive than adults to the memory-impairing effects of alcohol, as well as the impact of alcohol on brain functions that underlie memory formation. For instance, when treated with alcohol, adolescent rats perform worse than adults in spatial learning tasks that are known to require the functioning of the hippocampus. Alcohol also disrupts hippocampal function, and does so more potently in adolescents than adults. In contrast, adolescents appear to be far less sensitive than adults to both the sedative and motor impairing effects of alcohol. While research on this topic is still in its infancy, the findings clearly suggest that adolescence represents a unique stage of sensitivity to the impact of alcohol on behavior and brain function.

ACKNOWLEDGMENTS

This research was supported by NIAAA Grant #12478, a VA Senior Research Career Scientist award to H.S.S, and a grant from the Institute for Medical Research to A.M.W.

REFERENCES

1. LISTER, R.G., C. GORENSTEIN, D. FISHER-FLOWERS, *et al.* 1991. Dissociation of the acute effects of alcohol on implicit and explicit memory processes. Neuropsychologia 29:1205–1212.
2. RYBACK, R.S. 1970. Alcohol amnesia: observations in seven drinking inpatient alcoholics. Q. J. Stud. Alcohol 31: 616–632.
3. RYBACK, R.S. 1971. The continuum and specificity of the effects of alcohol on memory. Q. J. Stud. Alcohol 32: 995–1016.
4. WHITE, A.M., D. JAMIESON-DRAKE & H.S. SWARTZWELDER. 2002. Prevalence and correlates of alcohol-induced blackouts among college students: results of an e-mail survey. J. Am. Coll. Health 51: 117–131.
5. GOODWIN, D., J. CRANE & S. GUZE. 1969. Alcoholic "blackouts": a review and clinical study of 100 alcoholics. Am. J. Psychiatry 126: 191–198.
6. WHITE, A.M., D.B. MATTHEWS & P.J. BEST. 2000. Ethanol, memory and hippocampal function: a review of recent findings. Hippocampus 10: 88–93.
7. ZOLA-MORGAN, S., L.R. SQUIRE & D.G. AMARAL. 1986. Human amnesia and the medial temporal lobe region: enduring memory impairment following a bilateral lesion limited to field CA1 of the hippocampus. J. Neurosci. 16: 2950–2967.
8. BEST, P.J. & A.M. WHITE. 1998. Hippocampal cellular activity: a brief history of space. Proc. Natl. Acad. Sci. USA 95: 2717–2719.
9. WHITE, A.M. & P.J. BEST. 2000. Effects of ethanol on hippocampal place-cell and interneuron activity. Brain Res. 876: 154–165.
10. BLISS, T.V.P. & G.L. COLLINRIDGE. 1993. A synaptic model of memory: long-term potentiation in the hippocampus. Nature 361: 31–39.
11. MARTIN, S.J. & R.G.M. MORRIS. 2002. New life in an old idea: the synaptic plasticity and memory hypothesis revisited. Hippocampus 12: 609–636.
12. BLITZER, R.D., O. GIL & E.M. LANDAU. 1990. Long-term potentiation in rat hippocampus is inhibited by low concentrations of ethanol. Brain Res. 537: 203–208.
13. MORRISETT, R.A. & H.S. SWARTZWELDER. 1993. Attenuation of hippocampal long-term potentiation by ethanol: a patch-clamp analysis of glutamatergic and GABAergic mechanisms. J. Neurosci. 13: 2264–2272.
14. SCHUMMERS, J. & M.D. BROWNING. 2001. Evidence for a role for GABA(A) and NMDA receptors in ethanol inhibition of long-term potentiation. Brain Res. 94: 9–14.
15. MARKWIESE, B.J., S.K. ACHESON, E.D. LEVIN, *et al.* 1998. Differential effects of ethanol on memory in adolescent and adult rats. Alcohol. Clin. Exp. Res. 22: 416–421.
16. ACHESON, S., R. STEIN & H.S. SWARTZWELDER. 1998. Impairment of semantic and figural memory by acute alcohol: age-dependent effects. Alcohol. Clin. Exp. Res. 22: 1437–1442.
17. SWARTZWELDER, H.S., W.A. WILSON & M.I. TAYYEB. 1995. Differential sensitivity of NMDA receptor-mediated synaptic potentials to alcohol in immature vs. mature hippocampus. Alcohol. Clin. Exp. Res. 19: 320–323.
18. PYAPALI, G., D. TURNER, W. WILSON & H.S. SWARTZWELDER. 1999. Age- and dose-dependent effects of alcohol on the induction of hippocampal long-term potentiation. Alcohol 19: 107–111.
19. SWARTZWELDER, H. S., W.A. WILSON & M.I. TAYYEB. 1995. Age-dependent inhibition of long-term potentiation by alcohol in immature vs. mature hippocampus. Alcohol. Clin. Exp. Res. 19: 1480–1485.
20. LI, Q., W.A. WILSON & H.S. SWARTZWELDER. 2002. Differential effect of alcohol on NMDA receptor-mediated EPSCs in pyramidal cells in the posterior cingulate cortex of adolescent and adult rats. J. Neurophysiol. 87: 705–711.

21. LITTLE, P.J., C.M. KUHN, W.A. WILSON & H.S. SWARTZWELDER. 1996. Differential effects of alcohol in adolescent and adult rats. Alcohol. Clin. Exp. Res. **20:** 1346–1351.
22. SWARTZWELDER, H.S., R. RICHARDSON, B. MARKWIESE, *et al.* 1998. Developmental differences in the acquisition of tolerance to alcohol. Alcohol **15:** 311–314.
23. SILVERI, M. & L. SPEAR. 1998. Decreased sensitivity to hypnotic effects of alcohol early in ontogeny. Alcohol. Clin. Exp. Res. **22:** 670–676.
24. MOY, S., G. DUNCAN, D. KNAPP & G. BREESE. 1998. Sensitivity to alcohol across development in rats: comparison to [3H]zolpidem binding. Alcohol. Clin. Exp. Res. **22:** 1485–1492.
25. WHITE, A., M. TRUESDALE, J. BAE, *et al.* 2002. Differential effects of alcohol on motor coordination in adolescent and adult rats. Pharmacol. Biochem. Behav. **73:** 673–677.
26. WHITE, A., J. BAE, M. TRUESDALE, *et al.* 2002. Chronic intermittent alcohol exposure during adolescence prevents normal developmental changes in sensitivity to alcohol-induced motor impairments. Alcohol. Clin. Exp. Res. **26:** 960–968.
27. LILJEQUIST, S. & J. ENGEL. 1982. Effects of GABAergic agonists and antagonists on various alcohol-induced behavioral changes. Psychopharmacology **78:** 71–75.
28. MEREU, G. & G. GESS. 1985. Low doses of alcohol inhibit the firing of neurons in the substantia nigra, pars reticulara: a GABAergic effect? Brain Res. **360:** 325–330.
29. CHERUBINI, E., J. GAIARSA & Y. BEN-ARI. 1991. GABA: an excitatory transmitter in early postnatal life. Trends Neurosci. **14:** 515–519.
30. ZHANG, L., I. SPIGELMAN & P. CARLEN. 1991. Development of GABA mediated, chloride dependent inhibition in CA1 pyramidal neurons of immature rat hippocampal slices. J. Physiol. **444:** 25–49.
31. BEHRINGER, K., R. GAULT & R. SIEGEL. 1996. Differential regulation of GABA$_A$ receptor subunit mRNAs in rat cerebellar granule neurons: importance of environmental cues. J. Neurochem. **66:** 1347–1353.
32. XIA, Y. & G. HADDAD. 1992. Ontogeny and distribution of GABA$_A$ receptors in rat brainstem and rostral brain regions. Neuroscience **49:** 973–989.
33. AGUAYO, L., R. PEOPLES, H. YEH & G. YEVENES. 2002. GABA$_A$ receptors as molecular sites of alcohol action: direct or indirect actions? Curr. Top. Med. Chem. **2:** 869–885.
34. KAPUR, J. & R. MACDONALD. 1996. Pharmacological properties of GABA$_A$ receptors from acutely dissociated rat dentate granule cells. Mol. Pharmacol. **50:** 458–466.
35. KAPUR, J. & R. MACDONALD. 1999. Postnatal development of hippocampal dentate granule cell GABA$_A$ receptor pharmacological properties. J. Pharmacol. Exp. Ther. **55:** 444–452.
36. BECKER, H.C. & R.L. HALE. 1993. Repeated episodes of alcohol withdrawal potentiate the severity of subsequent withdrawal seizures: an animal model of alcohol withdrawal "kindling." Alcohol. Clin. Exp. Res. **17:** 94–98.
37. BROWN, M., R. ANTON, R. MALCOLM & J. BALLENGER. 1988. Alcohol detoxification and withdrawal seizures: clinical support for a kindling hypothesis. Biol. Psychiatry **23:** 507–514.
38. BOND, N.W. 1979. Impairment of shuttlebox avoidance learning following repeated alcohol withdrawal episodes in rats. Pharmacol. Biochem. Behav. **11:** 589–591.
39. WHITE, A.M., A.J. GHIA, E.D. LEVIN & H.S. SWARTZWELDER. 2000. Binge pattern alcohol exposure: differential impact on subsequent responsiveness to alcohol. Alcohol. Clin. Exp. Res. **24:** 1251–1256.
40. WEISSENBORN, R. & T. DUKA. 2003. Acute alcohol effects on cognitive function in social drinkers: their relationship to drinking habits. Psychopharmacology **165:** 306–312.
41. BROWN, A.S., S.F. TAPERT, E. GRANHOLM & D.C. DELIS. 2000. Neurocognitive functioning of adolescents: effects of protracted alcohol use. Alcohol. Clin. Exp. Res. **24:** 164–171.
42. DE BELLIS, M.D., D.B. CLARK, S.R. BEERS, *et al.* 2000. Hippocampal volume in adolescent-onset alcohol use disorders. Am. J. Psychiatry **157:** 737–744.
43. GRANT, K., P. VALVERIUS, M. HUDSPITH & B. TABAKOFF. 1990. Alcohol withdrawal seizures and the NMDA receptor complex. Eur. J. Pharmacol. **176:** 289–296.
44. HOFFMAN, P. & B. TABAKOFF. 1994. The role of the NMDA receptor in alcohol withdrawal. EXS **71:** 61–70.

45. SNELL, L., B. TABAKOFF & P. HOFFMAN. 1993. Radioligand binding to the NMDA receptor/ionophore complex: alterations by alcohol in-vitro and by chronic in-vivo alcohol ingestion. Brain Res. **602:** 91–98.
46. DOLIN, S.J. & H.J. LITTLE. 1989. Are changes in neuronal calcium channels involved in ethanol tolerance? J. Pharmacol. Exp. Ther. **250:** 985–991.
47. CREWS, F. & L. CHANDLER. 1993. Excitotoxicity and the neuropathology of alcohol. *In* Alcohol-Induced Brain Damage.W.A. Hunt & S.J. Nixon, Eds.: 355–371. NIH Publication No. 93-3549.
48. IORIO, K., L. REINLIB, B. TABAKOFF & P. HOFFMAN. 1991. NMDA-induced $[Ca^{2+}]^i$ enhanced by chronic alcohol treatment in cultured cerebellar granule cells. Alcohol. Clin. Exp. Res. **15:** 333.
49. IORIO, K., L. REINLIB, B. TABAKOFF & P. HOFFMAN. 1992. Chronic exposure of cerebellar granule cells to alcohol results in increased NMDA receptor function. Mol. Pharmacol. **41:** 1142–1148.
50. CREW, F., C. BRAUN, B. HOPLIGHT, *et al.* 2000. Binge ethanol consumption causes differential brain damage in young adolescent rats compared with adult rats. Alcohol. Clin. Exp. Res. **24:** 1712–1723.

The Use of Adolescent Nonhuman Primates to Model Human Alcohol Intake

Neurobiological, Genetic, and Psychological Variables

CHRISTINA S. BARR, MELANIE L. SCHWANDT, TIMOTHY K. NEWMAN, AND J. DEE HIGLEY

Laboratory of Clinical Studies, Primate Unit, Division of Intramural Clinical and Biological Research, National Institute on Alcohol Abuse and Alcoholism, Poolesville, Maryland 20837-0529, USA

ABSTRACT: Traits characteristic of type I and type II alcoholism are thought to relate to dysregulated central nervous system serotonin functioning. In this review, we discuss variables associated with high adolescent alcohol consumption and other risk-taking behaviors in a nonhuman primate model. Adolescent primates with low CSF concentrations of the serotonin metabolite 5-HIAA are more impulsive and exhibit increased levels of alcohol consumption. Both genetic and environmental factors contribute to alcohol-seeking behavior in adolescent macaques. Sequence variation within serotonin system genes, for example, a repeat polymorphism in the transcriptional control region of the monoamine oxidase gene (*MAOA-LPR*), increases the propensity for adolescent males to consume alcohol. Environmental factors, such as early life stress in the form of peer-rearing or early age of exposure to alcohol, are also associated with increased alcohol consumption. Peer-reared females, especially those exposed to alcohol during early adolescence, exhibit increased rates of alcohol consumption compared to those exposed to alcohol later in development. When genetic variables are also considered, there is an interaction between the low activity serotonin transporter gene promoter *s* allele (rh5-HTTLPR) and rearing condition on alcohol preference in females but not males, suggesting that the interactions between genes and the environment may be sexually dichotomous. By learning more about the interactions between genes, early experience, and alcohol intake in the adolescent nonhuman primate, we may be able to identify factors that contribute to the susceptibility, pathogenesis, and progression of impulse control disorders, such as alcoholism.

KEYWORDS: serotonin; primate; alcohol; stress; rearing; polymorphism; adolescent; GxE interaction

Address for correspondence: Christina S. Barr, V.M.D., Ph.D., Research Fellow, NIH Animal Center, Building 112, P.O. Box 529, Poolesville, MD 20837-0529. Voice: 301-496-9550; fax: 301-435-9278.

cbarr@mail.nih.gov

Ann. N.Y. Acad. Sci. 1021: 221–233 (2004). © 2004 New York Academy of Sciences.
doi: 10.1196/annals.1308.027

BACKGROUND

Alcoholism and alcohol abuse are relapsing, lifetime illnesses that are difficult to treat. Although they are complex disorders, with multiple subtypes and clinical pictures, one defining feature is the chronic use of alcohol, which leads to compulsive ethanol seeking, often in the face of negative social and psychological consequences. Both positive and negative reinforcement are thought to be critically involved in the transition from casual alcohol use to compulsive alcohol-seeking behavior.[1] While the positive reinforcing effects of alcohol are essential to the initiation and early maintenance of intake, recent studies suggest that alcohol-seeking behavior related to alleviation of symptoms during abstinence (negative reinforcement) is equally, if not more, effective in maintaining alcohol use.[2] Therefore, when considering risk factors for alcohol dependence, it is important to consider not only systems that are involved in alcohol reward, but those activated during withdrawal and abstinence.

A growing number of studies in nonhuman primates have been used to model some features of alcohol abuse and alcoholism.[3–8] Nonhuman primates are chosen as subjects primarily because they are neuroanatomically, socially, and genetically similar to humans. The majority of the alcohol research performed with nonhuman primates has involved studying macaques and other closely related Old World species, such as baboons and vervet monkeys.[5,8,10–12] Like humans, the typical macaque and other Old World species are socially oriented and live in complex societies with well-defined social roles, as well as frequent social stressors. As in humans, social context and social stress play critical roles in nonhuman primates' alcohol consumption.[6,13] We discuss studies from our laboratory that have shown that, as in humans, genetic influences also play a role. Because of these similarities, nonhuman primates are particularly well suited as subjects for research modeling the antecedents and concomitants of human alcohol-related problems.

REDUCED CNS SEROTONIN FUNCTIONING, RISK-TAKING BEHAVIORS, AND HIGH ALCOHOL CONSUMPTION

In his model, Cloninger identified two subtypes of alcoholism (type I and type II). Type I alcoholism is characterized by high levels of trait-like anticipatory anxiety. Individuals with type I alcoholism are postulated to consume alcohol primarily for its sedative and anxiolytic properties.[14,15] Type II alcoholism, on the other hand, is described in its original formulation as male-limited, early-onset, and sensation seeking and is characterized by impaired impulse control.[14] This impairment results in relatively unrestrained alcohol consumption as a consequence of loss of control once alcohol consumption begins. A cluster of unbridled behaviors related to impaired impulse control, similar to those described previously by Linnoila, such as physical aggression, risk taking, and social deficits, distinguishes individuals with type II alcoholism.[14,16] Historically, type II alcoholism has been attributed to serotonergic dysfunction, which is suggested by diminished cerebrospinal fluid concentrations of the major serotonin metabolite, 5-hydroxy-indole-acetic acid (CSF 5-HIAA).[17] Studies by Linnoila and his colleagues indicated that men with low CSF 5-HIAA concentrations frequently exhibit behavioral problems that may be indicative of impaired impulse control, such as suicide attempts, impulsive criminal acts, and violence.

Like humans, nonhuman primates with low CSF 5-HIAA concentrations are more likely to exhibit behaviors characteristic of impaired impulse control, such as spontaneous, long leaps at dangerous heights and repeated jumping into baited traps where they are captured and restrained.[18,19] Fairbanks and colleagues found that measures of impulsivity, such as latency to approach a potentially dangerous stranger, were correlated with CSF 5-HIAA concentrations and that treatment with the selective serotonin reuptake inhibitor, fluoxetine, reduced rates of impulsive behaviors.[20] A similar relationship between impulsivity and serotonin system dysfunction has been demonstrated in female vervet monkeys using the 5-HT agonist, fenfluramine, to assess net serotonergic system output.[21]

In humans and in nonhuman primates, impulsivity is higher during adolescence and young adulthood when compared to older aged subjects.[20] As in human males, for most male Old World nonhuman primates, adolescence is a period of high risk for injury and death.[22] Often, these deaths occur as a result of violence and accidents. Premature death in adolescent male macaques is strongly predicted by high levels of violent behavior and low CSF 5-HIAA concentrations,[22] indicating that these central differences in serotonin functioning have real-world consequences for adolescent well-being and overall risk for injury and death. Because they are impaired in controlling their impulses, we postulated that monkeys with low CSF 5-HIAA would exhibit high rates of alcohol consumption. This hypothesis is consistent with one of the postulates of Cloninger's tridimensional model of alcoholism,

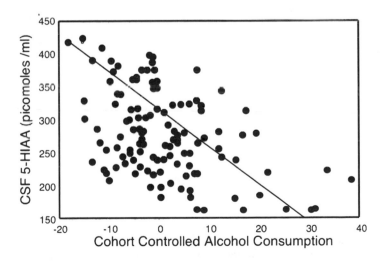

FIGURE 1. Relationship between CSF levels of 5-HIAA and voluntary alcohol consumption in rhesus macaques. Animals were given access to an 8.4% aspartame-sweetened alcohol solution and vehicle for 1 h/day for 4–7 weeks. Simple regression analysis demonstrated there to be an inverse relationship between CSF 5-HIAA and alcohol consumption ($r = -.48$, $P < .0004$).

that type II alcoholism is mediated by central serotonin deficits.[14,15] We have found an inverse correlation between CSF levels of 5-HIAA and voluntary alcohol consumption when rhesus are allowed free access to alcohol for 1 h/day (FIG. 1). To the degree that nonhuman primate findings can be extrapolated to the human condition, our results suggest that excessive alcohol consumption is associated with serotonin deficit.

POTENTIAL ETIOLOGICAL MECHANISMS: GENETIC AND ENVIRONMENTAL INFLUENCES

The serotonin system is among the systems involved not only in impulse control but in both the positive reinforcement of alcohol-induced reward and negative reinforcement of alcohol withdrawal. While serotonin release following consumption of alcohol is involved in activation of reward pathways, neuroadaptive diminutions in release during withdrawal can lead to pain, dysphoria, and depression.[23] As stated above, alcoholism is associated with dysregulated release, synaptic concentration, and metabolism of serotonin. Variations in many of the genes that encode receptors, enzymes, and transporters for serotonin have been studied in association with alcoholism.

The serotonin transporter is a protein critical to regulating serotonin function in the brain since serotonin's action in the synapse is terminated by reuptake. In mice, targeted disruption of the serotonin transporter gene results in increased adrenocorticotropic hormone (ACTH) and corticosterone responses to immobilization stress as well as increased anxiety during the elevated plus maze and light/dark exploration tasks.[24–27] In humans, there is a common polymorphism involving a repeat length variation in the promoter region of the serotonin transporter gene (SCL6A4, or 5-HTTLPR). The short (s) serotonin transporter allele contains an attenuated promoter segment and, as such, shows diminished transcription relative to that from the long (l) allele.[28] Variation of the serotonin transporter gene promoter is also associated with certain personality traits related to anxiety, depression, and aggression, such as neuroticism, harm avoidance, and disagreeableness.[28–30] Moreover, variation of the 5-HTTLPR has been associated with certain neuropsychiatric diseases, including type II alcoholism.[31,32] In rhesus, a 21-bp insertion/deletion polymorphism orthologous to the human serotonin transporter length variant, rh5-HTTLPR, has been shown to alter transcriptional efficiency,[33] resulting in decreased serotonin transporter mRNA levels in brains of l/s macaques.[34] Consistent with findings in humans, studies in our laboratory have demonstrated that adolescent and young adult rhesus macaques that are carriers of the s allele exhibit higher levels of alcohol preference than do l/l animals.[35]

Another gene that influences synaptic concentrations of serotonin is that encoding the enzyme, monoamine oxidase A (MAOA). A functional length variant in the transcriptional control region for the MAOA gene (MAOA-LPR) results in differential transcriptional activity.[36] The MAOA gene is located on the X chromosome and, therefore, polymorphisms in the transcriptional control region for this gene are likely to affect males and females differentially. In humans, the MAOA-LPR polymorphism has been associated with antisocial behavior in alcohol-dependent males,[37] and with impulsivity, hostility, and a lifetime history of aggression in a community sample of

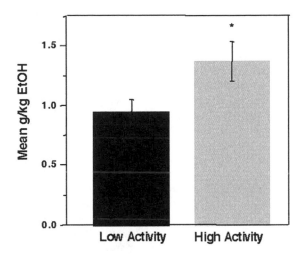

FIGURE 2. Association of a monoamine oxidase gene promoter length polymorphism (*MAOA-LPR*) with alcohol consumption in rhesus macaques. Data were analyzed by one-way ANOVA. Males carrying the high activity (HA) *MAOA-LPR* allele consumed significantly higher quantities of alcohol than did those with the low activity (LA) allele ($P < .02$).

men.[38] A recent study by Caspi and colleagues demonstrated a significant interaction between childhood maltreatment and reduced MAOA enzymatic activity in modulating the risk for antisocial behavior, aggressiveness, and violence during adolescence.[39] Because of the comorbidity of such disorders and traits with type II alcoholism, it is possible that *MAOA-LPR* genotype may also be associated with increased risk for alcoholism and related disorders.

As in humans, a length polymorphism has been identified in the transcriptional control region of the MAOA gene of numerous nonhuman primate species.[40] We have found that among adolescent and young adult male rhesus macaques the MAOA length polymorphism accounts for approximately 10% of the variance in alcohol consumption (FIG. 2). This suggests that MAOA gene promoter variation may confer risk to alcoholism among human adolescents. Because of the fact that males have only one copy of the MAOA gene, they may be particularly susceptible. This, and the fact that the *MAOA-LPR* polymorphism has previously been associated with antisocial behavior, suggests that MAOA gene promoter variation may specifically increase the risk for type II alcoholism in humans.

While genetic variation is known to be an etiological factor for alcoholism, not all children of alcoholics develop alcohol problems. Alcohol abuse and alcoholism are thought to be environmentally induced as well. Individuals who experience early life psychosocial stressors, such as abuse or loss of a parent, are at increased risk for anxiety and depression, known risk factors for alcoholism. Parental monitoring is also known to modulate the risk for alcohol abuse in adolescents.[41] It is, therefore, necessary to understand environmental and genetic factors and how they might interact when studying the pathogenesis of alcoholism. The obvious strength of animal studies is that environmental factors can be controlled, such that relative contributions or potential interactions between genes and environment can be examined.

One manipulation that has been widely used to study the effects of early experiences among monkeys is peer-only–rearing. In this rearing condition, subjects are removed from their parents at birth and reared with other age-matched infants, where they develop in the absence of adult influence. Peer-reared monkeys develop strong bonds with their age mates and use them as a secure base from which to explore.[42] Nevertheless, when they are compared to their mother-reared counterparts, peer-reared subjects exhibit evidence of nonsecure attachment bonds, higher levels of anxiety, and less exploration in novel settings when their attachment sources are present.[42] Peer-only–reared monkeys appear to exhibit deficits of impulse control. For example, when access to a baited, unfamiliar black box is presented, adolescent peer-reared monkeys are more likely to approach and sit close to the potentially dangerous device.[43] During aggressive episodes, contextually appropriate bouts of aggression are more likely to escalate into vicious and relentless aggressive encounters in adolescent peer-reared monkeys, when compared to parentally reared monkeys.[44] When they are provoked, peer-reared subjects are likely to become aggressive at inappropriate targets or in unexpected settings, and they are particularly prone to violently aggressive behaviors.[44–49]

There is evidence of other impulse control problems that are found in humans as well. In humans, parental loss from divorce early in life is associated with future excessive alcohol consumption in adults.[50,51] One of the landmark studies from our research demonstrated this to be true among rhesus monkeys as well. Those reared without adults as peer-reared subjects consume significantly higher volumes of alcohol and are more likely to drink to intoxication than those reared with their parents. Under baseline, nonstressful conditions, adolescent and young adult, parentally deprived peer-reared monkeys consume alcohol at rates that produce intoxication,[6] but when stress is induced using a social separation stressor, mother-reared monkeys increase their consumption to equal that among peer-reared subjects.[6] It is noteworthy that while peer-only–reared monkeys are typically more likely to consume alcohol in excess and exhibit severe aggression, administration of the serotonin reuptake inhibitor sertraline reverses these aberrant behaviors, reducing alcohol consumption, anxiety, and aggression.[52] Moreover, interindividual differences in CSF 5-HIAA concentrations predict subjects' response to sertraline, and thus suggests an underlying serotonin deficit.

In humans, the age of onset of alcohol use (i.e., the age at which individuals have their first "drink") appears to be an important factor in alcohol consumption and the potential for alcohol-related problems and abuse. Early exposure to alcohol, generally in the early teens, has been associated with increased frequency of drinking, increased amounts of alcohol consumed, increased rates of alcohol and/or other drug-related disorders, and increased likelihood of emotional, mental, and psychosomatic problems.[53–56] For the most part, these consequences are observed later in life, typically when these individuals are in their twenties or thirties. However, studies of the age of onset of alcohol use in humans raise the possibility of developmental variables contributing to early excessive drinking as well as to the development of alcohol-related problems later in life.

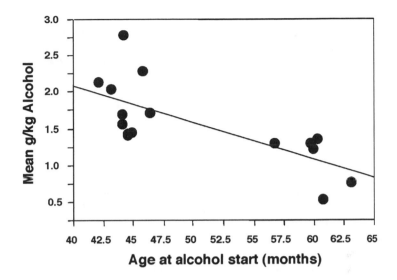

FIGURE 3. Peer-reared females in single-cage drinking condition. Data were analyzed using simple regression analysis. There was an inverse correlation between age of alcohol testing and alcohol consumption ($r = -.724$, $P = .0015$).

There are some important limitations of studies looking at age of onset of alcohol use in humans and its consequences. For example, there are a number of environmental factors that influence not only age of onset of alcohol use, but consumption patterns later in life. Two of the most common of these factors are positive attitudes towards alcohol among parents and friends, and use of alcohol and other drugs by peers.[56–61] In human subjects, it is often difficult to control for such environmental confounds when studying the effects of early exposure to alcohol on subsequent consumption patterns. This is especially important because such factors may actually account for the relationship between age at onset of alcohol use and the risk of developing alcohol-related problems.[62]

Results from rodent studies suggest that age-related biological factors may be involved in the propensity toward alcohol consumption. One possible mechanism is an age-related decrease in alcohol-induced release of dopamine and serotonin in specific areas of the brain associated with reward, such as the nucleus accumbens.[63] Yet another possibility is that alcohol may have a greater stimulatory effect on the hypothalamic–pituitary–adrenal (HPA) axis in younger animals compared to older animals, resulting in increased circulating levels of glucocorticoids, which are known to potentiate alcohol reward and reinforcement.[64,65] We have found that among adolescent macaques, there is an inverse correlation between age of exposure to alcohol and voluntary alcohol consumption, especially among females reared in peer-only groups (FIG. 3). This is interesting in light of the fact that peer-reared females have augmented HPA axis responses to alcohol relative to males or to females reared with their mothers.[66] Whatever the mechanisms, exposure to alcohol early in life may put individuals at risk for increased alcohol consumption at the time of onset, which in turn can increase risk for the development of alcohol-related disorders.

GENE BY ENVIRONMENT INTERACTIONS

There is accumulating evidence that genetic and environmental factors can interact, increasing one's susceptibility to psychosocial and mood disorders later in life.[39,67] Because their rearing environment can be tightly controlled, nonhuman primates are particularly useful for the study of gene–environment (GxE) interactions. Of particular interest for the study of GxE interactions is variation within regulatory or coding regions of genes likely to be influenced by a stressful environment or, alternatively, of genes involved in the behavioral response to stress. One of the neurotransmitters implicated in behavioral aberrations observed in animals exposed to early-life stress is serotonin, and serotonin plays a pivotal role in many forms of human adolescent psychopathology, with the selective serotonin reuptake inhibitors (SSRIs) and other serotonin-acting agents being some of the most widely prescribed psychotropic medications. During the early postnatal period, serotonin is involved in the development of the central nervous system,[68] and serotonin neurotransmission is involved in both activation and feedback control of the neuroendocrine stress axis.[69]

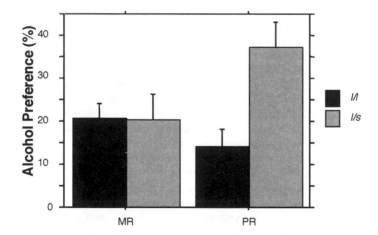

FIGURE 4. Interaction between a polymorphism in the serotonin transporter gene promoter region (rh5-HTTLPR) and rearing condition on alcohol consumption in rhesus macaques. Alcohol preference for female macaques with the *l/s* genotype was higher than that of *l/l* females (Fisher's PLSD, $P < .05$). In addition, there was an interaction between serotonin transporter genotype and rearing condition (FIG. 1, $F(1/31) = 5.3$, $P < .03$). Post hoc analysis demonstrated that peer-reared (PR) *l/s* animals consumed more alcohol than did PR *l/l* (Fisher's PLSD, $P < .005$) or mother-reared (MR) l/l animals (Fisher's PLSD, $P < .03$).

In turn, stress hormones are also involved in regulating the expression of certain serotonin system genes. The serotonin transporter gene promoter contains a glucocorticoid response element, making it responsive to stress-induced levels of corticosteroids, a phenomenon that is particularly evident among both human and rhesus carriers of the *s* allele.[34,70] This is interesting in light of the findings that 5-HTTLPR moderates the influence of life stress on depression.[67]

Using the rhesus macaque model, we have been able to demonstrate interactions between rearing experience and rh5-HTTLPR on many phenotypes of interest.[71] In three recent studies, we demonstrated that the *s* allele adversely affects neonatal responding[72] and increases alcohol sensitivity,[73] aggression,[71] and HPA axis activity during social separation stress,[74] but only among peer-reared animals. Monkeys reared by their mothers were not differentiated by genotype. Our first report of a GxE interaction demonstrated that rh5-HTTLPR genotype and rearing condition interact to influence cerebrospinal fluid concentrations of 5-HIAA.[33] Given the known relationship between 5-HIAA and alcohol consumption, it is not surprising that rh5-HTTLPR genotype and rearing also interact to influence alcohol preference (FIG. 4).

While it is accepted that there are additional factors, such as gender, that may increase an individual's sensitivity to adversity,[75] whether these factors modulate or contribute to the complex interactions between genes and early life stress has yet to be examined. As stated earlier, adolescent peer-reared female macaques are more likely to consume alcohol in excess if they are at a young age (just entering adolescence) than are older adolescents or young adults. Other studies in our laboratory have shown that peer-reared female macaques have augmented ACTH responses to acute intravenous alcohol and that elevated ACTH levels persist for weeks following

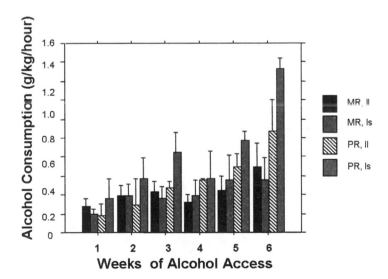

FIGURE 5. Interaction between weeks of exposure to alcohol and rearing condition [peer-reared (PR) vs. mother-reared (MR)] on alcohol consumption in female rhesus macaques (F(5/95) = 4, $P < .006$). The interaction between rearing condition and exposure to alcohol is especially evident among carriers of the rh5-HTTLPR *s* allele.

discontinuation of alcohol intake.[66] When segregated according to rh5-HTTLPR genotype and rearing condition, there is an interaction between early adverse experience and exposure to alcohol, such that while there is no effect of rearing condition on alcohol consumption during initial exposures to alcohol, females subjected to stress early in life demonstrate a progressive decline in consumption of sweetened vehicle but a marked increase in their levels of alcohol consumption with successive alcohol exposures (FIG. 5). This is especially evident among *s* allele carriers. Such a pattern could potentially be attributable to either accelerated development of tolerance to alcohol's intoxicating effects or, alternatively, increased sensitization to reinforcement (negative or positive) among peer-reared *l/s* females. This pattern is not present in males, suggesting that such GxE interactions may differ between the sexes.

SUMMARY

Traits characteristic of type I and type II alcoholism are thought to relate to dysregulated central nervous system serotonin functioning. To the extent that they generalize to humans, our findings suggest that the pathogenesis of alcohol dependence may have its origins, at least in part, in the interactive effect of early deleterious rearing experience and genetic factors. By learning more about the interactions between genes, early experience, and alcohol intake in the adolescent nonhuman primate, we may be able to identify factors that contribute to the susceptibility, pathogenesis, and progression of impulse control disorders, such as alcoholism.

REFERENCES

1. KOOB, G.F. & M. LE MOAL. 1997. Drug abuse: hedonic homeostatic dysregulation. Science **278:** 52–58.
2. KOOB, G.F. & M. LE MOAL. 2001. Drug addiction, dysregulation of reward, and allostasis. Neuropsychopharmacology **24:** 97–129.
3. CROWLEY, T.J. & A.E. ANDREWS. 1987. Alcoholic-like drinking in simian social groups. Psychopharmacology **92:** 196–205.
4. CROWLEY, T.J., C. WEISBARD & M.J. HYDINGER-MACDONALD. 1983. Progress toward initiating and maintaining high-dose alcohol drinking in monkey social groups. J. Stud. Alcohol **44:** 569–590.
5. ERVIN, F.R., R.M. PALMOUR, S.N. YOUNG, *et al.* 1990. Voluntary consumption of beverage alcohol by vervet monkeys: Population screening, descriptive behavior and biochemical measures. Pharmacol. Biochem. Behav. **36:** 367–373.
6. HIGLEY, J.D., M.F. HASERT, S.J. SUOMI, *et al.* 1991. Nonhuman primate model of alcohol abuse: Effects of early experience, personality, and stress on alcohol consumption. Proc. Natl. Acad. Sci. USA **88:** 7261–7265.
7. KRAEMER, G.W., C.R. LAKE, M.H. EBERT, *et al.* 1985. Effect of alcohol on cerebrospinal fluid norepinephrine in rhesus monkeys. Psychopharmacology **85:** 444–448.
8. KRAEMER, G.W. & W.T. MCKINNEY. 1985. Social separation increases alcohol consumption in rhesus monkeys. Psychopharmacology **86:** 182–189.
9. HIGLEY, J.D. 1996. Primates in alcohol research. Alcohol Health Res. World **19:** 213–216.
10. HIGLEY, J.D. & M. LINNOILA. 1997. A nonhuman primate model of excessive alcohol intake: Personality and neurobiological parallels of type I- and type II-like alcoholism. Recent Dev. Alcohol. **13:** 192–219.
11. MELLO, N.K. & J.H. MENDELSON. 1966. Factors affecting alcohol consumption in primates. Psychosom. Med. **28:** 529–550.

12. HENNINGFIELD, J.E., N.A. ATOR & R.R. GRIFFITHS. 1981. Establishment and maintenance of oral ethanol self-administration in the baboon. Drug Alcohol Depend. **7:** 113–124.
13. HIGLEY, J.D., S.J. SUOMI & M. LINNOILA. 1996. Progress toward developing a nonhuman primate model of alcohol abuse and alcoholism. J. Alcoholic Beverage Med. Res. Found. **7S:** 67–78.
14. CLONINGER, C.R. 1987. Neurogenetic adaptive mechanisms in alcoholism. Science **236:** 410–416.
15. CLONINGER, C.R. 1988. Anxiety and theories of emotion. *In* Handbook of Anxiety: Classification, Etiological Factors and Associated Disturbances. Vol. 2. R. Noyes Jr., M. Roth & G.D. Burrows, Eds.: 1–29. Elsevier. New York.
16. CLONINGER, C.R. 1986. A unified biosocial theory of personality and its role in the development of anxiety states. Psychiatr. Dev. **3:** 167–226.
17. LINNOILA, M., M. VIRKKUNEN, T. GEORGE, *et al.* 1997. Serotonin, violent behavior and alcohol. Experientia **71S:** 155–163.
18. HIGLEY, J.D., P.T. MEHLMAN, R.E. POLAND, *et al.* 1996. CSF testosterone and 5-HIAA correlate with different types of aggressive behaviors. Biol. Psychiatry **40:** 1067–1082.
19. MEHLMAN, P.T., J.D. HIGLEY, I. FAUCHER, *et al.* 1994. Low CSF 5-HIAA concentrations and severe aggression and impaired impulse control in nonhuman primates. Am. J. Psychiatry **151:** 1485–1491.
20. FAIRBANKS, L.A., W.P. MELEGA, M.J. JORGENSEN, *et al.* 2001. Social impulsivity inversely associated with CSF 5-HIAA and fluoxetine exposure in vervet monkeys. Neuropsychopharmacology **24:** 370–378.
21. MANUCK, S.B., J.R. KAPLAN, B.A. RYMESKI, *et al.* 2003. Approach to a social stranger is associated with low central nervous system serotonergic responsivity in female cynomolgus monkeys (*Macaca fascicularis*). Am. J. Primatol. **61:** 187–194.
22. HIGLEY, J.D., P.T. MEHLMAN, S. HIGLEY, *et al.* 1996. Excessive mortality in young free-ranging male nonhuman primates with low cerebrospinal fluid 5-hydroxyindoleacetic acid. Arch. Gen. Psychiatry **53:** 537–543.
23. KOOB, G.F. & F. WEISS. 1992. Neuropharmacology of cocaine and ethanol dependence. Rec. Dev. Alcohol **10:** 201–233.
24. LI, Q., C. WICHEMS, A. HEILS, *et al.* 1999. Reduction of 5-HT1A binding sites in 5-HT transporter knockout mice. J. Pharmacol. Exp. Ther. **291:** 999–1007.
25. LANFUMEY, L., C. MANNOURY LA COUR, N. FROGER, *et al.* 2000. 5-HT-HPA interactions in two models of transgenic mice relevant to major depression. Neurochem. Res. **25:** 1199–1206.
26. HOLMES, A., R. YANG, K.-P. LESCH, *et al.* 2004. Mice lacking the serotonin transporter exhibit 5-HT1A-mediated abnormalities in tests for anxiety-like behavior. Neuropsychopharmacology. In press.
27. WICHEMS, C.H., Q. LI, A. HOLMES, *et al.* 2000. Mechanisms mediating the increased anxiety-like behavior and excessive responses to stress in mice lacking the serotonin transporter. Soc. Neurosci. Abstr. **26:** 400.
28. LESCH, K.-P., D. BENGEL, A. HEILS, *et al.* 1996. Association of anxiety-related traits with a polymorphism in the serotonin transporter gene regulatory region. Science **274:** 1527–1531.
29. MAZZANTI, C.M., J. LAPPALAINEN, J.C. LONG, *et al.* 1998. Role of the serotonin transporter promoter polymorphism in anxiety-related traits. Arch. Gen. Psychiatry **55:** 936–940.
30. GREENBERG, B.D., F.J. MCMAHON & D.L. MURPHY. 1998. Serotonin transporter candidate gene studies in affective disorders and personality: promises and potential pitfalls. Mol. Psychiatry **3:** 186–189.
31. HALLIKAINEN, T., T. SAITO, H. LACHMAN, *et al.* 1999. Association between low activity serotonin transporter genotype and early onset alcoholism with habitual impulsive violent behavior. Mol. Psychiatry **4:** 385–388.
32. SAUNDER, T., H. HARMS, P. DUFEU, *et al.* 1998. Serotonin transporter gene variants in alcohol-dependent subjects with dissocial personality disorder. Biol. Psychiatry **43:** 908–912.

33. BENNETT A.J., K.-P. LESCH, A. HEILS, *et al.* 2002. Early experience and serotonin transporter gene variation interact to influence primate CNS function. Mol. Psychiatry **7:** 118–122.
34. LOPEZ, J.F. & J.D. HIGLEY. 2002. The effect of early experience on brain corticosteroid and serotonin receptors in rhesus monkeys. Biol. Psychiatry **51:** 294.
35. BARR, C.S., T.K. NEWMAN, S. LINDELL, *et al.* interaction between serotonin transporter gene variation and rearing condition in alcohol preference and consumption in female primates. Arch. Gen. Psychiatry. In press.
36. DECKERT, J., M. CATALANO, Y.V. SYAGAILO, *et al.* 1999. Excess of high activity monoamine oxidase A gene promoter alleles in female patients with panic disorder. Hum. Mol. Genet. **8:** 621–624.
37. SAMOCHOWIEC, J., K.-P LESCH, M. ROTTMANN, *et al.* 1999. Association of a regulatory polymorphism in the promoter region of the monoamine oxidase A gene with antisocial alcoholism. Psychiatry Res. **87:** 67–72.
38. MANUCK, S.B., J.D. FLORY, R.E. FERRELL, *et al.* 2000. A regulatory polymorphism of the monoamine oxidase-A gene may be associated with variability in aggression, impulsivity, and central nervous system serotonergic responsivity. Psychiatry Res. **95:** 9–23.
39. CASPI, A., J. McLAY, T.E. MOFFITT, *et al.* 2002. Role of genotype in the cycle of violence in maltreated children. Science **297:** 851–854.
40. NEWMAN, T.K., C.S. BARR, P. BABB, *et al.* Unpublished data.
41. KENDLER K.S., M.D. NEALE, R.C. KESSLER, *et al.* 1992. Childhood parental loss and adult psychopathology in women: A twin study perspective. Arch. Gen. Psychiatry **49:** 109–116.
42. HIGLEY, J.D., W.D. HOPKINS, W.W. THOMPSON, *et al.* 1992. Peers as primary attachment sources in yearling rhesus monkeys (*Macaca mulatta*). Dev. Psychol. **28:** 1163–1171.
43. BENNETT, A.J. & J.D HIGLEY. Unpublished data.
44. HIGLEY, J.D., M. LINNOILA & S.J. SUOMI. 1994. Ethological contributions: Experiential and genetic contributions to the expression and inhibition of aggression in primates. *In* Handbook of Aggressive and Destructive Behavior in Psychiatric Patients. M. Hersen, R.T. Ammerman & L. Sisson, Eds.: 17–32. Plenum Press. New York.
45. CAPITANIO, J.P. 1986. Behavioral pathology. *In* Comparative Primate Biology: Behavior, conservation and ecology. Vol. 2. G. Mitchell & J. Erwin, Eds.: 411–454. Liss. New York.
46. HIGLEY, J.D. & M. LINNOILA. 1997. A nonhuman primate model of excessive alcohol intake: Personality and neurobiological parallels of type I- and type II-like alcoholism. Recent Dev. Alcohol. **13:** 192–219.
47. MITCHELL, G. 1970. Abnormal behavior in primates. *In* Primate Behavior: Developments in field and laboratory research. R. Rosenblum, Ed. **1:** 195–249. Academic Press. New York.
48. SUOMI, S.J. 1982. Abnormal behavior and primate models of psychopathology. *In* Primate Behavior. J. Forbes & J. King, Eds.: 171–215. Academic Press. New York.
49. SUOMI, S.J. 1982. The development of social competence by rhesus monkeys. Ann. Ist. Super. Sanita **18:** 193–202.
50. HOPE, S., C. POWER & B. RODGERS. 1998. The relationship between parental separation in childhood and problem drinking in adulthood. Addiction **93:** 505–514.
51. KENDLER, K.S., M.C. NEALE, C.A. PRESCOTT, *et al.* 1996. Childhood parental loss and alcoholism in women: A causal analysis using a twin-family design. Psychol. Med. **26:** 79–95.
52. HIGLEY, J.D. & M. LINNOILA. 1997. Low central nervous system serotonergic activity is traitlike and correlates wit impulsive behavior: A nonhuman primate model investigating genetic and environmental influences on neurotransmission. Ann. N.Y. Acad. Sci. **836:** 39–56.
53. SCHUCKIT, M.A. & J.W. RUSSELL. 1983. Clinical importance of age at first drink in a group of young men. Am. J. Psychiatry **140:** 1221–1223.
54. DEWIT, D.J. *et al.* 2000. Age at first alcohol use: a risk factor for the development of alcohol disorders. Am. J. Psychiatry **157:** 745–750.

55. GRANT, B.F. *et al.* 2001. Age at onset of alcohol use and DSM-IV alcohol abuse and dependence: a 12-year follow up. J. Subst. Abuse **13**: 493–504.
56. HELLANDSJØ BU, E.T. *et al.* 2002. Teenage alcohol and intoxication debut: the impact of family socialization factors, living area, and participation in organized sports. Alcohol Alcohol. **37**: 74–80.
57. JESSOR, R. & S.L. JESSOR. 1975. Adolescent development and the onset of drinking: a longitudinal study. J. Stud. Alcohol **36**: 27–51.
58. MARGULIES, R.Z. *et al.* 1977. A longitudinal study of onset of drinking among high-school students. J. Stud. Alcohol **38**: 897–912.
59. FERGUSSON, D.M. *et al.* 1994. Childhood exposure to alcohol and adolescent drinking patterns. Addiction **89**: 1007–1016.
60. BARNES, G.M. & J.W. WELTE. 1986. Patterns and predictors of alcohol use among 7–12th grade students in New York State. J. Stud. Alcohol **47**: 53–62.
61. PEDERSEN, W. & A. SKRONDAL. 1998. Alcohol consumption debut: predictors and consequences. J. Stud. Alcohol **59**: 32–42.
62. PESCOTT, C.A. & K.S. KENDLER. 1999. Age at first drink and risk for alcoholism: a noncausal association. Alcohol Clin. Exp. Res. **23**: 101–107.
63. YOSHIMOTO, K., M. HORI, *et al.* 2002. Increase of rat alcohol drinking behavior depends on the age of drinking onset. Alcohol Clin. Exp. Res. **26**: 63S–65S.
64. SPENCER, R.L. & K.E. HUTCHISON. 1999. Alcohol, aging, and the stress response. Alcohol Res. Health **23**: 272–283.
65. PHILLIPS, T.J., A.J. ROBERTS & C.N. LESSOV. 1997. Behavior sensitization to ethanol: genetics and the effects of stress. Pharmacol. Biochem. Behav. **57**: 487–493.
66. BARR, C.S., T.K. NEWMAN, S. LINDELL, *et al.* 2004. Early experience and sex interact to influence LHPA-axis function following acute alcohol administration in rhesus macaques (*Macaca mulatta*). Alcohol Clin. Exp. Res. In press.
67. CASPI, A., K. SUGDEN, T.E. MOFFITT, *et al.* 2003. Influence of life stress on depression: moderation by a polymorphism in the 5-HTT gene. Science **301**: 386–389.
68. LAUDER, J.M. 1983. Hormonal and humoral influences on brain development. Psychoneuroendocrinology **8**: 121–155.
69. WEIDENFELD, J., M.E. NEWMAN, A. ITZK, *et al.* 2002. The amygdala regulates the pituitary-adrenocortical response and release of hypothalamic serotonin following electrical stimulation of the dorsal raphe nucleus in the rat. Neuroendocrinology **76**: 63–69.
70. GLATZ, K., R. MOSSNER, A. HEILS, *et al.* 2003. Glucocorticoid-regulated human serotonin transporter (5-HTT) expression is modulated by the 5-HTT gene-promoter-linked polymorphic region. J. Neurochem. **86**: 1072–1078.
71. CHAMPOUX, M., A.J. BENNETT, C. SHANNON, *et al.* 2002. Serotonin transporter gene polymorphism, differential early rearing, and behavior in rhesus monkey neonates. Mol. Psychiatry **7**: 1058–1063.
72. BARR, C.S., T.K. NEWMAN, C.C. PARKER, *et al.* 2003. The utility of the nonhuman primate model for studying gene by environment interactions in behavioral research. Genes Brain Behav. **2**: 236–240.
73. BARR, C.S., T.K. NEWMAN, M.L. BECKER, *et al.* 2003. Serotonin transporter gene variation is associated with alcohol sensitivity in rhesus macaques exposed to early-life stress. Alcohol Clin. Exp. Res. **27**: 812–817.
74. BARR, C.S., T.K. NEWMAN, C. SHANNON, *et al.* 2004. Interaction between the serotonin transporter gene promoter length variant and rearing condition in determining LHPA-axis responses to separation stress in rhesus macaques (*Macaca mulatta*). Biol. Psychiatry **55**: 733–738.
75. MCEWEN, B.S. 2001. Plasticity of the hippocampus; adaptation to chronic stress and allostatic load. Ann. N.Y. Acad. Sci. **933**: 265–277.

Adolescence and the Trajectory of Alcohol Use: Basic to Clinical Studies

SANDRA A. BROWN AND SUSAN F. TAPERT

Department of Psychology, University of California San Diego,
San Diego, California 92093, USA

ABSTRACT: Emerging findings from developmentally focused research indicates subtle but important neurocognitive disadvantages among adolescents with alcohol-use disorders (AUD) as compared to teens without AUD. Even after 3 weeks of abstinence AUD youth display a 10% decrement in delayed memory functions. Neuropsychological testing of youth followed at 4 and 8 years demonstrates that heavy drinking during adolescence is associated with diminished retrieval of verbal and nonverbal material, and poorer performance on tests requiring attention skills. Alcohol withdrawal over the teen years appears to uniquely contribute to deterioration in functioning in visuospatial tasks. Brain imaging studies suggest reduced hippocampal volumes, white matter microstructure irregularities, brain response abnormalities while performing challenging cognitive tasks, and enhanced brain response when viewing alcohol cues (i.e., alcohol advertisements) among adolescents with AUD. Family characteristics such as history of alcoholism and socioeconomic status as well as personal features, including adolescent psychopathology, gender, and age of onset must be carefully considered when investigating the influence of teenage drinking on neurocognition. Further research is needed to understand how age at onset of drinking and duration of abstinence at the time of assessment affect cognitive findings. Longitudinal studies are needed to clarify neuromaturational changes associated with early alcohol exposure and patterns of resiliency. Although the magnitude of alcohol-related effects observed in adolescents' neurocognition is relatively modest, the implications are major given the prevalence of alcohol involvement, and the important educational, occupational, and social transitions that occur during adolescence.

KEYWORDS: adolescence; alcohol; neurocogntition; fMRI; development

The present chapter highlights the relation of alcohol involvement among youth and neurocognitive functioning over the course of adolescent development. Following a brief review of adolescent alcohol use patterns and related problems, the chapter focuses on neurocognitive and neuroimaging studies from our research program. Emerging evidence demonstrates the cognitive and behavioral impact of early alcohol involvement and potential deleterious effects on brain functioning.

Address for correspondence: Sandra A. Brown, Ph.D., University of California San Diego, Department of Psychology, 9500 Gilman Drive, San Diego, CA 92093. Voice: 858-822-1887; fax: 858-822-1886.
sanbrown@ucsd.edu

Ann. N.Y. Acad. Sci. 1021: 234–244 (2004). © 2004 New York Academy of Sciences.
doi: 10.1196/annals.1308.028

BACKGROUND

Adolescence is the most common time for initiation of alcohol use. By the time high school students graduate, over 80% will have begun drinking alcohol. Heavy drinking (five or more drinks per occasion) is also prevalent, with 18% of tenth graders and 30% of twelfth graders reporting that they got drunk in the past month.[1] Approximately 6% of high school students consume quantities of alcohol and drink in problematic patterns such that they meet diagnostic criteria for alcohol abuse or dependence.[2] Alcohol is a contributor to the top causes of death for youth: accidents, suicides, and homicides.[3] For example, the leading cause of death for youth age 16-to-20 is unintentional injury, primarily related to motor vehicle accidents, of which one in three involve alcohol.[4]

The earlier alcohol use is initiated, the greater the risk for a variety of adverse consequences. Youth that begin drinking alcohol before age 14, have a 41% chance of developing alcohol dependence during their lifetime compared to individuals who wait to the legal drinking age of 21 when lifetime risk is reduced to 10%.[5] Early use of alcohol elevates risk for a multitude of mental health and social problems.[6] Rates of conduct disorder, antisocial personality disorder, nicotine dependence, and illicit drug abuse and dependence are significantly higher among youth that drink early.[7] Cross-culturally, studies also indicate that heavy adolescent alcohol use is associated with psychological distress, anxiety, and depression.[7] Youth with early problems such as school difficulties, personal difficulties (e.g., hyperactivity, impulsivity, and inattentiveness), or family problems are more likely of begin drinking early. Although alcohol use is prevalent among adolescents, those most disadvantaged, such as the homeless, abused, or neglected, evidence high rates of alcohol-use disorders (AUD), as well as behavioral and psychological symptoms.[6]

Youths with certain mental health disorders evident in early adolescence are more likely to initiate alcohol use and accelerate their use throughout adolescence. Disruptive disorders, including conduct problems and aggressive or oppositional behaviors, have been most consistently associated with the early onset of alcohol use and abuse.[7,8] In girls, early anxiety disorders may also accelerate alcohol involvement,[7] and girls appear more vulnerable to the adverse consequences under conditions of low parental monitoring.

HOW ALCOHOL AFFECTS ADOLESCENT BRAIN DEVELOPMENT

Despite the prevalence of alcohol use and related disorders in adolescence, we are just beginning to understand how protracted alcohol consumption during this period affects brain development and cognition. Central nervous system abnormalities including neurocognitive deficits, atrophy of several brain structures, abnormal electrophysiology, altered blood flow, abnormal brain function, and disruptive sleep have clearly been observed in adults with chronic heavy drinking histories (e.g., Refs. 9–11). Although it is less clear how adolescent brains are affected, mounting evidence from animal and human studies suggest a potentially greater impact of alcohol prior to full brain maturation. Understanding the neuromaturational implications of adolescent alcohol use is critical, since maladaptive patterns of alcohol use

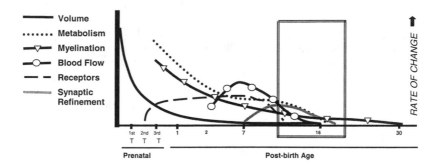

FIGURE 1. Human brain development patterns across development. (Adapted from Tapert & Schweinsburg.[30] Reproduced by permission.)

during adolescent development appears to limit educational, occupational, and social opportunities.

Adolescent Brain Development

To understand alcohol effects on adolescent brain development, it is helpful to briefly review the maturational processes unfolding during these years. As summarized in FIGURE 1, substantial neuromaturation continues throughout adolescence. Structural magnetic resonance imaging (MRI) studies have described disproportionate growth in the hippocampal region, and decreases in gray matter volume and density during adolescence, particularly in frontal and parietal brain regions, which underlies maturation of cognitive processing.[12–14] Neuronal myelination continues throughout adolescence and young adulthood[15,16] and is thought to be related to increases in cognitive efficiency. Stages of increased cerebral blood flow support periods of rapid brain growth.[17] Synaptic pruning occurs through midadolescence, varies in relation to environmental stimulation, and results in greater efficiency, as evidenced by decreased energy requirements and diminished glucose metabolism.[18,19] Changes in functional regional activity become increasingly evident and are indicative of regional specialization and maturation.[20]

Animal Studies

While human research on alcohol's impact on the brain has mushroomed over the past decade with the advent of more sensitive neuroimaging technology, animal studies have previously demonstrated that alcohol affects adolescent brain development processes in several ways.[21] In general, animal studies consistently show that adolescents appear to be more sensitive than adults to the learning and memory impairments produced by alcohol exposure, but less sensitive to the sedation and temperature regulation effects of this drug. For example, in a recent study investigators gave adolescent and adult rats multiple exposures of large quantities of alcohol, mimicking the binge drinking pattern characteristic of one-third of U.S. teens. Once rats reached adulthood, those who had been given alcohol during adolescence showed more impairments on a spatial learning memory task than those who had been given alcohol only as adults.[22] Furthermore, studies of adolescent and adult rats reveal that chronic alcohol use during adolescence alters sensitivity to alcohol-induced motor dyscoordination.[21] Another study examined the behavioral and neuroanatomical effects of a four-day alcohol binge on adolescent and adult rats. While significant brain damage was found in both groups during the autopsy, several frontal brain regions were damaged only in the adolescent exposed rats, suggesting that different brain regions vary in vulnerability to alcohol effects across development.[23]

Neuropsychological Studies

Through a series of studies we have longitudinally examined youths with and without alcohol abuse and dependence and monitored their alcohol and drug involvement into adulthood to investigate neurocognitive functioning over time. Neuropsychological studies of adults with AUD have consistently revealed visuospatial, executive functioning, psychomotor, and memory impairments secondary to heavy alcohol exposure.[6,24] However, until recently it was unclear whether the neurocognition of teenagers might be affected by protracted alcohol consumption. The limited number of studies that have examined neurocognition in adolescents with AUD have generally demonstrated modest functional decrements. For example, an early neuropsychological study by other investigators recruited teens with AUD from treatment centers, and demonstrated subtle deficits in verbal skills among youths with AUD compared to nonabusing controls, as well as problem-solving errors among girls with AUD relative to control girls.[25] Tarter and colleagues[26] examined cognition among 106 female youths with AUD, most of whom met criteria for other substance use disorders as well. Compared to 74 control girls, those with AUD performed poorly in several domains, including language, attention, perceptual efficiency, general intelligence, and academic achievement.

In a series of studies, our group has assessed AUD youths recruited from alcohol- and drug-treatment facilities and nonabusing control teens from the same communities who were matched for gender, age, socioeconomic status, and family history of alcohol and substance use disorders. In one study of 15–16 year olds with at least 100 episodes of heavy alcohol use ($M = 753$), youths with an AUD and three weeks of abstinence used fewer learning strategies to acquire new information and showed a 10% deficit in the ability to retrieve verbal and nonverbal information compared to control teens.[24] While both abusing and nonabusing youths were able to learn verbal and nonverbal (visual–spatial) information, as shown in FIGURE 2, delayed recall was reduced approximately 10% across tasks (e.g., Wechsler Memory Scale-Visual Reproduction, California Verbal Learning Test) for those with a history of AUD.

We followed samples of abusing and nonabusing youths longitudinally, and read-ministered a neurocognitive testing battery at 4 and 8 years subsequent to initial testing.[27,28] Among those who continued substance involvement after treatment, alcohol withdrawal symptoms experienced at any point during the follow-up period predicted poorer with visuospatial functioning at 4 years after treatment discharge, and those with recent use and a past history of withdrawal evidenced the poorest neurocognitive outcomes.[27] Further, at 8 years post-initial assessment (average age = 24 years) greater cumulative lifetime alcohol experiences predicted poorer attention

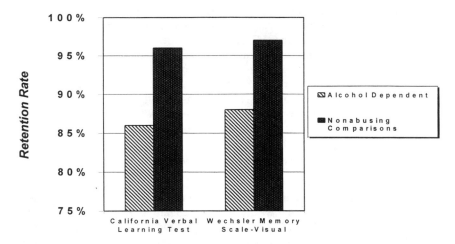

FIGURE 2. Neurocognition of detoxified alcohol-dependent teens. (From Brown *et al.*[24] Reproduced by permission.)

functioning as well as poorer working memory scores at the follow-up.[28] A history of alcohol withdrawal symptoms predicted reductions in visual–spatial functioning as measured by the Wechsler Memory Scale-Visual Reproduction as well as Rey-Osterrieth figure. These predictions remained significant even after excluding youths who had drank heavily (≥ 4 drinks/occasion for females, ≥ 5 drinks for males) and used other substances in the 28 days prior to testing. Together, these studies indicate that heavy alcohol involvement during adolescence is associated with cognitive deficits that worsen as drinking continues into late adolescence and young adulthood. Specifically, adolescents who by age 15–16 years of age have over 100 heavy drinking episodes and meet criteria for an AUD, use fewer strategies to learn new information and demonstrate significantly reduced memory skills. For those who continue alcohol involvement during the next 4 years and experience any withdrawal symptoms, deterioration in attention and visual–spatial functioning continues. By young adulthood these skills continue to deteriorate relative to nonabusing peers and their own baseline. These findings suggest that use and withdrawal differentially affect neurocognitive functioning across this stage of development.

As part of our longitudinal program of research we have examined the complex relationship between neurocognitive skills and onset and persistence of AUDs. Neurocognitive functioning appears to moderate outcome through its relation with coping skills and alcohol reinforcement expectancies. Adolescent coping skills significantly predict less alcohol and other drug use after treatment for those with lower levels of cognitive functioning, while coping skills do not predict outcomes for youths with higher levels of cognitive functioning.[23] In contrast, for youths with above average language skills, having more favorable alcohol expectancies predicted greater alcohol and drug use and dependence symptoms after treatment, whereas expectancies played a smaller role for young people with lower levels of language ability. These longitudinal investigations highlight changing neurocognitive functioning in relation to clinical course as well as the adverse cumulative effect of prolonged alcohol use during the course of adolescent development. Finally, neurocognition plays an active role in promoting or retarding alcohol involvement, depending on personal and environmental characteristics.

Brain-Imaging Studies

The recent advent of noninvasive neuroimaging techniques has provided unique opportunities to examine the influence of alcohol involvement on brain structure and function in adolescents. De Bellis and colleagues used MRI to quantify volumes of several brain structures among youths ages 13 to 21 years.[29] Those with adolescent-onset AUD had reduced hippocampal volumes, but similar cortical gray and white matter, amygdala, and corpus callosum sizes compared to controls. We have used diffusion tensor imaging to investigate corpus callosum microstructure integrity among teenagers with AUD and nonabusing controls.[30] All participants were free from psychiatric disorders, and had limited experience with other drugs. Preliminary results indicated that AUD youths exhibit subtle white matter abnormalities, particularly in the splenium of the corpus callosum. Thus, although adolescents with AUD show normal corpus callosum volumes, subtle abnormalities in white matter microstructure may represent the beginnings of a more profound disruption than is observed in chronic heavy drinking adults.

Functional brain changes have also been demonstrated among youths with AUD. Young women, ages 18–25, who started drinking heavily during adolescence and had a lifetime history of an AUD showed significantly diminished frontal and parietal functional MRI (fMRI) response as well as less accurate performance during a spatial working memory task relative to demographically similar young women with comparable family histories of alcoholism.[31] We used the same paradigm to examine brain activation among adolescents, ages 14–17, with little alcohol experience and age and gender-matched teens with AUD but without histories of other psychiatric disorders or heavy drug use. In contrast to our findings with young adult women, AUD boys and girls showed increased parietal response during spatial working memory compared to control teens, despite similar task performance.[30] These findings, if replicated, suggest that in the early stages of AUD, youth may be capable of compensating for subtle alcohol-induced neuronal disturbances by recruiting additional resources and more intense and widespread neuronal activation. However, the neurocognitive and fMRI findings among young adult women suggest that, as heavy drinking continues, neural injury may increase,[32] the brain may be less able to counteract alcohol-related disruption, and behaviors may begin to show signs of impairment.

Functional neuroimaging has also been used to evaluate response to alcohol cues among adults and adolescents with AUD.[33] In our study of 14–17 year olds, teens were shown pictures of alcoholic beverage advertisements and visually similar non-alcoholic beverage advertisements during fMRI. The images presented were individualized based on personal drinking experiences and preference in order to ensure familiarity with cues. Compared to youth with limited alcohol experience, teens with AUD demonstrated increased brain response to alcohol pictures in left anterior, limbic, and visual regions commonly associated with emotion, visual processing, and reward circuitry. Although family history of AUD was a significant predictor of re-

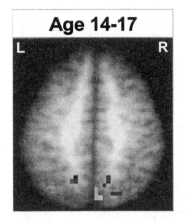
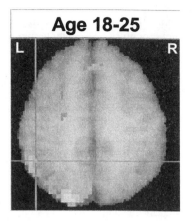

Task: Spatial Working Memory

AUD > Controls   *AUD < Controls*

FIGURE 3. Brain response to alcohol use in disordered adolescents and young adults: spatial working memory. (From Tapert *et al.*[30] Reproduced by permission.) (*Color figure shown in online version.*)

sponsivity, personal alcohol use was a stronger predictor of brain response to visual alcohol cues. Moreover, AUD teens reporting greater monthly alcohol consumption and more intense desires to drink showed the greatest extent of neural response to the alcohol advertisements. Given the strong neural response to alcohol beverage advertisements among teens with AUD, it is possible that these media images may influence continued drinking among teens with alcohol problems, and may interfere with effective coping strategies in youths attempting to stop using.

DEVELOPMENTAL CONSIDERATIONS

Several factors are critical in the consideration of alcohol's influence on the neurocognitive and neuroanatomical functioning of youth. First, while adverse behavioral and social trajectories are evident with the onset of AUDs during adolescence, it remains unclear whether the adolescent brain is ultimately more vulnerable to this toxin or will be more resilient and capable of recovery than adults (e.g., Refs. 6 and 24). Evidence with animals suggests greater vulnerability to adverse learning consequences and our human studies suggest cumulative neurocognitive impairment secondary to alcohol use over the course of middle to late adolescence. However, neuroimaging findings are consistent with early compensation, and only prospective longitudinal studies can resolve this apparent discrepancy.

Gender differences have been evident in studies of AUD adults, with females more susceptible to alcohol-related brain injury than males.[34] Hormonal fluctuations, differences in alcohol metabolism, and gender-specific drinking patterns, may partially account for the mounting evidence that adolescent girls suffer greater alcohol-related neurocognitive deficits than adolescent boys. Girls with AUDs show more perseveration errors than nonabusing girls, while boys with AUDs show *fewer* perseverative errors than control boys, suggesting that this component of frontal lobe functioning may be more adversely affected by heavy alcohol use in girls.[25] In our longitudinal research of 70 adolescents followed over 8 years, young women demonstrated more adverse cognitive effects related to alcohol and other drug use, especially in working memory and visuospatial functioning, whereas young men showed a greater relationship between verbal learning and substance involvement. Further, while alcohol withdrawal and hangovers were associated with poorer performance in both males and females, this effect was stronger in females.[28] Additionally, our recent fMRI spatial working memory investigations have shown greater magnitude of response change in girls than boys. Gender differences in fMRI response may reflect gender-specific disruptions in brain development related in part to hormonal changes or dysregulation in puberty,[35] which may ultimately influence subsequent neural development and functioning.

Studies of alcohol-related neurocognitive and neural sequelae need to consider other sources of abnormalities that may predate the onset of heavy drinking among youth. Two such factors are familial alcoholism and personal comorbid psychopathology, both of which are risk factors for developing an AUD and have been associated with unique neurocognitive features. Youths with multigenerational and dense family histories of alcoholism have shown modest neuropsychological differences compared to youths without such family histories independent of personal substance intake and maternal drinking during pregnancy.[36] Adolescent males who do not personally abuse alcohol or other drugs, but have family histories of alcohol dependence commonly perform worse on tests of language functioning and academic achievement, organization of new information, executive cognitive functioning, perseveration, working memory, nonverbal memory, visuospatial skills, and attention (e.g., Ref. 37). In our studies, family history of alcohol dependence and adolescent alcohol/substance use appear to operate as separate risk factors for poorer neuropsychological performance in youth.[36]

Disruptive disorders (e.g., conduct disorder, attention deficit hyperactivity disorder) and certain internalizing disorders are also associated with specific neurocognitive disadvantages that elevate risk for adolescent AUDs. Conduct disorder and related behavior disorders, characterized by disinhibition (e.g., ADHD) have been associated with poorer performance on academic achievement and IQ tests, and are more likely to show deficits on measures of executive functioning, including sequencing, cognitive flexibility, selective attention, and initiating planned strategies, including nonverbal tests.[38] Internalizing disorders,some of which parallel adolescent AUD results, have also been associated with alterations in cognitive performance and brain functioning in adolescents. Youths with familial alcoholism often show a low amplitude P3 component of the event-related potential, which has a slow rate of change during adolescence. However, in girls, this neurophysiological developmental pattern is also associated with childhood internalizing and externalizing psychopathology as well as psychiatric diagnoses in young adulthood.[39]

YOUTH RECOVERY OF NEUROCOGNITIVE ABILITIES

It remains uncertain to what extent the observed abnormalities in cognition of heavy drinking youth repair with sustained abstinence, and, if such abnormalities are repaired, how much sobriety is required until performance and brain integrity measures resume predrinking levels. Adults with histories of chronic heavy drinking have been shown to improve even after extended (i.e., multiple years) abstinence on neuropsychological testing, magnetic resonance spectroscopy, and brain volume indices (e.g., Refs. 43 and 44). In our studies, measurable memory deficits (10%) are evident after three weeks of abstinence, and neurocognitive functioning after 4 years of abstention appears comparable to baseline (e.g., Refs. 24 and 27). It remains to be seen if recoverability of brain integrity and cognitive function might be more complete in youth, whose brains are more plastic, or if recovery is less likely because neurotoxic insult may have adversely affected the course of neuromaturation.

REFERENCES

1. JOHNSTON, L.D., P.M. O'MALLEY & J.G. BACHMAN. 2003. The Monitoring the Future National Survey Results on Adolescent Drug Use: Overview of Key Findings, 2002. National Institute on Drug Abuse. Bethesda, MD.
2. ROHDE, P., P.M. LEWINSOHN & J.R. SEELEY. 1996. Psychiatric comorbidity with problematic alcohol use in high school students. J. Am. Acad. Child Adolesc. Psychiatry 35: 101–109.
3. NATIONAL CENTER FOR HEALTH STATISTICS. 1999. 10 leading causes of death, United States. Office of Statistics and Programming, National Center for Injury Prevention and Control, Center for Disease Control. Atlanta, GA.
4. HINGSON, R., T. HEEREN & M. WINTER. 2003. Age of first intoxication, heavy drinking, driving after drinking and risk of unintentional injury among U.S college students. J. Stud. Alcohol 64: 23–31.
5. GRANT, B.F. & D.A. DAWSON. 1997. Age at onset of alcohol use and its association with DSM-IV alcohol abuse and dependence: results from the National Longitudinal Alcohol Epidemiologic Survey. J. Subst. Abuse 9: 103–110.
6. BROWN, S.A., G.A. AARONS & A.M. ABRANTES. 2001. Adolescent alcohol and drug abuse. In Handbook Of Clinical Child Psychology, 3rd ed. C.E. Walker & M.C. Roberts, Eds.: 757–775. Wiley. New York.
7. ROSE, R.J. 1998. A developmental behavioral-genetic perspective on alcoholism risk. Alcohol Health Res. World, 22: 131–143.
8. COSTELLO, E.J., A. ERKANLI, E. FEDERMAN & A. ANGOLD. 1999. Development of psychiatric comorbidity with substance abuse in adolescents: effects of timing and sex. J. Clin. Child Psychol. 28: 298–311.
9. GRANT, I. 1987. Alcohol and the brain: neuropsychological correlates. J. Consult. Clin. Psychol. 55: 310–324.
10. NIXON, S.J., R. PAUL & M. PHILLIPS. 1998. Cognitive efficiency in alcoholics and polysubstance abusers. Alcohol. Clin. Exp. Res. 22: 1414–1420.
11. SULLIVAN, E.V. et al. 2003. Disruption of frontocerebellar circuitry and function in alcoholism. Alcohol. Clin. Exp. Res. 27: 301–309.
12. GIEDD, J.N. et al. 1999. Brain development during childhood and adolescence: a longitudinal MRI study. Nature Neurosci. 2: 861–863.
13. JERNIGAN, T.L. et al. 1991. Maturation of human cerebrum observed in vivo during adolescence. Brain 114(Pt. 5): 2037–2049.
14. GIEDD, J.N. et al. 1996. Quantitative magnetic resonance imaging of human brain development: ages 4-18. Cereb. Cortex, 6: 551–560.

15. SOWELL, E.R. *et al.* 2001. Improved memory functioning and frontal lobe maturation between childhood and adolescence: a structural MRI study. J. Int. Neuropsychol. Soc. **7:** 312–322.
16. COURCHESNE, E. *et al.* 2000. Normal brain development and aging: quantitative analysis at *in vivo* MR imaging in healthy volunteers. Radiology **216:** 672–682.
17. EPSTEIN, H.T. 1999. Stages of increased cerebral blood flow accompany stages of rapid brain growth. Brain Dev. **21:** 535–539.
18. HUTTENLOCHER, P.R. & A.S. DABHOLKAR. 1997. Regional differences in synaptogenesis in human cerebral cortex. J. Comp. Neurol. **387:** 167–178.
19. CHUGANI, H.T. 1998. A critical period of brain development: studies of cerebral glucose utilization with PET. Prev. Med. **27:** 184–188.
20. CASEY, B.J., J.N. GIEDD & K.M. THOMAS. 2000. Structural and functional brain development and its relation to cognitive development. Biol. Psychol. **54:** 241–257.
21. SPEAR, L.P. 2002. The adolescent brain and the college drinker: biological basis of propensity to use and misuse alcohol. J. Stud. Alcohol. Suppl. **14:** 71–81.
22. WHITE, A.M. *et al.* 2000. Binge pattern ethanol exposure in adolescent and adult rats: differential impact on subsequent responsiveness to ethanol. Alcohol. Clin. Exp. Res. **24:** 1251–1256.
23. CREWS, F.T. *et al.* 2000. Binge ethanol consumption causes differential brain damage in young adolescent rats compared with adult rats. Alcohol. Clin. Exp. Res. **24:** 1712–1723.
24. BROWN, S.A. *et al.* 2000. Neurocognitive functioning of adolescents: effects of protracted alcohol use. Alcohol. Clin. and Exp. Res. **24:** 164–171.
25. MOSS, H.B. *et al.* 1994. A neuropsychologic profile of adolescent alcoholics. Alcohol. Clin. Exp. Res. **18:** 159–163.
26. TARTER, R.E. *et al.* 1995. Cognitive capacity in female adolescent substance abusers. Drug Alcohol Depend. **39:** 15–21.
27. TAPERT, S.F. & S.A. BROWN. 1999. Neuropsychological correlates of adolescent substance abuse: four-year outcomes. J. Int. Neuropsychol. Soc. **5:** 481–493.
28. TAPERT, S.F. *et al.* 2002. Substance use and withdrawal: neuropsychological functioning over 8 years in youth. J. Int. Neuropsychol. Soc. **8:** 873–883.
29. DE BELLIS, M.D. *et al.* 2000. Hippocampal volume in adolescent-onset alcohol use disorders. Am. J. Psychiatry **157:** . 737–744.
30. TAPERT, S. F. & A. D. SCHWEINSBURG. The human adolescent brain and alcohol use disorders. *In* Recent Developments in Alcoholism, Vol. XVII: Research on Alcohol Problems in Adolescents and Young Adults. M. Galanter Ed. In press.
31. TAPERT, S.F. & S.A. BROWN. 1999. Gender differences in neuropsychological functioning of young adult substance abusers. Proc. Annu. Meet. of the American Psychological Association. Boston.
32. FEIN, G. *et al.* 1994. ^{1}H magnetic resonance spectroscopic imaging separates neuronal from glial changes in alcohol-related brain atrophy. *In* Alcohol and Glial Cells, F.E. Lancaster, Ed.: 227-241. National Institutes of Health. Bethesda, MD.
33. TAPERT, S.F. *et al.* 2003. Neural response to alcohol stimuli in adolescents with alcohol use disorder. Arch. Gen. Psychiatry **60:** 727–735.
34. HOMMER, D. *et al.* 2001. Evidence for a gender-related effect of alcoholism on brain volumes. Am. J. Psychiatry **158:** 198–204.
35. DE BELLIS, M.D. *et al.* 2001. Sex differences in brain maturation during childhood and adolescence. Cereb. Cortex **11:** 552–557.
36. TAPERT, S.F. & S.A. BROWN 2000. Substance dependence, family history of alcohol dependence, and neuropsychological functioning in adolescence. Addiction **95:** 1043–1053.
37. CORRAL, M.M., S.R. HOLGUÍN & F. CADAVEIRA. 1999. Neuropsychological characteristics in children of alcoholics: familial density. J. Stud. Alcohol **60:** 509–513.
38. MOFFITT, T.E. 1993. The neuropsychology of conduct disorder. Dev. Psychopathol. **5:** 135–151.
39. HILL, S.Y. & S. SHEN. 2002. Neurodevelopmental patterns of visual P3b in association with familial risk for alcohol dependence and childhood diagnosis. Biol. Psychiatry **51:** 621–631.

40. TAPERT, S. *et al.* 2002. Attention dysfunction predicts substance involvement in community youth. J. Am. Acad. Child. Adolesc. Psychiatry **41:** 680–686.
41. TAPERT, S.F. *et al.* 1999. The role of neurocognitive abilities in coping with adolescent relapse to alcohol and drug use. J. Stud. Alcohol **60:** 500–508.
42. TAPERT, S.F. *et al.* 2003. Influence of language abilities and alcohol expectancies on the persistence of heavy drinking in youth. J. Stud. Alcohol **64:** 313–321.
43. SCHWEINSBURG, B.C. *et al.* 2000. Elevated myo inositol in gray matter of recently detoxified but not long term abstinent alcoholics: a preliminary MR spectroscopy study. Alcohol. Clin. Exp. Res. **24:** 699–705.
44. BRANDT, J. *et al.* 1983. Cognitive loss and recovery in long-term alcohol abusers. Arch. Gen. Psychiatry **40:** 435–442.

Trajectories of Alcohol Use and Electrophysiological and Morphological Indices of Brain Development: Distinguishing Causes from Consequences

SHIRLEY Y. HILL

Department of Psychiatry, University of Pittsburgh School of Medicine, Pittsburgh, Pennsylvania 15213, USA

ABSTRACT: Alcoholism is a major public health problem. Patterns of drinking during adolescence can influence the likelihood of this outcome. Both environmental variation and familial/genetic susceptibility play important roles in this process. While there is some evidence to suggest that metabolic factors play a role in whether some individuals are protected from developing alcohol problems, there is substantial reason to look for cognitive factors that are associated with increased susceptibility. Developmental trajectories for information processing that can be reflected in P300 amplitude changes over time, as well as trajectories describing acquisition of postural control when compared in offspring from families with multiple cases of alcoholism or those with none or few, suggest that brain development provides a clue to why some individuals are more susceptible to becoming alcoholic. Finally, differences seen in amygdala volume between high- and low-risk adolescents suggest that functional differences seen in electrophysiological responding or neuropsychological test performance may have anatomical correlates.

KEYWORDS: alcoholism; alcohol dependence; familial/genetic susceptibility; P300; amygdala; brain laterality; longitudinal studies; multiplex families; adolescence

INTRODUCTION

Data from the National Comorbidity Survey, a nationally representative general-population survey of respondents (ages 15–54), suggests that men are twice as likely as women to meet lifetime criteria for alcohol dependence: 20.1% for men and 8.2% for women.[1]

Alcohol dependence has long been recognized to aggregate in families, with the morbid risk to relatives of alcoholics higher than the risk to individuals in the general population.[2] Currently, there are five adoption studies and fifteen twin studies that support the notion that there is a genetic influence in the development of alcohol de-

Address for correspondence: Dr. Shirley Y. Hill, Department of Psychiatry, University of Pittsburgh School of Medicine, 3811 O'Hara Street, Pittsburgh, PA 15213. Voice: 412-624-3505; fax: 412-624-3986.

syh50@imap.pitt.edu

Ann. N.Y. Acad. Sci. 1021: 245–259 (2004). © 2004 New York Academy of Sciences.

doi: 10.1196/annals.1308.029

pendence.[3] Comparing concordance for alcohol dependence in MZ and DZ twins in studies using relatively similar methodologies has provided estimates of heritability in males in the range of .49 (Ref. 4) to .64 (Ref. 5). Although estimates are based on fewer studies, it appears that heritability in females is within the range reported for males. Prescott et al.[6] has reported a heritability of .59 in women, while Kendler et al.[7] and Pickens et al.[8] reported a h^2 of .56 and .42, respectively. Also, there is evidence for genetic heterogeneity in women as noted by McGue et al.,[9] who found greater similarity in female twins with early onset (before age 20). Adoption studies find the risk to male offspring of alcoholics to be 2–3 times higher than offspring of male nonalcoholics,[10–13] with results mostly inconclusive for women because of relatively small samples.

In addition to twin and adoption methods, a strategy has been developed that recently has been shown to have especially good power for finding endophenotypic markers or genetic loci of risk for a particular disorder. This strategy involves selecting families for study on the basis of having multiple cases of the disorder of interest; such families are termed "multiplex." In the work from our laboratory to be described, families were selected for study if a minimum of two adult alcoholic brothers or alcoholic sisters were present in the family. Offspring from these families have been followed, in many cases, for over 10 years. Having multiplex families for study and incorporating neurobiological markers with good heritability and a known relationship to the disease of interest (alcohol dependence) as has been done in our laboratory, has led to identification of variation that may aid in uncovering some of the heterogeneity seen in alcoholism.

The alcoholism field has made significant progress in understanding how to match treatments to clients based on the salient characteristics of the clients (Project Match, NIAAA[14]). In contrast, prevention efforts designed to reduce levels of substance dependence among the youth have not distinguished between typical children/adolescents found in the general population and those who are at especially high risk because of their family background. The major obstacle in developing specialized methods for identification and intervention has been the almost exclusive study of factors predicting substance use problems in general-population samples largely drawn from schools. Our work and others' suggest that there are "survivors" even in high-density families of the type we have been studying for the past 18 years. Therefore, it is important to identify the predictors that protect or promote substance dependence among youth from high-risk families. We have taken major steps forward in this area in our studies of alcoholics and their multiplex families, finding a number of predictors of early onset drinking and psychiatric disorders during adolescence. Others have contributed substantially to this literature as well.[15,16]

PREDICTING EXCESSIVE USE OF ALCOHOL IN ADOLESCENCE AND BEYOND: THE ROLE OF FAMILIAL/GENETIC BACKGROUND, EXPECTANCIES, TEMPERAMENT

Familial/Genetic Background

The earlier that an adolescent begins regular drinking of alcohol, the higher the level of misuse[17] and alcohol dependence.[18] Hawkins et al.[17] recruited children between the ages of 10 and 11 and observed them for 7 years, finding greater misuse at ages 17 and 18 among those with earlier initiation. Using a large-scale population sample, Grant and Dawson[18] showed that age of onset of regular drinking predicted the likelihood of adult alcohol dependence. For those individuals younger than 14 years, the rate was 40%; for those age 20 and older, it was 10%. Similarly, in a nationally representative study in Britain, it was found that regular drinking at age 16 increased the risk fourfold for heavy drinking at age 23.[19] Using a longitudinal prospective design involving children and adolescents chosen for risk for alcohol dependence, based on their family constellation of alcoholism or lack of alcoholism among first- and second-degree relatives, high-risk children have been shown to have an earlier onset of drinking and an earlier onset of substance-dependence problems.[20] Specifically, using the number of affected first- and second-degree relatives with alcoholism provides a more precise measure of familial/genetic loading. These results appear to support a number of studies showing that familial risk for alcoholism, as defined by the presence of parental alcoholism, is a predictor of alcohol use and alcohol problems in adolescence.[21,22] Exposure to an alcoholic parent or older sibling may provide increased opportunity for an early onset that is independent of any assumed genetic loading. However, no effect of such exposure was reported in one study that specifically addressed this issue.[24]

Temperament

The heritability of human personality traits has been estimated to be between 30 and 60%, based on twin and adoption data.[25] The relationship between specific personality traits and alcohol dependence has been explored in a number of studies of adult alcoholics over the last two decades.[26,27] Among the more commonly studied personality characteristics are sensation seeking,[28] aggression,[29,30] alienation,[29] neuroticism,[31] and extraversion or sociability.[20,32] Because associations between specific personality characteristics and alcoholism have been seen in adult alcohol-

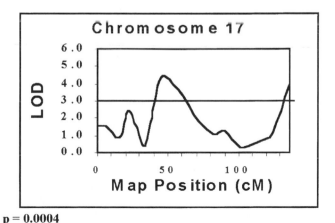

p = 0.0004

FIGURE 1. Linkage analysis of the alcoholism phenotype gives a LOD score significant at 0.0004 at marker D17S1857. This marker is within 3 cM of the 5-HTT gene.

ics, some interest has been seen in using these traits as predictors of alcohol use during adolescence. For example, college-age offspring of alcoholics have been evaluated using Eysenck's Neuroticism scale with both positive[23] and negative[33] findings. Using longitudinal data in which children/adolescents were queried annually about onset of drinking, Hill and colleagues[20] found the Extraversion scale of the Junior Eysenck Personality Inventory scores to predict onset. Prescott and colleagues[34] have also found extraversion to predict problem drinking in a population-based sample of twins.

Recent findings showing interindividual differences in cerebrospinal fluid (CSF) 5 hydroxyindoleacetic acid (5-HIAAA) variation in nonhuman primates that appears to be related to trait-like characteristics often seen in type II alcoholics (e.g., high levels of aggression) is of interest.[102] This analysis for genetic variation in the serotonin transporter gene supporting a relationship to aggressive behavior in nonhuman primates is particularly noteworthy. A recent genomewide search in our laboratory finds a substantial linkage result in this region (FIG. 1).

Alcohol Expectancies and Adolescence

Several studies have shown that alcohol-related expectancies are associated with drinking-related behavior in both adolescent and young adult populations.[35–37] The effect of family history of alcoholism on alcohol-related expectancies has been studied in early adolescents,[38] adolescents in treatment for alcohol abuse,[39] and in high school[40] and college students.[23,41] Using data from a prospective study of high- and low-risk children/adolescents, Shen and colleagues[42] found that during early adolescence having a high density of alcoholism in the family was associated with expectations of improvement in social functioning with alcohol use. In that study, positive expectancies concerning increases in social behavior and relaxation predicted age of onset to begin drinking. At each assessment, the offspring and one parent were administered the Alcohol Expectancy Questionnaire to assess similarities in expectations between parents and offspring. Here, high-risk offspring had beliefs that were similar to those of their parents. In contrast, low-risk offspring had beliefs about the effects of alcohol that were frequently quite dissimilar from those of their parents. Inasmuch as high-risk parents more often supported the positive effects of using alcohol (e.g., increased relaxation) than did control parents, the greater similarity between parents and offspring from high-risk families may facilitate transmission of alcohol dependence across generations.

NEUROBIOLOGICAL ANTECEDENTS AND CONSEQUENCES OF EXCESSIVE ALCOHOL USE

An extensive literature exists suggesting that children of alcoholics exhibit deficits in neuropsychological test performance.[23,43,44] Verbal performance has been reported to be diminished in children of alcoholics[43] as has nonverbal problem-solving skills including Block Design[23] and Halstead Category errors.[44] Additionally, children of alcoholics have been reported to have poorer school achievement than children of nonalcoholics,[23,43,45] though some studies have found no differences,[46,47] and others have found only limited achievement deficits for high-risk children who

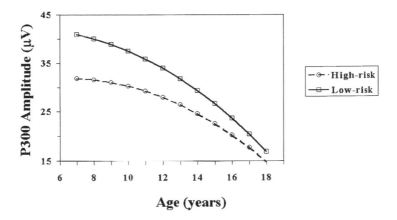

FIGURE 2. Developmental trajectories of P300 amplitude by risk group.

were well matched for SES and IQ to controls.[48] In that study, Wide Range Achievement Test scores were significantly lower for math, but spelling and reading scores were not significantly different.

The event-related potential (ERP), and particularly the amplitude of the P300 component of the ERP wave, has been studied as a possible neurocognitive marker of risk for developing alcohol dependence. Once alcohol use has begun, the distinction between antecedent and consequent conditions is, of course, blurred. However, a number of studies have used offspring of alcoholics that are young enough to have encountered minimal exposure to alcohol and other drugs. Differences in P300 amplitude between high- and low-risk for alcoholism offspring have frequently been observed.[49–52] Multiple studies have demonstrated that the amplitude of the P300 component of the ERP is smaller in high-risk child/adolescent offspring of alcoholics than in controls.[53] The meta-analysis performed by Polich *et al.*[53] found that, while P300 amplitude was reduced overall in high-risk compared to low-risk offspring, the differences were more pronounced in younger subjects and in those receiving a difficult visual discrimination task. Moreover, longitudinal data collected in our laboratory have identified electrophysiological differences between high- and low-risk children suggestive of developmental delays in cognitive development[54] (FIG. 2). Specifically, high-risk children/adolescents appear to be delayed in reaching age-appropriate P300 amplitude.[54] Using a longitudinal design, the children/adolescents were evaluated yearly with oddball tasks (two auditory paradigms and one visual) designed to elicit event-related potentials. Growth curves obtained for these children/adolescents (ages 8–18) studied showed differing patterns by modality (visual P300 shows a steady decline while auditory P300 shows an increase), with a consistent trend for the high-risk children to be delayed in reaching age-appropriate P300 levels when compared to controls.

Other evidence for subtle developmental delays in neurological capacity has been provided by longitudinal assessment of postural sway in these high- and low-risk children/adolescents.[55] Using a sensitive movement platform, children/adolescents were evaluated yearly to determine the amount of sway present when the participants

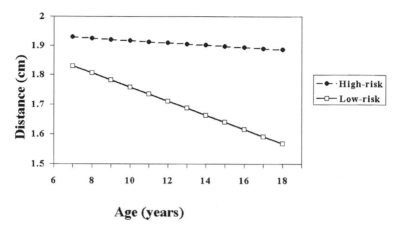

FIGURE 3. Developmental trajectories of body sway by risk group.

were asked to stand as steady as possible while assuming postural stances (heel-to-toe–bipedal, feet side to side–bipedal, monopedal). Age-related improvements in postural balance during childhood have been documented in our laboratory[55] and others.[56,57] Using cross-sectional analyses, several groups have found that high-risk children show greater body sway than do control children.[58–61] Follow-up of the same children at annual intervals during childhood and adolescence confirms that overall, in comparison to control children, high-risk children exhibit greater body sway, and moreover, appear to be delayed in achieving age-appropriate postural control.[55] (FIG. 3). Together, the neuropsychological, ERP, and postural results suggest that subtle differences in neurocognitive capacity may be characteristic of offspring from alcoholic families. To date, these domains have not been investigated further using either structural or functional imaging techniques to explore possible sources of identified developmental lags.

Although neuroimaging studies have become quite common in the alcoholism literature, the emphasis has been on either documenting brain pathologies in long-term adult alcoholics or more recently in uncovering neuropathologies thought to be the result of adolescent substance abuse.[62] DeBellis and colleagues[62] have reported that alcohol-dependent adolescents have significantly smaller hippocampal volume in comparison to age- and gender-matched controls. These differences have been interpreted as being the result of excessive use of alcohol, though the authors readily acknowledge that these structural differences may have been present before the initiation of drinking. Similarly, Brown et al.[63] have shown that alcohol-dependent adolescents show significantly poorer neuropsychological performance, including lower WISC-R Vocabulary, Information, Similarities and Coding scores and reduced reproduction retention rates, in comparison to controls. Also, recent work[103] has demonstrated that in comparison to low-exposure controls, late adolescent youth with at least 100 alcohol use episodes use fewer strategies when learning new information and retain less verbal and nonverbal information. Additionally, cumulative alcohol exposure and multiple episodes of alcohol withdrawal were associated with reduced visuospatial performance and attentional skill. FMRI studies with these adolescent alcohol abusers has revealed a lower BOLD response to spatial working memory tasks in multiple regions of interest. These observed differences in alcohol-dependent youth could be the result of alcohol use, or alternatively, may be neurobiological markers of vulnerability that are present before alcohol initiation.

NEUROBIOLOGICAL ANTECEDENTS: GROWTH AND DEVELOPMENT OF SUBCORTICAL BRAIN REGIONS DURING ADOLESCENCE/ POSSIBLE RELATIONSHIP TO ALCOHOL INTAKE

Based on the longitudinal data suggesting that high-risk children experience developmental delays in acquiring age-appropriate postural control,[55] and age-appropriate P300,[54] we hypothesized that brain areas that are changing rapidly during adolescence might show volumetric differences between high- and low-risk children/ adolescents. Both progressive and regressive processes are characteristic of adolescence.[64–73] In contrast to the decreases in cortical gray matter that is seen up to the age of 30, there is evidence for continued growth during the same developmental period in subcortical limbic structures including the septal area, hippocampus, and amygdala that show an increase in volume.[67]

The amygdala and hippocampus were targeted for volumetric analysis using a region-of-interest technique. This decision was based on four considerations. First, neural generators for P300 have been described in both cortical and subcortical regions,[74,75] including the hippocampus.[76,77] Although some have argued that the hippocampal formation may influence P300 only indirectly[78,79] through the interaction of hippocampal/temporal-parietal functioning with the frontal lobe, nevertheless, the hippocampus is thought to play a role in P300 production. Because P300 generation undoubtedly involves subcortical areas, we reasoned that the developmental changes in P300 previously observed[54] might reflect regressive or progressive events in subcortical anatomy during childhood and adolescence. Second, the amygdala has been directly implicated in the reinforcing effects of alcohol; microinjection of GABA and opioid antagonists in the central nucleus of the amygdala are quite effective in decreasing the acute reinforcing effects of ethanol.[80,81] Finally, as noted previously, adolescent substance abusers have been found to have smaller hippocampal volumes than do controls without substance abuse,[62] a finding that may reflect alcohol use during adolescence or, alternatively, greater familial loading of alcoholism in those individuals who become alcohol dependent by adolescence. If the latter interpretation is correct, familial/genetic differences in subcortical structures might be found when high- and low-risk for alcoholism offspring are compared. The study was designed to specifically address the issue of whether or not the hippocampus and amygdala varied in volume in high-risk offspring from high density for alcoholism families in comparison to controls.

Thirty-four high- and low-risk adolescents/young adults were selected for study who were well matched on age, SES, IQ, height, and weight. All were right-handed. Participants who were members of a longitudinal prospective study had been followed an average of 7.3 years (SD ± 2.1 years) with clinical information obtained at yearly intervals. This provided an opportunity to choose individuals for participation who had not begun to drink excessively or to use drugs extensively. Based on anal-

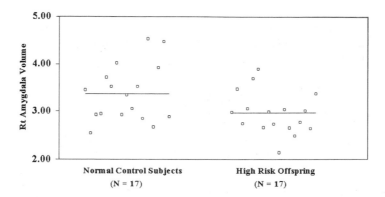

FIGURE 4. Right amygdala volume in high- and low-risk male participants. Individuals were matched for SES, IQ. Each high-risk individual was matched to an individual who was within one year of age. All were male and right handed.

ysis of all 34 cases, no significant differences in hippocampal volume were seen between the high- and low-risk offspring who had minimal alcohol exposure. This suggests that the finding observed by DeBellis et al.[62] in which smaller hippocampal volume was seen in adolescent alcohol abusers most likely reflects alcohol exposure.

In our study of youngsters with a high familial loading for alcohol dependence with low personal exposure to alcohol, of particular note was the significant difference in right amygdala volume when compared to controls ($F = 6.72$, $df = 1,32$, $P = .014$) (see FIG. 4). When this analysis was repeated using alcohol use in the past month as a covariate (information available for 22 individuals), the results remained significant ($F = 6.54$, $df = 1,19$, $P = .02$). There appears to be no evidence that the findings obtained were due to differences in alcohol consumption between the high- and low-risk groups. The correlation between drinking in the past month and right amygdala volume was nonsignificant.

NEURAL SUBSTRATES OF REWARD AND THEIR ROLE IN EXCESSIVE USE OF ALCOHOL: PREDICTING EXCESSIVE ALCOHOL USE IN ADOLESCENCE AND BEYOND

These findings of lateralized decreased amygdala volume in high-risk offspring is particularly interesting in view of speculations concerning the extended amygdala system that has been implicated in the etiology of drug and alcohol addiction.[82] Koob[82] has hypothesized that the acute reinforcing actions of drugs of abuse may be mediated by the striatopallidal and extended amygdala systems that include the shell of nucleus accumbens, the central nucleus of the amygdala, and the sublenticular extended amygdala. In this view, chronic administration of drugs of abuse leads to increasing dysregulation of brain reward systems. Changes in neurochemical components of the extended amygdala, including decreases in dopamine and serotonin neurotransmission in the nucleus accumbens and increases in corticotropin releasing factor in the central nucleus of the amygdala are thought to produce changes in the hedonic set point leading to compulsive drug seeking and drug use.[82]

The Amygdala and Emotional Facial Expression

Studies of animals[83] and brain-damaged patients[84,85] indicate a central role for the amygdala in emotional learning. Functional MRI studies of conditioned fear and extinction suggest that the amygdala contributes to both acquisition and extinction of associative emotional learning tasks in humans.[86] Additionally, the amygdala has been long recognized for its influence on social behavior.[87,88] Studies of subjects with complete bilateral amygdalar damage who are asked to judge faces for their "approachability and trustworthiness" fail in doing so when the cues provided are visual, but have normal judgment when characteristics are presented to them verbally.[85] The amygdala appears to be an important neural component that aids in the retrieval of socially relevant knowledge gained through appraisal of facial appearance.

Discrimination between stimuli on the basis of their acquired behavioral significance has been shown to be lateralized within the amygdala. The right amygdala appears to have a greater role in conditioning that occurs outside the individual's awareness.[89] Presentation of angry faces paired (CS+) or unpaired (CS−) with an unconditioned stimulus (UCS) (100-dB burst of white noise) revealed that following conditioning: CS+ and CS− faces presented sequentially in either a masked or unmasked condition (masking consisted of presentation of a neutral face that was either a target or nontarget) resulted in differential activation of the right or left amygdala using PET. A significant response in the region of the right amygdala (predominantly medial and inferior portion of the complex) was seen with the presentation of the masked CS+ faces with no response seen in the left amygdala to masked CS+ stimuli. The right amygdala response occurred to the masked conditioned faces (previous pairing with the UCS) that were not consciously perceived. In contrast, there was a left-sided activation with unmasked CS+ and CS− faces (subject was aware of the angry face). These findings illustrate the lateralization of amygdalar response that occurs as a function of the level of awareness of target stimuli. A similar specificity of response has been suggested by brain recordings in monkeys in which a similar lateralized region of the amygdala has been reported to contain units selective for faces and visually aversive cues.[90] The findings of Morris et al.[89] and Leonard et al.[90] are also consistent with previously published findings indicating a right-hemisphere advantage for processing emotional facial expressions.[91,92]

The Amygdala, Emotional Learning, and High-Risk Status

With amygdala volume showing reduction in offspring at high risk for alcohol dependence because of familial/genetic susceptibility, it is possible that deficits in emotional learning may precede the onset of alcohol dependence. Much of our social learning involves incidental memory and is often outside our conscious awareness. Adult alcoholics and their high-risk nonalcoholic adult relatives report higher levels of Alienation than do controls, as measured by scores on the Multidimensional Personality Questionnaire (MPQ).[29,93] Persons scoring at the highest end of the Alienation scale of the MPQ,[94,95] can be characterized as those who more often believe that they are mistreated, that others wish them harm, and similarly often feel betrayed and used by "friends."

Amygdala Volume and Addiction Potential/Relapse

Subjective reports of euphoria associated with saline injections have been noted among heroin abusers, especially when the injections take place in the abuser's usual injection environment.[96] Similarly, conditioned withdrawal has been reported for patients returning to environments associated with drug dependence.[97] Because the right amygdala appears to be activated more readily in association with stimuli for which the individual is unaware,[89] the potential number of neutral stimuli that can acquire reinforcer status may be much larger than those for which an individual has awareness and can, to some degree, control by limiting exposure. Relapse prevention programs that rely heavily on cognitive therapy utilize the individual's self-reported reinforcement history to target places, people, and situations that are known to be associated with relapse to train the individual in avoiding such stimuli or modifying the response to the cues.[98] However, neutral stimuli can become reinforcers without the individual's awareness. Acquisition of these reinforcers appear to be dependent on the functional integrity of the right amygdala. Results demonstrating that offspring from high-density for alcoholism families have smaller amygdalar volume suggest that this structural alteration may have implications for the development of addiction, possibly through the acquisition of reinforcers, many of which the individual may not be aware of, from among a large array of previously neutral visual stimuli.

P300 Developmental Trajectories and the Amygdala

The amygdala has been suggested as a possible source for P300 generation based on clinical data acquired in patients undergoing probing for epileptic foci in which endogenous potentials to infrequently occurring visual stimuli occurred in both hippocampus and the amygdala.[76] The amygdala has extensive connections with the orbital and medial prefrontal cortex (OMPFC),[99] which include limbic connections involved in eating behavior, guidance of behavior, and regulation of mood.[99] Also, the OMPFC overlaps the hippocampal/temporal–parietal regions currently thought to be involved in P300 generation.[100]

SUMMARY

Structural and functional alteration of specific brain regions may characterize those at increased risk for developing alcohol problems. These alterations are most readily identified in childhood and adolescence before the consequences of excessive use of alcohol occur. Future neuroimaging studies will enable us to distinguish those brain regions that are especially sensitive to the effects of alcohol, such as the hippocampus, as has previously been shown in adolescent alcohol abusers[62] and in animal studies as demonstrated by Swartzwelder.[101] The animal studies completed by Swartzwelder not only reaffirm that the hippocampal formation is sensitive to the acute and chronic effects of ethanol but also suggests that the hippocampus is uniquely responsive to ethanol during the periadolescent period. Work from our laboratory suggests that other brain regions may be "wired" differently in individuals with a high susceptiblity for developing alcohol problems due to their genetic background. Genes involved in those temperamental characteristics predisposing to alcohol dependence may also affect cognitive processing through pleiotropic effects of specific genes on brain development. Identification of such genes will ultimately provide better methods of identifying adolescents before alcohol problems become entrenched in their lifestyles, thereby preventing considerable suffering resulting from chronic alcohol dependence through adulthood.

ACKNOWLEDGMENTS

This work was supported by Grants AA05909, AA08082, AA11304 from the National Institute on Alcohol Abuse and Alcoholism. The author expresses appreciation to the families who took part in this study over the many years of follow-up and to the excellent collaboration offered by Drs. Steinhauer, DeBellis, Keshavan, and Weeks. Also, senior staff who deserve recognition include Jeannette Locke-Wellman and Lisa Lowers.

REFERENCES

1. KESSLER, R.C., R.M. CRUM, L.A. WARNER, et al. 1997. Lifetime co-occurrence of DSM-III-R alcohol abuse and dependence with other psychiatric disorder in the National Comorbidity Survey. Arch. Gen. Psychiatry 54: 3123–3321.
2. COTTON, N. 1979. The familial incidence of alcoholism: a review. J. Stud. Alcohol. 40: 89–116.
3. PRESCOTT, C.A. 2001. The genetic epidemiology of alcoholism: sex differences and future directions. In Alcohol in Health and Disease. D.P. Agarwal & H.K. Seitz, Eds.: 125–149. Marcel Dekker. New York.
4. CALDWELL, C.B. & I.I. GOTTESMAN. 1991. Sex differences in the risk for alcoholism: a twin study [Abstr.]. Behav. Genet. 21: 563.
5. HEALTH, A.C., K.K. BUCHOLZ, P.A.F. MADDEN, et al. 1997. Genetic and environmental contributions to alcohol dependence risk in a national twin sample: consistency of findings in women and men. Psychol. Med. 27: 1381–1396.
6. PRESCOTT, C.A., S.H. AGGEN & K.S. KENDLER. 1999. Sex differences in the sources of genetic liability to alcohol abuse and dependence in a population based sample of US twins. Alcohol. Clin. Exp. Res. 23: 1136–1144.
7. KENDLER, K.S., A.C. HEATH, M.C. NEALE, et al. 1992. A population-based twin study of alcoholism in women. JAMA 268: 1877–1882.
8. PICKENS, R.W., D.S. SVIKIS, M. MCGUE, et al. 1991. Heterogeneity in the inheritance of alcoholism. Arch. Gen. Psychiatry 48: 19–28.
9. MCGUE, M., R.W. PICKENS & D.S. SVIKIS. 1992. Sex and age effects on the inheritance of alcohol problems: a twin study. J. Abnorm. Psychol. 101: 3–17.
10. BOHMAN, M., S. SIGVARDSSON & C.R. CLONINGER. 1981. Maternal inheritance of alcohol abuse: cross-fostering analysis of adopted women. Arch. Gen. Psychiatry 38: 965–969.
11. CLONINGER, C.R., M. BOHMAN & S. SIGVARDSSON. 1981. Inheritance of alcohol abuse: cross-fostering analysis of adopted men. Arch. Gen. Psychiatry 38: 861–868.

12. GOODWIN, D.W., F. SCHULSINGER, L. HERMANSEN, *et al.* 1973. Alcohol problems in adoptees raised apart from alcoholic biological parents. Arch. Gen. Psychiatry **28:** 238–243.
13. CADORET, R.J., T.W. O'GORMAN & E. TROUGHTON. 1987. Genetic and environmental factors in alcohol abuse and antisocial personality. J. Stud. Alcohol. **48:** 1–8.
14. GORDIS, E. & R. FULLER. 1999. Project MATCH. Addiction **94:** 57–59.
15. STALLING, M.C., J.K. HEWITT, T. BERESFORD, *et al.* 1999. A twin study of drinking and smoking onset and latencies from first use to regular use. Behav. Genet. **29:** 409–421.
16. IACONO, W.G. 1999. Identifying psychophysiological risk for psychopathology: examples from substance abuse and schizophrenia research. Psychophysiology **35:** 621–637.
17. HAWKINS, J.D., J.W. GRAHAM, E. MAGUIN, *et al.* 1997. Exploring the effects of age of alcohol use initiation and psychosocial risk factors on subsequent alcohol misuse. J. Stud. Alcohol. **58:** 280–290.
18. GRANT, B.F. & D.A. DAWSON. 1997. Age at onset of alcohol use and its association with DSM-IV alcohol abuse and dependence: results from the National Longitudinal Alcohol Epidemiologic Survey. J. Subst. Abuse **9:** 103–110.
19. GHODSIAN, M. & C. POWER. 1987. Alcohol consumption between the ages of 16 and 23 in Britain: a longitudinal study. Br. J. Addict. **82:** 175–180.
20. HILL, S.Y., S. SHEN, L. LOWERS, *et al.* 2000. Factors predicting the onset of adolescent drinking in families at high risk for developing alcoholism. Biol. Psychiatry **48:** 265–275.
21. CHASSIN, L., F. ROGOSCH & M. BARRERA. 1991. Substance use and symptomatology among adolescent children of alcoholics. J. Abnorm. Psychol. **100:** 449–463.
22. CHASSIN, L., D.R. PILLOW, P.J. CURRAN, *et al.* 1993. Relation of parental alcoholism to early adolescent substance use: a test of three mediating mechanisms. J. Abnorm. Psychol. **102:** 3–19.
23. SHER, K.J., K.S. WALITZER, P.K. WOOD, *et al.* 1991. Characteristics of children of alcoholics: putative risk factors, substance use and abuse, and psychopathology. J. Abnorm. Psychol. **100:** 427–448.
24. BAHR, S.J., A.C. MARCOS & S.L. MAUGHAN. 1995. Family, educational, and peer influences on the alcohol use of female and male adolescents. J. Stud. Alcohol. **56:** 457–469.
25. PLOMIN, R., M.J. OWEN & P. McGUFFIN. 1994. The genetic basis of complex human behaviors. Science **264:** 1733–1739.
26. BARNES, G.E. 1983. Clinical and personality characteristics. *In* The Pathogenesis of Alcoholism: Psychosocial Factors, Vol 6. B. Kissin & H. Begleiter, Eds.: 113–196. Plenum Press. New York.
27. MULDER, R.T. 2002. Alcoholism and personality. Aust. N.Z. J. Psychiatry **36:** 44–52.
28. CLONINGER, C.R., S. SIGVRDSSON & M. BOHMAN. 1988. Childhood personality predicts alcohol abuse in young adults. Alcohol. Clin. Exp. Res. **12:** 494–505.
29. HILL, S.Y., J. ZUBIN & S.R. STEINHAUER. 1990. Personality resemblance in relatives of male alcoholics: a comparison with families of male control cases. Biol. Psychiatry **27:** 1305–1322.
30. VIRKKUNEN, M. & M. LINNOILA. 1997. Serotonin in early-onset alcoholism. Recent Dev. Alcohol. **13:** 173–189.
31. BARNES, G.E. 1979. The alcoholic personality: a reanalysis of the literature. J. Stud. Alcohol. **56:** 457–469.
32. JONES, M.C. 1968. Personality correlates and antecedents of drinking patterns in adult males. J. Consult. Clin. Psychol. **32:** 2–12.
33. SCHUCKIT, M.A. 1983. Extroversion and neuroticism in young men at higher or lower risk for alcoholism. Am. J. Psychiatry **140:** 1223–1224.
34. PRESCOTT, C.A., M.C. NEALE, L.A. COREY, *et al.* 1997. Predictors of problem drinking and alcohol dependence in a population-based sample of female twins. J. Stud. Alcohol **58:** 167–181.
35. GRUBE, J.W. & G.E. AGOSTINELLI. 1999. Perceived consequences and adolescent drinking: nonlinear and interactive models of alcohol expectancies. Psychol. Addict. Behav. **13:** 303–312.
36. RONNBACK, S.A., N.K. AHLLUND & R.E. LINDMAN. 1999. Confirmatory factor analysis of the AEQ-A questionnaire in Finland. Scand. J. Psychol. **40:** 11–19.

37. BROWN, S.A. 1985. Expectancies versus background in the prediction of college drinking patterns. J. Consult. Clin. Psychol. **53:** 123–130.
38. REESE, F.L., L. CHASSIN & B.S.G. MOLINA. 1994. Alcohol expectancies in early adolescents: predicting drinking behavior from alcohol expectancies and parental alcoholism. J. Stud. Alcohol **55:** 276–284.
39. BROWN, S.A., V.A. CREAMER & B.A. STETSON. 1987. Adolescent alcohol expectancies in relation to personal and parental drinking patterns. J. Abnorm. Psychol. **96:** 117–121.
40. MANN, L.M., L. CHASSIN & K.J. SHER. 1987. Alcohol expectancies and the risk for alcoholism. J. Consult. Clin. Psychol. **55:** 411–417.
41. LUNDAHL, L.H., T.M. DAVIS, V.J. ADESSO, et al. Alcohol expectancies: effects of gender, age, and family history of alcoholism. Addict. Behav. **22:** 115–125.
42. SHEN, S.A., J. LOCKE-WELLMAN & S.Y. HILL. 2001. Adolescent alcohol expectancies in offspring from families at high risk for developing alcoholism. J. Stud. Alcohol **62:** 763–772.
43. KNOP, J., T.W. TEASDALE, F. SCHULSINGER, et al. 1985. A prospective study of young men at high risk for alcoholism: school behavior and achievement. J. Stud. Alcohol **46:** 273–278.
44. DREJER, K., A. THEILGAARD, T. TEASDALE, et al. 1985. A prospective study of young men at high risk for alcoholism: neuropsychological assessment. Alcohol. Clin. Exp. Res. **9:** 498–502.
45. MARCUS, A.M. 1986. Academic achievement in elementary school children of alcoholic mothers. J. Clin. Psychol. **42:** 372–376.
46. REICH, W., F. EARLS, O. FRANKEL, et al. 1993. Psychopathology in children of alcoholics. J. Am. Acad. Child Adolesc. Psychiatry **32:** 995–1002.
47. VITARO, F., P.L. DOBKIN, R. CARBONNEAU, et al. 1996. Personal and familial characteristics of resilient sons of male alcoholics. Addiction **91:** 1161–1177.
48. HILL, S.Y., J. LOCKE, L. LOWERS, et al. 1999. Psychopathology and achievement in children at high-risk for developing alcoholism. J. Am. Acad. Child Adolesc. Psychiatry **35:** 725–733.
49. BERMAN, S.M., S.C. WHIPPLE, R.J. FITCH, et al. 1993. P3 in young boys as a predictor of adolescent substance abuse. Alcohol **10:** 69–76.
50. HILL, S.Y., S.R. STEINHAUER, J. PARK, et al. 1990. Event-related potential characteristics in children of alcoholics from high density families. Alcohol. Clin. Exp. Res. **14:** 6–16.
51. HILL, S.Y. & S. R. STEINHAUER. 1993. Assessment of prepubertal and postpubertal boys and girls at risk for developing alcoholism with P300 from a visual discrimination task. J. Stud. Alcohol **54:** 350–358.
52. HILL, S.Y., D. MUKA, S. STEINHAUER, et al. 1995. P300 amplitude decrements in children from families of alcoholic female probands. Biol. Psychiatry **38:** 622–632.
53. POLICH, J., V.E. POLLOCK & F.E. BLOOM. 1994. Meta-analysis of P300 amplitude from males at risk for alcoholism. Psychol. Bull. **115:** 55–73.
54. HILL, S.Y., S. SHEN, J. LOCKE, et al. 1999. Developmental delay in P300 production in children at high risk for developing alcohol-related disorders. Biol. Psychiatry **46:** 970–981.
55. HILL, S.Y., S. SHEN, J. LOCKE, et al. 2000. Developmental changes in postural sway in children at high and low risk for developing alcohol-related disorders. Biol. Psychiatry **47:** 501–511.
56. USUI, N., K. MAEKAWA & Y. HIRASAWA. 1995. Development of the upright postural sway of children. Dev. Med. Child Neurol. **37:** 985–996.
57. SHUMWAY-COOK, A. & M.H. WOOLLACOTT. 1985. The growth of stability: postural control from a developmental perspective. J. Mot. Behav. **17:** 131–147.
58. LIPSCOMB, T.R., J.A. CARPENTER & P.E. NATHAN. 1979. Static ataxia: a predictor of alcoholism? Br. J. Addict. **74:** 289–294.
59. HEGEDUS, A.M., R.E. TARTER, S.Y. HILL, et al. 1984. Static ataxia: a possible marker for alcoholism. Alcohol. Clin. Exp. Res. **8:** 580–582.
60. LESTER, D. & J.A. CARPENTER. 1985. Static ataxia in adolescents and their parentage. Alcohol. Clin. Exp. Res. **9:** 212.
61. HILL, S.Y. & S.R. STEINHAUER. 1993. Postural sway in children from pedigrees exhibiting a high density of alcoholism. Biol. Psychiatry **33:** 313–325.

62. DeBELLIS, M.D., D.B. CLARK, S.R. BEERS, *et al.* 2000. Hippocampal volume in adolescent-onset alcohol use disorders. Am. J. Psychiatry **157:** 733–744.
63. BROWN, S.A., S.F. TAPERT, E. GRANHOLM, *et al.* 2000. Neurocognitive functioning of adolescents: effects of protracted alcohol use. Alcohol. Clin. Exp. Res. **24:** 164–171.
64. COWAN, W.M., J.W. FAWCETT, D.D.M. O'LEARY, *et al.* 1984. Regressive events in neurogenesis. Science **225:** 1258–1265.
65. JERNIGAN, T.L., D.A. TRAUNER, J.R. HESSELINK, *et al.* 1991. Maturation of human cerebrum observed *in vivo* during adolescence. Brain **114:** 2037–2049.
66. JERNIGAN, T.L. & P. TALLAL. 1990. Late childhood changes in brain morphology observable with MRI. Dev. Med. Child Neurol. **32:** 379–385.
67. JERNIGAN, T.L. & E.R. SOWELL. 1997. Magnetic resonance imaging studies of developing brain. *In* Neurodevelopment and Adult Psychopathology. M.S. Keshavan & R.M. Murray, Eds.: 63–70. Cambridge University Press. New York.
68. GIEDD, J.N., J.W. SNELL, N. LANGE, *et al.* 1996. Quantitative magnetic resonance imaging of human brain development: ages 4–18. Cereb. Cortex **6:** 551–560.
69. GIEDD, J.N., A.C. VAITUZIS, S.D. HAMBURGER, *et al.* 1996. Quantitative MRI of the temporal lobe, amygdala, and hippocampus in normal human development: ages 4–18. J. Comp. Neurol. **366:** 223–230.
70. GIEDD, J.N., J. BLUMENTHAL, N.O. JEFFRIES, *et al.* 1999. Brain development during childhood and adolescence: a longitudinal MRI study. Nature Neurosci. **2:** 861–863.
71. PFEFFERBAUM, A., D.H. MATHALON, E.V. SULLIVAN, *et al.* 1994. A quantitative magnetic resonance imaging study of changes in brain morphology from infancy to late adulthood. Arch. Neurol. **51:** 874–887.
72. PAUS, T., A. ZIJDENBOS, K. WORSLEY, *et al.* 1999. Structural maturation of neural pathways in children and adolescents: *in vivo* study. Science **283:** 1908–1911.
73. THOMPSON, P.M., J.N. GIEDD, R.P. WOODS, *et al.* 2000. Growth patterns in the developing brain detected by using continuum mechanical tensor maps. Nature **404:** 190–193.
74. KROPOTOV, J.D. & S.C. ETLINGER. 1991. Human depth ERP in a visual threshold recognition task. Electroencephalogr. Clin. Neurophysiol. **79:** 45–51.
75. MECKLINGER, A., B. MAESS, B. OPITZ, *et al.* 1998. A MEG analysis of the P300 in visual discrimination tasks. Electroencephalogr. Clin. Neurophysiol. **108:** 45–56.
76. HALGREN, E., N.K. SQUIRES, C. WILSON, *et al.* 1980. Endogenous potentials in the human hippocampal formation and amygdala by infrequent events. Science **210:** 803–805.
77. YINGLING, C.D. & Y. HOSOBUCHI. 1984. A subcortical correlate of P300 in man. Electroencephalogr. Clin. Neurophysiol. **59:** 72–76.
78. MOLNAR, M. 1994. On the origin of the P300 event related potential component. Int. J. Psychophysiol. **17:** 129–144.
79. POLICH, J. 1998. P300 clinical utility and control of variability. J. Clin. Neurophysiol. **15:** 14–33.
80. HYYTIA, P. & G.F. KOOB. 1995. GABAA receptor antagonism in the extended amygdala decreases ethanol self-administration in rats. Eur. J. Pharmacol. **283:** 151–159.
81. HEYSER, C.J., A.J. ROBERTS, G. SCHULTEIS, *et al.* 1995. Central administration of an opiate antagonist decreases oral ethanol self-administration in rats. Soc. Neurosci. Abstr. **21:** 1698.
82. KOOB, G.F. 1999. The role of the striatopallidal and extended amygdala systems in drug addiction. Ann. N.Y. Acad. Sci. **877:** 445–460.
83. LEDOUX, J.E. 1956. The Emotional Brain. Simon and Schuster. New York.
84. BECHARA, A., D. TRANEL, H. DAMASIO, *et al.* 1995. Double dissociation of conditioning and declarative knowledge relative to the amygdala and hippocampus in humans. Science **269:** 1115–1118.
85. ADOLPHS, R., D. TRANEL & A.R. DAMASIO. 1998. The human amygdala in social judgment. Nature **393:** 470–474.
86. LABAR, K.S., J.C. GATEBY, J.C. GORE, *et al.* 1998. Human amygdala activation during conditioned fear acquistion and extinction: a mixed trial fMRI study. Neuron **20:** 937–945.
87. ROSVOLD, H.E., A.F. MIRSKY & K. PRIBRAM. 1954. Influence of amygdalectomy on social behavior in monkeys. J. Comp. Physiol. Psychol. **47:** 173–178.

88. KLING, A.S. & L.A. BROTHERS. 1992. The amygdala and social behavior. *In* The Amygdala: Neurobiological Aspects of Emotion, Memory and Mental Dysfunction. J.P. Aggleton, Ed.: 353–377. Wiley-Liss. New York.

89. MORRIS, J.S., A. OHMAN & R.J. DOLAN. 1998. Conscious and unconscious emotional learning in the human amygdala. Nature **393:** 467–470.

90. LEONARD, C.M., E.T. ROLLS, F.A. WILSON, *et al.* 1985. Neurons in the amygdala of the monkey with responses selective for faces. Behav. Brain Res. **15:** 159–176.

91. DEKOSKY, S.T., K.M. HEILMAN, D. BOWERS, *et al.* 1980. Recognition and discrimination of emotional faces and pictures. Brain Lang. **9:** 206–214.

92. GAZZANIGA, M.S. & C.S. SMYLIE. 1983. Facial recognition and brain asymmetries: clues to underlying mechanisms. Ann. Neurol. **13:** 536–540.

93. HILL, S.Y. 1993. Personality characteristics of sisters and spouses of male alcoholics. Alcohol. Clin. Exp. Res. **17:** 733–739.

94. TELLEGEN, A. 1985. Structure of mood and personality and their relevance to assessing anxiety, with an emphasis on self-report. *In* Anxiety and Anxiety Disorders. A.H. Tuma & J.D. Maser, Eds.: 681–706. Erlbaum. Hillsdale, NJ.

95. TELLEGEN, A., D.T. LYKKEN, T.J. BOUCHARD, JR., *et al.* 1988. Personality similarity in twins reared apart and together. J. Pers. Soc. Psychol. **54:** 1031–1039.

96. MIRIN, R.E. & S.M. MEYER. 1979. The Heroin Stimulus: Implications for a Theory of Addiction. Plenum Press. New York.

97. O'BRIEN, C.P. 1975. Experimental analysis of conditioning factors in human narcotic addiction. Pharmacol. Rev. **27:** 533–543.

98. MARLATT, G.A. 1990. Cue exposure and relapse prevention in the treatment of addictive behaviors. Addict. Behav. **15:** 395–399.

99. PRICE, J.L. 1999. Prefronal cortical networks related to visceral function and mood. Ann. N.Y. Acad. Sci. **877:** 383–396.

100. POLICH, J. & M. COMERCHERO. P3a from typical and novel visual stimuli. In press.

101. WHITE, A.M. & H.S. SWARTZWELDER. 2004. Hippocampal function during adolescence: a unique target of ethanol effects. Ann. N.Y. Acad. Sci. **1021:** 206–220. This volume.

102. BARR, C.S., M.L. SCHWANDT, T.K. NEWMAN & J.D. HIGLEY. 2004. The use of adolescent nonhuman primates to model human alcohol intake: neurobiological, genetic, and psychological variables. Ann. N.Y. Acad. Sci. **1021:** 221–233.

103. BROWN, S.A. & S.F. TAPERT. 2004. Adolescence and the trajectory of alcohol use: basic to clinical studies. Ann. N.Y. Acad. Sci. **1021:** 234–244.

Regulation of Sleep and Arousal

Introduction to Part VII

RUTH M. BENCA

Department of Psychiatry, University of Wisconsin–Madison,
Madison, Wisconsin 53705, USA

ABSTRACT: This paper introduces the theme of the relationship between sleep deprivation and behavior.

KEYWORDS: sleep deprivation; adolescent brain development

Of all possible insults to the adolescent brain, sleep deprivation is perhaps the most widespread. Although the precise functions of sleep are not yet known, mounting evidence suggests that sleep is critical for brain development and function. Children and adolescents require more sleep than adults, and maturational changes in sleep patterns are evident from early fetal life through the completion of adolescence.

Sleep deprivation and other disturbances of sleep have been linked with a number of negative outcomes in adults, including poorer quality of life, increased incidence of health problems and greater health care utilization, increased in accidents, and increased absenteeism.[1] Sleep deprivation has also been shown to result in dysregulation of neuroendocrine systems. It has been suggested that sleep loss may contribute to the increasing rates of obesity and diabetes.[2] Sleep-deprived teens are at greater risk for automobile accidents and substance abuse.[3]

The association between sleep and health appears to be strongest for psychiatric disorders. Sleep has been best studied in relation to mood disorders. Children and adolescents with sleep disturbances, like adults, have higher rates of depression and other psychiatric or behavioral problems. Conversely, adolescents with depression show significant subjective and objective changes in sleep. In adults, sleep disturbance has been shown to be highly predictive of an increased risk of depression in numerous studies, suggesting a potential causal relationship. The rise in rates of adolescent depression as our society has become progressively more sleep deprived may be more than mere coincidence.

Relatively little work has been done on the relationship of sleep loss to emotional and cognitive function during adolescence. Sleep deprivation impairs the ability of teens and young adults to perform simultaneous cognitive and postural balance tasks,[3] and ADHD-like symptoms have been reported to vary in relation to sleep deprivation. Studies in animal models have shown that sleep deprivation leads to in-

Address for correspondence: Ruth Benca, M.D., Ph.D., Department of Psychiatry, 6001 Research Park Boulevard, Madison WI 53705. Voice: 608-263-6162; fax: 608-263-0265.
rbenca@med.wisc.edu

Ann. N.Y. Acad. Sci. 1021: 260–261 (2004). © 2004 New York Academy of Sciences.
doi: 10.1196/annals.1308.030

creased motor activity, decreased persistence in performance tasks, and impaired ability to engage in defensive behaviors. On the basis of these data, it is tempting to speculate that sleep deprivation in adolescents may contribute to impulsive behavior, mood dysregulation, and attentional problems.

The papers in this section discuss the important developmental changes in the organization and timing of sleep that occur during adolescence. As we gain a better understanding of normal adolescent sleep, we may be better able to understand the impact of sleep abnormalities on adolescent brain function, including interactions with psychiatric and substance abuse disorders.

REFERENCES

1. BENCA, R.M. 2001. Consequences of insomnia and its therapies. J. Clin. Psychiatry **62:** 33–38.
2. DAHL, R.E. & D.S. LEWIN. 2002. Pathways to adolescent health sleep regulation and behavior. J. Adolesc. Health **31:** 175–184.
3. VAN CAUTER, E. & K. SPIEGEL. 1999. Sleep as a mediator or the relationship between socioeconomic status and health: a hypothesis. Ann. N.Y. Acad. Sci. **896:** 254–261.

Pubertal Development of Sex Differences in Circadian Function

An Animal Model

THERESA M. LEE,[a,b,d] DANIEL L. HUMMER,[a,d] TAMMY J. JECHURA,[c] AND MEGAN M. MAHONEY[d]

[a]Department Psychology, [b]Program in Neuroscience, and [d]Reproductive Sciences Program, University of Michigan, Ann Arbor, Michigan 48109, USA

[c]Department of Psychology, Bowling Green State University, Bowling Green, Ohio 43403, USA

ABSTRACT: The development of adult circadian function, particularly sexual dimorphism of function, has been well studied only in rapidly developed rodents. In such species development is complete by weaning. Data from adolescent humans suggest that significant development occurs during the pubertal period. We hypothesized that a more slowly developing rodent might better mimic the changes in circadian function around puberty in humans and allow us to determine the underlying neural changes. Entrained and free-running circadian rhythms were analyzed and correlated with pubertal development in male and female *Octodon degus* (degu) that remained gonadally intact or were gonadectomized at weaning. Brains were collected during development to measure androgen and estrogen receptors in the suprachiasmatic nuclei (SCN) Adult circadian period does not develop until 10–12 months of age in degus, long after the onset of gonadal maturation (3–5 months). The timing of circadian period maturation correlates with the appearance of steroid receptors in the SCN. Changes in free-running rhythms only occurred in gonadally intact degus. Adult phase angles of activity onset develop between 2 and 3 months of age (comparing results of two experiments), soon after the onset of pubertal changes. Conclusion: The development of sexually dimorphic adult circadian period occurs after gonadal puberty is complete and requires the presence of gonadal steroids. The delay in development until after gonadal puberty is likely due to the delayed appearance of steroid receptors in the SCN. Phase is not sexually dimorphic and changes in the absence of steroid hormones.

KEYWORDS: *Octodon degus*; degu; activity; phase angle; period; tau; development

Address for correspondence: Theresa M. Lee, Department of Psychology, University of Michigan, 525 E. University Avenue, Ann Arbor, MI 48109-1109. Voice: 734-936-1495; fax: 734-763-7480.
   terrilee@umich.edu

Ann. N.Y. Acad. Sci. 1021: 262–275 (2004). © 2004 New York Academy of Sciences.
doi: 10.1196/annals.1308.031

INTRODUCTION

The study of development of circadian rhythmicity in humans has a long history, beginning with the observations by Kleitman and Engelmann[1] that infants have essentially ultradian sleep/wake rhythms at birth that take approximately 8 weeks to begin producing night-time consolidation of sleep (see Ref. 2 for example). During the period of time that rhythmicity is developing, the parents also demonstrate altered sleep/activity patterns,[3] which frequently leads to sleep deprivation and the associated problems. However, many infants begin to demonstrate weak circadian rhythmicity within a few weeks of birth and parents quickly recover normal sleep/wake cycles. Work with altricial rodents suggests that this neonatal circadian pattern may be the result of maternal entrainment of the infant until the infant's own circadian system takes over completely, around the time of weaning.[4–7] Once the individual is independently producing robust circadian rhythms, it was long assumed that the system was stable until we became aged. Studies in both animal models and humans demonstrated that relatively old individuals have marked changes in expression of circadian rhythms (see Ref. 8 for review). Interestingly, very little work has been done to examine changes that may occur in the expression of circadian rhythms between weaning (and early independence) and the development of adult circadian rhythms. This is surprising, given the number of papers that have demonstrated that sex differences exist in the expression of numerous circadian rhythms for multiple species, including humans.[9–13] It is clear that at least some of these differences develop at puberty, and therefore something about circadian expression, if not the timing mechanism itself, must be changing during the transition from the juvenile to the adult state. The exception, of course, is Carskadon's data on sleep/wake regulation in adolescent humans, which does not appear to be sexually dimorphic, but clearly does change around the time of puberty (see Ref. 14 for review).

BRIEF REVIEW OF CIRCADIAN RHYTHMS AND THEIR IMPORTANCE

A circadian rhythm is defined as "an observed biological activity that oscillates under constant environmental conditions with a period length close to but not exactly equal to 24 h" (p. 15).[15] The circadian mechanism is the result of biochemical oscillation driven by feedback loops, providing an internal clock (or sense of time) for the individual. This clock may act to time events only within the tissue where it resides (e.g., the clock in the testes of the fly[16]) or it may provide information as a pacemaker to numerous other tissues. In mammals, the suprachiasmatic nucleus (SCN) is where the primary light-sensitive circadian pacemaker cells reside and co-ordinate their output signals. The endogenous period of pacemaker can be determined by housing an organism in constant conditions and measuring daily changes in one or more of the outputs, such as the rest/activity, body temperature, cortisol, or melatonin daily patterns. The free-running rhythm of these different behavioral and physiological measures will be the same and reflects the period (τ) of the SCN clock.

The non–24 h period of the endogenous circadian clock requires that outside information be obtained daily to synchronize the internal clock with the environment. The most important time cue (i.e., zeitgeber) is the light:dark cycle (LD), although many other non-photic cues can also act as weak cues on their own or can enhance the effect of the LD cycle (e.g., hot:cold cycles, daily periods of exercise, daily periods of social contact).[17-19] The process of synchronizing the endogenous circadian system to the environment is known as entrainment. Entrainment results from light (or other cues) altering the period of the endogenous clock. This occurs in a phase dependent manner, such that light exposure late in subjective day and early in subjective night causes a delay in the circadian oscillation and results in a lengthened period. Light signals during late subjective night and very early subjective day cause a phase advance in the oscillation and a shortening of the period. The relationship between the direction and size of phase shifts in response to zeitgeber signals at various times across the subjective day is known as the phase response curve (PRC). These phase shifts occur each day at times that shift the period by the difference between 24 h and the endogenous τ, resulting in synchrony between the 24-h period of the environment and the internal circadian mechanism.

As a result of entrainment, a specific relationship develops between the biological rhythm being measured and the entraining zeitgeber, described as the phase angle of entrainment. The phase angle of entrainment (ψ) is the difference between a specific phase of the biological rhythm being measured and a phase marker in the environmental zeitgeber. For example, activity onset for a diurnal organism may begin before, after, or at the same time that lights come on. The difference between activity onset and lights-on in hours or degrees of arc between the two reference points describes this relationship. When the zeitgeber controls the circadian rhythm very well (i.e., it is a "strong zeitgeber" because the individual is very sensitive to its effects), the ψ will remain constant unless the zeitgeber cycle is shifted, then the biological rhythm will also shift to regain proper alignment. This process of recovery is called reentrainment and the duration of the recovery period is positively correlated with the size of the shift. During the days of recovery the various behavioral and physiological rhythms recover at different rates resulting in the symptoms of circadian desynchronosis (or "jetlag"). If the zeitgeber is not very strong, then ψ will be unstable.

The phase angle of entrainment is influenced by two things: the endogenous period of the circadian pacemaker that needs to be adjusted to 24 h and the phase-response curve defining the effect of equal zeitgeber stimulation at various times. If two individuals have different free-running periods and the same PRC, then the phase angle of entrainment must differ to accommodate the difference in the circadian time when light must impinge on the system to entrain the endogenous mechanism. As we will see below, if ψ is the same in two individuals, it does not mean that the underlying period and PRC are the same, PRC differences may compensate for period differences. However, when ψ differs, then either τ or the PRC must also differ between individuals.

Why are circadian rhythms so important? Under the normal entrained state, circadian rhythmicity allows the organism to anticipate regular changes in the external environment and prepare to respond to them. If food or predators regularly appear soon after sunrise or sunset, anticipation of those events with appropriate physiological and behavioral responses can improve health and survival. Equally important is the internal coordination between different physiological events provided by the circadian system, such that appropriate combinations of physiological changes occur at the same time. For example, in preparation for meal time, the parasympathetic system controlling digestion, hunger drive, and intestinal motility are increased. At bedtime, heart rate, body temperature, and arousal all decline. During desynchrony of the circadian system, such as occurs during jetlag or shift work, the suites of rhythms are not well-coordinated and we suffer discomfort. Interestingly, the value of this circadian organization is particularly well reflected during early development in appropriately timed birth[20,21] and better growth patterns in pups synchronized with their mothers.[22-26] These findings carry over to comparisons of human infant growth patterns in different hospital nurseries where circadian signals vary from nearly absent to moderate.[27,28]

DEVELOPMENT OF CIRCADIAN RHYTHMS

Descriptive analysis of the development of circadian rhythms during infancy has been conducted in several species, including hamsters, rats, mice, and humans (see Ref. 2 for review). Studies of neonatal animals demonstrate that the expression of circadian rhythms is not fully developed at birth, even though the circadian mechanism in the suprachiasmatic nucleus (SCN) appears to be fully functioning.[29] The lack of fully developed rhythmicity at birth is likely due to the incomplete innervation of the SCN in altricial species, and the still developing output pathways from the SCN. At the time when circadian rhythms appear, they are initially of low amplitude, developing their full adult pattern only after days or weeks.[30] Thus, it is clear that the expression of circadian rhythmicity develops for some time after birth. Davis and Reppert argued, however, that while there are "systematic changes in sensitivity to stimuli and in amplitude, there is no evidence for a systematic change in the free-running period of circadian oscillations" (p. 257).[2] This is not to say that the environment can not affect the circadian mechanism, since it is clear that previous photoperiodic history can influence the free-running period (τ) for a very long time.[31] Similarly, it is clear that sex differences exist in the expression of circadian rhythms of adults and in SCN anatomy and function.[10-12] We present data below that demonstrate that the free-running period can be permanently altered postnatally and the change is dependent upon steroid hormones.

Sex Differences in Circadian Rhythms

A variety of species exhibit sex differences in circadian rhythms, including rats, mice, degus, hamsters, and humans. Sex differences are apparent in τ,[9,12,32-34] the amount and distribution of daily activity,[35] time spent sleeping,[34] the time and variability of activity onsets,[12] phase responses to light pulses,[12,36] the upper limits of entrainment,[12] susceptibility to splitting,[37] rates of reentrainment,[38] sensitivity to non-photic social cues during reentrainment,[39] and the age at which circadian rhythms first emerge.[40]

Some of the sex differences persist in the absence of circulating hormones in adulthood (organizing effects that are independent of adult hormones). For example, Zucker and colleagues[41] demonstrated that the circadian system of hamsters is sexually differentiated as a result of perinatal androgen exposure, such that period length in adult males is rendered insensitive to estrogen (E) exposure. That is, while E shortens τ in adult females, it fails to alter τ in adult males or adult females exposed perinatally to testosterone (T). Albers and colleagues[9] reported that perinatal exposure to T, either endogenously in male rats or exogenously in females, leads to an adult τ that is shorter than untreated females. In the absence of perinatal T exposure, exogenous E treatment shortens τ in adulthood. However, the same adult E treatment lengthens or shortens τ in males and perinatally androgenized females depending on the length of the animal's pretreatment period.[9]

Adult gonadal hormones also modulate the expression of circadian rhythms leading to some of the sex differences mentioned above (activational/reversible effects). Castration of males rapidly alters phase angles of activity entrainment (ψ) and rhythm amplitude (intensity of activity change across the day), but does not alter τ or PRC. Similarly, ovarian hormones modulate circadian rhythms in adult females. The amount and distribution of activity, amount and quality of sleep, ψ for activity onset, and τ fluctuate with the estrous cycle. Female hamsters phase advance and run significantly more during proestrous and estrus compared to other days of the cycle.[42–44] Rats exhibit earlier activity onsets, longer active phases (α), and shorter τ's on estrus.[45] Female degus increase activity and phase-advance activity onset during estrus, and then decrease activity and phase-delay activity onset the day after behavioral estrus.[33] Women sleep longer, have more REM, and experience fewer sleep disturbances during the luteal phase of the menstrual cycle than the follicular phase.[34] It seems that gonadal steroids are capable of rapidly influencing the circadian system, since many of these changes occur within hours of changes in peripheral hormone concentrations.[42]

These two sets of data suggest that sex differences in circadian rhythms may be due to organizational effects, that pubertal hormones may elicit sex differences, or an interaction between early organizational and later activational hormones may produce uniquely male and female circadian patterns. This latter possibility suggests that pre/perinatal exposure to steroid hormones may cause differences in expressed rhythms that are not apparent until pubertal hormones activate the differences. However, to date, no one has examined the timing of the development of sex differences in fundamental circadian properties of a precocial species or a more slowly developing species, with the exception of the data from humans.

OCTODON DEGUS: AN ANIMAL MODEL FOR CIRCADIAN DEVELOPMENT

Octodon degus is a moderate-sized, precocious, but slowly maturing, hystricomorph rodent from central Chile. We have used them to study a variety of questions about circadian rhythms in a diurnal mammal that readily adapts to most laboratory settings. They are born fully furred, eyes open, and are mobile within hours of birth. Teeth begin erupting within a few days, but they don't begin to consume significant solid food until two weeks of age and continue to nurse for 4–5 weeks. Although pubertal changes (measured by penile development and vaginal opening; Jechura, Hummer, and Lee, unpublished data) occur at 3 to 4 months of age (range is 10–14 weeks for males and 10–24 weeks for females) and reproductive activity is successful after 4.5 months for most animals, adult body size is not reached until 6–7 months of age (Young, Lee, and Rush, unpublished data). When compared with altricial myomorph rodents (e.g., hamsters, rats, mice) they have a slower pace of development marked by a relatively long juvenile period. In our laboratory we have routinely considered degus to be "adults" at 6 months and "elderly" at 4 years. The latter cut-off in a lifespan of 5-7 years was chosen as a marker of aging because female pregnancy rate drops off rapidly after 4 years (Lee, unpublished data).

Several sex differences have been described in the circadian system of degus, including rates of reentrainment,[38] the effect of social cues on reentrainment,[38,39] sensitivity to light intensity (Stimpson & Lee, unpublished data), the phase-response curve (PRC),[36] and τ.[32,33,36]

Adult male degus exhibit shorter free-running period lengths (23.2 ± 0.1 h)[32] than adult females (23.75 ± 0.1h)[33] Period does not vary as a function of ovariectomy (OVX) with or without hormone replacement[33] or castration[32] in adulthood. Rather, we hypothesized that the sex difference in τ probably results from a sex-specific organization of the brain earlier in development. In altricial species this organizational effect occurs pre- or perinatally. However, no one has looked at when sex differences might occur in a precocious species, particularly a relatively slowly developing and long-lived one. We also hypothesized that slower development might reveal the type of pubertal phase change in the circadian mechanism that Carskadon describes for the sleep/wake cycle of adolescent humans.[14] The three experiments described below explore the age-dependent change in phase angle of entrainment, timing of permanent sexual differentiation of circadian period, and a potential mechanism to explain the latter phenomenon.

AGE-RELATED CHANGES IN PHASE ANGLE OF ENTRAINMENT

For the studies described here only wheel-running activity was used as an indicator of circadian function. We also use core temperature rhythms in our circadian studies, but have not found any significant difference in τ, PRC, or rates of reentrainment between activity and core temperature. In the first experiment we tested the hypothesis that juvenile degus would have a different phase angle of entrainment than adults and that they would require more time to recover from a phase advance in the light cycle than do adults. The male and female pups were placed into cages with running wheels with their same-sex siblings on the day of weaning for 1 week to adapt to the environment. They were then housed individually with a running wheel and we collected 7 days of baseline data while they were entrained to LD 12:12 at 300 lux. Adult males and females were treated similarly. The light cycle was then phase advanced 6 hours and the animals were allowed to recover. We determined the phase angle of entrainment at 8 weeks of age for the pups and for the adults (age 1–3 years) and the rate of recovery from the phase shift.

The phase angle of entrainment did not differ between adult males and females, nor between male and female pups.[46] However, 8-week-old pups had a phase angle 50 min earlier than adults (F = 7.365, $P < 0.015$; FIG. 1). We found that juvenile pups required the same length of time to recover from a phase shift as the adults. These data are consistent with data comparing pre- and post-pubertal adolescents.

In a second experiment, phase angle of entrainment was determined in 3-, 6-, and 12-month-old animals that remained intact or were gonadectomized (GDX) at weaning. The GDX animals demonstrated a significant reduction in the phase angle ($P < 0.001$; FIG. 2) between 3 and 12 months, with data at 6 months intermediate between and not significantly different from the other two ages.[46] Interestingly, the intact animals do not show a significant change across these ages, which differs from the

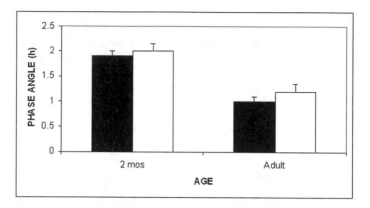

FIGURE 1. Entrained phase angles of activity onset (h) for 2-month-old pups and adults (1–3 years). Data are mean ± SEM time at which animals become active prior to lights on each day. Males are *dark bars* and females are *open bars*. Adults had significantly delayed phase angles compared with prepubertal juveniles.

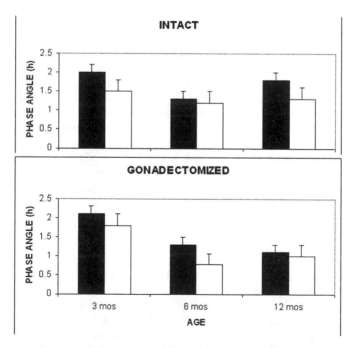

FIGURE 2. Mean ± SEM entrained phase angles of activity onset (h) at 3, 6, and 12 months of age for intact and gonadectomized male (*dark bars*) and females (*open bars*). Intact animals did not significantly change during the year, while both male and female gonadectomized animals significantly decreased the phase angle between 3 and 12 months.

comparison between 2-month-old and adult animals. This is most likely due to the effect of steroid hormones on phase, since we have found that gonadal steroids modify phase in both males and females.[32,33]

These two studies lead us to conclude that there is an age-dependent delay in the phase of activity onset that is steroid hormone independent. The change is equivalent in males and females. Intact adult animals are less delayed than they might otherwise be, because gonadal steroids slightly alter the phase. Interestingly, GDX of adult females results in no change in ψ (compared to females prior to estrus, when a large advance in ψ occurs). In contrast, GDX of adult males results in an advance of ψ for activity onset, which is not what one would expect from comparing 12-month-old animals that were intact or GDX since weaning. This would suggest that exposure to steroid hormones during the first six months also produces an organizational change in the underlying PRC that is steroid dependent.

GONADAL STEROID DETERMINED CHANGES IN PERIOD LENGTH

It is interesting that phase does not differ between adult males and females, because we have reported that period differs by an average of 36 min.[32,33] As noted above, GDX of adults does not alter τ, suggesting that organizational effects produce these differences. In the following study we tested the hypothesis that organization occurs during puberty. The free-running period of intact pups and pups GDX at 5 weeks of age was determined at 3, 6, and 12 months of age.[46] At 3 and 6 months of age, male and female degus, whether intact or GDX did not differ from each other and all had period lengths intermediate to those previously found in adult males and females. At 12 months of age, about 8 months after puberty onset, the sex difference in τ was evident for the intact animals ($P < 0.034$; Fig. 3 and 4). The decrease for intact males between 6 and 12 months was significant ($P < 0.03$), while τ did not change significantly for intact females from 3 to 12 months. In contrast, those GDX at 5 weeks demonstrated no difference in τ between males and females at 12 months and no change between 6 and 12 months of age. Intact and GDX male τ differed significantly at 12 months ($P < .048$). These data strongly suggested that gonadal hormones that increase during puberty were necessary for the development of the sex difference in τ, but that the difference actually appears long after the hormones began to increase and results from masculinization of the SCN. This poses an interesting dilemma. While there are other behaviors that first develop during puberty and take some time to become completely organized (e.g., male hamster sexual behavior),[47] we can find no report of another steroid-dependent behavior that is so delayed relative to the timing of puberty.

STEROID HORMONE RECEPTORS IN THE SCN

These data, of course, raised interesting questions about the precise timing of the post-pubertal change in τ and what might be happening in the SCN when the changes finally occur. The most obvious hypothesis was that steroid hormone receptors arrive in the SCN long after puberty, but at the time when τ changes. We repeated the earlier longitudinal study, but have examined the behavior of animals every 2 months

12-Month Male Representing Group Mean = 23.10±0.03

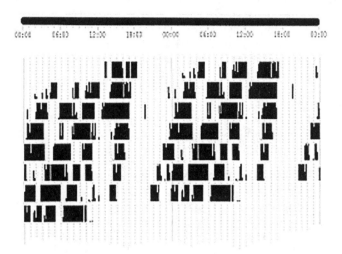

12-Month Female Representing Group Mean = 23.58±0.12

FIGURE 3. Example actograms of male and female 12-month-old degus housed in constant darkness. The free-running wheel-running activity of males is significantly faster than that of females. Prior to 12 months males and females alike had periods similar to the female in this example.

from 4–12 months of age. We found again that the sex difference does not emerge until 12 months of age. Brains have been collected from other animals between 3 and 12 months of age at monthly intervals. With the use of immunocytochemistry, we are determining whether and when androgen receptor-immunoreactivity (AR-ir) and estrogen receptor immunoreactivity (ER-ir) occurs in the SCN. Preliminary data from

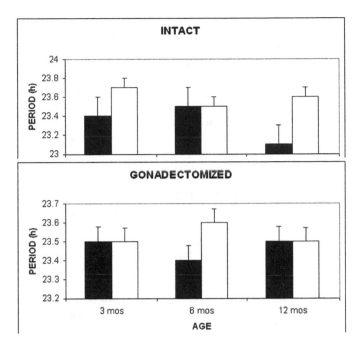

FIGURE 4. Mean free-running period (τ) ± SEM for intact and gonadectomized males and females at 3, 6, and 12 months of age. *Closed bars* represent males and *open bars* represent females. Gonadectomized animals do not change significantly and males do not differ from females. Intact females did not change, but males decreased the period significantly and differed from females at 12 months of age.

3, 7, and 12 month old males supports our hypothesis. There is essentially no AR-ir in the SCN of males at 3 months of age. At 7 months of age we find AR-ir in the SCN, primarily in the ventral area where retinohypothalamic tract neurons synapse on SCN neurons. This location for AR-ir would suggest a role for androgens in modulating the light input signal. We hypothesize that receptors in this area might modulate phase angle of entrainment, for example.

In the brains of 12-month-old males we found more AR-ir than at 7 months, and it was distributed into the dorsal SCN as well as the ventral area. In hamsters, the cells in the SCN that oscillate and also send axons to other areas of the brain are predominantly in the dorsal SCN. If the same were true for degus, the AR-ir we find in the dorsal SCN might be important for modulating output signals. More importantly, these late-appearing receptors may be those that permanently reduce τ in males.

We have also begun looking at ER-ir in females. A similar pattern appears to be emerging with virtually no ER-ir in the SCN at 3 months of age and stained cells evident in the ventral SCN at 7 months of age. There are far fewer ER-ir cells visible in the SCN of females than there are AR-ir cells in males. This may be because we are currently using an ERα antibody. Significant amounts of ERβ have been reported in the SCN of rats and humans,[48,49] but we have not yet identified an ERβ antibody that recognizes ERβ receptors in degus. It is entirely possible that female degus have as much ER-ir as males have AR-ir, but we are not yet visualizing the right protein. On the other hand, the behavioral data suggest that estrogen can modulate ψ in the adult intact females, which would be consistent with the emergence of ER receptors in the ventral SCN. We find few if any ER-ir–labeled cells in the dorsal SCN of females, again consistent with the apparent lack of change in τ during development that we find in females.

At this time, it is still unclear which steroid hormones cause the change in τ. It may be that males change τ in response to exposure to testosterone. Alternatively, androgens may only be modulating adult circadian rhythms, while estrogen is critical for reorganization of SCN function. This would follow the common hypothalamic sexual differentiation pattern of androgens being aromatized to estrogen, which then provides the organizational effect. If the latter is true, then we will need to explain why males and females respond differently to the same hormone. For example, this sort of effect might occur if there is an early pre- or perinatal period of organization that determines whether τ will shorten following exposure to aromatized T or E in adulthood. Thus, we have several important follow-up studies using replacement hormones (estrogen and dihydrotestosterone, which cannot be converted to estrogen) to determine which hormone is critical for the organizational effects, and/or for the activational responses, and at what age they have their effects. In addition, we will determine whether males also have ER in the SCN to allow aromatized testosterone to organize the SCN.

CONCLUSION

Our data reveal a somewhat surprising developmental program in the emergence of circadian sex differences in degus. We can find no other case where steroid hormones are necessary for an organizational change in behavior or physiology so long after adult hormone secretory patterns are constantly available. We do not know what triggers the rise in steroid receptors in the SCN since it is apparently not the rise in gonadal steroids per se. This model offers an opportunity to examine what cellular and genetic changes are occurring just prior to the rise in receptors. We hypothesize that the rise in receptors that leads to the change in τ is an age-dependent phenomenon that might also be related to the non-steroid–dependent changes that are occurring with phase angle of entrainment.

These data also offer us an opportunity to examine our understanding of the relationship between period, phase responses, and phase angles of entrainment—and how these may change as a function of age and hormone exposure.

ACKNOWLEDGMENTS

We wish to thank the lab manager, Amy Young, for her help with maintaining the laboratory, the animal colony, and assisting with many of these experiments. In addition, several University of Michigan undergraduates have assisted on these projects. They are Cheryl Stimpson, Jackie Walsh, Jonathan Flak, Jennifer Hsu, Anna Koniuch, David Cotter, Christine Endress, Nick Degrazia, Brent Densham, and Tristan Edwards. We also appreciate the expert care of the degu colony by Kathy Welch, Jim Donner and Julie Stewlow.

REFERENCES

1. KLEITMAN, N. & T.G. ENGELMANN. 1953. Sleep characteristics in infants. J. Appl. Physiol. **6:** 269–282.
2. DAVIS, F.C. & S.M. REPPERT. 2001. Development of mammalian rhythms. *In* Handbook of Behavioral Neurobiology, Vol 12: Circadian Clocks. J.S. Takahashi, F.W. Turek & R.Y. Moore, Eds.: 247–291. Kluwer Academic/Plenum Publishers. New York, NY.
3. WULFF, K. & R. SIEGMUND. 2002. Time pattern analysis of activity-rest rhythms in families with infants using actigraphy. Adv. Consciousness Res. **38:** 149–170.
4. DEGUCHI, T. 1975. Ontogenesis of a biological clock for serotonin: Acetyl coenzyme A N-acetyltransferase in pineal gland of rat. Proc. Natl. Acad. Sci. USA **72:** 2814–2818.
5. TAKAHASHI, K., C. HAYAFUJI & N. MURAKAMI. 1982. Foster mother rat entrains circadian adrenocortical rhythm in blinded pups. Am. J. Physiol. **243:** 443–449.
6. TAKAHASHI, K. & T. DEGUCHI. 1983. Entrainment of the circadian rhythms of blinded infant rats by nursing mothers. Physiol. Behav. **31:** 373–378.
7. VISWANATHAN, N. & M.K. CHANDRASHEKARAN. 1985. Cycles of presence and absence of mother mouse entrain the circadian clock of pups. Nature **317:** 530–531.
8. TUREK, F.W., K. SCARBROUGH, P. PENEV, *et al.* 2001. Characteristics of age-related changes in the circadian clock system. *In* Handbook of Behavioral Neurobiology, Vol 12: Circadian Clocks. J.S. Takahashi, F.W. Turek & R.Y. Moore, Eds.: 247–291. Kluwer Academic/Plenum Publishers. New York, NY.
9. ALBERS, H.E., F.C. DAVIS, J.M. DARROW & M. MENAKER. 1981. Gonadal hormones organize and modulate the circadian system of the rat. Am. J. Physiol. **241:** R62–R66.
10. CRITCHLOW, V. 1963. The role of light in the neuroendocrine system. *In* Advances in Neuroendocrinology. A.V. Nalbandov, Ed. University of Illinois Press. Urbana, IL.
11. DAAN, S. & C.S. PITTENDRIGH. 1976. A functional analysis of circadian pacemakers in nocturnal rodents. II. The variability of phase response curves. J. Comp. Physiol. **106:** 253–266.
12. DAVIS, F.C., J.M. DARROW & M. MENAKER. 1983. Sex differences in the circadian control of hamster wheel-running activity. Am. J. Physiol. **244:** R93–R105.
13. ZUCKER, I., K.M. FITZGERALD & L.P. MORIN. 1980. Sex differentiation of the circadian system in the golden hamster. Am. J. Physiol. **238:** R97–R101.
14. CARSKADON, M.A. & C. ACEBO. 2002. Regulation of sleepiness in adolescents: Updates, insights, and speculation. Sleep **25:** 606–614.
15. DUNLAP, J.C., J.J. LOROS, P.J. DECOURSEY, Eds. 2004. Chronobiology: Biological Timekeeping. Sinauer Associates, Inc. Publishers. Sutherland, MA.
16. GIEBULTOWICZ, J.M., J.G. RIEMANN, A.K. RAINA & R.L. RIDGWAY. 1989. Circadian system controlling release of sperm in the insect testes. Science **245:** 1098–1100.
17. ASCHOFF, J. 1979. Circadian rhythms: general features and endocrinological aspects. *In* Endocrine Rhythms. D.T. Krieger, Ed.: 1–61. Raven Press. New York, NY.
18. MRSOVSKY, N. 1996. Locomotor activity and non-photic influences on circadian clocks. Biol. Rev. **71:** 343–372.
19. GOVERNALE, M.M. & T.M. LEE. 2001. Olfactory social cues accelerate entrainment following phase shifts and entrain free-running rhythms in female *Octodon degus* (Rodentia). J. Biol. Rhythms **16:** 489–501.
20. HONNEBIER, M.B.O., D.F. SWAAB & M. MIRMIRAN. 1989. Diurnal rhythmicity during early human development. *In* Development of Circadian Rhythmicity and Photoperiodism in Mammals. S.M. Reppert, Ed.: 221–244. Perinatology Press. Ithaca, NY.
21. REPPERT, S.M. & G.R. UHL. 1987. Vasopressin messenger ribonucleic acid in supraoptic and suprachiasmatic nuclei: Appearance and circadian regulation during development. Endocrinology **120:** 2483–2487.

22. BARR, M.J. 1973. Prenatal growth of Wistar rats: Circadian periodicity of fetal growth late in gestation. Teratology **7:** 283–287.
23. DAVIS, F.C. 1989. Daily variation in maternal and fetal weight gain in mice and hamsters. J. Exp. Zool. **250:** 273–282.
24. MILLER, M.W. 1992. Circadian rhythm of cell proliferation in the telencephalic ventricular zone: Effect of in utero exposure to ethanol. Brain Res. **595:** 17–24.
25. HUDSON, R. & H. DISTEL. 1989. Temporal pattern of suckling in rabbit pups: A model of circadian synchrony between mother and young. *In* Development of Rhythmicity and Photoperiodism in Mammals. S.M. Reppert, Ed.: 83–102. Perinatology Press. Ithaca, NY.
26. JILGE, B. 1993. The ontogeny of circadian rhythms in the rabbit. J. Biol. Rhythms **8:** 247–260.
27. MANN, N.P., R. HADDOW, L. STOKES, *et al.* 1986. Effect of night and day on preterm infants in a newborn nursery: Randomised trial. Br. J. Med. **293:** 1265–1267.
28. MCMILLEN, I.C., J.S.M. KOK, T.M. ANDERSON, *et al.* 1991. Development of circadian sleep-wake rhythms in preterm and full-term infants. Ped. Res. **29:** 381–384.
29. WELSH, D.K., D.E. LOGOTHETIS, M. MEISTER & S.M. REPPERT. 1995. Individual neurons dissociated from rat suprachiasmatic nucleus express independently phased circadian firing rhythms. Neuron **14:** 697–706.
30. DAVIS, F.C. 1981. Ontogeny of circadian rhythms. *In* Handbook of Neurobiology, Vol. 4: Biological Rhythms. J. Aschoff, Ed.: 257–274. Plenum Press. New York, NY.
31. PITTENDRIGH, C.S. 1974. Circadian oscillations in cells and the circadian organization of multicellular systems. *In* The Neurosciences Third Study Program. F.O. Schmitt & F.G. Worden, Eds.: 437–458. MIT Press. Cambridge, MA.
32. JECHURA, T.J., J.M. WALSH & T.M. LEE. 2000. Testicular hormones modulate circadian rhythms of the diurnal rodent, *Octodon degus*. Horm. Behav. **38:** 243–249.
33. LABYAK, S.E. & T.M. LEE. 1995. Estrus- and steroid-induced changes in circadian rhythms in a diurnal rodent, Octodon degus. Physiol. Behav. **58:** 573–585.
34. LEIBENFLUT, E. 1993. Do gonadal steroids regulate circadian rhythms in humans? J. Affect. Disorders **29:** 175–181.
35. ROPER, T.J. 1976. Sex differences in circadian wheel running rhythms in the Mongolian gerbil. Physiol. Behav. **17:** 549–551.
36. LEE, T.M. & S.E. LABYAK. 1997. Free-running rhythms and light- and dark-pulse phase response curves for diurnal *Octodon degus* (Rodentia). Am. J. Physiol. **42:** R278–R286.
37. MORIN, L.P. & L.A. CUMMINGS. 1982. Splitting of wheelrunning rhythms by castrated or steroid treated male and female hamsters. Physiol. Behav. **29:** 665–675.
38. GOEL, N. & T.M. LEE. 1995. Sex differences and effects of social cues on daily rhythms following phase advances in *Octodon degus*. Physiol. Behav. **58:** 205–213.
39. GOEL, N. & T.M. LEE. 1995. Social cues accelerate reentrainment of circadian rhythms in diurnal female *Octodon degus* (Rodentia-Octodontidae). Chronobiol. Int. **12:** 311–323.
40. DIEZ-NOGUERA, A. & T. CAMBRAS. 1990. Sex differences in the development of motor activity circadian rhythms in rats under constant light. Physiol. Behav. **47:** 889–894.
41. ZUCKER, I., K.M. FITZGERALD & L.P. MORIN. 1980. Sex differentiation of the circadian system in the golden hamster. Am. J. Physiol. **238:** R97–R101.
42. MORIN, L.P., K.M. FITZGERALD & I. ZUCKER. 1977. Estradiol shortens the period of hamster circadian rhythms. Science **196:** 305–307.
43. RICHARDS, M.P.M. 1966. Activity measured by running wheels and observation during the oestrus cycle, pregnancy and pseudopregnancy in the golden hamster. Anim. Behav. **14:** 450–458.
44. TAKAHASHI, J.S. & M. MENAKER. 1980. Interaction of estradiol and progesterone: Effects on circadian locomotor rhythm of female golden hamsters. Am. J. Physiol. **239:** R497–R504.
45. ALBERS, H.E., A.A. GERALL & J.F. AXELSON. 1981. Effect of reproductive state on circadian periodicity in the rat. Physiol. Behav. **26:** 631–635.
46. JECHURA, T.J. 2002. Sex differences in circadian rhythms: Effects of gonadal hormones in *Octodon degus*. University of Michigan Doctoral Dissertation. Ann Arbor, MI.

47. ROMEO, R.D., H.N. RICHARDSON & C.L. SISK. 2002. Puberty and the maturation of the male brain and sexual behavior: A recasting of behavioral potentials. Neurosci. Biobehav. Rev. **26:** 381–391.
48. KRUIJVER, F.P.M. & D.F. SWAAB. 2002. Sex hormone receptors are present in the human suprachiasmatic nucleus. Neuroendocrinology **75:** 296–305.
49. WILSON, M.E., K.L. ROSEWELL, M.L. KASHON, *et al.* 2002. Age differentially influences estrogen receptor-alpha (ER alpha) and estrogen receptor-beta (ER beta) gene expression in specific regions of the rat brain. Mech. Ageing Dev. **123:** 593–601.

Regulation of Adolescent Sleep

Implications for Behavior

MARY A. CARSKADON, CHRISTINE ACEBO, AND OSKAR G. JENNI

E. P. Bradley Hospital Sleep Research Laboratory, Brown Medical School, Providence, Rhode Island 02906, USA

ABSTRACT: Adolescent development is accompanied by profound changes in the timing and amounts of sleep and wakefulness. Many aspects of these changes result from altered psychosocial and life-style circumstances that accompany adolescence. The maturation of biological processes regulating sleep/wake systems, however, may be strongly related to the sleep timing and amount during adolescence—either as "compelling" or "permissive" factors. The two-process model of sleep regulation posits a fundamental sleep-wake homeostatic process (process S) working in concert with the circadian biological timing system (process C) as the primary intrinsic regulatory factors. How do these systems change during adolescence? We present data from adolescent participants examining EEG markers of sleep homeostasis to evaluate whether process S shows maturational changes permissive of altered sleep patterns across puberty. Our data indicate that certain aspects of the homeostatic system are unchanged from late childhood to young adulthood, while other features change in a manner that is permissive of later bedtimes in older adolescents. We also show alterations of the circadian timing system indicating a possible circadian substrate for later adolescent sleep timing. The circadian parameters we have assessed include phase, period, melatonin secretory pattern, light sensitivity, and phase relationships, all of which show evidence of changes during pubertal development with potential to alter sleep patterns substantially. However the changes are mediated—whether through process S, process C, or by a combination—many adolescents have too little sleep at the wrong circadian phase. This pattern is associated with increased risks for excessive sleepiness, difficulty with mood regulation, impaired academic performance, learning difficulties, school tardiness and absenteeism, and accidents and injuries.

KEYWORDS: circadian rhythms; sleep homeostasis; puberty; melatonin; adolescent humans; MSLT

INTRODUCTION

The timing of sleep and wakefulness undergoes one of the most prominent behavioral changes that occur during adolescent development, a change that occurs in a

Address for correspondence: Mary A. Carskadon, Ph.D., E.P. Bradley Hospital Sleep Research Laboratory, Brown Medical School, 300 Duncan Drive, Providence, RI 02906 USA. Voice: 401-421-9440; fax: 401-453-357.
   mary_carskadon@brown.edu

Ann. N.Y. Acad. Sci. 1021: 276–291 (2004). © 2004 New York Academy of Sciences.
doi: 10.1196/annals.1308.032

majority of young people. Data collected from many countries have confirmed the strong trend for later bedtimes and later rising times during the teen years, for example, USA,[1,2] Canada,[3] Switzerland,[4] Italy,[5] Taiwan,[6,7] Brazil,[8,9] and South Africa.[10] In each instance, the temporal delay of sleep timing manifests most clearly on non-school nights (weekends and vacations); even when the school schedule constrains rising times, the bedtime delay remains apparent on school nights.[11]

Explanations for this developmental pattern are easy to identify in the changing adolescent psychosocial milieu. Such processes as the growing expression of autonomy, the increase in academic obligations and social opportunities, as well as the rising availability of late evening activities offered by access to telephone, television, and Internet—all contribute in a significant way to the behavioral regulation of adolescent sleep patterns.

In addition, however, sleep and waking are under regulatory control by intrinsic brain mechanisms. The most well-known model describing these mechanisms was first expressed by Borbély as the "two-process model,"[12] a model subsequently refined by Borbély and others.[13–16] In straightforward terms, the model posits a central mechanism providing homeostatic sleep regulation that interacts with the circadian timing mechanism. Anatomic, cellular, and molecular properties of the latter system have been described in great detail, as have the organizing principles of its function.[17] The anatomical structure of the homeostatic process is not yet known, however, nor has the specific nature of the neurochemical or neurocellular basis of this process yet been described, though adenosine regulation,[18] thalamocortical brain oscillations,[19,20] and changes in gene expression[21] have been hypothesized as specific features of the system. Nevertheless, the operational outputs of the homeostatic sleep-wake regulatory system such as quantitative measures of the EEG have been well described (for an overview see Ref. 22), and extensive modeling has successfully predicted outcomes.[23]

In brief, the homeostatic sleep-wake dependent process is modeled as "process S," which accumulates while awake and dissipates during sleep (FIG. 1).[12] Electrophysiological markers of process S include (1) stage 4 NREM sleep also known as slow wave sleep or SWS[24] and (2) EEG power density in the low frequency range (0.75–4.5 Hz) also known as slow wave activity or SWA.[25] The time course of process S delineated from SWA exhibits an exponential decay during sleep and an exponential rise during waking. Sleep occurring after a brief episode of waking (as in a daytime nap) shows relatively little stage 4 and low levels of SWA[26,27] as compared to these features during sleep that follows a normal or extended day length.[25,28] Thus, SWA levels during NREM sleep are determined by the duration of prior sleep and wakefulness. In addition, the speed of falling asleep (sleep latency) has been demonstrated to be a marker for sleep homeostasis.[29] For example, sleep restriction over several nights induces a progressive reduction of sleep latency.[30] Thus, faster sleep onsets can indicate greater accumulation of sleep homeostatic drive, familiar to us all, for example, when witnessing sleep deprived students or colleagues nodding off during the day.

The circadian timing system is essentially independent of prior waking and sleep.[31] It contributes to the timing of sleep by providing signals (the precise neurophysiological nature of which are unknown) interpreted as "sleep gates" occurring at some times and during other phases as "forbidden zones" for sleep.[13,32] Circadian sleep propensity reaches its maximal levels in the early morning and its trough in the

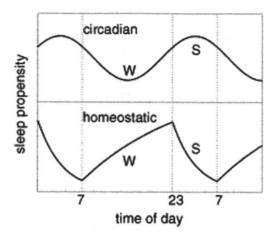

FIGURE 1. Schematic of the circadian and homeostatic process underlying sleep regulation. The rise of the homeostatic process yields a longer time constant then the decay reflecting the unbalanced amount of time spent awake and asleep. W, wakefulness; S, sleep. (Redrawn in part from Achermann & Bobély.[23])

evening (FIG. 1).[31] Current models include a concept in which the homeostatic and circadian systems normally operate as opponent processes that enable the consolidation of sleep and wakefulness.[16,31,33,34] In other words, an increasing circadian drive for arousal during the waking day is proposed to counteract the growing homeostatic sleep pressure in order to maintain the waking state.[14,16,33] Conversely, the declining NREMS sleep intensity or pressure during sleep opposes the increase in circadian sleep tendency across the night thereby maintaining consolidated sleep.[34]

Several additional features of the circadian timing system merit introduction (for an overview see Ref. 17). Although we do not have direct access to the clock mechanism itself in human participants, we are able to measure such parameters of the system as phase, period, amplitude, and phase angle through assessing peripheral signals. The timing of melatonin secretion is one of the most reliable of such measures and is eminently accessible in young humans through radioimmunoassay of melatonin from serial saliva samples. Thus, we can assess the phase of the circadian system as the onset, offset, midpoint, or peak phase of melatonin secretion. Phase preference (when it "feels good" to do various activities) can be assessed using standard self-assessment instruments.[35–37] The intrinsic period of the circadian timing system is more difficult to assess. In rodents, period is inferred from the timing of behaviors (usually wheel-running) over the course of many cycles under conditions of environmental isolation and constant darkness—not a testing environment available for human studies, particularly not for young humans. Instead, a method called forced desynchrony is used, wherein participants stay in the lab for a number of weeks under relatively low light conditions with sleep and waking scheduled at a day length that exceeds the range of entrainment of the circadian timing system, such as 20 or 28 hours.[38,39] Under these circumstances, the circadian timing system runs free from the sleep–wake process, and the intrinsic period of the rhythm can be assessed through the timing of daily phase markers. Coincidentally, this experimental paradigm is useful for analyses to identify the influences of the homeostatic and circadian processes independent from and interacting with one another.[31]

Our group has begun to apply these principles and methods to examine the development of intrinsic sleep-wake regulatory processes during adolescent development. Our aim is to determine the extent to which these processes undergo predictable changes in association with pubertal development and ultimately to identify how such changes may interact with the behavioral regulation of sleep. Intrinsic changes may either compel or control the adolescent phase delay, or they may be permissive of the phase delay. Thus, for example, a puberty-related delay in circadian phase might prevent older teens from falling asleep early and drive a later time for arousal; or a reduction in the build up rate of process S might permit or ease the way for older teens to stay up late. In addition, an important corollary of these biological systems is that certain aspects of the intrinsic regulatory processes may themselves respond to alterations of sleep and wakefulness associated with behavioral regulation. For example, behaviorally mediated changes in the timing of light–dark exposure directly interact with the phase resetting mechanism of the circadian timing system[40] and can reinforce or strengthen a tendency to phase delay. In this paper, we review findings that address these issues, identify the net effect on sleep patterns, and discuss briefly how the ultimate result of these processes may lay open vulnerable outcomes for adolescents.

THE HOMEOSTATIC PROCESS (PROCESS S) DURING ADOLESCENCE

The developmental alteration in slow wave sleep during adolescence has been known for a number of years. Feinberg[41] showed that SWS declined across the adolescent years using cross-sectional samples, as did the Williams group.[42,43] Karacan and colleagues[44] showed a pubertal decline in SWS in a longitudinal study where sleep was on the participants "usual" schedules, confirmed by Carskadon[45] in a longitudinal study that held sleep time constant. In the Carskadon report,[45] SWS declined by approximately 40% from Tanner stage 1 (ages 10 to 12 years) to Tanner stage 5 (ages 14 to 16 years). The fundamental question arises now whether the decline of SWS is reflected in altered sleep-wake processes as well. Several groups have presented data examining spectral EEG variables including SWA across adolescent development.[46,47] Gaudreau and colleagues,[47] for example, reported a similar nocturnal decline of SWA between children and adolescents.

Our group has begun to examine pubertal changes in the sleep EEG within the context of the homeostatic model. Sleep EEGs in 6 pre- or early pubertal (Tanner 1 or 2, ages 10.3 to 12.8 years, 5 girls) and 6 postpubertal adolescents (Tanner 5, ages 11.8 to 16 years, 3 girls) have been analyzed using spectral analysis.[48] We showed a significant reduction in EEG power density during NREM sleep at frequencies <2 Hz and 4–6 Hz for the mature versus the prepubertal participants. Total power in the low frequency band <2 Hz was reduced by 64% during NREM sleep. Furthermore, we saw an exponential overnight decay of SWA in both groups, with equal time constants of the decaying function. These findings converge to indicate that the homeostatic process involved in the dissipation of process S across sleep under controlled sleeping conditions does not manifest a maturational change across pubertal development. The substantially lower amount of SWS and low-frequency EEG power across adolescence may rather reflect changes in underlying brain structure (e.g., declining cortical synaptic density) as noted by Feinberg.[49,50]

The accumulation of process S, however, does appear to differ in its expression across adolescent development, based upon preliminary evidence. A test of this process requires assessment of the homeostatic markers under conditions that involve an alteration of the usual daily sleep-wake schedule, such as napping as suggested previously, or sleep deprivation. We have examined the speed of falling asleep (sleep latency) using standard methods in adolescents during 36 hours of sleep deprivation.[51] These data indicate that sleep latencies during initial hours of extended wakefulness were longer in more mature participants than in prepubertal children, indicating that accumulation of process S across the day may occur at a slower rate in more mature adolescents.

Our preliminary analyses of the EEG in the sleep episode following an extended waking interval of 36 hours showed the expected increase in low frequency EEG power during NREMS sleep in both groups.[48] The prepubertal children, however, manifested a less pronounced (30%) average increase of low frequency power comparing recovery to baseline versus the mature adolescents (70%). These data indicate that the younger child's brain quickly reaches the maximal capacity to generate low frequency activity during sleep. We are currently modeling the spectral EEG data from the nights following baseline and extended wakefulness to determine whether parameters that describe the accumulation of process S change as a function of pubertal development. Although the preliminary analysis of the sleep latency data hints at such a developmental change, we do not yet feel confident in drawing this conclusion.

The homeostatic sleep–wake process plays out in another manner when the adolescent delay in the timing of sleep produces chronic insufficient sleep in many youngsters. Chronic sleep restriction becomes manifest when we examine speed of falling asleep.[29] For example, we showed that tenth-grade students with a "first bell" at 7:20 AM were able to fall asleep in fewer than 5 minutes on morning tests of sleep latency, never rising above about 10 minutes; indeed, many showed REM sleep in brief morning naps, coinciding with the time of their second-period class.[11] These data illustrate a powerful effect of homeostatic sleep regulation, as well as the impact of the circadian timing system (vis-à-vis the REM sleep finding). To the extent that the bedtime delay in older adolescents is mediated by intrinsic processes, the requirement for early rising to attend school inevitably results in inadequate sleep.

THE CIRCADIAN TIMING SYSTEM (PROCESS C) DURING ADOLESCENCE

Our interest in the possibility that changes in the intrinsic circadian timing system accompany puberty stemmed from a self-report assessment of pubertal development and circadian phase preference in sixth graders.[37] These data showed that those children (particularly the sixth grade girls) who rated themselves as more physically mature also rated themselves as more "evening" type in their phase preference. We subsequently confirmed this circadian phase delay tendency in a laboratory study in which Tanner stage was assessed by physician evaluations and circadian phase was measured by salivary melatonin[a] levels. Again, pubertal stage correlated with the circadian phase marker, such that more mature children showed a later phase of melatonin secretion offset.[52] We here also report that melatonin onset phase measured in 27 adolescents after controlled sleep-wake schedules was positively correlated with Tanner stage ($r = .54$; $P = .003$). These findings provide convergent evidence that circadian phase undergoes a delay in association with puberty, even under conditions controlling for psychosocial influences on sleep-wake patterns.

We should note that an alteration of the amplitude of the daily melatonin secretory patterns across pubertal development has been known for many years. A decline in nocturnal plasma melatonin levels across puberty was shown in cross sectional samples.[53,54] This decline was initially thought to be part of the hormonal cascade initiating pubertal development. In fact, the earliest reports of the reduction of melatonin secretion in pubertal children led to a speculation that melatonin was a "trigger" for puberty,[55] which was disputed strongly by others (cf. Ref. 56). Other reports, however, indicated that no change occurred in total excretion of the melatonin urinary metabolite, 6-hydroxymelatonin sulfate (6-OHMS), across puberty. The pubertal change in plasma melatonin levels was attributed to a change in the distribution of secreted melatonin in the larger body mass of the more mature adolescents with no change in the production of melatonin per se.[57] Recently, Griefahn and colleagues[58] examined urinary 6-OHMS excretion in a longitudinal sample. Their data lead to the interpretation that body size is the mediating factor for the pubertal decline in plasma melatonin levels, not falling melatonin secretion. No studies are available that have assessed plasma and urinary concentrations of melatonin simultaneously.

We recently analyzed data from a cross-sectional sample of adolescents in whom salivary melatonin was collected at 30-minute intervals across 18 hours during a "constant routine" protocol.[59] The salivary melatonin profiles of 14 participants (ages 9.6 to 12.9 years, 7 girls) at Tanner stage 1 and 12 participants (ages 11.8 to 14.4 years, 6 girls) at Tanner stage 5 were collected. Linear regression analysis of melatonin levels (area under the curve) and amplitude (maximum) including age, body mass index, phase preference, and Tanner stage, showed a significant contribution only for Tanner stage. Furthermore, we found (as have others[60–62]) large individual differences in melatonin levels. Our analyses, based on data collected under very controlled conditions of sleep timing, again raise the possibility that pineal secretion of melatonin declines during pubertal development. We can only speculate that this developmental change—whether mediated centrally or by secondary developmental characteristics such as body size—may signal a pubertal reduction in feedback of melatonin to the circadian timing system, which could alter the circadian signal to the sleep-wake system.[63] Shanahan[64] hypothesized, for example, that low melatonin

---

[a]Pineal melatonin secretion is controlled by the circadian timing mechanism (and feeds back on this system) to rise during the brain's nighttime and nearly cease during the daytime of the brain. Hence, melatonin has been dubbed the "hormone of darkness." Melatonin secretion can be suppressed by light, and such suppression is thought to be one indicator of the extent to which light affects the timing system. We use melatonin levels to mark internal time as the "hands" of the intrinsic circadian clock.

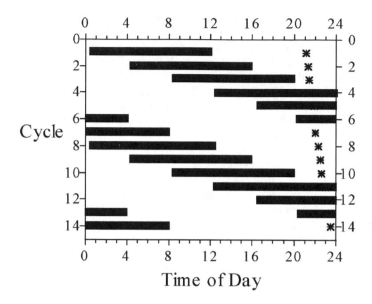

FIGURE 2. Schematic of the forced desynchrony protocol. Scheduled sleep episodes (*black bars*) are shown for a 28-hour day length for 14 consecutive cycles. Participants live in the laboratory under dim light conditions (~15 lux) so that dim-light melatonin onset (DLMO) can be determined from serial saliva samples. A hypothetical pattern of DLMO is shown by the *star symbols*, indicating that the circadian timing system is running free of the 28-hour day length at a period of about 24.2 hours.

amplitude reflects a diminished amplitude of the light-sensitive endogenous circadian pacemaker. Perhaps decreased melatonin amplitude in older adolescents plays a role in their tendency to manifest a delayed sleep phase.

Another mechanism predicted by circadian rhythms models is that a delay of circadian phase may be related to a lengthening of the period of the circadian clock, that is, a longer internal day length.[65] Under normal day-to-day circumstances, features of the environment that have a 24-hour period, particularly the light-dark cycle, entrain the internal clock to 24 hours. The phase angle with which the internal clock time aligns with the external day, however, is determined in part by the intrinsic circadian period: the phase angle of entrainment is delayed in parallel with the extent to which the internal day length exceeds 24 hours. Thus, we predicted that period of the circadian timing system may lengthen during puberty.

As mentioned previously, the method for measuring period is a bit arduous, involving prolonged laboratory stays under carefully controlled conditions. FIGURE 2 illustrates an experimental protocol we have used to assess period in adolescents by collecting serial measures of salivary melatonin onset and offset across 12 cycles on a 28-hour day(i.e., forced desynchrony). Our initial analysis of intrinsic period in adolescents showed that period appeared longer than reported by others in young adults, but we did not have adequate numbers of subjects to test the pubertal hypothesis.[66] We present here data from 27 participants who have completed the forced desynchrony protocol. We found no evidence of a pubertal change in period in this still rather small cross-sectional sample, but hope to acquire longitudinal data in order to re-examine this hypothesis. One of the major limitations of studying this phenomenon is the difficulty in making the measure in truly prepubertal participants because of the lengthy commitment to the laboratory stay. We compared the distribution of intrinsic period in our sample with samples of adults in whom period was also derived from melatonin phase markers in a 28-hour forced desynchrony paradigm.[67,68] The mean period of the circadian clock in adolescent participants (24.27 h) is significantly longer than in the adult samples (24.12 h). These comparisons are not conclusive, rather they are suggestive that longer internal day lengths may emerge in certain adolescents.

Another important feature of the circadian timing system is the phase-dependent sensitivity to light intrinsic to the clock resetting process.[69] Light occurring in the early part of the circadian night (evening and early nighttime) produces a delay resetting response in the clock, whereas light signals in the late night/early morning result in an advance resetting response (cf. Ref. 70). One marker of the effects of light on the circadian timing system is the suppression of melatonin levels by light.[40] We have hypothesized that the sensitivity of the circadian system to light may change during pubertal development in a manner that accentuates the tendency for a phase delay and have tested the hypothesis using melatonin suppression.[71] In brief, we suggest that a heightened sensitivity to evening light or a decreased sensitivity to morning light across pubertal development could result in the pubertal delay of sleep timing. An assessment of this hypothesis in 66 participants who received 4 levels of light on consecutive nights either in the late evening or early morning showed greater suppression to a low level of light administered in the morning for pre- and early pubertal participants than for late or postpubertal participants, and no differences in response to late night light.[72] These findings provide suggestive support for the hypothesis.

On the other hand, the most relevant assessment of the circadian response to light is actual phase realignment response to light signals. Thus, to what extent does the circadian timing mechanism actually reset its phase when an adequate light signal is given? We are currently evaluating this process by exposing adolescents who are Tanner stage 1 or Tanner stage 5 to a 2-hour light signal of 3,000 lux on two consecutive days. We administer light at times where the phase response curve predicts either a phase resetting delay or a phase resetting advance. Ultimately, we propose to acquire data across the entire phase response curve (PRC) for pre- and postpubertal adolescents, hypothesizing that the amplitude of the phase-resetting responses will be greater in the delaying direction or smaller in the advancing direction for the more mature group. If such developmental changes in PRC are operational, the permissive/responsive interaction of the behavioral and biological processes could set up a synergistic increase in pressure for adolescents to phase delay.

INTERACTION OF THE HOMEOSTATIC AND CIRCADIAN PROCESSES DURING ADOLESCENT DEVELOPMENT

A number of findings predict that a critical developmental outcome during adolescence may be a change in the phase angle of the homeostatic to the circadian tim-

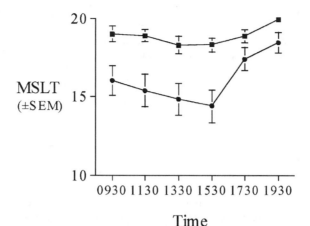

FIGURE 3. Sleep latency from Multiple Sleep Latency Tests (MSLT) in 25 pre-/early pubertal (Tanner stages 1 or 2; *squares*) and 27 mid-/late pubertal (Tanner stages 3, 4, or 5; *circles*) participants in a longitudinal sleep study.[29] Mean (± standard error) of sleep onset latencies indicate speed of falling asleep on tests scheduled at 2-hour intervals after 10-h nocturnal sleep episodes. More-mature participants fell asleep faster on the tests at 1530 and 1730, indicating augmented midday sleep tendency in spite of sleeping the same amount at night.[30]

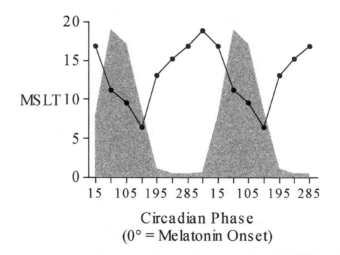

FIGURE 4. Circadian rhythm of sleep tendency as measured by MSLT on the background of averaged melatonin secretion (*gray shading*) from 10 adolescents studied in a 28-hour FD. The pattern displayed here is derived by averaging data from particular circadian phases (determined by the melatonin phase marker) irrespective of time awake.[74] As indicated in the text, the pattern appears paradoxical, since shortest sleep latency occurs at the end of the circadian night and long sleep latencies at the beginning of the circadian night. The rising latencies in the circadian day are conceptualized as indicating a clock-dependent alerting signal.

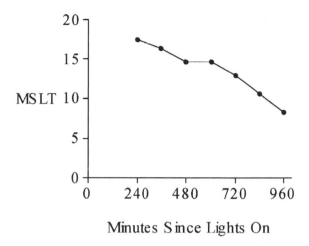

Minutes Since Lights On

FIGURE 5. The MSLT sleep tendency pattern from the study described in the legend for FIG. 4 was derived by the average of sleep latencies in reference to the length of time a participant was awake regardless of circadian phase.[74] This curve is conceptualized to indicate the homeostatic process accumulating as a growing sleep propensity across the waking day. As described in the text, the pattern of sleep propensity across an individual's waking day will depend upon the phase alignment of sleep/wake to the circadian timing system. Alterations of this phase alignment can facilitate late bedtimes when clock-dependent alerting rises late in the day. On the flip side, the phase angle of entrainment favoring late bedtime also is associated with difficulty waking in the morning.[74]

ing system. One of our earliest findings regarding sleep tendency during puberty[73] demonstrated a paradoxical increase in sleep tendency in adolescence at mid- to late puberty compared to pre- or early puberty. FIGURE 3 illustrates this finding, which was initially interpreted as an increase in sleep pressure, even though total sleep time had not changed. We also speculated that the changed pattern of diurnal sleep tendency might indicate a reorganization of central behavioral organization, for example, to favor a "siesta" in more mature humans.[73]

Recent conceptual advances in combination with data acquired in the context of forced desynchrony allow us to reinterpret this finding as a pubertal change in the phase angle of entrainment of sleep and waking to the circadian timing system.[74] We have shown, for example, that each of the two systems—when examined in isolation—provides counterintuitive findings with regard to circadian timing. As FIGURE 4 illustrates, the circadian signal demonstrates fastest sleep onsets (greatest sleep tendency) at the end of the circadian night (inferred from the melatonin secretory pattern) and slowest at the start of the circadian night. Taken at face value, however, these data are paradoxical, since most would assume that humans should fall asleep fastest at the beginning of the night rather than at night's end. The homeostatic process when examined separately from the circadian rhythm, builds to greater sleep tendency across time, thus faster sleep onsets occur the longer one is awake (FIGURE 5). Alignment of these two processes, however, as occurs during normally entrained conditions, solves the paradox: the circadian system, through "clock-dependent alerting," offsets the growing homeostatic pressure across the waking day. This association describes graphically the competing nature of these processes as described earlier.[74]

What is also apparent is that the alignment of these two processes will affect the balance of the two processes across the day. Thus, we now interpret our earlier findings of augmented midday sleep tendency in pubertal adolescents[73] to indicate a reorganization of the phase relationship of these processes. The mechanism underlying this realignment is not known, but it may be determined by the factors outlined above, such as alterations of intrinsic period or phase resetting properties of the clock mechanism. If the phase angle becomes realigned during late puberty, then the clock-dependent alerting later in the day can facilitate late sleep onset. Similarly, this phase realignment may manifest as a significant increase in the difficulty of waking in the morning. As more is learned about these underlying mechanisms and their association to the multiple behavioral influences on adolescent sleep timing, we may gain insights into opportunities for intervention.

CONSEQUENCES OF THE SLEEP DELAY FOR ADOLESCENT BEHAVIOR

In the United States in particular, as well as in a few other industrialized societies, the changing adolescent sleep–wake system exists in the context of a relatively unforgiving educational structure demanding earlier school attendance in older than younger children. Whether the delay of the timing of sleep in adolescents is exclusively attributable to the psychosocial milieu or receives contributions from changes in the intrinsic regulatory processes, we observe inadequate and ill-timed sleep in a large number, if not a majority of young people. Our group has found, for example, that the estimated amount of sleep accumulated during the school week in youngsters in grade 6 averages 500 minutes, in grade 8 is 473,[75] and in grade 10, the average is 452 and grade 12, 420 minutes based upon objective monitoring in the field. Laboratory data indicates that the sleep need in these youngsters is closer to 555 minutes per night.[45,76]

As we learn more about the effects of chronic insufficient sleep, concerns grow about the potential for negative impacts on adolescents. For example, rates of automobile crashes attributed to falling asleep while driving are markedly higher for the youngest drivers. Indeed, a retrospective analysis of over 4000 such occurrences showed that the drivers' ages in just over 50% of crashes were 16 to 25 years.[77] Growing evidence also indicates that adequate sleep plays an important role in memory consolidation and learning processes,[78–80] though research specific to adolescents is scarce. The preponderance of evidence from a variety of studies examining the association of sleep patterns with academic performance indicates that too little and poorly timed sleep has a negative impact in children, adolescents, and young adults.[81] Furthermore, tardiness, absenteeism, and high school graduation rates in adolescent students have been linked to sleep schedules and early school starting times.[82]

Mood regulation also suffers with inadequate sleep. Time and again, our studies—whether observational or experimental—have found depressed mood at greater rates in young people whose sleep is compromised (see Ref. 2, for example). Behavior disruption has also been noted as a concomitant of disturbed sleep in children with sleep disorders [83-86]; less is known about this association in adolescents.

Substance use, including caffeine, alcohol, and tobacco, is also greater in teens who sleep less.[87,88] Recent data in adults show that sleep is not simply for the mind, but affects metabolic processes as well.[89] Indeed, one epidemiologic study linked adolescent obesity with poor sleep patterns.[90] As sleep patterns are examined along with other lifestyle or medical outcomes, we can anticipate more negative associations of poor sleep to become apparent.

CONCLUSION

The robust tendency for the timing of sleep to delay during adolescent development is undeniably associated with the changed psychosocial environment of the developing teen and may also rely on developmental changes in fundamental regulatory processes. For many teens, this sleep delaying pattern cascades into a chronic pattern of insufficient school-day sleep, forced arousals at a biologically inappropriate time, and resulting negative impacts on adolescent performance, behavior, mood, and other processes. Countermeasures that are implemented on a personal, family, community, or societal level need to acknowledge all the factors contributing to the issue. We feel that primary among the countermeasures is an acknowledgement of a positive priority for sleep and a need for a better understanding of the sleep-wake regulatory process through education and research.

ACKNOWLEDGMENTS

We are grateful for the assistance of Peter Achermann, Ph.D., Susan Labyak, Ph.D., Ronald Seifer, Ph.D., Amy Wolfson, Ph.D., Barbara Tate, Ph.D., Daniel Taylor, Ph.D. We are also indebted to our research staff and our student research apprentices. This research was supported by the following grants: MH45945, NR04279, MH52415, MH01358 to Dr. Carskadon and 81ZH-068474 (Swiss National Science Foundation) to Dr. Jenni.

REFERENCES

1. CARSKADON, M.A. 1990. Patterns of sleep and sleepiness in adolescents. Pediatrician **17:** 5–12.
2. WOLFSON, A.R. & M.A. CARSKADON. 1998. Sleep schedules and daytime functioning in adolescents. Child Dev. **69:** 875–887.
3. LABERGE, L., *et al.* 2001. Development of sleep patterns in early adolescence. J. Sleep Res. **10:** 59–67.
4. STRAUCH, I. & B. MEIER. 1988. Sleep need in adolescents: a longitudinal approach. Sleep **11:** 378–386.
5. GIANOTTI, F. & F. CORTESI. 2002. Sleep patterns and daytime function in adolescence: an epidemiological survey of an Italian high school student sample. *In* Adolescent Sleep Patterns: Biological, social, and psychological influences. M.A. Carskadon, Ed.: 132–147. Cambridge University Press. Cambridge, UK.

6. GAU, S.F. & W.T. SOONG. 2003. The transition of sleep-wake patterns in early adolescence. Sleep **26:** 449–454.
7. GAU, S.F. & W.T. SOONG. 1995. Sleep problems of junior high school students in Taipei. Sleep **18:** 667–673.
8. ANDRADE, M.M. & L. MENNA-BARRETO. 2002. Sleep patterns of high school students living in Sao Paulo, Brazil. *In* Adolescent Sleep Patterns: Biological, social, and psychological influences. M.A. Carskadon, Ed.: 118–131. Cambridge University Press. Cambridge, UK.
9. ANDRADE, M.M. *et al.* 1993. Sleep characteristics of adolescents: a longitudinal study. J. Adolesc. Health **14:** 401–406.
10. REID, A., C.C. MALDONADO & F.C. BAKER. 2002. Sleep behavior of South African adolescents. Sleep **25:** 423–427.
11. CARSKADON, M.A. *et al.* 1998. Adolescent sleep patterns, circadian timing, and sleepiness at a transition to early school days. Sleep **21:** 871–881.
12. BORBÉLY, A.A. 1982. A two process model of sleep regulation. Hum. Neurobiol. **1:** 195–204.
13. DAAN, S., D.G. BEERSMA & A.A. BORBELY. 1984. Timing of human sleep: recovery process gated by a circadian pacemaker. Am. J. Physiol. **246:** R161–183.
14. BORBÉLY, A.A. *et al.* 1989. Sleep initiation and initial sleep intensity: interactions of homeostatic and circadian mechanisms. J. Biol. Rhythms **4:** 149–160.
15. ACHERMANN, P. *et al.* 1993. A model of human sleep homeostasis based on EEG slow-wave activity: quantitative comparison of data and simulations. Brain Res. Bull. **31:** 97–113.
16. ACHERMANN, P. & A.A. BORBELY. 1994. Simulation of daytime vigilance by the additive interaction of a homeostatic and a circadian process. Biol. Cybern. **71:** 115–121.
17. TUREK, F.W. & P.C. ZEE. 1999. Regulation of Sleep and Circadian Rhythms. Marcel Dekker, Inc. New York.
18. PORKKA-HEISKANEN, T. *et al.* 2002. Adenosine and sleep. Sleep Med. Rev. **6:** 321–332.
19. STERIADE, M., D.A. MCCORMICK & T.J. SEJNOWSKI. 1993. Thalamocortical oscillations in the sleeping and aroused brain. Science **262:** 679–685.
20. STERIADE, M. 1999. Coherent oscillations and short-term plasticity in corticothalamic networks. Trends Neurosci. **22:** 337–345.
21. CIRELLI, C. 2002. How sleep deprivation affects gene expression in the brain: a review of recent findings. J. Appl. Physiol. **92:** 394–400.
22. BORBÉLY, A.A. & P. ACHERMANN. 2000. Sleep homeostasis and models of sleep regulation. *In* Principles and Practice of Sleep Medicine. M.H. Kryger, T. Roth & W.C. Dement, Eds.: 377–390. W.B. Saunders, Co. Philadelphia.
23. ACHERMANN, P. & A.A. BORBÉLY. 2003. Mathematical models of sleep regulation. Front. Biosci. **8:** S683–693.
24. WEBB, W.B. & H.W. AGNEW. 1971. Stage 4 sleep: influence of time course variables. Science **174:** 1354–1356.
25. BORBÉLY, A.A. *et al.* 1981. Sleep deprivation: effect on sleep stages and EEG power density in man. EEG Clin. Neurophysiol. **51:** 483–493.
26. DIJK, D.J., D.G.M. BEERSMA & S. DAAN. 1987. EEG power density during nap sleep: reflection of an hourglass measuring the duration of prior wakefulness. J. Biol. Rhythms **2:** 207–219.
27. WERTH, E. *et al.* 1996. Dynamics of the sleep EEG after an early evening nap: experimental data and simulations. Am. J. Physiol. **271:** R501–510.
28. DIJK, D.J., D.P. BRUNNER & A.A. BORBÉLY. 1990. Time course of EEG power density during long sleep in humans. Am. J. Physiol. **258:** R650–R661.
29. CARSKADON, M.A. & W.C. DEMENT. 1982. Nocturnal determinants of daytime sleepiness. Sleep **5:** 73–81.
30. CARSKADON, M.A. & W.C. DEMENT. 1981. Cumulative effects of sleep restriction on daytime sleepiness. Psychophysiology **18:** 107–113.
31. DIJK, D.-J. & C.A. CZEISLER. 1995. Contribution of the circadian pacemaker and the sleep homeostat to sleep propensity, sleep structure, electroencephalographic slow waves, and sleep spindle activity in humans. J. Neurosci. **15:** 3526–3538.

32. STROGATZ, S.H. 1986. The Mathematical Structure of the Human Sleep-Wake Cycle. Springer-Verlag. New York.
33. EDGAR, D.M., W.C. DEMENT & C.A. FULLER. 1993. Effect of SCN lesions on sleep in squirrel monkeys: Evidence for opponent processes in sleep-wake regulation. J. Neurosci. **13**: 1065–1079.
34. DIJK, D.J. & C.A. CZEISLER. 1994. Paradoxical timing of the circadian rhythm of sleep propensity serves to consolidate sleep and wakefulness in humans. Neurosci. Lett. **166**: 63–68.
35. HORNE, J.A. & O.A. ÖSTBERG. 1976. A self-assessment questionnaire to determine morningness-eveningness in human circadian rhythms. Int. J. Chronobiol. **4**: 97–110.
36. SMITH, C.S., D. REILLY & K. MIDKIFF. 1989. Evaluation of three circadian rhythm questionnaires with suggestions for an improved measure of morningness. J. Appl. Psychol. **74**: 728–738.
37. CARSKADON, M.A., C. VIEIRA & C. ACEBO. 1993. Association between puberty and delayed phase preference. Sleep **16**: 258–262.
38. CZEISLER, C.A., J.S. ALLAN & R.E. KRONAUER. 1990. A method for assaying the effects of therapeutic agents on the period of the endogenous circadian pacemaker in man. *In* Sleep and Biological Rhythms: Basic mechanisms and applications to psychiatry. J. Montplaisir & R. Godbout, Eds.: 87–98. Oxford University Press. New York.
39. WYATT, J.K. *et al.* 1999. Circadian temperature and melatonin rhythms, sleep, and neurobehavioral function in humans living on a 20-h day. Am. J. Physiol. **277**: R1152–1163.
40. LEWY, A.J. *et al.* 1980. Light suppresses melatonin secretion in humans. Science **310**: 1267–1269.
41. FEINBERG, I., R. KORESKO & N. HELLER. 1967. EEG sleep patterns as a function of normal and pathological aging in man. J. Psychiatr. Res. **1**: 107–144.
42. WILLIAMS, R.L. *et al.* 1972. Sleep patterns of pubertal males. Pediatr. Res. **6**: 643–648.
43. WILLIAMS, R.L., I. KARACAN & C.J. HURSCH. 1974. Electroencephalography of Human Sleep: Clinical applications. John Wiley and Sons. New York.
44. KARACAN, I. *et al.* 1975. Longitudinal sleep patterns during pubertal growth: four-year follow up. Pediatr. Res. **9**: 842–846.
45. CARSKADON, M.A. 1982. The second decade. *In* Sleep and Waking Disorders: Indications and techniques. C. Guilleminault, Ed.: 99–125. Addison Wesley. Menlo Park, CA.
46. COBLE, P.A. *et al.* 1987. Electroencephalographic sleep of healthy children. Part II: Findings using automated delta and REM sleep measurement methods. Sleep **10**: 551–562.
47. GAUDREAU, H., J. CARRIER & J. MONTPLAISIR. 2001. Age-related modifications of NREM sleep EEG: from childhood to middle age. J. Sleep Res. **10**: 165–172.
48. JENNI, O.G., P. ACHERMANN & M.A. CARSKADON. 2003. Spectral analysis of the sleep EEG during adolescence: effects of pubertal stage and 36-h sleep deprivation. Sleep **26**: A189.
49. FEINBERG, I. 1982. Schizophrenia: caused by a fault in programmed synaptic elimination during adolescence? J. Psychiatr. Res. **17**: 319–334.
50. FEINBERG, I. *et al.* 1990. Gamma distribution model describes maturational curves for delta wave amplitude, cortical metabolic rate and synaptic density. J. Theor. Biol. **142**: 149–161.
51. TAYLOR, D., C. ACEBO & M.A. CARSKADON. 2003. MSLT across 36 hours of sleep loss in adolescents. Sleep **26**: A189.
52. CARSKADON, M.A. *et al.* 1997. An approach to studying circadian rhythms of adolescent humans. J. Biol. Rhythm **12**: 278–289.
53. WALDHAUSER, F. *et al.* 1984. Bioavailability of oral melatonin in humans. Neuroendocrinology **39**: 307–313.
54. CAVALLO, A. 1992. Plasma melatonin rhythm in normal puberty—interactions of age and pubertal stages. Neuroendocrinology **55**: 372–379.
55. KOLATA, G. 1984. Puberty mystery solved. Science **223**: 272.
56. KLEIN, D.C. 1984. Melatonin and puberty. Science **224**: 6.

57. TETSUO, M., M. POTH & S.P. MARKEY. 1982. Melatonin metabolite excretion during childhood and puberty. J. Clin. Endocrinol. Metab. **55:** 311–313.
58. GRIEFAHN, B. *et al.* 2003. Melatonin production during childhood and adolescence: a longitudinal study on the excretion of urinary 6-hydroxymelatonin sulfate. J. Pineal Res. **34:** 26–31.
59. ACEBO, C., S.E. LABYAK & M.A. CARSKADON. 2003. Dim light melatonin profiles during constant routines: amplitude and development. Sleep **26:** A113–114.
60. WALDHAUSER, F. & M. DIETZEL. 1985. Daily and annual rhythms in human melatonin secretion: role in puberty control. Ann. N.Y. Acad. Sci. **453:** 205–214.
61. ARENDT, J. 1988. Melatonin. Clin. Endocrinol. **29:** 205–229.
62. ZEITZER, J.M. *et al.* 1999. Do plasma melatonin concentrations decline with age? Am. J. Med. **107:** 432–436.
63. WALDHAUSER, F., J. KOVACS & E. REITER. 1998. Age-related changes in melatonin levels in humans and its potential consequences for sleep disorders. Exp. Gerontol. **33:** 759–772.
64. SHANAHAN, T.L. 1995. Circadian physiology and the plasma melatonin rhythm in humans. (Thesis). Harvard University, Boston, MA.
65. ASCHOFF, J. 1981. Free-running and entrained rhythms. *In* Handbook of Behavioral Neurology: Biological rhythms. J. Aschoff, Ed.: 81–93. Plenum Press. New York.
66. CARSKADON, M.A. *et al.* 1999. Intrinsic circadian period of adolescent humans measured in conditions of forced desynchrony. Neurosci. Lett. **260:** 129–132.
67. CZEISLER, C.A. *et al.* 1999. Stability, precision, and near-24-hour period of the human circadian pacemaker. Science **284:** 2177–2181.
68. WRIGHT, K.P. *et al.* 2001. Intrinsic near-24-h pacemaker period determines limits of circadian entrainment to a weak synchronizer in humans. Proc. Natl. Acad. Sci. USA **98:** 14027–14032.
69. DECOURSEY, P.J. 1960. Daily light sensitivity in a rodent. Science **131:** 33–35.
70. JOHNSON, C.H. 1990. PRC Atlas: An atlas of phase response curves for circadian and circatidal rhythms.
71. CARSKADON, M.A. *et al.* 2001. Melatonin sensitivity to light in adolescents: preliminary results. Sleep **24:** A190–A191.
72. CARSKADON, M.A., C. ACEBO & J.T. ARNEDT. 2004. Melatonin sensitivity to light in adolescent humans as a function of pubertal maturation. Neurosci. Lett. (Submitted for publication.)
73. CARSKADON, M.A. *et al.* 1980. Pubertal changes in daytime sleepiness. Sleep **2:** 453–460.
74. CARSKADON, M.A. & C. ACEBO. 2002. Regulation of sleepiness in adolescents: update, insights, and speculation. Sleep **25:** 606–614.
75. WOLFSON, A.R. *et al.* 2003. Actigraphically-estimated sleep patterns of middle school students. Sleep **26:** A126–127.
76. CARSKADON, M.A., C. ACEBO & R. SEIFER. 2001. Extended nights, sleep loss, and recovery sleep in adolescents. Arch. Ital. Biol. **139:** 301–312.
77. PACK, A.I. *et al.* 1995. Characteristics of crashes attributed to the driver having fallen asleep. Accident Anal. Prev. **27:** 769–775.
78. SMITH, C. 1996. Sleep states, memory processes and synaptic plasticity. Behav. Brain Res. **78:** 49–56.
79. MAQUET, P. 2001. The role of sleep in learning and memory. Science **294:** 1048–1052.
80. STICKGOLD, R. *et al.* 2001. Sleep, learning, and dreams: off-line memory reprocessing. Science **294:** 1052–1057.
81. WOLFSON, A.R. & M.A. CARSKADON. 2003. Understanding adolescent sleep patterns and school performance: a critical appraisal. Sleep Med. Rev. **7(6):** 491–506.
82. WAHLSTROM, K.L. 2002. Accomodating the sleep patterns of adolescents within current educational structures: an uncharted path. *In* Adolescent Sleep Patterns: Biological, Social, and Psychological influences. M.A. Carskadon, Ed. Cambridge University Press. Cambridge, UK.
83. ANDERS, T.F., M.A. CARSKADON & W.C. DEMENT. 1980. Sleep and sleepiness in children and adolescents. Pediatr. Clin. North Am. **27:** 29–43.

84. GUILLEMINAULT, C., R. KOROBKIN & R. WINKLE. 1981. A review of 50 children with obstructive sleep apnea syndrome. Lung **159:** 275–287.
85. BROUILLETTE, R. *et al.* 1984. A diagnostic approach to suspected obstructive sleep apnea in children. J. Pediatr. **105:** 10–14.
86. CHERVIN, R.D. *et al.* 2003. Conduct problems and symptoms of sleep disorders in children. J. Am. Acad. Child Adolesc. Psychiatry **42:** 201–208.
87. CARSKADON, M.A. 1990. Adolescent sleepiness: Increased risk in a high-risk population. Alcohol Drugs Driving **5/6:** 317–328.
88. TYNJALA, J., L. KANNAS & E. LEVALAHTI. 1997. Perceived tiredness among adolescents and its association with sleep habits and use of psychoactive substances. J. Sleep Res. **6:** 189–198.
89. SPIEGEL, K., R. LEPROULT & E. VAN CAUTER. 1999. Impact of sleep debt on metabolic and endocrine function. Lancet **354:** 1435–1439.
90. GUPTA, N.K. *et al.* 2002. Is obesity associated with poor sleep quality in adolescents? Am J. Human Biol. **14:** 762–768.

Regulation of Sleep and Arousal

Comments on Part VII

RONALD E. DAHL

*Psychiatry and Pediatrics, University of Pittsburgh Medical Center,
Pittsburgh, Pennsylvania 15213, USA*

ABSTRACT: This paper links the papers in this session and describes briefly how together they represent an ideal example of the kind of trans-disciplinary approach to understanding aspects of adolescent maturation that can have major clinical and social policy implications. The issues of adolescent sleep needs, circadian changes linked to pubertal maturation, the effects of sleep deprivation on adolescent health and behavior, and social controversies such as delaying the start times of high schools to address the problems of adolescent sleep deprivation all point to the need for additional empirical studies. This will require studies of normal human development as well as animal models to investigate the mechanisms underpinning these developmental changes in sleep and circadian regulation.

KEYWORDS: sleep deprivation; adolescent brain development; circadian; puberty; animal models

First I would like to thank David Dinges for his interesting and dynamic presentation at the conference, which stimulated a great deal of discussion about the importance of sleep across the lifespan and the implications of rampant sleep deprivation in individuals of all ages in our society; regrettably, it is not included in this volume.

As Ruth Benca made clear in her introduction, there is extensive empirical data indicating that sleep deprivation represents one of the most widespread sources of stress on the adolescent brain. Given the mounting data about the role of sleep in learning and memory from both animal and human studies, this raises some compelling questions about the consequences of insufficient sleep in adolescence—particularly in youth who also experiencing other sources of stress, challenge, and difficulties. The consequences range from the starkly obvious, such as the large number of deaths from auto accidents resulting from youth falling asleep at the wheel, to the wider range of complex but understudied effects of sleep deprivation on cognitive, emotional, and social functioning.

One important set of questions focuses on the *causes* of the high rates of sleep deprivation in adolescents. As highlighted in the paper by Mary Carskadon, a great

Address for correspondence: Ronald E. Dahl, M.D., Child and Adolescent Psychiatry, Pediatrics, University of Pittsburg Medical Center, 3811 O'Hara St., Rm. E724, Pittsburgh, PA 15213. Voice: 412-624-7740; fax: 412-624-0223.
dahlre@upmc.edu

Ann. N.Y. Acad. Sci. 1021: 292–293 (2004). © 2004 New York Academy of Sciences. doi: 10.1196/annals.1308.033

deal of scientific progress has been made in identifying the interactions between biological factors (such as the circadian shift at puberty toward becoming more "owl-like" in sleep patterns) and the social factors (including habits, the influence of culture, family, and peers, the lure of the Internet and other media, work and social schedules, and early school start times in high school) that oftenpush adolescent sleep schedules toward late and erratic bedtimes and insufficient numbers of hours for sleep—particularly on school days.

Several lines of investigation indicate that the biologic component of this complex behavioral and social problem is linked to pubertal influences on the biological timing systems, and these are likely to involve pubertal hormone effects on regions of the hypothalamus such as the suprachiasmatic nucleus (SCN) and related shifts in sleep and circadian regulation. However, one path to understanding the mechanisms of these pubertal changes, and to disentangle the specific biologic elements of these changes is by using animal models. Terri Lee's paper describes some elegant studies that are beginning to fill precisely this niche of knowledge.

The links between these animal and human studies, and the complementary nature of the work, provide an outstanding example of the principles that undergird this symposium on adolescent brain development. On one hand, the clinical and social policy aspects of adolescent sleep problems are enormously complex, and involve brain/behavior/social-context *interactions* that often spiral into very serious problems in youth. Yet key aspects of this complex problem—the puberty-specific changes in biological timing systems and the neuroendocrine mechanisms underlying these circadian shifts—are being investigated by studies in behavioral neuroscience, including those using animal models.

This is exactly the kind of transdisciplinary research that is needed to advance understanding of maturational changes in specific neurobehavioral systems in adolescence to inform clinical and social policy in ways that that have a positive impact on youth.

Adolescent Development and the Regulation of Behavior and Emotion

Introduction to Part VIII

RONALD E. DAHL

Psychiatry and Pediatrics, University of Pittsburgh Medical Center, Pittsburgh, Pennsylvania 15213, USA

ABSTRACT: This article introduces and identifies key issues in the articles in this section.

KEYWORDS: adolescent development; behavioral control; regulatory systems; neurobehavioral systems; self-regulation; cognitive control

As an introduction to the final section of this conference on Adolescent Brain Development, I will highlight a few points. First, this section will continue with the format that has been used throughout this volume: the integration of cross-disciplinary approaches. The first article, by Beatriz Luna, Ph.D., and John A. Sweeney, describes basic research focusing on the normal maturation of behavioral control in children and adolescents. This article includes behavioral and fMRI data addressing questions about the development of one regulatory system (voluntary control over eye movements), which are likely to have broad implications for the development of *other* self-regulatory capacities in adolescence. Moreover, the combination of behavioral data and functional imaging data provides information about the development of specific neurobehavioral systems underpinning these increased capacities for self-control in adolescents.

The second article, by Ann Masten, Ph.D., addresses much broader questions about social context in relation to positive and negative influences on adolescent development. More specifically, her article focuses on questions about risk and resilience and the importance of self-regulatory processes for youth trying to successfully navigate the complex environments of contemporary society.

One of the important concepts that Dr. Masten addresses is the idea of optimal social "scaffolding" in the life of adolescents. This term, *scaffolding*, which has come up a few times in this symposium, refers to the individuals and social structures that provide support, constraints, and monitoring of youth. Typically, this includes parents, teachers, coaches, schools, communities, and most importantly, the rules and behaviors of the adults that provide monitoring and a "safety net" for

Address for correspondence: Ronald E. Dahl, M.D., Staunton Professor of Psychiatry and Pediatrics, University of Pittsburgh Medical Center, 3811 O'Hara St., Rm. E-724, Pittsburgh, PA 15213. Voice: 412 246-5878; fax: 412-246-5880.

dahlre@upmc.edu

Ann. N.Y. Acad. Sci. 1021: 294–295 (2004). © 2004 New York Academy of Sciences.
doi: 10.1196/annals.1308.034

adolescents. The concept of an optimal balance in this scaffolding is one that does not weaken until the gradually increasing capacities for self-regulation have emerged during this period of development. In other words, social scaffolding holds up or supports individual adolescents until they are able to (reliably and responsibly) make all their own choices independently of any adult monitoring. In this way, it is analogous to the scaffolding that supports construction of a building—initially this is the primary support and eventually it is superfluous. However, in contrast to the optimal balance, or removing the scaffolding as the individual can manage without it, as Dr. Masten highlights, there are reasons to be concerned that particularly in some social contexts, there is very weak social scaffolding combined with very limited development of self-regulatory capacities, in a way that translates directly into vulnerability.

Together, these articles address the need to consider the neurobehavioral development of self-regulatory capacities (the work by Drs. Luna and Sweeney exemplifies one approach) with the changing challenges and demands upon these gradually developing capacities (as discussed in Dr. Masten's article). These papers are followed by comments by David Kupfer and Hermi Woodward, who discuss some of the implications of these articles, and the need for further work in these areas.

The Emergence of Collaborative Brain Function

fMRI Studies of the Development of Response Inhibition

BEATRIZ LUNA[a] AND JOHN A. SWEENEY[b]

[a]Laboratory of Neurocognitive Development, Department of Psychiatry, University of Pittsburgh, Pittsburgh, Pennsylvania, USA

[b]Center for Cognitive Medicine, Department of Psychiatry, University of Illinois at Chicago, Chicago, Illinois, USA

ABSTRACT: Adolescence marks the beginning of adult-level cognitive control of behavior supported by the brain maturation processes of synaptic pruning and myelination. Cognitive development studies on adolescence indicate that this period is characterized by improvements in the performance of existing abilities including speed and capacity of information processing and the ability to have consistent cognitive control of behavior. Although adolescents can behave at adult levels in some ways, brain imaging studies indicate that the functional organization of brain systems that support higher-cognitive processes are not fully mature. Synaptic pruning allows for more efficient local computations, enhancing the ability of discrete brain regions to support high-level cognitive control of behavior including working memory. Myelination increases the speed of neuronal transmission supporting the collaboration of a widely distributed circuitry, integrating regions that support top-down cognitive control of behavior. Functional brain imaging methods allow for the characterization of the relationship between cognitive development and brain maturation as we can map progressions in the establishment of distributed brain circuitry and its relation to enhanced cognitive control of behavior. We present a review on the maturation (as distinct from "development" in emphasizing the transition to maturity and stabilization) of response inhibition, brain structure, and brain function through adolescence. We also propose a model for brain-behavior maturation that allows for the qualitative changes in cognitive processes that occur during adolescence.

KEYWORDS: prefrontal cortex; inhibition; eye movements; antisaccades; maturation

Address for correspondence: Beatriz Luna, Ph.D., Laboratory of Neurocognitive Development, University of Pittsburgh Medical Center, 3501 Forbes Avenue, #743, Pittsburgh, PA 15213. Voice: 412-246-6138; fax: 412-246-6161.
lunab@upmc.edu

Ann. N.Y. Acad. Sci. 1021: 296–309 (2004). © 2004 New York Academy of Sciences.
doi: 10.1196/annals.1308.035

INTRODUCTION

There is a consensus that adolescence is a period of development distinct from both childhood and adulthood, yet, it has been difficult to identify the factors that make this period unique. In many aspects, adolescents behave much like adults. While they can perform complicated tasks, such as algebra, they are different from adults in their heightened risk-taking behavior and their decreased sense of consequences that is the basis of "responsible" behavior. The adult manner of interacting with the world is determined by both environmental and biological factors. Much work has been done identifying the environmental determinants of adolescent social behavior compared to relatively little work that has been done on the biological influences on cognition during this period. We propose that the emergence of adult-level cognitive control of behavior is directly linked to maturation of brain mechanisms during adolescence. Investigations characterizing the biological basis of adolescent behavior have focused primarily on pubertal changes, but minimal attention has been given to the possible contributions of brain maturation. Understanding the brain basis of the transition to adult-level cognitive control of behavior can provide us with important information regarding the constraints within which adolescent behavior need to be understood, and potentially about mechanisms of dysmaturation in psychiatric disorders.

Our understanding of the brain basis of cognition in adolescence has been limited for several reasons. Compared to the work on early cognitive development in childhood, little has been done to characterize these changes in adolescence. One reason may be that the cognitive changes in adolescence are not as significant and dramatic as the ones present in infancy and childhood since many abilities are in place early in development and adolescence marks a refinement, rather than an emergence, of these abilities. Second, work that has been done has utilized higher-order neuropsychological tasks that rely on multiple cognitive processes, limiting the ability to make brain-behavior links. Finally, only since the advent of functional brain imaging have we been able to directly study brain-behavior links in vivo in healthy pediatric populations.

We are now at a unique point where we can move beyond these limitations. First, functional magnetic resonance imaging (fMRI), a noninvasive neuroimaging method, allows the characterization of brain function *in vivo* at a high spatial resolution in pediatric samples in order to localize function and map brain systems underlying cognitive processing. Secondly, single-cell and non-human primate lesion studies have developed methods that allow direct links between brain mechanisms and cognition. These advances have put us in a position where we can make great strides in understanding the range and limitations of the maturation of interrelated brain and cognitive processes in adolescence.

The strategy that we have chosen is to probe brain processes underlying cognition using oculomotor tasks developed for single-cell non-human primate studies investigating the neuronal basis of cognition. These studies, as well as studies using these tasks with adult subjects in functional brain imaging studies, document that the cognitive control of attention and eye movements recruits circuitry underlying higher-order cognitive control of behavior. Basic neuroscience studies provide a detailed characterization of the physiology, anatomy, and neurochemistry of the cognitive control of eye movements, and this information encompasses a significant amount of what we know about the neuronal substrate of executive functions and the cognitive control of behavior supported by mechanisms in the prefrontal cortex. Importantly, oculomotor studies are particularly well-suited for developmental studies as the simple instructions (look or do not look at a visual stimulus) control for age differences in understanding task demands and they do not readily lend themselves to forming verbal strategies that could confound the results as can be the case with neuropsychological tests. While these tasks are simple, they require executive control of behavior and have the sensitivity to monitor changes in performance from childhood to adulthood. Developmental studies using oculomotor paradigms and fMRI have the potential to elucidate the mechanisms underlying cognitive and brain maturation.

COGNITIVE DEVELOPMENT: THE MATURATION
OF RESPONSE INHIBITION

Basic cognitive processes such as working memory and response inhibition, which are evident in infancy and improve throughout childhood,[1,2] continue robust development well into adolescence.[3-10] Cognitive development has been extensively studied in infancy and childhood as abilities are being acquired; however, systematic investigation of this maturation is limited after mid-childhood. A few studies have assessed a range of neuropsychological and executive processes after that period and have found that developmental improvements in cognitive control continue through early adolescence.[3-5,9-13] The most dramatic changes seem to be increases in information processing speed and capacity.[3-5] These results suggest that developmental changes in cognition during adolescence are distinct from those that occur earlier in infancy and childhood, as they involve improvements in existing capacities rather than the acquisition of new abilities. The tasks used in these studies include those that rely on working memory for numbers, such as the digit span tasks,[3] and those that require organization and planning skills as well as following set rules, such as the Contingency Naming Task and Tower of London.[4] The stimuli are primarily composed of numbers or words and sometimes geometrical figures, all of which involve symbolic knowledge for which strategies can be implemented that can reduce cognitive demands and undermine the ability to isolate dimensions of cognitive control. Responses using a separate domain, such as verbal or manual, require an added transformation across modalities. These factors can confound efforts to identify specific processes that continue to mature through adolescence. Finally, many studies assume that full maturity of function occurs by early adolescence and do not include comparison with adults, potentially missing continued development. We have taken the approach of using oculomotor paradigms to probe isolated dimensions of the cognitive control of behavior, such as working memory and response inhibition.

Essential to the executive control of goal-directed behavior, and consequently, for many forms of higher-order cognition, is the ability to voluntarily/cognitively choose what stimuli or ideas will guide our behavior, and to inhibit responses to competing ideas or events that could be less adaptive.[14-16] Voluntary response suppression is the process of exerting self-regulation to control task-irrelevant behavior through the stopping of planned or prepotent responses and the filtering of responses to potential distractors.[15,16] At a more basic level, inhibition underlies response selection as a multitude of alternative response plans compete in working memory that might serve to guide behavior.[14] Inhibition is used in the suppression of competing response plans previously associated with a given circumstance, cognitive processes activated for concurrent processes (dual processing), or distractions occurring at the time of responding. Response inhibition is present in every voluntary action we perform, since choosing a response necessitates not choosing other responses. Inhibition can be targeted to exogenous stimuli in the environment or to endogenous plans that are internally generated. Suppression is crucial for voluntary control of behavior from focusing of attention (attending to one conversation without being distracted by neighboring conversations), to higher-level processes such as in those underlying social behavior (the ability to stop aggressive tendencies in a heated situation). Investigating response inhibition is particularly relevant to understanding developmental advances in cognitive control that occur during adolescence. First, risk-taking behavior is acknowledged as characteristic of adolescence, and can be viewed as the inability to suppress prepotent responses, even if they may be less adaptive in the longer term, perhaps reflecting immaturity of inhibitory processes. Secondly, the brain circuitry underlying response inhibition involves high-order executive processing in the prefrontal cortex, and recruitment of distributed function for response planning and the top-down cognitive control of behavior.[17,18] Synaptic pruning and myelination may directly influence developmental advances in the maturation of cognitive control during adolescence because of the interdependency of effective functional communication across multiple brain regions. This means that extensive investigation of the maturation of response suppression may be useful for probing the interrelated maturation of cognitive and brain systems during adolescence.

The development of inhibition begins in infancy, when prepotent sensorimotor responses overrule cognitive plans.[1] Response inhibition continues to improve throughout childhood as demonstrated by the ability to retain visual fixation,[19] shift response set in the Go-No-Go task,[2,20] attend to the variable of interest in the Stroop task,[20,21] and interrupt a planned behavior in stop signal tasks.[12,24,25] It is also observed to diminish in the aged as demonstrated by the inability to inhibit responses to distractors.[25-27] In contrast, little is known regarding when and how this ability matures during adolescence. Although there is significant improvement throughout childhood in the performance of these tasks, maturity is not always established by the latest age of assessment in many developmental studies leaving a gap in the understanding of how we reach mature levels in adulthood.

Developmental studies characterizing advances in the cognitive control of eye movements have shown continued improvement in response inhibition that matures in mid-adolescence.[6-10] These studies used the antisaccade task, in which subjects are instructed to avoid looking at a suddenly-appearing peripheral target, and instead look in the mirror location (FIG. 1). One of the primary goals of the visual system is to guide foveation of visual stimuli of potential interest. Therefore, it takes great effort to override this hardwired sensorimotor response to immediately look to novel stimuli (referred to as the visual grasp reflex), and instead to generate a cognitively-driven eye movement to a calculated location away from the visual stimulus with no sensory guidance. Looking at the peripheral target indicates a failure of successful inhibition that is usually followed by redirecting fixation to the correct location indicating that the task instruction was understood but the task was not performed correctly. Children make approximately two to three times the number of response

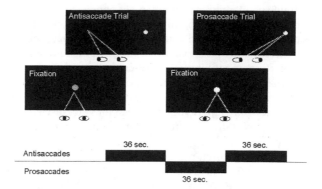

FIGURE 1. Stimuli presented during periods of antisaccade trials and prosaccade trials. When fixation was red (gray circle) subjects were instructed to avoid looking at the peripheral stimulus and instead direct their eyes in the mirror location. When the fixation target was green (white circle) subjects were instructed to look at the visual stimulus. Stimuli could appear at 3, 6, or 9 degrees of visual angle to the left or right of center. Each block of trials lasted 36 sec. Subjects performed 7.5 cycles of antisaccades alternating with prosaccades.

suppression errors as adults. There is a rapid decrease in the number of errors with age, with stabilization beginning in mid-adolescence.[6–10]

It is important to note that even children can perform isolated response inhibition trials correctly, indicating that the ability to inhibit a response is already present. What develops during adolescence is the ability to do so in a consistent manner. These results suggest that the brain circuitry supporting the ability to suppress a context-inappropriate response is in place by childhood, but the circuitry supporting the ability to sustain a state of cognitive control continues to mature through adolescence.

A distributed circuitry has been delineated to support response inhibition during the antisaccade task in monkeys[28–32] and in adult humans.[17,18,33–35] These areas include the frontal eye field (FEF), supplementary eye fields (SEF), dorsolateral prefrontal cortex (DLPFC), posterior parietal cortex, anterior cingulate cortex, basal ganglia, thalamus, and superior colliculus.

BRAIN MATURATION FROM LATE CHILDHOOD TO ADOLESCENCE

Paralleling cognitive development, brain maturation continues throughout adolescence (see articles by Giedd and colleagues and Lewis and colleagues, in this volume). The degree of cortical folding,[36] overall size, weight, and regional functional specialization of the brain is, for the most part, in adult form by early childhood.[37–39] Nonetheless, significant refinements of brain systems, including synaptic pruning, elaboration of dendritic arborization, and increased myelination, continue through adolescence and beyond.[40–44] Although these subtle structural changes in local brain circuitry are not evident in the gross anatomic resolution provided by *in vivo* structural brain imaging, they have a significant impact on brain function and behavior. In infancy, we develop an excess amount of synaptic connections that provide plasticity and are potentially the basis for early learning. The middle frontal gyrus, which matures later than visual cortex, reaches its peak of synaptogenesis by 1 year of age and does not stabilize until age 16.[41] It is at this time (1 year of age) that the earliest manifestations of working memory are seen in human infants.[1] Synaptic pruning of redundant connections during adolescence enhances the computational capacity of local circuitry, improving the ability to modulate activity and implement stop mechanisms in a prompt manner. During myelination, glial cell membranes wrap around axons, greatly speeding neuronal transmission. Myelination has been found to mature earlier in the visual cortex than the longer distance cortico-cortical connections of frontal, parietal, and temporal association areas, where it continues through adolescence.[42] Speeded neuronal transmission enhances local neuronal connections as well as the integration of widely distributed circuitry and the modulation of cortical and subcortical regions by frontal executive areas. These structural changes are believed to underlie the functional integration of frontal regions with the rest of the brain with development into adolescence.[45,46]

The formation of synapses equips brain regions to perform local computations, and significant synaptogenesis occurs in infancy when we see the emergence of the earliest manifestations of higher cognitive abilities. The continued improvement in executive function into adolescence, instead, is supported primarily by the elimination of redundant or unused synapses and the myelination of longer fiber tracks, both of which contribute to the progressive speeding of cognitive responses continually found in studies of this age period. The elimination of redundant synaptic connections supports more efficient and complicated regional neuronal computations. Myelination speeds neuronal transmission allowing distant brain regions to participate more efficiently in widely-distributed circuitry that supports top-down, executive control of behavior. Communication among cortical regions can ensure that the most adaptive and refined plans are generated, while improved cortico-subcortical communication enhances top-down modulation of response plan execution. This pattern suggests that fundamentally important maturation of brain systems occurring in adolescence are of a different nature than that of earlier development, and may support more effective integration of brain function across regions rather than improvements in the computational capacities of local brain function.

DEVELOPMENT OF BRAIN FUNCTION

Since synaptic pruning is not readily observable *in vivo* with conventional anatomic neuroimaging techniques, investigating brain function becomes especially important as a tool for advancing understanding of how the functional capacities of brain systems develop relative to their structure. Initial developmental studies investigating brain function used electroencephalography (EEG) and positron emission tomography (PET). Increased coherence of EEG activity was found across neocortical regions throughout adolescence, primarily between frontal and other cortical areas.[45] These findings were confirmed by PET results demonstrating changes in the local cerebral resting metabolic rates of frontal, parietal, and temporal regions throughout childhood that began to appear adult-like in adolescence.[46] These findings are important in indicating a late integration of the frontal lobe into widely distributed brain circuitry, however, these procedures have limited spatial resolution. Moreover, because of the invasive nature of PET, its use is restricted in healthy pediatric populations. In contrast, fMRI is a non-invasive neuroimaging procedure that also allows the *in vivo* investigation of brain activity that underlies cognitive function in pediatric populations and provides higher spatial resolution to localize brain function. fMRI provides an indirect assessment of neuronal activity by measuring the changes in blood oxygenation levels produced by increases in metabolic demands resulting from regional neuronal activity that supports the cognitive process of interest.

Several fMRI studies have compared brain function in children and adults during performance of response inhibition tasks. Increased activation of the prefrontal cortex in children compared to adults was found during the performance of a go-no-go task, suggesting it is a more effortful task for children.[47] When performance is matched between children and adults in a mixed go-no-go (inhibition of an established response) and flanker task (interference control), children have been found to have decreased recruitment of prefrontal cortex.[48] A similar reduction in prefrontal activation was demonstrated in 12–19-year-old subjects compared to 22–40-year-old subjects in a task requiring the suppression of an established response.[49] In contrast to adults, adolescents demonstrated increased activation in caudate and inferior frontal gyrus. Age-related increases in prefrontal function were also found during a Stroop interference task,[50] where, again, adolescents demonstrated mature parietal, but reduced prefrontal recruitment compared to adults. Finally, younger subjects were found to have increased activation of the inferior frontal gyrus, presumably because of the required effort to perform the task, and decreased activity of the middle frontal gyrus, possibly due to its specialized role in response inhibition.[51] Taken together, developmental fMRI studies indicate that the prefrontal cortex is involved in response inhibition early in childhood and that its relative participation changes with maturity.

However, it is the ability to inhibit responses consistently and not their emergence that characterizes the transition to mature performance, and it is this process that we propose may be subserved by other maturational factors underlying enhanced brain functional integration. It is worthy to note that many developmental studies of cognitive control have focused primarily on the role of prefrontal cortex and, thus, may have underestimated the developmental importance of larger-scale changes in widely distributed brain circuitry. While it is generally accepted that the prefrontal cortex plays a crucial role in higher-order cognition, it is also now well-established that these executive functions are subserved by widely distributed and integrated brain systems rather than by the prefrontal cortex alone.[52] As described above, EEG and PET studies[45,46] suggest that, in conjunction with developmental improvements in the intrinsic computational capacity of prefrontal cortex, there is increased integration of prefrontal cortex with other brain regions during adolescence.

We have focused on characterizing changes in the distribution of brain function from childhood through adolescence during the performance of a voluntary response suppression task.[53] We conducted an fMRI study of 36 healthy subjects ranging in age from 8–30 to model developmental changes in the brain substrate of antisaccade task performance (FIG. 1). Blocks of trials where a green cross hair indicated that subjects were to look toward peripheral targets (prosaccade trials) were compared to

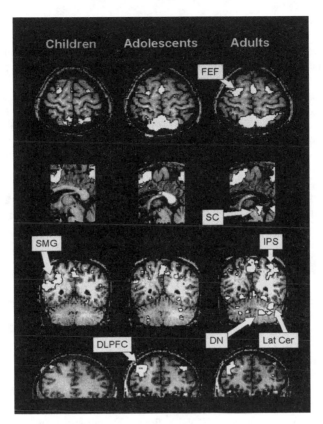

FIGURE 2. Group activation maps of regions activated ($t > 4.0$) during blocks of anti-saccade trials compared to blocks of prosaccade trials superimposed on the structural anatomic image of a representative subject (26-year-old female) warped into Talairach space. Columns show the average activation for each age group. FEF = frontal eye field; SC = superior colliculus; SMG = supramarginal sulcus; IPS = intraparietal sulcus; DLPFC = dorsolateral prefrontal cortex; Lat Cer = lateral cerebellum; and DN = dentate nucleus of the cerebellum. (From Luna et al.[53] Reprinted by permission.)

blocks of trials where a red cross indicated that eye movements to the mirror location of the cue were to be made (antisaccade trials). Activation across the whole brain was compared in children, adolescents, and adults. Results indicated that, across the age span, subjects recruited a widely distributed circuitry including the frontal, supplementary, and parietal eye fields, dorsolateral prefrontal cortex, thalamus, and striatum (FIG. 2). Adults demonstrated increased activation in regions known to play a role in the establishment of the preparatory state needed to successfully perform antisaccades, including frontal and parietal eye fields and the superior colliculus.[29,54] Additionally, only adults recruited regions in the lateral cerebellum that underlie cognitive processes related to timing and learning.[55] In contrast, adolescents demonstrated higher activation of DLPFC and striatum relative to children and adolescents, reflecting the increased difficulty in performing the task at adult levels and their ability to compensate by relying on the fronto-striatal circuitry that is accessible at this age. Children relied more on posterior parietal regions reflecting increased use of visuospatial processing. These results indicate that the increased integration of distant brain regions underlies improved efficiency with maturity in the cognitive control of behavior. The age-related changes we found in the prefrontal cortex support other studies indicating that the increased participation of brain regions supporting executive and attentional control are important in the maturation of voluntary response suppression. We extend these findings by proposing that the recruitment of regions underlying preparation and refined responses are also crucial to adult-level performance. Immature subjects are able to suppress prepotent responses and interference, but what improves with age is the consistency with which this behavioral state is maintained. We propose that this stage of maturation, encompassing adolescence, may be characterized by increased reliance on more widely distributed brain systems that incorporate regions not primarily involved in generating a voluntary response, but instead in the cognitive control, timing, and preparation of responses that improves the consistent control of behavior.

Developmental fMRI studies of voluntary response suppression indicate that brain function changes with increased age and improved behavioral performance. We still need to characterize the relative contributions of localized brain regions and identify those that are most dependent on the integration of whole brain processes and whose contributions are most essential to task performance. Our initial studies using an event-related design, allowing us to distinguish activation related to the preparation to inhibit a response from the response itself, indicate that adolescents are approximating the adult activation profile, but they do not yet activate the entire circuitry efficiently. Though adolescents may, at times, demonstrate mature response inhibition, the integration of brain circuitry supporting cognitively controlled behavior is still not working at adult levels.

The results indicating that adolescents' brain function is still not mature despite their improving performance suggests that this may be a vulnerable system that could fail under "hot" high demanding situations, where the circuitry is not sufficiently established to sustain adult-level cognitive control of behavior in the face of heightened states of affect or motivation, or distracting stimuli and competing tasks. This immature system may be particularly vulnerable to breaking down in neurodevelopmental psychiatric disorders, such as schizophrenia and attention deficit disorders, where the transition from localized to distributed function may become compromised and when other factors stress the system or in the context of abnormal brain maturation. With the background of methods and findings from normative psychological developmental research, we can now begin to explore possible failures in development that are associated with these neurodevelopmental psychiatric disorders.[56,57] Further, by studying populations at heightened familial risk for disorders, we can examine when the developmental dysmaturation of executive abilities begins to diverge from normal processes.

DISTRIBUTED BRAIN FUNCTION

Although regional specificity of computational capacities in the brain is well established, additional properties emerge from the interaction of different brain regions. The investigation of the brain basis of cognition has usually focused on neuronal computational capacity in specific brain regions, while functional integration has been viewed as the hierarchical processing of information through discrete regions. This view proposes that each brain region works at a different stage of the information processing stream from sensory to higher-level associations. This approach has lead to important discoveries regarding the neuronal basis of cognition including the characterization of neuronal circuits in prefrontal cortex with the capacity to maintain activation related to the maintenance and manipulation of information over time (delay-dependent cells supporting working memory).[58] However, we now know that these delay-dependent cells are also present in the medial dorsal nucleus of the thalamus as well as parietal cortex,[58] and anatomical studies indicate that most associational connections in neocortex are reciprocal, enabling the concurrent and recurrent activation of brain regions. The current view is that higher-order cognition is subserved by widely distributed, functionally integrated circuitry.[52] This theory has spawned a novel approach to the understanding of distributed brain function[59] that extends initial localization findings by focusing on the contributions of the coordination of brain function. In this view, cognitive control of behavior results from the reciprocal interactions among different regions of the brain, such as through periods of synchronized activity, instead of a hierarchical transformation of information. Synchronicity between occipital, parietal, and frontal regions has been found during face processing,[60] working memory,[61] and the acquisition and retrieval of memories.[62] This capacity for synchronous function across distant brain regions is supported by synaptic pruning and myelination allowing for the establishment of specific frequencies of activation that can be rapidly transmitted through a circuit supporting resonant and sustained integration. Synchronization could also support cognitive development during adolescence by improving distributed brain function and enhancing cognitive control of behavior.

THEORY OF COGNITIVE AND BRAIN MATURATION

Given our initial results, the brain maturational events of adolescence, and single-cell recording studies underscoring the importance of widely distributed circuitry, we propose that adolescence may be a period where there is an important transition to efficient brain collaboration. Traditional theory of cognitive and brain maturation suggests that higher-order cognitive development is due to a late maturation of frontal circuitry.[20,63–65] This viewpoint is based on early histological studies[41,42] showing a late stabilization of synaptic pruning and myelination in the frontal, relative to visual, cortex in humans and is not consistent with more recent non-human primate studies showing concurrent development throughout association areas of neocortex.[66] This view has implications on how we view cognitive development by suggesting that executive abilities do not emerge until the brain is fully mature in its ability to work in an integrated manner. A careful review of these studies, alongside recent MRI[67–69] and histological data,[70] demonstrates, contrary to the traditional theory, a dynamic late maturation throughout the neocortex,[58,71] that may provide the basis for increased control by prefrontal systems. We propose that the expansion of functional integration allows for the more efficient use of the widely distributed circuitry that is known to underlie adult-level higher-order cognition, and for prefrontal systems to play more effective roles in the cognitive control of behavior.[72] Adolescence may mark the beginning of a new stage in the brain-behavior relationship where newly established distributed brain function, in preference to more regional control, governs behavior. This parallels a transition from exogenous to endogenous control of behavior, or control of behavior by internal plans rather than external stimuli. This view of cognitive maturation suggests that, while development in childhood is characterized by gaining abilities, maturation in adolescence consists of a qualitative difference in the way existing capacities are functionally integrated. In this new framework, the emergence of some major psychiatric illnesses can be viewed, not as a loss of cognitive abilities, but as an inability to shift to this new mode of operation that would normally emerge in adolescence. Our investigations make an important contribution by laying out ideas and methodologies to investigate the coming on-line of widely distributed function in health and disease.

SUMMARY AND CONCLUSIONS

Adolescence marks the beginning of the adult-level consistent cognitive control of behavior, however, brain function is not yet operating at a mature level and increased effort is required due to the inefficient use of distributed brain systems. The lack of efficient brain integration may account for some behavioral characteristics of adolescence, such as being driven by external stimuli that overcome the still unstable systems for the voluntary control of behavior (impulsivity). This period of instability may be an inherent aspect of the natural progression to adulthood, as brain systems become more stabile and less plastic. In this theory, maturation is the ability to consistently control behavior, which is supported by established collaborative brain networks.

REFERENCES

1. DIAMOND, A. & P.S. GOLDMAN-RAKIC. 1989. Comparison of human infants and rhesus monkeys on Piaget's AB task: Evidence for dependence on dorsolateral prefrontal cortex. Exp. Brain Res. **74:** 24–40.
2. LEVIN, H.S., K.A. CULHANE, J. HARTMANN, et al. 1991. Developmental changes in performance on tests of purported frontal lobe functioning. Dev. Neuropsychol. **7:** 377–395.
3. DEMETRIOU, A., C. CHRISTOU, G. SPANOUDIS, et al. 2002. The development of mental processing: Efficiency, working memory, and thinking. Monogr. Soc. Res. Child Dev. **67:** 1–155; discussion 156.
4. ANDERSON, V.A., P. ANDERSON, E. NORTHAM, et al. 2001. Development of executive functions through late childhood and adolescence in an Australian sample. Dev. Neuropsychol. **20:** 385–406.
5. DAVIES, P.L. & J.D. ROSE. 1999. Assessment of cognitive development in adolescents by means of neuropsychological tasks. Dev. Neuropsychol. **15:** 227–248.
6. FISCHER, B., M. BISCALDI & S. GEZECK. 1997. On the development of voluntary and reflexive components in human saccade generation. Brain Res. **754:** 285–297.
7. MUNOZ, D.P., J.R. BROUGHTON, J.E. GOLDRING, et al. 1998. Age-related performance of human subjects on saccadic eye movement tasks. Exp. Brain Res. **121:** 391–400.
8. LUNA, B., K.E. GARVER, T.A. URBAN, et al. 2004. Child Dev. In press.

9. FUKUSHIMA, J., T. HATTA & K. FUKUSHIMA. 2000. Development of voluntary control of saccadic eye movements. I. Age-related changes in normal children. Brain Dev. **22:** 173–180.

10. KLEIN, C. & F. FOERSTER. 2001. Development of prosaccade and antisaccade task performance in participants aged 6 to 26 years. Psychophysiology **38:** 179–189.

11. ZALD, D.H. & W.G. IACONO. 1998. The development of spatial working memory abilities. Dev. Neuropsychol. **14:** 563–578.

12. WILLIAMS, B.R., J.S. PONESSE, R.J. SCHACHAR, et al. 1999. Development of inhibitory control across the life span. Dev. Psychol. **35:** 205–213.

13. SWANSON, H.L. 1999. What develops in working memory? A life span perspective. Dev. Psychol. **35:** 986–1000.

14. FUSTER, J.M. 1997. The Prefrontal Cortex. Raven Press. New York.

15. BJORKLUND, D.F. & K.K. HARNISHFEGER. 1995. The evolution of inhibition mechanisms and their role in human cognition and behavior In Interference and Inhibition in Cognition. F.N. Dempster & C.J. Brainerd, Eds.: 141–173. Academic Press, Inc. San Diego, CA.

16. DEMPSTER, F.N. 1992. The rise and fall of the inhibitory mechanism: Toward a unified theory of cognitive development and aging. Dev. Rev. **12:** 45–75.

17. GUITTON, D., H.A. BUCHTEL & R.M. DOUGLAS. 1985. Frontal lobe lesions in man cause difficulties in suppressing reflexive glances and in generating goal-directed saccades. Exp. Brain Res. **58:** 455–472.

18. SWEENEY, J.A., M.A. MINTUN, S. KWEE, et al. 1996. Positron emission tomography study of voluntary saccadic eye movements and spatial working memory. J. Neurophysiol. **75:** 454–468.

19. PAUS, T., V. BABENKO & T. RADIL. 1990. Development of an ability to maintain verbally instructed central gaze fixation studied in 8- to 10-year-old children. Int. J. Psychophysiol. **10:** 53–61.

20. LUCIANA, M. & C. NELSON. 1998. The functional emergence of prefrontally-guided working memory systems in four- to eight-year-old children. Neuropsychologia **36:** 273–293.

21. WISE, L.A., J.A. SUTTON & P.D. GIBBONS. 1975. Decrement in Stroop interference time with age. Percept. Mot. Skills **41:** 149–150.

22. TIPPER, S.P., T.A. BOURQUE, S.H. ANDERSON, et al. 1989. Mechanisms of attention: a developmental study. J. Exp. Child Psychol. **48:** 353–378.

23. RIDDERINKHOF, K.R., G.P.H. BAND & G.D. LOGAN. 1999. A study of adaptive behavior: effects of age and irrelevant information on the ability to inhibit one's actions. Acta Psychol. **101:** 315–337.

24. GREENBERG, L.M. & I.D. WALDMAN. 1993. Developmental normative data on the test of variables of attention (T.O.V.A.). J. Child Psychol. Psychiatry **34:** 1019–1030.

25. SWEENEY, J.A., C. ROSANO, R.A. BERMAN, et al 2001. Inhibitory control of attention declines more than working memory during normal aging. Neurobiol. Aging **22:** 39–47.

26. OLINCY, A., R.G. ROSS, D.A. YOUNG, et al. 1997. Age diminishes performance on an antisaccade eye movement task. Neurobiol. Aging **18:** 483–489.

27. HASHER, L., E.R. STOLTZFUS, R.T. ZACKS, et al. 1991. Age and inhibition. J. Exp. Psychol. Learn. Mem. Cogn. **17:** 163–169.

28. BURMAN, D.D. & C.J. BRUCE. 1997. Suppression of task-related saccades by electrical stimulation in the primate's frontal eye field. J. Neurophysiol. **77:** 2252–2267.

29. EVERLING, S., M.C. DORRIS, R.M. KLEIN, et al. 1999. Role of primate superior colliculus in preparation and execution of anti-saccades and pro-saccades. J. Neurosci. **19:** 2740–2754.

30. FUNAHASHI, S., M.V. CHAFEE & P.S. GOLDMAN-RAKIC. 1993. Prefrontal neuronal activity in rhesus monkeys performing a delayed anti-saccade task. Nature **365:** 753–756.

31. GOTTLIEB, J. & M.E. GOLDBERG. 1999. Activity of neurons in the lateral intraparietal area of the monkey during an antisaccade task. Nature Neurosci. **2:** 906–912.

32. SCHLAG-REY, M., N. AMADOR, H. SANCHEZ, et al. 1997. Antisaccade performance predicted by neuronal activity in the supplementary eye field. Nature **390:** 398–401.

33. MURI, R.M., O. HEID, A.C. NIRKKO, et al. 1998. Functional organisation of saccades and antisaccades in the frontal lobe in humans: a study with echo planar functional magnetic resonance imaging. J. Neurol. Neurosurg. Psychiatry **65:** 374–377.

34. DORICCHI, F., D. PERANI, C. INCOCCIA, *et al.* 1997. Neural control of fast-regular saccades and antisaccades: an investigation using positron emission tomographytomography. Exp. Brain Res. **116:** 50–62.
35. O'DRISCOLL, G.A., N.M. ALPERT, S.W. MATTHYSSE, *et al.* 1995. Functional neuroanatomy of antisaccade eye movements investigated with positron emission tomography. Proc. Natl. Acad. Sci. USA **92:** 925–929.
36. ARMSTRONG, E., A. SCHLEICHER, H. OMRAN, *et al.* 1995. The ontogeny of human gyrification. Cereb. Cortex **5:** 56–63.
37. CAVINESS V.S., *et al.* 1996. The developing human brain: A morphometric profile. In Developmental Neuroimaging: Mapping the development of brain and behavior. R.W. Thatcher et al, Eds.: 3–14. Academic Press. New York.
38. GIEDD, J.N., A.C. VAITUZIS, S.D. HAMBURGER, *et al.* 1996. Quantitative MRI of the temporal lobe, amygdala, and hippocampus in normal human development: ages 4-18 years. J. Comp. Neurol. **366:** 223–230.
39. REISS, A.L., M.T. ABRAMS, H.S. SINGER, *et al.* 1996. Brain development, gender and IQ in children. A volumetric imaging study. Brain **119:** 1763–1774.
40. CHANGEUX, J.P. & A. DANCHIN. 1976. Selective stabilisation of developing synapses as a mechanism for the specification of neuronal networks. Nature **264:** 705–712.
41. HUTTENLOCHER, P.R. 1990. Morphometric study of human cerebral cortex development. Neuropsychologia **28:** 517–527.
42. YAKOVLEV P.I. & A.R. LECOURS. 1967. Regional Development of the Brain in Early Life. Blackwell Scientific. Oxford.
43. JERNIGAN, T.L., D.A. TRAUNER, J.R. HESSELINK, *et al.* 1991. Maturation of human cerebrum observed in vivo during adolescence. Brain **114:** 2037–2049.
44. PFEFFERBAUM, A., D.H. MATHALON, E.V. SULLIVAN, *et al.* 1994. A quantitative magnetic resonance imaging study of changes in brain morphology from infancy to late adulthood. Arch. Neurol. **51:** 874–887.
45. THATCHER, R.W., R.A. WALKER & S. GIUDICE. 1987. Human cerebral hemispheres develop at different rates and ages. Science **236:** 1110–1113.
46. CHUGANI, H.T. 1998. A critical period of brain development: studies of cerebral glucose utilization with PET. Prev. Med. **27:** 184–188.
47. CASEY, B.J., R.J. TRAINOR, J.L. ORENDI, *et al.* 1997. A developmental functional MRI study of prefrontal activation during performance of a go-no-go task. J. Cogn. Neurosci. **9:** 835–847.
48. BUNGE, S.A., N.M. DUDUKOVIC, M.E. THOMASON, *et al.* 2002. Immature frontal lobe contributions to cognitive control in children: evidence from fMRI. Neuron **33:** 301–311.
49. RUBIA, K., S. OVERMEYER, E. TAYLOR, *et al.* 2000. Functional frontalisation with age: mapping neurodevelopmental trajectories with fMRI. Neurosci. Biobehav. Rev. **24:** 13–19.
50. ADLEMAN, N.E., V. MENON, C.M. BLASEY, *et al.* 2002. A developmental fMRI study of the Stroop Color-Word task. NeuroImage **16:** 61–75.
51. TAMM, L., V. MENON & A.L. REISS. 2002. Maturation of brain function associated with response inhibition. J. Am. Acad. Child Adolesc. Psychiatry **41:** 1231–1238.
52. GOLDMAN-RAKIC, P.S. 1988. Topography of cognition: parallel distributed networks in primate association cortex. Annu. Rev. Neurosci. **11:** 137–156.
53. LUNA, B., K.R. THULBORN, D.P. MUNOZ, *et al.* 2001. Maturation of widely distributed brain function subserves cognitive development. NeuroImage **13:** 786–793.
54. EVERLING, S. & D.P. MUNOZ. 2000. Neuronal correlates for preparatory set associated with pro-saccades and anti-saccades in the primate frontal eye field. J. Neurosci. **20:** 387–400.
55. KIM, S.G., K. UGURBIL & P.L. STRICK. 1994. Activation of a cerebellar output nucleus during cognitive processing. Science **265:** 949–951.
56. LUNA, B. & J.A. SWEENEY. 1999. Cognitive functional magnetic resonance imaging at very-high-field: eye movement control. Top. Magn. Reson. Imaging **10:** 3–15.
57. LUNA, B., N.J. MINSHEW, K.E. GARVER, *et al.* 2002. Neocortical system abnormalities in autism: An fMRI study of spatial working memory. Neurology **59:** 1–7.
58. GOLDMAN-RAKIC, P.S. 1987. Development of cortical circuitry and cognitive function. Child Dev. **58:** 601–622.

59. VARELA, F., J.P. LACHAUX, E. RODRIGUEZ, et al. 2001. The brainweb: phase synchronization and large-scale integration. Nature Rev. Neurosci. **2**: 229–239.
60. RODRIGUEZ, E., N. GEORGE, J.P. LACHAUX, et al. 1999. Perception's shadow: long-distance synchronization of human brain activity. Nature **397**: 430–433.
61. SARNTHEIN, J., H. PETSCHE, P. RAPPELSBERGER, et al. 1998. Synchronization between prefrontal and posterior association cortex during human working memory. Proc. Natl. Acad. Sci. USA **95**: 7092–7096.
62. BUZSAKI, G. 1996. The hippocampo-neocortical dialogue. Cereb. Cortex **6**: 81–92.
63. HUDSPETH, W.J. & K.H. PRIBRAM. 1990. Stages of brain and cognitive maturation. J. Educ. Psychol. **82**: 881–884.
64. STUSS, D.T. 1992. Biological and psychological development of executive functions. Brain Cogn. **20**: 8–23.
65. DIAMOND, A. & C. TAYLOR. 1996. Development of an aspect of executive control: development of the abilities to remember what I said and to "do as I say, not as I do". Dev. Psychobiol. **29**: 315–334.
66. RAKIC, P., J.P. BOURGEOIS, M.F. ECKENHOFF, et al. 1986. Concurrent overproduction of synapses in diverse regions of the primate cerebral cortex. Science **232**: 232–235.
67. GIEDD, J.N., J. BLUMENTHAL, N.O. JEFFRIES, et al. 1999. Brain development during childhood and adolescence: a longitudinal MRI study. Nature Neurosci. **2**: 861–863.
68. SOWELL, E.R., P.M. THOMPSON, K.D. TESSNER, et al. 2001. Mapping continued brain growth and gray matter density reduction in dorsal frontal cortex: Inverse relationships during postadolescent brain maturation. J. Neurosci. **21**: 8819–8829.
69. PAUS, T., A. ZIJDENBOS, K. WORSLEY, et al. 1999. Structural maturation of neural pathways in children and adolescents: in vivo study. Science **283**: 1908–1911.
70. BENES, F.M. 1998. Brain development, VII. Human brain growth spans decades. Am. J. Psychiatry **155**: 1489.
71. DENNIS, M. 1991. Frontal lobe function in childhood and adolescence: a heuristic for assessing attention regulation, executive control, and the intentional states important for social discourse. Dev. Neuropsychol. **7**: 327–358.
72. GOLDMAN-RAKIC, P.S., M. CHAFEE & H. FRIEDMAN. 1993. Allocation of function in distributed circuits. In Brain Mechanisms of Perception and Memory: From Neuron to Behavior. T. Ono et al., Eds.: 445–456. Oxford University Press. New York.

Regulatory Processes, Risk, and Resilience in Adolescent Development

ANN S. MASTEN

Institute of Child Development, University of Minnesota,
Minneapolis, Minnesota 55455-0345, USA

ABSTRACT: This article highlights the potential of developmental psychopathology as a useful integrative perspective for the challenging task of linking the study of brain development and adolescent behavior in context; it considers clues from behavioral research on resilience on the nature of regulatory processes as risks and assets, or vulnerabilities and protective factors for the development of competence and psychopathology in adolescence; and it advocates more integrative neurobehavioral research on risk and resilience in adolescent development.

KEYWORDS: developmental psychopathology; resilience; regulatory processes; adolescents

Understanding successful and unsuccessful pathways through adolescence is clearly vital to the sciences concerned with human development in all its forms at all levels, and also to the stakeholders in the health and well-being of adolescents and the citizens they will become—parents, practitioners, policy-makers, communities, society, and young people themselves. At the beginning of the 21st century, we stand at an exciting and challenging juncture in the effort to illuminate the processes that account for normative and deviant patterns of development entering and leaving adolescence and the strategies that may work to alter pathways in more favorable directions. This volume highlights the potential of advances in the neurobehavioral sciences to elucidate processes that contribute to successful development and psychopathology in adolescence. At the same time, it is clear we have a long way to go not only in charting basic brain development in adolescence, but in understanding the complex interplay of individual adolescents and the contexts in which their development unfolds. Adolescent brain development is inextricably embedded in a much larger network of interacting systems that profoundly influence how the brain develops and how adolescents put their brains to use as they make their way through life.

This article has three goals: (1) to highlight the potential of developmental psychopathology as a useful integrative perspective for the challenging task of linking the study of brain development and adolescent behavior in context, and (2) to consider clues from behavioral research on resilience on the nature of regulatory pro-

Address for correspondence: Ann S. Masten, Institute of Child Development, 51 East River Road, Minneapolis, MN 55455-0345. Voice: 612-624-0215; fax: 612-624-6373.
amasten@umn.edu

Ann. N.Y. Acad. Sci. 1021: 310–319 (2004). © 2004 New York Academy of Sciences.
doi: 10.1196/annals.1308.036

cesses as risks and assets, or vulnerabilities and protective factors for the development of competence and psychopathology in adolescence; and (3) to advocate for more integrative neurobehavioral research on risk and resilience in adolescent development.

DEVELOPMENTAL PSYCHOPATHOLOGY AND THE ADOLESCENT

The developmental psychopathology perspective, reinforced by theory and data from studies of risk and resilience, underscores the importance of a dynamic systems model of development that embeds adolescent development, including individual brain development, in a larger network of social and cultural systems. Interactions of individuals and the systems in which development unfolds not only serve regulatory functions for individual behavior but also shape and are shaped by brain development.

Developmental psychopathology is an integrative approach to understanding behavior problems in the full context of human development, with a focus on variations in adaptation, the processes that account for that variation, and how patterns of maladaptation may be prevented or ameliorated. This perspective emerged over the past three decades as theory and research on child development and psychopathology converged.[1-4] This perspective has several key implications for understanding the role of brain development in adolescence.

First, developmental transitions are important. Periods of rapid or dramatic transformation in organism or context or both, which clearly is the situation both for the transition into and out of adolescence, are likely hot spots for observing onset or offset of psychopathology, and also periods when changes in vulnerabilities and opportunities may arise and redirect the course of development. A number of disorders and symptoms of psychopathology, including depression, self-injury behavior, substance abuse, eating disorders, bipolar disorder, and schizophrenia have striking developmental patterns corresponding to transitions in early and late adolescence.[5] Developmental transitions represent reorganization in multiple systems in response to changes within the organism, the context, and their many interactions. Brain development and physical maturation trigger some of these changes; however, experiences (some of them occurring as a result of adolescent decision making or cultural traditions or age-graded role transitions) also may set off cascades of change that influence gene expression and brain organization.

Second, psychopathology is assumed to arise from complex interactions of organism and the multiple systems in which the life of the organism is embedded.[6,7] Observable changes in behavior are likely to result from multiple causes (the principle of multicausality), at multiple levels of interaction, reflecting the co-action of organism and environment from genes to society. As a result, common endpoints and final pathways can emerge from diverse beginnings (the principle of equifinality) and individuals who start down the same path can end up going down many different roads over time (the principle of multifinality). From this perspective, the same problem of adolescence, whether it be violence, pregnancy, alcohol use or smoking, or self-injurious behavior is assumed to have multiple causes and arise in diverse kinds of people for diverse reasons. Similarly, the same genetic vulnerability or injury in a developing brain can result in a diverse array of subsequent phenotypes and functional variations in behavior.

This multi-systems perspective highlights the importance of connecting multiple levels of analysis and the multidisciplinary collaborators necessary to do so.[8] Developmental psychopathology increasingly reflects the integration of biological and neuroscience models and methods with the disciplines more traditionally focused on behavior and psychosocial models and methods.[9–11] In this respect, this volume exemplifies the new face of developmental psychopathology in the 21st century.

Third, the organism is an active agent in development. Individuals recruit, elicit responses, and in other ways choose and influence the contexts that in turn contribute to their development. Adolescents can choose to hang around with antisocial peers that accelerate their deviant behavior.[12] They choose to attend school or do their homework instead of attending a party. As access to electronic tools expand, adolescents can actively interact with diverse media and people all over the world, and increasingly control their interactions and exposure to people and information.[13,14] It is unclear how the "virtual worlds" of adolescents, where context can be individualized to an unprecedented degree, are influencing brain development.[5]

Fourth, the developmental psychopathology perspective assumes transactional influences between individual and other systems.[15] Individuals and their peers, families, teachers, and all the many other people they interact with in the contexts of daily life reciprocally influence each other. Adolescents behave in ways that are engaging, manipulating, off-putting, and sometimes alarming to other people in their lives, with many consequences. Moreover, the people in their lives are also interacting, such that there can be indirect consequences of adolescent behavior on others who in turn will take actions that alter subsequent adolescent experiences. Getting into trouble with peers may lead to police or school authorities interacting with parents, with subsequent consequences for the lives of adolescents. From a transactional perspective, we have just begun to chart the symphony of co-regulation that may govern the course of behavior among adolescents and the people in their lives.

Moving up to a more macro-system level of interaction, adolescents, through their collective purchasing power in modern societies also influence the clothes, movies, music, TV, food, and other products that are made and how they are marketed. Concomitantly, marketers actively recruit adolescents to buy and choose their products. Increasingly, advertising appears to be deliberately couched in regulatory terms addressing the needs and concerns of adolescents: this product will help you feel better, look better, attract sexual interest, make friends, or be cooler.

Fifth, developmental psychopathology assumes that research on positive and deviant functioning and development are mutually informative. It is crucial to understand not only pathways to problems but also the pathways away from problems. Thus, developmental psychopathology encompasses the study of good and poor adaptation, competence and symptoms, risks and assets, vulnerabilities and protective factors. It is assumed that a full understanding of psychopathology and problems requires a deep understanding of normative and deviant processes that may be involved in etiology and prevention. Studies of naturally occurring pathways are important, as are studies to experimentally manipulate the direction of development.

Sixth, the developmental psychopathology perspective emphasizes the importance of longitudinal studies for understanding the interplay of genes, individual and context, at multiple levels, in shaping development. Variations in the causes, tempo, context, and timing of development within and across systems, within and across individuals can create very misleading conclusions in cross-sectional studies, as noted by theorists and statisticians.[16] Moreover, hindsight has a habit of leading one to misguided conclusions about continuity and change in development. Prospective, longitudinal studies are quintessential developmental psychopathology because they are much more likely to reveal unexpected pathways toward and away from the behavior of interest.

The importance of a longitudinal perspective obtains for experimental studies of intervention as well as for studies of naturally occurring pathways in development. An important illustration of this point can be found in the Seattle Social Development Project.[17–19] Utilizing data from a large prospective panel study of antisocial behavior, these investigators have illustrated pathways toward and away from serious antisocial behavior and examined the predictors of those pathways, utilizing innovative methods of growth curve analysis and identification of developmental trajectories popularized by Nagin[20] and others. Utilizing data from a longitudinal panel study, they have examined divergence and convergence of pathways from various starting levels of antisocial behavior at age 13, in search of the predictors of pathways and change. Beginning from a moderate level of juvenile offenses, for example, desisting versus escalating pathways are predicted by individual characteristics (aggression, internalizing symptoms) and also neighborhood qualities (drug availability). Beginning with low levels of offenses, escalating pathways (late onset offending) versus holding the positive course of no offending are forecasted by greater antisocial peer involvement, lower school bonding, and more drug availability in the neighborhood. Other kinds of risky behavior (such as teen pregnancy and drug problems) are also predictable from similar risk or protective factors in the adolescent or environment in this study.

As part of the same project, these investigators have embedded an experimental intervention into a subgroup of the children in this study, all residents of risky neighborhoods for antisocial behavior. Based on their social development model, they designed an intervention targeting processes believed to influence movement onto prosocial or antisocial pathways, including school bonding. There were three groups compared in this longitudinal intervention trial, with schools assigned to different treatment conditions: a full treatment group who received a multifaceted intervention throughout elementary school, a late treatment group that received only the late elementary school years of the program, and a comparison group with no intervention participating in the panel study. Results are compelling in several ways. First, the intervention worked to reduce multiple kinds of risky behavior as assessed years later.[19] Second, the intervention resulted in greater school bonding, a key hypothesized mediator of pathways toward or away from antisocial behavior. Third, the treatment effects could be attributed to school bonding. Generally their results are consistent with the idea that school bonding is a protective factor in the battle against antisocial development and that efforts to create stronger bonds by intervening in elementary school can work.

However, the data are quite interesting in another way. The treatment effects evident for the full treatment group are clear at age 13 (a year after the treatment had concluded) and then disappear for several years (ages 14 to 16) only to re-emerge later in adolescence. If the follow-up assessment for this prevention study had been limited to one assessment at age 15, conclusions would be quite different about whether and how it worked. It is intriguing to consider the possibility that treatment effects were temporarily swamped by the noise of developmental change during the early teen years. It is also conceivable that acting "unbonded" to school is normative during the early secondary school years, whereas open involvement and attachment to school is normative later on in high school. In any case, these data underscore the important of longitudinal data for a clear picture of change over the course of adolescent development.

RESILIENCE RESEARCH IN DEVELOPMENTAL PSYCHOPATHOLOGY

Hints about Regulatory Processes Implicating Brain Development in Adolescence

The study of behavioral resilience phenomena in developmental psychopathology may offer some important clues about the significance of regulatory processes for successful passages through adolescence and the corresponding role of brain development and processes in regulating affect, arousal, and behavior. The study of resilience had its beginnings in the study of populations at risk for psychopathology, as part of an effort to study etiological processes.[20–24] Prospective developmental studies of children at risk for problems led to the observation that there are diverse outcomes (i.e., multifinality) among groups of children considered to be a risk due to their status as a member of a known risk group (with elevated probability of some undesired outcome) or their known exposure to psychosocial adversities strongly associated with problems, such as family violence or poverty. The striking phenomenon of individuals with successful development among groups of very high-risk children inspired a pioneering group of investigators to study the processes that could account for such apparent resilience. This body of work, encompassing a vast array of risk factors, outcomes, and possible mediating or moderating processes, from diverse situations and cultures, consistently points to a "short list" (TABLE 1) of factors linked to better outcomes in adolescence and more successful transitions from childhood to adolescence and adolescence to adulthood.[25–28] This list may reflect the operation of fundamental human adaptation systems common to all or many human lives that play a central role in psychosocial development.[22] Some of these systems can be located at a given time in the adolescent (such as cognitive abilities and executive functioning) and some of which are located in the context (such as effective parenting and good schools). However, all of these systems develop and change over time, and therefore must reflect the dynamic interactions of all the systems involved in development. The most damaging hazards in human development may be the ones that damage or alter these adaptive systems. Children can and do overcome horrible experiences; however, there are situations that have lasting consequences mediated by alterations in important adaptive systems, including brain damage or deviations resulting from maltreatment, malnutrition, or neglect. These systems also may be influenced by genes or genetic defects that constrain development (e.g., Down syndrome) or genetic vulnerabilities that impair the development of adaptive systems under certain conditions, as postulated in diathesis-stressor models of mental disorders (e.g., schizophrenia).

It is worth noting that the most widely implicated factors associated with maladaptation versus resilience in adolescents all implicate what might be termed regulatory capital. A speculative list is provided in TABLE 2. Like "human capital," some

TABLE 1. The "short list" of widely reported correlates and predictors of resilience in youth

One or more effective parents

Connections to other competent and caring adults

Cognitive, attention, and problem-solving skills

Effective emotion and behavior regulation

Positive self-perceptions (of efficacy, worth)

Beliefs that life has meaning; hopefulness

Religious faith and affiliations

Aptitudes and characteristics valued by society (e.g., talent, attractiveness)

Prosocial friends

Socioeconomic advantages

Effective school, school bonding

Effective community (e.g., safe, with emergency services, recreation centers)

TABLE 2. Regulatory processes implicated by studies of resilience

Executive functioning

Emotion regulation

Attachments to adults who monitor and support youth effectively

Relationships with peers who up- or down-regulate others effectively

Bonding to prosocial socializing and community organizations

Opportunities for regulatory capacity-building

of these resources are attributes of the individual and how well the central nervous system is operating to direct successful behavior, such as intellectual skills, quality of executive functioning, or good concentration skills. Others, like "social capital," are resources derived from connections to other people, and draw on the regulatory effectiveness of these relationships or people, such as effective parenting or strong mentoring relationships. Still others reflect connections to social and cultural organizations that provide structure, rules, expectations, and support, such as schools, sport teams, clubs, and religious organizations. Sampson and colleagues[29] have described neighborhoods high on this type of social and regulatory capital as high in "collective efficacy," a measurable neighborhood attribute that is associated with fewer problems in youth.

These systems could operate in a number of ways. Some children appear to enter the challenging period of adolescence with poor regulatory skills, reflecting earlier processes and experiences: they do not have what is required for safe negotiation of the challenges of adolescence, particularly in the risky environments they are likely to face. In other cases, adolescents appear to have adequate regulatory capacity, but it becomes misdirected (from society's point of view) toward negative aims or even co-opted by antisocial peers and adults. This may occur as a result of bad neighborhoods or peer influences, real and perceived oppression or discrimination, war, etc.

Still other adolescents may flourish despite risky environments or faulty brain function, through compensatory processes. Thus, this literature hints that for some adolescents, the problem is poor regulatory skills in the organism, for others the core problem is availability of contextual resources, and for others, the core issue is how they choose to deploy perfectly adequate regulatory capacity. Clearly, it will be important to distinguish poor skills from poor applications of skills in studies to link brain development and function to behavior in adolescence. Nonetheless, the resilience literature generally suggests that good regulatory capacity, utilized effectively toward achieving competence in age-salient developmental tasks, holds the key to successfully negotiating the adolescent transition.

There are also hints in the literature on resilience that "late blooming" occurs, that there are adolescents who appear to be off-course in development, who then regroup and become successful young adults.[23,30] The processes by which this might occur are a matter of speculation; the possibilities, however, have intriguing implications for the study of brain development. One possibility is that the transition to adulthood offers greater freedom of action and more opportunities for life-altering changes in context (e.g., military service, marriage, moving to job opportunities, college). The other possibility is that a *developmental* change occurs in cognition or motivation that leads to an awakening or epiphany about the direction needed in one's life and subsequent actions to correct that course. These developmental changes in thinking and planning may result from brain developments that make it possible to reflect, plan, delay gratification, and coordinate one's motivation, behavior, and life in new ways, as referred to by Keating at this symposium, just as new opportunities are becoming available in the environment, providing chances for course correction in development as adolescents transition to adult life.

Despite many hints that regulatory processes are central to positive developmental pathways through adolescence in the resilience literature, very little work in this framework has integrated brain development and its implications into the story. Only recently are scientists undertaking explicit neurobehavioral approaches to resilience.[10,31,32]

Three waves of research are evident in the history of behavioral research on resilience developmental psychopathology.[33] The first wave, which began about three decades ago and is waning now, was characterized by identifying among young people at risk for diverse reasons the correlates and predictors of good adaptation—attributes of the individuals, their families, and communities that seem to make a difference. The second wave that ensued and continues to build is focused on identifying the processes and mechanisms "behind the factors" that may explain how resilience occurs naturally. The second-wave work is focused on mediators and moderators of adaptation in the context of risk or adversity. The third wave of work, which is just beginning, is focused on creating resilience through intervention, to put hypothesized processes to the test in experimental designs based on a risk/resilience framework. The Seattle Social Development Project[19] illustrates how all three stages of research can be combined. In their panel study, as described above, they identified predictors of good versus undesirable outcomes. One of these predictors was school bonding, a process hypothesized to mediate the pathways to good outcomes among high risk youth. In the intervention study, they attempted to moderate this mediation process (through their intervention program) to create resilience among high risk children.

The biology and neuroscience of resilience is just getting underway, thus there is likely to be some lag in the integration of brain processes into the ongoing waves of work on resilience. Hopefully, the shift from descriptive correlates to processes will progress quickly for two reasons: first, behavioral scientists have provided clues about correlates and possible processes at a behavioral level; and second, neuroscientists are rapidly advancing the basic understanding of brain processes pertinent to adaptive functioning and behavioral development.

EMERGING TRENDS IN THE DEVELOPMENTAL PSYCHOPATHOLOGY OF ADOLESCENCE

This volume reflects a transformation occurring in contemporary models of adolescent development that is also evident in the research on risk and resilience and likely results from mergers and collaborations across disciplines concerned with young people and their well-being. There is a shift to models that encompass multiple systems and multiple levels, integrating developmental theory, general systems theory, developmental epidemiology and psychiatry, behavioral genetics, molecular genetics, and neuroscience. As a result, models are more dynamic and complex. Research has moved beyond individual and family influences to address peer, neighborhood, school, cultural, and media effects as well as their joint effects on the course of individual development. At the same time, there is increasing effort to add deeper models within the organism that connect more levels of neurocircuitry, molecular genetics, and biological processes to cognitive behavior, action, or adaptive outcomes. There is growing interest in "biological embedding" and related topics focused on how experience is carried forward by the individual in development but also how the organism may compensate for deficiencies in function or right itself and how brain plasticity works. There are more urgent calls for research that addresses issues of great concern to society and moves beyond understanding to preventing violence, substance abuse and binge drinking, driving accidents, obesity, self-injurious behavior, and other problems strongly associated with adolescence and with the regulation of affect, arousal, and behavior. There are questions about modern cultures and societies and how they may contribute to or prevent such problems. The continuing shift of puberty onset to earlier ages, particularly in girls, coupled with the emergence of a prolonged transition period to establish full-fledged adulthood in many societies[5,34] is raising a host of questions about the interactions of biology and context and the way we live and scaffold the development of our children on the road to adulthood and self-regulation.

It is clear that there are casualties along the way to maturity, often manifesting during transition periods, at school entry, the transition to adolescence, or the transition to adulthood. However, it is important to remember that most children become capable adults well-adapted to their society and that the road to success can be bumpy or circuitous. Periods of rapid change or development in capacity or expansion in opportunity, such as occur during the entry years into adolescence as well as the exit years, may herald a risky passageway until the regulatory capacity develops to manage new skills, opportunities, or impulses. We want adolescents to learn to drive safely, to have good friends, to effectively navigate the electronic world, and to be happy while making wise decisions about the ways they raise or lower their arousal and the contexts in which they spend their time. If, as suggested here, regulatory processes play a central role in resilience among children at risk due to adversity and disadvantage, and many of these youth do not have adequate personal or social regulatory capacity operating in their favor, then it is imperative to understand the processes by which regulatory capital can be promoted, protected, and recovered in development.

A better science of adolescent brain development is going to illuminate the processes of risk and resilience that threaten and protect young people as they navigate the years from childhood to adulthood. Eventually, our efforts to promote success and prevent casualties through these passages should provide benefits. Meanwhile, nurturing this new scientific enterprise is going to take patience, painstaking work at many levels of inquiry, collaboration among scientists from diverse fields of training, new ways of thinking and training, and thoughtful funding to facilitate the science, the training, and the collaboration that will be required.

REFERENCES

1. CICCHETTI, D. 1990. An historical perspective on the discipline of developmental psychopathology. *In* Risk and Protective Factors in the Development of Psychopathology. J. Rolf, Ed.: 2–28. Cambridge University Press. New York.
2. MASTEN, A.S. & W.J. CURTIS. 2000. Integrating competence and psychopathology: Pathways toward a comprehensive science of adaptation in development. Dev. Psychopathol. **12:** 529–550.
3. CUMMINGS, E.M., P.T. DAVIES & S.B. CAMPBELL. 2000. Developmental Psychopathology and Family Process. Guilford. New York.
4. SROUFE, L.A. & M. RUTTER. 1984. The domain of developmental psychopathology. Child Dev. **55:** 17–29.
5. STEINBERG, L., R. DAHL, D. KEATING & A.S. MASTEN. 2004. The study of developmental psychopathology in adolescence: integrating affective neuroscience with the study of context. *In* Handbook of Developmental Psychopathology, 2nd ed. D. Cicchetti & D. Cohen, Eds. Wiley. New York.
6. CICCHETTI, D. & F.A. ROGOSCH. 1996. Equifinality and multifinality in developmental psychopathology. Dev. Psychopathol. **8:** 597–600.
7. SAMEROFF, A.J. 2000. Developmental systems and psychopathology. Dev. Psychopathol. **12:** 297–312.
8. CICCHETTI, D. & G. DAWSON, Eds. 2002. Multiple levels of analysis [Special Issue]. Dev. Psychopathol. **14:** 477–666.
9. COWEN, E.L. & J.A. DURLAK. 2000. Social policy and prevention in mental health. Dev. Psychopathol. **12:** 815–834.
10. CURTIS, W.J. & C.A. NELSON. 2003. Toward building a better brain: Neurobehavioral outcomes, mechanisms, and processes of environmental enrichment. *In* Resilience and Vulnerability: adaptation in the context of childhood adversities. S. Luthar, Ed.: 463–488. Cambridge University Press. New York.
11. NELSON, C.A., F.E. BLOOM, J.L. CAMERON, *et al.* 2002. An integrative, multidisciplinary approach to the study of brain-behavior relations in the context of typical and atypical development. Dev. Psychopathol. **14:** 499–520.
12. DEATER-DECKARD, K. 2001. Annotation: Recent research examining the role of peer relationships in the development of psychopathology. J. Child Psychol. Psychiatry **42:** 565–579.
13. BROWN, J.D. 2000. Adolescents' sexual media diets. J. Adolesc. Health **27S:** 35–40.
14. BROWN, J.D. & E.W. WITHERSPOON. 2002. The mass media and American adolescents' health. J. Adolesc. Health **31:** 153–170.
15. SAMEROFF, A.J. & M.J. MACKENZIE. 2003. Research strategies for capturing transactional models of development: The limits of the possible. Dev. Psychopathol. **15:** 613–640.

16. KRAEMER, H.C., J.A. YESAVAGE, J.L. TAYLOR & D. KUPFER. 2000. How can we learn about developmental processes from cross-sectional studies, or can we? Am. J. Psychiatry 157: 163–171.
17. CHUNG, I.-J., K.G. HILL, J.D. HAWKINS, et al. 2003. Childhood predictors of offense trajectories. J. Res. Crime Delinq. 39: 60–90.
18. HAWKINS, J.D., R.F. CATALANO, R. KOSTERMAN, et al. 1999. Preventing adolescent health-risk behavior by strengthening protection during childhood. Arch. Pediatr. Adolesc. Med. 153: 226–234.
19. HAWKINS, J.D., B.H. SMITH, K.G. HILL, et al. 2003. Understanding and preventing crime and violence. In Taking Stock of Delinquency: An overview of findings from contemporary longitudinal studies. T.P. Thornberry & M.D. Krohn, Eds.: 255–312. Kluwer Academic Press. New York.
20. NAGIN, D. 1999. Analyzing developmental trajectories: Semi-parametric, group-based approach. Psychol. Methods 4: 139–170.
21. GARMEZY, N. 1985. Stress-resistant children: The search for protective factors. In Recent Research in Developmental Psychopathology: Journal of Child Psychology and Psychiatry Book Supplement #4. J.E. Stevenson, Ed.: 213–233. Pergamon Press. Oxford.
22. MASTEN, A.S. 2001. Ordinary magic: Resilience processes in development. Am. Psychol. 56: 227–238.
23. MASTEN, A.S. & J.L. POWELL. 2003. A resilience framework for research, policy, and practice. In Resilience and Vulnerability: Adaptation in the context of childhood adversities. S.S. Luthar, Ed.: 1–25. Cambridge University Press. New York.
24. RUTTER, M. 1990. Psychosocial resilience and protective mechanisms. In Risk and Protective Factors in the Development of Psychopathology J. Rolf et al. Eds.: 181–214. Cambridge University Press. New York.
25. LUTHAR, S.S., Ed. 2003. Resilience and Vulnerability: Adaptation in the context of childhood adversities. Cambridge University Press. New York.
26. MASTEN, A.S., K.M. BEST & N. GARMEZY. 1990. Resilience and development: Contributions from the study of children who overcome adversity. Dev. Psychopathol. 2: 425–444.
27. MASTEN, A.S. & J.D. COATSWORTH. 1998. The development of competence in favorable and unfavorable environments: Lessons from successful children. Am. Psychol. 53: 205–220.
28. RUTTER, M. 2000. Resilience reconsidered: Conceptual considerations, empirical findings, and policy implications. In Handbook of Early Intervention, 2nd edit. J.P. Shonkoff & S.J. Meisels, Eds.: 651–681. Cambridge University Press. New York.
29. SAMPSON, R.J., S.W. RAUDENBUSH & F. EARLS. 1997. Neighborhoods and violent crime: A multilevel study of collective efficacy. Science 277: 918–924.
30. MASTEN, A.S., K. BURT, G.I. ROISMAN, et al. 2004. Resources and resilience in the transition to adulthood: continuity and change. Dev. Psychopathol. In press.
31. CHARNEY, D.S. 2004. Psychobiological mechanisms of resilience and vulnerability: Implications for the successful adaptation to extreme stress. Arch. Gen. Psychiatry 161: 195–216.
32. CURTIS, W.J. & D. CICCHETTI. 2003. Moving research on resilience into the 21st century: Theoretical and methodological considerations in examining the biological contributors to resilience. Dev. Psychopathol. 15: 773–810.
33. WRIGHT, M O'D. & A.S. MASTEN. 2004. Resilience processes in development: Fostering positive adaptation in the context of adversity. In Handbook of Resilience in Children. S. Goldstein & R. Brooks, Eds. Kluwer/Academic/Plenum. New York. In press.
34. ARNETT, J.J. 2000. Emerging adulthood: A theory of development from the late teens through the twenties. Am. Psychol. 55: 469–480.

Adolescent Development and the Regulation of Behavior and Emotion

Comments on Part VIII

DAVID J. KUPFER AND HERMI R. WOODWARD

Western Psychiatric Institute and Clinic, Department of Psychiatry, Pittsburgh, Pennsylvania 15213, USA

In this session, we have focused on two presentations that highlight the advances we are making, both experimentally and conceptually, toward a better, more integrated understanding of adolescent development and the regulation of behavior and emotions. Drs. Beatriz Luna and John Sweeney have provided a particularly elegant example of how neuroscientists are identifying the neurosubstrates that underlie the emergence of new behaviors and regulatory skills during adolescence. Their findings indicate that by age 15, adolescents perform nearly at adult levels in a task involving response suppression, but suggest that major differences exist between adolescents and adults in what brain regions are engaged to accomplish this task. "Adult" or mature suppression is marked by an orchestration of processes in different brain regions into "collaborative brain function" that serves to accomplish the desired outcome. In adolescents, the same process requires more effortful "work," as evidenced by the imaging data showing increased DLPFC activation in adolescents, but a relative lack of collaborative function as compared to adult subjects.

Aside from the elegance of the experiments, this study also can serve as an example of how neuroscience can stimulate further conceptual development. It represents a beautiful model for operationalizing a specific component of something that all of us who have raised children through adolescence, or who have worked with adolescents, know to be true: Response suppression—the ability to control behavior according to instruction or rational understanding—is difficult to do for adolescents, and particularly so in the presence of compelling alternative forces, such as strong impulses or emotions. Behavioral control requires huge effort, and while it can be accomplished, it is less likely to be accomplished consistently during adolescence. Consistency in carrying through with intended or planned choices develops gradually and increases for most individuals as they enter later adolescence and make the transition into adulthood. What Drs. Luna and Sweeney's findings elucidate are the neurosubstrates that may underlie this developmental change: the increasing integration of brain regions involved in response suppression, and the resultant emerging efficiency in response planning and behavioral control.

Address for correspondence: David J. Kupfer, M.D., Western Psychiatric Institute and Clinic, Department of Psychiatry, 3811 O'Hara Street, Pittsburgh, PA 15213. Voice: 412-624-2353; fax: 412-624-8015.

kupferdj@msx.upmc.edu

Ann. N.Y. Acad. Sci. 1021: 320–322 (2004). © 2004 New York Academy of Sciences.
doi: 10.1196/annals.1308.037

What makes this increasing integration possible? Is it brain development unfolding on an "automatic" time line? No, more likely the continued synaptic pruning and myelination occurring during adolescence is driven by experience of adolescence, or, in other words, by the continued "practicing" of response patterns in the face of everyday life and decision making that is required during this transition. In healthy individuals, emotions and cognition become increasingly integrated as adolescents "practice" by living through the emotional and practical consequences of some bad decisions and by experiencing the exhilaration of having succeeded at producing a desired outcome through response planning and behavioral control.

Dr. Ann Masten's presentation focused on how contexts need to be viewed, not as dynamic "outside" forces that shape an adolescent's further development, but as the shapers of the very experiences that provide the practice grounds for emergent regulatory skills. Her article reminds us to what degree our conceptual models have now integrated both neuroscience approaches and context-focused research. No longer do we question whether the forces that drive adolescent behavior are highly influenced by biological factors, such as those inherent in the pubertal transition, or whether it is the biological processes of puberty that give rise to a whole new set of emotions and motivations never experienced earlier in life. Conversely, there is increasing acknowledgment that the physical transformation of a child going through puberty also sets the stage for altered contextual processes—the young adolescent treats the world differently, but is also treated differently by it. Thus, the stage is set for an all-new and ever-expanding world of experiences, both within and outside the individual. These new experiences require new regulatory skills and, at the same time, provide the very practice ground on which emergent regulatory skills can be honed and matured to adult-level functioning. Drawing on the long-term research on adolescent resilience, Dr. Masten highlights the importance of supportive contexts to provide scaffolding for the developing adolescent in this process of developing regulatory competence, particularly during the early part of adolescence when new biology and new contexts challenge regulatory skills that are emergent, but still highly immature.

Both authors have stressed the importance of this period of development as a window of both risk and opportunity. The emergence of adolescent regulatory skills and their maturation to adult levels requires a solid foundation. Dr. Masten states that children who enter adolescence with weak regulatory skills are at risk for developing problems during the transition from childhood into adulthood. Drs. Luna and Sweeney give us insight into the same problem from a brain perspective: The emergence of "collaborative brain function" requires the individual to draw on and integrate activity in different regions of the brain, to "orchestrate" brain function across regions. If any of the constituent "parts" playing in this orchestra are weak, the entire performance can be compromised. In turn, consistent failure in reaching a level of integration that is required and demanded by adolescent contexts, such as school, job, or social group, can lead to a spiral of dysfunction that may surface as mental health problems or psychopathology.

Despite much progress, we have many challenges in front of us as we move forward in our quest to understand adolescent brain and behavioral development, and specifically the emergence of regulatory skills, the cognitive/emotional integration that is an essential requirement for successful adolescent development. Given the wide range of perspectives we are seeking to integrate, it is not surprising that we still have a long way to go. One of the most critical issues is that of making experimentally accessible what is the essence of adolescence life and experience. The elegance of Drs. Luna and Sweeney's experiments not withstanding, the antisaccade task is still a very far cry from capturing the complex reality of adolescents' lives. How to bridge the enormous divide between what are the most pressing questions about healthy and/or derailed adolescent development and what we can investigate with rigorous neuroscientific tools is still an open question. Some of our brightest talents are devoting their efforts to developing tasks that begin to simulate real-life experiences and are amenable to being applied in a neuroimaging environment. We will make further progress over the next few years, but may never be able to bridge the gap altogether. However, other emergent methodologies may allow us to fill in some of the remaining divide. For example, time-sampling methods have made inroads into a more profound understanding of adolescents' day-to-day (or, perhaps more accurate for adolescents' perceptions of the passing of time, hour-to-hour) experience in real life and with the real people that constitute their social reference points. New, more portable, and less restrictive neuroscientific tools may also be developed to give us insight into the behaving brain and make it easier to chart the developmental course of specific regulatory functions over the course of the transition from childhood into adulthood.

Introduction to Short Papers

CHERYL KIRSTEIN,[a] AARON WHITE,[b] AND KYLE FRANTZ[c]

[a]University of South Florida, Department of Psychology,
Tampa,Florida 33620, USA

[b]Duke University Medical Center, Department of Psychiatry,
Durham, North Carolina 27710, USA

[c]Georgia State Univerity, Department of Biology,
Atlanta, Georgia 30303, USA

KEYWORDS: adolescence; neurobehavior; adolescent vulnerabilities; adolescent brain function; adolescent substance use

The short paper presentations at the conference reflected the wide range of innovative research programs on adolescent vulnerabilities. Both human and nonhuman studies addressed topics ranging from the molecular basis of adolescent brain function to the long-term neurobehavioral consequences of adolescent substance use. Although all of the short papers were extremely informative, the following describe those studies noted especially for their significant impact across the nascent field of research on adolescence.

Address for correspondence: Cheryl Kirstein, Ph.D., University of South Florida, Department of Psychology, 4202 E. Fowler Avenue, PCD 4118G, Tampa, FL 33620. Voice: 813-974-1958; fax: 813-974-4617.
kirstein@chuma1.cas.usf.edu

Ann. N.Y. Acad. Sci. 1021: 323 (2004). © 2004 New York Academy of Sciences.
doi: 10.1196/annals.1308.038

Development of Error-Monitoring Event-Related Potentials in Adolescents

PATRICIA L. DAVIES,[a] SIDNEY J. SEGALOWITZ,[b] AND WILLIAM J. GAVIN[c]

[a]Department of Occupational Therapy, Colorado State University, Fort Collins, Colorado 80523, USA

[b]Department of Psychology, Brock University, St. Catharines, Ontario, L2S 3A1, Canada

[c]Department of Speech, Language, and Hearing Sciences, University of Colorado, Boulder, Colorado 80309, USA

ABSTRACT: In order to study the maturation of neurobehavioral systems involved in affect regulation and behavioral choices during adolescence, we examined brain activity associated with response monitoring and error detection using event-related potentials (ERPs). In a visual flanker test, trials with incorrect responses elicit ERP components including an error-related negativity (ERN) and a later error-positivity (Pe). We examined the amplitude and latency of the ERN and Pe of incorrect responses in 124 children from 7 to 18 years of age. The ERN amplitude in error trials increased with age although this was qualified by a nonlinear change. The quadratic distribution of the ERN indicated an initial drop in amplitude (lowest at age 10 for girls; age 13 for boys) with a subsequent rise through adolescence. The Pe amplitude did not change with age. Results are discussed with respect to continued maturation of the anterior cingulate cortex and possible influences on adolescent behaviors.

KEYWORDS: error-related negativity (ERN); error monitoring; prefrontal cortex (PFC); anterior cingulate cortex (ACC); gender differences

Of particular interest in the study of adolescent behavior is the maturation of neurobehavioral systems involved in affect regulation and behavioral choices. Relevant to this area of research is event-related potential (ERP) technology, which allows the evaluation of brain activity associated with response monitoring and error detection. In a target-discrimination task, trials with incorrect responses elicit ERPs that include two components—an error-related negativity (ERN) and a later error-positivity (Pe). Substantial evidence points to the anterior cingulate cortex (ACC) as the source generator of the ERN, and the ERN is thought to be dopaminergically driven.[1] The ACC is a major part of the limbic system with massive connections to the prefrontal cortex (PFC).[2] Given the continued maturation of the ACC, PFC, and dopaminergic systems into young adulthood, our aim was to investigate the development of ERPs to correct and incorrect (error) responses.

Address for correspondence: Patricia L. Davies, 219 Occupational Therapy, Colorado State University, Fort Collins, CO 80523. Voice: 970-491-7294; fax: 970-491-6290.
pdavies@lamar.colostate.edu

Ann. N.Y. Acad. Sci. 1021: 324–328 (2004). © 2004 New York Academy of Sciences.
doi: 10.1196/annals.1308.039

METHOD

ERPs to correct and incorrect responses were recorded during a standard 480-trial visual flanker task in 124 children from 7 to 18 years of age. The electroencephalogram (EEG) was recorded from 29 scalp sites and two bipolar electro-oculograms (EOGs). Although the ERN has been shown to be strongest at FCz, some partici-

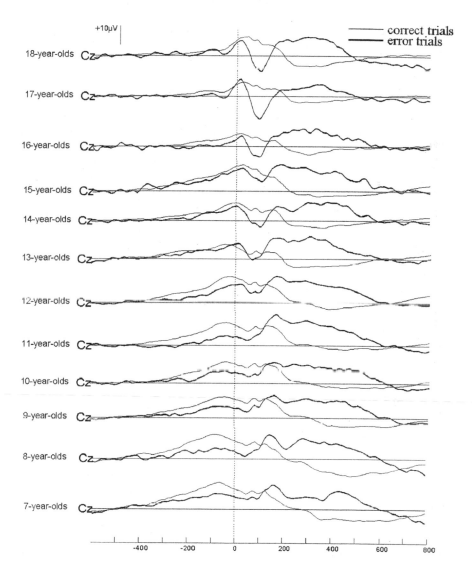

FIGURE 1. Grand average response-locked ERPs for each age group at Cz for correct trials (*thin line*) and error trials (*thick line*). The vertical hashed line represents the response. ERPs are presented relative to a 200-ms baseline, 600 to 400 ms prior to the response.

pants missed FCz so we scored the ERPs at Cz. The EEG was recorded at 500 samples/s (0.23 to 30-Hz bandpass; re-referenced offline to averaged ears; trials with EOGs greater than ±100 µV were eliminated).

The ERP was elicited during a visual flanker task that consisted of two congruent arrays, HHHHH and SSSSS (80 trials each), and two incongruent arrays, SSHSS and HHSHH (160 trials each).[3] One array appeared on each trial and the participant's task was to press the key corresponding to the central letter, either an S or an H. The stimulus duration was 250 ms and the interstimulus interval was 1 s for older children (age 10 to 18 years) and 1.5 s for younger children (ages 7 through 9 years). For more details, see Davies, Segalowitz, and Gavin.[4]

RESULTS

ERP components on error trials were measured relative to an early baseline (600 to 400 ms prior to the response) and had a P3 to the stimulus ($M = 11.2$ µV at Cz) peaking at 31 ms before the response, an ERN ($M = -0.7$ µV at Cz) peaking at 67 ms after the response, and a Pe ($M = 17.9$ µV at Cz) 248 ms after the response. See FIGURE 1 for the grand averages. ERN amplitude was measured as a difference from the positive P3 peak to the negative ERN peak. Linear and quadratic age effects accounted for 20.4% and 9.5% of the variance in the ERN, respectively, $F(1,122) = 31.2$, $P < .001$ and $F(1,121) = 16.4$, $P < .001$. A clear reduction in ERN amplitude at

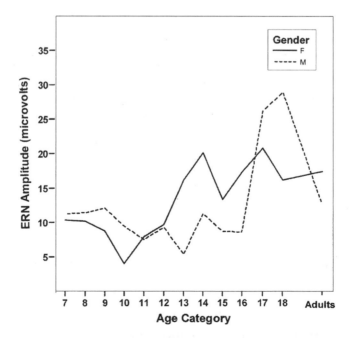

FIGURE 2. Age × Gender interaction in ERN amplitude measured peak-to-peak (P3-to-ERN) in µV. Adult values are included for reference.

age 10 years and subsequent fluctuations through adolescence are suggestive of pubertal effects, so we examined the interactions with gender. Data were subjected to a regression analysis with age and age-squared on the first step, gender on the second step, and the two interactions with gender on the third. The interaction step was significant, $F(2,118) = 4.8$, $P = .01$. The ERN quadratic distribution indicated an initial drop in amplitude with a subsequent rise through adolescence. The girls have a minimum value at age 10 years while for the boys the lowest value is at age 13 years (FIG. 2). In contrast to the ERN, the Pe amplitude did not change with age, $r = -.08$, n.s.

DISCUSSION

The results of this study support a developmental model of the ERN, which does not reach adult levels until late teen years. Given that the likely generator of the ERN is the ACC,[5] our results support the concept of a continued physiological maturation of the ACC. This contrasts with the development of the Pe component, found to be very robust, even in the young children in this study.

Recent research shows that the ACC has dense projections to the motor cortex and spinal cord, reciprocal cortico-cortical projections with the PFC, and massive input from the thalamus and brainstem nuclei involved in motivation and drive.[6] Also, extensive connections between the ACC and the amygdala have been implicated in social functioning[7] because the amygdala mediates primitive behaviors, such as aggression, fear, and sexual activity.[8] All of these major connections with the ACC indicate that the integration of movement, cognition, emotion, drive, and motivational functions occur in the ACC, and this may account for the ACC's involvement in translating intentions to action, willed control of behavior, and self-evaluation of responses and action.[6, 9]

While changes within the brain during adolescence may establish the foundation for the maturation of normal and adaptive behaviors leading to independence, they may also trigger the onset of abnormal forms of behavior or psychopathologic states including psychosis, depression, substance abuse, violence, and suicide.[10] Investigations of developmental alterations in the neural systems associated with performance monitoring during adolescence will provide a unique opportunity for increasing our understanding of both normal and abnormal behaviors manifested during this critical stage of cognitive and emotional development.[11] Thus the ERN/Pe paradigm may provide insights to the manifestation of these complex developmental changes which may lead to maladaptive behaviors. For example, the ERN has been shown to be smaller in patients with schizophrenia.[12] Given that adolescence is a period of social adaptation, emotional turmoil, impulsivity, and stress,[13] further investigations of the response-monitoring ERP components (ERN and Pe) especially as they relate to stress, socialization, and hormone levels, may provide insights into this vulnerable period in the transition from childhood to adulthood.

ACKNOWLEDGMENTS

This research was funded in part by Grant 1 K01 HD01201-01A1 from the National Institute of Child Health and Human Development to P.L.D. and in part by

Grant 122222-98 from the Natural Sciences and Engineering Research Council of Canada to S.J.S.

REFERENCES

1. HOLROYD, C.B. & M.G. COLES. 2002. The neural basis of human error processing: reinforcement learning, dopamine, and the error-related negativity. Psychol. Rev. **109:** 679–709.
2. VOGT, B.A. 1993. Structural organization of cingulate cortex: Areas, neurons, and somatodendritic transmitter receptors. *In* Neurobiology of Cingulate Cortex and Limbic Thalamus: A Comprehensive Handbook. B.A. Vogt & M. Gabriel, Eds.: 19–70. Birkhauser. Boston.
3. ERIKSEN, B.A. & C.W. ERIKSEN. 1974. Effects of noise letters upon the identification of a target letter in a nonsearch task. Percept. Psychophys. **16:** 143–149.
4. DAVIES, P.L., S.J. SEGALOWITZ & W.J. GAVIN. 2004. Development of response-monitoring ERPs in participants 7 to 25 years old. Dev. Neuropsychol. **25:** 355–376.
5. LUU, P. *et al.* 2003. Electrophysiological responses to errors and feedback in the process of action regulation. Psychol. Sci. **14:** 47–53.
6. PAUS, T. 2001. Primate anterior cingulate cortex: where motor control, drive and cognition interface. Nature Rev. Neurosci. **2:** 417–24.
7. MACLEAN, P.D. 1985. Brain evolution relating to family, play, and the separation call. Arch. Gen. Psychiatry **42:** 405–417.
8. LEDOUX, J.E. 1995. Emotion: clues from the brain. Annu. Rev. Psychol. **46:** 209–325.
9. GEHRING, W.J., J. HIMLE & L.G. NISENSON. 2000. Action-monitoring dysfunction in obsessive-compulsive disorder. Psychol. Sci. **11:** 1–6.
10. SPEAR, L.P. 2000. The adolescent brain and age-related behavioral manifestations. Neurosci. Biobehav. Rev. **24:** 417–463.
11. CUNNINGHAM, M.G., S. BHATTACHARYYA & F.M. BENES. 2002. Amygdalo-cortical sprouting continues into early adulthood: implications for the development of normal and abnormal function during adolescence. J. Comp. Neurol. **453:** 116–130.
12. MATHALON, D.H. *et al.* 2002. Response-monitoring dysfunction in schizophrenia: an event-related brain potential study. J. Abnorm. Psychol. **111:** 22–41.
13. SPEAR, L.P. 2000. Neurobehavioral changes in adolescence. Curr. Dir. Psychol. Sci. **9:** 111–114.

ERP Correlates of Action Monitoring in Adolescence

CECILE D. LADOUCEUR, RONALD E. DAHL, AND CAMERON S. CARTER

Department of Psychiatry, School of Medicine, Western Psychiatric Institute and Clinic, University of Pittsburgh, Pittsburgh, Pennsylvania 15213, USA

ABSTRACT: This study examines the development of action monitoring in adolescence by measuring the N200, the ERN (error-related negativity) and the P_E (error positivity), which are event-related potentials (ERPs) that appear to be generated in the anterior cingulate cortex (ACC) and reflect action-monitoring processes. We predicted that amplitude would be significantly greater in late compared to early adolescence. Participants consisted of 11 adolescents that were divided into early (age 9–14) and late (age 14–17) adolescence groups. ERPs were recorded during an 840-trial arrow-flanker task and using 128-channel dense array EEG. Results indicated that there were no differences in P_E amplitude but that N200 and ERN amplitudes were greater in the late adolescence group. According to the conflict monitoring hypothesis, this suggests that the ability to detect error-related conflict, which is involved in the modulation of cognitive control, appears to be fully developed later in adolescence and may be linked to the maturation of the ACC.

KEYWORDS: ERN; P_E; N200; action monitoring; adolescence

Recently, studies in adults have identified event-related potentials (ERPs) that appear to be generated in the anterior cingulate cortex (ACC) and reflect action-monitoring processes.[1–3] Given important changes in the regulation of behavior during adolescence, the goal of this study was to examine the developmental changes in these action-monitoring ERPs (i.e., N200, error-related negativity [ERN], and error positivity [P_E]) in a group of adolescents. The prefrontal cortex undergoes important maturational changes during adolescence.[4] Therefore, we predicted that these action-monitoring ERPs would be significantly greater during late compared to early adolescence. Additional analyses were conducted to examine the relationship between ERN amplitude and post-error slowing in order to investigate the functional role of the ERN in the development of cognitive control. Given the suggested monitoring role of the ERN in cognitive control processes,[5] we hypothesized that ERN amplitude would be associated with trial-to-trial performance adjustments.

Address for correspondence: Cecile D. Ladouceur, Ph.D., Department of Psychiatry, School of Medicine, Western Psychiatric Institute and Clinic, University of Pittsburgh, Pittsburgh, PA 15213. Voice: 412-246-5872; fax: 412-246-5880.

ladouceurcd@upmc.edu

Ann. N.Y. Acad. Sci. 1021: 329–336 (2004). © 2004 New York Academy of Sciences.
doi: 10.1196/annals.1308.040

METHODS

A total of 11 adolescents between 9 and 17 years of age (mean age = 14.18 years, SD = 2.44; 7 girls and 4 boys) participated in this study. Based on the median age, subjects were separated into two groups: early adolescence (n = 5, mean age = 12.20 years, SD = 2.17; 2 girls and 3 boys), and late adolescence: (n = 6, mean age = 15.83 years, SD = 0.98; 5 girls and 1 boy). Participants were screened for neurological and psychiatric disorders, and for visual accuracy. The University of Pittsburgh Institutional Review Board approved the study. To participate, children and their parents were required to sign assent and informed consent forms, respectively.

PROCEDURE

EEG measures were taken while subjects performed an arrow version of the Eriksen flanker task[6] with congruent (e.g., →→→→→) and incongruent (e.g., ←←→←←) conditions. The probability of each stimulus array was .25. The task comprised a total of 7 blocks with 120 trials each and one practice block of 60 trials. Subjects were asked to respond to the arrow in the center with either their right or left index finger, depending on the direction of the arrow. They also received specific instructions encouraging them to respond as quickly and as accurately as possible. To manipulate motivation further, participants were told at the beginning of the task that they could win a "cash bonus" depending on their performance (all received an extra $5).

EEG Data Acquisition and Analyses

The EEG data were recorded with a 128-channel Geodesic Sensor Net.[7] Impedance measures were below 50 KΩ. The EEG was digitized at 250 samples per second with a 0.1–100-Hz bandpass filter and digitally filtered offline using a 0.3–30-Hz bandpass filter. The EEG was segmented −400 to +800 ms for response-locked trials and −300 to +800 ms for stimulus-locked trials. Channels were interpolated if fast average amplitude was 200 μV, differential amplitude was greater than 100 μV, or if a channel had 0 variance or was bad more than 20% of the time. Segments were eliminated if they contained more than 10 bad channels, or if eye blinks or movements (greater than 70 μV) were detected. A spherical spline interpolation was used to correct bad channels. Channels were referenced to the vertex during data acquisition and re-referenced to the average and using a spherical spline interpolation (PARE Correction). Amplitude and latency were measured at Cz for the ERN, P_E, and N200 and at Pz for the P300; all were measured relative to an early prestimulus (N200, P300) or preresponse baseline (ERN, P_E) (−150 to −50 ms).

RESULTS

Behavioral Data

As expected, reaction times were significantly faster in the late- relative to the early-adolescence group, ($F(1, 9) = 5.79$, $P < .05$, partial $\eta^2 = .39$) (FIG. 1). Across

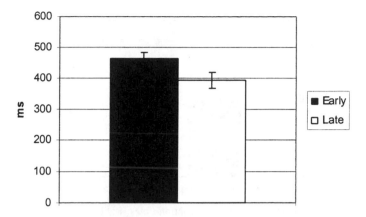

FIGURE 1. Overall reaction times.

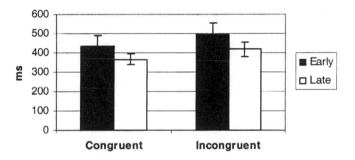

FIGURE 2. Reaction times in congruent and incongruent trials.

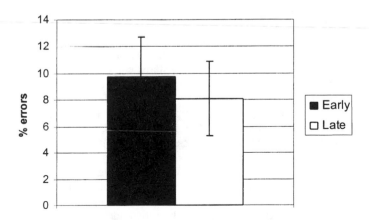

FIGURE 3. Overall percentage of errors.

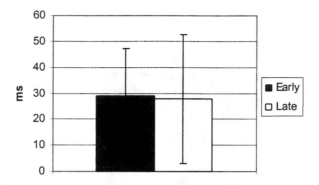

FIGURE 4. Post-error reaction times (Rabbitt effect).

age groups, reaction times were significantly slower in the incongruent relative to the congruent condition, (F(1, 9) = 197.62, $P < .001$, partial $\eta^2 = .96$) (FIG. 2) and faster on error ($M = 361$ ms, SD = 60 ms) compared to correct trials ($M = 438$ ms, SD = 64 ms) (F(1, 9) = 53.36, $P < .001$, partial $\eta^2 = .86$), which is consistent with results in adult studies.[3] In addition, there were no group differences in the percentage of errors, $t(9) = .98$, n.s.(FIG. 3) and in post-error slowing $t(9) = .98$, n.s. (FIG. 4), which is consistent with previous findings and suggests that performance was similar across age groups.

ERP Data

As shown in FIGURE 5, results revealed significantly greater P_E amplitude (F(1, 9) = 20.07, $P < .01$, partial $\eta^2 = .69$) and latency (F(1, 9) = 30.76, $P < .001$, partial $\eta^2 = .77$) in error relative to correct trials for both age groups. FIGURE 5 also reveals a significant trial type by age-group interaction (F(1, 9) = 24.37, $P < .01$, partial $\eta^2 = .73$) regarding ERN amplitude. Post hoc analyses indicated that ERN amplitude was greater in error compared to correct trials in late-, $t(5) = 5.04$, $P < .01$, but not in early adolescence, $t(4) = -1.96$, n.s.. In addition, as shown in FIGURE 6, N200 amplitude was significantly greater in incongruent relative to congruent trials in late-, $t(5) = 2.95$, $P < .05$, but not in early adolescence, $t(4) = 1.45$, n.s.. The trial type by age-group interaction did not reach statistical significance threshold, most likely owing to a lack of statistical power (F(1, 9) = 1.42, $P = .26$, partial $\eta^2 = .26$). No age-related differences were found associated with ERN or N200 latency. Moreover, both groups showed significantly larger P300 amplitude (F(1, 9) = 15.97, $P < .01$, partial $\eta^2 = .64$) and latency (F(1, 9) = 22.31, $P < .01$, partial $\eta^2 = .71$) in incongruent compared to congruent trials. These results, coupled with the similarity in morphology of the P_E component across groups, rules out the possibility that differences in ERN and N200 amplitude were attributable to overall smaller ERPs in early adolescence. In order to examine the functional role of the ERN in trial-to-trial performance adjustment, we separated error trials as a function of fast and slow reaction times in post-error correct trials within each participant and measured ERN amplitude and latency. After removal of one outlier in the older group, results revealed sig-

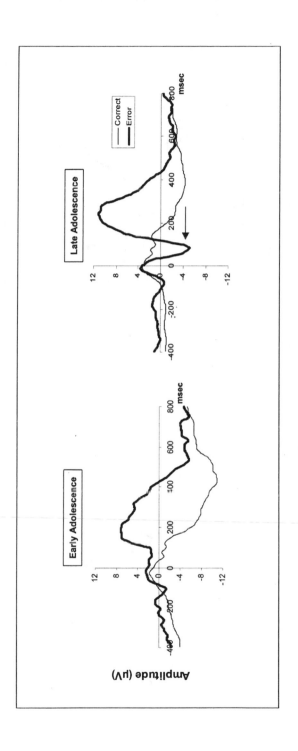

FIGURE 5. Response-locked waveforms.

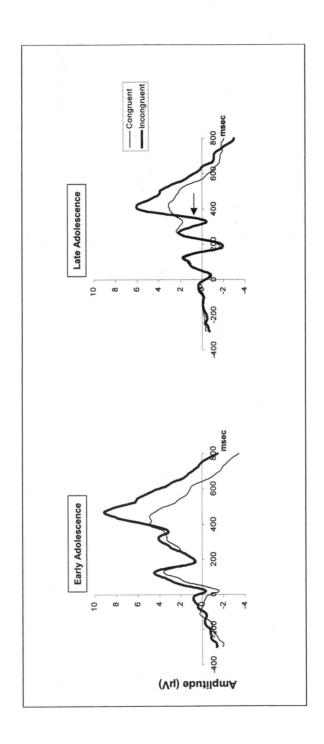

FIGURE 6. Stimulus-locked waveforms.

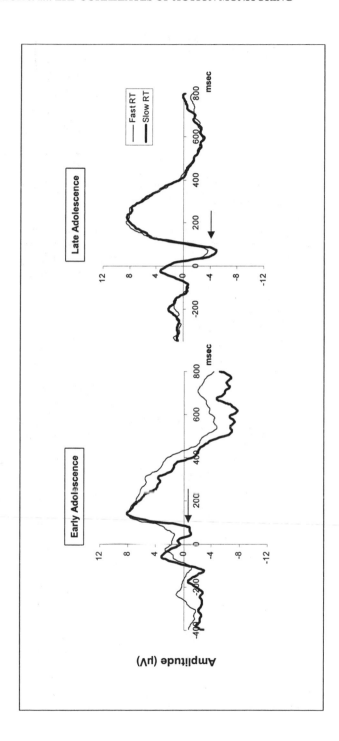

FIGURE 7. Response-locked waveforms as a function of post-error adjustments in performance.

nificantly larger ERN amplitudes in slow compared to fast trials in both age groups $(F(1, 8) = 11.21, P < .05,$ partial $\eta^2 = .58)$.

DISCUSSION

Although P_E was present in early and late adolescence, the N200 and ERN did not seem to appear until late adolescence. According to the conflict-monitoring hypothesis,[3,5] this suggests that although awareness of having committed an error is present early on, the ability of detecting error-related conflict, which is involved in the modulation of cognitive control, develops later in adolescence. Like the older group, the young adolescents did, however, show greater negativity in erroneous trials associated with post-error adjustment. This implies that the presence of ERN in early adolescence may be contingent upon performance adjustment, which would support the role of the ERN in the modulation of cognitive control.[5] Given that the N200 and ERN have been localized in the ACC,[3] these results suggest that the development of action monitoring, which is involved in the regulation of behavior, is linked to the maturation of the ACC during adolescence.[8]

Future research will involve replicating these results with a larger sample of adolescents, estimating the neural generators of these components using source localization analyses, and examining individual differences related to gender, puberty, and mood.

ACKNOWLEDGMENTS

This study was supported by NIMH Grant MH041712 and by a fellowship awarded to C.D.L. from the Canadian Institutes of Health Research (CIHR).

REFERENCES

1. FALKENSTEIN, M., J. HOHNSBEIN, J. HOORMAN, et al. 1991. Effects of crossmodal divided attention on late ERP components. II. Error processing in choice reaction tasks. Electroencephalogr. Clin. Neurophysiol. **78:** 447–455.
2. GEHRING, W.J., B. GOSS, M.G.H. COLES, et al. 1993. A neural system for error detection and compensation. Psychol. Sci. **4:** 385–390.
3. VAN VEEN, V. & C.S. CARTER. 2002. The timing of action-monitoring processes in the anterior cingulate cortex. J. Cognit.Neurosci. **14:** 593–602.
4. LUNA, B. & J.A. SWEENEY. 2001. Studies of brain and cognitive maturation through childhood and adolescence: a strategy for testing neurodevelopmental hypotheses. Schizophrenia Bull. **27:** 443–455.
5. BOTVINICK, M.M., C.S. CARTER, T.S. BRAVER, et al. 2001. Conflict monitoring and cognitive control. Psychol. Rev. **108:** 624–652.
6. ERIKSEN, C.W. & E.A. ERIKSEN. 1979. Target redundancy in visual search: do repetitions of the target within the display impair processing? Percept. Psychophysiol. **26:** 195–205.
7. TUCKER, D.M. 1993. Spatial sampling of head electrical fields: the geodesic sensor net. Electroencephalogr. Clin. Neurophysiol. **87:** 154–163.
8. CASEY, B.J., R. TRAINOR, J. GIEDD, et al. 1997. The role of the anterior cingulate in automatic and controlled processes: a developmental neuroanatomical study. Devel. Psychobiol. **30:** 61–69.

Individual Differences in Executive Attention Predict Self-Regulation and Adolescent Psychosocial Behaviors

LESA K. ELLIS,[a,b] MARY K. ROTHBART,[b] AND MICHAEL I. POSNER[b]

[a]Westminster College, Salt Lake City, Utah 84105, USA

[b]University of Oregon, Eugene, Oregon, USA

ABSTRACT: This study examined temperament, executive attention, parental monitoring and relationships, and involvement in pro- and antisocial behaviors in an ethnically diverse sample of adolescents. We sought to relate parent- and self-reported effortful control to performance on measures of executive attention and to better understand the relative contributions of individual-difference variables and environmental variables in predicting behaviors in adolescence. The results indicated a relationship between poor executive attention and mother-reported effortful control. Inclusion of individual-difference variables significantly increased prediction of problem-behavior scores, suggesting the importance of including such variables in studies of adolescent deviance.

KEYWORDS: adolescence; temperament; executive attention; self-regulation; psychosocial behaviors; individual differences

While a number of studies have illustrated the role of environmental factors such as poor parental discipline and monitoring in predicting adolescent deviance, others have examined risk factors associated with individual differences. One important source of individuality during adolescence is the interaction between temperamental emotional reactivity and self-regulation. Emotional reactivity is thought to arise from evolutionarily conserved affective-motivational systems in the brain and, as such, individual differences in emotional reactivity can be seen as resulting from individual differences in the neural structures and neurochemistry subserving such systems. Conversely, self-regulation refers to the capacity for effortful control of action and emotion. We view this effortful control as reflecting functioning of a neurally based executive attention system that allows an individual to choose between competing response tendencies and, when necessary, to suppress an inappropriate response.[1]

While individual differences in temperament may be evident from an early age, we believe that temperament itself develops over time and both shapes, and is shaped by, the environment. The current study examined temperament, executive attention, parental monitoring and relationships, and involvement in both pro- and an-

Address for correspondence: Dr. Lesa K. Ellis, Department of Psychology, Westminster College, 1840 South 1300 East, Salt Lake City, UT 84105. Voice: 801-832-2425.
lellis@westminstercollege.edu

Ann. N.Y. Acad. Sci. 1021: 337–340 (2004). © 2004 New York Academy of Sciences.
doi: 10.1196/annals.1308.041

tisocial behaviors in an ethnically diverse sample of adolescents. We sought both to relate parent- and self-reported effortful control to performance on measures of executive attention and to better understand the relative contributions of individual difference variables and environmental variables in predicting problem behaviors in adolescents.

METHODS

Participants included 104 ethnically diverse 16- to 17-year old adolescents (63 female; 41 male) and his or her parent(s), and represented a subsample from a larger longitudinal intervention study taking place in the area of Portland, Oregon. The original sample was recruited from three area middle schools in a part of the city with a high crime rate. At the time participants were originally recruited, teacher ratings were used to identify low-risk, at-risk, and high-risk youth. The current sample included 26 adolescents in the low-risk group (11 female; 15 male), 35 in the at-risk group (19 female; 16 male), and 43 in the high-risk group (31 female; 12 male).

MEASURES

Adolescent and parent participants completed the Early Adolescent Temperament Questionnaire—Revised, an instrument designed to assess individual differences in emotional reactivity, including Surgency, Affiliativeness, and Negative Affectivity, as well as Effortful Control.[2] Participants also completed the Child and Family Center Questionnaire—Child Form (CFCQ-C), an adaptation of an instrument designed to measure parenting constructs and antisocial peer associations and behaviors.[3] Only youth report was utilized in the current study. Antisocial peer association and behavior scores were combined to provide a problem-behavior composite score.

Participants completed the Attention Network Test (ANT), a computerized task designed to test the efficiency of the alerting, orienting, and executive attention systems.[4] While alerting and orienting scores were calculated, only the executive effect scores were utilized in the current analysis and will be described here. Executive attention in the ANT is assessed via a flanker paradigm, in which participants are asked to identify the direction of a centrally presented arrow on a computer screen by pressing a mouse button. The arrow is flanked on either side by two arrows pointing in the same direction (congruent condition), or in the opposite direction (incongruent condition). The executive attention effect was calculated by subtracting the mean RT of congruent conditions from the mean RT of incongruent conditions; thus, a higher score reflected relatively greater interference caused by presentation of incongruent flankers.

Participants also completed the Counting and Emotional Stroop task, a variant of measures developed by Bush and Whalen and associates for use in fMRI.[5] Participants were presented a word in the middle of the screen either one, two, three, or four times. Stimuli words were chosen from a corpus of words generated by children and adolescents for use in such tasks,[6] and were categorized as neutral, incongruent number (e.g., "four" presented three times), or negatively valenced emotion words.

TABLE 1. Hierarchical multiple regression to predict Problem Behavior score

Block 1			R^2	Sig.		Beta	t	Sig.
			.24	.000	Family Conflict	.31	2.88	.005
					Parental Monitoring	−.33	−2.67	.009
					Risk Group	.02	.17	.861
					Prosocial Behavior	.10	.85	.396
Block 2	$R^2\Delta$	Sig.	R^2	Sig.		Beta	t	Sig.
	.21	.000	.045	.000	Family Conflict	.17	1.73	.088
					Parental Monitoring	−.23	−2.10	.039
					Risk Group	−.10	−1.11	.270
					Prosocial Behavior	.19	1.75	.084
					Effortful Control	−.46	2.78	.007
					Effortful Control (mother-report)	−.25	−2.72	.008
					Total Interference	.25	2.78	.007
					Surgency	.16	1.78	.079

Counting interference scores were calculated by subtracting RTs for neutral words from incongruent number RTs, and emotion interference scores were calculated by subtracting neutral word RTs from emotion words RTs. The three interference scores were then combined to provide a measure of total interference.

RESULTS

No significant relations were found between self-reported Effortful Control and performance on the attention tasks; however, there was a modest but significant correlation between mother-reported Effortful Control and total interference scores ($r = −.31$, $P <.01$), the direction of which indicated that individuals experiencing more difficulty with the cognitive tasks were lower in mother-reported Effortful Control. In addition, multiple regression analyses were performed to examine the relative ability of environmental and individual difference variables to predict the problem-behavior composite scores (TABLE 1). In Block One, CFCQC Parental Monitoring/ Rule Making, Family Conflict and Prosocial Behavior scores, along with Teacher Risk Rating, were entered simultaneously as predictors of Problem Behavior composite scores. This model was significant in its ability to predict Problem Behavior scores ($r^2 = .24$, $F (3, 85) = 5.66$, $P < .001$). In a second block, Total Interference scores, mother- and self-reported Effortful Control scores, and Surgency scores were entered simultaneously. When Block 2 variables were entered, significant additional variance was gained ($r^2 \Delta = .21$, $F \Delta (4, 81) = 7.589$, $P < .001$). The overall model remained significant ($r^2 = .45$, $F(8, 81) = 8.29$, $P < .001$). Both self-report Effortful Control ($t = −4.09$, $P < .001$) and mother-report Effortful Control ($t = −2.02, P < .05$)

contributed significantly to prediction of Problem Behavior scores, as did Total Interference ($t = 2.948$, $P < .01$).

DISCUSSION

The results indicated a relationship between poor executive attention and mother-reported Effortful Control, in accordance with our hypothesis. Further, inclusion of individual-difference variables significantly increased prediction of Problem Behavior scores, suggesting the importance of including such variables in studies of adolescent deviance. Future studies will seek to replicate these findings, as well as to explore development of executive attention during the adolescent period.

REFERENCES

1. ROTHBART, M.K. & J.E. BATES. 1998. Temperament. *In* Handbook of Development, Social, Emotional and Personality Development, Vol. 3, 5th ed. N. Eisenberg, Ed. :105–176. John Wiley. New York.
2. ELLIS, L.K. & M.K. ROTHBART. Revision of the early adolescent temperament questionnaire. Manuscript in preparation.
3. METZLER, C.W. *et al.* 1998. The stability and validity of early adolescents' reports of parenting constructs. J. Fam. Psychol. **12:** 600–619.
4. FAN, J. *et al.* 2002. Testing the efficiency and independence of attentional networks. J. Cogn. Neurosci. **14:** 340–347.
5. BUSH, G. *et al.* 1998. The counting Stroop: an interference task specialized for functional neuroimaging: validation study with functional MRI. Hum. Brain Mapp. **6:** 270–282.
6. DOOST, H.T.N. *et al.* 1999. The development of a corpus of emotional words produced by children and adolescents. Pers. Individ. Dif. **27:** 433–451.

Positive and Negative Affect in Depression

Influence of Sex and Puberty

ERIKA E. FORBES, DOUGLAS E. WILLIAMSON, NEAL D. RYAN,
AND RONALD E. DAHL

*Western Psychiatric Institute and Clinic, University of Pittsburgh School of Medicine,
Pittsburgh, Pennsylvania 15213, USA*

ABSTRACT: To examine adolescent depression as a model for unusual emotion
regulation, the current study considered the influence of gender, pubertal development, and cortisol on self-reported mood. Children and adolescents with
major depressive disorder ($n = 35$, mean age 12.5 years) were compared with
psychiatrically healthy children and adolescents ($n = 36$, mean age 10.5 years).
During a three-day assessment, participants rated their mood at three time
points, pubertal development was determined through physical examination,
and plasma cortisol was sampled during the second night. Depressed participants experienced less positive affect and more negative affect than did controls. Diagnostic group, gender, and pubertal status interacted to predict
negative affect, with depressed adolescent girls experiencing especially high
levels of negative affect. Cortisol was generally unrelated to depression and
mood. Findings are consistent with emotion-based models of depression and
with the literature on depression and emotion regulation during adolescence.

KEYWORDS: depression; emotion regulation; gender differences; adolescence;
cortisol

Adolescence involves important changes in affect regulation and, ostensibly, in appetitive brain systems. Affect increases in intensity and duration, and rates of depressive disorders increase dramatically.[1,2] Adolescent depression, with its
characteristic low levels of mood, pleasure, energy, and motivation, and its prevalence during this life period, may be viewed as an extreme form of adolescent affective variation. For this reason, it may be considered a model for understanding affect
and affect regulation in normal development.

Three issues related to affect regulation in adolescent depression merit examination. One issue is whether adolescent depression involves unusual levels of both positive affect and negative affect. Emotion-based theories of psychopathology posit
that depression is characterized by increased negative affect and decreased positive
affect.[3,4] This model has been supported in research with adults,[5] and studies of affect and adjustment have now begun to consider its relevance to children and ado-

Address for correspondence: Erika E. Forbes, Western Psychiatric Institute and Clinic, University of Pittsburgh School of Medicine, 3811 O'Hara St., Pittsburgh, PA 15213. Voice: 412-
246-5871; fax: 412-246-5880.
    forbese@upmc.edu

Ann. N.Y. Acad. Sci. 1021: 341–347 (2004). © 2004 New York Academy of Sciences.
doi: 10.1196/annals.1308.042

lescents.[6–8] The relation of negative affect and positive affect to adolescents with major depressive disorder has not been examined, however. This is especially important for positive affect because abnormal levels of this type of affect are postulated to be a central feature of depressive states.[9]

A second issue is whether positive and negative affect in adolescent depression may be influenced by sex and pubertal status. For girls, hormonal changes that occur during puberty increase the risk of developing depression.[10,11] Thus, it is possible that pubertal girls may be especially likely to experience heightened negative affect or diminished positive affect.

A third issue involves the relation between cortisol and affect. Cortisol, which reflects function of the hypothalamic pituitary adrenal axis, has been found to be elevated in adult depression.[12] Some studies have reported that elevated cortisol level around sleep onset characterizes adolescent depression[13] and predicts recurrence of the disorder.[14] Cortisol thus plays a role in affective disturbance and may influence affect during depressive states.

The current study examined sex, pubertal status, and cortisol in relation to mood in adolescent depression. We predicted that children with depression would experience higher negative affect and lower positive affect than would control children; that the high negative affect/low positive affect pattern for depression would be especially pronounced in pubertal girls; and that baseline cortisol would be positively related to negative affect and inversely related to positive affect for both depressed and control children.

METHOD

Participants

Children in the study were a subsample of participants in a longitudinal study of the psychobiology of early-onset depression.[15] The depressed group comprised 35 children (19 female, mean age 12.5 years, 20 mid–late pubertal) with diagnoses of major depressive disorder. The control group comprised 36 low-risk normal children (13 female, mean age 10.5 years, 5 mid–late pubertal) who were free of psychopathology. For participants in the control group, the lifetime history of affective disorder was negative for all first-degree relatives and at least 80% of second-degree relatives. Diagnoses were made using the K-SADS-PL,[16] a structured diagnostic interview. Pubertal development was assessed by physical examination. Children with Tanner scores of 1–2 were classified as *pre–early pubertal* ($n = 46$), and those with Tanner scores ≥ 3 were classified as *mid–late pubertal* ($n = 25$).

Procedure

The laboratory assessment involved a 3-day laboratory visit. Affect was measured at three time points: 8 PM on day 2, 8 AM on day 3, and 8 PM on day 3. Participants used a self-report visual analogue scale to rate their experience of eight affective states: happy, sad, drowsy, calm, energized, alert, lethargic, and tense. Affect data were reduced using a principal-components analysis with varimax rotation, which extracted two factors: *Positive affect*, which accounted for 16.6% of the total variance, had positive loadings for happy, calm, alert, and energized, and a negative loading for sad. *Negative affect*, which accounted for 39.6% of the total variance, had positive loadings for sad, drowsy, lethargic, tense, and energized. Plasma cortisol was sampled every 20 min during the night of day 2. The cortisol data included in the current study were mean plasma levels during the period from 1 hour before to 1 hour after sleep onset, as defined by polysomnography measures.

RESULTS

The depressed group was older than the control group ($F(1,69) = 21.03, P < .001$), and consequently age was included as a covariate in tests of group differences.

Depression and Positive and Negative Affect

Random effects regression models for positive affect and negative affect with participant as a random effect and time as a repeated measure indicated that the depressed group experienced less positive affect and more negative affect than did the control group ($F(1,198) = 30.92, P < .001$ and $F(1,197) = 34.71, P < .001$, respectively). Group means are depicted in FIGURE 1. A repeated measures analysis of variance (ANOVA) for positive affect and negative affect over the three time points indicated a marginally significant group × time interaction effect for positive affect ($F(2,56) = 3.11, P = .05$). Analyses of linear trends in positive affect within each group indicated that the depressed group experienced a decrease in positive affect during the lab visit ($F(1,26) = 5.91, P < .05$) while the control group did not experience a change in positive affect ($F(1,31) = .82, P > .35$). Mean positive affect over time is depicted in FIGURE 2. The group × time interaction effect for negative affect was nonsignificant ($F(2,56) = 1.48, P > .20$).

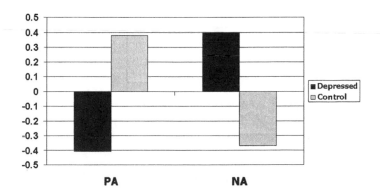

FIGURE 1. Positive affect (PA) and negative affect (NA) factor scores for adolescents with major depressive disorder (depressed) and low-risk normal adolescents (control).

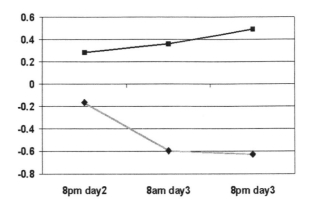

FIGURE 2. Positive affect over 3 time points for adolescents with major depressive disorder (depressed, *lower line*) and low-risk normal adolescents (control, *upper line*).

Puberty and Sex Effects on Affect

A repeated measures ANOVA with time as a repeated measure indicated a group $\times$ sex $\times$ pubertal status interaction for negative affect ($F(2,52) = 7.01$, $P < .01$). Means for the depressed and control groups, divided by sex and pubertal status, are displayed in FIGURE 3. Follow-up ANOVAs to examine this interaction were guided by the prediction that pubertal girls in the depressed group would be especially likely to display abnormally high negative affect. ANOVAs indicated a significant sex $\times$ pubertal status interaction in the depressed group, but not the control group ($F(2,27) = 6.45$, $P < .01$ and $F(2,22) = 1.28$, $P > .25$, respectively). Furthermore, a comparison of mid–late pubertal girls and boys in the depressed group indicated a marginally significant difference, with girls experiencing more negative affect than boys ($F(1,12) = 4.69$, $P = .05$). The depressed group $\times$ sex $\times$ pubertal status interaction for positive affect was nonsignificant ($F(2,51) = .90$, $P > .40$).

Cortisol and Affect

The depressed and control groups did not differ in their cortisol levels ($F(1,66) = .57$, $P > .45$), and for the sample overall, cortisol level was uncorrelated with positive affect and negative affect ($r = -.09$ and $r = .09$, respectively). Correlation analyses within the depressed and control groups revealed that for the control group only, cortisol level was inversely related to mean levels of both positive affect and negative affect (rs $= -.32$ and $-.33$, respectively, Ps $< .05$).

DISCUSSION

The current study found that the affective characteristics of adolescent depression involve both positive affect and negative affect and are influenced by sex and pubertal status. As predicted, children with depression experienced lower positive affect

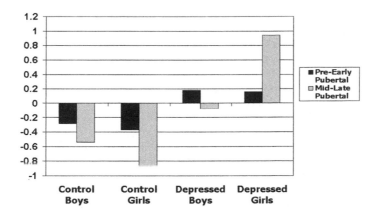

FIGURE 3. Negative affect in adolescents with major depressive disorder (depressed) and low-risk normal adolescents (control), divided by sex (boys, girls) and pubertal stage (pre–early, mid–late).

and higher negative affect than did control children, and group differences in affect were moderated by sex and pubertal status. Specifically, depressed girls who were mid–late pubertal experienced more negative affect than did depressed boys, non-depressed girls, and depressed pre-early pubertal girls.

An examination of cortisol and depression indicated that the depressed and control groups did not differ in plasma cortisol level around sleep onset. The two groups differed in the relation of cortisol to affect, however. Cortisol was unrelated to affect for the depressed group, but was inversely related to both positive affect and negative affect for the control group. This pattern of findings was not consistent with our prediction that cortisol would be positively correlated with negative affect and inversely correlated with positive affect for both groups. However, the lack of relation between cortisol and affect for the depressed group is in agreement with findings of abnormal physiological responses to emotional contexts in adult depression.[17,18] The lack of relation between cortisol and affect in the depressed group also suggests that affect during depression, while not necessarily unrelated to cortisol, may be determined by a more complex set of factors than is typical affect.

Our findings on positive and negative affect support emotion-based models of depression[3,4] and suggest that children with depression experience patterns of affect similar to those found in adults with depression.[5] As predicted by literature on the emergence of sex differences in depression and by models of affect regulation during adolescence,[9,10] depression-related differences in negative affect were especially pronounced for pubertal girls.

An analysis of change in affect across assessments revealed that the depressed and control groups also differed in their pattern of positive affect over time. Whereas the control group experienced a steady level of positive affect, the depressed group experienced a decline. The adolescents in the depressed group might have experienced the typical affective response of interest or excitement when encountering a new and unusual environment, but their positive affect dropped once they became accustomed to that environment. This finding suggests that depression involves difficulty in sustaining or regulating positive affect, not merely abnormal mean levels of positive affect. In addition, the finding highlights the importance of measuring affect at multiple time points in order to understand how the process of affect regulation goes awry in depression.

It will be valuable for future work on affect and childhood depression to address the multiple pathways to affect disturbance and to elucidate the role that dysregulation of both positive affect and negative affect may play in this disorder. In addition, the relation between positive affect and negative affect in childhood depression merits further examination. A limitation of the current study is that it did not examine adolescents' affect over time or in comparison with affect in adults or younger children. In order to understand both normal and abnormal changes in affect during adolescence, it will be useful to investigate age differences in cross-sectional and longitudinal samples over broad age ranges.

ACKNOWLEDGMENT

This study was supported by NIMH Grant MH041712 to N.D.R.

REFERENCES

1. LEWINSOHN, P.M., et al. 1993. Adolescent psychopathology: I. Prevalence and incidence of depression and other DSM-III-R disorders in high school students. J. Abnorm. Psychol. 102: 133–144.
2. BIRMAHER, B., et al. 1996. Childhood and adolescent depression: a review of the past 10 years. Part I. J. Am. Acad. Child Adolesc. Psychiatry 35: 1427–1439.
3. CLARK, L.A. & D. WATSON. 1991. Tripartite model of anxiety and depression: psychometric evidence and taxonomic implications. J. Abnorm. Psychol. 100: 316–336.
4. DEPUE, R.A. & W.G. IACONO. 1989. Neurobehavioral aspects of affective disorders. Annu. Rev. Psychol. 40: 457–492.
5. WATSON, D., et al. 1995. Testing a tripartite model: II. Exploring the symptom structure of anxiety and depression in student, adult, and patient samples. J. Abnorm. Psychol. 104: 15–25.
6. JOINER, T.E., JR., et al. 1996. Tripartite structure of positive and negative affect, depression, and anxiety in child and adolescent psychiatric inpatients. J. Abnorm. Psychol. 105: 401–409.
7. LONIGAN, C.J., et al. 1999. Positive and negative affectivity in children: confirmatory factor analysis of a two-factor model and its relation to symptoms of anxiety and depression. J. Consult. Clin. Psychol. 67: 374–386.
8. LONIGAN, C.J., et al. 2003. Relations of positive and negative affectivity to anxiety and depression in children: evidence from a latent variable longitudinal study. J. Consult. Clin. Psychol. 71: 465–481.
9. ALLEN, N.B. & P.B.T. BADCOCK. 2003. The social risk hypothesis of depressed mood: evolutionary, psychosocial, and neurobiological perspectives. Psychol. Bull. 129: in press.
10. ANGOLD, A., et al. 1999. Pubertal changes in hormone levels and depression in girls. Psychol. Med. 29: 1043–1053.
11. ANGOLD, A., et al. 1998. Puberty and depression: the roles of age, pubertal status, and pubertal timing. Psychol. Med. 28: 51–61.
12. HALBREICH, U., et al. 1985. Cortisol secretion in endogenous depression. I. Basal plasma levels. Arch. Gen. Psychiatry 42: 904–908.

13. DAHL, R.E., *et al.* 1991. 24-hour cortisol measures in adolescents with major depression: a controlled study. Biol. Psychiatry **30:** 25–36.
14. RAO, U., *et al.* 1996. The relationship between longitudinal clinical course and sleep and cortisol changes in adolescent depression. Biol. Psychiatry **40:** 474–484.
15. DAHL, R.E., *et al.* 2000. Low growth hormone response to growth hormone-releasing hormone in child depression. Biol. Psychiatry **48:** 981–988.
16. KAUFMAN, J., *et al.* 1995. Schedule for Affective Disorders and Schizophrenia in School-Aged Children—Present and Lifetime Version (K-SADS–PL). Pittsburgh, PA: Western Psychiatric Institute and Clinic.
17. ALLEN, N.B., *et al.* 1999. Affective startle modulation in clinical depression: preliminary findings. Biol. Psychiatry **46:** 542–550.
18. ROTTENBERG, J., *et al.* 2003. Vagal rebound during resolution of tearful crying among depressed and nondepressed individuals. Psychophysiology **40:** 1–6.

Sex Differences in the Effects of Pubertal Development on Responses to a Corticotropin-Releasing Hormone Challenge

The Pittsburgh Psychobiologic Studies

LAURA R. STROUD,[a] GEORGE D. PAPANDONATOS,[b]
DOUGLAS E. WILLIAMSON,[c] AND RONALD E. DAHL[c]

[a]*Centers for Behavioral and Preventive Medicine, Brown Medical School, Providence, Rhode Island 02903, USA*

[b]*Center for Statistical Sciences, Brown University, Providence, Rhode Island, USA*

[c]*University of Pittsburgh School of Medicine, Pittsburgh, Pennsylvania, USA*

ABSTRACT: We propose that sex differences in HPA regulation may emerge during puberty and help to explain sex differences in depression. In this study, we examined sex differences in cortisol responses to CRH challenge across pubertal stages in carefully screened control subjects from the Pittsburgh Psychobiologic Studies. Participants were 7–16 years of age, physically healthy, and had no personal or family history of psychiatric disorder. Physician-rated Tanner staging was conducted, followed by CRH challenge sessions including 30–40 minutes pre-infusion baseline, 1 μg/kg CRH infusion, 90–180 minutes of post-infusion measures, and 9–10 plasma cortisol samples. Girls showed increasing total cortisol responses to CRH across Tanner stages, explained by slower recovery from peak cortisol levels, while boys showed similar total responses across Tanner stages. Results show subtle sex differences in the influence of puberty on HPA regulation at the pituitary level, which may represent one factor underlying the emergence of girls' greater rates of depression during this time.

KEYWORDS: CRH challenge; cortisol; sex differences; puberty; adolescents; children

Across nations and cultures, women of reproductive ages are approximately two times as likely to suffer from depressive symptoms, syndromes, and disorders as men.[1] Girls' greater rates of both depressive symptoms and depressive disorders appear to emerge during adolescence, with the majority of studies showing the female

Address for correspondence: Laura R. Stroud, Ph.D., Centers for Behavioral and Preventive Medicine, Brown Medical School, Coro-West, Suite 500, One Hoppin Street, Providence, RI 02903. Voice: 401-793-8194; fax: 815-346-1070.

Laura_Stroud@brown.edu

Ann. N.Y. Acad. Sci. 1021: 348–351 (2004). © 2004 New York Academy of Sciences.
doi: 10.1196/annals.1308.043

preponderance to emerge around age 13–14 years.[2] That this age coincides approximately with the mid-point of pubertal development has led to a growing body of research supporting the role of pubertal processes in the emergence of sex differences in depression.

In adults, depression has been associated with multiple abnormalities along the limbic-hypothalamic pituitary adrenal (LHPA) axis, including increased basal cortisol levels, dexamethasone nonsuppression, and increased central CRH drive. Although associations are less consistent, depression in adolescents has also been associated with alterations along the HPA axis, particularly increased basal cortisol prior to sleep onset,[3] alterations in free cortisol,[4] and dexamethasone nonsuppression in certain patients.[5] Given links between depression and alterations along the hypothalamic pituitary adrenal (HPA) axis, we propose that sex differences in HPA regulation may emerge over puberty and help to explain sex differences in depression.

Consistent with our hypothesis, preclinical research has shown consistent sex differences in HPA responses. Female rats consistently show greater basal and stress levels of the HPA hormones compared to males.[6] Further, similar to sex differences in depression, sex differences along the HPA axis appear to emerge during puberty, with males showing few differences over puberty, but females showing increases in corticosterone, ACTH, CRF and corticosterone-binding globulin.[7] In humans, there is some evidence for gender and pubertal effects on *basal* levels of HPA hormones over puberty; however, little research has examined the influence of gender and pubertal development on HPA *response to challenge* in humans. In the present study, we had the unique opportunity to examine sex differences in cortisol responses to a CRH challenge across pubertal stages in carefully screened control subjects pooled from three phases of the Pittsburgh Psychobiologic Studies.

METHOD

Seventy-eight participants (58% boys, 42% girls) ranging in age from 6 to 16 years completed the study. Participants were carefully screened controls recruited over three phases of the Pittsburgh Psychobiologic Studies. All were physically healthy and had no current, personal, or family history of psychiatric disorder. Pubertal development was determined by Tanner staging conducted by a physician. Sessions began at either 4:00 or 5:00 PM, and included 30–40 minutes pre-infusion baseline, 1 μg/kg CRH infusion, 90–180 minutes of post-infusion measures, and 9–10 plasma cortisol samples per session. A total of 211 sessions were completed, with 39 participants completing the CRH session only once, and 39 participating twice or more (range, 2–7 sessions), with at least 12 months between sessions.

We developed a nonlinear mixed model to fit the data, then examined the influence of gender and Tanner stage on model parameters. A simplified version of a one-compartment oral dose model best fit the data: Mean Response = $\Theta_0 + \Theta_1 *$ Time + $\Theta_2 * T*e^{-\Theta_3 * T}$. Time was standardized so that CRH infusion occurred at time 0, whereas $T = \max (0, \text{time})$ such that the nonlinear departure from baseline only operated in the post-infusion phase. In the model, Θ_0 represents baseline cortisol at the time of infusion, Θ_1, slope of the linear approximation of the diurnal rhythm over the study, Θ_2, magnitude of peak change from baseline, and Θ_3, the reactivity and recovery rate. The peak change in cortisol from the linearly declining baseline is

TABLE 1. Model parameters over puberty in boys and girls

	Sex	Estimate (Standard Error)		
		Tanner 1/2	Tanner 3	Tanner 4/5
Peak change (μg/dL)	Female	8.7 (0.3)	8.5 (0.3)	8.4 (0.5)
	Male	9.9 (0.3)	10.1 (0.3)	10.2 (0.5)
Time to peak (min)	Female	29.9 (1.0)	35.2 (1.3)	41.4(2.7)
	Male	33.3 (1.0)	32.2 (0.9)	31.2 (1.4)
Reactivity rate (μg/dL/min)	Female	.033(.001)	.028 (.001)	.024(.002)
	Male	.030 (.001)	.031 (.001)	.032 (.001)
Total response (μg/dL)	Female	709 (34)	819 (43)	945 (84)
	Male	898 (39)	881 (33)	865 (54)

$(\Theta_2/\Theta_3)^* e^{-1}$, reached at $T_{max} = 1/\Theta_3$. Area under the curve (AUC) is given by Θ_2/Θ_3. Heteroscedasticity in the data was also estimated in the model.

RESULTS

Means and standard deviations for model parameters in boys and girls over puberty are shown in TABLE 1, with predicted curves in FIGURE 1. Significant gender by Tanner interactions emerged for magnitude of peak change from baseline, time to peak response, reactivity rate, and total cortisol response to CRH ($Ps < .05$). Specifically, girls showed decreases in magnitude of peak change over puberty, while boys showed increases over puberty. Girls also showed slower time to peak cortisol responses and slower reactivity rates over puberty while boys showed little change in these parameters. For total cortisol responses to CRH, girls showed increases over puberty explained by slower recovery from peak cortisol levels, while boys showed similar total responses across Tanner stages. No significant interactions emerged for baseline slope. To control for effects of age and body mass index (BMI), we examined Tanner by BMI and Tanner by age interactions stratifying on gender. No significant effects emerged.

DISCUSSION

Although recent studies show increases in *basal levels* of cortisol over puberty, few have examined HPA *responses to challenge*. We found subtle changes in cortisol responses to CRH challenge over puberty in girls. Specifically, girls showed slower recovery, increases in total cortisol response, but slower time to peak cortisol following CRH challenge over puberty, while boys showed little change in cortisol responses. Thus, even in carefully screened controls, this preliminary study shows that pubertal changes may alter HPA regulation. Given links between depression and dysregulation of the HPA axis, it is possible that subtle changes in HPA regulation in girls across puberty may be one factor underlying the emergence of girls' greater rates of depression during this time. Future research should examine whether more or less pronounced sex

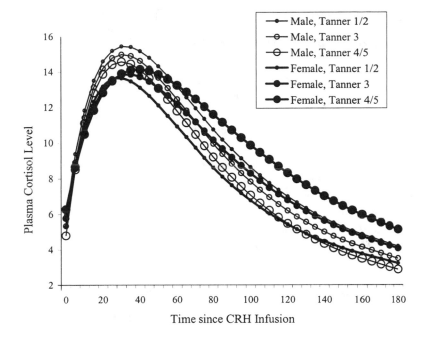

FIGURE 1. Predicted cortisol responses to CRH infusion by gender and pubertal stage.

differences emerge in depressed or high-risk adolescents and whether responses to psychological challenges show similar changes over puberty.

REFERENCES

1. NOLEN-HOEKSEMA, S. 1990. Sex Differences in Depression. Stanford University Press. Stanford, CA.
2. NOLEN-HOEKSEMA, S. & J.S. GIRGUS. 1994. The emergence of gender differences in depression during adolescence. Psychol. Bull. **115:** 424–443.
3. DAHL, R.E., N.D. RYAN, J. PUIG-ANTICH, *et al.* 1991. 24-hour cortisol measures in adolescents with major depression: a controlled study. Biol. Psychiatry **30:** 25–36.
4. GOODYER, I.M., J. HERBERT, A. TAMPLIN, *et al.* 2000. Recent life events, cortisol, dehydroepiandrosterone and the onset of major depression in high-risk adolescents. Br. J. Psychiatry **177:** 499–504.
5. DAHL, R.E., J. KAUFMAN, N.D. RYAN, *et al.* 1992. The dexamethasone suppression test in children and adolescents: a review and a controlled study. Biol. Psychiatry **32:** 109–126.
6. ATKINSON, H.C. & B.J. WADDELL. 1997. Circadian variation in basal plasma corticosterone and adrenocorticotropin in the rat: sexual dimorphism and changes across the estrous cycle. Endocrinology **138:** 3842–3848.
7. CRITCHLOW, V., R.A. LIEBELT, M. BAR-SELA, *et al.* 1963. Sex difference in resting pituitary-adrenal function in the rat. Am. J. Physiol. **205:** 807–815.
8. LEGRO, R.S., H.M. LIN, L.M. DEMERS, *et al.* 2003. Urinary free cortisol increases in adolescent caucasian females during perimenarche. J. Clin. Endocrinol. Metab. **88:** 215–219.

Sleep Hygiene and Sleep Quality in Italian and American Adolescents

MONIQUE K. LeBOURGEOIS,[a] FLAVIA GIANNOTTI,[b] FLAVIA CORTESI,[b] AMY WOLFSON,[c] AND JOHN HARSH[d]

[a]Sleep and Chronobiology Research Laboratory, E.P. Bradley Hospital/Brown Medical School Department of Psychiatry and Human Behavior, Providence, Rhode Island 02906, USA

[b]Center of Pediatric Sleep Disorders, Department of Developmental Neurology and Psychiatry, University of Rome "La Sapienza," Rome, Italy

[c]Department of Psychology, College of the Holy Cross, Worcester, Massachusetts 01610, USA

[d]Department of Psychology, The University of Southern Mississippi, Hattiesburg, Mississippi 39406, USA

ABSTRACT: This study investigated cross-cultural differences in adolescent sleep hygiene and sleep quality. Participants were 1348 students (655 males; 693 females) aged 12–17 years from public school systems in Rome, Italy (n = 776) and Southern Mississippi (n = 572). Participants completed the Adolescent Sleep-Wake Scale and the Adolescent Sleep Hygiene Scale. Reported sleep hygiene and sleep quality were significantly better for Italian than American adolescents. A moderate linear relationship was observed between sleep hygiene and sleep quality in both samples (Italians: R = .40; Americans: R = .46). Separate hierarchical multiple regression analyses showed that sleep hygiene accounted for significant variance in sleep quality, even after controlling for demographic and health variables (Italians: R^2 = .38; Americans: R^2 = .44). The results of this study suggest that there are cultural differences in sleep quality and sleep hygiene practices, and that sleep hygiene practices are importantly related to adolescent sleep quality.

KEYWORDS: adolescence; sleep hygiene; sleep quality

INTRODUCTION

Previous research has shown that sleep difficulties are common during adolescence. Furthermore, poor or inadequate sleep is associated with negative outcomes, including daytime sleepiness, emotional dysfunction, and behavioral problems.[1] Sleep hygiene may be importantly related to adolescent sleep quality; however, this relationship has not been well explored. The purpose of the present study was to (1)

Address for correspondence: Monique K. LeBourgeois, Ph.D., E.P. Bradley Hospital/Brown Medical School, Sleep and Chronobiology Research Laboratory, 300 Duncan Drive, Providence, RI 02906. Voice: 401-421-9440; fax: 401-453-3578.
monique_lebourgeois@brown.edu

Ann. N.Y. Acad. Sci. 1021: 352–354 (2004). © 2004 New York Academy of Sciences.
doi: 10.1196/annals.1308.044

TABLE 1. Sample characteristics for Italian and American students ($N = 1348$)

	Italian ($n = 776$)	American ($n = 572$)	Statistics
Age[a]	14.6 (1.60)	14.6 (1.60)	
Sex (% male)	54.5	41.2	$\chi^2 = 29.1, P < .001$
Race (% Caucasian)	99.6	21.7	$\chi^2 = 887.2, P < .001$
SES[a,b]	4.5 (1.40)	5.1 (0.61)	$t = 6.3, P < .001$
Medications (%)	5.5	18.2	$\chi^2 = 58.9, P < .001$
Illnesses/disabilities (%)	8.6	16.8	$\chi^2 = 20.5, P < .001$
Pubertal status[a]	3.1 (0.56)	3.2 (0.56)	
Circadian preference[a]	26.3 (4.12)	26.0 (4.36)	

NOTE: SES = socioeconomic status.
[a]Mean (Standard Deviation).
[b]Occupational scoring for head of household (1 = unskilled to 9 = professional)

compare the sleep hygiene practices and sleep quality of adolescents from two industrialized societies, Italy and the United States; and (2) investigate the relationship between sleep hygiene and sleep quality in both samples.

METHODS

Participants were 1348 adolescents (655 males; 693 females) aged 12–17 years (M = 14.6; SD = 1.6). Data were collected from public school systems in Rome, Italy ($n = 776$; response rate = 83.3%) and Southern Mississippi ($n = 572$; response rate = 57.4%). As shown in TABLE 1, samples did not statistically differ in mean age, pubertal status, and circadian preference. Participants completed the following pencil-and-paper self-report measures:

(a) *Self-Rating Scale for Pubertal Development*[2]—This 5-item scale provides an overall measure of physical maturation. Pubertal Development Scale scores range from 1 (not yet started) to 4 (seems complete).

(b) *Morningness/Eveningness Scale*[3]—This 10-item measure of circadian preference produces scores ranging from 10 (extreme evening) to 43 (extreme morning).

(c) *Adolescent Sleep-Wake Scale (ASWS)*—The ASWS is a 28-item measure of the following sleep quality domains: Going to Bed, Falling Asleep, Maintaining Sleep, Reinitiating Sleep, Returning to Wakefulness. Sleep quality scores range from 1 (very poor) to 6 (very good).

(d) *Adolescent Sleep Hygiene Scale (ASHS)*—The ASHS includes 33 items that assess sleep hygiene practices along several conceptual domains (Physiological, Cognitive, Emotional, Sleep Environment, Substances, Bedtime Routine, Daytime Sleep, Sleep Stability, and Bed Sharing). Sleep hygiene scores range from 1 (very poor) to 6 (very good).

RESULTS

Reported sleep hygiene was significantly better ($P < .001$) for Italian (M = 4.5, SD = .57) than American adolescents (M = 4.0, SD = .61). Likewise, Italian students reported significantly better ($P < .001$) sleep quality than American students (M = 4.4, SD = .53; M = 4.0, SD = .71, respectively). A moderate linear relationship was observed between sleep hygiene and sleep quality in both samples (Italians: $R = .40$, $P < .01$; Americans: $R = .46, P < .01$). Separate hierarchical multiple regression analyses were performed on the samples to control for variables that may account for these relationships. The variables entered in step 1 included demographic characteristics [age, sex, race (Americans only)], SES, medication/illness status, pubertal status, and circadian preference. For both samples, variables in step 1 explained a significant proportion ($P < .001$) of the variance in sleep quality [Italians: $R^2 = .18$, $F(7, 747) = 24.09$; Americans: $R^2 = .25$, $F(8, 553) = 23.13$]. Sleep hygiene (ASHS) scores were added in step 2. The total variance explained was significantly increased [Italians: $R^2 = .35$, $F(9, 738) = 21.52$; Americans: $R^2 = .41$, $F(9, 544) = 16.12$]. Sleep hygiene was responsible for significant variance above that accounted for by variables entered in step 1 (17% for Italians; 16% for Americans). A final hierarchical multiple regression analysis with all cases (both samples combined) showed that geographic location (Italy vs. the United States) only explained an additional 1% of the variance in ASWS scores after controlling for sleep hygiene and all other variables.

DISCUSSION

This study suggests cultural differences in sleep quality and sleep hygiene practices during adolescence. The results also indicate that sleep hygiene practices are importantly related to sleep quality. Further research is needed to determine if practicing good sleep hygiene will result in improved sleep quality, reduced daytime sleepiness, and better daytime functioning during adolescence.

REFERENCES

1. ROBERTS, R.E., C.R. ROBERTS & I. G. CHEN. 2002. Impact of insomnia on future functioning of adolescents. J. Psychosom. Res. **53:** 561–569.
2. CARSKADON, M.A. & C. ACEBO. 1993. A self-administered rating scale for pubertal development. J. Adolesc. Health **4:** 190–195.
3. CARSKADON, M.A., R. SEIFER & C. ACEBO. 1991. Reliability of six scales in a sleep questionnaire for adolescents. Sleep Res. **20:** 421.

Cognitive and Emotional Components of Frontal Lobe Functioning in Childhood and Adolescence

ISABELLE M. ROSSO,[a,b] ASHLEY D. YOUNG,[a] LISA A. FEMIA,[a]
AND DEBORAH A. YURGELUN-TODD[a,b]

[a]McLean Hospital, Cognitive Neuroimaging Laboratory,
Belmont, Massachusetts 02478, USA

[b]Harvard Medical School, Boston, Massachusetts 02115, USA

ABSTRACT: Frontal lobe functions include a range of cognitive, emotional, and social abilities that enable goal-directed behavior. Although a number of studies have plotted the development of frontal lobe functions in childhood, few have extended into the adolescent years. There is also little information on which cognitive and emotional components of frontal functioning may be correlated. The aims of this study were to identify and compare age effects on different components of frontal functioning in childhood and adolescence and to examine whether abstract reasoning skills were associated with levels of emotional intelligence and social sensitivity. Twenty children (ages 9–18) were recruited from the local community for a study of normal adolescent brain development. All subjects were free of psychiatric or developmental disorders, as determined by a structured interview. Subjects completed a comprehensive neuropsychological test battery, as well as self-report measures of social sensitivity (anxiety) and emotional intelligence. Significant age effects were found for measures of abstract reasoning, response inhibition, and attentional set shifting. Levels of social anxiety increased moderately with age, although not significantly at this sample size. Abstract reasoning skills correlated positively with levels of social anxiety but not emotional intelligence. The pattern of results suggests differential developmental trajectories across various cognitive and emotional domains of frontal lobe functioning in childhood and adolescence. Increased abstract reasoning ability may be associated with increased vulnerability to social anxiety during this period.

KEYWORDS: adolescence; development; cognition; emotion; anxiety

INTRODUCTION

Frontal lobe functioning encompasses a number of cognitive and emotional faculties that show a protracted developmental course, beginning in infancy and continuing at least until early adolescence.[1] Developmental changes in cognitive

Address for correspondence: Isabelle M. Rosso, Ph.D., McLean Hospital, Brain Imaging Center, 115 Mill Street, Belmont, MA 02478. Voice: 617-855-2607; fax: 617-855-3713. irosso@hms.harvard.edu

Ann. N.Y. Acad. Sci. 1021: 355–362 (2004). © 2004 New York Academy of Sciences.
doi: 10.1196/annals.1308.045

components of frontal functioning include gains in attentional control, working memory capacity, response inhibition, as well as a gradual shift from relatively concrete to increasingly abstract thinking.[2–7] The maturation of socio-emotional components of frontal functioning includes improved abilities to identify, express, and manage emotions[8]—skills that are elements of the broader construct of "emotional intelligence."[9] There is also a developmental progression in the nature or content of childhood fears, from separation anxiety in early childhood to social-evaluative concerns in early adolescence.[10] Most previous developmental studies of frontal functions, however, have focused on the prepubertal years, with few extending into adolescence and young adulthood. Thus, it is unclear which aspects or components of frontal functioning continue to change or progress into adolescence and which components are stable at this stage of development.

It is also unclear which cognitive and emotional aspects of frontal functioning are correlated versus independent in childhood and adolescence. Information processing models of social anxiety and emotional intelligence suggest that both may be mediated in part by inferential thinking about the mental states of other people.[11,12] An ability to make inferences about others' thoughts may relate to levels of social anxiety, while an ability to deduce others' feelings may relate to levels of emotional intelligence. We suggest that both types of abilities require abstract reasoning skills, specifically a metacognitive or abstract awareness of "self" and "other." We therefore hypothesized that abstract reasoning skills would be associated with higher levels of social anxiety and emotional intelligence in childhood and adolescence.

This study had two main aims. The first was to examine whether increasing age in a sample of children and adolescents was associated with improving scores on tasks tapping different cognitive and emotional dimensions of frontal lobe functioning. The second was to examine whether emotional intelligence and social anxiety were correlated with performance on a neurocognitive measure of abstraction.

METHODS

The participants in this study were 20 children and adolescents (10 male, 10 female) aged 9 to 18 years, from middle class families of the local community. All spoke English as their first language and none had a history of developmental disorder, learning disability, neurological disorder, or Axis I psychiatric disorder. They received standardized psychiatric interviews (KSADS), self-report personality inventories, and a comprehensive two-hour neuropsychological test battery. This report focuses on the tests of frontal lobe functioning shown in TABLE 1.

We conducted Spearman's correlations (rho) to evaluate associations between age and the frontal lobe measures. We also qualitatively examined the trajectories of age-related differences in frontal measures with graphs dividing the sample into three age groups, which were chosen based on Levin and colleagues[4] (preadolescence, ages 9–12, $N = 6$; early adolescence, ages 13–15, $N = 7$; late adolescence, ages 16–19, $N = 7$). Finally, we examined the relationship of emotional intelligence and social anxiety with abstract reasoning ability with Spearman's rho: first using the raw scores of each measure and then using the residual values from regressions that removed the effects of age on each of the three measures.

TABLE 1. Measures of cognitive and emotional components of frontal functioning

Functional domain and measure	Variable
Verbal working memory	
Digit Span, Backwards (WAIS-III)	Total correct
Abstraction	
Matrix Reasoning (WAIS-III)	Total correct
Response inhibition	
Stroop, Color-Word Interference	Time to complete interference subtest—Time to complete color-naming subtest
Stroop, Color-Word Interference	Total errors on interference subtest
Verbal fluency	
Phonemic, COWA	Total words
Semantic, Animal Naming	Total words
Cognitive flexibility	
Trail Making Test, B–A (HRB)	Time to complete condition "B"—Time to complete condition "A"
Emotional intelligence	
Emotional quotient, Bar-On Test	Raw score, total emotional quotient
Social sensitivity	
MASC	Raw score, social anxiety scale

NOTE: WAIS-III, Wechsler Adult Intelligence Scale, Version III; COWA, Controlled Oral Word Association Test; HRB, Halstead Reitan Battery; MASC, Multidimensional Anxiety Scale for Children.

TABLE 2. Spearman's correlations (rho) of age with cognitive and emotional measures of frontal functioning

	rho	P
Emotional intelligence	−0.04	.88
Social anxiety	0.35	.14
Digit Span backward	0.27	.25
Stroop interference	−0.39	.09
Stroop errors	−0.63	.003
COWA fluency	0.06	.79
Semantic fluency	−0.01	.97
Matrix reasoning	0.51	.02
Trail making B–A	−0.46	.04

RESULTS

TABLE 2 displays the correlations of age and each of the measures of frontal functioning. Increasing age was significantly associated with better performance on measures of abstract reasoning, attentional set shifting, and response inhibition (FIGS. 1A, 2A, 3A). FIGURES 1B, 2B, and 3B show the mean and standard error for these three neuropsychological domains across the three age groups. We did not see the hypothesized age effects on emotional intelligence quotients, although social

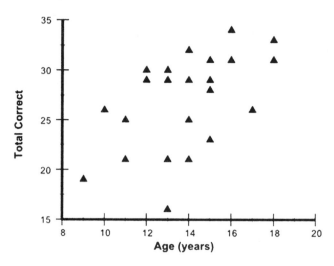

FIGURE 1. (A) Abstract reasoning scores and increasing age.

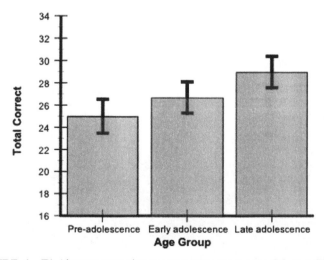

FIGURE 1. (B) Abstract reasoning scores across age groups (Mean ± SEM).

anxiety levels did show a moderate age-related increase that may become statistically significant with a larger sample.

Spearman's correlations revealed a significant association between matrix reasoning performance and social anxiety levels (rho = 0.46, P = .04), which retained trend significance level after removing the contribution of age (rho = 0.40, P = .09). Emotional intelligence was not associated with matrix reasoning scores either before (rho = 0.12, P = .61) or after (rho = 0.21, P = .38) partialling out the effects of age.

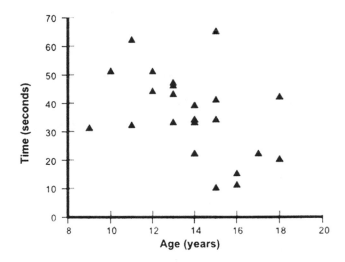

FIGURE 2. (A) Attentional shifting and increasing age.

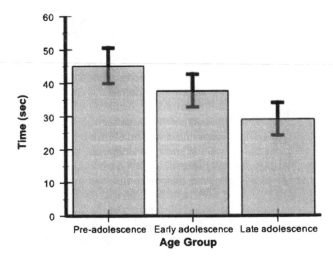

FIGURE 2. (B) Attentional shifting scores across age groups (Mean ± SEM).

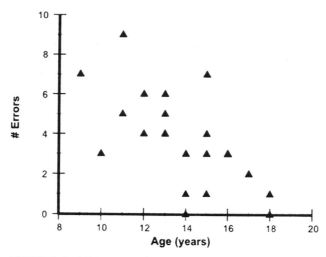

FIGURE 3. (A) Response inhibition errors and increasing age.

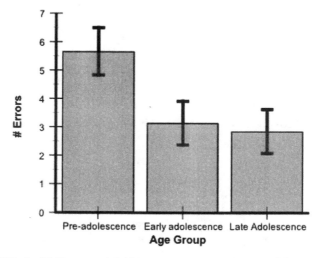

FIGURE 3. (B) Response inhibition errors across age groups (Mean ± SEM).

CONCLUSIONS

These findings suggest differential rates or timelines of development across various cognitive and emotional domains of frontal lobe functioning through late childhood and adolescence. Indices of verbal fluency, verbal working memory, and emotional intelligence did not show significant age-related trends. In contrast, there were statistically significant age effects on measures of abstract reasoning, attentional set shifting, and response inhibition. Abstraction and set-shifting abilities improved at a constant rate throughout the age range, while response inhibition performance seemed to level off by early adolescence. Finally, social anxiety levels increased moderately with age, although this did not reach statistical significance at this sample size.

To our knowledge, this is the first study to report an association between adolescents' levels of social anxiety and their abstract reasoning skills. This relationship is interesting in light of theories whereby social anxiety results in part from constructing a (negative) image of how one appears to others during a social encounter.[11,12] We suggest that taking this "observer perspective" on the self may require developmental gains in abstract reasoning skills. If so, the maturation of abstract reasoning abilities may be an enabling factor in the increased vulnerability to social anxiety disorder during adolescence. Alternatively, it is possible that social anxiety appears independently of abstract reasoning skills, but that it is maintained or exacerbated by higher levels of abstraction ability.

Limitations of this study include the small sample size and the cross-sectional nature of the analyses. Consequently, we anticipate verifying these patterns of findings as the sample of this ongoing study increases, and as the subjects return for follow-up longitudinal assessments. The resultant increase in statistical power will also enable us to examine possible moderating effects of gender.

Strengths of this study include its potential relevance to neuropsychiatric disorders that show an increase or peak in risk for onset during adolescence, including social anxiety disorder and schizophrenia. Specifically, characterizing normal maturational changes in frontal functions may help elucidate the pathophysiology of illnesses whose manifestation may be mediated in part by deviations in peri-adolescent frontal lobe development.

REFERENCES

1. STUSS, D.T. & B. LEVINE. 2002. Adult clinical neuropsychology: lessons from studies of the frontal lobes. Annu. Rev. Psychol. **53:** 401–433.
2. ANDERSON, V.A. *et al.* 2001. Development of executive functions through late childhood and adolescence in an Australian sample. Dev. Neuropsychol. **20:** 385–406.
3. KLENBERG, L., M. KORKMAN & P. LAHTI-NUUTILA. 2001. Differential development of attention and executive functions in 3- to 12-year-old Finnish children. Dev. Neuropsychol. **20:** 407–428.
4. LEVIN, H.S. *et al.* 1991. Developmental changes in performance on tests of purported frontal lobe functioning. Dev. Neuropsychol. **7:** 377–395.
5. LUCIANA, M. & C.A. NELSON. 1998. The functional emergence of prefrontally-guided working memory systems in four- to eight-year-old children. Neuropsychologia **36:** 273–293.
6. SPEAR, L.P. 2000. The adolescent brain and age-related behavioral manifestations. Neurosci. Biobehav. Rev. **24:** 417–463.
7. WILLIAMS, B.R. *et al.* 1999. Development of inhibitory control across the life span. Dev. Psychol. **35:** 205–213.
8. KOLB, B., B. WILSON & L. TAYLOR. 1992. Developmental changes in the recognition and comprehension of facial expression: implications for frontal lobe function. Brain Cogn. **20:** 74–84.
9. BAR-ON, R. 1997. The Bar-On Emotional Quotient Inventory (EQ-i): a test of emotional intelligence. Multi-Health Systems. Toronto, Canada.

10. PINE, D.S. 2001. Affective neuroscience and the development of social anxiety disorder. Psychiatr. Clin. North Am. **24:** 689–705.
11. SPURR, J.M. & L. STOPA. 2002. Self-focused attention in social phobia and social anxiety. Clin. Psychol. Rev. **22:** 947–975.
12. CLARK, D.M. & F. MCMANUS. 2002. Information processing in social phobia. Biol. Psychiatry **51:** 92–100.

Trajectories of Adolescent Emotional and Cognitive Development

Effects of Sex and Risk for Drug Use

MARISA M. SILVERI, [a,b] GOLFO K. TZILOS,[a] PATRICIA J. PIMENTEL,[a]
AND DEBORAH A. YURGELUN-TODD[a,b]

[a]Cognitive Neuroimaging Laboratory, McLean Hospital,
Belmont, Massachusetts 02478, USA

[b]Harvard Medical School, Cambridge, Massachusetts 02478, USA

ABSTRACT: Adolescence has been widely accepted as a time for notable alterations in brain functioning. The objective of this longitudinal study was to compare trajectories of emotional and cognitive development in adolescent girls and boys with low- versus high-risk for future drug use. Nineteen healthy adolescents (aged 13.9 ± 2.0 years; 10 girls), stratified into low- and high-risk groups based on family history of drug abuse, were examined at baseline and after one year. Emotional intelligence was assessed using the Bar-On Emotional Quotient Inventory, the Multidimensional Anxiety Scale for Children, and the Perceived Stress Scale. The neurocognitive test battery was designed to evaluate academic achievement, executive function, verbal memory and learning, and included the Wide Range Achievement Test, Stroop Color-Word Interference Test, Rey Auditory Verbal Learning Test, and Digit Span and Digit Symbol subtests of the Wechsler Adult Intelligence Scale-Revised. Improvements in academic achievement, executive function, and working memory were observed at the one-year follow-up. Notable sex differences also were evident in emotional intelligence, academic achievement, and memory. Interestingly, these sex-related differences interacted with risk status; improvement in cognitive performance in boys and low-risk girls was generally superior to high-risk girls, who tended to show modest, if any, improvement at the one-year follow-up. These preliminary findings provide evidence of sex differences in emotion intelligence and cognitive function. Furthermore, these data also suggest that history of familial drug abuse may have a more pronounced impact on emotional and cognitive development in adolescent girls than boys.

KEYWORDS: adolescent; development; cognition; family history; substance abuse; emotion

Adolescence is a time for notable alterations in brain structure and re-organization, accompanied by changes in emotional and cognitive function.[1–4] The onset of substance use often occurs during this critical developmental period and is a reliable

Address for correspondence: Marisa M. Silveri, Ph.D., Cognitive Neuroimaging Laboratory, Brain Imaging Center, McLean Hospital, 115 Mill Street, Belmont, MA 02478. Voice: 617-855-2920; fax: 617-855-2770.

msilveri@hms.harvard.edu

Ann. N.Y. Acad. Sci. 1021: 363–370 (2004). © 2004 New York Academy of Sciences.
doi: 10.1196/annals.1308.046

predictor of future drug-related problems.[5] Accordingly, developmental studies may help determine if alterations in cerebral structure and/or function in drug-dependent adults are a consequence of chronic drug use during development or the result of vulnerabilities present prior to initiation of drug use.

Previous studies have determined that exposure to family substance use disorders (family history positive (FH+) status) during adolescence also predicts future substance abuse.[6] To date, previous FH adolescent studies documenting the negative effects of family history status and/or adolescent drug use on cognition mainly have focused on boys, or have included children with Axis I diagnoses.[7,8] Furthermore, empirical studies of children with familial substance abuse histories have not included measures of emotional development. Thus, the goal of the present longitudinal study was to examine developmental changes in adolescent girls and boys, FH– or FH+, for substance abuse, on measures of emotional intelligence, academic achievement, and cognitive functioning.

METHODS

Subjects

Participants included 19 healthy adolescent volunteers (10 girls) (TABLE 1). Adolescents were stratified into FH– or FH+ based on structured interviews with the accompanying parent, in which family (parent and/or grandparent) history of alcohol or drug abuse was obtained. Subjects completed baseline and one-year follow-up visits, and were free of Axis I diagnoses, neurological illness, severe medical problems, and psychoactive substance use. Subjects were recruited via local advertisement and all received monetary compensation for their participation. All subjects and their parent(s) or guardian(s) provided written informed consent prior to study participation.

Clinical Assessments

Trained research technicians administered all assessments. These assessments included the structured clinical psychiatric interview using the Kiddie-Schedule for Affective Disorders and Schizophrenia (K-SADS) and for emotional intelligence, the Bar-On Emotional Quotient Inventory, the Multidimensional Anxiety Scale for Children (MASC), and the Perceived Stress Scale (PSS, data only available at follow-up).

TABLE 1. Subject demographics

	Girls FH+ (N = 5)	Girls FH– (N = 5)	Boys FH+ (N = 5)	Boys FH– (N = 4)
Age ± SD (years)	12.8 ± 2.3	14.2 ± 2.2	15.0 ± 2.3	13.0 ± 0.8
Education ± SD (years)	7.2 ± 2.1	8.6 ± 2.0	9.4 ± 2.0	7.0 ± 0.8
Handedness	4R, 1L	5R	5R	4R

Academic and Cognitive Screening Tests

An abbreviated battery of academic and intellectual screening tests was administered to all subjects. These tests included the Wide Range Achievement Test (WRAT-R; Reading, Spelling and Arithmetic subtests), Stroop Color-Word Interference test, Rey Auditory Verbal Learning Test (RAVLT), and Wechsler Adult Intelligence Scale-Revised (WAIS-R; Digit Span and Symbol subtests).

Data Analyses

Separate 2(Sex) × 2(FH+ vs. FH–) × 2(Baseline vs. 1 year) repeated measures analyses of variance (ANOVAs) and Fishers post hoc tests were used to examine emotion, academic and cognitive measures. All significant ANOVAs are reported ($\alpha = .05$).

RESULTS

Emotional Intelligence

Bar-On Adaptability. There was a main effect of risk, $F(1,14) = 4.68, P < .05$, with FH+ adolescents displaying significantly higher adaptability scores than FH– adolescents (Fig. 1). A significant effect of time, $F(1,14) = 5.45, P < .05$, which interacted with sex, $F(1,14) = 7.24, P < .02$, was observed for the Total Emotional Quotient; only girls declined significantly over time. MASC: Significant effects of risk, $F(1,14) = 12.33, P < .005$, and time, $F(1,14) = 5.23, P < .05$, along with a time × risk interaction, $F(1,14) = 9.49, P < .01$, were observed, with the FH+ group displaying significantly lower anxiety scores across both testing times. PSS: There was a significant sex effect observed at follow-up, $F(1,14) = 4.92, P < .05$, with girls (14.7 + 1.9, mean + SEM) exhibiting significantly higher perceived stress scores than boys (9.9 ± 0.9).

Academic Achievement

WRAT-R. There was a significant sex × risk interaction, $F(1,15) = 9.05, P < .01$, for the reading subtest; FH+ girls exhibited significantly lower reading scores than boys and FH– girls (Fig. 2). There also was a trend for a main effect of sex for the reading subtest ($P = .06$). Significant effects of sex, $F(1,15) = 8.15, P < .05$, and time, $F(1,15) = 9.83, P < .01$, were observed for the spelling subtest, along with a trend for a sex × risk interaction ($P = .09$). Post hoc test revealed that boys had significantly higher spelling scores than girls, especially when compared with FH– girls. Adolescents also improved spelling performance significantly over time. Similarly, a sex × risk interaction, $F(1,15) = .01, P < .03$, and a main effect of time, $F(1,15) = 8.63, P < .02$, were observed for the arithmetic subtest. Boys and FH– girls had significantly higher arithmetic scores than FH+ girls. Adolescents also improved significantly over time.

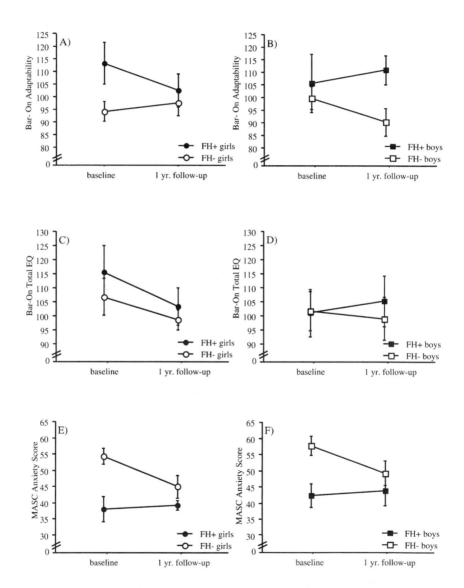

FIGURE 1. Measures of emotional intelligence: Bar-On Adaptability in (**A**) girls and (**B**) boys; Bar-On Total Emotional Quotient in (**C**) girls and (**D**) boys; MASC in (**E**) girls and (**F**) boys. FH+ adolescents are indicated as *closed symbols* and FH− adolescents are indicated as *open symbols*. All data represent the mean ± SEM.

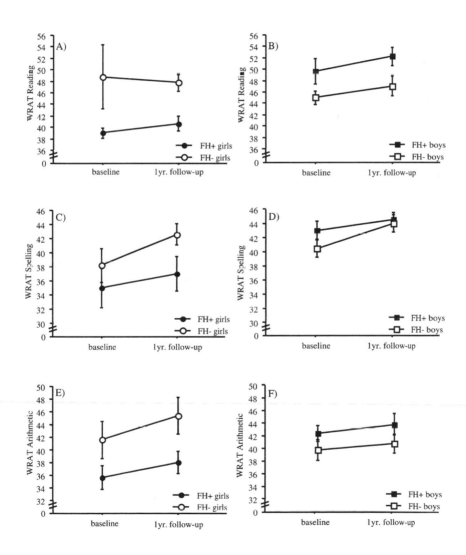

FIGURE 2. Measures of academic achievement on the WRAT: Reading subtest in (**A**) girls and (**B**) boys; Spelling subtest in (**C**) girls and (**D**) boys; Arithmetic subtest in (**E**) girls and (**F**) boys. FH+ adolescents are indicated as *closed symbols* and FH− adolescents are indicated as *open symbols*. All data represent the mean ± SEM.

TABLE 2. Stroop Color-Word Interference Task

Test	Girls FH+ ($N = 5$)	Girls FH− ($N = 5$)	Boys FH+ ($N = 5$)	Boys FH− ($N = 4$)
Color Naming	-5.6 ± 1.5	-9.2 ± 7.0	-3.5 ± 2.5	-8.2 ± 1.9
Word Reading	0.4 ± 1.9	-5.2 ± 1.3	-3.8 ± 2.2	-2.2 ± 1.9
Interference	-18.4 ± 1.3	-14.8 ± 3.5	-29.3 ± 17.7	-25.0 ± 5.1

NOTE: Data represent mean change from baseline to follow-up ± SEM (sec).

Cognitive Performance

Stroop Color-Word Interference Test. There were main effects of time for Color Naming ($F(1,15) = 10.63$, $P < .006$), Word Reading ($F(1,15) = 8.88$, $P < .01$), and Interference ($F(1,15) = 29.54$, $P < .0001$); adolescents showed significant improvement from baseline to follow-up (TABLE 2). There also was a sex × risk interaction for Interference, $F(1,15) = 5.30$, $P < .04$, with FH+ girls exhibiting the smallest improvement compared to FH− girls and boys.

Rey Auditory Verbal Learning Task (RAVLT; Total Number Correct). There was a significant sex × risk interaction, $F(1,15) = 4.63$, $P < .05$, with FH− girls recalling significantly fewer words than FH+ girls; this pattern was not observed in boys (FIG. 3). There also was a trend ($P = .08$) towards improvement between baseline and 1 year follow-up.

Digit Symbol (WAIS-R). There was a significant sex × risk interaction, $F(1,15) = 5.09$, $P < .05$, with FH− girls outperforming FH+ girls, and the opposite pattern being observed for FH+ boys, who performed better than FH− boys (FIG. 3). There also was a main effect of time, $F(1,15) = 28.24$, $P < .0001$, demonstrating that adolescents show significant improvement in performance from baseline to follow-up.

DISCUSSION

This is the first longitudinal examination of changes in emotional, academic, and cognitive capacity in adolescent girls and boys, FH+ or FH− for substance abuse. Not surprisingly, all subjects showed improvement in spelling and arithmetic and on performance of the Stroop and Digit Symbol tasks from baseline to one-year follow-up. There was a significant influence of FH status on our measures with FH+ girls displaying poorer academic performance when compared to FH− girls and boys, and FH+ adolescents scoring significantly higher on the adaptability scale and significantly lower on the MASC. In addition, sex differences included boys outperforming girls in academic measurements of reading and spelling and girls reporting higher levels of perceived stress than boys.

Our findings are consistent with previous cognitive studies examining the effects of FH for substance abuse during adolescence. Those studies found elementary school–aged sons of alcoholics exhibited poorer intellectual functioning than sons of nonalcoholics,[7] as well as deficits on measures of language and attention.[8] Taken together, these findings indicate drug use is not necessary for FH+ adolescents to exhibit decreased cognitive performance, perhaps highlighting the importance of risk

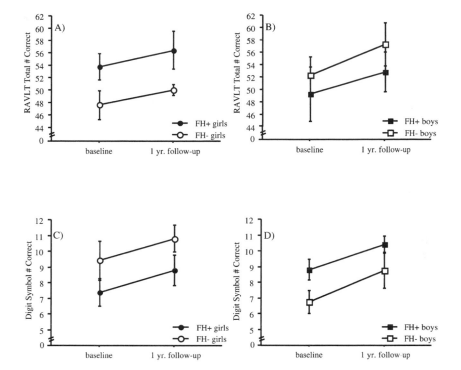

FIGURE 3. Measures of cognitive performance: RAVLT, total number correct across five trials, in (**A**) girls and (**B**) boys; WAIS-R Digit Symbol subtest, total number correct, in (**C**) girls and (**D**) boys. FH+ adolescents are indicated as *closed symbols* and FH− adolescents are indicated as *open symbols*. All data represent the mean ± SEM.

as a factor leading to cognitive impairments, even prior to drug use. These preliminary data are limited by the small sample size and minor differences in age. These data suggest a need for early intervention, as poor cognitive and emotional development may compromise educational attainment and delay healthy psychosocial development.

ACKNOWLEDGMENTS

This study was supported by the Charles H. Hood Foundation (D.Y.T.) and the National Institute on Drug Abuse grant DA12483 (D.Y.T.).

REFERENCES

1. GIEDD, J.N., *et al.* 1996. Quantitative magnetic resonance imaging of human brain development: ages 4–18. Cereb. Cortex **6:** 551–560.

2. PFEFFERBAUM, A., *et al.* 1994. A quantitative magnetic resonance imaging study of changes in brain morphology from infancy to late adulthood. Arch. Neurol. **51:** 874–887.
3. SPEAR, L.P. 2000. The adolescent brain and age-related behavioral manifestations. Neurosci. Biobehav. Rev. **24:** 417–463.
4. YURGELUN-TODD, D. *et al.* 2002. Sex differences in cerebral tissue volume and cognitive performance during adolescence. Psych. Rep. **91:** 743–757.
5. BATES, M.E. & E.W. LABOUVIE. 1997. Adolescent risk factors and the prediction of persistent alcohol and drug use into adulthood. Alcohol. Clin. Exp. Res. **21:** 944–950.
6. BIEDERMAN, J., *et al.* 2000. Patterns of alcohol and drug use in adolescents can be predicted by parental substance use disorders. Pediatrics **106:** 792–797.
7. POON, E., *et al.* 2000. Intellectual, cognitive, and academic performance among sons of alcoholics, during the early school years: differences related to subtypes of familial alcoholism. Alcohol. Clin. Exp. Res. **24:** 1020–1027.
8. TAPERT, S.F. & S.A. BROWN. 2000. Substance dependence, family history of alcohol dependence and neuropsychological functioning in adolescence. Addiction **95:** 1043–1053.

The Human HPLC Column

"Minds-On" Neuroscience for the Next Generation

KYLE J. FRANTZ

Department of Biology, Georgia State University, and the Center for Behavioral Neuroscience, Atlanta, Georgia 30303-3088, USA

ABSTRACT: Science education researchers have suggested that neuroscientists can play an important role in science education programs for adolescents by creating "minds-on" teaching and learning modules for scientists and teachers to use in classrooms. Effective educational partnerships between teachers and visiting scientists not only ignite student interest but also provide opportunities for scientist and teacher professional development. The aim of the present teaching module was threefold: (1) to introduce adolescents to the acute neurochemical effects of psychomotor stimulant drugs and their analysis using high performance liquid chromatography (HPLC), (2) to spur maturation of analytical reasoning skills among adolescents, and (3) to spark enthusiasm for science education.

KEYWORDS: adolescents; science education; analytical reasoning; learning module

INTRODUCTION

During the school year, adolescents spend approximately one-third of their time in school, making the school environment key to their cognitive, social, and physical maturation.[1] With specific reference to the development of critical thinking and skills related to science literacy, early science classes influence abilities and interests in fields such as neuroscience.

To increase science literacy, it is crucial to change current trends in education. Only 26% of U.S. high school seniors are predicted to perform at a C-level or better in undergraduate courses.[2] Initiatives in education reform emphasize inquiry-based active learning and real-world relevance.[3,4] These approaches yield rapid intellectual development[5] and may increase interest and motivation to learn science.[4] One highly relevant topic for adolescents is the impact of drug abuse on the nervous system. Out of 43,700 U.S. secondary school students surveyed, more than half will have tried an illicit drug by the time they complete high school.[6] Neuroscientists who study this and other relevant topics are therefore prime candidates to assist in education reform.

Address for correspondence: Kyle J. Frantz, Department of Biology, MSC 8E 0698, 33 Gilmer Street SE Unit 8, Georgia State University, Atlanta, GA 30303-3088. Voice: 404-651-1487; fax: 404-651-3929.
kfrantz@gsu.edu

Ann. N.Y. Acad. Sci. 1021: 371–375 (2004). © 2004 New York Academy of Sciences.
doi: 10.1196/annals.1308.047

Neuroscientists already visit schools to discuss educational paths and career goals. As per recommendations of science education researchers, neuroscientists can help further by creating "minds-on" teaching and learning modules for scientists and teachers to use in classrooms.[7] Effective educational partnerships between teachers and visiting scientists not only ignite student interest but also provide mutually beneficial opportunities for scientist and teacher professional development.[3]

The aim of the present teaching module was threefold: (1) to introduce adolescents to the acute neurochemical effects of psychomotor stimulant drugs and their analysis using high performance liquid chromatography (HPLC), (2) to spur maturation of analytical reasoning skills among adolescents, and (3) to spark enthusiasm for science.

METHODS

The use of HPLC was placed in the context of drugs of abuse and their effects on brain neurochemistry. First, basic brain anatomy and reward circuitry were presented. Second, neurotransmission was reviewed, with a focus on dopamine release and

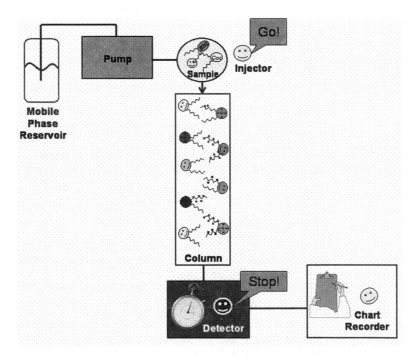

FIGURE 1. The human HPLC column actively involved adolescents in their own science exploration. They played roles including solid phase particles and analyte molecules in a sample.

its facilitation by psychomotor stimulant drugs. Finally, recording *in vivo* neuro-chemical events using microdialysis coupled with HPLC was introduced. Visual aides for background materials were obtained in part from the National Institute on Drug Abuse Slide Teaching Packets (www.nida.nih.gov).

Once familiar with a context for HPLC, students became a "human HPLC column." They acted out components of the column and its stationary phase, regulated passage of "molecules" (other students) down the column, collected data on retention time for different types of molecules (e.g., dopamine and its metabolites), and graphed the results. Specifically, six to eight volunteers were recruited to serve as "solid phase" by lining up facing one another and waving their arms as though the arms were hydrocarbons attached to a silanol surface on the silica beads comprising the solid phase (FIG. 1). Three to six "analyte" volunteers, labeled as dopamine, co-caine, or benzoylecgonine (metabolite of cocaine), gathered at the top of the "column" awaiting further instructions. An "injector" volunteer initiated "sample injection" by saying "Go!" to the "analyte" lined up at the head of the column.

Different molecular interactions between solid phase and analytes were modeled as follows: "Dopamine" students progressed down the "column" freely, by walking between the "solid phase" students waving their arms. "Cocaine" students pro-gressed down the "column" waving their own arms, causing brief contact with the "solid phase" students still waving their arms. "Benzoylecgonine" students pro-gressed down the "column" shaking hands with each "solid phase" student, simulat-ing intermolecular attractions between analyte and solid phase.

When each "analyte" reached the end of the column, a "detector" volunteer an-nounced the completion of the run by saying "Stop!" A "timer" volunteer noted "re-tention time" by recording the number of seconds required for each molecule to progress down the column. A "chart recorder" volunteer placed retention times on a table he or she created on the chalkboard.

Data were plotted with retention time on the *x*-axis and amount of analyte (i.e., number of students of the assigned type of molecule) on the *y*-axis (FIG. 2). This graphing exercise aided in student review of graphing techniques and enabled stu-dents to create a type of chromatogram. Students were then challenged to consider and graph changes in the data that would follow administration of a higher dose of a stimulant or repeated administration of the same dose (i.e., elevations in brain levels

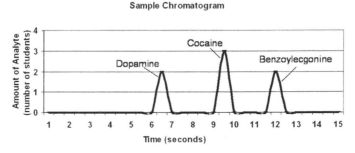

FIGURE 2. A sample "chromatogram" from the activity.

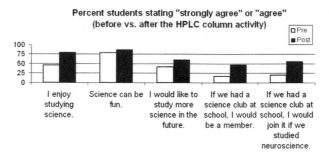

FIGURE 3. Attitudes toward science improved after the activity, as measured by answers to questions including those abbreviated on the columns.

of dopamine, cocaine, and benzoylecgonine after cocaine intake, or increase in dopamine response after repeated cocaine). Advanced students were led in a discussion of limitations of the model. For example, there was no mobile phase; the intricacies of chemical detection following the separation were ignored, and dopamine, cocaine, and benzoylecgonine are not likely to be separated and detected on the same HPLC system.

RESULTS

Attitudes toward science improved after the HPLC column activity, according to surveys of 10–12th grade students conducted before and after the HPLC column activity ($N = 25$; FIG. 3). "Being active and creating models" was the "top favorite" way of learning for 33% of students in 10–12th grade ($N = 32$; data not shown). (Notably, 41.7% ranked "listening to my teacher talk" as their least favorite way of learning.) Over 90% of students stated that they "had fun" in class that day.

DISCUSSION

The human HPLC column created an active learning environment while teaching a relatively complex concept in analytical chemistry. Future educational endeavors should combine and evaluate this and other activities in order to describe progress in reasoning skills among adolescents who participate consistently in such "minds-on" neuroscience modules.

REFERENCES

1. STEINBERG, L. 2002. Adolescence, 6th edit. McGraw-Hill Higher Education. New York.
2. AMERICAN COLLEGE TESTING. 2003. ACT High School Profile Report High School Graduating Class 2003. ACT, Inc. Iowa City.
3. CAMERON, W. & E. CHUDLER. 2003. A role for neuroscientists in engaging young minds. Nature Rev. Neurosci. **4:** 1–6.

4. MORENO, N. 1999. K-12 science education reform-a primer for scientists. BioScience **49:** 569–576.
5. ALLEN, D. & K. TANNER. 2003. Approaches to cell biology teaching: mapping the journey-concept maps as signposts of developing knowledge structures. Cell Biol. Educ. **2:** 133–136.
6. JOHNSTON, L.D., P.M. O'MALLEY & J.G. BACHMAN. 2003. Monitoring the Future national survey results on drug use, 1975–2002. Volume I: Secondary school students (NIH Publication No. 03-5375). National Institute on Drug Abuse. Bethesda, MD.
7. NATIONAL ACADEMY OF SCIENCES. 1996. National Science Education Standards. National Academy Press. Washington, DC.

Significance of Adolescent Neurodevelopment for the Neural Circuitry of Bipolar Disorder

HILARY P. BLUMBERG,[a,b] JOAN KAUFMAN,[b] ANDRÉS MARTIN,[c] DENNIS S. CHARNEY,[d] JOHN H. KRYSTAL,[a,b] AND BRADLEY S. PETERSON[e]

[a]VA Depression Research Center (REAP), VA Connecticut Healthcare System (116-A), West Haven, Connecticut 06516, USA

[b]Department of Psychiatry, Yale University School of Medicine, New Haven, Connecticut 06511, USA

[c]Yale Child Study Center, Yale University School of Medicine, New Haven, Connecticut 06520-7900, USA

[d]Mood and Anxiety Disorders Research Program, National Institute of Mental Health, Bethesda, Maryland 20892-1381, USA

[e]Department of Psychiatry, Columbia College of Physicians & Surgeons, New York, New York 10032, USA

ABSTRACT: The deficits of executive control of emotions and impulses of adult BD implicate involvement of a ventral prefrontal cortex (VPFC) neural system that subserves these functions that include the VPFC, as well as its subcortical connection sites of amygdala, striatum, and thalamus. Differences in the timing of major developmental changes in the structures within this neural system suggest that abnormalities in particular components of this neural system may emerge during critical developmental epochs during the course of the illness. Our recent neuroimaging data suggest that abnormalities in the subcortical components of VPFC neural systems may be evident by early adolescence in BD, whereas VPFC deficits progress over the course of adolescence and may be difficult to detect prior to late adolescence or early adulthood. This potential neurodevelopmental model for BD could have important implications for the recognition of early signs of the disorder and for age-specific treatment strategies.

KEYWORDS: bipolar disorder; magnetic resonance imaging; child development

The influences of the neurodevelopmental trajectories of cortico-limbic structures in adolescence on bipolar disorder (BD) are not known, yet they may have important implications for the recognition of early signs of the disorder and for treatment strategies to target features specific to adolescents with the disorder. In adolescents, BD

Address for correspondence: Hilary P. Blumberg, M.D., Department of Psychiatry, Yale University School of Medicine, VA Depression Research Center (REAP), VA Connecticut Healthcare System (116-A), 950 Campbell Avenue, West Haven, CT 06516. Voice: 203-932-5711, Ext. 4376; fax: 203-937-3886
hilary.blumberg@yale.edu

Ann. N.Y. Acad. Sci. 1021: 376–383 (2004). © 2004 New York Academy of Sciences.
doi: 10.1196/annals.1308.048

symptoms may be less clear than in adults and may show greater phenotypic overlap with other disorders of impulse control such as attention-deficit hyperactivity disorder (ADHD).[1] Early misdiagnosis may place adolescents with BD at risk for negative outcomes. For example, stimulant exposure in individuals with BD may be associated with a worsened course.[2] Moreover, brain structures that are identified as vulnerable to the development of neuropathology during adolescence in BD could be targeted for treatment interventions that may positively influence the course of the disorder.

The deficits of executive control of emotions and impulses of adult BD implicate involvement of a ventral prefrontal cortex (VPFC) neural system that subserves these functions that include the VPFC, as well as its subcortical connection sites of

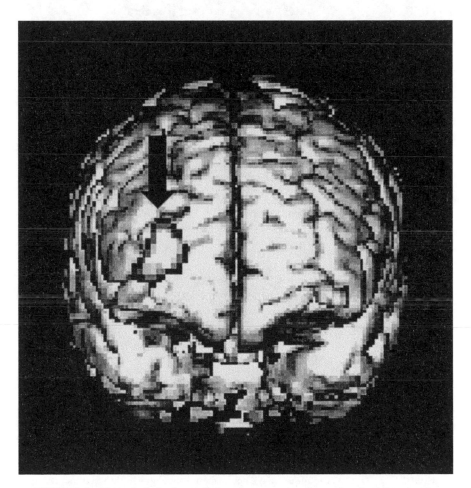

FIGURE 1. This whole-brain rendering demonstrates the region in right rostral prefrontal cortex where activation was relatively decreased during performance of a word-generation task in mania as compared to euthymia in BD.[16] (Figure reprinted with the permission of the *American Journal of Psychiatry.*)

amygdala, striatum, and thalamus.[3] However, differences in the timing of major developmental changes in the structures within this neural system suggest that abnormalities, in particular components of this neural system, may emerge during critical developmental epochs during the course of the illness.

Subcortical structures, such as amygdala, basal ganglia, and thalamus, are thought to be relatively complete in their structural and functional maturity by puberty.[4,5] In contrast, the prefrontal cortex undergoes substantial structural and functional developmental changes during adolescence. Studies of nonhuman primates

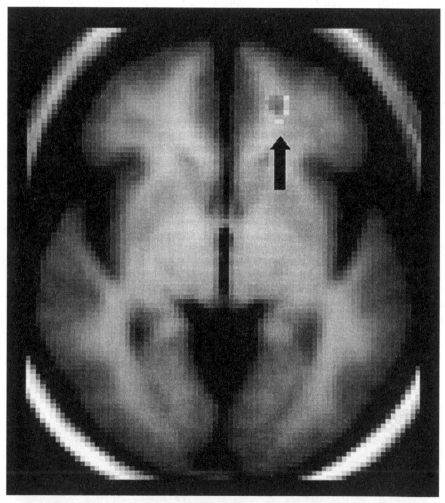

FIGURE 2. This axial-oblique image demonstrates the region of left-ventral prefrontal cortex where activation was relatively decreased during performance of an event-related color-naming Stroop task in individuals with BD in elevated, depressed, and euthymic mood states as compared to healthy comparison subjects.[17] (Figure reprinted with the permission of the American Medical Association.)

demonstrate progressive synaptic changes prior to puberty, followed by substantial regression of synaptic varicosities in prefrontal cortex during adolescence.[6,7] Structural magnetic resonance imaging (MRI) studies in healthy humans provide data consistent with this regional sequence of development of preadolescent increases, and postadolescent decreases, in cortical gray matter.[8–10] This sequence of structural brain development may contribute to a shift over adolescence in the dependence on subcortical to prefrontal structures to accomplish goal-dependent behavior.[11] Functional MRI (fMRI) studies provide evidence in adolescents for increased dependence on prefrontal cortex relative to subcortical structures for task performance, such as increased frontal relative to striatal engagement for tasks that require the inhibition of inappropriate motor responses,[12,13] and increased frontal relative to amygdala engagement during emotional face processing.[14]

Neuroimaging studies of BD in adults[15–17] demonstrate prominent structural and functional abnormalities in VPFC present during acute BD episodes (FIG. 1), as well as across episodes (FIG. 2), suggesting that VPFC abnormalities are a pervasive "trait" feature of the disorder in adults. Cellular abnormalities found on postmortem cytological study of VPFC in BD provide further support for neural abnormalities in this brain region in adult BD.[18] There is scant published data on brain abnormalities in juveniles with BD. The sequence of neurodevelopment suggests that as subcortical structures are relatively complete in their development by puberty, abnormalities in these structures may already be evident by early adolescence in BD. In contrast, the vulnerability to abnormalities in VPFC may not be fully expressed until late adolescence or early adulthood, when VPFC maturation is anticipated to be complete. That is, VPFC structure and function may progressively diverge between healthy individuals and those with BD, such that significant structural and functional differences may not be apparent until later in adolescence or early adulthood.

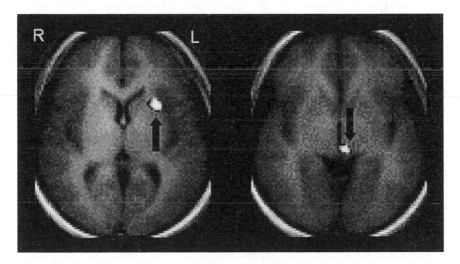

FIGURE 3. This axial-oblique image demonstrates increased activation in left putamen (*left image*) and thalamus (*right image*) in adolescents with BD compared to healthy adolescents.[20] (Figure reprinted with the permission of the *American Journal of Psychiatry.*)

TABLE 1. Adolescent brain development and bipolar disorder

	Clinical features	Impacted brain structures	Neuroimaging abnormalities
Adolescents with bipolar disorder	Symptoms common to childhood disorders of impulse	Subcortical	Amygdala volume decreases; striatal and thalamic activity increases
Adults with bipolar disorder	Deficits in executive regulation of emotion and behaviors	Ventral prefrontal	Ventral prefrontal deficits

Our recent neuroimaging data support the presence of subcortical structural and functional abnormalities, and developing VPFC abnormalities, in adolescents with BD (TABLE 1). In a structural MRI experiment, we observed significant amygdala volume deficits in both adolescents with BD ($N = 14$) and adults with BD ($N = 22$) as compared to healthy adolescent ($N = 23$) and adult ($N = 33$) comparison subjects ($P < .001$).[19] Thus, structural abnormalities in amygdala appear to be an early and stable feature of BD. We investigated potential functional abnormalities in adolescents with BD in an experiment that employed fMRI methods to study 10 adolescents with BD and 10 healthy comparison adolescents during the performance of a color-naming Stroop task. The fMRI data demonstrated activity increases of greater magnitude in left striatum and thalamus in adolescents with BD than in the healthy comparison group ($P < .005$) (FIG. 3).[20] These data also demonstrated age-related increases in VPFC activity in healthy adolescents (FIG. 4), consistent with the progressive prefrontal engagement over adolescence observed by other groups.[12–14] This progressive engagement of VPFC during task performance was not observed in the adolescents with BD. These data suggest that abnormalities in the development of VPFC functional maturity over adolescence in BD may contribute to VPFC abnormalities observed in adults with the disorder.

The structural and functional MRI data in adolescents with BD, considered in the context of the putative sequence of neurodevelopment described herein, suggest that abnormalities in the subcortical components of VPFC neural systems may be evident by early adolescence in BD, whereas VPFC deficits progress over the course of adolescence and may be difficult to detect prior to late adolescence or early adulthood. Clinical implications for BD could include consideration of biological markers and behaviors more closely related to subcortical mechanisms in order to detect BD earlier in its course, and of treatment strategies adjusted to target subcortical mechanisms that may have the potential to influence the development of VPFC. Consideration of this neurodevelopmental sequence may help to explain difficulties in differentiating neuropsychiatric disorders in youth. Abnormalities in the regulation of attention, psychomotor behavior, and impulse control are common to youths with BD and youths with other neuropsychiatric disorders that are typically recognized prior to puberty, such as ADHD and Tourette syndrome (TS) (see Ref. 21). This suggests overlap in abnormalities of subcortical function common to these disorders prior to puberty. However, after puberty, the majority of children with ADHD and TS improve, suggesting salutary effects of developing prefrontal influences,

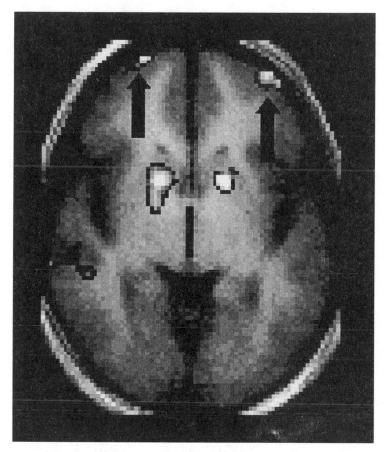

FIGURE 4. This axial-oblique image demonstrates the age-related increases in VPFC activation in healthy adolescents as they performed an event-related color-naming Stroop task.[20] (Figure reprinted with the permission of the *American Journal of Psychiatry.*)

whereas in BD abnormalities in the development of VPFC are reflected in the emergence of disturbances in complex emotional and planning behaviors characteristic of adult presentations of the disorder.

It should be noted that these developmental interpretations should be considered with caution, as data on the development of VPFC neural systems in humans are limited and preliminary neuroimaging samples are small and cross-sectional. Longitudinal within-subject studies of brain changes within BD and healthy comparison subjects are needed. However, this preliminary evidence suggests a potential model for considering neurodevelopmental influences on the expression of BD in adolescence.

ACKNOWLEDGMENTS

The authors were supported by research grants from the Stanley Medical Research Institute, Bethesda, MD (H.P.B.), National Alliance for Research in Affective Disorders and Schizophrenia, Great Neck, NY (H.P.B.), The Ethel F. Donaghue Women's Investigator Program at Yale, New Haven, CT (H.P.B.), and Charles A. Dana Foundation, New York (B.S.P.), the Suzanne Crosby Murphy Endowment at Columbia University College of Physicians and Surgeons, New York (B.S.P.), the Department of Veterans Affairs Research Career Development (H.P.B.), Merit Review (H.P.B.) and Research Enhancement Award Program (R.E.A.P.) (H.P.B., J.H.K.) Awards, Alcohol Research Center (J.H.K.), and Clinical Neurosciences Division of the National Center for PTSD (J.K., J.H.K.),and the National Institute of Mental Health Mental Health Clinical Research Center (H.P.B., J.H.K.), MH01232 (B.S.P.), MH59139 (B.S.P.), MH01792 (A.M.), and National Institute on Alcohol Abuse and Alcoholism KO2AA 00261-01 (J.H.K.).

REFERENCES

1. KAUFMAN J. & H. BLUMBERG. 2003. Neurobiology of early onset mood disorders. *In* Pediatric Psychopharmacology: Principles and Practice. A. Martin, L. Scahill, J. Leckman & D. Charney, Eds. Oxford University Press. Oxford
2. DELBELLO, M.P., C.A. SOUTULLO, W. HENDRICKS, *et al.* 2001. Prior stimulant treatment in adolescents with bipolar disorder: association with onset. Bipolar Dis. **3:** 53–57.
3. BLUMBERG, H.P., D.S. CHARNEY & J.H. KRYSTAL. 2002. Frontotemporal neural systems in bipolar disorder. Semin. Clin. Neuropsychiatry **7:** 243–254.
4. YAKOVLEV P.I. & A. LECOURS. 1967. The myelogenetic cycles of regional maturation in the brain. *In* Regional Development of the Brain in Early Life. A. Minowski, Ed.: 3–65. Blackwell. Oxford.
5. MACHADO, C.J. & J. BACHEVALIER. 2003. Non-human primate models of childhood psychopathology: the promise and the limitations. J. Child Psychol. Psychiatry **44:** 64–87.
6. BOURGEOIS, J.P., P.S. GOLDMAN-RAKIC & P. RAKIC. 1994. Synaptogenesis in the prefrontal cortex of rhesus monkeys. Cereb. Cortex **4:** 78–96.
7. LEWIS, D.A. 1997. Development of the prefrontal cortex during adolescence: insights into vulnerable neural circuits in schizophrenia. Neuropsychopharmacology **16:** 385–398.
8. GIEDD, J.N., J. BLUMENTHAL, N.O. JEFFRIES, *et al.* 1999. Brain development during childhood and adolescence: a longitudinal MRI study. Nat. Neurosci. **2:** 861–863.
9. PASSE, T.J., P. RAJAGOPALAN, L.A. TUPLER, *et al.* 1997. Age and sex effects on brain morphology. Prog. Neuro-Psychopharmacol. Biol. Psychiatry **21:** 1231–1237.
10. PFEFFERBAUM, A., D. MATHALON, E.V. SULLIVAN, *et al.* 1994. A quantitative magnetic resonance imaging study of changes in brain morphology from infancy to late adulthood. Arch. Neurol. **51:** 874–887.
11. ALEXANDER G.E. & P.S. GOLDMAN. 1978. Functional development of the dorsolateral prefrontal cortex: an analysis utilizing reversible cryogenic depression. Brain Res. **143:** 233–249.
12. LUNA, B., K.R. THULBORN, D.P. MUNOZ, *et al.* 2001. Maturation of widely distributed brain function subserves cognitive development. NeuroImage **13:** 786–793.
13. RUBIA, K., S. OVERMEYER, E. TAYLOR, *et al.* 2000. Functional frontalisation with age: mapping neurodevelopmental trajectories with fMRI. Neurosci. Biobehav. Rev. **24:** 13–19.
14. KILLGORE, W.D., M. OKI & D.A. YURGELUN-TODD. 2001. Sex-specific developmental changes in amygdala responses to affective faces. NeuroReport **12:** 427–433.

15. DREVETS, W.C., J.L. PRICE, J.R. SIMPSON, *et al.* 1997. Subgenual prefrontal cortex abnormalities in mood disorders. Nature **386:** 824–827.
16. BLUMBERG, H.P., E. STERN, S. RICKETTS, *et al.* 1999. Rostral and orbital prefrontal dysfunction in the manic state of bipolar disorder. Am. J. Psychiatry **156:** 1986–1988.
17. BLUMBERG, H.P., H.C. LEUNG, P. SKUDLARSKI, *et al.* 2003. A functional magnetic resonance imaging study of bipolar disorder: state- and trait-related dysfunction in ventral prefrontal cortices. Arch. Gen. Psychiatry **60:** 599–607.
18. RAJKOWSKA, G. 2002. Cell pathology in mood disorders. Semin. Clin. Neuropsychiatry **7:** 281–292.
19. BLUMBERG, H.P., J. KAUFMAN, A. MARTIN, *et al.* 2003. Amygdala and hippocampus volumes in adolescents and adults with bipolar disorder. Arch. Gen. Psychiatry **60:** 1201–1208.
20. BLUMBERG, H.P., A. MARTIN, J. KAUFMAN, *et al.* 2003. Frontostriatal abnormalities in adolescents with bipolar disorder: preliminary observations using functional MRI. Am. J. Psychiatry **160:** 1345–1347.
21. SPESSOT, A.L., K.J. PLESSON & B.S. PETERSON. 2004. Neuroimaging of developmental psychopathologies: the importance of self-regulatory and neuroplastic processes in adolescence. Ann. N. Y. Acad. Sci. **1021:** 86–104.

Impact of Cannabis Use on Brain Function in Adolescents

LESLIE K. JACOBSEN,[a] W. EINAR MENCL,[b] MICHAEL WESTERVELD,[a,c,d] AND KENNETH R. PUGH[a]

Departments of [a]Psychiatry and Pediatrics , [c]Neurosurgery , and [d]Child Study, Yale University School of Medicine, New Haven, Connecticut, USA

[b]Haskins Laboratory, New Haven, Connecticut, USA

ABSTRACT: Cannabis is the most common illicit substance used by adolescents. This paper reports results of a pilot study using fMRI and a working memory task to compare brain function of adolescent cannabis users to that of two control groups, one matched for tobacco use and the other for nonsmokers.

KEYWORDS: cannabis; fMRI; brain function

BACKGROUND

Cannabis remains the most commonly used illicit substance by adolescents: recent survey data indicate that nearly half of all U.S. 12th graders report a lifetime history of cannabis use <http://monitoringthefuture.org/data/02data.html>.

Animal studies have demonstrated that Δ^9-tetrahydrocannabinol (THC), the primary psychoactive constituent of cannabis, disrupts learning and memory.[1] Human studies of cognitive functioning in acutely abstinent adult cannabis users have demonstrated deficits in verbal learning and memory,[2] selective and sustained attention,[3] speed of processing,[3] executive cognitive functioning,[4] and declines in IQ.[5] Although these deficits may remit with prolonged abstinence in adults,[2] both human and animal data suggest that early onset of cannabis use may result in more severe deficits that do not remit with abstinence.[6–9]

Few systematic examinations of the impact of cannabis use on brain function in teenagers have been reported. In the present pilot study, we used functional magnetic resonance imaging (fMRI) to compare brain function of adolescent cannabis users to that of two control groups, one matched for tobacco use and one group of nonsmokers.

Address for correspondence: Leslie K. Jacobsen, M.D., Department of Psychiatry, Yale University School of Medicine, New Haven, CT. Voice: 203-764-8480; fax: 203-764-8484.
leslie.jacobsen@yale.edu

Ann. N.Y. Acad. Sci. 1021: 384–390 (2004). © 2004 New York Academy of Sciences.
doi: 10.1196/annals.1308.053

TABLE 1. Pilot sample of 7 cannabis users, 7 tobacco smokers, and 7 nonsmokers

	Cannabis Users (C)	Tobacco Only (T)	Non-smokers (NS)	t, P C vs. T	t, P C vs. NS
Age (yr)	17.4±1.0	17.1±0.9	16.8±1.4	$t = 0.6$ $P = 0.58$	$t = 1.0$ $P = 0.32$
Ratio of males to females	3/4	3/4	2/5	$\chi^2 = 0.0$ $P = 1.0$	$\chi^2 = 0.3$ $P = 0.58$
Cigarettes per day	11.8±9.8	12.4±9.8	0	$t = 0.1$ $P = 0.91$	–
FTND	2.1±1.5	3.4±2.8	–	$t = 1.1$ $P = 0.27$	–
No. of days of cannabis use (range)	282.8±523.1 (24–1460)	0.6±0.5 (0-1)	0	–	–
Months since last use (range)	10.1±10.2 (1.5–24)	13.0±8.2 (4-24)	–	$t = 0.37$ $P = 0.72$	–
Age at onset of cannabis use	13.8±1.9	–	–	–	–
Lifetime no. of drinks	71.2±31.1	46.6±40.7	26.6±67.6	$t = 1.3$ $P = 0.23$	$t = 1.6$ $P = 0.14$
Years of education	10.3±1.1	10.3±0.8	10.0±1.2	$t = 0.0$ $P = 1.0$	$t = 0.5$ $P = 0.64$
Years of parent education	12.4±1.3	14.0±1.6	15.6±2.9	$t = 2.0$ $P = 0.07$	$t = 2.6$ $P = 0.02$
Weeks of prenatal exposure to tobacco	30.5±20.4	24.7±20.8	24.4±20.5	$t = 0.4$ $P = 0.7$	$t = 0.4$ $P = 0.67$
WJR Letter SS	98.1±15.8	95.1±8.2	97.7±6.4	$t = 0.4$ $P = 0.66$	$t = 0.1$ $P = 0.95$
KBIT composite	97.0±10.9	91.4±11.0	103.2±9.6	$t = 0.9$ $P = 0.34$	$t = 1.1$ $P = 0.27$

NOTE: FTND = Fagerstrom Test for Nicotine Dependence; WJR = Woodcock-Johnson Revised Test of Achievement Letter-Word Identification subtest; SS = standard score; KBIT = Kaufman Brief Intelligence Test.

METHODS

Subjects

Seven cannabis users who also smoked tobacco were compared with 7 tobacco smokers with minimal history of cannabis use and 7 nonsmokers with no history of cannabis use who were similar in age and gender. Demographics and drug-use history of this pilot sample are presented in TABLE 1.

All subjects were free of medical and psychiatric disease and were free of illicit substance use other than cannabis. Subjects underwent urine toxicology test at screening and prior to cognitive assessment. Two cannabis users had detectable concentrations of cannabinoids in their urine at the time of screening. All subsequent urine toxicology screens from these subjects were negative. The minimum length of time between screening and cognitive assessment and scanning was 4 weeks. Four subjects in the tobacco group reported having tried cannabis once. No subject in the nonsmoker group had ever used cannabis. The groups did not differ in symptoms of depression (Beck Depression Inventory), anxiety (the Multidimensional Anxiety Scale for Children), inattention (Conners-Well's Adolescent Self-Report Scale), or stressful life events.

Assessment of Selective, Divided, and Sustained Attention

Sustained attention was assessed using the Conners Continuous Performance Test. Selective and divided attention were assessed using a slightly modified version of a previously described computerized word recognition task.[17]

Assessment of Brain Function

Brain function was assessed using fMRI while subjects performed an auditory n-back task with two levels of working memory load (1- and 2-back), and two levels of selective attention load (binaural and dichotic stimulus presentation). Stimuli were consonant-vowel-consonant (CVC) nonwords.

Given the small sample size and preclinical and clinical evidence that THC modulates hippocampal function, we focused our analysis of the imaging data on the hippocampus. Data were acquired perpendicular to the long axis of the hippocampus, and were analyzed using a mixed-model repeated-measures Analysis of Variance (ANOVA) on a voxel-by-voxel basis with group as a between-subjects factor and memory and selective attention load as within-subjects factors. Significant activations were defined by at least 8 contiguous voxels and $\alpha = 0.01$.

RESULTS

Selective, Divided, and Sustained Attention

There was a significant effect of group on the percentage of button presses that were correct during the CPT ("percent hits"; F = 3.83, $P = .04$). Post hoc t-tests revealed that cannabis users had a significantly lower percentage of hits than did nonsmokers. The difference between cannabis users and tobacco smokers did not achieve statistical significance ($P = .12$). Although the relationship between total number of episodes of cannabis use and percent hits was not significant ($r = -0.10$, $n = 7$, $P = .84$), there was a trend for greater number of episodes of cannabis use to be positively correlated with the number of incorrect button presses during the CPT ("false alarms"; $r = 0.72$, $n = 7$, $P = .07$).

There were no significant effects of group on either accuracy or reaction time on selective or divided attention tasks.

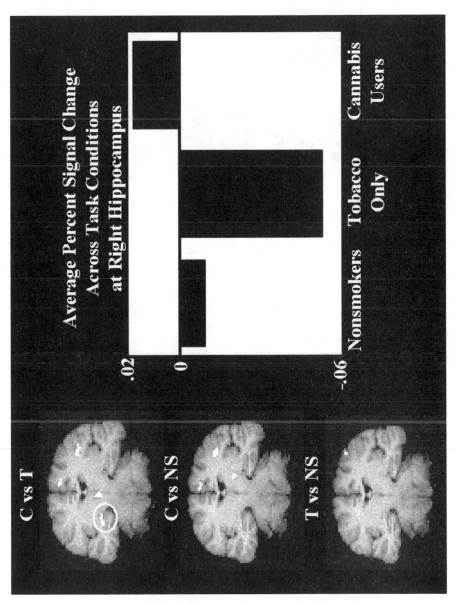

FIGURE 1. *See following page for legend.*

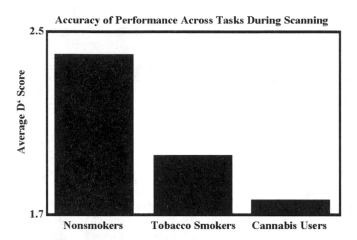

FIGURE 2. Average D′ score across tasks for nonsmokers, tobacco smokers, and users of both tobacco and cannabis.

Brain Function

A significant main effect of group was observed at the right hippocampus (Talairach coordinates: $x = 26.4$, $y = -22.7$, $z = -5.0$). FIGURE 1 (left) presents ANOVA results showing the main effect of group for each of the three group contrasts at the same level of the hippocampus. Functional data have been projected onto a standardized T1 weighted image of the brain; images are displayed with the right side of the brain on the left side of the figure. FIGURE 1 (right) presents plots of average percent signal change observed at the encircled, functionally defined, region of the right hippocampus across all task conditions for each group.

ANOVA of behavioral data collected while subjects performed the task during scanning revealed a main effect of group on accuracy of performance (measured by computing D′ for each task condition; $F = 4.90$, $df = 2,18$, $P = .02$), but no significant group by memory load effects on performance. Average D′ score across tasks for each group is plotted in FIGURE 2.

Post hoc t-tests indicated that, across tasks, performance accuracy of cannabis users was significantly lower than that of nonsmokers, while performance accuracy of tobacco smokers did not differ from that of nonsmokers. During the dichotic 2-back task, the most difficult task condition, performance accuracy of cannabis users

---

FIGURE 1. *Left:* ANOVA results showing the main effect of group for each of the three group contrasts at the same level of the hippocampus. Functional data have been projected onto a standardized T1 weighted image of the brain; images are displayed with the right side of the brain on the left side of the figure. *Right:* plots of average percent signal change observed at the encircled, functionally defined, region of the right hippocampus across all task conditions for each group. C = users of cannabis and tobacco; T = users of tobacco only; NS = nonsmokers, nonusers of cannabis.

was significantly worse than that of nonsmokers, and was worse than that of tobacco smokers at a trend level ($t = 1.94$, df $= 12$, $P = .07$), while accuracy of tobacco smokers and nonsmokers did not differ. Measures of cannabis exposure were not significantly correlated with performance accuracy.

Measures of cannabis use and performance accuracy were not significantly correlated with right hippocampal activity.

DISCUSSION

In this pilot study, abstinent adolescent cannabis users had deficits in sustained attention and performed a working memory task less accurately than controls. Across working memory task conditions, adolescent cannabis users also failed to deactivate the right hippocampus.

Recent work has underscored the role of inhibition of hippocampal neurons during mnemonic processing.[10–12] Data presented in FIGURE 1 suggest that while both nonsmokers and tobacco smokers deactivate the right hippocampus across task conditions, cannabis users fail to deactivate this structure. Given that all conditions in this task involve some degree of mnemonic processing (remembering the word presented either 1-back or 2-back), failure to reduce hippocampal activation during task performance may therefore reflect dysfunction of inhibitory interneurons within the hippocampus in cannabis users during mnemonic processing.[13] This effect may be mediated by cannabis-induced inhibition of neurotransmitter release disrupting hippocampal synaptic plasticity or by cannabis-induced apoptosis of hippocampal neurons.[14–16]

ACKNOWLEDGMENTS

This work was supported by Grant DA14655 from the National Institute on Drug Abuse.

REFERENCES

1. VARVEL, S.A., R.J. HAMM, B.R. MARTIN & A.H. LICHTMAN. 2001. Differential effects of delta-9-THC on spatial reference and working memory in mice. Psychopharmacology **157:** 142–150.
2. POPE, H.G., A.J. GRUBER, J.I. HUDSON, *et al.* 2001. Neuropsychological performance in long-term cannabis users. Arch. Gen. Psychiatry **58:** 909–915.
3. SOLOWIJ, N., P.T. MICHIE & A.M. FOX. 1995. Differential impairments of selective attention due to frequency and duration of cannabis use. Biol. Psychiatry **37:** 731–739.
4. POPE, H.G. & D. YURGELUN-TODD. 1996. The residual cognitive effects of heavy marijuana use in college students. JAMA **275:** 521–527.
5. FRIED, P., B. WATKINSON, D. JAMES & R. GRAY. 2002. Current and former marijuana use: preliminary findings of a longitudinal study of effects on IQ in young adults. Canad. Med. Assoc. J. **166:** 887–891.
6. EHRENREICH, H., T. RINN, H.J. KUNERT, *et al.* 1999. Specific attentional dysfunction in adults following early start of cannabis use. Psychopharmacology **142:** 295–301.

7. POPE, H.G., A.J GRUBER, J.I. HUDSON, et al. 2003. Early-onset cannabis use and cognitive deficits: what is the nature of the association? Drug Alcohol Depend. **69:** 303–310.

8. SCHWARTZ, R.H., P.J. GRUENEWALD, M. KLITZNER & P. FEDIO. 1989. Short-term memory impairment in cannabis-dependent adolescents. Am. J. Dis. Child. **143:** 1214–1219.

9. STIGLICK, A. & H. KALANT. 1985. Residual effects of chronic cannabis treatment of behavior in mature rats. Psychopharmacology **85:** 436–439.

10. KAHANA, M.J., R. SEKULER, J.B. CAPLAN, et al. 1999. Human theta oscillations exhibit task dependence during virtual maze navigation. Nature **399:** 781–784.

11. FREUND, T.F. & G. BUZSAKI. 1996. Interneurons of the hippocampus. Hippocampus **6:** 347–470.

12. FELL, J., P. KLAVER, K. LEHNERTZ, et al. 2001. Human memory formation is accompanied by rhinal-hippocampal coupling and decoupling. Nature Neurosci. **4:** 1259–1264.

13. FREUND, T.F. & A.I. GULYAS. 1997. Inhibitory control of GABAergic interneurons in the hippocampus. Canad. J. Physiol. Pharmacol. **75:** 479–487.

14. KIM, D. & S.A. THAYER. 2001. Cannabinoids inhibit the formation of new synapses between hippocampal neurons in culture [abstract]. J. Neurosci. **21:** RC 146.

15. HOFFMAN, A.F. & C.R. LUPICA. 2000. Mechanisms of cannabinoid inhibition of GABA(A) synaptic transmission in the hippocampus. J. Neurosci. **20:** 2470–2479.

16. CHAN, G.C., T.R. HINDS, S. IMPEY & D.R. STORM. 1998. Hippocampal neurotoxicity of Δ^9-tetrahydrocannabinol. J. Neurosci. **18:** 5322–5332.

17. SHAYWITZ, B.A., S.E. SHAYWITZ, K.R. PUGH, et al. 2001. The functional neural architecture of components of attention in language-processing tasks. Neuroimage **13:** 601–612.

An fMRI Study of Response Inhibition in Youths with a Family History of Alcoholism

ALECIA D. SCHWEINSBURG,[a] MARTIN P. PAULUS,[b,c] VALERIE C. BARLETT,[d]
LAUREN A. KILLEEN,[e] LISA C. CALDWELL,[d] CARMEN PULIDO,[f]
SANDRA A. BROWN,[a–c] AND SUSAN F. TAPERT[b,c]

[a]Department of Psychology and [b]Department of Psychiatry,
University of California San Diego, San Diego, California 92161, USA

[c]Veterans Administration San Diego Healthcare System,
San Diego, California 92161, USA

[d]Veterans Medical Research Foundation, San Diego, California 92161, USA

[e]Department of Psychology, Pennsylvania State University,
University Park, Pennsylvania 16802, USA

[f]Joint Doctoral Program in Clinical Psychology, University of California San Diego and
San Diego State University, San Diego, California 92161, USA

ABSTRACT: Disinhibition among alcoholics may precede or result from alcohol use disorders (AUDs). It remains unclear how disinhibition might contribute to AUD risk among youths with a family history of alcoholism (FHP). We used functional magnetic resonance imaging (fMRI) to explore inhibition-related neural risk factors for AUD. Participants were 12- to14-year-old nondrinkers, including 12 FHP youths and 14 youths with no family history of alcoholism (FHN). Youths performed a go/no-go task during fMRI acquisition. At a conservative threshold, FHN youths showed less inhibitory response than FHP youths in the left middle frontal gyrus, despite similar task performance between groups. Using a more liberal threshold, FHP youths also demonstrated less response in additional frontal regions. These preliminary findings suggest that FHP youths show less inhibitory frontal response than FHN youths. Altered neural activation among FHP youths may underlie subsequent disinhibition and could be related to the AUD risk.

KEYWORDS: adolescence; response inhibition; alcoholism; family history; fMRI

Previous studies of adults with alcohol dependence have described electrophysiological abnormalities during response inhibition.[1,2] However, it is unclear whether these difficulties precede or are a consequence of alcohol use disorders (AUD). Youths with a family history of AUD are at high risk for developing AUD them-

Address for correspondence: Susan Tapert, Ph.D.,VA San Diego Healthcare System (116B), 3350 La Jolla Village Drive, San Diego, CA 92161. Voice: 858-552-8585, Ext. 2599; fax: 858-642-6474.
stapert@ucsd.edu

Ann. N.Y. Acad. Sci. 1021: 391–394 (2004). © 2004 New York Academy of Sciences.
doi: 10.1196/annals.1308.050

TABLE 1. Participant demographic characteristics

	FHP M (SD) or % ($N = 12$)	FHN M (SD) or % ($N = 14$)
Age	13.55 (0.92)	13.77 (0.75)
% Female	42%	64%
% Caucasian	83%	79%
Annual family income (thousands)	66.75 (47.93)	88.77 (43.81)
Grades completed	6.83 (0.94)	7.21 (0.80)
Vocabulary T-score	61.46 (5.82)	58.57 (6.26)

selves,[3] yet it remains unclear how disinhibition among these youths might contribute to this susceptibility. Young adult children of alcoholics demonstrated reduced electrophysiological response during an inhibition task, suggesting inhibitory deficits that may precede the development of alcoholism.[4] Further, behavioral inhibition and reduced frontal lobe neuropsychological performance predict future drinking problems among individuals with a family history of AUD.[5] We used functional magnetic resonance imaging (fMRI) to investigate response inhibition among young adolescents with a family history of AUD in order to further understand the neural correlates of vulnerability to AUD. We hypothesized that youths with family histories of AUD would show less frontal lobe brain response during a go/no-go task that assesses response inhibition and typically activates frontal brain systems in youths and adults.[6]

Participants were 12–14-year-old boys and girls who had not previously used alcohol or drugs. Twelve family history–positive (FHP) youths had at least one parent or two second-degree relatives on the same side of the family with AUD, and 14 family history–negative (FHN) youths had no first or second degree relatives with alcohol or other drug use disorders. Exclusionary criteria included left-handedness; history of head injury, medical or neurological illness, and psychiatric disorders; and use of psychotropic medications. Groups were similar on demographics, including age, gender, ethnicity, and family income (TABLE 1).

During fMRI acquisition, youths performed a go/no-go task in which they were presented one of four different solid blue shapes every 1.5 seconds (total time = 6 minutes, 25 seconds). The shapes were a small square, a large square, a small circle, and a large circle. Participants were asked to respond with a button press as quickly as possible to the presentation of each shape except for the small square. A high-resolution structural image was acquired for anatomical standardization and structure localization. In addition to imaging, youths received a comprehensive battery of neuropsychological tests and mood assessments.

fMRI analyses contrasted no-go trials (small blue square) against go trials (other shapes) for each participant, converted time series data to standard Talairach space,[7] and compared groups with an independent samples t-test. We created a mask to examine group differences specifically in the frontal lobe. To control for Type I error, we required that significant clusters surpass a volume threshold of $\geq 815 \, \mu L$ ($\alpha < .05$).

Groups performed with similar accuracy and reaction time on go and no-go trials during fMRI scanning. FHN youths demonstrated 91% accuracy on go trials and 83% accuracy on no-go trials, while FHP youths performed with 99% accuracy on go trials and 87% accuracy on no-go trials (ns). Group differences were found for the Delis-Kaplan Executive Function System[8] Color-Word subtest, on which FHN

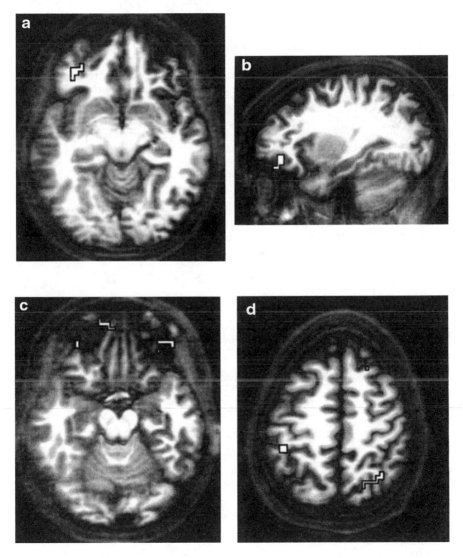

FIGURE 1. Group differences in go/no-go brain response. *White clusters* represent regions where FHP youths showed less brain response than FHN youths. At a conservative threshold, FHP youths showed less brain response than FHN youths in the left middle frontal gyrus (**a** and **b**). At a more liberal volume threshold, FHP youths showed less brain response than FHN youths in additional frontal (**c**) and parietal (**d**) regions.

youths performed better than FHP youths on the Inhibition versus Color Reading Scaled Score, and FHP youths performed better than FHN youths on the Inhibition/ Switching versus Inhibition Scaled Score ($P < .05$). No other group differences in neuropsychological functioning or in mood state were observed.

At our conservative cluster volume threshold, FHP youths showed less go/no-go brain response than FHN youths in the left middle frontal gyrus (cluster volume = 900 µL; FIG. 1a and b). Using a more liberal cluster volume threshold, FHP youths also demonstrated less go/no-go response than FHN youths in several additional frontal regions: left medial/superior frontal, bilateral middle frontal, right superior frontal, and right inferior frontal gyri (FIG. 1c). Extending analyses outside the frontal lobe revealed that FHP youths also showed less response than FHN youths in the right superior temporal gyrus, right precuneus/superior parietal lobule, and bilateral inferior parietal lobule (FIG. 1d).

This preliminary study indicates that FHP youths show less brain activation while trying to withhold a response relative to FHN youths, despite similar levels of task performance between groups. This attenuated activation pattern in the presence of response inhibition among FHP youths may be related to subsequent problems with disinhibition and impulsive behaviors. Inadequate activation in prefrontal cortex during response inhibition could relate to resisting alcohol use opportunities and developing AUD. Further investigations, including longitudinal studies of youths with family histories of AUD and examination of gender differences, are needed to delineate the neural underpinnings of vulnerability to AUD.

REFERENCES

1. COHEN, H.L., et al. 1997. Neurophysiological correlates of response production and inhibition in alcoholics. Alcohol. Clin. Exp. Res. **21:** 1398–1406.
2. FALLGATTER, A.J., et al. 1998. Event-related correlates of response suppression as indicators of novelty seeking in alcoholics. Alcohol Alcohol. **33:** 475–481.
3. SCHUCKIT, M.A. 1985. Studies of populations at high risk for alcoholism. Psych. Dev. **3:** 31–63.
4. COHEN, H.L., et al. 1997. Neuroelectric correlates of response production and inhibition in individuals at risk to develop alcoholism. Biol. Psychiatry **42:** 57–67.
5. DECKEL, A.W. & V. HESSELBROCK. 1996. Behavioral and cognitive measurements predict scores on the MAST: a 3-year prospective study. Alcohol. Clin. Exp. Res. **20:** 1173–1178.
6. CASEY, B.J., et al. 1997. A developmental functional MRI study of prefrontal activation during performance of a go-no-go task. J. Cogn. Neurosci. **9:** 835–847.
7. TALAIRACH, J. & P. TOURNOUX. 1988. Coplanar stereotaxic atlas of the human brain. Three-dimensional proportional system: An approach to cerebral imaging. Thieme. New York.
8. DELIS, D.C., E. KAPLAN & J.H. KRAMER. 2001. Examiner's manual for the Delis-Kaplan Executive Function System. Psychological Corporation. San Antonio, TX.

A Comparative Developmental Study of Impulsivity in Rats and Humans

The Role of Reward Sensitivity

JATIN G. VAIDYA, ANGELA J. GRIPPO, ALAN KIM JOHNSON, AND DAVID WATSON

Department of Psychology, University of Iowa, Iowa City, Iowa 52242, USA

ABSTRACT: The present study was conducted to test the hypothesis that differences in reward sensitivity between adolescents and adults account for differences in impulsivity. In a comparative study, we examined preferences for various concentrations of sucrose solutions as an operational measure of reward sensitivity in adolescent and adult rats and humans. Humans also completed self-report measures of impulsivity and reward sensitivity. There was some indication that adolescents preferred sweeter solutions compared to adults. Also, adolescents scored substantially higher on impulsivity. However, adolescents and adults did not differ in self-ratings of reward sensitivity and personality scores were not consistently related to sucrose preferences. The data highlight some of the benefits and issues that arise with developing comparative measures in humans and animals. Future comparative research using alternative behavioral paradigms is necessary to determine if and how changes in reward sensitivity influence developmental shifts in impulsivity.

KEYWORDS: impulsivity; anhedonia; reward sensitivity; adolescent development; rats; humans

A great deal of research from both human and animal studies supports the commonsense view that adolescents are substantially more impulsive than adults.[1-3] Recently, Spear[4] has theorized that changes in neural circuitry make adolescents less sensitive to rewards compared to adults. Due to this "adolescent anhedonia," adolescents must engage in high risk, thrill-seeking activities to receive the same amount of pleasure an adult may receive from a much more mundane task. While intriguing, little developmental research has been conducted to date that behaviorally examines potential shifts in reward sensitivity from adolescence to adulthood.

In the present study, we examined sucrose preferences in humans and rats as an operational measure of reward sensitivity. Sucrose intake is commonly used as a measure of reduced reward sensitivity or anhedonia in animal studies of depression.[5] We expected adolescent rats and humans to show preferences for sweeter solutions

Address for correspondence: Jatin Vaidya, E11 SSH, Department of Psychology, University of Iowa, Iowa City, IA 52242. Voice: 319-335-0268; fax: 319-335-0191.
jatin-vaidya@uiowa.edu

Ann. N.Y. Acad. Sci. 1021: 395–398 (2004). © 2004 New York Academy of Sciences.
doi: 10.1196/annals.1308.051

compared to adults, and that sucrose preferences would be correlated with measures of impulsivity and reward sensitivity in humans.

METHODS

Rats

Sixteen male Sprague-Dawley rats, ages 5–6 weeks (adolescents) and 11–12 weeks (adults) were housed in a light- and temperature-controlled environment. In two series (ascending and descending by concentration), rats were allowed ad libitum access to four different sucrose concentrations (6%, 14%, 22%, and 30%) in addition to water (0%), each available for 48 hours. Bottle positions were counterbalanced, and intakes were measured every 24 hours. Sucrose intake was also measured 4 hours after the presentation of each concentration during the first series as a measure of novelty seeking (i.e., an operational definition of impulsivity).

Humans

Human participants consisted of 33 adolescents (average age 13.8 years) and 23 adults (average age 39.7 years), and were roughly equivalent in gender composition. Participants initially completed a current mood questionnaire (Positive and Negative Affect Schedule),[6] consisting of two scales measuring positive affect (PA) and negative affect (NA). Participants then completed either the remaining questionnaires or the sucrose test portion, followed by the other, in a counterbalanced manner.

Participants completed the General Temperament Survey,[7] which consists of three scales: Positive Temperament, Negative Temperament, and Disinhibition (i.e., Impulsivity). The Positive Temperament scale is conceptually related to other individual differences measures of approach motivation and reward sensitivity.[8] Participants also completed the anhedonia-related items from the Mood and Anxiety Symptoms Questionnaire.[9]

In a pseudorandomized design, participants tasted, without swallowing, four different sucrose concentrations (6%, 14%, 22%, and 30%) and water (0%), and rated their preferences on a six-point scale (1 = extremely unpleasant, 6 = extremely pleasant). Subjects then tasted each solution once more and ranked the solutions from least pleasant to most pleasant.

RESULTS

Rats

FIGURE 1 shows the averaged fluid intake from the ascending and descending series, corrected for body weight, in both groups at each concentration. There was a main effect of group [$F(1,70) = 30.9, P < .05$) and sucrose concentration [$F(4,70) = 57.7, P < .05$], and an interaction [$F(4,70) = 6.7, P < .05$]. Adolescents drank significantly more 6% [$t(14) = 4.6, P < .05$] and 30% [$t(14) = 3.5, P < .05$] sucrose than adults. Four hours following initial presentation of the sucrose, adolescents drank significantly more of the 6% sucrose (the first concentration presented in the ascending series) than adults [$t(14) = 2.4, P < .05$].

Humans

Current PA or NA was not correlated with sucrose preferences nor did adolescents and adults differ in their current affective states. Adolescents scored higher than adults on the Impulsivity questionnaire [$t(54) = 3.4, P < .01$], but did not differ on the remaining scales. Adolescents and adults did not significantly differ in their ratings of the sucrose. However, adolescents ranked the more concentrated solutions as being more pleasant, whereas the adults rated the less concentrated solutions as more pleasant (FIG. 2). In general, personality ratings were not correlated with su-

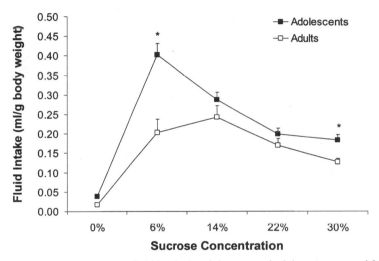

FIGURE 1. Mean (± SEM) fluid intake in adolescent and adult rats, corrected for body weight.

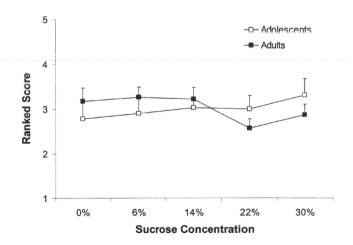

FIGURE 2. Mean (± SEM) sucrose rankings in adolescent and adult humans (5 = most pleasant).

crose preferences. However, Positive Temperament was positively correlated with ratings of the 30% solution ($r = .36$, $P < .01$).

DISCUSSION

The current study was a comparative developmental investigation of reward sensitivity and impulsivity in adolescent and adult rats and humans. As we hypothesized, both adolescent rats and humans showed a preference for sweeter solutions relative to adults, suggesting that adolescents may require greater intensity to derive pleasure from a putatively pleasurable stimulus. Further, consistent with previous research,[1,3] rat and human adolescents were more impulsive than adults in the present study, as indicated by higher scores on the Impulsivity scale in humans and the increased early consumption of a novel substance in rats. However, reward sensitivity was not significantly related to impulsivity in humans. It is possible that sucrose preference is a different construct than anhedonia *per se*, as sucrose preferences were also unrelated to Anhedonia scores in humans.

It is interesting to note the similarities found between adolescent rats and humans in the current study, in both sucrose preferences and impulsivity. Changes in brain development may mediate reward sensitivity and impulsive behavior during adolescence. The current study is a first step in examining developmental differences in reward sensitivity and impulsivity and can serve as a foundation for further investigations of the important biological and behavioral changes that occur during adolescence. Future studies should consider cross-species comparisons to gain a better understanding of the mechanisms of reward sensitivity and impulsive behavior in adolescents.

REFERENCES

1. ARNETT, J. 1992. Reckless behavior in adolescence: a developmental perspective. Dev. Rev. **12:** 339–373.
2. ZUCKERMAN, M. *et al.* 1978. Sensation seeking in England and America: cross-cultural, age, and sex comparisons. J. Consult. Clin. Psychol. **46:** 139–149.
3. LAVIOLA, G. *et al.* 2003. Risk-taking behavior in adolescent mice: psychobiological determinants and early epigenetic influence. Neurosci. Biobehav. Rev. **27:** 19–31.
4. SPEAR, L.P. 2000. The adolescent brain and age-related behavioral manifestations. Neurosci. Biobehav. Rev. **24:** 417–463.
5. GRIPPO, A.J. *et al.* 2002. Cardiovascular alterations and autonomic imbalance in an experimental model of depression. Am. J. Physiol. Regul. Integr. Comp. Physiol. **282:** R1333–R1341.
6. WATSON, D. *et al.* 1988. Development and validation of brief measures of positive and negative affect: the PANAS scales. J. Pers. Soc. Psychol. **54:** 1063–1070.
7. CLARK, L.A. & D. WATSON. The General Temperament Survey. Unpublished manuscript. Southern Methodist University. Dallas.
8. WATSON, D. & L.A. CLARK. 1997. Extraversion and its positive emotional core. *In* Handbook of Personality Psychology. R. Hogan & S. Briggs, Eds. Academic Press. San Diego, CA.
9. WATSON, D. & L.A. CLARK. The Mood and Anxiety Symptoms Questionnaire. Unpublished manuscript. University of Iowa. Iowa City.

Developmental Differences in Nicotine Place Conditioning

TRACY A. TORRELLA,[a] KIMBERLY A. BADANICH,[b] REX M. PHILPOT,[b] CHERYL L. KIRSTEIN,[b] AND LYNN WECKER[c,d]

[a]Honors College, University of South Florida, Tampa, Florida 33620, USA

[b]Department of Psychology, Cognitive and Neural Sciences, University of South Florida, Tampa, Florida 33620, USA

[c]Department of Pharmacology and Therapeutics, University of South Florida College of Medicine, Tampa, Florida 33612, USA

ABSTRACT: To understand the motivations and implications of the prevalence of smoking, studies have compared the behavioral effects of nicotine, the psychoactive drug in tobacco, in adolescent and adult animals. The present study used a biased three-chambered conditioned-place preference procedure without prior habituation to examine the potential rewarding and anxiolytic effects of nicotine across adolescence and adulthood to assess the presence of age-dependent differences in response to nicotine.

KEYWORDS: conditioned place preference; nicotine; adolescence; anxiolytic

BACKGROUND

In the United States, the rate of smoking among adolescents (12–17 years of age) continues to increase and has not declined in the past 20 years.[1] The use of tobacco products begins predominantly in early adolescence, and with the prevalence of earlier ages of initiation in adolescence there may be increased risk for nicotine addiction and the eventual regular use of tobacco.[2,3] Indeed, it is believed that people who begin smoking at an early age are more likely to develop severe levels of dependence with significantly higher rates of addiction than are adults who start at a later age.[4,5]

To understand the motivations and implications of the prevalence of smoking, studies have compared the behavioral effects of nicotine, the psychoactive drug in tobacco, in adolescent and adult animals. The conditioned place preference (CPP) paradigm is a procedure commonly used to determine the rewarding property of drugs. Additionally, the use of the biased CPP procedure allows for assessment of the anxiolytic action of drugs. To date, only one study has compared the potential rewarding and anxiolytic effects of nicotine in adolescents and adults.[6] This study demonstrated that a low dose of nicotine bitartrate (0.6 mg/kg) had anxiolytic activ-

Address for correspondence: Lynn Wecker, Department of Pharmacology and Therapeutics, USFCOM, MDC Box 9, 12901 Bruce B. Downs Boulevard, Tampa, FL 33612-4799. Voice: 813-974-3823; fax: 813-974-3081.

lwecker@hsc.usf.edu

Ann. N.Y. Acad. Sci. 1021: 399–403 (2004). © 2004 New York Academy of Sciences.
doi: 10.1196/annals.1308.052

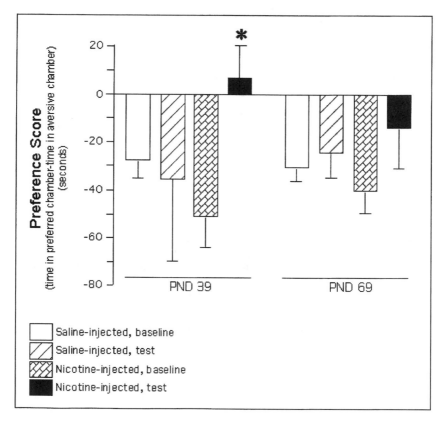

FIGURE 1. Age-dependent effects of nicotine on place aversion. Rats PND 30–39 and PND 60–69 were assigned randomly to either the saline- or nicotine-injected groups, and tested for differences in response to nicotine utilizing a biased three-chambered CPP paradigm. The preference score was determined by subtracting the time spent in the aversive chamber from the time spent in the preferred chamber both prior to and following an 8-day training period. *Bars* represent group mean values (± SEM) of determinations from 7 to 12 rats per group. The *asterisk* denotes a significant (*P* < .05) difference from corresponding baseline values.

ity and induced CPP in adolescent subjects, whereas only anxiolytic activity was manifest by adult subjects. However, this study used an initial three-day pre-training habituation to the injections and a two-chambered CPP apparatus (lacking a neutral zone) was utilized.

The two-chambered CPP apparatus introduces a confound in the interpretation of preference scores. Traditionally, a place preference has been viewed as resulting from classically conditioned associations between the drug-paired context and the rewarding properties of the drug.[7] Thus, the preference for the drug-paired chamber following training is assumed to be motivated by the acquired appetitive value of the drug conditioned stimuli, that is, it represents the rewarding efficacy of the drug itself. However, the use of a two-chambered CPP apparatus does not allow for the experimenter to distinguish between an acquired tendency to approach a rewarding context and an acquired tendency to avoid an aversive context. Therefore, a CPP may be interpreted as a drug-induced reward, when in fact the drug serves primarily as an anxiolytic whose properties are selectively paired with only one environment subsequently reducing experimental- and context-related stress within that compartment exclusively. The use of a three-chambered apparatus minimizes the potential influence of a conditioned aversion on the interpretation of the results by providing an alternative for avoidance of the aversive compartment. Thus, increased time spent in the drug-conditioned compartment represents, more reliably, the rewarding efficacy of the drug, and in the biased procedure, allows for the assessment of the anxiolytic effects of the drug, that is, reducing baseline aversion to the drug-paired compartment. The present study used a biased three-chambered CPP procedure without prior habituation to examine the potential rewarding and anxiolytic effects of nicotine across adolescence and adulthood to assess the presence of age-dependent differences in response to nicotine.

METHODS

Subjects

This study used Sprague-Dawley (Harlan Sprague Dawley, Inc.) rats at postnatal day (PND) 30–39 (mean weight males = 145 g, females = 110 g) and PND 60–69 (mean weight males = 330 g, females = 210 g), with a range of weights from 85 g to 380 g. Animals from multiple litters were used with no more than one male and one female per litter for each experimental condition. Animals were assigned randomly to either the saline- (control) or nicotine-injected group, and animal care was in accordance with the guidelines set forth by the National Institutes of Health.

Apparatus

The apparatus consisted of a three-chambered box made of black Plexiglas with a clear Plexiglas cover. A large neutral chamber (21 cm wide × 36 cm long × 21 cm high), separated two compartments (21 cm wide × 15 cm long × 21 cm high) by removable walls on either end. The two end chambers provided distinct visual and tactile cues to establish an association when paired with either saline or nicotine. One chamber had blue, checkered pattern wallpaper with a wire mesh floor, while the other had a flowered pattern wallpaper with a rubber mat floor.

Training and Testing

The model for this study utilized a biased CPP paradigm. Animals were tested on PND 30 or PND 60 in the CPP apparatus for 5 minutes with the walls removed for free access to all three chambers to determine an initial preference for either the checkered or the flowered chamber. Per the biased design, the end chambers were designated *post hoc* as preferred or aversive, based on which compartment the animal spent the most and least time in, respectively. Following baseline recording, the animals were trained over a period of eight days (PND 31–38 or PND 61–68). Each morning (between 0900 and 1100 h) the animals received a subcutaneous (s.c.) injection of either saline or nicotine bitartrate (0.6 mg/kg) and were confined to the preferred or aversive chambers for 5 minutes, respectively. Each afternoon (between 1400 and 1600 h) the control animals received a second injection of saline and were confined to the aversive chamber for 5 minutes, while the drug group received an injection of saline and were confined to the preferred compartment for 5 minutes. On PND 39 or PND 69, approximately 24 hours after their last injection, animals were placed in the apparatus with the walls removed and tested for 5 minutes to determine the conditioned effects of nicotine injections. Before each trial and test period, the apparatus was cleaned with Quatricide (Pharmacal Research Laboratories Inc.) to remove any lingering odor cues. A video-based tracking system (EthoVision, Noldus Information Technologies) was used to record and quantify the data. Groups were compared using SuperANOVA (Abacus Concepts). A two-way ANOVA [Age (2) × Dose (2)] with repeated measures [Time (2)] was used; in those instances where significant main effects were noted, individual group differences were determined by Fisher's PLSD.

RESULTS

In general, rats from both age groups preferred the flowered chamber relative to the checkered chamber, and no significant differences were noted between the two age groups (see Fig. 1). Analysis of Baseline versus Test using raw chamber preference revealed a significant Trial × Treatment interaction [$F(1,35) = 4.396, P < .05$]. For saline-injected rats, the 8-day training period did not affect the preference for either age group tested, that is, the time spent in the preferred and aversive chambers did not differ between baseline testing and corresponding post-training testing. In contrast, 8 days of training with nicotine paired to the aversive side increased the time spent in the aversive chamber and correspondingly decreased the time spent in the preferred chamber for PND 39 rats, but not PND 69 animals. *Post hoc* analysis revealed a significant increase relative to baseline in time spent on the aversive side for only the PND 39 animals following nicotine conditioning [$t = -3.43, P < .05$].

DISCUSSION

The present data reveal an age-dependent effect of nicotine, in that nicotine produced anxiolytic effects in adolescent rats and not in adults. Data indicate that the time spent in the aversive chamber increased in adolescent animals, but not in adults, following nicotine injections. Thus, the anxiolytic properties of nicotine were manifest by PND 30–39 animals using the three-chambered biased CPP procedure. However, CPP was not exhibited by either adolescent or adult animals. These results are in contrast to those reported demonstrating a nicotine-induced CPP in adolescent Sprague-Dawley rats using a two-chambered apparatus and a habituation period.[6] The apparent discrepancy between results obtained in the present study and those reported may be attributed to the design of the experimental apparatus. In a two-chambered apparatus, a preference may be manifest due to avoidance of the alternate compartment, that is, the preferred compartment may be favored merely because it is less aversive rather than preferred. A traditional interpretation of an observed CPP in this paradigm would be that preference is an indicator of the reward efficacy of the drug. However, the present data suggest that it is the ability of nicotine to reduce stress that mediates the observed preference in the two-chambered paradigm.

The present results reveal a unique responsiveness of adolescent animals to the anxiolytic properties of nicotine. Specifically, in adolescence, repeated pairings of nicotine with an aversive context results in a redistribution of behavior indicative of the reduced aversion. In other words, through associative processes, nicotine removes the aversive quality of the context. When considered from a learning perspective, these data are powerful indicators of an increased risk of addiction for adolescence, particularly in the presence of significant psychological stressors. Because nicotine is anxiolytic, the reduction in stress produced by its use may reinforce the future use of the drug. Further, because nicotine's anxiolytic properties are apparent in adolescents, but not adults, there is a greater risk for the establishment of such associations and the development of addictive behavior. This hypothetical predisposition may explain why individuals who begin smoking during adolescence may be more prone to addiction than their adult counterparts, and suggests a potential developmental difference in the nature of nicotinic receptors and/or the biological systems they influence.

ACKNOWLEDGMENT

This work was supported by The Robert Wood Johnson Foundation: Tobacco Etiology Research Network.

REFERENCES

1. NELSON, D.E., G.A. GIVINO, D.R. SHOPLAND, *et al.* 1995. Trends in cigarette smoking among US adolescents, 1974 through 1991. Am. J. Public Health **85:** 34–40.
2. ESCOBEDO, L.G., S.E. MARCUS, D. HOLTZMAN & G.A. GIOVINO. 1993. Sports participation, age at smoking initiation, and the risk of smoking among US high school students. J. Am. Med. Assoc. **269:** 1391–1395.
3. TAIOLI, E. & E.L. WYNDER. 1991. Effect of the age at which smoking begins on frequency of smoking in adulthood. N. Engl. J. Med. **325:** 968–969.
4. KANDEL, D.B. & K. CHEN. 2000. Extent of smoking and nicotine dependence in the United States: 1991–1993. Nicotine Tobacco Res. **2:** 263–274.
5. CHEN, J. & W.J. MILLAR. 1998. Age of smoking initiation: implications for quitting. Health Rep. **9:** 39–46.
6. VASTOLA, B.J., L.A. DOUGLAS, E.I. VARLINSKAYA & L.P. SPEAR. 2002. Nicotine-induced conditioned place preference in adolescent and adult rats. Physiol. Behav. **77:** 107–114.
7. BARDO, M.T. & R.A. BEVINS. 2000. Conditioned place preference: What does it add to our preclinical understanding of drug reward? Psychopharmacology **153:** 31–43.

Age and Experience Affect the Recruitment of New Neurons to the Song System of Zebra Finches during the Sensitive Period for Song Learning

Ditto for Vocal Learning in Humans?

LINDA WILBRECHT AND FERNANDO NOTTEBOHM

Laboratory of Animal Behavior, Rockefeller University, New York, New York 10021, USA

ABSTRACT: Vocal learning in songbirds and humans is a complex learned skill with sensory, motor, and social aspects. It culminates in the imitation of sounds produced by other, usually older individuals. Song learning and language learning may differ in their cognitive content, but both require coordination of auditory feedback and fine motor control, which may be supported by similar brain structures. Vocal learning in birds as in humans requires the use of forebrain networks; in songbirds these networks are thought to be related, in part, to the frontal association cortex-basal ganglia loops that mature in humans at adolescence.

KEYWORDS: vocal learning; songbirds; forebrain networks; adolescence

Vocal learning in songbirds and humans is a complex learned skill with sensory, motor, and social aspects. It culminates in the imitation of sounds produced by other, usually older individuals. Song learning and language learning may differ in their cognitive content, but both require coordination of auditory feedback and fine motor control, which may be supported by similar brain structures. Vocal learning in birds as in humans requires the use of forebrain networks. In songbirds these networks are thought to be related, in part, to the frontal association cortex-basal ganglia loops that mature in humans at adolescence.[1–6]

Vocal learning has been much studied in zebra finches, a songbird native to Australia that breeds readily in the laboratory. Male zebra finches acquire their song by imitating that of another bird with which they can interact socially.[7–9] This process normally starts approximately 30 days after hatching, after the young birds have left the nest and have started to feed on their own; it ends at sexual maturity, some 90 days after hatching. The song mastered by that time is the same song the zebra finch will sing for the rest of its life.[7,8]

Address for correspondence: Fernando Nottebohm, Rockefeller Field Research Center, Millbrook, NY 12545. Voice: 845-677-3059; fax: 212-327-8312.

nottebo@rockefeller.edu

Ann. N.Y. Acad. Sci. 1021: 404–409 (2004). © 2004 New York Academy of Sciences.
doi: 10.1196/annals.1308.049

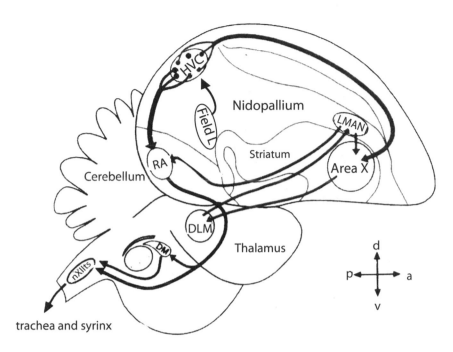

FIGURE 1. Schematic drawing of a sagittal section of a songbird brain in relation to the high vocal center (HVC). Ascending auditory information enters the song system via Field L of the nidopallium. Two pathways are distinguished within the song system by different projections from HVC: (1) an anterior pathway necessary for the acquisition of song starts from HVC and then goes through three relays (Area X, DLM, and LMAN) before reaching RA; and (2) a posterior pathway that links HVC with one relay, (RA), to the hypoglossal motor neurons (nXIIts) that innervate the muscles of the vocal organ (syrinx). RA, robust nucleus of the arcopallium; DLM, medial nucleus of the dorsolateral thalamus; LMAN, lateral magnocellular nucleus of the anterior nidopallium.

Birds that imitate sounds have evolved a telencephalic "song system" that appears to be specialized for the acquisition and production of learned song. FIGURE 1 shows a schematic diagram of the zebra finch song system. Nucleus HVC is part of two pathways: a posterior one necessary for the production of song and an anterior one necessary for the acquisition but not for the production of song.[10–13] HVC neurons that project to Area X in the avian striatum are born before the bird hatches, but production of other HVC neurons continues after hatching and into adulthood.[14–16]

In experimental animals new neurons can be visualized by labeling them with cell birth markers, such as BrdU or tritiated-thymidine, which are incorporated into newly synthesized DNA. The HVC volume of male zebra finches does not change significantly after day 90, nor does the total number of its neurons, yet new neurons continue to be recruited to HVC, albeit at a lower rate than in juveniles (FIG. 2).[16,17] The new neurons replace older ones that died earlier, so that the total count remains the same.[13,18] As the adults grow older, the rate of addition declines further.[19] Though the song of a 90-day-old zebra finch is roughly as stereotyped as that of a 3-

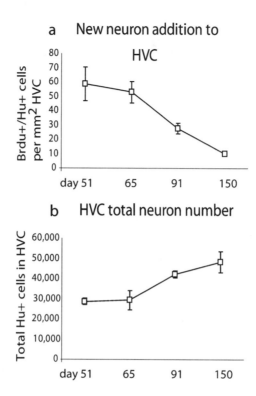

FIGURE 2. (a) Animals of different ages were injected with a cell-birth marker, bromodeoxyuridine (BrdU) for 5 days and killed 30 days after the first injection. New neurons were identified in HVC using antibodies for BrdU and a neuronal protein Hu. The number of new neurons found in HVC declined as birds matured and the sensitive period for song learning ended. (b) HVC grew in total neuron number throughout development and stabilized around 4 to 5 months of age.

year-old bird, when older birds are deafened their songs deteriorate much more slowly than in young adults.[20] This suggests that the rate of incorporation of new neurons to HVC is correlated with the stability of the underlying motor or auditory memory[19,21] and the number of new neurons in HVC may determine a bird's ability to modify its songs.

Recent results suggest why turnover of HVC neurons may be particularly relevant for song learning potential. Individual HVC → RA-projecting neurons fire once, in a brief 6 ms burst at exactly the same time during each rendering of a male zebra finch's song motif and different HVC → RA neurons fire at different times.[22] Given the average length of song and number of HVC → RA neurons, this means that 40–80 cells of this kind are responsible for executing successive 6-ms portions of the learned pattern.[22] Interestingly, these are the cells that account for a majority of the neurons added to HVC during song ontogeny.[15,16]

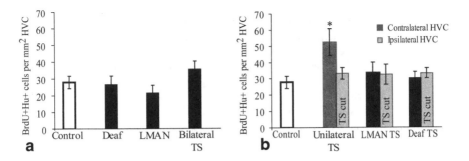

FIGURE 3. (a) Animals of with different treatments were injected with a cell-birth marker, BrdU, on days 61–65 after hatching, and they were killed 30 days after the first injection. New neuron counts in HVC were similar for controls and birds that could not imitate a song because of deafening, lesion of LMAN, or bilateral denervation of the syrinx at day 26. TS, tracheo-syringeal nerve. (b) When the same protocol was followed but birds received only unilateral denervation of the syrinx at day 26, we found more new neurons in the HVC of their intact hemisphere (contralateral) than on their operated (ipsilateral) side. They also had significantly more new neurons than controls, and both were able to imitate song comparably well. If the unilaterally denervated birds were also deafened or received LMAN lesions at day 26, disrupting their ability to imitate a song, then the difference in new neuron counts between the two HVCs disappeared.

Clearly, there is a positive relation between times when many new neurons are added to HVC and times when vocal learning is particularly robust, but what is the nature of this relation? Vocal imitation can be blocked in a number of different ways, such as deafening, bilateral denervation of the syringeal muscle (vocal organ), or bilateral lesion of the forebrain nucleus LMAN at the end of a male zebra finch's first month of life. In all these cases, though, the pattern of new neuron addition observed in juveniles and the number of neurons present in the adult HVC did not differ between controls and operated birds (FIG. 3a). However, it would be a mistake to conclude, from this, that the program that guides the development of HVC is impervious to experience. Early unilateral denervation of the syrinx results in the atrophy of syringeal muscles on the denervated side. Birds treated in this manner are still able to imitate a song model with the intact syringeal half and they recruit a greater number of new neurons to the intact hemisphere's HVC during song ontogeny when compared to intact controls (FIG. 3b). Interestingly, this difference disappears if, in addition to unilateral denervation, the birds are deafened or have LMAN lesioned on both sides (FIG. 3b). Perhaps, the asymmetry in recruitment induced by unilateral denervation of one syringeal half is related to the bird's effort to learn a new song with the intact side.[17,23] This may be due to differential use of the intact side or a delay in the closure of the sensitive period for song learning caused by slowing (but not blocking) of the animal's ability to make a satisfactory imitation. However, even in unilaterally denervated birds, the total number of HVC neurons present in adults was very similar to that in intact controls (data not shown). Thus, though the total number of neurons present in the adult HVC is not determined by experience, the rates of recruitment and turnover of these cells are.

In summary, the recruitment and incorporation of new neurons in HVC probably provides part of the circuit plasticity that underlies the sensitive period for vocal learning. This recruitment of neurons, which occurs even when imitation is blocked, can be magnified or extended when learning load is increased. Clearly, much more remains to be done,[17,23] but if the parallels between vocal learning in birds and humans are to be fully explored to better understand the human condition, then we suggest that the search should be on for neuronal recruitment and replacement in the parts of the juvenile and adult brain responsible for the acquisition and production of speech and language.

ACKNOWLEDGMENTS

The authors would like to thank Daun Jackson, Sharon Sepe, Helen Ecklund, and the Rockefeller University Field Research Center staff for assistance with animal care. This research was funded by a Public Health Service grant, Mr. Howard Phipps, the Mary Flagler Cary Charitable Trust, and a National Science Foundation Graduate Research Fellowship (L.W.).

REFERENCES

1. KARTEN, H.J. 1997. Evolutionary developmental biology meets the brain: the origins of mammalian cortex. Proc. Natl. Acad. Sci. USA **94:** 2800–2804.
2. DIEKAMP, B., O. GAGLIARDO & O. GUNTURKUN. 2002. Nonspatial and subdivision-specific working memory deficits after selective lesions of the avian prefrontal cortex. J. Neurosci. **22:** 9573–9580.
3. METZGER, M., S. JIANG & K. BRAUN. 1998. Organization of the dorsocaudal neostriatal complex: a retrograde and anterograde tracing study in the domestic chick with special emphasis on pathways relevant to imprinting. J. Comp. Neurol. **395:** 380–404.
4. SCHARFF, C. & F. NOTTEBOHM. 1991. A comparative study of the behavioral deficits following lesions of various parts of the zebra finch song system: implications for vocal learning. J. Neurosci. **11:** 2896–2913.
5. BRAINARD, M.S. & A.J. DOUPE. 2000. Interruption of a basal ganglia-forebrain circuit prevents plasticity of learned vocalizations. Nature **404:** 762–766.
6. WILBRECHT, L. & F. NOTTEBOHM. 2003. Vocal learning in birds and humans. Ment. Retard. Dev. Disabil. Res. Rev. **9:** 135–148.
7. IMMELMANN, K. 1969. *In* Bird Vocalizations. R.A. Hinde, Ed.: 64–74. Cambridge University Press. Cambridge.
8. ARNOLD, A.P. 1975. The effects of castration on song development in zebra finches (*Poephila guttata*). J. Exp. Zool. **191:** 261–325.
9. BOEHNER, J. 1990. Early acquisition of song in the zebra finch, *Taeniopygia guttata*. Anim. Behav. **39:** 369–374.
10. NOTTEBOHM, F., T.M. STOKES & C.M. LEONARD. 1976. Central control of song in the canary, *Serinus canaria*. J. Comp. Neurol. **165:** 457–486.
11. NOTTEBOHM, F., D.B. KELLEY & J.A. PATON. 1982. Connections of vocal control nuclei in the canary telencephalon. J. Comp. Neurol. **207:** 344–357.
12. BOTTJER, S.W. & A.P. ARNOLD. 1984. Forebrain lesions disrupt development but not maintenance of song in passerine birds. Science **224:** 901–903.
13. SCHARFF, C., J.R. KIRN, M. GROSSMAN, et al. 2000.Targeted neuronal death affects neuronal replacement and vocal behavior in adult songbirds. Neuron **25:** 481–492.
14. GOLDMAN, S.A. & F. NOTTEBOHM. 1983. Neuronal production, migration and differentiation in a vocal control nucleus of the adult female canary brain. Proc. Natl. Acad. Sci. USA **80:** 2390–2394.

15. ALVAREZ-BUYLLA, M. THEELEN & F. NOTTEBOHM. 1988. Birth of projection neurons in the higher vocal center of the canary forebrain before, during, and after song learning. Proc. Natl. Acad. Sci. USA **85:** 8722–8726.
16. NORDEEN, K.W. & E.J. NORDEEN. 1988. Projection neurons within a vocal motor pathway are born during song learning in zebra finches. Nature **334:** 149–151.
17. WILBRECHT, L., A. CRIONAS & F. NOTTEBOHM. 2002. Experience affects recruitment of new neurons but not adult neuron number. J. Neurosci. **22:** 825–831.
18. KIRN, J., B. O'LOUGHLIN, S. KASPARIAN & F. NOTTEBOHM. 1994. Cell death and neuronal recruitment in the high vocal center of adult male canaries are temporally related to changes in song. Proc. Natl. Acad. Sci. USA **91:** 7844–7848.
19. WANG, N., P. HURLEY, C. PYTTE & J.R. KIRN. 2002. Vocal control neuron incorporation decreases with age in the adult zebra finch. J. Neurosci. **22:** 10864–10870.
20. LOMBARDINO, A.J. & F. NOTTEBOHM. 2000. Age at deafening affects the stability of learned song in adult male zebra finches. J. Neurosci. **20:** 5054–5064.
21. SCOTT, L.L., E.J. NORDEEN & K.W. NORDEEN. 2000. The relationship between rates of HVc neuron addition and vocal plasticity in adult songbirds. J. Neurobiol. **43:** 79–88.
22. HAHNLOSER, R.H., A.A. KOZHEVNIKOV & M.S. FEE. 2002. An ultra-sparse code underlies the generation of neural sequences in a songbird. Nature **419:** 65–70.
23. WILBRECHT, L., T. PETERSEN & F. NOTTEBOHM. 2002. Bilateral LMAN lesions cancel differences in HVC neuronal recruitment induced by unilateral syringeal denervation. Lateral magnocellular nucleus of the anterior neostriatum. J. Comp. Physiol. A Neuroethol. Sens. Neural Behav. Physiol. **188:** 909–1015.

REFERENCES NOT CITED IN TEXT

EALES, L.A. 1987. Song learning in female-raised zebra finches: another look at the sensitive phase. Anim. Behav. **35:** 1356–1365.
EALES, L.A. 1985. Song learning in zebra finches: some effects of song model availability on what is learnt and when. Anim. Behav. **33:** 1293–1300.
MORRISON, R.G. & F. NOTTEBOHm. 1993. Role of a telencephalic nucleus in the delayed song learning of socially isolated zebra finches. J. Neurobiol. **8:** 1045–1064.
NOTTEBOHM, F. & M.E. NOTTEBOHM. 1976. Left hypoglossal dominance in the control of the canary and white-crowned sparrow song. J. Comp. Physiol. **108:** 171–192.
WILBRECHT, L. 2003. The recruitment of new neurons to the song system during the sensitive period for song learning in the zebra finch. Thesis Dissertation. The Rockefeller University. New York
ZANN, R.A. 1996. The Zebra Finch. Oxford University Press. New York.

Nicotine Administration Significantly Alters Accumbal Dopamine in the Adult but Not in the Adolescent Rat

KIMBERLY A. BADANICH[a] AND CHERYL L. KIRSTEIN[a,b]

Departments of [a]Psychology, and [b]Pharmacology & Therapeutics, University of South Florida, Tampa, Florida 33620, USA

ABSTRACT: Many drug-dependent adults began using drugs during adolescence. In fact, adolescent drug users are more likely to become drug-dependent adults than those abstaining from drug use until after the age of 18. Because of this, recent research has begun to investigate the consequences of adolescent drug use. Specifically, research has begun to focus on the behavioral effects of drugs on the developing brain and the development of drug addiction. The present study examined the responsiveness of the mesolimbic dopamine (DA) pathway during development through the use of *in vivo* microdialysis. Specificall, it was determined whether nicotine-induced accumbal DA release differs between adolescent and adult rats. To assess nicotine's effects across age, animals received acute or repeated nicotine at early adolescence (postnatal day (PND) 35), late adolescence (PND 45), or young adulthood (PND 60). Findings suggest that there are significant differences between adolescent and adult animals in their dopaminergic response to nicotine. Adult animals had an enhanced DA response to acute nicotine challenge, an effect absent in adolescence. Additionally, this nicotine-induced increase in adults was not apparent after repeated nicotine treatment. These results provide insight into how the adolescent brain responds to nicotine and may also provide evidence as to how prolonged nicotine use affects normal brain development and responsiveness.

KEYWORDS: adolescent rat; nicotine; nucleus accumbens; development; addiction

INTRODUCTION

Cigarette smoking is prevalent during adolescence. Fifty percent of U.S. high school students have tried cigarettes at least once in their lifetime.[1] Of those adolescents who have tried a cigarette, 25% progressed to daily smoking during adolescence.[1] Ninety percent of all adult smokers initiated smoking cigarettes during adolescence.[2] However, when compared to younger age groups, those who abstain from smoking until after the age of 18 are least likely to continue smoking as adults.

Address for correspondence: Cheryl L. Kirstein, Ph.D., Psychology Department, PCD 4118G, University of South Florida, 4202 E. Fowler Avenue, Tampa, FL 33620. Voice: 813-974-9626; fax: 813-974-4617

kirstein@luna.cas.usf.edu

Ann. N.Y. Acad. Sci. 1021: 410–417 (2004). © 2004 New York Academy of Sciences.
doi: 10.1196/annals.1308.054

Nicotine, the active ingredient in cigarettes, has been suggested to produce its rewarding properties through several mechanisms. Nicotine research has focused physiologically on the functioning of the mesolimbic system after nicotine administration in adult animals.[4–7] A considerable body of evidence indicates that activation of the mesolimbic system produces the rewarding effects associated with nicotine as well as other drugs of abuse (alcohol, cocaine, stimulants, opiates).[8–12] The mesolimbic system, which consists of dopamine (DA) neurons originating in the ventral tegmental area (VTA) and terminating in the nucleus accumbens septi (NAcc), has been shown to mediate drug-associated reward.[12] In general, drugs of abuse produce their rewarding properties by enhancing the efficacy of this dopaminergic pathway through stimulation of mesolimbic DA neurons and the induction of phasic firing. Phasic firing of mesolimbic DA neurons causes enhanced DA release in the NAcc shell.[8,10] It is this sudden efflux of DA into the NAcc shell that produces the rewarding effects associated with drug use. Administration of DA antagonists completely blocks nicotine-induced conditioned place preference.[13] Taken together, these results suggest that DA and the mesolimbic system are integral components in expressing the rewarding properties of nicotine in adult animals.

Nicotine binds to nicotinic acetylcholine (nACh) receptors located in the VTA, NAcc, and in the prefrontal cortex (PFC).[14] These receptors are located on the cell bodies and terminals of both dopaminergic, glutamatergic, and GABAergic neurons.[14–16] Stimulation of nAChR's in the VTA increases phasic firing of DA neurons.[17] Additionally, stimulation of nAChR's in the PFC facilitate glutamatergic synapses on mesolimbic DA neurons and elicit DA release. Responsivity of nicotine-induced accumbal DA release has been measured in adult animals using *in vivo* microdialysis. Many studies have shown that acute and repeated nicotine significantly increase accumbal DA; however, repeated administration has been shown to reduce subsequent nicotine-induced increases in DA for adult animals.[4–7]

To date, investigations of nicotine's effects on the mesolimbic system have been conducted in adults despite the fact that this system undergoes unique physiological and functional change during adolescence (for review, see Ref. 18). In summary, the mesolimbic system undergoes marked change during adolescence, which may influence how this system responds to nicotine. It may be this difference that drives adolescents to be highly susceptible to nicotine dependence. To determine if the mesolimbic system responds differently to nicotine treatment during development, the present study used *in vivo* microdialysis to examine the effects of acute or repeated nicotine administration in adolescent and adult rats.

MATERIALS AND METHODS

Animals

Forty-four Sprague-Dawley (Harlan) rats derived from breeding pairs in our laboratory were used as subjects. No more than one male and one female per litter were used in a given condition. Animals were derived from 21 different litters. Average weights at the time of surgery for each age were as follows: PND 35 = 127.5 g, PND 45 = 186.67 g, and PND 60 = 275.0 g. In all respects, maintenance and treatment of the animals were within the guidelines for animal care by the National Institutes of Health.

Pretreatment

Early adolescence (PND 35), late adolescence (PND 45), or young adults (PND 60) received acute or repeated nicotine. For 4 days prior to the target age (i.e., PND 35, 45, or 60), animals received twice-daily injections of either nicotine (0.6 mg/kg) or saline. Nicotine bitartrate was obtained from Sigma, dissolved in saline and adjusted for pH (pH = 7.0). Nicotine dose was expressed as the salt.

Surgical Procedures and In Vivo Microdialysis

Animals were anesthetized on either PND 34, 44, or 59 using a ketamine/xylazine cocktail (1.0 and 0.15 mg/kg/ip). An incision was made over the skull and the rat was mounted on a stereotaxic instrument for surgery. Three holes were drilled in the skull (two for skull screws and one for the guide cannula). The guide cannula was lowered to the NAcc shell[19] and affixed to the skull with cranioplast. The probe was immediately lowered into the NAcc. Animals were singly housed with *ad libitum* food and water in a BAS Raturn system. Probes were perfused continuously at a flow rate of 0.2 µL/min with artificial cerebrospinal fluid (145 mM NaCl, 2.4 mM KCl, 1.0 mM MgCl, 0.2 mM ascorbate, pH = 7.4) for 12 hours prior to the start of sampling. On either PND 35, 45, or 60, dialysates were collected at a flow rate of 1.0 µL/min at 10-minute intervals into refrigerated microcentrifuge tubes containing 2.5 µL of 0.25 M perchloric acid ($HClO_4$). Six baseline samples were taken, after which animals received an injection of either nicotine or saline and samples collected for an additional 120 minutes. Dialysate samples (12.5 µL) were either run immediately or stored at −80°C until analyzed. Drop sites were verified histologically to ensure placement in the NAcc shell region.

Neurochemical Analyses

Analyses of dialysate samples were performed with a reverse-phase high-performance liquid chromatography system (BAS) coupled with electrochemical detection (HPLC-EC) set to oxidize DA and its two major metabolites 3,4-dihydroxyphenylacetic acid (DOPAC) and homovanillic acid (HVA) (750 mV). An amperometric detector with an LC-4C carbon working electrode referenced to an Ag/AgCl electrode was used. The mobile phase consisted of 75 mM sodium phosphate, 1.4 mM octane sulfonic acid, 10 uM EDTA, and 10% v/v acetonitrile (pH 2.9) set at a flow rate of 100 µL/min. Samples (6 µL) were injected onto a C-18 microbore column for peak separation. Data were recorded and quantified by Chromgraph on a Dell Dimension 2100.

Data Analysis

Change in DA levels post nicotine challenge were analyzed using area under the curve followed by a 3 (PND 35, 45, 60) × 3 (acute, repeated, saline control) ANOVA with Fisher's least significant difference for post hoc analyses of age and treatment effects.

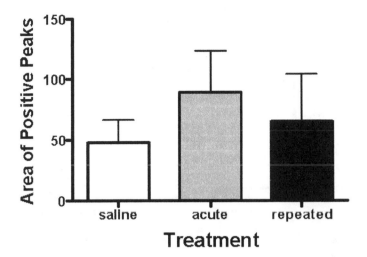

FIGURE 1. Nicotine administration in early adolescents (PND 35). Neither acute (*gray bar*) nor repeated (*black bar*) nicotine administration significantly elevated DA.

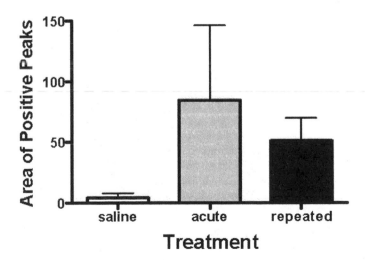

FIGURE 2. Nicotine administration in late adolescents (PND 45). Neither acute (*gray bar*) nor repeated (*black bar*) nicotine administration significantly elevated DA.

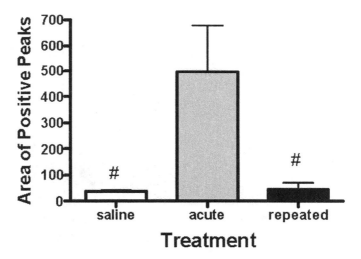

FIGURE 3. Nicotine administration in adults (PND 60). Acute nicotine administration significantly elevated DA (*gray bar*). Adult animals showed tolerance after repeated administration (*black bar*). # = differs from PND 60 acute.

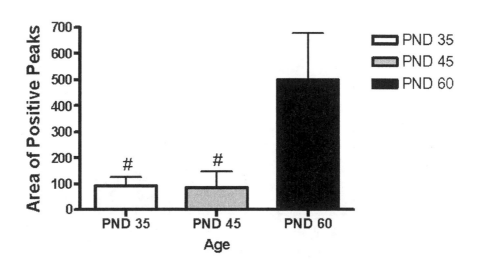

FIGURE 4. Acute nicotine challenge across age. Acute nicotine challenge significantly elevated DA in adult (*black bar*) but not in adolescent (*white and gray bars*) animals. # = differs from PND 60 acute.

RESULTS

The effects of acute versus repeated nicotine administration on accumbal DA levels post nicotine challenge are significantly different across age. Data are expressed as area under the curve. A positive peak was defined as an elevation in DA above the mean of the first three baseline samples that was sustained for at least two time points. A 3×3 (Age $\times$ Treatment) ANOVA indicated Age ($F(2, 33) = 5.90, P < .05$) and Treatment ($F(2, 33) = 11.36, P < .05$) had a significant effect on DA overflow, in addition to a significant interaction between Age and Treatment ($F(4, 33) = 5.65, P < .05$).

Both early and late adolescent animals failed to express a nicotine-induced dopaminergic response irrespective of condition (FIGS. 1 and 2).

Although both adolescent ages failed to express a significant increase in DA, a trend toward enhanced DA overflow for the acute condition is evident. In contrast, adult animals receiving an acute nicotine challenge had elevated DA levels in comparison to adult saline controls (FIG. 3).

Adult DA levels in response to repeated nicotine treatment were significantly lower than in the acute condition (FIG. 3). Importantly, when comparing adolescent and adult animals, DA levels were significantly elevated in adults after an acute nicotine challenge (FIG. 4).

Overall, there were no significant differences between the early and late adolescent ages, nor were there sex differences. Basal DA levels in the NAcc across age were unaffected by systemic pretreatment with nicotine.

DISCUSSION

The present findings suggest that the mesolimbic dopaminergic system responds differently to nicotine across development. Adult animals had an enhanced DA response to acute nicotine challenge, an effect absent in adolescents. Additionally, this response to nicotine in adults was not apparent after repeated nicotine treatment. These data suggest that the dopaminergic response evident in adult animals after one injection of nicotine is significantly blunted in animals receiving repeated nicotine treatment. DA levels that return to baseline levels may quite possibly be indicative of neurological adaptation and the development of physiological tolerance. These DAergic differences between adolescent and adult animals may be influenced by substantial differences in mesocorticolimbic circuitry across development.

Enhanced dopaminergic response in adult animals may be influenced by stimulation of nACh receptors located on dopaminergic (VTA), glutamatergic (PFC), and GABAergic (NAcc) neurons.[16,20] These neurons synapse with GABAergic medium spiny (MS) neurons[16,21,22] and affect GABAergic activity in the NAcc. When stimulated, MS neurons inhibit the ventral pallidum, initiating altered activity of the mediodorsal nuclei of the thalamus and also the prefrontal cortex, thus completing the mesocorticolimbic loop.[23] Therefore binding of nicotine to nACh receptors in any of the aforementioned areas would activate the mesocorticolimbic pathway. Stimulation of nACh receptors potentiates the activity of the mesocorticolimbic pathway. Because the PFC also sends excitatory projections to the VTA,[24] activity of this pathway is again potentiated and results in the release of DA in the NAcc.

In contrast, adolescents did not express a nicotine-induced DA response, which may be explained by the ontogeny of the mesocorticolimbic pathway. Excitatory projections from the PFC undergo refinement during adolescence.[25] These excitatory projections from the PFC to the NAcc may not yet be fully developed.

Another possibility is that there also may be an overproduction and pruning of cholinergic synapses and nACh receptors located in the NAcc. The activity of the cholinergic neurons may predominate if the cholinergic system has not yet entered the pruning stage for the adolescent ages chosen in the present study. As a result, nicotine binding to nACh receptors located on GABAergic interneurons would cause an inhibition of MS neurons and a disruption of information flow through the mesocorticolimbic pathway. This would be in contrast to adults who have fully developed neural circuitry and the resulting potentiation of mesolimbic DA neuron activity.

Recent work in our lab using a biased conditioned place preference paradigm has shown that adolescents spend more time in the previously nonpreferred (aversive) chamber following repeated nicotine pairings.[26] Vastola et al.[27] also found that adolescent animals spend more time in the previously nonpreferred chamber after repeated pairings of nicotine. Adolescent animals in this study exhibited a preference for the paired chamber, an effect absent in adults. In spite of the lack of nicotine-induced DA release in the accumbens, it is clear that adolescents find the properties of nicotine reinforcing to some extent. These data suggest that the anxiolytic properties of nicotine may be a more critical factor in adolescent animals and perhaps smoking. Adolescents have a bounty of factors that could attribute to increased anxiety, such as peer pressure, teachers, and parents, along with their increased striving for independence. Adolescents go through this time period with anxiety; many strive and succeed without turning to smoking cigarettes as a coping mechanism. It is this vulnerable point during adolescence that future research, both clinical and experimental, should explore further.

ACKNOWLEDGMENTS

This work has been supported by a grant from the Robert Wood Johnson Foundation: The Teenage Etiology Research Network (TERN). The authors thank Rex M. Philpot for his technical assistance.

REFERENCES

1. THE YOUTH RISK BEHAVIOR SURVEY. 2001. Trends in cigarette smoking among high school students. Center for Disease Control and Prevention. Washington, D.C.
2. AMERICAN LUNG ASSOCIATION. 2003. Adolescent smoking statistics. <http://www.lungusa.org/press/tobacco/not_stats.html>
3. U.S. DEPARTMENT OF HEALTH AND HUMAN SERVICES. 1994. Preventing tobacco use among young people: a report of the Surgeon General. USDHHS, PHS, CDCP. Office on Smoking and Health. Washington, D.C.
4. VEZINA, P. et al. 1992. Nicotine and morphine differentially activate brain dopamine in prefrontocortical and subcortical terminal fields: effects of acute and repeated injections. J. Pharmacol. Exp. Ther. **261:** 484–490.
5. BENWELL, M.E. & D.J. BALFOUR. 1992. The effects of acute and repeated nicotine treatment on nucleus accumbens dopamine and locomotor activity. Br. J. Pharmacol. **105:** 849–856.

6. IMPERATO, A., A. MULAS & G. DI CHIARA. 1986. Nicotine preferentially stimulates dopamine release in the limbic system of freely moving rats. Eur. J. Pharmacol. **132:** 337–338.
7. BENWELL, M.E., D.J. BALFOUR & H.M. LUCCHI. 1993. Influence of tetrodotoxin and calcium on changes in extracellular dopamine levels evoked by systemic nicotine. Psychopharmacology **112:** 467–474.
8. PEOPLES, L.L. *et al.* 1998. Phasic firing time locked to cocaine self-infusion and locomotion: dissociable firing patterns of single nucleus accumbens neurons in the rat. J. Neurosci. **18:** 7588–7598.
9. GRACE, A.A. 2000. The tonic/phasic model of dopamine system regulation and its implications for understanding alcohol and psychostimulant craving. Addiction **95**(Suppl. 2): S119–128.
10. CADONI, C. & G. DI CHIARA. 2000. Differential changes in accumbens shell and core dopamine in behavioral sensitization to nicotine. Eur. J. Pharmacol. **387:** R23–R25.
11. SINGER, G., M. WALLACE & R. HALL. 1982. Effects of dopaminergic nucleus accumbens lesions on the acquisition of schedule induced self injection of nicotine in the rat. Pharmacol. Biochem. Behav. **17:** 579–581.
12. WISE, R.A. & M.A. BOZARTH. 1982. Action of drugs of abuse on brain reward systems: an update with specific attention to opiates. Pharmacol. Biochem. Behav. **17:** 239–243.
13. ACQUAS, E. *et al.* 1989. SCH 23390 blocks drug-conditioned place-preference and place-aversion: anhedonia (lack of reward) or apathy (lack of motivation) after dopamine-receptor blockade? Psychopharmacology **99:** 151–155.
14. VIDAL, C. 1996. Nicotinic receptors in the brain. Molecular biology, function, and therapeutics. Mol. Chem. Neuropathol. **28:** 3–11.
15. CLARKE, P.B. & A. PERT. 1985. Autoradiographic evidence for nicotine receptors on nigrostriatal and mesolimbic dopaminergic neurons. Brain Res. **348:** 355–358.
16. DE ROVER, M. *et al.* 2002. Cholinergic modulation of nucleus accumbens medium spiny neurons. Eur. J. Neurosci. **16:** 2279–2290.
17. MEREU, G. *et al.* 1987. Preferential stimulation of ventral tegmental area dopaminergic neurons by nicotine. Eur. J. Pharmacol. **141:** 395–399.
18. SPEAR, L.P. 2000. The adolescent brain and age-related behavioral manifestations. Neurosci. Biobehav. Rev. **24:** 417–463.
19. PHILPOT, R.M., S. MCQUOWN & C.L. KIRSTEIN. 2001. Stereotaxic localization of the developing nucleus accumbens septi. Brain Res. Dev. Brain Res. **130:** 149–153.
20. MUSEO, E. & R.A. WISE. 1990. Microinjections of a nicotinic agonist into dopamine terminal fields: effects on locomotion. Pharmacol. Biochem. Behav. **37:** 113–116.
21. CHAO, S.Z. *et al.* 2002. D1 dopamine receptor stimulation increases GluR1 surface expression in nucleus accumbens neurons. J. Neurochem. **83:** 704–712.
22. CARR, D.B. & S.R. SESACK. 2000. Projections from the rat prefrontal cortex to the ventral tegmental area: target specificity in the synaptic associations with mesoaccumbens and mesocortical neurons. J. Neurosci. **20:** 3864–3873.
23. CHURCHILL, L., D.S. ZAHM & P.W. KALIVAS. 1996. The mediodorsal nucleus of the thalamus in rats—I. Forebrain gabaergic innervation. Neuroscience **70:** 93–102.
24. COOPER, D.C. 2002. The significance of action potential bursting in the brain reward circuit. Neurochem. Int. **41:** 333–340.
25. LEWIS, D.A. 1997. Development of the prefrontal cortex during adolescence: insights into vulnerable neural circuits in schizophrenia. Neuropsychopharmacology **16:** 385–398.
26. TORRELLA, T.A. *et al.* 2003. Developmental differences in nicotine place conditioning. This volume.
27. VASTOLA, B. *et al.* 2002. Nicotine-induced conditioned place preference in adolescent and adult rats. Physiol. Behav. **77:** 107–114.

Grid Crossing: Inability to Compare Activity Levels between Adolescent and Adult Rats

J. L. VILA,[a] R. M. PHILPOT,[a,b] AND C. L. KIRSTEIN[a,b]

Department of [a]Psychology: Cognitive and Neural Sciences, and
[b]Department of Pharmacology and Therapeutics, University of South Florida,
Tampa, Florida 33620, USA

ABSTRACT: Traditionally, studies measuring behavioral activity have used male adult animals and grid crossings (GCs) as a representative measure of activity in lieu of total distance moved (TDM). However, using GCs as the dependent measure may not be effective for comparing the activity of animals during development, as they vary significantly in size. The present study examines the reliability of GCs as opposed to TDM as an indicator of locomotor activity for comparisons during ontogeny using a computerized behavioral tracking system (Noldus). Rats (postnatal day[PND] 35, PND 60) were tracked for a period of 3 minutes inside a closed runway. GCs and TDM were measured for the recorded tracks. It was determined that GCs were positively correlated with TDM in the behavioral apparatus, suggesting that GCs is a reliable measure of an individual animal's activity. Using GCs as the dependent measure, no significant differences in activity were observed across age or sex. However, using TDM indicates adolescent rats are significantly more active than their adult counterparts. These data indicate that although the number of GCs is predictive of total activity, the slope of the relationship varies significantly with age, therefore making it inappropriate to use GCs when comparing across ages. Studies that use animals of differing age must be sensitive to baseline differences in locomotor activity.

KEYWORDS: adolescence; locomotor activity; behavior; grid crossing

Historically, neuroscience research has been conducted using adult male animals. In recent years the importance of adolescent research in the area of drug abuse has received increased attention—particularly research focusing on the neurochemical and behavioral aspects of adolescence. These studies are leading to a growing understanding of the unique aspects of the adolescent brain and behavior. Many important developmental changes occur within the adolescent time period.[1]

Investigations of the activational effects of psychomotor compounds traditionally have utilized locomotor activity as a behavioral measure and demonstrate that more active animals exhibit a greater propensity to self-administer drugs of abuse.[2] In these studies animals are tested drug free and subsequently categorized based on to-

Address for correspondence: Dr. C.L. Kirstein, University of South Florida, Department of Psychology: Cognitive and Neural Sciences, and Department of Pharmacology and Therapeutics, 4202 E. Fowler, PCD 4118-G, Tampa, Fl 33620. Voice: 813-974-9626; fax: 813-974-4617.
Kirstein@chuma1.cas.usf.edu

Ann. N.Y. Acad. Sci. 1021: 418–421 (2004). © 2004 New York Academy of Sciences.
doi: 10.1196/annals.1308.055

tal activity in the apparatus. These developmental behavioral studies often compare obtained results to studies using adults in an attempt to describe the behavioral changes occurring across age.

In the past, in order to simplify quantification, the trial area used for testing was often divided into quadrants or grids. Occurrences of line crossings were tallied as an indicator of TDM during the trial.[3] More recently, photobeams and cells have been used to construct an invisible matrix, and a computer records the number of beam breaks registered. Although more sophisticated, this process is fundamentally an electronic measure of GCs. Currently, activity measures can be obtained using computerized behavioral tracking systems. In addition to eliminating experimenter bias these programs can provide more direct behavioral data, such as TDM.

The main objective of this study was to determine the reliability of GCs as opposed to TDM when comparing activity levels between adolescent and adult male and female rats. Additionally, recordings were analyzed to determine if activity levels and distribution of movement within the closed runway remain constant between groups.

METHOD

Subjects

Twenty-six Sprague-Dawley rats (Harlan) derived from breeding pairs in our colony were used in this experiment. Behavioral recordings took place between 11:00 and 13:00 h. No more than one male and female per litter were placed in any given condition. Animal care was in accordance with the guidelines set forth by the National Institutes of Health.

Locomotor Recording

Animals at PND 35 and PND 60 were placed inside a closed runway (32" × 8.5") for a 3-minute trial. The runway consisted of black Plexiglas with a clear Plexiglas cover. Testing was done on an elevated platform, centered in a sound-attenuated room. Prior to each session, the box was cleaned with quatracide to remove olfactory cues. The computer video-based tracking system EthoVision (Noldus, Leesburg, VA) was used for automated acquisition and analysis of data. With this program the runway was divided into 16 grids (2" × 4.5"). GCs, time spent moving, distribution of movement, and TDM were measured from the recorded tracks.

RESULTS

When comparing GCs as a measure of activity, adolescent rats did not differ from adults [AGE, $F(1,22) = 2.6$, $P > 0.05$]. In contrast, TDM of the same animals revealed that adolescents were significantly more active than the adults [AGE, $F(1,22) = 5.24$, $P < 0.05$]. However, time spent moving did not distinguish between ages [AGE, $F(1,22) = 0.04$, $P > 0.05$] or sexes [SEX, $F(1,22) = 0.48$, $P > 0.05$]. Using TDM instead of GCs exposed trends across males and females that were not revealed using GCs. Specifically, using TDM females displayed a trend towards elevated activity relative to same-aged males [SEX, $F(1,22) = 3.04$, $P = 0.095$].

GCs and TDM were correlated ($r = 0.69$). This correlation was strong at PND 35 ($r = 0.72$) and PND 60 ($r = 0.57$) (FIG. 1). However, the slope of the regression line across ages differed significantly (PND 35 m = 3.24, PND 60 m = 2.87, t (22) = 4.06). Subsequent analysis revealed that adult males had a significantly lower slope than all other trend lines (FIG. 2).

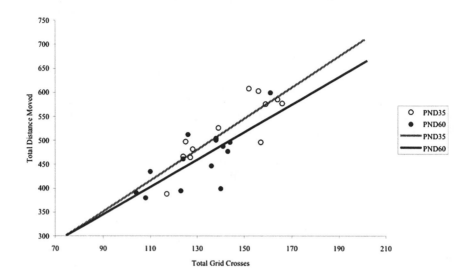

FIGURE 1. Grid crossings by total distance moved between ages.

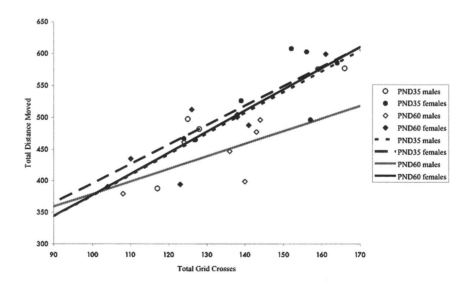

FIGURE 2. Grid crossings by total distance moved between age and sex.

DISCUSSION

The present findings suggest that GCs cannot be utilized to compare animals across age or sex. Total time spent moving and distribution of movement within the closed runway was similar between adults and adolescents and across sex. These findings indicate that the procedure used for this study is an appropriate approach when comparing animals across age. Prior studies have indicated that adolescent rats are more active than their adult counterparts.[4] However, in the present study increased activity reached significance only when analyzing TDM. This finding suggests that there is a loss of experimental sensitivity produced when GCs were utilized as an indicator of activity.

Overall, GCs were positively correlated with TDM, indicating that GCs are representative of TDM. However, this relationship is not held constant across development or sex. Adult male animals exhibited less TDM per GC. This indicates a weakness in the predictability of GCs in relation to TDM across development. Specifically, GCs will tend to overestimate total activity in adult male animals when compared to adolescent or female adult animals (FIG. 2). Therefore, comparing females across development may be unbiased, but comparison between developing males is a biased evaluation. These findings are not due to the size of the animal given that the Noldus program follows the center of gravity, not the whole animal. The points tracked for both ages are identical in size, signifying that the adolescents move more per grid crossed regardless of how grid size was defined. These results indicate that the increase in activity within each GC was most reasonably due to additional exploring per grid in the adolescent animals.

Together, these findings suggest that TDM is a more sensitive measure than GCs and that it should be used when making comparisons across age and sex. Prior studies that failed to obtain significance in activity across development may, in fact, have shown a difference using the more sensitive TDM. Future studies should strive to use the most precise methods of tracking TDM to achieve more accurate comparisons across development.

ACKNOWLEDGMENT

This study was supported by NIDA RO1DA14024.

REFERENCES

1. KABBAJ, M. & H. AKIL. 2001. Individual differences in novelty-seeking behavior in rats:a C-*Fos* study. Neuroscience **106:** 535–545.
2. PIAZZA, P.V., J. DEMINIERE, M. LEMOAL & H. SOMON. 1989. Factors that predict individual vulnerability to amphetamine self-administration. Science **245:** 1511–1513.
3. SPEAR, L., I.A. SHALABY & J. BRICK. 1980. Chronic administration of haloperidol during development: behavioral and psychopharmacological effects. Psychopharmacology **70:** 47–58.
4. SPEAR, L. 2000. The adolescent brain and age-related manifestations. Neurosci. Biobehav. Rev. **24**(4): 417–463.

Developmental Differences in the Accumbal Dopaminergic Response to Repeated Ethanol Exposure

REX PHILPOT AND CHERYL KIRSTEIN

Departments of Psychology and Pharmacology, University of South Florida, Tampa, Florida 33620, USA

ABSTRACT: Recent research indicates that alcohol use/abuse is often initiated during the adolescent period and that brain reinforcement pathways (e.g., the mesolimbic dopamine [DA] pathway) are undergoing developmental transition. Our research focuses on the effects of ethanol administration on neural mechanisms associated with addiction in preadolescent (postnatal day [PND] 25), adolescent (PND 35, PND 45), and young adult (PND 60) animals. Using conditioned place preference (CPP) testing, we have shown that adolescent animals are unique in their responses to ethanol. Since CPP has been associated with contextually conditioned incentive motivation, our results suggest that younger animals may be more vulnerable to addiction. The present data reveal that adolescent animals are neurochemically distinct in response to ethanol's effects. Using *in vivo* microdialysis within the nucleus accumbens septi (NAcc), we have determined the DAergic response across development. Results reveal that basal levels of DA transition during the adolescent period and differ from preadolescent or adult animals. Specifically, PND 45 animals exhibited significantly higher, and PND 25 significantly lower, basal DA levels than all other ages examined. Further, repeated exposure to ethanol elevated basal DA levels significantly regardless of age or dose. Basal 3,4-dihydroxyphenylacetic acid (DOPAC)/DA ratio also differed as a function of age, with PND 35 and PND 60 animals demonstrating the highest ratios, and PND 45 animals producing the lowest baseline levels. Repeated ethanol exposure produced significant changes in basal ratios as a function of age. Interestingly, PND 45 animals exhibited no change in ratios with repeated exposure, while all other ages demonstrated a dose-dependent rise in DOPAC/DA ratios. These data indicate an age-dependent difference in the homeostatic alterations of mesolimbic systems in response to repeated ethanol treatment, an effect that may manifest itself as differences in behavioral responsivity and conditionability to the drug and the drug's effects.

KEYWORDS: adolescence; dopamine; nucleus accumbens septi; ethanol; development

Adolescence is a complex developmental period involving increased socialization, risk taking, cognitive and sexual development, and rapid growth. This period is char-

Address for correspondence: Cheryl Kirstein, Ph. D., University of South Florida, 4202 East Fowler Ave., PCD 4118-G, Tampa, FL 33620. Voice: 813-974-1958; fax: 813-974-4617.
kirstein@chuma1.cas.usf.edu

Ann. N.Y. Acad. Sci. 1021: 422–426 (2004). © 2004 New York Academy of Sciences.
doi: 10.1196/annals.1308.056

acterized by exploring potentials and challenging protective barriers to transition from a dependent to an independent organism. A natural consequence of adolescence is tremendous experimentation and risk taking,[1] a pattern that, in the arena of drug abuse, often manifests itself as first-time drug use and the potential for drug abuse.[2] Drug use typically begins early in the maturational process, increasing dramatically in adolescence. By the twelfth grade, approximately 80.3% of U.S. adolescents have used alcohol at some time, an increase from 51.7% for 8th graders.[3] Adult lifetime prevalence data indicate that 81.3% have had some experience with alcohol, a rate only slightly higher than that reported for 12th graders, suggesting that during adolescence most individuals have their first experience with the drug. Of particular importance, the rate of initiation of alcohol use among the 12–17 year old age group has increased in recent years.[4]

Developmental changes in the mesolimbic system, which projects from the ventral tegmental area (VTA) to the nucleus accumbens septi (NAcc), may mediate the behavioral changes associated with adolescence, consequently increasing the probability of drug-use initiation as well as potentiating the likelihood of abuse. It is clear that in both human and rodent populations, mesolimbic dopamine (DA) systems are undergoing a tremendous transition. Basal DA synthesis in the NAcc is lower in postnatal day (PND) 30 than in PND 40 rats, and turnover rates for PND 30 animals are less than those reported in adults.[5] DA receptor populations also change, exhibiting a pattern of overproduction and pruning across adolescence.[5–7] This pattern is similar in humans as well.[8] In rats, the density of D1, D2, and D4 receptors in the NAcc increases to a peak at PND 28 and then declines significantly to adult levels at PND 60.[9] Parallel with these changes, DA transporter levels are undergoing substantial change, increasing in concentration in the NAcc to adult levels through adolescence.[10,11]

The dynamic changes in the mesolimbic DA system during adolescence suggests that processes mediated by this system are unlikely to manifest themselves similarly in adults. Across adolescence there may be tremendous transitions in reactivity to stimuli (e.g., drugs) that act on these systems. Particularly, developmental transitions in this pathway may mediate the increased likelihood of engaging in drug use initiation (risk taking) during adolescence. Thus, drugs of abuse may exhibit unique profiles of action in these systems during adolescence and, as a result, increase the probability of the development of addiction among adolescents.

To examine the influence of ethanol exposure on NAcc DA, animals were placed into one of two treatment conditions—acute or repeated ethanol—and administered one of five doses: saline, 0.2, 0.5, 1.0, or 2.0 g/kg ethanol (17% v/v). Neurochemical responses to treatment were measured using *in vivo* microdialysis following 4 days of treatment. Coordinates for probe placement in the NAcc of PND 25, 35, 45, and 60 animals were determined using weight-based regression lines established in a prior study.[12] All animals received injections (b.i.d.) at one of 4 age ranges: PND 21–24 (preadolescent), 31–34, 41–44 (periadolescent), or 56–59 (young adult) to examine developmental differences in response profiles. Four to eight animals were used per group, for a total of 315 animals.

The probe was perfused with artificial cerebrospinal fluid (145 mM NaCl, 2.4 mM KCl, 1.0 mM $MgCl_2$, 1.2 mM $CaCl_2$, and 0.2 mM ascorbate, pH = 7.4) at a flow rate of one μL/min and inserted (under anesthesia). Animals were placed within a BAS Raturn Apparatus (Bioanalytical Systems, West Lafayette, VA) overnight to allow for elimination of anesthetic. Sampling began 24 h following placement of the probe. Samples were collected (1 μL/min) every 10 min using a refrigerated fraction collector (BAS) and acidified with 0.25 N HClO$_4$. A total of six baseline samples were collected, the final three of which were used for the calculation of baseline levels. Drop sites were verified histologically to ensure placement in the NAcc shell region.

Extracellular levels of DA, and 3,4-dihydroxyphenylacetic acid (DOPAC) were determined using HPLC-EC. Direct injections of dialysis samples were separated by a Microbore HPLC system (BAS) with a mobile phase consisting of monochloroacetic acid (0.15 M), sodium octyl sulfate (0.50 mM), EDTA (1.0 mM), and acetonitrile (4.0%) (pH = 2.9). Peaks were detected using a BAS LC-4C electrochemical detector coupled to a radial flow electrode referenced at 0.800 V. Data were analyzed using a 4 (Age) × 2 (Treatment) × 4 (Dose) ANOVA with subsequent simple effects analyses and Fisher LSDs to isolate effects.

The present findings indicate late adolescent animals (i.e., PND 45) produce substantially greater quantities of DA in extracellular fluid than younger and older animals (FIG. 1). Given evidence suggesting that NAcc DA is related to both responsiveness to novel stimuli and drug abuse liability, and that these two factors are correlated, it is reasonable to assume that differences in basal DA activity in the NAcc may manifest itself as transitional differences in behavior. The developmental elevation in DA may serve to produce the increased exploratory behavior and risk taking typically observed in adolescence.

The present study shows a lack of alteration in DOPAC/DA turnover at this age (PND 45; FIG. 2), suggesting a failure to adapt to repeated ethanol use or, at a minimum, a unique fashion of adaptation at this age that may result in increased reactivity to ethanol following repeated use relative to other ages. Further, the unique status of the DA system during this time, coupled with its unique response to repeated ethanol use, may result in a system that develops differentially as a result of alcohol ex-

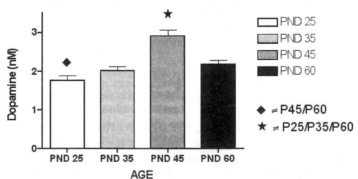

FIGURE 1. Analysis of basal DA revealed a significant main effect of Age 3,279 $F = 17.171$, $P < 0.05$. Post hoc analysis revealed that PND25 animals exhibited significantly less basal DA in dialysate than PND 45 or PND 60, while PND 45 animals demonstrated higher basal levels than all other ages examined.

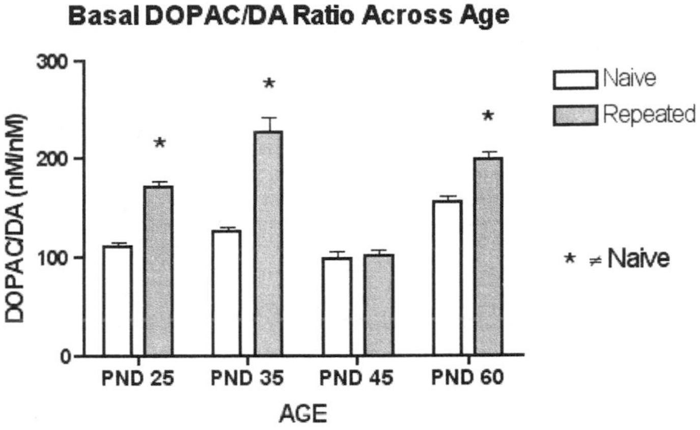

Basal DOPAC/DA Ratio Across Age

FIGURE 2. Analysis of basal DOPAC/DA ratio revealed a significant Age × Pretreatment interaction 3,279 $F = 7.637$, $P < 0.05$. Analysis of simple effects in naive animals revealed that PND 60 animals produce higher DOPAC/DA ratios than all other ages, and that PND 45 animals exhibit lower ratios than all other ages. With repeated exposure, PND 25 animals exhibit lower turnover values than PND 35 or PND 60, and PND 45 animals exhibited lower turnover than all ages. Importantly, PND 45 animals failed to demonstrate an elevation in DOPAC/DA ratio following repeated ethanol exposure.

posure during adolescence. This may, in turn, increase the likelihood of long-term ethanol use, abuse, and dependence.

ACKNOWLEDGMENT

This work was supported by NIAAA Grant AA11820.

REFERENCES

1. SPEAR, L.P. 2000. The adolescent brain and age-related behavioral manifestations. Neurosci. Biobehav. Rev. **24**(4): 417–463.
2. ZUCKERMAN, M. 1974. The sensation seeking motive. Prog. Exp. Pers. Res. **7**: 79–148.
3. JOHNSTON, L.D. 2000. Monitoring the future: national survey results on drug use, 1975–1999. National Institute on Drug Abuse, U.S. Dept. of Health and Human Services, National Institutes of Health. Bethesda, MD.
4. SAMHSA. 1999. Summary of findings from the 1998 national household survey on drug abuse: 128. U.S. Dept. of Health and Human Services. Rockville, MD.
5. ANDERSEN, S.L., et al. 1997. Sex differences in dopamine receptor overproduction and elimination. Neuroreport **8**(6): 1495–1498.
6. TEICHER, M.H., S.L. ANDERSEN & J.C. HOSTETTER, JR. 1995. Evidence for dopamine receptor pruning between adolescence and adulthood in striatum but not nucleus accumbens. Brain Res. Dev. Brain Res. **89**(2): 167–172.
7. ANDERSEN, S.L. & M.H. TEICHER. 2000. Sex differences in dopamine receptors and their relevance to ADHD. Neurosci. Biobehav. Rev. **24**(1): 137–141.

8. SEEMAN, P., *et al.* 1987. Human brain dopamine receptors in children and aging adults. Synapse **1**(5): 399–404.

9. TARAZI, F.I. & R.J. BALDESSARINI. 2000. Comparative postnatal development of dopamine D(1), D(2) and D(4) receptors in rat forebrain. Int. J. Dev. Neurosci. **18**(1): 29–37.

10. COULTER, C.L., H.K. HAPPE & L.C. MURRIN. 1996. Postnatal development of the dopamine transporter: a quantitative autoradiographic study [published erratum appears in Brain Res. Dev. Brain Res. 1996. Jan 2; **98**(1): 150]. Brain Res. Dev. Brain Res. **92**(2): 172–181.

11. COULTER, C.L., H.K. HAPPE & L.C. MURRIN. 1997. Dopamine transporter development in postnatal rat striatum: an autoradiographic study with [3H]WIN 35,428. Brain Res. Dev. Brain Res. **104**(1–2): 55–62.

12. PHILPOT, R.M., S. MCQUOWN & C.L. KIRSTEIN. 2001. Stereotaxic localization of the developing nucleus accumbens septi. Brain Res. Dev. Brain Res. **130**(1): 149–153.

Age-Related Differences in Elevated Plus Maze Behavior between Adolescent and Adult Rats

TAMARA L. DOREMUS, ELENA I. VARLINSKAYA, AND LINDA PATIA SPEAR

Center for Developmental Psychology, Department of Psychology,
Binghamton University, Binghamton, New York 13902, USA

ABSTRACT: Adolescence is a time of considerable transformations, often associated with increases in risk taking and novelty-seeking behaviors. Little is known of a possible age-dependent expression of anxiety-related behaviors in novel or potentially dangerous situations. The present study explored age differences in anxiogenic and anxiolytic stimuli between adolescent and adult Sprague-Dawley rats using the elevated plus maze (EPM). Data were compared across several experiments using factor analysis of multiple EPM measures. Under some circumstances, adolescents revealed a relatively low behavioral anxiety profile compared to adults, whereas in other situations results revealed the opposite pattern. Characteristics of the pretest circumstances altered considerably the nature of the conclusions reached regarding age-related changes in anxiogenic and anxiolytic stimuli. In general, anxiety measures in adolescents were less affected by variations in pretest conditions compared to the same variables in adults, suggesting possible adolescent immaturity of brain mechanisms involved in the regulation of anxiety.

KEYWORDS: adolescence; anxiety; elevated plus maze; factor analysis

Although previously thought to be a period unique to humans, adolescence is a transition seen across many mammalian species.[1] In addition to hormonal, neural, and psychosocial transformations, increases in risk-taking and novelty-seeking behaviors are also common during adolescence.[1] These behaviors may be associated with developmental alterations in anxiety, although available data are mixed, with reports of elevated,[2] decreased,[3] and no changes[4] in anxiety during adolescence. The elevated plus maze (EPM) has been validated pharmacologically and widely used as a model of anxiety in adult animals.[5] Results from our laboratory have shown surprisingly variable age differences in EPM anxiety when compared across studies. The present analyses were conducted to better understand age differences in EPM behavior across varying test conditions in both adolescent and adult rats.

Address for correspondence: Dr. Linda Spear, Department of Psychology, Binghamton University, P.O. Box 6000, State University of New York, Binghamton, NY 13902-6000. Voice: 607-777-2825; fax: 607-777-6418.
lspear@binghamton.edu

Ann. N.Y. Acad. Sci. 1021: 427–430 (2004). © 2004 New York Academy of Sciences.
doi: 10.1196/annals.1308.057

METHODS AND RESULTS

Subjects were adolescent (postnatal day [PND] 33–35) and adult (PND 70–75) male and female Sprague-Dawley rats raised in our colony. Non-drug-treated animals from three different experiments were included in these analyses. In all studies, 5- min EPM test sessions were conducted under dim light with a white noise generator and recorded by a video camera mounted above the apparatus. An experienced observer later scored tapes. Separate apparatuses were used for each age, with the adolescent EPM (30 × 8.9-cm open arms with 20.3-cm walls on closed arms) scaled to 3/4 of the adult dimensions (48.3 × 12.7-cm open arms with 29.2-cm walls on closed arms) based on crown–rump length and gait-width analyses. Across the three experiments, three different conclusions were drawn regarding age-related alterations in anxiety levels.

Experiment 1 assessed the effect of prior social isolation or exposure to a novel environment on EPM performance and observed that adolescent animals were overall less anxious than adults. Examination of saline-treated animals in a study of ethanol hangover (Exp. 2) found adolescent males to be more anxious than adult males, with a more subtle age difference in females. When assessing saline-injected animals from a study designed to examine EPM behavior after acute ethanol exposure (Exp. 3), no age-related differences were seen in anxiety levels.

Slight changes in pretest conditions across each of these studies may have contributed to these contradictory conclusions. To assess the contribution that variations in pretest conditions may have had on consequent EPM behaviors, each of the seven different pretest conditions used across the three studies were ranked according to their degree of perturbation: homecage; 30 min of social isolation; 30 min in a novel breeder tub with a partner; a small saline injection and 30 min in a novel environment with a partner; small saline injection and 30 min of isolation in a novel environment; large saline injection and 30 min social isolation with restraint; large saline injection and 30 min of isolation in a novel environment. In adults, anxiety levels were strongly related to the level of pretest perturbation, with adults demonstrating lower levels of anxiety as pretest perturbation increased. Adolescents, however, showed no clear relationship between pretest conditions and anxiety behaviors. These results demonstrate the importance of pretest circumstances in influencing age-related comparisons in the EPM and raise the question as to whether the EPM test is measuring the same underlying components of behavior in both adolescent and adult rats. Factor analysis was used to assess this issue.

Principal components analysis (PCA) was employed using an orthogonal (varimax) rotation on factors displaying an Eigenvalue of 1 or greater in both adolescent and adult animals from each of the three experiments. Because the data analyzed in each study reflect only saline-treated animals, sampling adequacy was marginal, yet adequate to conduct the analyses reported. Consistent with previous factor analyses of EPM behavior in adult male rodents,[6,7] measures thought to reflect anxiety (i.e., open arm activity, protected head dips, and protected stretched attend postures) loaded highly on factor 1 for both age groups in all three experiments. At both ages, behaviors loading onto factor 2 appeared to be generally activity-related (i.e., closed arm entries and total arm entries); whereas those most consistently loading on factor 3 (percent of time in the central square, total number of stretched attend postures, and rears) appeared likely to reflect what others have termed risk assessment.[8] The percent of variance accounted for by each of the three factors was approximately equal across age groups and experiments, accounting for a total variance of 78–84% in each analysis. Similar PCA conducted to compare males and females in each experiment also revealed three-factor solutions, with the loading of behaviors on the three factors in females similar to those seen in the age analyses (anxiety, activity, risk assessment). In males, however, activity-related behaviors loaded most consistently on factor 3, with the percent of variance accounted for by this component lower in males than in females. These data are consistent with other studies reporting stronger activity-driven behavior in females in the EPM,[6] and even in other behavioral tests of anxiety.[9]

DISCUSSION

The factor analysis results provide evidence that the EPM measures similar components of behavior in adolescent and adult animals, and hence is an appropriate behavioral test of anxiety for making age-related comparisons in both adolescent and adult animals. Nonetheless, subtle differences in pretest characteristics, previously thought to be innocuous, may alter considerably the nature of the conclusions reached regarding age-related changes in anxiogenic and anxiolytic stimuli. It is therefore critical that implications of a particular pretest condition for EPM behavior be considered at each age when assessing the ontogeny of responsiveness to anxiolytic and anxiogenic stimuli. Use of the EPM to compare the sexes in responsiveness to anxiety manipulations should be done conservatively, regardless of age, given that male and female rats differ in the amount of variance accounted for by activity-related behaviors.

ACKNOWLEDGMENT

This work was supported by NIAAA Grants R37-AA12525 and RO1 AA12150 to L.P. Spear

REFERENCES

1. SPEAR, L.P. 2000. The adolescent brain and age-related behavioral manifestations. Neurosci. Biobehav. Rev. **24:** 417–463.
2. DOREMUS, T.L., S.C. BRUNELL, E.I. VARLINSKAYA & L.P. SPEAR. 2003. Anxiogenic effects during withdrawal from acute ethanol in adolescent and adult rats. Pharmacol. Biochem. Behav. **75:** 411–418.
3. IMHOF, J.T., Z.M.I. COELHO, M.L. SCHMITT, *et al.* 1993. Influence of gender and age on performance of rats in the elevated plus maze apparatus. Behav. Brain Res. **56:** 177–180.
4. VARLINSKAYA, E.I. & L.P. SPEAR. 2002. Acute effects of ethanol on social behavior of adolescent and adult rats: role of familiarity of the test situation. Alcohol Clin. Exp. Res. **26:** 1502–1511.
5. PELLOW, S., P. CHOPIN, S.E. FILE & M. BRILEY. 1985. Validation of open:closed arm entries in an elevated plus-maze as a measure of anxiety in the rat. J. Neurosci. Methods **14:** 149–167.

6. FERNANDEZ, C., M.I. GONZALEZ, C.A. WILSON & S.E. FILE. 1999. Factor analysis shows that female rat behaviour is characterized primarily by activity, male rats are driven by sex and anxiety. Pharmacol. Biochem. Behav. **64:** 731–738.
7. RODGERS, R.J. & A. DALVI. 1997. Anxiety, defence and the elevated plus-maze. Neurosci. Biobehav. Rev. **21:** 801–810.
8. WALL, P.M. & C. MESSIER. 2001. Methodological and conceptual issues in the use of the elevated plus-maze as a psychological measurement instrument of animal anxiety-like behavior. Neurosci. Biobehav. Rev. **25:** 275–286.
9. JOHNSTON, A.E. & S.E. FILE. 1991. Sex differences in animal tests of anxiety. Physiol. Behav. **49:** 245–250.

The Cellular Basis for Volume Changes in the Rat Cortex during Puberty: White and Gray Matter

JANICE M. JURASKA[a] AND JULIE A. MARKHAM[b]

[a]Neuroscience Program and [a,b]Department of Psychology, University of Illinois, Champaign, Illinois 61820, USA

ABSTRACT: We have found that developmental changes through the adolescent period in the rat cerebral cortex provide parallels to those seen in the human cortex. Like humans, the rat cerebral white matter increases during this time due to increases in the number of axons that become myelinated even while the total number of axons decreases. We have preliminary evidence that estrogen decreases the rate of myelination, which results in a sex difference in adult rats. Another parallel to the human cortex is the nonlinear changes in the size of the cortex. We have found that in some cortical regions, female rats show decreases in cortical volume and number of neurons across the time of puberty, and removal of the ovaries stops these decreases. The rat cortex may serve as a model for the cellular changes underlying the volume changes seen in adolescent humans.

KEYWORDS: puberty; cerebral cortex; neuron number; corpus callosum; myelination; axon number; prefrontal cortex; rat

Imaging studies during human adolescence have revealed cortical changes including increases in the size of the corpus callosum[1] and decreases in the volume of the frontal cortex.[2,3] The cellular basis for these gross size changes are difficult-to-impossible to obtain from human tissue. This makes it especially relevant that we have found parallel changes in the rat cerebral cortex around the time of puberty, which begins between 30 and 40 days of age. The rats we are examining are Long Evans hooded (pigmented) rats.

THE CORPUS CALLOSUM AND WHITE MATTER

The callosal region that we have concentrated on is the splenium, which we have shown is composed of axons chiefly from the visual cortex with a small number from the temporal cortex in the rat.[4,5] The splenium increases in size between 25 and 60 days of age in rats of both sexes.[5] In an electron microscope study, the gross size

Address for correspondence, Dr. Janice M. Juraska, Neuroscience Program, University of Illinois, 603 E. Daniel, Champaign, IL 61820. Voice: 217-333-8546; fax: 217-244-5876. jjuraska@s.psych.uiuc.edu

Ann. N.Y. Acad. Sci. 1021: 431–435 (2004). © 2004 New York Academy of Sciences. doi: 10.1196/annals.1308.058

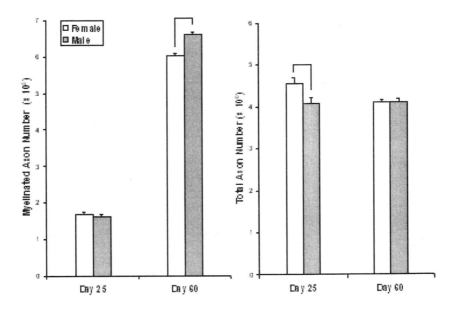

FIGURE 1. The number of myelinated axons and the total number of axons (myelinated plus unmyelinated) axons in the rat splenium. In addition to the labeled significant sex differences, there was a significant effect of age for myelinated axons. For the total number of axons, only the females showed a significant difference between ages. (Modified from Kim & Juraska.[5])

increase was found to be driven by sizable increases in the number of myelinated axons, in spite of the continuing loss of axons overall in females (FIG. 1).[5] The number of myelinated axons has a substantial effect on gross size because they are considerably larger, on average, than unmyelinated axons even without their myelin sheaths.[4,5] There are sex differences that appear for the first time following puberty that indicate a potential role for the rise of gonadal hormone secretions associated with puberty. By 60 days of age, males have a greater number of myelinated axons in the splenium even as the sex difference found at day 25 (female > male) in the total number of axons disappears (FIG. 1).[5] We have preliminary data that the removal of the ovaries in females before puberty (day 25) results in an increase in the number of myelinated axons in the splenium and that this increase is reversed with chronic exposure to estrogen.[6] Thus estrogen appears to influence the myelination process. The increase in myelination that do occur in intact females during this time indicate that estrogen is only a modulating variable.

We have found significant stepwise increases in the volume of the white matter under the frontal cortex between 20, 35, and 90 days of age.[7] Comparable to the increase in frontal white matter found during human adolescence, males increase more than females, which results in a sex difference by adulthood.[1,7] The increase in both sexes is probably due to myelination, as we have shown in the corpus callosum.

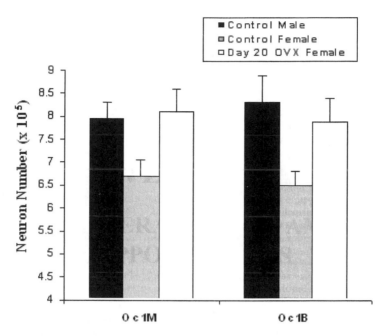

FIGURE 2. The number of neurons in the binocular (Oc1B) and monocular (Oc1M) portions of the primary visual cortex of adult rats. Control females have significantly fewer neurons than both control males and females with ovaries removed at 20 days of age. (Modified from Nunez *et al.*[9])

GRAY MATTER

We have mounting evidence that neurons are lost in the cortex around the time of puberty in female rats. First, we found that female rats continue to undergo a late developmental wave (day 25) of apoptosis in the visual cortex, which male rats do not experience. This was quantified using both pyknotic cells and TUNEL as markers of cell death.[8] Next, the removal of the ovaries in females at day 20 abolished the sex difference (male > female) in neuron number in the visual cortex that is seen in adulthood (FIG. 2).[9] Removal of the testes in males of the same age did not alter adult neuron number. Last, we have preliminary data from an ongoing study of the ventral prefrontal cortex (infralimbic and prelimbic, comparable to Brodmann areas 25 and 32). Here parcellated volume of this area significantly decreased between ages 35 (peripuberty) and 90 (adulthood) in female, but not in male, rats.[10] Ongoing counts of neuron number (illustrated by individual animal means on FIG. 3), quantified through unbiased stereology, indicate that neuron number is stable across these ages in males but appears to decrease in females (FIG. 3).[10]

The human cortex undergoes regional decreases during adolescence in both sexes,[2,3] while in rats the loss of volume and neurons has thus far been restricted to females. However, the work on rats demonstrates that neurons can be lost this late in the lifespan and that pubertal hormones are a modulator of these decreases. This im-

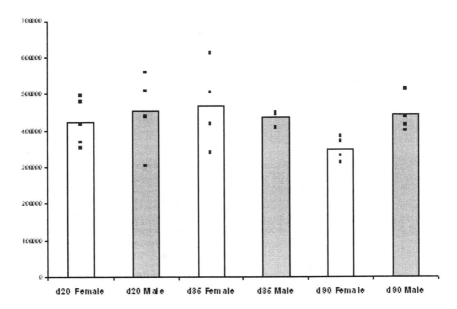

FIGURE 3. The number of neurons in the ventral medial prefrontal cortex of the rat at 20, 35, and 90 days of age. *Bars* are group means; the individual animals are represented as *small squares*.

plies the adolescent brain may be vulnerable to other agents that can promote cell death and that the rat may serve as a model for this vulnerability.

ACKNOWLEDGMENT

This work has been supported by NSF, most recently by Grant IBN 01-36468.

REFERENCES

1. GIEDD, J.N., *et al.* 1996. Quantitative magnetic resonance imaging of human brain development: ages 4–18. Cereb. Cortex **6**: 551–560.
2. SOWELL, E.R., *et al.* 1999. In vitro evidence for post-adolescent brain maturation in frontal and striatal regions. Nat. Neurosci. **2**: 859–861.
3. GIEDD, J.N., *et al.* 1999. Brain development during childhood and adolescence: a longitudinal MRI study. Nat. Neurosci. **2**: 861–863.
4. KIM, J.H.Y., A. ELLMAN & J.M. JURASKA. 1996. A re-examination of sex differences in axon density and number in the splenium of the rat corpus callosum. Brain Res. **740**: 47–56.
5. KIM, J.H.Y. & J.M. JURASKA. 1997. Sex differences in the development of axon number in the splenium of the rat corpus callosum from postnatal day 15 through 60. Dev. Brain Res. **102**: 77–85.
6. PYCH, J.C., S. WEBB & J.M. JURASKA. 2001. Estrogen alters the amount and pattern of myelination in the rat corpus callosum. Soc. Neurosci. Abstr. **27**: 370.

7. MARKHAM, J.A., *et al.* 2002. Sex, development, and aging influence the volume of white matter underlying rat frontal cortex. Program No. 33.17. Society for Neuroscience. Washington, DC.

8. NUNEZ, J.L., D.M. LAUSCHKE & J.M. JURASKA. 2001. Cell death in the development of the posterior cortex in male and female rats. J. Comp. Neurol. **436:** 32–41.

9. NUNEZ, J.L., J. SODHI & J.M. JURASKA. 2002. Ovarian hormones after postnatal day 20 reduce neuron number in the rat primary visual cortex. J. Neurobiol. **52:** 312–321.

10. MARKHAM, J.A., J.R. MORRIS & J.M. JURASKA. 2003. Development and aging of neuron number in the rat medial prefrontal cortex: influence of sex. Program No. 149.11 Society for Neuroscience. Washington, DC.

13-*cis* Retinoic Acid (Accutane) Suppresses Hippocampal Cell Survival in Mice

YASUO SAKAI,*a* JAMES E. CRANDALL,*a* JACOB BRODSKY,*b*
AND PETER McCAFFERY*a*

a UMMS/E. K. Shriver Center, Waltham, Massachusetts 02452, USA

b University of Massachusetts Medical School, Worcester, Massachusetts, USA

ABSTRACT: Use of the acne drug Accutane (13-*cis* retinoic acid, [13-*cis* RA])
has been associated with severe depression. This association has been considered controversial because no causative link has been found between 13-*cis* RA
and this disorder. A recent hypothesis has suggested that atrophy of the hippocampus can result in depression. We now show, in a mouse model, that endogenous RA generated by synthetic enzymes in the meninges acts on hippocampal
granule neurons, and chronic (3-week) exposure to a clinical dose of 13-*cis* RA
may result in hippocampal cell loss. In humans this may be conjectured to be
the mechanism by which Accutane contributes to depression.

KEYWORDS: depression; vitamin A; neurogenesis; dentate gyrus; BrdU; sub-
granular zone; meninges; RALDH2

INTRODUCTION

Accutane is an effective antiacne drug for which, in the year 2000, nearly 2 million prescriptions were dispensed.[1] The active agent of the drug is 13-*cis* retinoic
acid (13-*cis* RA). This is probably metabolized systemically to its all-*trans* isomer
and binds to its specific nuclear receptor, which activates the transcription of a large
number of genes.[2] In general, the action of RA is to induce differentiation of immature, proliferating cells to become mature cells.[2] This function likely results in many
of the side effects of Accutane that are directed towards proliferating cells in the
adult such as in the skin, gut, and bone.[3] One controversial side effect, however, is
on behavior. Several reports have suggested a link between Accutane use and severe
depression with suicidal ideation.[3–5] Given that RA's potent effect is on immature
cells, it would be predicted that the predominant effect of this drug on the brain
would be on the regions of proliferation and neural birth, which are limited to only
two regions—the subventricular zones adjacent to the lateral ventricles and the dentate gyrus of the hippocampus. There has been great interest in the events of proliferation and neural birth in the hippocampus, in part because of a recent hypothesis
proposing that a breakdown in such processes can contribute to depression.[6–9] If 13-

Address for correspondence: P. McCaffery, UMMS/E.K. Shriver Center, 200 Trapelo Rd.,
Waltham, MA 02452. Voice: 781-642-0172; fax: 781-642-0116.
peter.mccaffery@umassmed.edu

Ann. N.Y. Acad. Sci. 1021: 436–440 (2004). © 2004 New York Academy of Sciences.
doi: 10.1196/annals.1308.059

cis RA repressed the number of new neurons born in the hippocampus, this could result in a decline in hippocampal function and, in turn, contribute to depression. In this study we first show that RA is normally synthesized in the hippocampus, where it promotes transcription in the granule cells of the dentate gyrus. Three weeks' exposure to a clinical dose of 13-*cis* RA results in a change in this signal. We go on to show that this same regime of 13-*cis* RA exposure results in a significant decline in the survival of newly born granule cells, suggesting that chronic exposure to 13-*cis* RA may result in hippocampal cell loss.

RESULTS AND DISCUSSION

Hippocampal plasticity is under the control of several hormones that regulate gene transcription via nuclear receptors, including estrogen and the glucocorticoids. RA also regulates gene transcription via members of this receptor family and is probably important for the generation of synaptic plasticity.[10] FIGURE 1a shows that a major source of RA for the hippocampus is likely to be from the RA-synthesizing enzyme RALDH2 that is present in the meninges overlaying the brain adjacent to the ventral (infrapyramidal) blade of the dentate gyrus. This would presumably create an asymmetrical distribution of RA across the hippocampus. This asymmetry can be seen using a transgenic RA reporter mouse line to detect RA-activated transcription in which RA signaling is visualized by expression of the beta-galactosidase reporter gene, identified by detection with a specific antibody (FIG. 1b).[11] The endogenous RA signal is predominantly localized to the infrapyramidal blade closest to the meningeal source of RA. Daily exposure to an exogenous source of RA, in the form of Accutane, would be expected to change this pattern. Mice were injected intraperitoneally with 13-*cis* RA at a dose of 1 mg/kg/day, the typical treatment dose used for acne. FIGURE 1c illustrates induction of the RA reporter gene in the dentate gyrus after 3 weeks of 13-*cis* RA treatment. The increase is most pronounced in the suprapyramidal (dorsal) blade of the dentate gyrus, changing the balance of RA signaling with a more uniform RA reporter response in the blades.

What are the consequences of this change in RA signaling after exposure to 13-*cis* RA? RA regulates neural differentiation in the developing CNS[2] and may be expected to normally control neurogenesis in the hippocampus. Excess amounts of RA would be predicted to deregulate these processes. We investigated the effects of 3 weeks' RA treatment on the survival of hippocampal cell precursors. These cells were labeled at the beginning of the 3-week period with bromodeoxyuridine

---

FIGURE 1. Normal RA signaling in the dentate gyrus of the hippocampus and its change as a result of 13-*cis* RA exposure. One source of RA for the hippocampus is likely to be meninges, which express the RA synthesizing enzyme RALDH2, as detected by immunohistochemistry **(a)**. Normal RA signaling in the hippocampus is localized to the neurons of the dentate gyrus, as indicated by the induction of a RAREhsplacZ RA reporter gene, and is predominantly in the infrapyramidal blade, identified using antibodies against the beta-galactosidase RA reporter protein **(b)**. The greater induction in this lower blade is likely due to the source of RA from RALDH2 in the meninges below. After 21 days of injection of 13-*cis* RA the number of cells in the dentate gyrus that express beta-galactosidase (indicating RA signaling) increased and was more uniformly distributed between the two blades **(c)**.

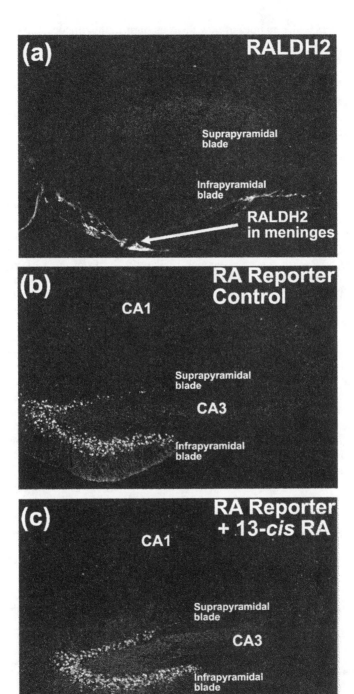

FIGURE 1. *See previous page for legend.*

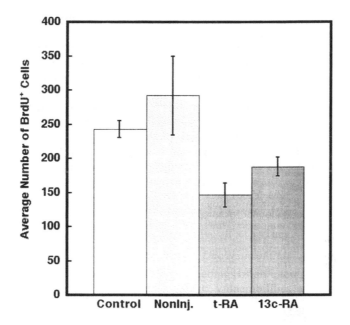

FIGURE 2. The decline in number of BrdU-positive cells remaining in the hippocampus and hippocampal SGZ after 21 days of exposure to 13-*cis* or all-*trans* RA. If proliferating cells are labeled with BrdU and RA treatment is initiated and continued over 21 days, then a significant reduction (23–40%) in the average number of BrdU-positive cells is evident throughout the hippocampal formation with either the all-*trans* or 13-*cis* isomer of RA. It is likely that both isomers act to reduce hippocampal cell survival via the same mechanism utilizing the RA receptor, implying that 13-*cis* RA is isomerized to the all-*trans* isomer that binds to the receptor to activate transcription. Average number of BrdU-positive cells ± standard error of the mean are given below for each group. Control (vehicle-injected) = 243 ± 13, noninjected control = 292 ± 58, *t*RA = 146 ± 18, *t* = 4.56, *P* = 0.011 compared to control (vehicle-injected) by two-tailed *t*-test 13*cis*-RA = 188 ± 14, *t* = 2.9, *P* = 0.044 compared to control (vehicle-injected) by two-tailed *t*-test.

(BrdU),[12] and each day the animals were vehicle injected (50% DMSO, 50% saline), noninjected, or injected with all-*trans* or 13-*cis* RA. In humans, Accutane (13-*cis* RA) is used orally between 0.5–2.0 mg/kg/day over a 4-month treatment period, predominantly in a teenage population in whom the rate of neurogenesis would be predicted to be relatively high.[13] To parallel these conditions, our studies were performed on young adult CD-1 mice, an age and strain with relatively high levels of neurogenesis.[13,14] After 3 weeks the number of BrdU-labeled cells were counted throughout the hippocampal formation in every 12th 40-μm section, taking the average of 3 mice per group (see FIG. 2). Although there was a slight decrease in survival over 3 weeks in the control-injected animals versus uninjected animals, the average number of BrdU-labeled neurons was comparable. However, both all-*trans* and 13-*cis* isomers of RA significantly decreased the number of surviving cells by 40% and 23%, respectively. Because all-*trans* RA is the isomer that activates the RA receptors, this result suggests that 13-*cis* RA is isomerized to the all-*trans* isomer to have its suppressive effect on cell survival.

In short, our results suggest that RA may be a local regulator of cell birth in the hippocampus. Excess RA, in the form of Accutane (13-*cis* RA) or all-*trans* RA, reduces the survival of new cells born in the dentate gyrus of the hippocampus. The increasing evidence that deficits in hippocampal neurogenesis play a role in the etiology of depression[6–9] implies that deregulation of the normal pathway of RA signaling may be an underlying cause of Accutane-induced depression.

[NOTE ADDED IN PROOF: Treatment of mice with 13-*cis* RA has recently been shown by Crandall *et al.*[15] to result in a reduction in hippocampal cell proliferation, neurogenesis, and hippocampus-dependent learning.]

REFERENCES

1. WYSOWSKI, D.K., J. SWANN & A. VEGA. 2002. Use of isotretinoin (Accutane) in the United States: rapid increase from 1992 through 2000. J. Am. Acad. Dermatol. **46:** 505–509.
2. MCCAFFERY, P. & U.C. DRAGER. 2000. Regulation of retinoic acid signaling in the embryonic nervous system: a master differentiation factor. Cytokine Growth Factor Rev. **11:** 233–249.
3. HULL, P.R. & C. DEMKIW-BARTEL. 2000. Isotretinoin use in acne: prospective evaluation of adverse events. J. Cutan. Med. Surg. **4:** 66–70.
4. SCHEINMAN, P.L., *et al.* 1990. Acute depression from isotretinoin. J. Am. Acad. Dermatol. **22:** 1112–1114.
5. JOSEFSON, D. 1998. Acne drug is linked to severe depression. Br. Med. J. **316:** 723.
6. SHELINE, Y.I., *et al.* 1996. Hippocampal atrophy in recurrent major depression. Proc. Natl. Acad. Sci. USA **93:** 3908–3913.
7. MALBERG, J.E., *et al.* 2000. Chronic antidepressant treatment increases neurogenesis in adult rat hippocampus. J. Neurosci. **20:** 9104–9110.
8. KEMPERMANN, G. 2002. Regulation of adult hippocampal neurogenesis—implications for novel theories of major depression. Bipolar Disord. **4:** 17–33.
9. VYTHILINGAM, M., *et al.* 2002. Childhood trauma associated with smaller hippocampal volume in women with major depression. Am. J. Psychiatry **159:** 2072–2080.
10. MISNER, D.L., *et al.* 2001. Vitamin A deprivation results in reversible loss of hippocampal long-term synaptic plasticity. Proc. Natl. Acad. Sci. USA **98:** 11714–11719.
11. ROSSANT, J., *et al.* 1991. Expression of a retinoic acid response element-hsplacZ transgene defines specific domains of transcriptional activity during mouse embryogenesis. Genes Dev. **5:** 1333–1344.
12. MILLER, M.W. & R.S. NOWAKOWSKI. 1998. Use of bromodeoxyuridine-immunohistochemistry to examine the proliferation, migration and time of origin of cells in the central nervous system. Brain Res. **457:** 44–52.
13. KUHN, H.G., H. DICKINSON-ANSON & F.H. GAGE. 1996. Neurogenesis in the dentate gyrus of the adult rat: age-related decrease of neuronal progenitor proliferation. J. Neurosci. **16:** 2027–2033.
14. KEMPERMANN, G., H.G. KUHN & F.H. GAGE. 1997. Genetic influence on neurogenesis in the dentate gyrus of adult mice. Proc. Natl. Acad. Sci. USA **94:** 10409–10414.
15. CRANDALL, J., *et al.* 2004. 13-*Cis*-retinoic acid suppresses hippocampal cell division and hippocampal-dependent learning in mice. Proc. Natl. Acad. Sci. USA **101:** 5111–5116.

The Effects of Ethanol on Spatial and Nonspatial Memory in Adolescent and Adult Rats Studied Using an Appetitive Paradigm

P. RAJENDRAN AND L. P. SPEAR

Center for Developmental Psychobiology, Department of Psychology,
Binghamton University, Binghamton, New York, 13902-6000,USA

ABSTRACT: Adolescent rats have been reported to be less sensitive than adults to many acute ethanol effects, including ethanol-induced sedation and motor impairment, but conversely more sensitive to ethanol-induced disruptions in spatial memory in a Morris water maze (Markwiese *et al.*, 1998). The present study examined adolescent and adult rats trained for 6 days under spatial or nonspatial versions of a presumably less stressful sand box maze. Moderately food-deprived animals were given 0, 0.5, or 1.5 g/kg ethanol intraperitoneally 30 min before training each day, but were tested without ethanol or reinforcer on test day. Spatial acquisition was impaired by 1.5 g/kg in adults but not adolescents, with no ethanol impairment on the nonspatial task at either age. These results are opposite the ontogenetic profile reported by Markwiese *et al.*, (1998) and may reflect differential activation of prefrontal cortex or other stress-sensitive forebrain regions by the two tasks across age.

KEYWORDS: alcohol; adolescence; spatial; learning; memory; development; stress; sand box; Morris water maze; appetitive; aversive

INTRODUCTION

Alcohol abuse is endemic, particularly among adolescents and young adults. Eighty percent of high schoolers have at least tried alcohol, and 50 % of all 12th graders reported using alcohol in the month to the survey.[1] In studies of adolescence using a rodent model, adolescents have been shown to be less sensitive to many of the acute effects of ethanol exposure, including ethanol-induced sedative, motor-impairing, and anxiolytic effects.[2–5] In contrast, adolescent rats have been reported to be more sensitive to certain restricted effects of ethanol, including an ethanol-induced disruption of spatial memory when assessed in a Morris water maze.[6,7] Given that adolescents have sometimes been found to be more sensitive than nonadolescents to stressful situations,[8] the present study examined whether the enhanced sensitivity of adolescents to ethanol-induced disruption in spatial memory acquisition

Address for correspondence: Dr. Linda Spear, Department of Psychology, Binghamton University, P.O. Box 6000, State University of New York, Binghamton, NY 13902-6000. Voice: 607-777-2825; fax: 607-777 6418.
lspear@binghamton.edu

Ann. N.Y. Acad. Sci. 1021: 441–444 (2004). © 2004 New York Academy of Sciences.
doi: 10.1196/annals.1308.060

and performance seen in an aversive escape task (the Morris water maze) would also be seen in an appetitive situation (a sand box task).[9]

METHOD

The subjects were male Sprague-Dawley rats bred in our breeding colony, and pair-housed with male siblings at weaning on postnatal day (PND) 21. Beginning on PND 26–27 in the adolescent group and on PND 68–70 in the adult group, rats were singly housed and restricted to 85 % of their targeted (adolescent) or original (adult) body weights by varying the chow provided.

A 2 (age) × 2 (condition) × 3 (dose) paradigm was used. "Dose" refers to ethanol injected ip—0, 0.5, or 1.5 g/kg, using 12.6 % ethanol in 0.9 % saline 30 min before training; "condition" refers to whether animals were tested in a spatial or nonspatial version of the sand box task. The sand box used consisted of a plastic circular chamber 1 m in diameter and 15 cm high containing sand to a depth of 6 cm in which an appetitive reinforcer, Froot Loops (FLs), could be hidden. Spatial cues were placed on the walls of the testing room. In the nonspatial paradigm a metal pipe 10 cm long, with a rubber stopper hidden under the sand to hold it in place, was used to mark the location of the FLs. A camera suspended from the ceiling of the room monitored and video recorded each session. A white noise generator (60 db at 100 cm) attenuated superfluous sounds. Animals were given 1 trial per day duing all 6 days of training.

In the nonspatial groups, each day the FLs were placed in 1 of 6 positions, about 5 cm from the wall of the box, with the steel tube marking the position of the FLs. In the spatial paradigm, the FLs were placed at the same position throughout the experiment, with only spatial cues on the walls available to help the animal reach the target location. Start positions for all animals varied across days. Following 1 day of habituation to the sand box for 30 min in the absence of reinforcer, animals were given 3 days of shaping, during which the FLs were gradually buried across days, and 3 days of training with buried FLs. Ethanol or saline were administered 30 min before each session of shaping and training. Training sessions continued until the animal either found the FLs or 5 min had elapsed, whichever occurred earlier. If the animal was not able to locate the buried FLs within the requisite time, the experimenters exposed the location. On all days, powdered FLs were mixed in the sand to ensure that the odor permeated the maze. The sand was raked after each animal was tested. Twenty-four hours after the last day of training, all animals were tested for latencies to dig and find target location 30 min after being given saline injections. No FL was buried at the target location on this day.

RESULTS

Acquisition Data

In general, adolescents and adults learned the task at similar rates, although adults took significantly longer to find the FLs on the first day of shaping. Ethanol influenced the latency to approach/dig and latency to find measures only in adults, with the lower dose decreasing these latencies on day 4 in the nonspatial condition relative to saline treatment, whereas the higher dose increased latencies on both measures in the spatial condition on day 5. Adolescents reared significantly more than adults. Regardless of age, the higher dose of ethanol suppressed rearing, with animals given 1.5 g/kg of ethanol rearing less than those receiving either saline or 0.5 g/kg of ethanol. Animals reared least on the first day of shaping (day 2), most on day 4 (the last day the object was visible), and declined in their rearing behavior thereafter.

Test Day Data

On test day, only an age effect was seen in the rearing data, with adolescents again rearing more than adults. For both the latency to approach/dig and the latency to find target location measures, there was a significant dose effect only in the adult spatial group, with adults trained under the higher dose during training in the spatial condition showing considerably longer latencies on test day than those given saline during training.

DISCUSSION

The higher dose of ethanol (1.5 g/kg) impaired spatial learning and memory in adults but not adolescents in the sand box maze, affecting both the latency to approach/dig and the latency to find/find target location measures during both the acquisition and test phases. Such an impairment was not seen in animals performing the nonspatial task, suggesting that ethanol impairs spatial learning in adults, without affecting nonspatial learning or general performance variables. This ethanol-induced spatial impairment was not seen at the training doses (0.5 and 1.5 g/kg) in adolescents. Ethanol also reduced rearing during acquisition but had no residual effects on the drug-free test day in the groups earlier injected with ethanol.

Our data suggest that in a nonstressful sand box task it is adults who are more sensitive than adolescents to ethanol-induced disruption of performance in a spatial memory task. These results contrast with the results of Markwiese et al.,[6] who showed that adolescents trained under the influence of moderate doses of ethanol (1–2 g/kg) were more impaired than similarly treated adults when tested in a presumably more stressful water maze task. Although caution is necessary when comparing across experiments, it is possible that adolescent-associated development of stress-sensitive regions involved in spatial learning may have contributed to the differences observed between the current study and that of Markwiese et al.[6]

ACKNOWLEDGMENT

This work was supported by NIAAA Grants R37 AA 12525 and RO1 AA 12150 to L. P. Spear

REFERENCES

1. JOHNSTON, L.D., P.M. O'MALLEY & J.G. BACHMAN. 2001. National Survey Results on Drug Use from the Monitoring the Future Study, 1975–2000., Vol. I: Secondary

School Students (NIH Publication No. 01-4924). National Institute on Drug Abuse. Bethesda, MD.

2. WHITE, A.M., *et al.* 2001. Differences in EtOH-induced motor impairments and EtOH metabolism in adolescent and adult rats. Alcohol. Clin. Exp. Res. **25** (Suppl.): 109A.

3. VARLINSKAYA, E.I. & L.P. SPEAR. 2002. Acute effects of ethanol on social behavior of adolescent and adult rats: role of familiarity of the test situation. Alcohol Clin. Exp. Res. **26:** 1502–1511.

4. SILVERI, M.M. & L.P. SPEAR. 1998. Decreased sensitivity to the hypnotic effects of ethanol early in ontogeny. Alcohol Clin. Exp. Res. **22:** 670–676.

5. LITTLE, P.J., *et al.* Differential effects of ethanol in adolescent and adult rats. Alcohol. Clin. Exp. Res. **20:** 1346–1351.

6. MARKWIESE, B.J., *et al.* 1998. Differential effects of ethanol on memory in adolescent and adult rats. Alcohol. Clin. Exp. Res. **22:** 416–421.

7. PYAPALI, G.K., *et al.* 1999. Age- and dose-dependent effects of ethanol on the induction of hippocampal long-term potentiation. Alcohol **19:** 107–111.

8. STONE, E.A. & D. QUARTERMAIN. 1997. Greater behavioural effects of stress in immature as compared to mature male mice. Physiol. Behav. **63:** 143–145.

9. HANSON, G.R. & D.C. RICCIO. 2001. The sand maze: an appetitive alternative to the Morris water maze. Presented at the Midwestern Psychological Association Poster Session, May 2001.

Adolescent Ethanol Sensitivity: Hypothermia and Acute Tolerance

R. C. RISTUCCIA AND L. P. SPEAR

Binghamton University Psychology Department, and
Center for Developmental Psychobiolology and Department of Psychology,
Binghamton University, Binghamton, New York 13902, USA

ABSTRACT: A two-injection paradigm was used to assess acute (within-session) tolerance to ethanol in telemetry-implanted adolescent and adult rats. Male rats were intragastrically pretreated with either 1.0 g/kg of ethanol or water and then challenged with 2.0 g/kg of ethanol or water when blood alcohol levels (BALs) of ethanol-pretreated animals were anticipated to approach zero. Adults showed more rapid and sustained ethanol-induced hypothermia than adolescents. Acute tolerance to ethanol-induced hypothermia did not emerge clearly with the two-injection paradigm; ethanol-pretreated animals of both ages generally did not differ from those pretreated with water in their hypothermic response to ethanol despite higher BALs after the second intubation. Housing condition (paired or isolated) had little influence on ethanol-induced hypothermia. The adolescent attenuation of ethanol-induced hypothermia in this experiment was not associated with greater expression of within-session (acute) tolerance.

KEYWORDS: ethanol hypothermia; ethanol sensitivity; acute tolerance; adolescence; body temperature; activity; telemetry; Sprague-Dawley rat

Adolescence is a time of increased vulnerability to drug use and abuse with a steady increase in ethanol use occurring during this period.[1] While the exact cause of this heightened vulnerability is not completely understood, much current research has focused on the differences in the way adolescents respond to ethanol and the rate at which they develop tolerance. It is possible that decreased sensitivity and faster development of tolerance serve as permissive factors that allow adolescents to consume more ethanol than adults.[2]

Sensitivity to acute ethanol exposure varies during ontogeny. Although adolescents are more sensitive than adults to certain restricted ethanol effects (e.g., ethanol-induced memory impairment and ethanol-induced disruption of long-term potentiation[3]), younger animals through adolescence are generally less sensitive than adults to most effects of ethanol, including ethanol-induced sedation, motor impairment, and anxiolysis.[2] The data for ethanol-induced hypothermia are more mixed.[4–6]

Address for correspondence: Robert D. Ristuccia, Binghamton University Psychology Department, Science IV, Vestal Parkway East, Binghamton, NY 13902. Voice: 607-777-2578; fax: 607-777-6418.
rristuccia@yahoo.com

Ann. N.Y. Acad. Sci. 1021: 445–447 (2004). © 2004 New York Academy of Sciences.
doi: 10.1196/annals.1308.061

These ontogenetic differences in sensitivity to acute ethanol exposure may be related in part to developmental alterations in the expression of acute (within session) tolerance. Acute tolerance (AT) is defined as a decrease in sensitivity to the effects of ethanol that occurs within a single exposure. When compared to a time point earlier in the same ethanol exposure session, AT can be observed as decreased impairment at equivalent blood alcohol levels (BALs) or indirectly as equivalent impairment at significantly higher BALs. AT has been reported to decline ontogenetically, at least in terms of sedative effects.[7] Developmental differences in stressor responsivity may also influence ontogenetic assessments of ethanol sensitivity, with, for instance, adolescents being more sensitive to the stress of isolate housing than adults,[8] and stress is known to influence ethanol sensitivity.[9]

Therefore, the purpose of this study was to investigate age differences in sensitivity to ethanol hypothermia and the expression of acute tolerance to this effect. Core body temperature and activity changes in response to ethanol administration in isolate- and pair-housed adolescent and adult rats were examined by means of implanted telemetry probes using a two-intubation procedure derived from Ponomarev and Crabbe[10] to assess acute tolerance.

METHODS

The design of this experiment was a 2 (age) × 2 (housing) × 3 (pretreatment) factorial using 88 male Sprague-Dawley rats. On the day of surgery, half of the animals were pair-housed, while the other half were housed in isolation. Body temperature and activity were monitored continuously in the home cage by telemetry probes (DSI model #TA10TA-F20).

Adolescent and adult animals were implanted with telemetry probes on postnatal day 35 (P35) and P70, respectively. Ethanol administration began 48 h after surgery. Using the basic method of Ponomarev and Crabbe,[10] AT was assessed using a two-intubation paradigm. The ethanol-pretreated animals received two intragastric intubations of 18.9% ethanol, first 1.0 g/kg at 1030 h and then 2.0 g/kg at 1120 h. While not sufficient to induce hypothermia, the first ethanol intubation was intended to initiate adaptations associated with AT, and was hypothesized to result in an attenuated reaction to the second intubation relative to animals receiving their first ethanol intubation at that time. Water-pretreated animals received isovolumetric water as their first intubation and ethanol as the second, whereas water-only controls received two water intubations. To assess BALs, a tail blood sample was taken at 1250 h.

RESULTS AND DISCUSSION

While adolescents and adults showed the same maximum hypothermic response at the same time following the second intubation, there were significant age differences in the duration of ethanol-induced hypothermia. Adults showed a more rapid hypothermic response after the second intubation that lasted much longer than in the adolescents, results reminiscent of other studies reporting a relative adolescent insensitivity to ethanol-induced hypothermia.

No direct evidence of AT was observed given that ethanol-pretreated animals did not show attenuated hypothermia relative to water-pretreated animals. Indeed, while the initial ethanol intubation did not induce hypothermia itself, it left ethanol-pretreated animals vulnerable to future hypothermic challenges. At best, indirect evidence for AT was obtained, with the ethanol-pretreated animals maintaining significantly higher BALs than their water-pretreated counterparts, but only showing significantly lower temperatures at a few time bins. Based on these results, the two-intubation paradigm appears to be an inadequate method of assessing AT to ethanol hypothermia.

Housing condition did not interact with ethanol sensitivity or AT expression at either age, although pair-housed animals were generally more active than isolate-housed animals. Adolescents were significantly more active than adults, as well as significantly more reactive to the stresses of intubation and blood sampling. Ethanol did not alter activity, perhaps due to floor effects related to testing in the homecage during the light phase of the diurnal cycle.

These results provide strong confirming evidence that adolescents are less sensitive than adults to the hypothermic effects of ethanol. Adolescent animals were also more reactive than adults to the stress associated with the intubation and blood-sampling procedures. The stress of isolate housing did not influence ethanol responsivity at either age, although pair-housed animals were more active than isolate-housed animals at both ages. Together, these findings indicate that, while more sensitive to procedural stress, adolescents are less sensitive to the effects of ethanol on body temperature.

ACKNOWLEDGMENTS

This work was supported by NIAAA R37-AA12525 and RO1 AA12150 to L.P.S.

REFERENCES

1. YOUNG, S.E., R.P. CORLEY, M.C. STALLINGS, et al. 2002. Substance use, abuse and dependence in adolescence: prevalence, symptom profiles, and correlates. Drug Alcohol Depend. **68:** 309–322.
2. SPEAR, L.P. 2000. The adolescent brain and age-related behavioral manifestations. Neurosci. Biobehav. Rev. **24:** 417–463.
3. WHITE, A.M. & H.S. SWARTZWELDER. 2004. Hippocampal function during adolescence: a unique target of ethanol effects. Ann. N.Y. Acad. Sci. **1021:**
4. SILVERI, M.M. & L.P. SPEAR. 2000. Ontogeny of ethanol elimination and ethanol-induced hypothermia. Alcohol **20:** 45–53.
5. BRASSER, S.M. & N.E. SPEAR. 2002. Physiological and behavioral effects of acute ethanol hangover in juvenile, adolescent, and adult rats. Behav. Neurosci. **116:** 305–320.
6. SWARTZWELDER, H.S., R.C. RICHARDSON, B. MARKWIESE-FOERCH, et al. 1998. Developmental differences in the acquisition of tolerance to ethanol. Alcohol **15:** 311–314.
7. SILVERI, M.M. & L.P. SPEAR. 1998. Decreased sensitivity to the hypnotic effects of ethanol early in ontogeny. Alcohol. Clin. Exp. Res. **20:** 670–676.
8. STONE, E.A. & D. QUARTERMAIN. 1997. Greater behavioral effects of stress in immature as compared to mature male mice. Physiol. Behav. **63:** 143–145.
9. MEZEY, E. 1998. Stress and ethanol metabolism. Alcohol Alcohol. **33:** 310.
10. PONOMAREV I. & J.C. CRABBE. 2002. NMDA receptor involvement in very rapid adaptation to ethanol-induced sedation. Poster presented at the Annual Meeting of the Research Society on Alcoholism, San Francisco.

Long-Term Neurobehavioral Effects of Alcohol or Nicotine Exposure in Adolescent Animal Models

CRAIG J. SLAWECKI, ANNIKA THORSELL, AND CINDY L. EHLERS

The Scripps Research Institute, Department of Neuropharmacology,
La Jolla, California 92037, USA

ABSTRACT: Adolescent alcohol and nicotine abuse is common, but its neurodevelopmental consequences remain unclear. This laboratory utilized adolescent rodent models to assess the hypothesis that adolescents are highly susceptible to the effects of alcohol and nicotine. Rats were exposed to ethanol for 10–14 days using an intermittent vapor inhalation paradigm. Rats were continuously exposed to nicotine for 5 days using Nicoderm CQ™ transdermal patches. Alcohol or nicotine exposure altered neurobehavioral function when assessed after 3–7 weeks of abstinence. Alcohol-induced changes include increased electroencephalographic (EEG) frequency, decreased amplitude of the cortical N1 and hippocampal P3 event-related potential (ERP) components, enhanced anxiety-like behavior, and enhanced depressive-like behavior. Nicotine-induced changes include decreased slow-wave cortical EEG power, increased cortical N1 ERP amplitude, decreased motor activity, and increased anxiety-like behavior. These findings support the hypothesis that adolescents are uniquely susceptible to the effects of chronic alcohol and nicotine exposure.

KEYWORDS: adolescence; alcohol; nicotine

The 1998 National Household Survey on Drug Abuse reported that roughly 20% of teens between 12 and 17 years of age currently use alcohol and/or nicotine. Preexisting genetic susceptibility, increased risk-taking behavior, and impaired self-regulatory behavior all may contribute to the adolescent initiation of alcohol and nicotine use. However, ongoing neurodevelopmental changes may also increase susceptibility of the adolescent brain to the effects of chronic alcohol and nicotine exposure. Adolescent rats (i.e., a 28–45-day-old rat) serve as good models to study alcohol and nicotine abuse, because they undergo comparable behavioral and neuroanatomical development as do adolescent humans. The global hypothesis driving our studies is: *Adolescents are uniquely susceptible to the detrimental neurobehavioral consequences of alcohol and nicotine exposure.* In exploring this hypothesis, neurobehavioral profiles of adult rats exposed to alcohol or nicotine as adolescents have been explored.

Address for correspondence: Craig J. Slawecki, The Scripps Research Institute, Department of Neuropharmacology, CVN14, 10550 North Torrey Pines Road, La Jolla, CA 92037. Voice: 858-784-7240; fax 858-784-7475.
cslawecki@scripps.edu

Ann. N.Y. Acad. Sci. 1021: 448–452 (2004). © 2004 New York Academy of Sciences.
doi: 10.1196/annals.1308.062

ADOLESCENT ALCOHOL EXPOSURE

As described previously,[2,3] in our model, adolescent or adult rats are exposed to ethanol vapor for 10–14 days using an intermittent 12-h/day schedule that mimics cyclical patterns of alcohol consumption. Blood alcohol levels are maintained at 250 mg/dL. At the start of ethanol exposure, adolescent rats are 30–31 days old and adult rats are >60 days old.

Ten days of alcohol exposure alters neurophysiological function in rats exposed as adolescents, but not as adults, after >7 weeks of abstinence.[2,3] Neurophysiological function in rats exposed to ethanol during adolescence is characterized by increased cortical and hippocampal electroencephalographic (EEG) frequency and decreased amplitude of the cortical N1 and hippocampal P3 components of the auditory event-related potential (ERP).[2] It is speculated that the decreased N1 and P3 amplitudes are indicative of deficits in attention and memory function, as reported in clinical studies of adolescent alcohol abusers.[4] In addition, adult rats exposed to ethanol during adolescence demonstrate decreased neurobehavioral responses to acute ethanol challenges relative to controls.[3] Additional behavioral data reveal enhanced anxiety-like and depressive-like behavior more than 3 weeks after adolescent ethanol exposure ends. In the Light-Dark Box, a significantly $[F(1,11) = 5.91, P = .033]$ more rapid retreat to the dark side of the test box by ethanol-exposed rats is suggestive of increased anxiety-like behavior (FIG. 1A). In the Porsolt swim test, a

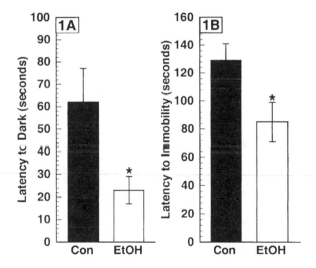

FIGURE 1. Adolescent ethanol exposure increases (**1A**) anxiety-like behavior in the Light-Dark Box, and (**1B**) depression-like behavior in the Porsolt Swim Test. *Light-Dark Box behavior* was assessed during a 10-min test session. The light side was illuminated at a level of 50 lux. *Latency to dark* represents the time taken to retreat to the dark side of the apparatus after being placed in the light side at the start of the test. *Porsolt Test behavior* was assessed during a 5-min session. The apparatus was a plastic tub (diameter = 34 cm, depth = 48 cm) filled with 24 ± 2°C water. *Latency to immobility* represents the time taken to stop swimming after the start of the test. Ethanol-exposed (EtOH, *n* = 6). Control (Con, *n* = 7). Data are the group mean ± SEM. *Asterisks* (*) = different from control (*P* < .05).

significant $[F(1,11) = 6.76, P = .025]$ decrease in the latency of ethanol-exposed rats to become immobile is suggestive of enhanced depressive-like behavior (FIG. 1B). It is currently unclear if these neurobehavioral changes enhance the abuse liability of alcohol, as increased ethanol self-administration has not been observed in adult rats exposed to ethanol during adolescence using this model.[5]

ADOLESCENT NICOTINE EXPOSURE

The nicotine exposure model developed in our laboratory utilizes Nicoderm CQ™ transdermal patches as a delivery system.[6-8] Nicotine-exposed rats and age-matched controls are between 35 and 40 days old during the treatment period. Each day during the 5-day treatment, a portion of a nicotine patch that delivers 5 mg/kg/day is placed on a shaved portion of the rat's back. This nicotine dose produces average blood levels of 90 ng/mL nicotine and 650 ng/mL cotinine.[6] During nicotine treatment, increased motor activity and biphasic changes in water intake (i.e., an early suppression followed by a later enhancement) are also observed.[6,8]

Five days of adolescent nicotine exposure has lasting effects on behavior and neurophysiological function that can be observed >6 weeks after exposure has ended.[6-8] Robust and persistent decreases in motor activity develop 1 week after the cessation of exposure.[6,8] Decreased motor activity and increased anxiety-like behavior in the standard open field and the modified open field is observed in nicotine-exposed rats 2–3 weeks after exposure has ended.[8] Neurophysiological recordings obtained >6 weeks after exposure ends demonstrate decreased slow-wave cortical EEG

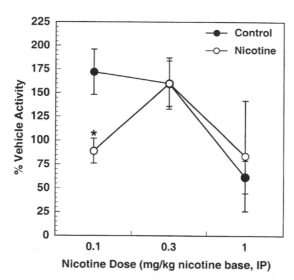

FIGURE 2. Nicotine's stimulatory effects are attenuated in adult rats exposed to nicotine as adolescents (Nicotine, $n = 9$; Control, $n = 11$). Activity assessment began 5 minutes after saline or nicotine administration. Each assessment lasted for 20 minutes. Activity level is presented as percent of saline: [(Nicotine condition/vehicle condition)*100]. Data are the group mean ± SEM. *Asterisks* (*) = different from control ($P < .05$).

power and increased cortical N1 ERP amplitude in nicotine-exposed rats.[6] Furthermore, cortical neurophysiological responses to CRF are reduced in nicotine-exposed rats,[7] and the stimulatory effect of low-dose nicotine is reduced in rats exposed to nicotine during adolescence. For example, 0.1 mg/kg nicotine significantly [$F(2,36)$ = 3.32, $P < .048$] enhances motor activity relative to vehicle in age-matched control rats, but not nicotine-exposed rats (FIG. 2).

SUMMARY AND CONCLUSIONS

These findings add to a growing literature demonstrating that adolescents are uniquely susceptible to the lasting neurobehavioral effects of chronic alcohol and nicotine exposure. Indices of impaired attention and memory, enhanced anxiety-like and depressive-like behavior, and decreased sensitivity to ethanol challenge during adulthood are found in our adolescent ethanol exposure model. In the adolescent nicotine model, neurobehavioral patterns indicative of anxiety and neurophysiological hyperarousal are observed. These nicotine-induced changes are associated with decreases in responsivity to nicotine and corticotropin-releasing factor. Increased anxiety, the onset of depression, or decreased sensitivity to alcohol or nicotine could all partially contribute to adult alcohol or nicotine abuse. While it is unclear if the neurobehavioral changes described earlier enhance the abuse potential of alcohol or nicotine, further studies will prove useful in expanding our understanding of how adolescent alcohol or nicotine use contributes to adult cognitive impairment, neuropsychiatric disorders, and substance abuse.

ACKNOWLEDGMENTS

This work was supported by K01 AA00298 to C.J.S. and AA06420 to Dr. George Koob from the NIAAA, 10RT-0334 to C.L.E. from the State of California TRDRP. Thanks are extended to Maury Cole, Tess Kimber, and Antonio Sweeney for maintaining departmental ethanol vapor chambers. Jennifer Roth and Ashley Rowinski are thanked for aiding in the data collection and analysis.

REFERENCES

1. SPEAR, L.P. 2000. The adolescent brain and age-related behavioral manifestations. Neurosci. Biobehav. Rev. **24**: 417–463.
2. SLAWECKI, C.J., M. BETANCOURT, M. COLE & C.L. EHLERS. 2001. Periadolescent alcohol exposure has lasting effects on adult neurophysiological function in rats. Brain Res. Dev. Brain Res. **128**: 63–72.
3. SLAWECKI, C.J. 2002. Altered EEG responses to ethanol in adult rats exposed to ethanol during adolescence. Alcohol. Clin. Exp. Res. **26**: 246–54.
4. TAPERT, S.F., E. GRANHOLM, N.G. LEEDY & S.A. BROWN. 2002. Substance use and withdrawal: neuropsychological functioning over 8 years in youth. J. Int. Neuropsychol. Soc. **8**: 873–883.
5. SLAWECKI, C.J. & M. BETANCOURT. 2002. Effects of adolescent ethanol exposure on ethanol consumption in adult rats. Alcohol **26**: 23–30.

6. SLAWECKI, C.J. & C.L. EHLERS. 2002. Lasting effects of adolescent nicotine exposure on the electroencephalogram, event related potentials, and locomotor activity in the rat. Brain Res. Dev. Brain Res. **138:** 15–25.
7. SLAWECKI, C.J. & C.L. EHLERS. 2003. Blunted cortical EEG responses to CRF in adult rats exposed to nicotine during adolescence. Neuropeptides **37:** 66–73.
8. SLAWECKI, C.J., A. GILDER, J. ROTH & C.L. EHLERS. 2003. Increased anxiety-like behavior in adult rats exposed to nicotine as adolescents. Pharmacol. Biochem. Behav. **75:** 355–361.

An Animal Model of Sensation Seeking: The Adolescent Rat

KIRSTIE H. STANSFIELD,^{a} REX M. PHILPOT,^{a} AND CHERYL L. KIRSTEIN^{b,c}

Departments of ^{a}Psychology, ^{b}Cognitive and Neural Sciences, and ^{c}Pharmacology and Therapeutics, University of South Florida, Tampa, Forida 33620, USA

ABSTRACT: Previous research has established a strong relationship between a rodent's preference for novelty and sensitivity to psychomotor stimulants. Rats with greater sensitivity to the motoric effects of amphetamine exhibit higher preferences for novelty. Additionally, animals with high novelty preference scores are more easily drug conditioned and are more sensitive to, and can more accurately discriminate, amphetamine doses. Novelty preference in animals has been compared to sensation seeking in humans and is strongly correlated with drug use and addiction vulnerability. Thus, the present studies employed a playground maze procedure to measure changes in novelty preference across age following either four or eight habituation trials using eight distinct objects. Early-adult (postnatal day [PND] 59) animals did not exhibit a significant preference for a novel object regardless of total number of habituation trials. Early-adolescent animals (PND 34) exhibited a preference for the novel object in fewer than four habituation trials, but exhibited no preference with increased habituation trials. These results are counterintuitive and may demonstrate an overgeneralization of the habituation trials specific to adolescent animals. Given that adolescence is a period of heightened exploration, one would expect adolescent animals to demonstrate an enhanced preference for novel stimuli using this paradigm. However, it is possible that the complexity of the task, as presented, reveals differences in the establishment and behavioral manifestation of associations during adolescence. To address this issue, a separate novelty paradigm was implemented using an open-field habituation procedure followed by the introduction of a single novel object during the testing period. This revised design provides the foundation needed to better assess novelty-induced locomotor activity and novelty preference in adolescent rats.

KEYWORDS: novelty preference; sensation seeking; adolescence; development

INTRODUCTION

Adolescence is a time of high-risk behavior and increased exploration. It is also a period when the brain is undergoing many complex changes that can exert long-term influences on decision making and cognitive process.[1] Adolescence is also marked by a greater probability to initiate drug use and is associated with an in-

Address for correspondence: Cheryl L. Kirstein, Ph.D., Psychology Department–PCD 4118G, University of South Florida, 4202 E. Fowler Avenue, Tampa, FL 33620. Voice: 813-974-9626; fax: 813-974-4617.

Kirstein@luna.cas.usf.edu

Ann. N.Y. Acad. Sci. 1021: 453–458 (2004). © 2004 New York Academy of Sciences.
doi: 10.1196/annals.1308.063

creased risk to develop addiction and dependency in adulthood. Specifically, Estroff has reported that most illicit drug use begins at approximately age 12, with peak periods of initiation between ages 15 and 19.[2] In fact, more than half (54%) of high school seniors have had at least one experience with an illicit compound.[3] During the 1990s, there was a steady rise in the frequency of drug use in teenagers, and by 2001, 4.3% of eighth graders, 5.7% of tenth graders, and 8.2% of high school seniors reported using cocaine at least once in their lifetime.[4] The fact that illicit drug use is so dramatic during the adolescent period is of particular concern given that the escalation of use appears more rapidly among teenagers than adult users, suggesting a greater addictive potential during adolescence than in adulthood.[2]

Arnett has shown a relative predisposition toward sensation seeking in adolescence, a factor that Zuckerman associates with increased likelihood of risk-taking behaviors, including drug use or initiation.[5,6] Measures of sensation seeking are highly correlated with approach to novelty or novelty preference in humans, indicating that preference for novelty is a valid measure of risk-taking behavior probability, specifically the initiation of drug use.[7]

Similar to humans, animals have been shown by numerous studies to have a strong correlation between novelty preference/novelty reactivity and drugs, specifically the rewarding efficacy of psychomotor stimulants and self-administration rates.[8] High novelty–preferring rats (HP) show higher rates of amphetamine and cocaine-induced locomotor activity and will self-administer these drugs more readily than low novelty–preferring (LP) rats.[9] Moreover, HP rats seem to participate in far greater risk-taking behaviors and to show much higher behavioral and neurochemical responses in reaction to environmental stressors or pharmacological challenges than LP rats.[10] These data suggest a strong relationship between sensation-seeking and novelty-seeking, making it more likely that adolescents will become involved in risky behaviors including drug use and initiation. The present study examined responses to novelty and novelty-induced locomotor activity as a sensitive measure of individual differences across age, in order to determine whether adolescents are uniquely susceptible to drugs of abuse as measured by novelty preference.

METHODS

Eighty-three Sprague-Dawley (Harlan) rats postnatal day (PND) 34 ($\mu = 134g$) and PND 59 ($\mu = 293.13g$) at the time of testing were used as subjects in these experiments. No more than one male per litter per age was used in a given condition. Pups were "sexed" and culled to 10 pups per litter on PND 1. Pups remained housed with their respective dams in a temperature- and humidity-controlled vivarium on a 12:12h light: dark cycle (07:00 h/19:00 h) until PND 21, after which pups were weaned and group-housed. Animal care was in accordance with the guidelines set forth by the National Institutes of Health.

Paradigm 1

Animals were tested on a plastic circular platform (216 cm in diameter) standing 70 cm from the ground. Eight black circles (28 cm in diameter) were evenly spaced outlining the perimeter of the apparatus. Eight different plastic figurines were adhered to the middle of each black circle with Velcro.

Rats were handled on either PND 31 or 56 for one 3-minute session to minimize stress levels due to handling. For the next three consecutive days (PND 32–34 or 57–59) each rat was placed on the playground maze facing away from the experimenter; the experimenter then left the room, while the animal could freely explore the novel environment for 3 minutes. Each day, the eight figurines were randomly distributed among the black circles.

On the fourth day, rats were placed in the familiar apparatus for 3 minutes and removed for 1 minute while a novel object was placed instead of a random familiar object; their behavior was recorded for 3 minutes.

Paradigm 2

Habituation trials were doubled and occurred two times per day over 4 days, for a total of eight habituation trials followed by the behavioral test.

Paradigm 3

Animals were tested in an enclosed environment, and their behavior was recorded. Over a period of 4 consecutive days, twice a day each rat (PND 31–34 and 56–59) was placed on the open field in one of four randomly selected zones to freely explore the novel environment for 5 minutes. On the fourth consecutive day (trial 8), rats were placed in the familiar apparatus for 5 minutes, and then removed for 1 minute while a single novel object (approximately 6.5 inches high and 4 inches wide) was attached to the center of the table with a magnet. Novelty preference and novelty-induced locomotion were determined using the Noldus Behavioral Tracking System.

RESULTS

Novelty Testing Using Eight Objects and Four Trials (Paradigm 1)

There was a significant main effect of AGE in raw preference score, $t(18) = 5.730, P < 0.0001$ (FIG. 1). Early-adolescent animals showed a greater preference for novelty, while adults did not.

Novelty Testing Using Eight Objects and Eight Trials (Paradigm 2)

Using twice the number of trials, there were no significant differences for AGE in raw preference score, $t(41) = 1.750, P > 0.05$ (FIG. 2). Neither early-adolescent nor adult animals demonstrated a preference for novelty with more exposures.

Novelty Testing Using One Object after Eight Habituation Trials (Paradigm 3)

There was a significant main effect of total duration in the novel zone across Trials, $F(1,42) = 54.29, P < 0.001$; however, there were no significant differences across Age $F(1,42) = 0.0474, P > 0.05$ (FIG. 3), suggesting a preference for novelty regardless of age.

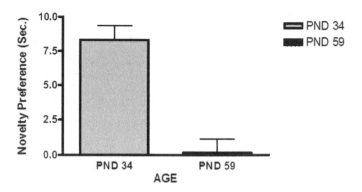

FIGURE 1. Adolescent animals (PND 34) exhibited a preference for novelty when tested under an 8-object, 4-trial paradigm.

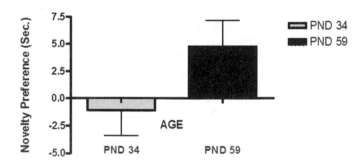

FIGURE 2. Adolescent (PND 34) and adult animals (PND 59) do not exhibit a novelty preference under an 8-object and 8-trial paradigm.

Animals failed to demonstrate a change in total distance moved in the presence of a novel object across TRIAL, $F(1,42) = 0.9271$, $P > 0.05$, and AGE $F(1,42) = 1.127$, $P > 0.05$. Additionally, no significant changes in total time spent moving in response to a novel object across TRIAL, $F(1,42) = 0.4124$, $P > 0.05$, or across AGE $F(1,42) = 0.0343$, $P > 0.05$, were detected.

Comparative Analyses of Paradigm 2 and 3

A 2×2 analysis of variance (ANOVA) indicated no significant differences across AGE in total distance moved between paradigm 1 and 2, $F(1,22) = 0.6869$, $P > 0.05$. However, a subsequent t-test, collapsing across AGE, showed a significant difference in total distance moved between the two paradigms, $t(44) = 3.729$, $P < 0.05$, with animals in paradigm 3 exhibiting more activity. Analysis of the variability about the mean indicated that the variances between the paradigms differed significantly, $F(22,22) = 3.108$, $P < 0.05$.

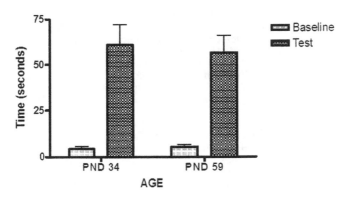

FIGURE 3. Both PND 34 and PND 59 animals spend more time in the novel zone from baseline compared to test day.

DISCUSSION

The present studies used several paradigms to determine an accurate way to assess novelty preference in adolescent and adult animals. The results indicate a significant difference between the three behavioral paradigms. Manipulation of trials revealed that early adolescent animals show a greater preference for novelty than do adult animals when four habituation trials are used, an effect that was lost with eight exposures. The findings suggest the habituation period plays an important role in the behavioral response of adolescent animals to novel objects. It is possible adolescent animals may overgeneralize when repeatedly exposed to the environment and experience with objects in general. In contrast, the adult animals either do not learn about the objects on the playground maze regardless of exposures or simply do not prefer novel objects. To test this idea of overgeneralization when multiple objects are used, animals were habituated to the environment only. Adolescent and adult animals were comparable in total distance moved and total time spent moving, from baseline to test, indicating that the presence of a novel object did not change activity levels. Both ages exhibited a novelty preference (i.e., increase in total time spent in the novel zone from baseline to test). Taken together, the results suggest that both adolescents and adults tend to exhibit a preference for novelty, but that variations of learning (i.e., trials/exposures) can mask these tendencies. Habituating animals to the environment and subsequently introducing a novel object provides a reliable approach for assessing novelty preference across age.

ACKNOWLEDGMENTS

This work is funded by Grant DA14024 from the National Institute of Drug Abuse, NIH.

REFERENCES

1. SPEAR, L.P. 2000. The adolescent brain and age-related behavioral manifestations. Neurosci. Biobehav. Rev. **24:** 417–463.
2. ESTROFF, T.W., et al. 1989. Adolescent cocaine abuse: addictive potential, behavioral and psychiatric effects. Clin. Pediatr. **28:** 550–555.
3. WALLACE, J.M., JR., et al. 2003. Gender and ethnic differences in smoking, drinking and illicit drug use among American 8th, 10th and 12th grade students, 1976–2000. Addiction **98:** 225–234.
4. JOHNSTON, L.D. 2001. Monitoring the Future: National Survey Results on Drug Use, 1975–1999. National Institute of Drug Abuse, U.S. Department of Health and Human Services, National Institute of Health. Bethesda, MD.
5. ARNETT, J.J. 1999. Adolescent storm and stress, reconsidered. Am. Psychol. **54:** 317–326.
6. ZUCKERMAN, M. 1986. Sensation-seeking and the endogenous deficit theory of drug abuse. NIDA Res. Monogr. **74:** 59–70.
7. MCCOURT, W.F., et al. 1993. Sensation-seeking and novelty-seeking. Are they the same? J. Nerv. Ment. Dis. **181:** 309–312.
8. KLEBAUR, J.E., et al. 2001. Exposure to novel environmental stimuli decreases amphetamine self-administration in rats. Exp. Clin. Psychopharmacol. **9:** 372–379.
9. HOOKS, M.S., et al. 1991. Response to novelty predicts the locomotor and nucleus accumbens dopamine response to cocaine. Synapse **9:** 121–128.
10. KLEBAUR, J.E., et al. 2001. Individual differences in behavioral responses to novelty and amphetamine self-administration in male and female rats. Behav. Pharmacol. **12:** 267–275.

Changes in Sensitivity to Ethanol-Induced Social Facilitation and Social Inhibition from Early to Late Adolescence

ELENA I. VARLINSKAYA AND LINDA P. SPEAR

Center for Developmental Psychobiology, Department of Psychology, Binghamton University, Binghamton, New York 13902-6000, USA

ABSTRACT: Adolescent rats are more sensitive than adults to ethanol-induced social facilitation, but are less sensitive to the suppression of social interactions seen at higher ethanol doses. Given recent findings that point to age differences in ethanol responsiveness, even within the adolescent period, the present study assessed acute effects of low to moderate doses of ethanol on social behavior of early, mid- or late adolescent rats. Age-related changes in responsiveness to the effects of ethanol on social behavior were apparent even within the adolescent period, with early adolescents being more sensitive to ethanol-induced social facilitation and less sensitive to ethanol-induced social inhibition than mid- and late adolescents. Given that ethanol-induced social facilitation as well as a lower sensitivity to the adverse effects of ethanol may contribute to heavy drinking, this pattern of early adolescent responsiveness to ethanol's social consequences may put them at higher risk for extensive alcohol use.

KEYWORDS: adolescence; ethanol; social behavior; rat

Adolescence is a time of acquiring new social skills and a period of rapid hormonal and neural changes.[1] It is also a period during development when the risk for extensive alcohol use is elevated. An important quality of ethanol that may contribute to heavy drinking in human adolescents is its ability to produce social facilitation by enhancing the effectiveness of interactions with peers.[2] Unique neural alterations that occur during adolescence influence adolescents' responsiveness to ethanol in a way that differs from adult responding. Adolescent rats, but not their adult counterparts, exhibit an ethanol-induced facilitation of social behavior, an effect seen under familiar test circumstances after low doses of ethanol. Adolescents, conversely, are less sensitive than adults to the inhibition of social interactions seen after moderate ethanol doses.[3] Given recent findings in our laboratory[4] and others[5] that point to age differences in ethanol responsiveness even within adolescence, the present study assessed potential age-related alterations in ethanol sensitivity during the adolescent period when indexed in terms of the activating and suppressing effects of ethanol on social behavior.

Address for correspondence: Elena I. Varlinskaya, Psychology Department, Binghamton University, Binghamton 13902, NY. Voice: 607-777-7164.
varlinsk@binghamton.edu

Ann. N.Y. Acad. Sci. 1021: 459–461 (2004). © 2004 New York Academy of Sciences.
doi: 10.1196/annals.1308.064

TABLE 1. Activation effects of low doses of ethanol on adolescent social behaviors

Adolescent period	Dose of ethanol (g/kg)			
	0	0.25	0.5	0.75
Early (P28)	182.5 ± 7.4	193.6 ± 10.4	236.5 ± 8.1*	219.7 ± 11.5*
Mid (P35)	157.6 ± 9.8	172.0 ± 9.6	203.8 ± 3.1*	157.9 ± 7.9
Late (P42)	157.1 ± 7.0	187.1 ± 7.6	183.8 ± 12.2	147.5 ± 13.4

NOTE: Asterisks indicate significant differences (increase in overall social activity) from corresponding saline-treated controls, $P < 0.05$.

TABLE 2. Suppressing effects of moderate doses of ethanol on adolescent social behavior

Adolescent period	Dose of ethanol (g/kg)				
	0	1.0	1.25	1.5	1.75
Early (P28)	179.3 ± 11.5	181.6 ± 12.2	137.7 ± 23.3	51.2 ± 11.6*	33.6 ± 6.6*
Mid (P35)	153.4 ± 5.6	102.2 ± 10.9*	52.9 ± 7.4*	34.2 ± 8.4*	22.2 ± 6.7*
Late (P42)	150.7 ± 8.4	73.0 ± 13.6*	39.9 ± 3.8*	28.5 ± 5.0*	13.2 ± 2.1*

NOTE: Asterisks indicate significant differences (decrease in overall social activity) from corresponding saline-treated controls, $P < 0.05$.

Acute effects of low (0, 0.25, 0.5, and 0.75 g/kg) to moderate (0, 1.0, 1.25, 1.5, and 1.75 g/kg) doses of ethanol on social behavior of early (postnatal day [P] 28), mid- (P35) or late (P42) adolescent male and female Sprague-Dawley rats were investigated in two separate experiments using a modified social interaction test ($n = 5$ animals/sex/ethanol dose). Ethanol was administered intraperitoneally as a 12.6% (v/v) solution in physiological saline. One day before testing, experimental subjects were placed into the two-compartment testing chamber for 20 min to make the testing situation familiar for them. On the next day, each subject was injected with the appropriate test solution and placed individually in a holding cage for 30 min before the test. At the onset of testing, each animal was placed into a testing chamber and immediately exposed, for 10 min, to a non-manipulated, unfamiliar peer of the same sex and age. Test sessions were videotaped for later scoring by an observer uninformed as to the treatment condition of each animal. Overall social activity (i.e., the sum of social investigation, contact behavior, and play fighting frequencies) was scored and analyzed.

Overall social activity was enhanced in early adolescents (P28) by 0.5 and 0.75 g/kg ethanol and in mid-adolescents (P35) by 0.5 g/kg. No activating effects of ethanol were evident in P42 animals (TABLE 1). Social behavior did not differ as a function of gender, so data are collapsed across this variable in TABLES 1 and 2. After administration of the higher dose range, early adolescents were less sensitive to the ethanol-associated suppression of social interactions than mid- or late adolescents. Overall social activity in P28 rats was suppressed only by a dose of 1.5 g/kg ethanol or higher, whereas even 1 g/kg suppressed social activity in P35 and P42 animals (TABLE 2).

These results demonstrate that age-related changes in responsiveness to the effects of ethanol on social behavior are apparent even within the adolescent period, early adolescents being more sensitive to ethanol-induced social facilitation and less sensitive to ethanol-induced social inhibition than mid- and late adolescents. No significant sex differences in sensitivity to the activating and suppressing effects of ethanol were found at any of the ages in the present study, despite other evidence for more rapid maturation in adolescent females than males.[6] Early adolescent animals showed a unique pattern of responsiveness to the social consequences of ethanol: apparent social facilitation was evident in these animals after low doses of ethanol, whereas social inhibition after higher ethanol doses was less pronounced than in their older counterparts. To the extent that these data are applicable to human adolescents, and given that ethanol-induced social facilitation and low sensitivity to the adverse effects of ethanol may contribute to heavy drinking, the unique pattern of early adolescent responsiveness to the effects of ethanol on social activity may put them at a higher risk for extensive alcohol use.

ACKNOWLEDGMENTS

The research presented in this paper was supported by Grants R37 AA12525 and R01 AA12150 to Linda P. Spear and R01 AA12453 to Elena I. Varlinskaya from the National Institute of Alcohol Abuse and Alcoholism.

REFERENCES

1. SPEAR, L.P. 2000. The adolescent brain and age-related behavioral manifestations. Neurosci. Biobehav. Rev. **24:** 417–463.
2. BECK, K.H., D.L. THOMBS & T.G. SUMMONS. 1993. The social context of drinking scales: construct validation and relationship to indicants of abuse in an adolescent population. Addict. Behav. **18:** 159–169.
3. VARLINSKAYA, E.I. & L.P. SPEAR. 2002. Acute effects of ethanol on social behavior of adolescent and adult rats: role of familiarity of the test situation. Alcohol. Clin. Exp. Res. **26:** 1502–1511.
4. VARLINSKAYA, E.I & L.P. SPEAR. 2003. Age- and time-dependent effects of ethanol on social interactions: implications for the ontogeny of acute tolerance [abstract]. Alcohol. Clin. Exp. Res. **27:** 131A.
5. PHILPOT, R.M., K.A. BADANICH & C.L. KIRSTEIN. 2003. Place conditioning: age-related changes in the rewarding and aversive effects of alcohol. Alcohol. Clin. Exp. Res. **27:** 593–599.
6. ODELL, W.D. 1990. Sexual maturation in the rat. *In* Control of the Onset of Puberty. M.M. Grumbach, P.C. Sizonenko & M.L. Aubert, Eds.: 183–210. Williams and Wilkins. Baltimore, MD.

Adolescent and Adult Rats' Aversion to Flavors Previously Paired with Nicotine

CARRIE E. WILMOUTH AND LINDA P. SPEAR

Center for Developmental Psychology, Department of Psychology, Binghamton University, Binghamton, New York 13902-6000, USA

ABSTRACT: Despite the high prevalence of adolescent smoking, few studies have examined nicotine sensitivity during this developmental period. In the present study we examined adolescent and adult rats' preference/aversion for a flavor previously paired with nicotine. Paired (nicotine + Kool-Aid) and unpaired (Kool-Aid) solutions were presented in the home cage on alternating nights, with water given during the light phase for six days. A choice test was conducted 24 hr after the last night of conditioning, with both flavors presented simultaneously during the dark cycle. On test day, although the flavor previously paired with nicotine was not preferred at either age, adolescent rats consumed significantly more of the paired flavor than adults. These results suggest that adolescent rats are less sensitive to the aversive properties of nicotine. This finding taken together with adolescents' increased sensitivity to the rewarding properties of nicotine, may result in an increased vulnerability to nicotine dependence.

KEYWORDS: adolescent; nicotine; conditioned taste aversion; rats

Despite the high prevalence of smoking in adolescents, little research has examined the rewarding properties of nicotine during this developmental period. Previous research in our lab has demonstrated that adolescent rats are more sensitive to nicotine's rewarding properties than their adult counterparts in a conditioned place preference paradigm.[1] We have also found adolescent rats to consume more nicotine than do adults in home-cage, two-bottle choice tests.[2] Similarly, during early adolescence male mice show a preference for nicotine solution in a two-bottle choice test, while older animals do not.[3]

To further explore potential age differences in the rewarding properties of nicotine, the present study determined whether adults and adolescents differ in their preference for or aversion to a flavor previously paired with nicotine over an equally familiar flavor that was presented alone.

Address for correspondence: Dr. Linda Spear, Department of Psychology, Binghamton University, Binghamton, NY 13902-6000. Voice: 607-777-2825; fax: 607-777-6418.
lspear@binghamton.edu

Ann. N.Y. Acad. Sci. 1021: 462–464 (2004). © 2004 New York Academy of Sciences.
doi: 10.1196/annals.1308.065

EXPERIMENT 1

Methods

Adult (P60) and adolescent (P28) male Sprague-Dawley rats were individually housed at the onset of testing and acclimated for 2 days prior to the start of conditioning. Paired and unpaired solutions were presented on alternating nights, with water given during the light phase for six days. On the first night of conditioning, rats were given access in their home cage to one bottle containing saccharin-sweetened Kool-Aid solution (cherry or grape) paired with nicotine (0.002%). During the following dark cycle, rats were presented with the alternative favor of Kool-Aid (unpaired solution). Flavors paired with nicotine were counterbalanced across subjects. A choice test was conducted 24 h after the last night of conditioning, with both unadulterated flavors presented simultaneously during the 10-hr dark cycle.

Results

During conditioning, adolescents' nicotine intake (mg/kg) decreased across sessions, but remained significantly higher than adults' (average intake/day for adolescents: 2.3 mg/kg; adults: 1.7 mg/kg). Adolescent but not adult animals also demonstrated a suppression of fluid intake (mL/kg) when presented with the nicotine-containing solution (135.9 ± 10.3) as compared to nonpaired Kool-Aid solutions (164.5 ± 9.7) or water (184.4 ± 6.6). On test day, both adult and adolescent rats demonstrated an aversion for the flavor previously paired with nicotine (adolescent: $-25.3\% \pm 13.8$; adult: $-55.4\% \pm 12.8$), but no effect of age was observed.

EXPERIMENT 2

Given that adolescents suppressed their intake of the nicotine-containing solution in Experiment 1, while subsequently increasing water consumption during the light phase, animals were not given access to water during the light phase in Experiment 2.

Results

When access to water was not permitted during the light cycle, adolescents did not demonstrate a suppression of intake when presented with nicotine-containing solutions. Again, adolescents consumed significantly more nicotine (3.5 mg/kg ± 0.09) than did adults (1.6 mg/kg ± 0.05) throughout the conditioning sessions.

On test day, both age groups consumed considerably less of the nicotine-paired flavor than the flavor that had been presented alone; again, no significant effect of age was observed (adolescent: $-51.3\% \pm 9.6$; adult: $-56.7\% \pm 10.2$). Thus, despite adolescents' elevated nicotine intake during conditioning, they did not develop a stronger aversion to the nicotine-paired flavor than adults.

EXPERIMENT 3

In light of adolescents' higher nicotine intake relative to that of adults observed in Experiments 1 and 2, the concentration of nicotine solution was adjusted for each age in this experiment in an attempt to produce equivalent mg/kg nicotine intake across ages. The concentration of nicotine solution presented to adolescents was reduced to 0.0015%, while the concentration for adults was increased to 0.003%.

Results

Adolescent (2.9 ± 0.1) and adult (2.2 ± 0.3) rats consumed comparable amounts of nicotine (mg/kg) during the conditioning phase. During testing, adults demonstrated a significantly greater aversion (−72.0 % ± 2.8) to flavors previously paired with nicotine when compared to adolescents (−50.6 % ± 9.4) rats.

DISCUSSION

Many self-administered drugs are known to have both reinforcing and aversive properties.[4] The aversive properties may be more easily associated with taste, while there may be a predisposition to associate rewarding properties with environmental cues. The current study demonstrates that when mg/kg nicotine exposure is equated across age, adolescent rats demonstrate a reduced aversion for flavors paired with nicotine when compared to adults. Taken together with prior studies from our laboratory,[1] these findings suggest that while adolescents are more sensitive to the reinforcing and stimulatory properties of nicotine, they possess a blunted sensitivity to the aversive properties of nicotine. Acting together these factors may contribute to the increased vulnerability to tobacco dependence observed among individuals who initiate smoking during adolescence.

REFERENCES

1. VASTOLA, B.J., L.A. DOUGLAS, E.I. VARLINSKAYA & L.P. SPEAR. 2002. Nicotine-induced conditioned place preference in adolescent and adult rats. Physiol. Behav. 77: 1–8.
2. WILMOUTH, C.E. & P.L. SPEAR. 2002. Oral nicotine self-administration in rats during adolescence (abstr.). Drug Alcohol Depend. 66: S195.
3. ADRIANI, W., S. MACRI, R. PACIFICI & G. LAVIOLA. 2002. Peculiar vulnerability to nicotine oral self-administration in mice during early adolescence. Neuropsychopharmacology 27: 212–224.
4. WISE, R.A., R.A. YOKEL & H. DEWIT. 1976. Both positive reinforcement and conditioned aversion from amphetamine and from apomorphine in rats. Science 191: 1273–1274.

The Effects of Methylphenidate on Novel Object Exploration in Weanling and Periadolescent Rats

CHARLES J. HEYSER, MARSHA PELLETIER, AND JENNIFER S. FERRIS

Department of Psychology, Franklin & Marshall College,
Lancaster, Pennsylvania 17604, USA

ABSTRACT: Methylphenidate (Ritalin®) is used in the treatment of attention-deficit hyperactivity disorder. Surprisingly, little research has been conducted on the effects of methylphenidate during early development. Therefore, the present study was conducted to examine the effects of methylphenidate on object exploration in developing rats. Male and female weanling (21-day-old) and periadolescent (34-day-old) Sprague-Dawley rats were tested after acute or chronic treatment with methylphenidate. In weanling rats, chronic methylphenidate (5.0 mg/kg) increased locomotor activity and disrupted novel object exploration. In periadolescent rats, methylphenidate disrupted exploration of the novel object, but had no effect on locomotor activity at any dose tested. Periadolescent rats appear to be less sensitive to methylphenidate-induced changes in activity compared to weanling animals, whereas methylphenidate disrupted novel object exploration in both ages. Our results suggest that methylphenidate may alter recognition memory and/or reactivity to or preference for novelty.

KEYWORDS: methylphenidate (MPH); early development; exploration; rats; Ritalin

INTRODUCTION

Methylphenidate (MPH; Ritalin®) is widely used in the treatment of attention-deficit hyperactivity disorder (ADHD).[1] However, it is clear that healthy children are taking MPH, including those misdiagnosed with ADHD and those taking the drug illegally. Until recently, surprisingly little research had been conducted on the effects of MPH during early development, despite its widespread availability for several decades.[1] For example, the administration of MPH to 3–11 day old CD-1 mice resulted in an increase in locomotor activity, but had no effect on neuromuscular development.[2] In rats, exposure to MPH during adolescence [postnatal day (P) 35–42] facilitated the acquisition of cocaine self-administration in adult animals,[3] whereas exposure during preadolescence (P20–35) decreased the rewarding effects of cocaine in adulthood as measured by conditioned place preference.[4] The results of

Address for correspondence: Charles J. Heyser, Franklin & Marshall College, Department of Psychology, Lancaster, PA 17604. Voice: 717-291-3834; fax: 717-291-4387.
  cheyser@fandm.edu

Ann. N.Y. Acad. Sci. 1021: 465–469 (2004). © 2004 New York Academy of Sciences.
doi: 10.1196/annals.1308.066

these studies indicate short-term effects of MPH and the potential for long-lasting effects of early exposure.

The present study was conducted to further characterize the effects of MPH on exploratory behavior in weanling and adolescent rats. The adolescent period in rodents has been characterized by elevated levels of novelty seeking, risk taking, as well as reduced behavioral and hormonal response to stress.[5,6] In addition, there are several reports of reduced sensitivity to the effects of an acute administration of psychostimulants during this age period.[7] Exploratory behavior is typically assessed by observing animals in an empty open field and recording only the number of line crosses and/or rears.[8] It is our contention that, although useful, this represents a restrictive view of "exploratory behavior." Therefore we have begun to focus on tasks that provide the animals with additional opportunities for exploration (e.g., objects).[9,10] The advantages to the object exploration task are that there is no explicit need for any food or water restriction and several behavioral end points can be obtained, including general activity, along with measures of learning (e.g., habituation and recognition memory).[9] The object exploration task was also selected, given that previous reports have shown a decrease in preference for novelty following the administration of MPH in adult rats.[11]

METHODS

Subjects were offspring derived from Sprague-Dawley (Harlan, Inc.) rats bred in our laboratory. Offspring were weaned on P21 and housed in same-sex groups of 4–5 per cage with a 12-h light/dark cycle (lights on at 8:00 AM). Food and water were available *ad libitum*. Male and female rats were randomly assigned to either an acute or chronic treatment group. Rats in the chronic treatment group were given twice daily intraperitoneal (ip) injections of saline or MPH (2 or 5 mg/kg) for 7 days. These doses were selected from studies showing and increase in activity in adult animals.[12] Injections were separated by an interval of 8 h, with the first injection occurring at 9:00 AM. Weanling rats were injected from postnatal day 15 (P15) to P21 and periadolescent rats from P28 to P34. Rats in the acute treatment group were given a single ip injection of saline or MPH (2 or 5 mg/kg) on P21 or P34. Each rat was tested 30 min after the last injection for object exploration.

Object exploration was conducted in a circular open field (80 cm × 40 cm). Testing consisted of four 6-min trials, with a 3-min intertrial interval between each trial. There were no objects in the arena during trial 1, which served as a baseline/familiarization period to the novel environment. In trial 2, two identical pink plastic cups with green covers were placed into the open field. These objects were of sufficient height and weight so that they could not be climbed or moved. The objects were positioned equidistant from the walls and from each other. The same two objects remained in the open field during trial 3. In trial 4, one of the (familiar) objects was replaced with a novel object (a metal box). The behavior of each animal was videotaped and scored later by trained observers blind to the treatment conditions. Only the line cross and duration of contact with each object data will be presented in this brief report. All procedures were conducted in accordance with the guidelines established by the National Institutes of Health *Guide for the Care and Use of Laboratory Animals*.

RESULTS

As can be seen in FIGURE 1, the acute administration of MPH (5 mg/kg) significantly increased the number of line crosses in weanling rats. A further increase in line crosses was observed in weanling rats treated chronically with 5 mg/kg MPH (i.e., a sensitized response). In contrast, there was no effect of MPH administration on line crossing at any dose in the periadolescent (P34) animals (see FIG. 1).

The results of the object exploration are shown in FIGURE 2. A discrimination index (DI) was calculated for each animal using the duration of contact for each object

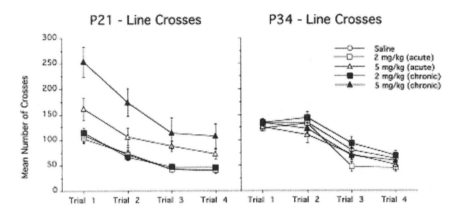

FIGURE 1. Mean number of line crosses for weanling (P21) and periadolescent (P34) rats during the four 6-min trials.

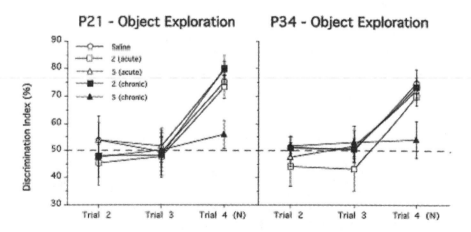

FIGURE 2. Mean discrimination index of object exploration for weanling (P21) and periadolescent (P34) rats. If the objects are equally explored, the discrimination index will be 50% (as indicated by the *dashed line*). In trial 4 (N), object 1 was replaced with a novel object.

using the following formula: DI = $((T1/(T1 + T2))*100)$, where T1 and T2 equal the duration of contact for object 1 and 2, respectively. If the objects are equally explored, then the discrimination index will be 50%. In trial 4, object 1 was replaced with a novel object. As expected, both weanling and periadolescent rats treated with saline showed preferential exploration of the novel object in the last trial. In contrast, all animals treated chronically with MPH (5 mg/kg) showed equal exploration of the novel and familiar object in trial 4. This disruption in novel exploration was not observed in animals given an acute dose of MPH.

DISCUSSION

The results of the present study show that the behavioral response to MPH is significantly influenced by the age of the animal. In weanling rats (P21), chronic administration of MPH (5 mg/kg) increased locomotor activity and disrupted novel object exploration. In periadolescent rats (P34), MPH disrupted exploration of the novel object at the same dosing regime, but had no effect on locomotor activity at any dose tested. Taken together with previous reports, periadoescent rats (P34) appear to be less sensitive to MPH-induced changes in activity compared to weanling animals (PD21) and adult rats given similar doses.[12] The finding that MPH disrupted novel object exploration in both ages suggests that MPH may alter recognition memory and/or reactivity to or preference for novelty. This finding is particularly interesting given that MPH had no effect on locomotor activity in periadolescent rats. These results confirm previous reports showing a decreased preference for novelty in adult animals (Hughes) and extend these effects to younger animals. These data also add to a growing literature showing a hyposensitivity to the behavioral effects of psychostimulants during the adolescent period in rodents.[5–7]

REFERENCES

1. SOLANTO, M.V. 1998. Neuropsychopharmacological mechanisms of stimulant drug action in attention-deficit hyperactivity disorder: a review and integration. Behav. Brain Res. **94:** 127–152.
2. PENNER, M.R., et al. 2001. Effects of chronic and acute methylphenidate hydrochloride (Ritalin) administration on locomotor activity, ultrasonic vocalizations, and neuromotor development in 3- to 11-day-old CD-1 mouse pups. Dev. Psychobiol. **39:** 216–228.
3. BRANDON, C.L., et al. 2001. Enhanced reactivity and vulnerability to cocaine following methylphenidate treatment in adolescent rats. Neuropsychopharmacology **25:** 651–661.
4. ANDERSEN, S.L., et al. 2002. Altered responsiveness to cocaine in rats exposed to methylphenidate during development. Nature Neurosci. **5:** 13–14.
5. SPEAR, L.P. 2000. The adolescent brain and age-related behavioral manifestations. Neurosci. Biobehav. Rev. **24:** 417–463.
6. LAVIOLLA, G., et al. 2003. Risk-taking behavior in adolescent mice: psychobiological determinants and early epigenetic influence. Neurosci. Biobehav. Rev. **27:** 19–31.
7. BOLONAS, C.A., S.J. GLATT & D. JACKSON. 1998. Subsensitivity to dopaminergic drugs in periadolesence rats: a behavioral and neurochemical analysis. Dev. Brain Res. **111:** 25–33.
8. HUGHES, R.N. 1997. Intrinsic exploration in animals: motives and measurement. Behav. Processes **41:** 213–226.

9. ENNACEUR, A. & J. DELACOUR. 1988. A new one trial test for neurobiological studies of memory in rats. 1. Behav. Brain Res. **33:** 197–207.
10. SAVE, E., *et al.* 1992. Object exploration and reactions to spatial and nonspatial changes in hooded rats following damage to parietal cortex or hippocampal formation. Behav. Neurosci. **106:** 447–456.
11. HUGHES, R.N. & L.A. SYME. 1972. The role of social isolation and sex in determining effects of chlordiazepoxide and methylphenidate on exploratory behavior. Psychopharmacologia **27:** 359–306.
12. GERASIMOV, M.R., *et al.* 2000. Comparison between intraperitoneal and oral methylphenidate administration: a microdialysis and locomotor activity study. J. Pharmacol. Exp. Ther. **295:** 51–57.

Index of Contributors